OPTION FOR THE POOR AND FOR THE EARTH

Revised Edition

FROM LEO XIII TO POPE FRANCIS

OPTION FOR THE POOR AND FOR THE EARTH

Revised Edition

FROM LEO XIII TO POPE FRANCIS

Donal Dorr

ORBIS BOOKS
Maryknoll, New York 10545

ORBIS BOOKS
Maryknoll, New York 10545

Fathers and Brothers
MARYKNOLL™

Founded in 1970, Orbis Books endeavors to publish works that enlighten the mind, nourish the spirit, and challenge the conscience. The publishing arm of the Maryknoll Fathers and Brothers, Orbis seeks to explore the global dimensions of the Christian faith and mission, to invite dialogue with diverse cultures and religious traditions, and to serve the cause of reconciliation and peace. The books published reflect the views of their authors and do not represent the official position of the Maryknoll Society. To learn more about Maryknoll and Orbis Books, please visit our website at www.maryknollsociety.org.

First published 1983.
Revised and expanded edition 2012.
Further revised and expanded edition 2016.

Library of Congress Cataloging-in-Publication Data
Names: Dorr, Donal, author.
Title: Option for the poor and for the eart : from Leo XIII to Pope Francis
/ by Donal Dorr.
Description: Revised edition. | Maryknoll : Orbis Books, 2016. | Includes
bibliographical references and index.
Identifiers: LCCN 2015045818 (print) | LCCN 2015050016 (ebook) | ISBN
9781626981621 (pbk.) | ISBN 9781608336296 (ebook)
Subjects: LCSH: Christian sociology—Catholic Church—History of doctrines. |
Catholic Church—Doctrines—History.
Classification: LCC BX1753 .D66 2016 (print) | LCC BX1753 (ebook) | DDC
261.8088/282—dc23
LC record available at http://lccn.loc.gov/2015045818

Contents

Preface

In the four years since the previous edition of this book was published in 2012 there has been a notable change in the emphasis and tone of official Catholic social teaching. Pope Francis became pope early in 2013. From the very beginning of his pontificate he called for a poor church at the service of poor and excluded people—and in his own actions and lifestyle he made it clear that for him this was no empty formula. His actions, his speeches and documents, and his off-the-cuff comments all show that he is committed to making an option for the poor in a quite radical and even dramatic manner. He is more blunt and uncompromising than previous popes in his challenge to the present exploitative and unsustainable model of economic development. Furthermore, he insists strongly on the close link between concern for the fragile Earth and concern for poor and vulnerable people, insisting repeatedly that the first and main victims of climate change are the poor. And he is the first pope to devote an encyclical to the topic of ecology. So his is an option not just for the poor but also for the Earth.

For these reasons it seems appropriate, even necessary, to issue a newly revised and expanded edition of this book rather earlier than would normally be the case. In the present edition I have added two new chapters (chapters 19 and 20) devoted to the teaching of Pope Francis. In the first of the new chapters I give an account of Francis's teaching on justice and the poor, as well as on actions by him which lend credibility to what he has written and said. In the second new chapter I offer an account of his teaching on ecology in the first two years of his papacy and then more extensively in his ecology encyclical, *Laudato Si'*, adding a commentary and evaluation of this major document. I have also completed a major revision and expansion of my final chapter. In addition, I have made some changes and updates to the text of earlier chapters, mainly to take account of recent studies that were not available in 2012 when the previous edition was published. The primary bibliography has been extended to include details of the documents and statements of Pope Francis and other relevant recent material. Finally, I have added bibliographical details of the more recent books and articles to which I have referred in the text of the book. The index of the book has also been updated. In order to ensure that the book would not become unduly long, I have shortened some of the chapters of the previous edition, summarizing some of the less significant material in them.

The 2012 edition was itself a greatly expanded and at times radically updated version of a book on the option for the poor that I had published twenty years earlier. That 2012 edition included five new chapters covering such topics as justice for women, ecology, and an extended treatment of the teaching of John Paul during the later years of his papacy, as well as the teaching and significant actions of Pope Benedict up to the final months before he resigned.

I take this opportunity to thank once again Trócaire (the Irish Catholic Agency for World Development) and the theology faculty of Maynooth College, who cooperated in establishing the Cardinal Conway Research Fellowship in the Theology of Development. My research for the first book was done partly while I was the holder of this fellowship. My research, some years later, for a new and enlarged edition of this book was carried out under the sponsorship of the Irish Missionary Union and of Trócaire. I thank Orbis Books and their editors Sue Perry and Jim Keane for inviting me to write this book and, more recently, to add the new material in the present edition, as well as for their painstaking editing of the text. I also say a heartfelt thanks to my sister Ben Kimmerling, my brothers Noel and Frank, and my sister-in-law Eileen Lynch—each of them for unfailing support and for inspiration as well as for help in relation to the content of various parts of what I have written here.

The sheer length of this book may perhaps deter some would-be readers from reading it straight through. I venture to suggest that they might find it helpful to read the first chapter, then the short summaries at the end of each of chapters 2 to 18, and then read the final three chapters in their entirety. They might then wish to return to one or more of the earlier chapters which deal with topics or periods in which they have a special interest.

I am particularly grateful to the many friends and fellow workers—in East, West, Central, and Southern Africa, as well as in Brazil, Ireland, England, Scotland, the United States, and Australia—who took part with me in workshops or courses about justice, development, and human liberation. They gave me new life and helped me grow in understanding and commitment to issues of justice and ecology. I have written this book not just for scholars and students but also for those fellow workers and for people like them in many parts of the world—Christians who feel called to work for justice and who turn to church social teaching for inspiration and for guidance about how to answer the call.

Donal Dorr
October 28, 2015

Abbreviations

AAS	*Acta Apostolicae Sedis*
ASS	*Acta Sanctae Sedis*
BP	*Actes de Léon XIII, Encycliques, Moto Proprio, Brefs, Allocutions, Actes de Dicastrères etc.* Paris: Bonne Presse, n.d.
CA	*Centesimus Annus*
CC	*Casti Connubi*
CiV	*Caritas in Veritate*
D1–D32	Thirty-two numbered addresses of Pius XII. See Bibliography of Primary Sources.
DCE	*Deus Caritas Est*
DM	*Dives in Misericoria*
DR	*Divini Redemptoris*
EG	*Evangelii Gaudium*
EV	*Evangelium Vitae*
EN	*Evangelii Nuntiandi*
FC	*Familiaris Consortio*
Gilson	*The Church Speaks to the Modern World: The Social Teaching s of Leo XIII*, edited by Étienne Gilson
Great Ency.	*The Great Encyclical Letters of Pope Leo XIII (with a preface by John J. Wynn).*
GS	*Gaudium et Spes*
JW	*"Justice in the World"*
LE	*Laborem Exercens*
L'Oss. Rom	*L'Osservatore Romano*
LS	*Laudato Si'*
Medellín	Sixteen documents from the Second General Conference of Latin American Bishops, Medellín, 1968
MD	*Mulieris Dignitatem*
MM	*Mater et Magistra*
Movements	Address to the Participants of the World Meeting of Popular Movements, October 28, 2014
OA	*Octogesima Adveniens*
PG	*Pastores Gregis*

1

Context

In this book I trace the historical development of the social teaching of the Catholic Church over a period of 135 years, from the time of Pope Leo XIII up to the end of 2015. However, the book is much more than a history. I venture to suggest that it can be used as a textbook about the main themes of social justice. I believe that this is a better way of learning about social justice, and of teaching it, than if one were to adopt a schematic or systematic approach which divides the material under headings and sub-headings. Furthermore, I think that it is not sufficient or appropriate just to present an uncritical exposition of official Catholic social teaching, as was done as recently as 2011 by Jean-Yves Naudet in his book *La doctrine social de l'église*. Instead, as I give an account of the teaching that has emerged over the years, I offer a serious evaluation and critique of it, both in the light of issues that were current at the time each document was published and also in relation to subsequent developments up to the present in the sciences, politics, and theological reflection. My aim is to discuss the major issues not just as items of past history but as serious contemporary challenges.

Key issues of social justice emerged in each of the time spans covered in this book. Here are just some of the more obvious examples taken from the twenty-one chapters of the book.

- In the present chapter I explain what is meant by an option for the poor and for the Earth. Then I raise the issue of whether one gains a new perspective by making an option in favor of people who are poor and an option to protect our environment—and I suggest that it is only from that perspective that one can come to a proper understanding of all the fundamental issues of social justice.
- My treatment of the encyclicals of Leo XIII (chapter 2) raises the perennial question of how far people who are poor and oppressed are entitled to go in challenging and resisting a government that is serving only the interests of those who are rich and powerful. It also raises the issue of the need for trade unions and the role they can play in working for justice in society.

- My account of the encyclicals of Pius XI (chapter 3) raises a number of important current issues: the distinction between personal injustice and structural injustice—and the relation between them; the concept of subsidiarity; whether workers should have a share in both the profits and the management of the enterprises in which they are working; the issue of whether or to what extent the capitalist system is compatible with Christianity; and finally, the very nature of social justice.
- The study of the many writings and talks of Pius XII (chapter 4) leads one to look at the question of how an excessively bureaucratic government puts unacceptable limits to personal freedom. It also raises the issue of the moral limits to the right to private property.
- The account of the encyclicals of John XXIII (chapter 5) offers us the opportunity to examine the advantages and disadvantages of a "welfare state" approach to dealing with the issue of poverty. It also raises the very practical question of whether Church leaders should adopt positions that ally them more with left-wing campaigners or with those who defend right-wing views.
- The study of "The Church in the Modern World" issued by Vatican II (chapter 6) deepens one's understanding of the issue of the limits to the right to private property. It also raises the issue of the Catholic conception of personal human rights—and the ways in which the Christian emphasis on social solidarity broadens one's understanding of the nature of rights.
- Paul VI's *Populorum Progressio* (chapter 7) leads one to examine the issue of social justice at the international level. It also raises crucial questions about the nature of human development, about whose task it is to bring it about, and about whether it is ever legitimate to use violence in the struggle for justice.
- The Medellín documents of the Latin American bishops and the response of Pope Paul in *Octogesima Adveniens* (chapter 8) offer the opportunity to explore the value of an inductive approach to social morality, starting from the situation on the ground in the various continents and leading to different solutions in different parts of the world.
- The synod 1971 document "Justice in the World" (chapter 9) raises the vital issue of whether commitment to justice is so central to preaching the gospel that there can be no true evangelization if it is neglected. It also raises two other crucial issues—ecological justice and justice in the Church itself, particularly justice for women.
- Study of the 1975 document "Evangelization in the Modern World" (chapter 10) invites us to examine the notion of liberation in its political, economic, and cultural-religious aspects—and to see how

this relates to the more traditional concepts of salvation and evangelization.

- In chapter 11 we have an examination of the humanistic vision of John Paul II as outlined in his first encyclical and in his major addresses during the early years of his pontificate.
- Chapter 12 raises the issue of the sense in which the Christian and the Church are called to *struggle* for justice—and they invite us to engage in a serious dialogue with the more liberal strands of Marxism on such issues as struggle and alienation. They encourage us to reflect on the related issue of the extent to which Church leaders should set out to empower those who are poor and oppressed and to encourage them to actively resist.
- Chapter 13 has an examination of two later social encyclicals of John Paul that lead us to explore the concept of solidarity and to look closely at the topic of the welfare state.
- In chapter 14 we have the opportunity to see how the Church moved from insisting that "a woman's place is in the home" to defending the equality of women with men and the right of women to take part in public life—and to explore the controversial concept of the complementarity of women and men, and how it relates to the issue of the ordination of women.
- Pope Benedict's first encyclical *Deus Caritas Est* (chapter 15) raises a major issue about the proper role of the development agencies of the Church: Should they draw back from promoting justice, focusing instead mainly on charitable relief? It also explores the question of whether Church leaders should ever become politically involved in openly challenging oppressive governments.
- Benedict's encyclical *Caritas in Veritate* (chapter 16) asks us to look again at the issue of the relationship between justice and love—and invites us to explore ways in which the present soulless economic system can be challenged by an "economy of communion."
- Chapter 17 examines various reactions to *Caritas in Veritate* and goes on to give an account of an important document from the Pontifical Council for Justice and Peace.
- Chapter 18 on ecology offers us the opportunity to examine the growing awareness by Church authorities that environmental issues have become an integral aspect of the justice agenda. We go on to consider whether it may be necessary to relocate all the issues of economic and political justice within the wider context of the ecological crisis that we face today.
- Chapter 19 deals with the teaching and actions of Pope Francis on the issue of poverty and justice, including the issue of how radical Catholic social teaching should be in protesting against the injustices

that seem inseparable from the way the present version of capitalism operates in practice. It also deals with Francis's stance in relation to the crucial issue of structural justice in the Church.

- Chapter 20 gives an account of the teaching of Pope Francis on ecological issues, including a detailed commentary and evaluation of his encyclical on ecology in the light of recent developments in ecological theology.
- Chapter 21 looks at the issue of whether there is an organic or coherent tradition of social teaching in the Catholic Church. Then it lists a wide variety of strengths and weaknesses in this teaching. Finally it offers an extended account of what is involved in an option for the poor and for the Earth.

THE VIEW FROM BELOW

In choosing to write about an option in favor of people who are poor or marginalized, I am not just selecting one particular aspect of Catholic social teaching and leaving aside other important issues of social justice. My belief is that choosing to be in solidarity with those who are poor and opting to work with them for justice gives one a new *perspective* on the other elements of Catholic social teaching such as property rights, human rights, solidarity, subsidiarity, and participation. When a person or group makes this option authentically, they find it possible and necessary to view the world "from the underside." They feel called to shape their lives in the light of this point of view—one that is quite different from the perspective of those who are wealthy and powerful. From my own experience of having lived for some years with poor people in what are (often inaccurately) called "developing countries," I know that all the issues of justice, power, and poverty are seen quite differently when looked at "from below." Many of the actions that seem necessary and sensible to the people "at the top" are experienced by those "at the bottom" as quite outrageously unjust, oppressive, and wrong. As a result, those who make an option for the poor soon find that they have new friends and allies—and new opponents and adversaries.

What is even more important from a Christian point of view is our belief that God "chose what is weak in the world to shame the strong; God chose what is low and despised in the world" (1 Cor. 1:27–28). This implies that those who are weak, poor, marginalized, or disadvantaged are privileged instruments of God in sharing in the saving work of Jesus. This in turn indicates that the poor and the disadvantaged have a privileged role in the prior reading of the "signs of the times," which enables people to discern God's will for themselves, for their communities, and for the wider world. Here then is the biblical basis for saying that Catholic social thought and teaching will be inadequate or distorted unless it gives particular weight to the experience of poor or disadvantaged people.

This scriptural insight is reinforced by the psychological insight that those who have power or higher social status often fail to understand or appreciate the views and feelings of those who are "under" them; and this can blind them to the reality of the world around them (cf. Mindell 1995, 58; also Curran 2002, 184–85). Furthermore, people who are highly educated by Western standards, and who come from countries that have a high degree of economic development, are often infected with a certain cultural arrogance. This causes them to assume that, when they come to deal with poor people or poor countries, they know better than the local people themselves what is good for these poor people or poor countries (cf. Dorr 2007, 256–60). My conclusion from all this is that, if we are to develop an authentic body of Catholic social thought as a basis for Catholic social teaching, it is important that we choose to live in solidarity with the poor and to share in their struggle for justice.

AN ECOLOGICAL PERSPECTIVE

In chapters 18 and 20 of this book I trace the growing awareness in the world and in the Church of the urgency of the ecological issue and the appalling consequences if we fail to take effective action within the next few years to keep the rise in global temperature below two degrees centigrade. The damage that has already been done to our environment is causing major problems to some of the poorest people in our world. Here I mention just three of the more obvious problems. Island countries in the Pacific are already largely submerged in the sea and their inhabitants have to be evacuated—and the same will soon apply to the low-lying parts of densely populated countries like Bangladesh. The melting of the glaciers in the Himalayas poses a huge threat to the millions who live downstream. The pattern of rainfall in a large stretch of eastern and southern Africa has been so disrupted that millions of people have become "famine refugees."

The question of *ecojustice* must now be treated as an overriding issue of the social justice agenda, the background against which all international and national planning decisions about economics need to be taken. In addition to the huge problems that global warming and damage to the environment are causing for the people of today, there is the issue of "intergenerational justice." Our present actions, decisions, and lifestyle are leaving a dreadful legacy for those who come after us. In effect, we are stealing the resources of the people of future generations. Many politicians and other decision makers simply ignore the reality of global warming and ecological damage. Others accept it notionally but fail to take it seriously in practice. Furthermore, some billionaire businesspeople and powerful corporations are funding "think tanks" to provide arguments for denying or playing down the seriousness of ecological issues.

Our own personal decisions about our lifestyle need to be taken in the light of the ecological issue and that of intergenerational justice. The temperature of the air in our homes and places of work, the kind of transport we use to travel to work, the places where we go on holidays, even the kind of food we eat—all these affect the amount of carbon that is spewed into the atmosphere. Obviously, the problems will not be solved unless there is determined political action at the governmental and intergovernmental levels. But we cannot avoid the personal moral challenge by leaving it to our governments to deal with the issue. The problems will not be solved unless there are major changes in our personal lifestyles and in the values we choose to stand for in electing our politicians.

It has become increasingly obvious that even our most pressing economic and political problems need to be situated within the context of the ecological issues that threaten life on Earth as we have come to know it. This is the background against which we need to deal with all the other issues of the social justice agenda. It is for this reason that I have chosen to broaden the title I have given to this book, calling it *Option for the Poor and for the Earth*.

A WIDER BODY OF SOCIAL TEACHING AND SOCIAL THOUGHT

The corpus of official Catholic social teaching is, of course, much wider than the material covered in these documents; there are also many official documents issued by various conferences of bishops in different parts of the world. A comprehensive study of official Catholic social teaching would have to take serious account of this material (cf. Verstraeten 2011, 322–24). The limitations of space and of my own knowledge do not allow me to do so in this book. So I have confined my attention mainly to Vatican teaching. However, I have dealt with documents issued by some bishops' conferences where these are significant for the Church as a whole and especially where they have had an impact on Vatican teaching. For instance, I have given an account of the main thrust of the Medellín and Puebla documents from Latin America and referred more briefly to the pastoral letters on social issues issued by the US Bishops' Conference and to the Basel document issued in 1989 by the Conference of European Churches.

It is important also to emphasize that I am not attempting here to give a full account of Catholic social *thought*. This includes a whole body of theological reflection and writing by theologians on issues of social justice, development, reconciliation, and ecology. Just as importantly, it includes the shared experience and reflection of "on the ground" social activists in organizations such as YCW (Young Christian Workers), Pax Christi, national and local justice-and-peace groups, the Jesuit Refugee Service, Sant'Egidio, and other socially active "new movements," as well as Christian activists not attached to any specific organization (cf. Verstraeten 2011, 326; Coleman 2005, 525). Other important components in Catholic social thought are the principles and guidelines that, over the years, have been worked out and adopted by Catholic agencies that fund and support development and justice work and engage in raising awareness among the wider public and in advocacy and lobbying on these issues (cf. Hogan 2000, 183–90). Not only that, but there is also the ongoing reflection of the leaders and staff of these Catholic relief and development agencies and what Susy Brouard calls the "operant theology" embodied in their actual practice (Brouard 2011, 8–9). So there is "a complex living tradition of practice and thought, a continuing learning process at the point of intersection of gospel with life" (Verstraeten 2011, 314). All this practice and reflection is the matrix from which the official teaching emerges, although very little of it is ever acknowledged in the official documents.

The main material covered in this book is the teaching of the popes, the Second Vatican Council, and various Vatican bodies. In commenting on and evaluating this material I have, however, to the best of my ability and within the limits of the available space, attempted to take account of the wider body both of official teaching of bishops and of the various strands of Catholic social thought to which I have referred in the previous paragraph. The period that I am covering stretches from 1878 to mid-2015. My general aim is to examine how Vatican social teaching developed over that period and to determine in what sense, and to what extent, a consistent, organic tradition has been developed. The more specific aim is to examine the extent to which, during this period, the official teaching of the Vatican was a defense of the poor and powerless in society and an encouragement to them in the struggle for justice.

I have used the phrase "option for the poor" as a convenient way to focus these questions. Since this term is relatively new, it would, of course, be anachronistic to expect to find a clear expression of it in the earlier stages of the teaching of the past 135 years. But it is important to get behind the *term* "option for the poor," so as to look at the *reality* that is designated by the term. That is what I have tried to do throughout this book. I have examined the stances taken by different popes, and by Vatican II, in relation to issues of poverty, injustice, and oppression in society. To what extent were they on the side of the poor and the powerless in the struggle against injustice? That is the key issue—and it arose long before the term "option for the poor" was coined. The advantage of using the concept of an option for the poor is that it provides a standard by which one can assess the reality and thoroughness of the official Church's frequently expressed concern for the poor.

In recent years a number of activists who live and work with poor people object to the use of the term "the poor." They prefer to use the phrase "people who are poor," since this puts the emphasis on the fact that the most important point is that these are *people* and that the fact that they happen to be poor is not what defines them. I think this is an important point, not just a matter of being "politically correct." However, the term "option for the poor" has by now been so widely accepted that I feel it is best to continue to use it, with this brief apology for doing so.

A RESPONSE TO STRUCTURAL INJUSTICE

The term "option for the poor" only came into common usage during the 1970s. Since then it has become the most controversial religious term since the Reformers' cry, "Salvation through faith alone." Hostile critics dismiss the notion as an unlikely cross between Latin American Catholicism and Marxism. But most of those who favor the idea believe that the Church is called to make an option for the poor not merely in Latin America but everywhere else as well. Furthermore, they find the basis for such an option in the Bible rather than in Marx—and they were saying this long before the collapse of the Marxist-inspired governments of Eastern Europe.

The notion of an option for the poor developed in Latin America, as Church leaders there began to implement the renewal sparked off by Vatican II. At the heart of this option were three basic elements:

- First, there was a commitment by Church leaders not to collude with oppressive regimes but to campaign actively for structural justice in society and to take the risk of throwing the authority of the official Church behind efforts to resist oppression and exploitation.
- Second, there was a belief that the key agents in bringing about such change must be the poor, the oppressed, and the marginalized themselves, and therefore a commitment to work "from below" for and with these groups, actively supporting and empowering them.
- Third, there was a commitment to ensure that the Church itself becomes more just and participative. In this way poor and oppressed groups and individuals could have their dignity and value recognized

by being listened to and could have a practical experience of being empowered by participating in decision making at least in the Church. The commitment to justice in the Church itself would also ensure that Church people would have credibility in working for justice in society.

Some people are uneasy about the notion of an option for the poor on the grounds that it implies a rejection of the rich and is therefore incompatible with the Christian message that is intended for all. But, as Albert Nolan pointed out, "The option for the poor is not a choice about the *recipients* of the gospel message, *to whom* we must preach the gospel; it is a matter of *what gospel* we preach to anyone at all. It is concerned with the *content* of the gospel message itself" (Nolan 1986, 18).

An option for the poor is a commitment by individual Christians and the Christian community at every level to engage actively in a struggle to overcome the social injustices that mar our world. To be genuine it must come from a real experience of solidarity with the victims of our society. This means that one aspect of an option for the poor has to do with sharing in some degree in the lives, sorrows, joys, hopes, and fears of those who are on the margins of society. Without this, the attempt to serve the interests of "the poor" will be patronizing—and it will make them feel more powerless and dependent than ever. But an option for the poor is not primarily the choice of a less affluent lifestyle by individuals or groups. It is a commitment to resist the *structural injustice* that marks our world. The person who makes such an option is undertaking to work to change the unjust economic, social, and political structures that determine how power and resources are shared out in the world—and also in the Church. The aim is to bring about a just society.

The word "option" suggests a personal choice. While continuing to put emphasis on this personal aspect, I would want to insist that the choice in question is not essentially an act of private asceticism or even of face-to-face compassion for a poor person. It is specifically a response directed toward change at the level of the wider society as a whole, a response to the unjust ordering of society. Therefore, it makes sense only in the context of an awareness of how society is, in fact, structured.

We live in a stratified society where certain economic, political, cultural, and religious structures maintain and promote the dominance of the rich and powerful over the mass of ordinary people and peoples. These structures operate through agencies and institutions that are staffed mainly by middle-class people—those who provide the professional and commercial services of society. Whatever their private loyalties and values, these service people contribute to structural injustice through the kind of work they are doing. The possibility of making an option for the poor arises for such people, and it is mainly to them that the challenge is issued. Some of the services provided by the churches are an integral part of the institutions of society, for instance, educational or medical institutions in various countries. Those who are working in, or responsible for, Church services of this kind are asking themselves whether their work, however good it may be in itself, is an adequate embodiment of the Church's commitment to justice in society.

An option for the poor, in the sense in which it is intended here, means a series of choices, personal or communal, made by individuals, by communities, or even by corporate entities such as a religious congregation, a diocese, or a Church (as represented by its central administration, and, in varying degrees, by its ordinary members). It is the choice to disentangle themselves from serving the interests of those at the "top" of society and to begin instead to come into solidarity with those at or near the bottom. Such solidarity means commitment to working and living within structures and agencies that promote the interests of the less-favored sectors of society. These would include those who are economically poor, the groups that are politically marginalized or oppressed, people discriminated against on sexual grounds, peoples that have been culturally silenced or oppressed, and those who have been religiously disinherited or deprived.

What about people who are themselves poor? They too have to make a choice. We should not think only of an option *for* the poor by those who are not themselves poor. There is need also for an option *by* the poor. Many of them may at times be tempted to overcome their poverty by taking advantage of others—perhaps by turning to extortion and crime. For poor and oppressed people the option that faces them is whether they will choose to work in solidarity with others to challenge the unjust structures of society.

In the final pages of chapter 21 I have offered a fairly comprehensive systematic account of what is involved in an option for the poor and for the Earth; and I have also included some clarification on the topic as part of chapter 12. I have written more extensively on the topic elsewhere, with special reference to how the more experiential aspect of such an option (sharing the life of "the poor") might be fitted together with the more organizational aspects (building alternative structures) (Dorr 1984, 1990, and 1991). I have also set out to clarify the distinction between a biblically based option for the poor and the Marxist concept of "a class option" (Dorr 2000, 250–53).

In recent years many earnest Christians who have been trying to discern "the signs of the times" in renewal courses and assemblies find themselves challenged to make an option for the poor. Yet, having worked with many groups of this kind, I have come to believe that many of those who are faced with this challenge do not really know what it involves. Some find the term "option for the poor" both confusing and threatening, for it puts a question mark over their present way of life and previous commitments. Fears and guilt create an aura of ambiguity around the term as well as some selective blindness. Frequently the most helpful approach is to provide some kind of biblical background and to trace the recent development in Church action, reflection, and teaching. This allows people space to answer the questions for themselves.

There is a close link between the concept of an option for the poor and the practice of liberation theology. It is no coincidence that both emerged at the same time in the same Latin American milieu. One of the main reasons why many Church people in the West have difficulties in relation to option for the poor is that they have no real sympathy with the whole project of liberation theology. This applies to three different categories of Christians in the West.

- The first category of these are people who see an option for the poor as a version of the Marxist class option or are opposed to it on the grounds that it is a politicization of the faith. These people are not at all opposed to helping the poor. But they see liberation theology as a dangerous threat to the stability of society and to the teaching authority of Church leaders.
- In the second category are religious communities or individual Christians who feel guilty about the poverty all round them and want to share the life of the poor. They may revise their constitutions or their personal ideals by undertaking an option for the poor. But they may have very little understanding of the *political* aspects of such an option. They may also fail to advert to the fact that what is in question is not just living poorly, but an empowering of "the poor" through searching *with* them for the meaning of Christian faith in our world. If such individuals or groups are to come to a more authentic understanding of what is meant by an option for the poor, they need to get some sense of the whole project that is liberation theology—not as a set of theories but as a way of exploring with "ordinary" people the relevance of Jesus to our daily lives. This can soon lead to effective challenges to the power structures of state or Church.
- The third category includes many of those who feel called to struggle for justice in the economic and political spheres. They see this as part of their Christian vocation, but they assume that it is to be carried out according to the usual Western model of political organization or lobbying. Frequently, then, they end up organizing *on behalf of* the poor but not really working very effectively *with* them. For them, too, the project that is liberation theology can open up an entirely

new way of being with "ordinary" or marginalized people; out of this comes a better understanding of what is meant by an option for the poor.

THE BIBLICAL CONCEPT OF POVERTY

In the Old Testament, the term "the poor" refers especially to those groups of people who are economically deprived, who have no social status, who are treated unjustly by foreign rulers or by the authorities in their own land. These people are oppressed because they are poor and are therefore at the mercy of the unscrupulous. Furthermore, they are poor because they are oppressed: they have been further impoverished by being cheated and deprived of their rights. Some groups of "the poor" are doubly oppressed. They are the people who are at risk not only because they are economically poor, but also because they happen to be widows, orphans, or resident aliens—categories of people who have nobody to defend them against exploitation.

The Old Testament leaves us in no doubt that God has a special care for "the poor." The oppression of God's people in Egypt moved Yahweh to save them, as the Book of Exodus recounts. After the Israelites had settled in "the Promised Land" the poor among them found themselves oppressed by the wealthy and powerful of their own people. Time after time God sent the prophets to protest against this injustice and to proclaim God's care for the poor.

The New Testament deepens our understanding of what it means to be poor. In some important respects, Jesus himself should be seen as one of "the poor." Having "emptied himself" to share our humanity (Phil. 2:7), he became a native of a despised village (John 1:46) and was known as a carpenter's son (Matt. 13:55). He resisted the temptation to carry out his mission through the use of glory and power (Matt. 4:5–10). He was the innocent victim of persecution and was executed as a criminal after an unjust trial.

The Bible makes it clear that religious leaders can also exercise power unjustly. The reaction of Jesus to the scribes and Pharisees, as portrayed in the New Testament, suggests that he sees them as oppressors, imposing their will on the mass of ordinary believers (e.g., Matt. 15:3–20, 23:4–38). In challenging this abuse of power, Jesus was standing in the tradition of Moses and the prophets who cried out against economic injustice and political oppression. Defense of the poor includes standing up for those who are powerless before religious authorities who abuse their power.

Some Christians today hold that the New Testament is more concerned about "poverty of spirit" than about material poverty. However, a study of the theme of poverty in the Bible suggests that it is not helpful to make too sharp a distinction between "the poor" and those who are "poor in spirit." The scriptures indicate that those who are poor and defenseless have nobody to turn to but God. God has a special care for the victims of injustice and those who are poor; and they in turn can more easily accept the divine care and protection. Of course, poor people can also turn *away* from God—through bitterness and lack of hope. But in general it is more likely that those who are economically and politically poor will also be "poor in spirit," dependent on God and open to God. Of course, rich people may also turn to God; but so long as they remain attached to wealth and rely on their own power, it is almost impossible for them to be "poor in spirit" and to enter God's realm (cf. Matt. 19:24).

These brief points from scripture go some way toward clarifying what an option for the poor means—and what it does not mean. Such an option, seen in a biblical perspective, would mean some special care or preference for people or groups who are marginalized in human society. It is quite true that there is a sense in which *everybody* is "poor before God." But this idea can be invoked as a way of evading the central thrust of the biblical teaching about poverty. The meaning of the word "poor" can be extended and redefined to a point where the challenge of the scriptural position gets lost. In chapter 12 of this book the question of the meaning of the word "poor" is treated in a little more detail, and there I examine the different senses in which one might speak of the "poverty" of rich people.

MY APPROACH

In this study I have not limited myself to looking at the most formal Church documents such as papal encyclicals. In order to present the teaching of some popes, especially Pius XII and John Paul II, I found it necessary to take account of many of the more important addresses that represent the thinking of the popes. I take it that the various documents and statements represent the considered views of their official authors, no matter who may have prepared the drafts. So I have not devoted much attention to the question of who drafted the various documents. But where information on this matter is available, I have taken account of it.

Up to the time in 1961 when Pope John XXIII issued his encyclical *Mater et Magistra*, most Catholic commentaries on the social encyclicals treated them as quite beyond any overt criticism—though in practice each commentator interpreted them in the light of his or her own viewpoint. Since 1961, however, papal teaching is no longer assured of a welcome even from all Catholics. Some liberal theologians and commentators criticize them, at times unfairly. However, many conservatives comment on them with a certain sycophantic fundamentalism while picking out and emphasizing the parts that fit in with their own viewpoint and ig- noring or playing down other parts. The result, of course, is that the real message of these important documents can become distorted before it reaches many ordinary Christians. There is need for a serious and objec- tive evaluation of these documents, and my hope is that this book will contribute to such a study.

In evaluating the views and actions of Church leaders, I have tried to take account of their historical situation. In this way I hope to provide a background to present-day issues and to throw light on the overall pat- tern of the Church's teaching. But the book is intended to be theology as much as history. I do not think it is possible to write history from some totally detached or uncommitted point of view. Objectivity is not attained by abandoning all commitment; and commitment to social justice is part of the Christian faith in the light of which I have carried out this study. This faith has affected my choice of data and my understanding and evaluation of the material.

My faith has even had an effect on the way I have written the book. I have tried to take account of the fact that the social teaching of the Church is a personal challenge to each of us. This challenge can get lost if the presentation is unduly academic. Academic accounts of Catholic social teaching can easily give the impression of complacency, as though the Church were outside history, sitting in judgment on various social systems (e.g., Charles 1982; Herr 1991). I know from experience that many Christians who are working for justice are eager to study the Church's social teaching. But they want it presented in a way that relates it to practical commitment. And they would like the presentation to be not only objective, but also challenging and even inspirational. My hope is that readers will find some enlightenment and some inspiration in at least some chapters of the book.

In this book I use the phrase "social teaching." This calls for a brief com- ment. Up to the 1960s the term "Catholic social doctrine" was commonly used. However, toward the end of Vatican II this term fell into theological disrepute. Some theologians felt it smacked of a timeless dogmatism that would be particularly inappropriate in matters of social morality where the emphasis of Church teaching has changed so much over the years. Others objected to the notion of a "Catholic social doctrine" or even a "Catholic social teaching" on the grounds that this phrase suggests that the Church has a body of principles and a model of society that amount to a "third way," that is, an alternative to the capitalist and socialist models; this they considered unacceptable.

In chapter 11 of the book I have discussed these issues. Here it suffices to say that Pope John Paul II and, following him, Pope Benedict XVI have succeeded to some extent in reinstating the term "social doctrine," using it alongside "social teaching" and similar terms. But this does not mean a return to the situation of the 1930s when many Catholics thought the Church had a blueprint for society. For these popes, social "doctrine" or teaching does not mean an immutable set of truths. They see it rather as an organic tradition of teaching by the Church on social issues. This tradition is open to development; and each of these popes believes that he has made his own contribution to it. They do not see it primarily as a matter of laying down rules for how society should be organized. They believe rather that the Church has a duty to teach and witness certain basic truths about the human person and certain fundamental human values that ought to be respected in society. It is within the context of such an organic tradition of social teaching that the notion of an option for the poor can best be understood.

* * *

SUMMARY

This study of Catholic social teaching examines the extent to which the Church's teaching is an effective defense of the poor and powerless in society and an encouragement to them in the struggle for justice as well as an effective response to the pressing issue of environmental justice. The concept of an option for the poor is a standard by which one can assess the depth and effectiveness of the Church's concern for the poor. It also provides a unique point of view that throws light on all the other topics dealt with in Catholic social teaching. Furthermore, it has now become clear that there is a close link between justice for those who are poor and respect for our environment. In the course of this historical study, the main themes of that teaching come to the fore; and they are dealt with not just as matters of history but as challenges that still face us today.

An option for the poor is a commitment to struggle against structural injustice. Those who make such an option are in solidarity with the victims of our society, and with them they set out to work for a more equitable sharing of power and resources in society and in the Church. This commitment has a solid base in the biblical teaching about the attitude of God toward injustice, oppression, and poverty.

The notion of an option for the poor gives rise to confusion or a sense of threat in those who do not have a sympathetic understanding of the approach of the liberation theologians. These theologians try to be with "ordinary" people, especially people who are poor or disadvantaged, in their struggle to make the world and the Church more just and more humane. A crucial aspect of an option for the poor is a commitment to work with people who are poor or oppressed, helping them explore and articulate the relation between their faith and the reality of their lives.

This study of the Church's teaching seeks to interpret our history in the light of a faith commitment and to combine objectivity with challenge.

QUESTIONS FOR REVIEW

1. *What are the political aspects of an option for the poor and for the Earth?*
2. *What is meant by "the view from below"?*
3. *What more is involved in an "option for the poor and for the Earth" over and above political action?*
4. *To whom does the term "the poor" apply in the Bible?*
5. *What connection is there between revelation and the experience of the poor?*
6. *Is it anachronistic to examine the social teaching of a hundred years ago in the light of the concept of an option for the poor and for the Earth?*

QUESTIONS FOR REFLECTION

1. *What would it mean to engage in a project of liberation theology in your country? Who are attempting such a project?*
2. *Who are "the poor" and who are "the powerful" in the world today, in your own country, in the Church?*

ISSUES FOR FURTHER STUDY

1. *The poor and the oppressed in the Bible. Read Tamez 1982.*
2. *Jesus and liberation theology. Read Sobrino 1989.*

2

Pope Leo XIII and *Rerum Novarum*

In 1891 Pope Leo XIII issued *Rerum Novarum,* the first of the great social encyclicals. In it he protested strongly against the harsh conditions that industrial workers had to endure. It is sometimes cynically suggested that Leo was moved to issue it more by the loss to the Church of the working classes of Europe than by their exploitation and suffering. No doubt he was anxious to ensure that the Church should not be rejected by the mass of the new urban poor. But that is no reason to cast doubt on the genuineness of his protest about their treatment. This protest did not spring from Leo's own firsthand experience, for he had not previously been actively involved in a campaign on behalf of workers; he was more of a scholar and diplomat than an activist. It would be wrong to suggest that *Rerum Novarum* represents an entirely new beginning, for there is a good deal of coherence between it and papal teaching of the previous 150 years (see Coleman 1991, 3–4). Nevertheless it represents a significant turning point in the tradition.

The encyclical was written in response to a strong and constantly growing pressure from many sources, including distinguished Church leaders in Europe and America whose views were respected by Leo.[1] They wanted an authoritative statement from the pope partly because it would be a powerful support to all who were protesting against the exploitation of workers and partly because it would make Catholics less likely to adopt the "extreme" views put forward by various champions of the working classes (for background, see Molony 1991, 8–63).

Anybody who reads *Rerum Novarum* today, more than 120 years after it was written, may feel that the changes it calls for are not radical and

---

[1]For a helpful overview of the economic, political, and religious background of the period, see Shannon (2005, 127–34). Shannon's commentary also has a full account of the writing of the document and the changes in its different drafts. See also Molony 1991, 64–105; Duncan 1991, 69–70; and Naudet 2011, 251–52. In an interesting article, Michael Walsh (2012, 157–59) emphasizes the highly conservative milieu out of which the encyclical came to be written and particularly the corporatist philosophy that was favored by most of those who were calling for an intervention by the pope.

that it is rather vague in regard to how they should be brought about. Clearly, it does not go nearly as far as the encyclicals of recent popes in articulating the requirements of social justice and in offering specific criticisms of the structures and practices that lead to poverty and oppression. Nevertheless, it lays a solid foundation on which the later social encyclicals and other Church documents could build.

Though the content of Leo's encyclical was important and remains important, what was perhaps most important was the character of the document as a cry of protest against the exploitation of poor workers. It is not so much the detail of what Leo had to say that was significant but the fact that he chose to speak out at that time, intervening in a most solemn way in a burning issue of the day. His intervention meant that the Church could not be taken to be indifferent to the injustices of the time. Rather, it was seen to be taking a stand on behalf of the poor.

That Catholic Church leaders since that time have frequently spoken out strongly on issues of social injustice makes it difficult to appreciate just how significant it was that Pope Leo should issue his encyclical at that time. An analogy may help. Suppose the present pope were to issue an encyclical maintaining that it is quite immoral for any nation or individual to make or handle nuclear weapons. Commentators might say that this was simply an application of known principles of morality. But the document would have enormous significance as an intervention that committed the Vatican firmly to a specific practical application of general moral principles. It would put the pope firmly on the side of the nuclear disarmers and against those who hold that nuclear weapons are necessary. In a somewhat similar way, *Rerum Novarum* represents a definite moral stance by the pope. It committed the Catholic Church officially to a rejection of a central thesis of the liberal capitalism of the Western world, namely, that labor is a commodity to be bought at market prices determined by the law of supply and demand rather than by the human needs of the worker (e.g., *RN* 16–17, 33–34).[2] So already in this first of the social encyclicals, there was a strong protest against the prevailing order.

It is clear that Leo XIII intended his encyclical to be a major intervention in defense of the poor. He solemnly and firmly proposed his teaching as a remedy for the social problems of the time (*RN* 13), at the heart of which were "the misery and wretchedness pressing so unjustly on the majority of the working class" (*RN* 2); and he saw such an intervention as necessary because "a small number of very rich people have been able

---

[2]It should be noted that the numbering of the paragraphs used at present in the English-language version of *Rerum Novarum* on the Vatican website is different from the more widely used numbering that I use here.

to lay upon the teeming masses of the laboring poor a yoke little better than that of slavery itself" (*RN* 2).

Looked at from the point of view of its effect, this first of the social encyclicals must be seen as a significant move of the Church toward the side of the poor. It ensured that social issues could no longer be treated as marginal or secondary to the mission of the Church or as an "optional extra." This applied not merely in the sphere of official teaching but also in practical commitment. *Rerum Novarum* gave great encouragement to those of the clergy and laity who had been working for years to get the Catholic Church involved in social issues; and it had the long-term effect of greatly increasing the numbers of such committed activists. So if one judges in terms of the effects over a considerable period of years, it is correct to say with Alec Vidler that the encyclical "had a truly epoch-making effect in driving home the idea that Catholics must have a social conscience" (Vidler 1964, 127). But this did not happen overnight. Practical and theological obstacles made for uneven and slow progress in some sectors of society. In fact, the encyclical was at first largely ignored by many of the people with whom it was most directly concerned—employers, industrial workers, and even some churchmen. In some places, such as Latin America, it was scarcely read at all. Where it was read, it was not always accepted. It gave rise to some scandal, not only in society but even within the Church itself (cf. Chenu 1979, 15, 18; Molony 1991, 123–29; Murray 1953c, 551; McGovern 1980, 99; Pius XI, *QA* 14).

The reason for this shocked reaction and the resistance that accompanied it was not so much any specific course of action proposed by the pope. It was rather the much more fundamental point that he challenged the current assumption that the "laws" of economics should be treated as though they were laws of nature and therefore the basis for morality. Pope Leo issued this challenge at the most obvious point of all, which is also the most sensitive point: he questioned the sacrosanct nature of the wage contract. He rejected the assumption that the employer's obligations in justice can be taken to have been fulfilled once the agreed-upon wage has been paid. Leo insisted that "there underlies a dictate of natural justice more imperious and ancient than any bargain between one person and another, namely that wages ought not to be insufficient to support a frugal and well-behaved wage-earner" (*RN* 34). He drew the conclusion that if "through necessity or fear of a worse evil," the worker accepts a wage less than that required for frugal living, then "that person is made the victim of force and injustice" (*RN* 34; cf. Shannon 2005, 138–39). None of this involved any radical new departure in Catholic moral theology. For instance, the same general principles were applied by moral theologians of that period in their assessment of the morality of "secret compensation": they judged that it was morally acceptable for workers to supplement an unjust wage by petty pilfering. Nevertheless, in the atmosphere of the time, it was really quite shocking that Leo should bluntly apply these general principles to a situation that was so widespread. It amounted to a clear and outspoken contradiction of the taken-for-granted views of those who held power in the Western world.

The basic principle behind Leo's stance is that human labor cannot be treated simply as a commodity because to do so is to deny human dignity and reduce the worker to the status of a thing. Needless to say, there is nothing startling in Leo's assertion that it is shameful and inhuman to treat people as though they were things. But for a pope to invoke this principle in defense of underpaid workers was quite startling—shocking for some and inspiring for others. That is why it can be claimed that the importance of *Rerum Novarum* is to be measured not merely in terms of its contribution to the body of teaching (or "doctrine") of the Catholic Church but also in terms of its impact as an intervention on the side of the poor: that is what we may call the "effective" meaning of the document in contrast to its "doctrinal" meaning.

REJECTION OF SOCIALISM AND
OF LAISSEZ-FAIRE CAPITALISM

It is only in the context of this overriding purpose and effective meaning of *Rerum Novarum* that we can understand properly the point of the fairly lengthy section of the encyclical that is devoted to a treatment of socialism (*RN* 16). It is sometimes assumed that the main purpose of *Rerum Novarum* was to condemn socialism and that the encyclical is "the Church's answer to socialism." This view was given a particular credibility in the English-speaking world by the fact that the standard English translation gave a rather free rendering of the very first words of the encyclical. It spoke of "a desire for revolutionary change." This phrase evoked fears of the turmoil of revolution and could convey the impression that the main aim of the pope was to speak out against the revolutionary ideas of Marx. In fact, the official Italian text makes it clear that, in using the words "*Rerum Novarum*," the pope was speaking of the "burning desire for change" that was characteristic of the period (cf. Molony 1991, 102–3). Leo's main purpose was to speak out not against Marxist revolution but against the exploitation of workers carried out in the name of liberal capitalism. As the historian John Molony (1991, 103) says, "Then or later, to caricature the encyclical by a free translation of its first line as merely another condemnation of socialism was to cast a gloss on its meaning which Leo never intended, despite the trenchant criticism of socialism which it contained."

Leo was undoubtedly concerned about socialism. This is evident from the fact that he had already condemned it on a number of occasions. In *Rerum Novarum* he set out not merely to reject it, but also to refute it (*RN* 3–12), but it must be said that his account does scant justice to the views of moderate socialists of the time. It is clear that Leo considered this part of the encyclical to have an importance in its own right: it warned off the small but significant number of radical Catholics who were flirting with socialist ideas. However, his formal rejection of socialism also served a different and wider purpose. It gave Leo the freedom to condemn the abuses within the existing capitalist system without leaving himself open to the accusation that he favored socialism.

Despite its strong rejection of socialism, the encyclical must have appeared to many to be tainted with socialist principles on one vital issue—the question of intervention by the state. Leo was already radically challenging the principles of liberal capitalism by his insistence on the need for the state to intervene at times in economic affairs (cf. Molony 1991, 123; also Shannon 2005, 141); to many of the people of his time, his adoption of this stance meant that he had already gone over to socialism. It is true that in the early part of the document, the pope lays down very strict limits to the right of the state to intervene in the affairs of the individual and the family (*RN* 6, 9, 10, 11).[3] But later on in the encyclical, he makes particular mention of the duty of the state to be concerned for the interests of the working classes, that is, the poor (*RN* 27). He explains his position as follows: "When there is question of defending the rights of individuals, the poor and badly-off have a claim to especial consideration. The richer class have many ways of shielding themselves . . . whereas the mass of the poor . . . must chiefly depend upon the assistance of the State" (*RN* 29). In later paragraphs the pope specifies various ways in which the state should protect workers from abuse and exploitation (*RN* 32–34). This whole approach involved a rejection of the principles of laissez-faire capitalism, especially as expounded by the Manchester school.

From the point of view of its doctrine, *Rerum Novarum* can be seen as a balanced statement of general principles that rejects the two extremes—socialism, on the one hand, and uncontrolled capitalism, on the other. But when one considers its effective meaning as an intervention by the pope in the social issues of the time, it is clear that it is an attempt to place the Catholic Church on the side of the poor—or of the working class, which at that time was more or less the same thing.[4] It succeeded

---

[3]For a helpful account of Leo's position on the limits of the state's competence and duty of intervention in economic affairs, see Murray 1953, 552–56.

[4]In *RN* 29 Leo contrasts the "richer class" with "the mass of the poor" and adds that wage earners "mostly belong to that class" (i.e., the poor).

in doing so to a considerable extent—at least insofar as it was the first major official step in a long process that has been continuing, with some ups and downs, up to the present.

However, a clarification is called for at once: the encyclical did not attempt to put the Church on the side of the working class against another class. What it was against was not a group or class but simply the reality of exploitation. So it did not represent a "class option" in the usual sense of the term. In fact, a major concern of the pope was to bridge the gap between the classes of society. For instance, he said that in a state it is "ordained by nature that these two classes should dwell in harmony and agreement" (*RN* 15); and later in the encyclical he expressed his aim: "The gulf between vast wealth and sheer poverty will be bridged over, and the respective classes will be brought nearer to one another" (*RN* 35). Nevertheless, this in no way detracts from Leo XIII's firm stand in this encyclical on the side of the mass of exploited workers in the society of the time. It would be overstating the case to claim that *Rerum Novarum* represents or calls for "an option for the poor" in the sense in which that term is generally understood today, but it indicates that the pope had a particular concern for the poor and that, as we look back, it can be seen as a major step on the road that eventually led to such an option.

I must add at once that the spirituality enshrined in *Rerum Novarum* is quite different from that which is associated with the making of an option for the poor. A clue to Leo's spirituality is to be found in the changes that were made to the text of *Rerum Novarum* while it was being composed. In the first draft of the encyclical the opening words presented the pope as speaking on behalf of "the God who wants to be present in the poor." But this was edited out in later versions, and the tone was changed so that the pope was presented instead as the one who puts before the world the truth that has been entrusted to the Church. Furthermore, the later drafts included a strong insistence on Christian resignation that had been absent from the first draft (cf. Molony 1991, 67, 79, 81). As I shall point out, Pope Leo advocated a spirituality that would now be seen as "escapist"; he encouraged the poor to put up with their lot by reminding them of the rewards of the life to come.

THE PROPOSED REMEDY

Pope Leo gave the impression that in *Rerum Novarum* he was putting forward the Church's "remedy" (*RN* 12) for the social problem. The encyclical suggests that if this remedy were applied, it would eliminate the grave injustices of the existing system and bring harmony to the social and economic order. But was the pope actually proposing a realistic solution? Granted that he was seeking to defend the poor against exploitation, was he also proposing a coherent program that could bring this about in practice? Or was there a gap between the aim he wished to attain and the means he proposed?

What kind of changes does Leo XIII have in mind? As already noted, *Rerum Novarum* insists on the duty of the state to protect the poor (*RN* 29). This amounts to a call for a major change in the role that the state had been playing in society in Leo's time. In order to understand and assess the pope's call, it is helpful to consider an issue frequently overlooked by moralists—the relation between economic power and political power.

We can look briefly at two contrasting views of the role of the state in society. (By "the state" I understand here the apparatus of government that has power to control the way people act in society.) First, there is the classical theory of liberal capitalism. It held that the state should mainly confine itself to "political" matters, such as defending society from external aggression and ensuring internal order and stability; normally the government should not "interfere" in the economic sphere but should rather allow private enterprise, open competition, and the forces of the market to operate freely. The assumption here is that the state and its agencies (the judiciary, the security forces, the civil service, etc.) are "neutral" and independent in relation to any economic rivalries or conflicts that take place in society; their task is to provide the framework within which economic activity can take place peacefully and effectively.

In sharp contrast to this is the Marxist theory. It holds that, in fact, the state is not neutral; political power is normally held by those with economic power—and, as one might expect, they use the apparatus of the state to further their own interests; the lower classes find that the laws and the security forces are being used to oppress them and to ensure that they cannot escape from the economic exploitation practiced by those who control the wealth.

What was the view of Leo XIII? He disagreed with both of the above views. But in speaking about the role of the state in *Rerum Novarum* he comes fairly close to each of the two views at different times. His ideal of what the state ought to be, though it differs significantly from that of liberal capitalism, nevertheless shares with the latter the assumption that the state is neutral and "above" economics. But Leo's account of what happens *in practice* is closer to the Marxist view.

According to the principles laid down by Leo, economic power ought not to overlap with political power. In society as it ought to be, the wealthy would not control the apparatus of the state. Instead, the state would be above the interests of all classes and would keep a balance between them (*RN* 26–27). Leo maintains that cooperation rather than conflict is to be the basis of the social order: "The great mistake . . . is to take up the notion that class is naturally hostile to class, and that the wealthy and working-classes are intended by nature to live in mutual conflict" (*RN* 15). The reason this mistaken view was held, the pope believed, lay in the failure to appreciate the design of nature for the body politic, a design that he described in organic terms: "Just as the symmetry of the human frame is the result of the suitable arrangement of the different parts of the body, so in a state is it ordained by nature that these two classes should dwell in harmony and agreement, so as to maintain the balance of the body politic. Each needs the other: Capital cannot do without Labour, nor Labour without Capital" (*RN* 15). In Leo's view the institutions of the state have the task of preserving and fostering the cooperation of the different classes. This means that, in principle, the state is neutral; it is not the instrument of the richer class.

However, a quite different account of the state is suggested by the actual situation as it had evolved up to the time when the encyclical was written. Looking at what had taken place all around him, Pope Leo did not gloss over the obvious fact that in practice the rich were the ones who held the effective power, a power that extended into the apparatus of the state: "On the one side there is the party which holds power because it holds wealth; . . . which manipulates for its own benefit . . . all the sources of supply, and which is even represented in the councils of the State itself. On the other side there is the needy and powerless multitude" (*RN* 35).

Faced with this reality, Leo proposed his long-term solution: the gulf between the classes should be narrowed by enabling as many workers as possible to become owners of property (*RN* 35). This indicates that he recognized that, in practice, so long as wealth is concentrated in the hands of the few, these few are likely to have undue political power and will use this power for their own benefit. In other words, so long as most of the wealth of the nation is in the hands of one sector of society, the state will be hindered in playing its proper role of protecting the rights of the poor. Leo was well aware that this was actually happening; that is why he insisted so strongly on the need for the state to protect the rights of workers and why he went on to list several of these rights (*RN* 26–34).

We have now noted two of the key changes that Leo proposed as a remedy for the social problem: immediate action by the state to protect the interests of the working classes and a long-term effort to distribute ownership of property much more widely. The next question is who or what are to be the agents of change that can ensure that the remedy is really applied and the changes take place? How can one make sure that those who have the power to make the changes have the will to do so—and that those who want the changes are in a position to bring them about?

Pope Leo gives a double answer to this question. First, he insists on the vital role that the Church has to play in society. Second, he defends the right of workers to band together in trade unions or other associations for their own protection (*RN* 36). Unfortunately, however, each of these two sources or agents of change is open to serious challenge in the form in which it is presented in *Rerum Novarum*. In the following two sections of this chapter, I shall consider each point in turn.

HOW PROPHETIC CAN THE CHURCH DARE TO BE?

First of all, Leo insists strongly on the right of the Church to play a major role in shaping society; in fact, this is one of the vital points on which he challenges the assumptions of liberal capitalism (cf. Molony 1991, 123). The "liberal" view was that religion is largely a private affair. Leo, in contrast, held that religion is the most powerful intermediary of all in drawing the rich and the working class together; and he saw the Church as the spokesperson for religion in reminding each class of its duties to the other and especially of the obligations of justice (*RN* 16). In Leo's view the Church has a task that would nowadays be called "prophetic"—that of challenging each of the classes of society to meet its obligations in justice to the others. But how can the Church best promote cooperation and respect, combined with justice, in the relations between the classes? Leo's view—and his difficulties—can best be understood by looking at two contrasting strategies.

One possible approach is to call the rich and powerful to conversion, while exhorting the poor and powerless to be patient—and especially to respect public order in the way they seek their rights. In this approach those who hold power would be encouraged not merely to change their hearts but also to change the structures of society so that injustice would be eliminated.

A different strategy would be to animate the poor to demand their rights. They would be encouraged not simply to wait patiently for justice but rather to confront the rich and powerful when this proves necessary. The Church could assure them that God is the God of the poor, who supports those who feel called to act like Moses in challenging the injustice of the powerful.

Are the two policies mutually exclusive? Partly, but not entirely. It is possible for Church leaders to appeal to the rich while animating the poor. But the two strategies differ fundamentally on one major point— whether the poor ought to be encouraged to wait patiently or to engage where necessary in active confrontation. The difference between the two approaches is based above all on the different degree of importance each of the two approaches gives to the value of stability in society. In the first approach, stability is seen as a very high value, so indispensable that one dare not put it at risk. In the second approach, stability is seen as an important value but not one of overriding importance. It is seen as a value that must at times be risked in order to ensure justice in society; furthermore, it is considered that the best guarantee of long-term stability is to ensure that society is just.

How does Leo's approach relate to these two possible strategies? It must be said that he adopted a position much nearer to the first approach than to the second—and this was because he was so convinced of the importance of stability in society. There is no doubt that he wanted major changes. But what he had in mind was change "from the top down" rather than "from the bottom up." He issued a ringing call to conversion to the people who held economic power. But what if this call goes largely unheeded? Then it appears that, for Leo, those who are part of the poor working class have little option but to put up with their sad situation. Toward the end of this chapter I consider various encyclicals and writings of Leo in order to provide a background against which his approach in *Rerum Novarum* can be understood more clearly. But *Rerum Novarum* itself throws quite a lot of light on the pope's attitude, both in what it says and in what it fails to say.

A central paragraph in the encyclical lists the reciprocal duties of employers and workers, duties of which the Church reminds them in order to promote harmony and justice. First, those of the employers:

> The following duties bind the wealthy owner and the employer: not to look upon their work-people as their bondsmen but to respect in every person his or her dignity and worth. . . . They are reminded that . . . to misuse people as though they were things in the pursuit of gain . . . is truly shameful and inhuman. . . . Furthermore, employers must never tax their work-people beyond their strength, or employ them in work unsuited to their sex and age. Their great and principal duty is to give every one what is just. . . . To gather one's profit out of the need of another, is condemned by all laws human and divine. . . . Lastly, the rich must religiously refrain from cutting down the workers' earnings, whether by force, by fraud, or by usurious dealing. (*RN* 16–17)

This whole passage constitutes a very moving call for conversion—and not just a change of heart but significant changes in business practice and standards of behavior in the economic world. However, there is an element of unrealism in it, for, unfortunately, Leo is making a rhetorical statement rather than one that is literally true when he says that "all laws human and divine" condemn those who "gather [their] profit out of the need of another." In his own time, as well as before and after his time, there have been some human laws that allow such exploitation. It is precisely at this point that a wide gap exists between the laws governing business in an unbridled liberal capitalist society and what the Church sees as the divine law.

What if this gap still remains, in spite of Pope Leo's eloquent appeal? What is the pope's response if employers continue to neglect the duties he has listed, if they fail to respect their workers, if they still fail to pay a just wage, and if they tax them beyond their strength? What if the wealthy continue to make a profit out of the need of the poor? Above all, what if the laws of the state continue to allow this exploitation to take place and if the law courts and security forces fail to offer the poor adequate protection against these injustices? These are not hypothetical questions. The pope was well aware that injustices of this kind were a permanent feature of the social situation of his time. One is entitled, therefore, to ask what action he recommends to workers in the face of such abuses.

The following is a list of some of the duties that *Rerum Novarum* lays down for workers: "fully and faithfully to perform the work which has been freely and equitably agreed upon; never to injure the property, nor outrage the person, of an employer; never to resort to violence in defending their own cause, nor to engage in riot or disorder; and to have nothing to do with people of evil principles, who ... excite foolish hope" (*RN* 16). This catalogue gives very little encouragement to activism on the part of workers in the struggle for rights. Not merely does it not give any guidelines by which workers might determine how far they could go in a situation of confrontation, but it does not appear to envisage that they might be entitled to engage in any serious confrontation. For instance, workers are told that they must not injure the property of an employer. It is not clear whether Leo adverted to the implications of this teaching. If taken strictly, it would seem to imply that a strike is wrong whenever it causes damage to the property of an employer. Did the pope really want to go as far as that?

In a later paragraph of the encyclical he says that when a strike poses an imminent threat of public disturbance, the law may be invoked to protect the peace (*RN* 29). This implies, of course, that a strike may be lawful where it does not pose such a threat. But it is significant that Leo's main emphasis is on circumstances that would make a strike wrong rather than on those that would justify it. Two paragraphs later he acknowledges that strikes occur, points out their causes and consequences, but does not make an explicit judgment about their morality (*RN* 31).

Leo XIII was well aware that insistence by workers on their rights in the economic sphere could quickly spill over into the political area and give rise to a threat to public order. His reluctance to encourage the working class to press militantly for their rights stems from his belief that nothing should be done that might cause such a "disturbance." The pope wanted to preserve a clear line of distinction between the socioeconomic sphere and the political sphere,[5] so that his challenge to the status quo in the economic order would not be taken as an incitement to confrontation in the political field.

Was Leo entitled to rely on this distinction between the economic sphere and the political sphere? Perhaps the best answer is to say that the distinction is very useful in principle but that in the late nineteenth century it could be used to evade difficult social issues. It is certainly useful to carve out a clearly defined area called "the economic" as distinct from the area called "the political." Within this economic area a certain clash of interest and a struggle between competing groups can then be accepted and "contained." But this presupposes that the richer classes are not allowed to use their economic power to exert political pressure on others. A limited degree of struggle in the economic area is tolerable if the state can ensure that its laws and institutions remain neutral, so as to serve all classes with impartial justice. In the time of Leo XIII this political impartiality was not maintained. As he himself pointed out, the wealthy exercised undue political power (*RN* 35). In practice this meant that key institutions of the state—its laws, courts, and police—showed a greater or lesser degree of bias against the poor. Such a bias is not merely something personal, but a structural imbalance.

In this situation only political changes could ensure that the economic rights of the poor were protected. To confine the struggle of workers to the purely economic order would frequently mean condemning them to futility, for as soon as an effective economic weapon was developed (e.g., a general strike), it could at once be countered by political means. For instance, if the wealthy classes found that their dominant position was under threat as a result of a general strike, they could use their power over the institutions of the state to ensure that such a strike was banned by law or was made subject to crippling restrictions.

Suppose Church authorities in these circumstances were to say that the poor are not entitled to work for major political changes, structural changes. This would amount to an option against the poor. It would be giving ideological support to those who were oppressing the poor. Leo XIII did not make such an option—at least not explicitly. But he failed to

---

[5]In the very first sentence of the encyclical (*RN* 1) the pope distinguishes between "the sphere of politics" and "the cognate sphere of practical economics." The Latin text reads as follows: "ut commutationum studia a rationibus politicis in oeconomicarum cognatum genus aliquando defluerent." See Antonazzi (1957, 78); cf. Leo XIII, *Praeclara Gratulationis* (BP IV 102) where he distinguishes between the social question and the political question and says he has treated the former in an earlier encyclical (i.e., *Rerum Novarum*) and then he goes on to speak of the political question (cf. also Leo XIII, *Graves de Communi*).

give clear guidelines for political and quasi-political action by the working class; and this was the only kind of action that was likely to bring about the changes that would ensure justice in society. He allowed such words and phrases as "disorder" (*RN* 16) and "danger of disturbance to the public peace" (*RN* 29) to remain vague in meaning and therefore capable of being invoked to cover almost any situation that threatened the interests of the rich and powerful. He did not distinguish clearly between, on the one hand, an altogether unacceptable level of violent or disruptive action and, on the other hand, a certain level of disturbance and instability that may be necessary if structural injustices are to be overcome despite the resistance of powerful groups. In other words, he failed to develop guidelines for confrontation.

Pope Leo set up an ideal of harmony in society that was so exalted and perfect that it remained abstract and unreal. Instead of envisaging a whole series of possible situations, approximating in a greater or lesser degree to the ideal, he seemed to consider only two alternatives to his ideal. The first of these was "disorder" or "disturbance"; and this was something he felt he had to condemn. The second alternative was the existing state of what we would now call "structural injustice." This was the situation where the institutions of the state supported and reinforced the gap between rich and poor. This too was something that he had to condemn. But when this condemnation had little or no practical effect, then it seemed as though the Church would have to acquiesce reluctantly in the existing unjust situation rather than opt for "disorder." This acquiescence, reluctant though it was, gave a considerable degree of religious support to a society that was structurally unjust. It undoubtedly diminished the effectiveness of *Rerum Novarum* as a cry of protest and a call for justice on behalf of the poor.

To understand why Leo XIII found himself in this awkward position we must look beyond *Rerum Novarum* to the writings in which he presented his teaching on political questions. But before moving on to that study, there is one further important point in *Rerum Novarum* itself that needs to be looked at.

WORKERS' ORGANIZATIONS

In the previous section I have been considering religion and the Church as a possible agent of change in society, a force that might be able to bring about the transformation required to make it a structurally just society. In this section I go on to examine more closely the teaching of *Rerum Novarum* on the other possible agent of major social change that has to be considered in the present context, namely, the trade union movement.

(For the pope entirely ruled out revolutionary movements as acceptable agents of change; and in *Rerum Novarum* he did not consider the question of political change brought about by democratic action—that did not enter into the socioeconomic question with which he was concerned in this encyclical.)[6] I have already noted that the pope was reluctant to encourage workers to take organized militant action to secure their rights. What then was his teaching in regard to trade unions or other associations that could give some power to the workers?

At the beginning of *Rerum Novarum* there is a perceptive passage in which the pope points to one of the basic reasons why workers at that time could be so exploited. He says, "The ancient workers' guilds were abolished in the last century, and no other protective organization took their place" (*RN* 2). This statement has sometimes been dismissed as a pointless pining for an outdated social order. No doubt there is a certain nostalgia there. But what the pope says immediately afterward shows that this passage contains one of the most important insights in the whole encyclical. The pope adverts to the fact that, partly as a result of the abolition of the guilds, "workers have been surrendered, isolated and helpless, to the hard-heartedness of employers and the greed of unchecked competition" (*RN* 2).[7]

The point to note here is that the plight of the workers is not attributed simply to the hard-heartedness and greed of employers and their unchecked competition against each other. Rather the problem arises because the workers no longer have protective organizations or other defenses. It is this lack of protection that has now left them "isolated and helpless" at the mercy of employers. Greed and competition remain "unchecked" precisely because of the workers' lack of any organization to defend their interests. At this point the pope is not saying whether he considers that employers are more hard-hearted and greedy than they were in the past. Instead, he is focusing attention on the safeguards that society offers, or fails to offer, to workers; and this is a question of the structures of society, rather than a purely moral matter such as how virtuous the employers are.

This passage indicates that Leo XIII had gone some way toward analyzing the structures of the society of his time and pinpointing the relationship

---

[6]Toward the end of this chapter I examine Leo's teaching on this question of working for change by democratic means.

[7]Cf. Vidler (1964, 144); also Calvez and Perrin (1961, 353): "It would be foolish to conclude . . . that Leo XIII entertained any romantic attachment to the past. The men of the last years of the eighteenth century were blameworthy, not because they had destroyed the 'ancient working-man's guilds,' but because they had put no other organization in their place."

between poverty and the powerlessness of workers. So it would not be quite fair to suggest, as Chenu does, that *Rerum Novarum* fails entirely to offer a "structural analysis" of the causes of poverty (Chenu 1979, 25). What is true, however, is that there is little coherent development of the basic insight about the need for protective organizations for workers. Perhaps even more important is that Leo's prophetic voice seemed to falter when it came to drawing practical conclusions from his insight about the importance of trade unions.

The history of Western countries over the past 180 years shows how major changes can be brought about in society by an effective trade union movement. Through the unions, workers have been able to bargain with employers from a position of some strength. The trade unions have often ensured that the solidarity of workers is not weakened by the use of non-union labor to break strikes. More recently, trade unions have also had some involvement in the shaping of government policy. This quasi-political role is a necessary check on the political influence that can be exerted on government by the employers. The result is that there is a somewhat better chance that the state will protect the interests of workers, as Pope Leo wished (*RN* 29). The result so far of all this leaves much to be desired, both with regard to the internal organization of Western countries and in their relationship with developing and undeveloped countries. But it represents a considerable advance on the society of Leo's time insofar as the internal structures of these countries are concerned; it goes some way toward achieving that balance in the body politic that Leo considered to be essential (*RN* 15).

The central point that emerges from this brief look at the role of trade unions is that major social injustices can be overcome even if the rich and powerful are not "converted." The greed and hard-heartedness of employers may still be present. But now they are no longer "unchecked," to use Leo's word (*RN* 2). Workers are no longer "isolated and helpless." They have a structure that protects them. It is a good example of what is meant when people say that social injustice must be dealt with at the structural level, not merely by working for the moral conversion of the oppressors.

Since Leo had noted the disastrous effect of the loss of the workers' guilds, one might have expected that he would go on to point out the need for strong and united movements of workers. He could have recommended such organizations in order to ensure adequate protection against the hard-heartedness and greed of employers, and particularly to protect workers in the face of that cutthroat competition that often "forces" employers to treat their workers unjustly. Despite the obvious advantages of such an approach, *Rerum Novarum* did not come out clearly in favor unions. This may have been partly owing to an inability of Leo XIII and his advisers to anticipate how the trade union movement would develop. But it would appear that it was at least partly due to hesitation about giving encouragement to any kind of movement that could bring about significant structural change. The practical proposals put forward by the pope fall far short of recommending a strong and united workers' movement that would confront employers and actively campaign for a just society.

The pope defends the basic right of workers to form associations. The most important of these, he says, are "Working-people's Unions" (*RN* 36). But the encyclical goes on to speak about associations in such vague and general terms that what he says could scarcely be applied to trade unions in the modern sense. These paragraphs (*RN* 36–44) refer to a wide variety of associations ranging from sodalities to trade unions, and it is difficult if not impossible to know which of Leo's remarks are intended to refer to which type of organization.[8] Having said that working-people's unions are the most important form of association, the pope immediately speaks in very general terms about unions or associations, some of which are open in their membership to employers as well as workers (*RN* 36). When he goes on to speak of organizations that aim to promote the cause of workers, he carefully avoids the use of such militant phrases as "struggling for rights"; his main emphasis is on self-restraint and harmony. Working-people's associations, he says, must give their "chief attention to the duties of religion and morality," and their concept of social betterment should have this chiefly in view (*RN* 42). Indeed, there is no clear evidence in the encyclical that the pope approved of the idea of a trade union as presently understood, namely, an organization that has limited goals of a secular nature and is confined in its membership to "workers" as distinct from employers or management.

The reluctance of the pope to dissociate spiritual from temporal welfare is important. He wanted to ensure that Catholic workers would not be "led astray" by associations that were not explicitly Catholic. So he encouraged Catholic workers to form their own associations as an alternative to those that might expose their religion to peril (*RN* 40).[9] There were

---

[8]For the various words used in the original Italian drafts and in successive Latin texts, see Antonazzi (1957, 157–75). Michael Walsh (2012) goes so far as to claim that it is a myth that Catholic trade unions owe their inspiration to *Rerum Novarum.* I would qualify this statement. I agree that the type of association that Leo favored was not a trade union in the modern sense. I would maintain, nevertheless, that in subsequent years, his encyclical had the effect of providing support for Catholic trade unions.

[9]In an address that he gave six years before *Rerum Novarum,* Leo had followed a similar line. He called for unity—but what he had in mind was that Catholics should unite with each other rather than with others; see Leo XIII, *C'est avec* in *The Pope and the People: Select Letters and Addresses on Social Questions by Pope Leo XIII, Pope Pius X, Pope Benedict XV and Pope Pius XI* (1929; London: CTS, 1937), 68–69, abbreviated *Pope and People.* Some years later (in 1895) in a letter to the bishops of the United States, Leo reluctantly acknowledged that religiously neutral trade unions may sometimes be

two unfortunate results of this policy. In the first place it contributed notably to a fragmentation of the trade union movement. Instead of uniting with other activists in a strong united workers' movement, many socially oriented Catholics in various European countries formed Catholic trade unions. This had the effect of greatly weakening the solidarity of workers, for, inevitably, the different unions began to compete with each other and adopted different policies and strategies on particular issues. A second result of Leo's policy was that it diminished the influence that Catholic social activists could have on those of other churches, or of no church, and vice versa; so the Catholic social movements remained rather cut off from similar movements outside the Church, while the emerging "secular" trade unions tended to become secularist and even at times anti-Catholic.

There was, then, a clear disparity between the kind of workers' associations that Leo XIII was actually recommending and the kind of workers' movement that would have a real chance of bringing about the major structural changes required if society were to become just. The main reason for this seems to be that Leo XIII was not prepared to take the risks involved in calling for, and actively supporting, a united militant workers' movement. The encyclical itself indicates some of the pope's reservations. He believed that many of the existing unions were "in the hands of secret leaders and . . . managed on principles ill-according with Christianity and the public well-being" (*RN* 40). Furthermore, he was convinced that these unions and their leaders were trying to bring about what would now be called a "closed shop"—a situation where only those who joined that union would be able to get a job. The combination of these two features was seen by the pope as posing a grave danger for Catholic workers, for he felt that for them to be forced to join such unions would put their faith, and therefore their salvation, at risk (*RN* 40). There can be little doubt that the principles, which he saw as incompatible with Christianity, were socialist and revolutionary ones—the two being, for Leo, more or less inseparable.

The attitude of Leo XIII to trade unions was largely determined by two of his major concerns. On the one hand, he wanted to vindicate the right of the individual to free association in the protection of personal interests; so he affirmed the basic right of the worker to join a union or form a new one. But, on the other hand, the pope had an overriding concern for public order. It was this that led him to oppose any movement that sought to change the social structures of society by vigorous action "from below." If an assessment of *Rerum Novarum* is to be fair, it must take account of both of these points. It must not play down the impor-

---

necessary—see *Longinqua Oceani* in *Great Ency.* (372): "Unless forced by necessity to do otherwise, Catholics ought to prefer to associate with Catholics."

tance of the pope's vindication of the right to form trade unions. But it must also acknowledge that Leo was a very long way from encouraging militant action by workers to reconstruct society.

AN ESCAPIST SPIRITUALITY

Leo had a conception of civil authority that required that he emphasize the duty of obedience and submission.[10] For him, one of the purposes of Catholic associations was to discourage militancy on the part of workers. It is not surprising, then, to find in his 1881 encyclical, *Diuturnum*, the statement that the Church strengthens the authority of rulers and helps it in many ways (BP I, 158).

In 1885, in his classic encyclical *Immortale Dei*, on the Christian constitution of states, Pope Leo said, "All public power must proceed from God" (BP II, 18; *Great Ency.* 109). Four years later, in the encyclical *Quamquam Pluries*, he suggests that not only is God the source of political power in a general way but also that God's support is given to whatever particular form of government has emerged in a given country—for this is attributed to God's providence.

The significant feature of Leo's approach here is the way in which he quite consciously links economics and politics with life after death. He maintains that religion pacifies the poor very effectively by promising them rewards in heaven proportionate to the miseries they have endured patiently on Earth.

This spirituality was applied by Pope Leo even in situations where rulers abuse their God-given authority. In his early encyclical *Quod Apostolici Muneris*, directed against socialism, communism, and nihilism, the pope makes it clear that abuses by rulers give subjects no right to rebel:

> Should it, however, happen at any time, that in the public exercise of
> authority rulers act rashly and arbitrarily, the teaching of the Catholic

---

[10] In his encyclical *Libertas Praestantissimum* (BP II, 194–96; *Great Ency.* 151) Leo said that since religion "derives the prime origin of all power directly from God Himself . . . it admonishes subjects to be obedient to lawful authority as to the ministers of God . . . forbidding all seditious and venturesome enterprises calculated to disturb public order and tranquillity." It is on this basis that Leo claims that religion of its essence is wonderfully helpful to the state. In a helpful study of Pope Leo's teaching, John Courtney Murray notes that his polemical bias led him closer to absolutist conceptions than to Christian and medieval ones; so he put the emphasis "on the duty of the people to consent to the king's legislation, rather than on the duty of the king to obtain the consent of the people" (see Murray 1953a, 23; Murray 1952, 546n50).

Church does not allow subjects to rise against them without further warranty, lest peace and order become more and more disturbed, and society run the risk of greater detriment. And when things have come to such a pass as to hold out no further hope, she teaches that a remedy is to be sought in the virtue of Christian patience and in urgent prayer to God. (BP I, 34; *Great Ency.* 28)

However, there are certain qualifications to be made. The first of these concerns a situation where a ruler commands something that is evidently wrong, opposed to the law of God or the will of God. One is then entitled—and indeed obliged—not to obey the command (*Diuturnum*, BP I, 148). But those who resist can use only lawful means of doing so. Leo approved only of those forms of political representation or activity that do not challenge the legitimacy of the authority of those in power.

A second qualification is this: Leo accepted that once a regime has been overthrown and a new authority has taken over, then the people should obey the new rulers. However, the crucial point is this: the legitimacy of the new government does not depend on the legitimacy of the rebellion against the previous regime. The neatness of Leo's teaching on this issue is that it explains the legitimacy of postrevolutionary governments without offering any moral justification or support to attempts to bring about such a transition!

Leo held that if citizens cannot obtain justice within the existing system, they may not take the further step of trying to topple it by means declared illegal by the regime itself. At that point the limit has been reached; injustice must then be endured, for to challenge the system, even in defense of justice, is to challenge the authority of God himself.

When spelled out in this blunt fashion, Pope Leo's teaching on political authority may seem shockingly pragmatic. Does this mean that the pope subordinated the value of justice to the values of order and stability? To put the question in this way is hardly fair to the pattern of his thinking. As he would see it, public order is not an alternative to justice in society. Rather, stability and order constitute a fundamental precondition for justice and might even be called an integral part of the just society. This explains why they have an overriding importance in his teaching, so much so that other instances of injustice have to be tolerated rather than have the order of society disturbed.

Leo was quite within the Catholic tradition in giving a high priority to order and stability in society. But he departed from the traditional teaching worked out by the scholastics in giving overriding importance to stability and order: he held that any resistance that transgressed against the laws of the regime can never be countenanced, no matter how unjust the regime may be.

FEAR OF REVOLUTION

Leo was worried about the danger of revolution. He had an almost neurotic fear of social disorder—so much so that nearly every other social value was in practice subordinated to the values of stability and harmony in society. One of his worst fears was that the Catholic Church should be identified in any degree with something that might smack of revolutionary change. Furthermore, he generally linked socialism with revolution. He seems to have thought of socialism as the summit and source of practically every social evil one could imagine. His fear of "socialism" led him to modify an earlier draft of *Rerum Novarum* in which the right to private property had been subordinated to the wider principle that the goods of the Earth are for the common good (Chenu 1979, 22).[11] He felt, it seems, that a statement of this kind would be, or would appear to be, too close to the socialist view. So he gave a very restrictive interpretation to the traditional teaching that "God has granted the earth to humankind in general"; this simply means, he says, "that no part of it was assigned to anyone in particular, and that the limits of private possession have been left to be fixed by people's own industry, and by the laws of individual races" (*RN* 7). This was quite a different emphasis from that of traditional scholastic teaching (cf. Shannon 2005, 135, 142). Charles Curran (2002, 177–78) gives an interesting account of how "Leo XIII absolutizes the right to private property." The departure by Leo from earlier Catholic teaching can be linked to the departure that I have already noted—his refusal to accept that rebellion could ever be justified. It too came from his concern for stability and his fear of revolution.

INADEQUATE SOLUTION—BUT A MAJOR ADVANCE

Pope Leo did not advert to the inconsistency in his own position. He was defending the existing political order while condemning the existing economic order—despite his acknowledgment that the two were so closely interlinked that the rich could use the machinery of the state to promote their interests at the expense of the poor.

It was quite unrealistic of Leo to expect that the rich and powerful

---

[11]Laurentin (1972, 96–97), refers to a growing misunderstanding of the teaching of Saint Thomas, a misunderstanding that affected the drafting of *Rerum Novarum* (cf. Camp 1969, 55).

could be persuaded by moral exhortations to relinquish their privileged position. If they chose to be intransigent, his teaching offered little remedy. One must therefore conclude that what Leo XIII presented as the official Church teaching on sociopolitical questions did not measure up to the deeply Christian instinct that led him to cry out against mistreatment of the poor. One could go further and say that the attitudes and spirituality that were reflected in his teaching contributed to the failure of the Church to gain the confidence of the mass of industrial workers.

Nonetheless, it must not be forgotten that *Rerum Novarum* was a major intervention by the pope in defense of the poor. As such, it helped put the Church firmly on their side. It laid a solid basis for the emergence of the concept of "social justice"—a term that was not used regularly in papal documents until much later. The notion of social justice was implicit in Leo's teaching. What seems to emerge is that it is a matter of justice (not "merely" of charity) to ensure that the social order does not facilitate the exploitation of the poor. In this way it laid a foundation for the eventual development of the notion of an "option for the poor"—and a spirituality that would embody such an option.

Taken as a whole, the economic, social, and political teaching of Leo XIII represents a major achievement. Despite the weaknesses or inadequacies that have been noted, it is a powerful synthesis, comprehensive and systematic. While rooted in tradition, it offers an opening to the new situation, a situation that included the emergence of democratic governments, the reality or threat of political revolution, and the development of an industrial proletariat ground down by poverty. It is not surprising, then, that Leo's teaching has remained the basis of the official Catholic position on social issues. Later popes constantly referred to the teachings of Leo XIII and seldom attempted to change them.

* * *

SUMMARY

Leo XIII's *Rerum Novarum* was the first major step by the Vatican toward putting the Church on the side of the poor and the working class. Its impact came not so much from its content as from the fact that by issuing an encyclical on this topic, the pope was seen to be coming to the defense of the poor. The encyclical expresses deep concern for the plight of the poor, makes a strong protest on their behalf, and calls for changes in society. But Leo failed to make a clear option for the poor in the technical sense. However, the encyclical can be seen as the beginning of a process that eventually led Church leaders to approve of the notion of an "option for the poor." The crucial point is the pope's insistence that the worker as a person must take precedence over the so-called laws of economics. By asserting this principle, Pope Leo was challenging the dominant liberal capitalist ideology of the time. He also strongly attacked the socialist position and in this way sought to find a middle way between individualism and collectivism.

Leo called for major changes in the socioeconomic order. He maintained that the state has a duty in the short term to protect workers against exploitation and in the long term to ensure that the ownership of property is much more widely distributed. But Leo wanted these changes to be initiated "from the top down," that is, by the very people or classes who were benefiting from the existing liberal-capitalist order. If they failed to introduce a more equitable society, Leo was not prepared to encourage the poor or workers to engage in confrontation. He defended the right of workers to form trade unions, but he did not want the unions to play a political role in changing society. Nor did he want Catholics to join with other workers in the kind of strong united trade union movement that could bring about major social change.

He was so convinced of the importance of order in society, and so concerned about the evil effects of revolution, that he built his political theology around stability as the key value. He insisted that political power derives from God and that to disobey civil authority is to rebel against God. He did not follow the older Catholic tradition, which held that it is lawful to resist a tyrannical abuse of power. He refused to accept that rebellion could sometimes be justified. Where changes could not be brought about without a threat to social order, he expected Christians to put up with injustice.

Leo's spirituality was in line with his theology. It was of a kind that actively discouraged the poor from confronting the wealthy to claim their rights; he asked the victims of oppression and injustice to put up with their suffering in the hope of a reward in the next life.

QUESTIONS FOR REVIEW

1. *What aspects of capitalism was Leo opposed to and what aspects did he approve of?*
2. *What was Leo's position about the role of trade unions? About strikes?*
3. *What did Leo hold about the role of the Church in society?*
4. *What kind of resistance to injustice did Leo approve of, and what kind did he forbid?*

QUESTIONS FOR REFLECTION

1. *Is capitalism today worse or better than in the time of Leo XIII?*
2. *If* Rerum Novarum *were being rewritten today, what categories of people should it focus on as being the poorest and most oppressed? Why has this change occurred?*
3. *Contrast your own spirituality with that of Leo in relation to social and political activity.*
4. *Are there times when it is better to endure injustice than to resist it?*

ISSUES FOR FURTHER STUDY

1. *Leo's position about the worker's right to a family wage. Read Molony 1991.*
2. *Why did the Church in Leo's time lose the working classes in Europe and not in America or Australia? Read Church histories of the period.*
3. *What is the role of the trade union movement in your own country today? What is the relationship between the Church and the trade unions?*

3

Pius XI and a New Social Order

There was an interval of forty years between Pope Leo's *Rerum No-varum* and the second major social encyclical, *Quadragesimo Anno*, issued by Pope Pius XI in 1931. The intervening period included the papacy of two other popes. The first of these was Pius X who was pope from 1903 to 1914. He was seen as a very holy man who was canonized as a saint many years later, but he was extremely authoritarian in his approach. The Church retreated into a defensive mode, and many biblical scholars and theologians were treated very harshly. One could hardly say that the Catholic Church provided a model of justice during the papacy of Pius X. There was an abandonment of the relative openness to the contemporary world that had begun in the time of Leo.

The most notable document issued by Pius X on social questions was the motu proprio of 1903 called *Fin Dalla Prima*. It consists mainly of a schematic summary of major points from the teaching of Leo XIII, with references to Pope Leo's documents. The style of the document, as well as the points that Pius X chose to emphasize, gives it the character of a manual of discipline. Notably absent is any sense of Leo's passionate concern for the plight of the working classes; the concern of Pius X seemed to be to ensure unity within the Church and stability in society.

Fin Dalla Prima differs subtly but significantly from *Rerum Novarum* on one important point, which it mentions twice:

> VI. To calm the strife between rich and poor, it is necessary to distinguish between justice and charity. Only when justice has been violated is there a right to make a claim, in the strict sense of the word. . . .
>
> XIX. Finally, let Catholic writers, while upholding the cause of the people and of the poor, beware of using language that may inspire the masses with hatred of the upper classes of society. Let them not talk of claims and of justice, when it is a question of mere charity. (*ASS [Acta Sanctae Sedis]*, 341–42, 344; *Pope and People*, 184, 187, translation slightly emended)

In the first of these passages, paragraph VI, a reference is given to the text of *Rerum Novarum*. But although the latter encyclical undoubtedly speaks both of obligations of justice and of obligations of charity, it does not by any means draw the same conclusions that Pope Pius X draws.[1]

The way in which Pius X applies the distinction between justice and charity is unfortunate. He says that there is a "claim, in the strict sense of the word," only when justice has been violated. When this is put together with paragraph XIX, the effect is to suggest that it is "merely" an obligation of charity to bring about an equitable social order. This set back the emerging concept of "social justice" to which *Rerum Novarum* had made such a notable contribution. It gave the impression that any social obligation that could not be specified in the strict interpersonal terms of commutative justice was less compelling or could be ignored with greater impunity.

Benedict XV, who was pope from 1914 to 1922, was much more liberal in approach than Pius X. He curbed the excesses of antimodernism and began to open up the Catholic Church to a cautious dialogue with the modern world. In the field of sociopolitical activity he allowed Catholics to play a more active role in Italian political life, thus opening the way for a rapprochement between church and state. Benedict's concern with trying to make peace during World War I and with Italian political affairs led him to pay less attention to the socioeconomic aspects of "the social question." He did not speak very often about socioeconomic matters, and, when he did, his statements were conservative in tone and content.

In his encyclical *Ad Beatissimi Apostolorum*, written in 1914, Benedict said, "The poor who strive against the rich as though they had taken part of the goods of others, not merely act contrary to justice and charity but also act irrationally, particularly as they themselves by honest industry can improve their fortunes if they choose" (*AAS* [*Acta Apostolicae Sedis*] 6, 571–72; *Pope and People*, 208, translation emended).

This passage shows the extent to which the pope had come to accept the belief that, more than anything else, gives a moral legitimation to the capitalist system. This is the belief that under such a system everybody, or at least nearly everybody, has a reasonable chance to "make good," since everybody has more or less an equal chance, at least in principle. It is rather unfortunate that Benedict XV should have lent his authority as pope to what might be called "the mythological basis of the liberal capitalist order." It represented a backward step from *Rerum Novarum*,

---

[1] A footnote in the English translation says tactfully that Leo's documents do not "explicitly" state what Pius says (see *Pope and People*, 184). *The Pope and the People: Select Letters and Addresses on Social Questions by Pope Leo XIII, Pope Pius X, Pope Benedict XV and Pope Pius XI* (1929; London: CTS, 1937) is a collection of papers as the subtitle indicates. It is abbreviated here as *Pope and People*.

where Leo had pointed out that the system is biased against the poor.

In a letter written in 1920 to the bishop of Bergamo, Pope Benedict insisted that a diversity of classes in society was part of the natural order and was willed by God. Although he encouraged Catholics to help the poor, he wanted the poor to be imbued with a spirituality that would discourage them from seeking vainly for a higher situation than they could reach and from trying to escape from evils they could not avoid; they should rather be encouraged to put up with their troubles peacefully in the hope of the good things of heaven (*AAS* 12, 111).

A NEW POPE

Benedict XV died in 1922, and the new pope was Pius XI, whose papacy lasted from 1922 to 1939. In 1931 he issued the second of the great social encyclicals. It was written to commemorate the fortieth anniversary of Leo XIII's *Rerum Novarum,* so it is known as *Quadragesimo Anno.* The usual English title is "The Social Order."[2] In this chapter I examine the contribution to Catholic social teaching made by Pius XI in *Quadragesimo Anno* and some of his other encyclical letters. But I shall be doing this from a particular point of view. My main emphasis will not be on the topics that are usually associated with Pius XI, namely, on his development of the concept of "social justice" and his emphasis on the principle of subsidiarity.[3] I propose to focus on a prior question: Did the pope commit the Church to supporting a radical transformation of the structures of society, an alternative to the capitalist or free enterprise model, and, if so, how far was he prepared to go in challenging the existing order?

Quadragesimo Anno is a worthy successor to *Rerum Novarum.* It has the same sense of moral outrage at the suffering of the poor (e.g., *QA* 59, 112) as one finds in Leo's encyclical and the same kind of criticism of economic liberalism, which had caused that suffering (e.g., *QA* 10, 88). Moreover, Pius's encyclical, like that of his predecessor, rejects communism and socialism (*QA* 112, 117–20). Pius, like Leo, sees himself as presenting a "middle way" between economic liberalism and socialism.

The new social encyclical sets out to vindicate and develop the teaching of *Rerum Novarum.* But then it goes on to look at current social issues in a radical way, with the aim of showing how they can be tackled according

---

[2]For background on the writing of the encyclical, see Hinze (2005, 152–55) and Duncan (1991, 113–24); for a contemporary commentary, see Action Populaire (1931, 81–108). The Jesuit Oswald von Nell-Breuning was the main drafter of the encyclical, but as I note later, the pope himself insisted on adding the key paragraphs *QA* 91–97.

[3]Hinze (2005, 151–74) has a valuable treatment of these and other elements in the encyclical in her careful and comprehensive study.

to Christian principles. Pius XI was conscious that major changes had taken place over the previous forty years. He wanted to ensure that the Church's social teaching was fully up to date and clearly relevant to the actual situation of the time (*QA* 40, 117). In his view there were several particularly urgent reasons why the Church should be actively involved in social issues at that time:

- Wealth had come to be concentrated in the hands of a relatively small number of people (*QA* 105; cf. *Divini Redemptoris* 8; also Pius XI's 1932 encyclical *Caritate Christi Compulsi*: "that unjust distribution of goods, the effect of which is to concentrate the wealth of the nations in the hands of a small group of private citizens who . . . regulate the markets of the world according to their choice, to the great detriment of the mass of humankind" (*AAS* 24, 179, my translation).
- This concentration of wealth had led to a concentration of economic power and even of political power (*QA* 105–8).
- Although the condition of the workers in the West had improved since the time of Leo, there was now, in the Americas and in the Far East, a vast increase in the number of very poor industrial workers "whose groans rise from earth to heaven"; there was also "the immense army of agricultural wage earners whose condition is depressed in the extreme" (*QA* 59).
- There was the further problem of widespread unemployment at the time the encyclical was written (*QA* 74; cf. encyclical *Nova Impendat, AAS* 23, 393–97).

Pius XI was not content merely to repeat, develop, and apply the teaching of Leo XIII. As the French theologian Marie-Dominique Chenu rightly remarks, he was concerned not just with the condition of workers, but with the whole socioeconomic order of society (Chenu 1979, 35).[4] He introduced into official Church teaching the phrase "social justice" (*QA* 88), relating it to the common good and giving general guidelines for how it should be realized in society. Charles Curran (2002, 189) has a helpful account of the elements included in the concept of social justice. Pius XI also insisted that social justice alone is not enough; it has to be supplemented by social charity. Christine Firer Hinze (2005, 167) helpfully suggests that the connection, which Pius XI made among the common good, social justice, and social charity, provides a background against which, many years later, Pope John Paul II developed his teaching on solidarity.

---

[4]It should be noted that the paragraph numbering system used by Chenu is quite different from that used in the English translations.

Above all, Pius focused attention on the basic causes of injustice and poverty. He was prepared to go much further than Leo in doing what would now be called a "structural analysis" of society, locating the inadequacies and built-in injustices in its structures. He avoided the mistake of adopting a purely "moralizing" approach, an attitude that explains social evils in terms of the sinfulness of individuals.

He also avoided the opposite mistake, namely, that of putting the blame for all the ills of the world on the structures of society. I cannot fully agree with Charles Curran (2002, 46) when he says that "the documents of Catholic social teaching do not give central importance to the change of heart"—though admittedly Pius refers more to a change of conduct than a change of heart. *Quadragesimo Anno* insists on the need for both "a reform of social institutions" and "the improvement of conduct" (*QA* 77; cf. *QA* 97, 98, 127). The encyclical treats these two aspects of the problem separately for the most part. But at one point it comes close to expressing an important insight about the relationship between the two, namely, that evil conduct can solidify into a set of practices and traditions that are themselves real "structures" of society, affecting the more obvious political, social, and economic structures. The pope does not quite say this. But he gives an impressive account of how moral standards tend to become eroded in the existing economic order (*QA* 132–35).

A NEW SPIRITUALITY

The main concern of this study is with what Pius had to say about the structures of society and the need for radical change in them. But before moving on to this question, it is worthwhile to consider one point about the reform of conduct. Perhaps the most effective way in which the Church can influence human behavior is by promoting a particular kind of spirituality. Leo XIII had encouraged what might be termed "a spirituality of stability." He laid emphasis on obedience to lawful authorities to a point that in the last analysis people were asked to endure gross injustices rather than overthrow the regimes that perpetrated them. The promise of future reward was held out to those who were patient in this way. Pius XI seems to give less emphasis to this kind of spirituality. The author of *Quadragesimo Anno* is clearly aware of the Marxist accusation that the Church condones injustice by offering happiness in the next life as a reward for patience in the face of oppression in this life. He responds by denying that the Church in general does this, though he admits that some people in the Church do so. The pope condemns the conduct of those who "abuse religion itself, trying to cloak their own unjust impositions under its name" (*QA* 125).

It is true that Pius XI maintains that workers should not feel "discontent at the position assigned them by divine Providence in human society" (*QA* 137). But that comment should not be taken to indicate that he sees stability in society as something to be promoted at all costs. His remark is simply an expression of his concern that feelings of envy and hatred should be overcome through a theology and spirituality of human work (*QA* 137). In general, there is a slight but noticeable shift in emphasis from an "escapist" to a "worldly" spirituality, as one moves from *Rerum Novarum* to *Quadragesimo Anno*. This is a good example of how the "doctrinal" continuity between Leo and Pius XI is combined with subtle but significant changes.

One can sense in *Quadragesimo Anno* the emergence of a new spirituality of social justice, but it has not yet fully succeeded in maintaining its autonomy. On some occasions it almost seems as though the pope's concern for justice is little more than a means to the end of bringing workers into the Church or ensuring that they are not led astray (cf. *Divini Redemptoris* 61, 63, 70; *Firmissimum* 22). But *Quadragesimo Anno* shows that its author does see concern for social justice as a fundamental value in its own right. It speaks, for instance, of choosing people who "show themselves endowed with a keen sense of justice, ready to oppose with manly constancy unjust claims and unjust actions" (*QA* 142). The pope goes on to add that such people should show great prudence and should above all be filled with the charity of Christ (*QA* 142). Here we find linked together four major virtues—justice, courage, prudence, and the love of Christ; for Pius XI these constitute the heart of a Christian spirituality of justice.

THE NEED FOR STRUCTURAL CHANGE

However important a change of heart and conduct may be, Pius XI was well aware that it is not sufficient on its own to overcome modern social problems. He believed that well-meaning employers were often trapped by the system, by structures in society that embodied injustice and created further injustice: "We turn again in a special way to you, Christian employers and industrialists, whose problem is often so difficult for the reason that you are saddled with the heavy heritage of an unjust economic regime whose ruinous influence has been felt through many generations" (*Divini Redemptoris* 50).

One instance of the difficulty is that competition might be so keen that individual employers know that any increase in their costs would put them out of business. Consequently, they find themselves unable to pay their employees a just wage. The pope insisted that in this kind of situation, there is an obligation to establish structures or institutions designed to limit the competition that causes the injustice (*Divini Redemptoris* 53). When Pius XI turns his attention in *Quadragesimo Anno* to the question of the reform of the structures of society, he points out the key factor: wealth gives power. He goes much further than his predecessors in recognizing that in a capitalist society, the state is largely controlled by a wealthy group (cf. Calvez and Perrin 1961, 350), in such a way that "its resources and authority may be abused in economic struggles" (*QA* 108): "The State which should be the supreme arbiter, ruling in regal fashion far above all party contention, intent only upon justice and the common good, has become instead a slave" (*QA* 109). Earlier in the encyclical Pius had said, "The open violation of justice is sometimes not merely tolerated but even ratified by legislators" (*QA* 4).

Pius makes a radical criticism of the capitalist system as it has developed since the time of Leo XIII: "Free competition has destroyed itself; economic domination has taken the place of the open market" (*QA* 109). Here the pope is pointing to a fatal weakness in capitalism, the point where it fails to be what it essentially claims to be. It begins as free enterprise; and this includes free competition. But a "natural result" (*QA* 107) of the competition is that only the toughest survive. Before long the free competition is only a myth and an ideology; the reality is the elimination of competition and the securing of economic and even political domination by the most ruthless (see R. Miller 1947, 233). That is why Pius XI insists that "the proper ordering of economic life cannot be left to free competition"; it must be "subjected to and governed by a true and effective guiding principle" (*QA* 88). Public authorities must ensure that free competition is kept within just and definite limits and that economic power is kept under control (*QA* 110).[5] If such a degree of interference by the state in "the market" were implemented, it would amount to a radical change in the structures that had shaped the Western world.

In dealing with the question of the restructuring of society, the pope is quite subtle. His encyclical cleverly combines the advantages of being broad and general with the advantages of being rather specific. Three paragraphs give a specific and fairly detailed account of the type of corporative state that was being introduced at that time in Italy by Mussolini

---

[5]In reference to this development of capitalism into a system where domination replaces competition, Christine Gudorf (1980, 10) maintains that "Pius XI placed the blame . . . not on any natural direction of the system of capitalism, but on the lack of moral restraint of the individuals concerned." It is true, of course, that the pope blamed capitalists for lack of restraint. But his main point here is the need for some limits to be imposed on free competition, and these limits are to be not merely moral but structural since they are to be imposed by public authorities.

(*QA* 92–94; for historical background, see R. Miller 1947, 190–97). But the pope does not identify this as his own position. Instead he lists some of its advantages and disadvantages. In this way he succeeds in distancing himself somewhat from the model of society adopted by the Italian fascists while he outlines its main features with a measure of what he himself called "benevolent attention."[6] It is interesting to note that Oswald von Nell-Breuning (1936, 254–57), in a commentary on the encyclical, gave a very different interpretation of *QA* 92–94. In that commentary, the original German version that was written in the year after the encyclical, he professed to see delicate irony and understated criticism in the pope's references to the Italian system. Since Nell-Breuning was the principal drafter of the encyclical, his interpretation would, in normal circumstances, have to be taken very seriously. However, nearly forty years later Nell-Breuning (1986, 60–62) wrote a revealing account of the drafting of the encyclical in which he acknowledged that the pope himself had insisted on having these paragraphs added into the draft;[7] the implication is that Pius XI *did* intend to convey some degree of approval of the Italian system. It is clear that Nell-Breuning himself strongly disapproved of such a system; so his earlier commentary on this topic might be termed an exercise in "damage limitation," an effort to tone down the meaning of what the pope had insisted on saying.

Before his account of the Italian fascist system, Pius had already made his own proposals (which were in fact drafted by Nell-Breuning). In them he carefully avoids details and specific applications. Instead, he gives general norms such as the following:

- "The aim of social policy must . . . be the re-establishment of vocational groups" (*QA* 82).
- Professional corporations may take a variety of different forms (*QA* 86).
- Wages should be determined not with a view to private advantage but on the basis of providing employment for as many as possible (*QA* 74).
- No larger or higher association should "arrogate to itself the functions

---

[6]The phrase "benevolent attention" was used by Pius XI two weeks after he had issued *Quadragesimo Anno* to describe its attitude toward the Italian system. See his address of May 31, 1931, *AAS* 23, 231: "nella Enciclica *Quadragesimo anno* tutti hanno facilmente riconosciuto un cenno di benevola attenzione agli ordinamenti sindacali e corporativi italiani." For general background on the relationship between Pius XI and Mussolini, see Kertzer (2014).

[7]Hinze (2005, 162) notes that paragraphs 91–97 "were written in Italian in Pius XI's own hand."

which can be performed efficiently by smaller and lower societies"
(*QA* 79). (This important statement is the first clear formulation
in papal teaching of the principle of subsidiarity that has become
central to Catholic social thought.)

Pius XI reaffirmed the right of workers to form voluntary trade unions
(*QA* 30, 34, 35, 87).[8] He even had strong words of criticism for those who
were reluctant to acknowledge this right (*QA* 30–31; *Divini Redemptoris*
50). A comparison of the descriptions of the role of trade unions in *Rerum
Novarum* and *Quadragesimo Anno* shows an interesting shift of emphasis.
There is an almost militant ring to what Pius says about unions, a tone
quite different from that of Leo. Pius XI emphasizes the importance of
unions as a means by which workers can protect themselves against oppression (*QA* 30, 34). He implies that the trade unions are the defenders
and champions of the lowly and oppressed (*QA* 31). He even sees them
as having what would now be called a consciousness-raising role insofar
as it was through unions that workers "learned to defend their temporal
rights and interests energetically and efficiently, retaining at the same time
a due respect for justice" (*QA* 33).

Nevertheless, Pius XI did not see workers' organizations as the solution
to the social problem. The whole bent of his thinking was in a different
direction. He envisaged the elimination or minimizing of the division of
society into classes (upper, middle, and lower). This would be brought
about by ensuring that the main divisions would be on the basis of the
different sectors of society, such as agriculture, transport, and the various
branches of industry (*QA* 82–85). These "vocational" structures would
cut across class lines. Within each vocational sphere there could be opportunities for employers and employees to meet separately on occasion
(*QA* 85). But the whole order of society would be designed to ensure
that there would be no opposition or confrontation between the class of
workers as a whole and the class of employers. The division into vocational sectors would not be so rigid and total that it would give rise to
the kind of destructive competition and group selfishness it was supposed
to eliminate. In fact, it was simply an application of the general principle
of subsidiarity that Pius XI considered to be a "fixed and unshaken"
principle of social philosophy (*QA* 79). Pius suggests that "workers and
executives become sharers in the ownership or management [of business
enterprises] or else participate in some way in the profits" (*QA* 65). This
proposal would seem more realistic in a society organized on vocational
lines than in a capitalistic world.

---

[8]For background information on the development of trade unions, see Somerville (1933).

REJECTION OF CAPITALISM

Pope Pius XI, like Leo XIII, was concerned to lessen hostility between the classes of society (*QA* 81–83; *RN* 15, 35, 41). His teaching, following that of Leo, proposed a conception of society as an ordered harmony rather than a battleground where workers and employers confront each other (*QA* 83–84; *RN* 15). But Pius went further than Leo in indicating how this was to be brought about. Leo had relied mainly on a reform of conduct rather than proposing any major change in the structures of society. Pius XI wanted structural changes as well as moral ones. As I have noted, a basic feature of the restructured society he proposed was that its main components would not be classes but vocational groups (*QA* 82). Such a society would, he believed, be more natural than one stratified into different classes (*QA* 83). Harmonious relationships could be expected to develop both within the vocational groups and between them (*QA* 85).

The pope did not go into detail about how these groupings should be organized or how their internal and external relationships should be structured. In fact, he specifically said that people could choose for themselves the form they wished the professional groups to take (*QA* 86). But even though *Quadragesimo Anno* does not give a blueprint covering such details, nevertheless it is clear that the type of society Pius was calling for would involve a major change in any country where capitalism was in operation. The question therefore arises whether he was definitively rejecting the capitalist system. This calls for a nuanced answer.

When the encyclical insists that "the proper ordering of economic life cannot be left to free competition" (*QA* 88), this is more than an objection to abuses of the system. It is a repudiation of the central principle of capitalism—its ideological foundation. At the heart of capitalist thinking is the belief that market forces should be the determining factor in the economic order. It is the market that has the central role in regulating prices, profits, and wages—as well as in determining which enterprise succeeds and which fails. In rejecting this principle, Pius was rejecting capitalism not just in its contemporary form but in its essential nature. I cannot agree with the view of Jean Villain that the Church "does not condemn the principles of capitalism but condemns the liberalism which in fact has vitiated the working and evolution of capitalism, and consequently condemns 'actual' capitalism" (Villain 1953, 233, my translation). This distinction between economic liberalism and the principles of capitalism is too strained; it cannot be maintained so long as the word "capitalism" retains its proper meaning.

However, a certain qualification must be added at once. Capitalism has an attenuated meaning that might be summed up as "a system in which individuals and groups have a right to own property and engage in business enterprises of various kinds." Insofar as the word is understood in this sense, the pope was certainly not rejecting it.[9] Indeed, he explicitly stated that a system where capital and labor are normally provided by different people is not in itself to be condemned and certainly is not evil of its very nature (*QA* 100–101). Pius also held that free competition is "justified and certainly useful provided it is kept within certain limits" (*QA* 88, R. Miller 1947 translation). He did not favor the extreme corporatist position that, paradoxically, had certain similarities to socialism, especially in the matter of restrictions on the use of private property (cf. Camp 1969, 65, 97).

The attitude of Pius may be expressed by saying that he did not want capitalism in the strict sense, but he undoubtedly wanted a large measure of free enterprise. He wanted people to be free to own and use land and free to found and conduct businesses without undue interference by either public authorities or capitalistic monopolies. Furthermore, he believed that such regulation and control as was required should be carried out at a lower rather than a higher level; it should as far as possible be done through a vocational structure rather than by the state. All this is clear from the general principles he lays down (especially *QA* 61–90). It is supported by the tenor of the critical comments he makes about the fascist-corporative system. In fact he does not present this criticism as his own; instead, he notes that some people consider the system to be excessively bureaucratic and see it as giving the state a role that should be left to private initiative (*QA* 95).

AMBIVALENCE

It has been said with some justification that Pius XI was ambivalent in regard to the capitalist system of his time (Camp 1969, 40). There is no doubt that some of his statements give the impression that he wanted a reform of the system, whereas in other statements it seems as though he wanted the system to be entirely replaced. A good deal of the confusion can be removed by invoking the distinction I have made above between "free enterprise" and "capitalism"; one might say that the pope wanted the former to be reformed and the latter to be replaced. But I must add that even this distinction does not clear up the sense of ambivalence entirely. However, such ambivalence is not necessarily a bad thing. If the pope had opted unambiguously in favor of one particular socioeconomic

---

[9]A rather similar distinction between two meanings of capitalism and a similar conclusion about the attitude of Pius XI may be found in John A. Ryan (1935, 181; cf. Hinze 2005, 167–68).

system, he would have been going beyond his proper role and his competence. Perhaps, then, the element of ambivalence should be seen as a virtue rather than a fault!

In order to clarify the issue further it is helpful to distinguish between two different questions that frequently have not been clearly distinguished from each other. The first question is the one we have been considering, namely, did Pius XI reject capitalism—or, more accurately, in what sense did he reject it? The second question is what economic system does *Quadragesimo Anno* propose? It has sometimes been assumed that one should answer this second question first, and in this way the first question will also be answered. But, in fact, there is no answer to the second question. The view of Pius XI was that an economic system would include "technical" economic details that are outside the competence and mission of the Church (*QA* 41). He held that "economic science" covers a sphere distinct from that of "moral science," even though the two are closely related to each other (*QA* 42).[10]

This means that the pope could not be expected to teach that a given economic system is *the* correct one. Rather he set out to lay down general principles to which any system should conform, and he used these principles to assess and criticize existing or proposed systems, namely, capitalism, communism, different varieties of socialism, and the fascist-corporatist system. Anybody who expects the encyclical to say clearly and explicitly which is the correct system will certainly, like Camp, find its statements about capitalism a cause of "bewilderment" and open to different interpretations (Camp 1969, 40). But if we adopt a restricted conception of the role and competence of the teaching authority of the Church, then the apparent ambivalence of the encyclical will be seen as simply an indication that Pius XI resisted the temptation to exceed his competence as a moral teacher by making a pronouncement on a "technical" issue of economics. In other words, it will show that he was correct in refusing to be dogmatic on a matter where uncertainty and openness was the appropriate response.

It would be an exaggeration, however, to claim that all this was quite clear in the encyclical or even in the mind of the pope himself. In fact, the way in which he treated the relationship between economic science and moral science (*QA* 42) is not entirely satisfactory. There is a suggestion of a kind of dualism and a reduction of economics to a purely instrumental role. The distinction Pius XI made between the proper object of papal

---

[10]In the CST translation the Latin phrases "oeconomica res" and "moralis disciplina" are rendered as "economic life" and "moral conduct," respectively; for the translation of the two Latin phrases that I have used in the text, I have taken the Nell-Breuning rendering of the first term and the Miller version of the second term (see Nell-Breuning 1936, 77; Miller 1947, 42).

teaching and the "technical aspects"[11] of economics (*QA* 41) was made only in passing and was not fully developed.

This distinction made by the pope was important, because it entitled him to refrain from giving specific teaching on technical matters. But it was only a first step because its frame of reference is too static. It divides the issues too neatly into those that lie within the technical sphere and those in the moral sphere, in which the pope sees himself as having the right and the duty to make pronouncements. The real life situation is by no means so amenable to such a clear distinction.

Church leaders, moral theologians, and the Church as a community have to assess concrete situations in the light of Christian experience and the principles that distill and express the wisdom of the past and the present. The distinction between technical matters and moral issues, insofar as it exists, is itself an end product of such assessment rather than a ready-made self-evident framework whose application is obvious and almost automatic. Furthermore, the dividing line between the two is a shifting one, since moral issues can open up in matters that had seemed to be purely technical. Because of this complexity, Church authorities must recognize that it may be necessary to live with a good deal of uncertainty; at times, the most they can do is commit themselves to searching for the best way forward.

DESIRE FOR CERTAINTY

At the time of *Quadragesimo Anno*, and for thirty years afterward, it was not easy for the Catholic community or its leaders to experience themselves as uncertain and searching on important social issues. There was considerable pressure on Church authorities to present themselves as "having the answers." A lot of this pressure came from the believing community who looked to the leadership for clear and authoritative teaching on all issues that had a moral dimension (*QA* 7, 8, 41, 117, 122). There were two good reasons why the pope should offer such authoritative teaching. First, it gave the Catholic Church as a whole a clear sense that it had a message for the non-Catholic world. Second, it provided the Catholic clergy and laity with the assurance that they had a teaching authority to guide them. It is understandable, then, that many clergy and laity—and even the Vatican itself—came to speak about *Quadragesimo Anno* as though it had provided a definitive answer to the social question.

---

[11]The Latin text that I have translated as "technical aspects" is "*quae artis sunt*"; the CTS translation ("in matters of technique") is less satisfactory.

For those who saw the encyclical as providing the answer or the solution to the social problem, it was a very short step to interpreting this to mean that it offered its readers "the correct system." The unanswered questions, the deliberate vagueness, and the slightly different emphases in different parts of the encyclical were then no longer seen as indications of searching and uncertainty. No, the truth must be there; it had only to be brought forth by means of a careful exegesis of the text.

It is not surprising, then, that controversy sprang up on certain key issues—above all on the question of whether corporatism was being proposed as *the* Catholic solution (see, e.g., Nell-Breuning 1936, 21–32, 256). Because the text of the encyclical was presumed to contain "the truth," the controversy tended to center on the proper interpretation of the text rather than on the arguments for or against corporatism. In this way, the prevailing theology and spirituality of the authority of the teaching Church led to a playing down of the fact that the pope did not commit himself on some important socioeconomic issues.[12] The effect was that this reserve, which was an important feature of the encyclical, was not appreciated for what it was; instead it became the occasion for a rather fruitless exegetical controversy.

WHY WAS PIUS XI SO RADICAL?

Quadragesimo Anno has been understood by some to be proposing an alternative socioeconomic system, a replacement for the capitalist system. But it is more accurate to see the encyclical as laying down some fundamental principles of social morality, using these as a basis for evaluation, and concluding that they rule out the acceptance of socialism in any form (cf. Hinze 2005, 164), and of capitalism both in its basic ideological principles and in its actual historical development. If this account is correct (and a fortiori if the encyclical were proposing a specific socioeconomic system as some have assumed) then Pius XI was reacting against Western capitalism in a much more radical way than his predecessor (see O'Brien 1991, 19). Why was he less inhibited than Leo had been forty years earlier, in calling for an abandonment of the system on which modern Europe and America had been built?

Three factors may be mentioned as likely to have encouraged Pius XI to go much further than his predecessor:

---

[12]Even the balanced treatment of the topic by John A. Ryan seems to presuppose that the pope had "the answer" (J. Ryan 1935, 174–78).

- The economic collapse and the Great Depression of the time had raised questions about the viability of the capitalist economic system.[13]
- Since the time of Leo XIII the inevitable and "natural" consequences of the capitalist system had had the opportunity to emerge and develop further. Particularly significant, as I noted earlier, was that the system had to a considerable extent ceased to be what it claimed to be, namely, one of free enterprise. Instead of giving most people a chance to become entrepreneurs, the system actually concentrated wealth and power in the hands of a privileged few (*QA* 105–9).
- The liberal capitalist system no longer seemed to be the only effective alternative to communism or socialism. At this time, Italy and Portugal had adopted a corporatist-fascist model of society.

The situation had changed in two respects since Leo's time. On the one hand, there was no guarantee that the capitalist order as it had developed could, in fact, ensure social and political stability. On the other hand, it seemed possible that there was an alternative socioeconomic model that could ensure stability and could, at the same time, be more equitable. The effect of all this was that it could no longer be presumed that the Catholic Church would, in the last analysis, provide support for the status quo rather than take the risk of being an agent of major sociopolitical change.

AUTHORITY AND SUBVERSION

Although one can make a distinction between economics and politics, the two are closely interrelated. To seek to change the economic structures of society is itself a political action. So the question arises whether or to what extent Pius XI had thought through the political implications of his call for new socioeconomic structures. This issue scarcely arises in *Quadragesimo Anno*.

However, in three major encyclicals issued in March 1937 Pius XI confronted the question of obedience to civil authorities. In the first, *Mit brennender Sorge*, he made an outspoken attack on the Nazi regime in Germany (§§41–42, 47). But the pope said nothing that could in any way be taken as an incitement to subversion.

---

[13]O'Brien (1991, 20) sees the position of Pius XI as guided by "an ideology of counterattack and Catholic restoration." He goes on to claim that "it was a utopia, and a dangerous one." There is a good deal of truth in this view, but it seems to me to be somewhat one-sided, playing down unduly the aspects of Pius's teaching that were related to the economic and political circumstances of his time.

The second of the three encyclicals, *Divini Redemptoris*, is dated five days later than the first. In this encyclical he strongly condemns communism (§33). But he does not really address himself to the dilemma of allegiance faced by those who have to live under a communist government, for his main concern was not with such people but with the threat of communism to the Western world.

The issue of allegiance was, however, taken up by Pius XI just nine days later in the third of these encyclicals. This was entitled *Firmissimum*, and it dealt with the situation of Catholics in Mexico. Toward the end of it there are a few paragraphs where the pope bluntly faces the question of active resistance to the civil authorities. He maintained that in certain circumstances "there would appear no reason to condemn citizens for uniting to defend the nation and themselves by lawful and appropriate means against those who make use of the power of the State to drag the nation to ruin" (§35). The context makes it clear that when Pius uses the phrase "by lawful and appropriate means" (*licita atque idonea auxilia*) he is not leaving it to the oppressive regime itself to define what is "lawful" or "unlawful."

This was a sharp break with the past, a notable departure from what had been taught by Leo XIII, Pius X, Benedict XV, and by Pius XI himself up to that time (see Coste 1963, 200–201). Since the time of Leo XIII (and before) the effect of papal teaching had been to give a notable measure of canonization to the status quo, despite the protests of popes about injustices. That had now changed, at least in this one instance. And what is perhaps most significant is that the change was a return to an older tradition, according to which the possibility of a legitimate rebellion was considered. So the statement of Pius XI cannot easily be dismissed as a temporary aberration. Its effect is to put on the agenda of Catholics seeking social reform a question that Leo XIII and his successors had deliberately closed off. That question is whether a particular regime is so utterly unjust that the obligation of allegiance may be superseded by a more primordial obligation. Could it be legitimate to rebel? Could it even be a duty to do so, in order to replace an incorrigibly corrupt or unjust regime with one that would promote justice and the common good?

Almost six years intervened between *Quadragesimo Anno* and *Firmissimum*. But there is a link between the two. The first represents a major challenge to the existing socioeconomic order, but it gives little guidance on the political question of how these changes could be brought about. The later encyclical opens up the possibility of disobedience and resistance to civil authorities and even a justified rebellion in certain exceptional circumstances. It would be contrived and historically inaccurate to suggest that the pope intended *Firmissimum* to "give teeth" to his earlier encyclical. But the radical quality of his views on the political issue is of a piece with that of his position on the socioeconomic question. In this sense, at least, each of the two encyclicals supports and complements the other.

CONCLUSION

The experience of the years since the pontificate of Pius XI suggests that it would be unwise of Church leaders today to identify themselves closely with the views he espoused on socioeconomic and political issues. In both of these areas he showed sympathy for right-wing thinking that went significantly beyond traditional conservatism. This approach is quite out of tune with the main thrust of post–Vatican II Catholic social teaching. But if we go behind these historically conditioned opinions, we reach a fundamental level where Pope Pius XI has a lot to offer.

In the encyclical *Quadragesimo Anno* he took a prophetic stand on economic questions. In the encyclical *Firmissimum* he took an equally prophetic stand on a political issue. By doing so, he showed very clearly that the official Church does not always have to play a conservative role in society. Concern for stability is important, but stability is not the only social value or even the highest. Justice ranks higher. There may be times when the value of justice calls the Christian community and its leaders to take a risky stand on political, social, and economic issues. They may feel called to challenge the basic economic and political structures that are widely assumed to be necessary for the survival of our society—and even for the world as we know it. In taking such a radical stance, they may be encouraged by the example of Pope Pius XI, who, while staying within the tradition of Catholic social teaching, nevertheless gave that tradition a distinctly prophetic emphasis and laid a solid foundation for the challenging and prophetic stands taken by later popes and other Church leaders.

* * *

SUMMARY

Pius X was much more conservative than Leo XIII on social issues; the result was that the Church moved backward from Leo's fairly advanced position and pushed back the emerging concept of social justice. Benedict XV was more liberal and flexible in his attitudes and policies; but his statements on social issues were quite like those of Pius X. So there was little advance in social teaching during his papacy.

In 1931, forty years after *Rerum Novarum*, the first social encyclical, Pius XI issued *Quadragesimo Anno*. Among its contributions to Catholic social teaching were its use of the term "social justice" and its articulation of the principle of subsidiarity. This encyclical challenged the capitalist model of society much more strongly and more specifically than Leo's encyclical had done. Though Pius XI spoke out against the existing type of capitalism, the pope wanted to retain a good deal of free enterprise. He favored a corporatist-vocational model of society.

This encyclical convinced many Catholics that the Church has a "blueprint" for the ideal society and that this requires major sociopolitical changes in the structures of society. So it could no longer be assumed that the Church was, in the final analysis, a conservative force. The later encyclical of Pius XI, *Firmissimum*, issued in 1938, represented a break with the political theology of Leo XIII on the vital question of loyalty to an unjust regime; it suggested that, in an extreme situation, resistance and rebellion could be justified.

These encyclicals of Pius XI were issued at a time when the Vatican was leaning more to the right than to the left. But more important than this political orientation is the fact that these encyclicals helped the Church have a clearer understanding of the radical and prophetic role it is called to play in society.

QUESTIONS FOR REVIEW

1. *In what ways did Pius X and Benedict XV back-track on the social teaching of Leo?*
2. *How had the economic situation of the world changed between the time of Leo and the time of* Quadragesimo Anno?
3. *What is the principle of subsidiarity?*
4. *What is meant by a vocational or corporatist ordering of society?*
5. *In what way did Pius XI depart from Leo's teaching about resistance to oppression?*

QUESTIONS FOR REFLECTION

1. *Does the Church have an ideal of how society should be organized?*
2. *Is the principle of subsidiarity valid today?*

ISSUES FOR FURTHER STUDY

1. *How has the Lateran Treaty affected the way in which the Catholic Church exists in, and relates to, the world?*

4

Pius XII: Anticommunism
and Decolonization

In 1939 Eugenio Pacelli became pope and took the title Pius XII. He took charge of a Church that was highly centralized, not merely administratively but also in the sphere of theology and spirituality. His style as pope fostered this centralization. He produced an almost endless stream of addresses and documents in which he gave a "teaching" on a very wide range of issues. Social, economic, and political questions were among the many topics on which he made pronouncements. But in his teaching he tended to concentrate more on political issues than on strictly economic ones. The reason for this was the situation in which he found himself—and perhaps also his own character and interests.

In the first section of this chapter I examine the teaching of Pius XII on the traditional issues of the social justice agenda that he had inherited from Leo XIII and Pius XI. In the second section I take up an issue that came to the fore only during the pontificate of Pius XII—the question of the Church's attitude to colonialism and decolonization.

ANTICOMMUNISM AND MODERATED CAPITALISM

All through the first years of the papacy of Pius XII the world was dominated by World War II. This was the background against which the pope's major addresses of that time were delivered. Pius was deeply concerned not only about the Nazi threat but also about the dangers of communism. In the light of the immediacy of these political struggles it is understandable that socioeconomic questions seemed less pressing and were given less prominence. Furthermore, the war had the effect of forcing governments to exercise an exceptionally high degree of control of economic, social, cultural, and political life. The effect of this in the noncommunist world was to bring about a notable shift from a "free enterprise" model of society toward a bureaucratic model, and this was done in a climate that dampened down social tensions.

The Preoccupations of Pius XII

In the years following the war, the dominant issue was once again political rather than overtly economic. Relations between East and West had quickly deteriorated into the Cold War, and in Asia there was open, but localized, war. No doubt economic and social questions were very much at stake in the East–West struggle. After all, the differences between communism and capitalism are primarily concerned with such economic issues as who should own the means of production. But, ironically, the struggle between communism and capitalism was now identified with an international political conflict between East and West. This is evident in the pope's Christmas message of 1950 (D21, 55–59),[1] in which part 3 of the message is concerned with internal peace whereas part 4 deals with peace between peoples. The former treats some economic issues whereas the latter refers mostly to political rather than economic matters.

Preference for Democracy

In his later teaching, Pius XII showed a clear preference for democracy over other forms of political organization. As the war drew toward its close, the pope moved on from his earlier position of neutrality in relation to different forms of government (cf. Langan 2005, 182). In his Christmas message of 1944 he took democracy as his theme (D10). He even went so far as to say that "a democratic form of government is considered by many today to be a natural postulate of reason itself," precisely because the modern state is so deeply involved in the lives of people (D10, ¶12)—and because people want an effective share in shaping their lives and society (D10, ¶8; cf. Moody 1953, 71). It is clear, however, that democracy as such was by no means an absolute for the pope; what he was concerned about was the needs of a healthy community. These, he said, can also be met under other legitimate forms of government (see D14, 258). So one

---

[1]In order to avoid cumbersome references to the works of Pius XII, I have given full bibliographical references to twenty-seven of his documents (in chronological order) in the bibliography at the end of this book and have given each of them a reference number—D1, D2, D3, and so on. I have used these abbreviations whenever I refer to the works of Pius XII; e.g., in the present references "D2" refers to his Christmas address of 1939, and "D4" refers to his radio message for Christmas 1941. Numbers following the "D" number refer to the pages of the relevant document except in cases where I refer to a paragraph using the symbol ¶.

must agree with Langan (2005, 182) that "the papal endorsement of democracy, while real and significant, is qualified and cautious."

The leaning of Pius XII toward democracy had what would now be called a geopolitical dimension: it identified the pope with "the West" in the struggle against communism as a world power. It is hardly surprising therefore that Pius XII was not inclined at this time to make sweeping condemnations of the capitalist order, for it was on this foundation that "the free world" rested.

In some respects the situation facing Pius XII was more like that facing Leo XIII than the situation at the time of *Quadragesimo Anno*. There appeared to be only one realistic alternative to capitalism. That was communism—and the pope (like many other Church leaders) saw this as the ultimate abomination in the political order. His Christmas message of 1954 (D27, 25) even raised a doubt whether communist governments had the moral authority to command their citizens; it also questioned whether communist governments were capable of entering into morally binding international agreements.

The "third way," represented by fascist-inspired corporatism, had been greatly discredited by World War II (cf. Camp 1969, 40). It is true that Spain and Portugal still retained something of this approach. But it no longer seemed a realistic or attractive option for "the West" as a whole. However, the capitalist system had survived the economic crisis of the 1930s—though it had done so only by following the economic policies proposed by John Maynard Keynes and allowing a good deal of tampering by the state with the market economy. The war itself gave an important boost to the capitalist system—and proved that the system could flourish in much closer partnership with a bureaucratic state than had been envisaged in its earlier ideology. After the war, a crucial aspect of the Marshall Plan was massive US investment in Europe; this contributed to a quick recovery of capitalism in Europe (and considerable inroads by US companies into the European market). Within a few years of the ending of the war, Japan became the new showpiece for the "free enterprise" system.

The result of all this was that capitalism could again present itself as the system that works, that brings progress. In its new guise it could even claim to have gone most of the way toward solving the traditional social problem, namely, the poverty of the working class. This apparent success seemed so obvious that by 1952 Pius XII was inclined to accept that, essentially, the problem had been solved, at least in Western society.[2]

---

[2]D24, 791–92: "Die Not des Proletariats und die Aufgabe, diese den Zufälligheiten der wirtschaftlichen Konjuktur schutzlos preisgegebene Menschenklasse emporzuheben zu einem den anderen gleichgeachteten Stand mit klar umschribenen Rechten. Diese Aufgabe ist, jedenfalls im Wesentlichen, gelöst" (cf. D27, 20).

However, what made it particularly difficult for the pope to challenge the capitalist system in any radical way was the fact that it was seen as the economic face of political democracy.

At no time did he condone capitalist abuses; in fact, he spoke out at various times against the subordination of the common good to private greed (e.g., D9, 252–53; D16, 435–36; D5, 16–17). But his tone is rather closer to that of Leo XIII than to that of Pius XI. It is significant that he refers far more frequently to *Rerum Novarum* than to *Quadragesimo Anno*. The radio message in which he commemorated the fiftieth anniversary of Leo's encyclical (D3) paid surprisingly little attention to *Quadragesimo Anno*, which of course had its tenth anniversary at the same time.

Pius XII invoked in a rather vague and general way the principles laid down in *Quadragesimo Anno*. But he was notably less specific than Pius XI in regard to how these general principles are to be put into effect in practice. He was perhaps more aware that there is no easy formula that would be *the* practical solution to the social problem.

In one interesting and significant passage of an address given in 1949 he refers explicitly to the professional organizations so favored by Pius XI. He says they offered a "concrete and opportune formula." He defends this formula against the accusation that it was a surrender to fascism—and also against the suggestion that what Pius XI proposed meant a return to medievalism. But then Pius XII goes on to say that this section of *Quadragesimo Anno* must now be seen as an instance of *an opportunity missed*, because it was not seized on at the opportune time (D19, 284). This is a good example of how Pius XII preserved a "doctrinal" consistency with his immediate predecessor while changing the emphasis and the practical implications to a significant extent.

It is clear that, by the time he made this statement in 1949, Pius XII felt that it would be unrealistic and perhaps even counterproductive for the Church to commit itself unreservedly to working for the acceptance of a corporative type state in most Western countries. For the foreseeable future the most realistic approach for the Church seemed to him to be to rest content with a tempered version of capitalist society while working for a further tempering of its obnoxious features.

Concern for Personal Freedom

Having referred to the "missed opportunity" to implement the kind of society Pius XI would have wished, Pius XII goes on to address himself to the possibilities and dangers of the current situation. He expresses concern about excessive nationalization of the means of production. He recalls the teaching of *Quadragesimo Anno* that some degree of this may be acceptable. But he maintains that the economy is not of its nature an institution of the state; the role of the public authorities is not to replace private rights and initiative but rather to serve them (D19, 285). It soon becomes clear that by the year 1949 the chief concern of the pope was not so much the dangers of capitalism but rather the threat of the erosion of free enterprise through excessive nationalization.

This resistance to nationalization is an indication that his basic concern was to defend the social value of personal freedom. Unlike his predecessor, he was not campaigning eagerly for the replacement of the capitalist order by some alternative system, for he believed that the problem was not chiefly the iniquity of one system over another. Rather it was that all the massive systems of the modem world tend to swallow up the individual person. He defended individual freedom, rights, and responsibilities, insisting that it is the will of God that humans have a sphere of rights that are immune to all arbitrary attack (D5, 5–24). In doing so, he laid a foundation for the later emphasis on human rights adopted by Pope John XXIII, especially in *Pacem in Terris*. Pius rejected the great systems of the left and the right, noting that slavery of the person could result from the tyranny of private capital as well as from the power of the state.[3] By 1950 he had become concerned that the power of trade unions would increase to a point where the freedom of the individual worker would almost be lost (D20, 487).

By 1952 Pius XII saw a particular danger that the Cold War between East and West could lead to restrictions of the freedom of the person "in what is called the free world" (D25, 42). Clearly, the pope was aware of the dangers of what later came to be called "the national security state" and the ideology on which it is based. Fear of enemies abroad and of subversives within the state give rise to serious intrusions into the lives of citizens with the curtailment, infringement, and outright denial of human rights.

Distribution of Goods

A significant contribution of Pius XII to the body of social teaching or doctrine of the Catholic Church has to do with the question of the ownership and distribution of property. It came quite early in his pontificate, in the broadcast (D3) that he made in 1941 to commemorate the fiftieth anniversary of *Rerum Novarum*. There are two important points in this message. The first is that economic prosperity is not to be measured purely in material or quantitative terms. Furthermore, and perhaps even

---

[3]D5, 17: "Che questa servitù derivi dal prepotere del capitale privato o dal potere dello Stato, l'effetto non muta"; cf. D8 252–53.

more significantly, the pope insists that there must be an equitable distribution of whatever goods are available. He holds that no matter how much wealth there may be in a given area, the country cannot be said to be economically prosperous if its people do not have the opportunity to share equitably in its wealth (D3, 200–201).

In defining economic prosperity in this way, Pius XII was well ahead of the economists and planners of his time. During the years when he was pope, and for many years afterward, it was widely held that the best way for a country to become economically prosperous and for it to develop as quickly as possible was to subordinate equitable distribution to rapid growth of the gross national product. Indeed, this view still prevails among many politicians and decision makers. They believe that the national "cake" is to be enlarged first; later on will be the time to consider a fair distribution. In recent years this assumption is being questioned widely. The results of a major research project carried out in the Department of Health Sciences of the University of York were published in a controversial book titled *The Spirit Level* (Wilkinson and Pickett 2010). This provided fairly convincing prima facie evidence that societies where wealth is unevenly divided are more likely to have greater social and environmental problems, not only among the poor, but in the whole society. Drug problems, obesity, high crime levels, lower levels of literacy, higher levels of mental illness, long working hours, and many other problems are less frequent in societies where there is less of a gap between the richest and the poorest in the population. As one might have expected, these conclusions were questioned on various grounds by some other scientists—particularly those associated with right-wing "think tanks" (Saunders 2010; Cohen 2010; see Wilkinson and Pickett 2010, 277–78 in response). But it is widely accepted (e.g., Atkinson 2015, 301) that the research goes some way toward providing empirical evidence for what many people have sensed to be the case—a view quite similar to the one put forward in 1941 by Pius XII.

In his radio message of 1941 Pius XII made a second major contribution to the socioeconomic teaching of the Church; it concerns private property. Like his predecessors, he insisted on the right and value of private ownership. But in contrast to Leo XIII, he did not hesitate to give the first priority to the general right of all people to the use of the goods of the Earth. The right of the individual to a particular item of private property does not negate the more general and fundamental right; rather it is to be a means of actualizing the right of all to the use of material goods (D3, 198–99). He went on to spell this out explicitly:

Undoubtedly the natural order, deriving from God, demands also private property. . . . But all this remains subordinated to the natu-

ral scope of material goods and cannot be independent of the first
and fundamental right which concedes their use to all people; but
it should rather serve to make possible the actuation of this right in
conformity with its scope. (D3, 221, my translation; cf. D3, 198–99)

This way of treating the question of private property represents an important development in Catholic social teaching, because it is clearer and more explicit than the treatment of private property in *Quadragesimo Anno* (*QA* 45–46) and provides a significant corrective to the treatment of the topic in *Rerum Novarum* (*RN* 19).

The acceptance of the idea that the right to private ownership is subordinate to the general right of all people to the goods of the Earth provides a solid basis for recent teaching. Later popes and the Council Fathers at Vatican II referred to the teaching of Pius XII and drew out the practical implications in a way that attracted the attention of the world and shifted the focus of Catholic social teaching.

The most notable feature of the approach of Pius XII to socioeconomic issues was his realism, that is, his practical acceptance, especially in the second half of his pontificate, of a capitalistic society. He did not repudiate the call of Pius XI for major restructuring of the social order along lines that would be at least vaguely corporative or vocational. But it would seem that this ideal never appeared to Pius XII to be feasible in practice during the years that he was pope. So the corporative ideal came to have what one might call an eschatological character—something that was to come about in an indefinite future (D19, 284). Indeed, in 1952 Pius XII sharply rejected the idea of implementing one of his predecessor's proposals (namely, a degree of co-management) on the grounds that this was one element in an integral scheme and was therefore not to be separated from the whole (D23, 1670; cf. an address of June 1950—D20, 487). This means in effect that while giving formal approval to the proposal for radical reform of existing structures, he was, in practice, resisting an important step toward a piecemeal implementation of such restructuring.

It would appear that the practical ideal of Pius XII would have been a nonbureaucratic free enterprise economy, with noncentralized agencies to facilitate cooperation between various sectors of the economy. The state would play an unobtrusive "watchdog" role to ensure that the common good would be served. The pope believed that this ideal was threatened in Western countries not only by overgrown unbridled capitalism but particularly by socialistic tendencies—especially by nationalization of the means of production and the introduction of the welfare state.

The pope believed in the possibility of gradual and peaceful improvement of the existing system. He held that justice can be promoted not through revolution but through a harmonious evolution (D6, 175). He believed that the Western economic system had gone a long way toward overcoming poverty. In practice, then, it offered the best hope for the future—not an ideal best but the best available at the present time. Consequently, his stance represents a practical option of support for a capitalist order, with the qualification that he disapproved of certain aspects of it. In the socioeconomic area, therefore, he effectively (though not doctrinally) retreated from the call of Pius XI for a fundamental restructuring of society and even from Leo XIII's outraged protest against the capitalist system.

There is a danger that one might stop at this point and conclude that if an option for the poor meant anything to Pius XII, it was largely confined to charitable works rather than the transformation of society. But that would be to overlook the fact that "the poor" is a term that applies not merely to those who have little wealth, but also to those who find themselves powerless. In other words, there is a political as well as a socioeconomic connotation to the word. The kind of deep concern that was aroused in Leo XIII by the plight of the mass of the industrial workers crushed by economic poverty was awakened in Pius XII by the thought of masses of ordinary people deprived of the possibility of taking personal responsibility for many aspects of their daily lives.

Pius spoke out strongly and repeatedly about this powerlessness, just as Leo had spoken out about economic poverty. In this sense, he was on the side of the poor. But, again like Leo, he could do little more than protest. He saw what was wrong, and he proposed an ideal in which people would have all the freedoms of a genuine democracy, unencumbered by bureaucracy. But he did not focus attention on any really practical and effective steps that could be taken toward the overcoming of powerlessness and the achievement of real participation and freedom. As Langan (2005, 187) remarks, he continued the tradition of "expressing universal truths" and "incorrigible generality." The concern of Pius about the danger of communism was so great that he was unwilling to take the risk of posing an explicit and detailed challenge to the many inadequacies of Western governments in implementing in practice their professed commitment to freedom and democracy.

FROM COLONIALISM TO INTERNATIONAL DEVELOPMENT

After World War II, two major struggles were played out on the world stage: the struggle between East and West and the struggle against colonialism by the peoples of what came to be called the Third World. In the preceding section I looked at how the first of these struggles affected the social teaching of Pius XII. Now I move on to look at the second issue.

Many former colonies gained political independence during the pontificate of Pius XII, so this is an appropriate place to begin to examine the attitude of the Church to colonialism and the process of decolonization. The issue of colonization was given very little attention in the social teaching of the Catholic Church in the late nineteenth and early twentieth centuries. Now, however, the question of the relationship between "the North" and "the South" (or, in older terminology, between "the developed world" and "the developing world") has been moving more and more to the center of the social justice agenda of churches. In order to have a proper grasp of this issue, it is essential to have some understanding of how the Church saw colonialism and what it had to say about the early stages of the process of decolonization.

During the four hundred years of European colonial expansion, almost all Church authorities accepted a theology that could justify colonization under certain circumstances. In 1659, Pope Alexander VII alluded to a principle that would allow the colonial powers to see themselves as performing a service to humankind insofar as they were understood to be occupying uninhabited or underpopulated areas and tapping unused resources of the Earth (Alix 1967, 19). There were only a few prophetic figures like Bishop Bartolomé de Las Casas who were so outraged that they could not be silenced when they cried out against the exploitation that was taking place under the guise of colonization and evangelization (see Williamson 1992). Despite the occasional protests of Church leaders against abuses, and the insistence of the Vatican that what missionaries should bring from Europe was only the faith (Alix 1967, 20–21, 73–74), there can be no doubt that the Church gave a certain legitimacy to political and economic colonialism by its day-to-day cooperation with the occupying powers.

In the early colonial period there seems to have been little or no suggestion that the whole process of European colonization was morally repugnant, although there were occasional protests by Church authorities against particular barbarities or gross injustices. Perhaps the main reason why they did not speak out against colonialism was because, like most of their contemporaries, they could scarcely imagine an end to the colonial era.

The myth of Western superiority was not seriously undermined by the fact that many Latin American nations had become independent. This was because their struggle for independence was led not by the indigenous peoples of Latin America but almost entirely by people of European stock, the descendants of the colonists, or by people of racially mixed stock who had been culturally assimilated, at least to the extent of adopting Spanish or Portuguese as their mother tongue.

In the late nineteenth and early twentieth centuries the current theology and spirituality were marred by a dualism that greatly exaggerated the gap between secular matters and the religious sphere. In attempting to be neutral or "above politics," Church leaders often condoned, in practice, social and political injustices. They made little attempt to challenge the policies of the imperial powers—except in cases where these clashed with the rights or interests of the Church. Indeed, Pope Leo XIII did not even give backing to the independence struggles of Catholic peoples like the Poles and the Irish—even though the usual justification for colonialism could scarcely apply in these cases (cf. Alix 1967, 23, 80–81).

In 1926, Pius XI in his mission encyclical, *Rerum Ecclesiae* (*AAS* [*Acta Apostolicae Sedis*]18, 65–83), referred to what he called the "unlikely case" in which a native population would seek to gain its freedom and drive out not only the colonial administration, but also the foreign missionaries of the occupying power. He did not address the question of whether such a struggle for freedom would be justified; instead, he confined himself to pointing out the disastrous position in which the Church would find itself in such a situation. There is no indication that he was moved by the growing cry being raised by poor and exploited peoples from many parts of the non-Western world. Like his predecessors, he failed to throw the Church firmly on the side of the subject peoples who were making new or renewed efforts to shake off the oppressive and exploitative domination of the imperial powers. Church leaders and theologians in Europe did not seem to realize that the liberation struggles of the colonized peoples would soon come to the center of the world's stage.

The process of decolonization speeded up enormously in the wake of World War II. Nevertheless, in the late 1940s and the 1950s—and even into the 1960s—the Catholic Church still seemed quite unprepared to address such issues as the morality of a war of liberation; indeed it even seemed uninterested in such questions. Pius XII, who gave addresses on almost every conceivable political topic, had very little to say on this issue—though it had become a burning question for millions of Catholics all over the world.

The End of the Colonial Era

Shortly after the end of World War II it became obvious to very many people that the colonial era was indeed drawing to a close. Pius XII recognized that the process of decolonization was irreversible. Nevertheless, he was quite circumspect about giving support to those engaged in the struggle for independence. This was partly because of his fear that communist governments would come to power in the newly independent nations. In 1945 he made a statement supporting the right of nations great and small to take their destiny into their own hands (D13). The obvious reference was to the European nations, but the principle could be taken to apply also to the colonies (cf. Alix 1967, 30–31). At that time the pope preferred not to be too specific. So long as the struggles for liberation in the colonies were still going on, he did not openly throw the support of the Church behind them. But as soon as any particular war of liberation was successfully completed, the Vatican was quick to recognize the newly independent nation and to seek an exchange of diplomatic representatives with it. This policy was in line with that laid down by Leo XIII, which I noted in chapter 2.

By the mid-1950s Pius XII was becoming much more explicit: he began to emphasize the right of colonized peoples to their independence (D27; D29). The Vatican policy of the time was a highly pragmatic one; it was following events rather than seeking to lead them by a prophetic challenge to the injustice of colonialism (cf. Alix 1967, 38). Having laid down general principles about the right of people to self-determination, the pope could in good faith decide that it was not for him to make the political judgment about whether the various conditions had been fulfilled in any particular case.

In 1957 Pius XII issued an encyclical titled *Fidei Donum* on the mission of the Church in Africa (D31; Hickey 1982, 110). Here we find the pope placing the Church in the position of a wise, experienced, and somewhat distanced observer of the international political order. From this high ground the pope went on at once to warn the colonial powers not to deny "a just and progressive political freedom" to the peoples who seek it.

In this encyclical Pius XII took a highly favorable view of the good effects of the colonial occupation. He suggested that those who were struggling for freedom ought "to credit Europe with their progress, for without its influence in all fields, they could have been led by a blind nationalism to hurl themselves into chaos and slavery." He went on to call for a collaboration that would extend to the people of the newly emergent nations "the true values of Christian civilization, which have already borne so many good fruits in other continents" (Hickey 1982, 111, translation slightly emended).

From the mid-nineteenth century to the mid-twentieth most Western-educated people took it for granted that the countries of the West were more richly endowed by nature or providence than other countries. This view was shared by Pius XII (e.g., D28; D32). The assumption is, of course, quite unwarranted. The disparity in wealth between, say, Holland and its former colony Indonesia is clearly not due to the bounty of nature but to the history of European colonial and postcolonial history. It is not too much to say that the myth that the West was more blessed by nature served as a cover-up for the real story of European imperial expansion and exploitation.

It is interesting to note that in the 1940s and 1950s the assumption that the West was more endowed by nature gradually gave way to another assumption, namely, that the West is more "advanced" or "developed" than other parts of the world. This too is based on a myth—the myth that there is just one single path or ladder of development that is open to all nations and that some are further up the ladder than others. Like the myth that the wealthy nations owe their prosperity to the bounty of nature, the myth of development served the interests of the West. It led people to assume that because Western countries are wealthy and technologically advanced, they are also more civilized.

The modern notion of development began to come to the fore in the 1940s. As early as 1941 Pius XII spoke of the right of small states to economic development (D3, 16–17). In 1955 he suggested that one reason for the gap between rich and poor nations was due to the fact that the former had reached a more advanced stage of civilization and development (D28). However, this question of development remained rather peripheral for Pius XII; it was only in the time of later popes that it became a central issue. I take it up again in later chapters.

* * *

SUMMARY

The position of Pius XII was much less radical than that of his predecessor. In his concern about the dangers of communism, Pius XII took a strong stand on the side of Western democracy. During his pontificate the Catholic Church gave strong religious and ideological support to those who opposed communism and socialism at the international, national, and local levels. Pius XII apparently considered that it was no longer realistic to work for a corporatist model of society. He gave tacit support to the capitalist economic model that went hand in hand with the Western political system. He held that the worst excesses of capitalism had already been curbed in the Western world, and he believed that further gradual reforms were possible. While expressing misgivings about certain aspects of the free enterprise approach, he apparently felt that it was the best available option in his time; he saw it as more effective in overcoming poverty and safeguarding human freedom and dignity than the likely alternatives. His chief concern about the new developments in society related not so much to economic poverty as to the powerlessness that arises when people are subjected to bureaucratic structures of any kind. In protesting strongly against this powerlessness of ordinary people, Pius could be said to be taking the side of the poor. From a doctrinal point of view, the main contribution of Pius XII to Catholic social teaching was his insistence that the right of private property is subordinate to the general right of all people to the goods of the Earth.

The Church acquiesced in, and gave religious support to, the colonial expansion of the European powers into other continents, although a small number of outstanding Church people put up a strong resistance to exploitation and oppression by the colonial powers. After the first period, colonialism scarcely featured for three hundred years as a social justice issue for the Church. In the late nineteenth and early twentieth centuries, the Church gave little or no support to indigenous peoples struggling for independence.

Many former colonies gained political independence during the pontificate of Pius XII. He recognized the right of colonized peoples to become independent and to become "developed." He tacitly assumed that the Western nations were more advanced. He gave little encouragement to those who were struggling for liberation. But as soon as the struggle was won in any given area, he was keen to establish diplomatic relations with the newly independent state.

QUESTIONS FOR REVIEW

1.   *Why was Pius XII more favorable toward democracy than previous popes?*
2.   *What was the main difference between the social teaching of Pius XI and that of Pius XII?*
3.   *What was the teaching of Pius XII about private property?*
4.   *What did Pius say about equal distribution of income in a population?*
5.   *What was the attitude of Pius XII toward the struggle for freedom in the colonies?*

QUESTIONS FOR REFLECTION

1.   *Is the Church's commitment to democracy a fundamental part of its social teaching?*
2.   *In what ways was the Church guilty of cultural and religious imperialism during the great missionary age, and in what ways did it resist this temptation? To what extent has it changed today in this regard?*
3.   *Why was Catholic social teaching so slow to address effectively the issues of the struggle for liberation in the colonies?*

ISSUES FOR FURTHER STUDY

1. *What was the relationship between church and state in your own country during the time of the papacy of Pius XII? Did the Church favor one sector of society?*
2. *To what extent did the Church collude in the oppression and exploitation of the peoples of Latin American, Asia; and Africa? Read Williamson 1992; Boff and Elizondo 1991; Pakenham 1991.*

5

Pope John XXIII—A New Direction?

Pius XII died in 1958, and Angelo Roncalli became pope, taking the title John XXIII. It is generally agreed that he made a major contribution to the social teaching of the Catholic Church. My main purpose in this chapter is to examine whether, or in what sense, he gave a new direction to Catholic social teaching. There are two sections in the chapter. In the first, I hope to show that in one sense his position was by no means a radical one, nor did it represent any major departure from the direction set by earlier popes, especially by Pius XII. In the second section, I suggest that, in another sense (and despite what has just been said), Pope John had a major role to play in giving the Catholic Church a significantly new direction in social teaching and policy.

A SUPPORTER OF THE STATUS QUO?

There was an extraordinary freshness about Pope John XXIII, both in his style and in his two major encyclicals on social issues—*Mater et Magistra*, issued in 1961 and *Pacem in Terris*, issued in 1963.[1] Those who like to categorize everybody as either a liberal or a conservative have little difficulty in seeing "good Pope John" as a liberal, in sharp contrast to his predecessor. This is, of course, an oversimplification, but as a journalistic generalization, it contains a good deal of truth, especially insofar as it refers to the style of the pope. In his teaching, however, there is much more continuity with Pius XII. The trouble with the labels "liberal" and

---

[1]For an account of the various translations of these two documents, see the bibliography of official documents at the end of this book. When giving references to these two encyclicals I shall use the abbreviations *MM* and *PT* followed by the paragraph number. Marvin L. Mich (2005, 191–216) offers a detailed and careful study of *Mater et Magistra*. The first pages of Mich's study give a good account of the background to the writing of the encyclical. Drew Christiansen (2005, 217–43) provides a detailed commentary on *Pacem in Terris*. The first pages of his commentary give a good account of the background to the writing of the encyclical.

"conservative" is not so much that they are inaccurate as that many people assume that between them they are exhaustive. The fact is that there is room for at least one other label—"the radical"—which cannot be reduced to either "liberal" or "conservative." The word "radical" has been given a remarkably wide variety of meanings in history (see Raymond Williams 1976, 209–11; also Holland and Henriot 1983, 37–45). In using it here, I take it to mean a readiness to work for a fundamental change in the structures of society. The radical person may be liberal on some issues and conservative on others. In many cases, however, the radical has an outlook that is entirely different from both the liberal and the conservative—one that shows just how much the other two have in common.

On social issues Pope John was not a radical. On the question of the fundamental restructuring of society, his approach was not very different from that of Pius XII, and in some ways Pius XI was more radical than either of them. The similarities and the differences between Pius XII and John XXIII can be found in a significant passage near the end of *Pacem in Terris*, written shortly before John died:

> There are, indeed, generous souls who . . . burn with desire to put everything right and are carried away by such an ungovernable zeal that their reform becomes a sort of revolution.
>
> To such people we would suggest that it is in the nature of things for growth to be gradual and that therefore in human institutions no improvement can be looked for which does not proceed step by step and from within. The point was well put by our predecessor Pius XII: "Prosperity and justice lie not in completely overthrowing the old order but in well planned progress. Uncontrolled passionate zeal always destroys everything and builds nothing." (*PT* 161–62, Waterhouse version adapted)

Pope John's statement lacks the acerbity of his predecessors. He shows understanding and sympathy for the "generous souls" who are not satisfied with a step-by-step reform. But, despite this, he, in fact, reaffirms the gradualist approach of Pius XII. This is no mere verbal acceptance made in the interests of assuring a kind of doctrinal continuity. Pope John was an optimist (cf. Cronin 1964a, 242) who really believed that the necessary improvements could come "step by step and from within," without any radical disruption of the system.

Optimism about the World

This optimism of John XXIII has to be teased out, so as to disentangle various elements in it. First of all, it represents a new theology of the world. It would perhaps be more accurate to speak of a new spirituality of commitment to the world, a spirituality that contains the seed of a new theology. Marvin Mich puts it well when he says that Pope John "moved away from a spirituality of detachment and replaced it with a spirituality of engagement that asked Christians to be creatively engaged in the world as a chief characteristic of their spiritual journey" (Mich 2005, 204). During the Second Vatican Council the seed of a new theology planted by Pope John sprouted very rapidly indeed. John's distinctive spirituality can be detected mostly as a difference of tone. To document it, one would have to note what he omits more than what he says. What comes through is the fact that he is not afraid that commitment to the world and its values will cause people to neglect the highest spiritual values. One significant point in *Mater et Magistra* is the optimistic way in which he speaks about human work in general (*MM* 107) and especially about agricultural work (*MM* 149). Two years later, in *Pacem in Terris*, the new approach is rather more explicit, especially in his call for a "synthesis" between scientific and spiritual values (*PT* 150), an "interior unity" between religious faith and action in the temporal sphere (*PT* 152).

One important element in Pope John's conception of the world is his insistence that people have to work together for the common good and that this collaboration is to be facilitated by the civil authorities. On this point there is a clear doctrinal continuity between what he says and the teaching of Leo XIII, but nevertheless there is a difference in tone that has important practical implications. Like his predecessors, John XXIII insists that human authority is derived from God. But, significantly, he immediately adds a text from Saint John Chrysostom, which shows that it is not that a particular ruler is appointed by God, but rather that the authority exercised by the ruler comes from God (*PT* 46). So in this first paragraph of his teaching on the question, Pope John is distinguishing between authority and the officeholder. In the next paragraph he insists that human authorities are subject to a higher authority (*PT* 47). He goes on to say that civil authorities can impose an obligation in conscience only insofar as their authority is intrinsically linked to the authority of God (*PT* 49). If civil authorities make demands contrary to the moral order, or fail to acknowledge human rights, their authority no longer exists, and so the citizen is not bound to obey (*PT* 51, 61). Indeed, as Christiansen says, "The backbone of the document is its teaching on human rights. Morality, political authority, international relations, and the world community are all interpreted in light of the rights of human beings" (Christiansen 2005, 223). Christiansen goes on to point out the extent to which this was a departure from the approach of Pius IX in the "Syllabus of Errors" of 1864 and later Catholic thinking (Christiansen 2005, 224, 233–36).

According to Pope John, the whole purpose of political authority is the promotion of the common good (*PT* 84). The pope, following Leo XIII, insisted that authorities are bound to be particularly concerned for the poor; but it is significant that John XXIII expressed this in terms of human rights, saying that the less fortunate members of the community are less able to defend or assert their rights (*PT* 56). The denial by a government of the right of the individual to an area of personal freedom is branded by Pope John as "a radical inversion of the order of human society" (*PT* 104, Campion version). These statements indicate that John was emphasizing a different aspect of authority from that stressed by Leo XIII. The latter was afraid of anarchy, so he insisted that when human authorities make demands on citizens, they do so with the authority of God; only reluctantly and minimally did Leo take note of the cases where human authorities forfeited the right to unquestioned obedience. John XXIII, like Pius XII, was more concerned lest individual freedom be stifled by authoritarian rulers or bureaucracies. So he paid more attention to the duty of authorities to fulfill their proper role, namely, the service of the common good and the respecting of human rights. For him, human authority ceases to be real authority when it fails in this regard.

Quite clearly, this approach leaves much greater scope for the individual to assess whether those in power are, in fact, exercising a lawful authority. Pope John is not, of course, encouraging political dissent, still less any kind of organized resistance. But evidently his conception of human society is that of a community of persons who voluntarily submit to civil authority in order to attain the common good. He does not hold that democracy is the only valid form of government (*PT* 52), but the values he promotes are those to which democracy at its best is committed and that it should embody.

The general optimism of Pope John about the world finds expression in his teaching about political organization and authority. He believes people can cooperate successfully not only at the local and national levels but also at the international level (*MM* 155–65, 170–77; *PT* 80–145). The whole presupposition of his two great social encyclicals was that people need only to be encouraged and animated to cooperate more fruitfully. He presumes not merely the ability to cooperate but the fundamental willingness of people and nations to cooperate even at the cost of personal, sectional, or national sacrifice. Although this presupposition might easily be overlooked, it is important to note it, for it explains why John XXIII addressed himself mainly to the following question: What improvements are needed in economic, social, and political affairs in order that people may live with greater human dignity? He did not concentrate on another issue that may be equally or more important: How can these changes be brought about, especially where many of those who hold power are reluctant to accept reforms that would curb their power?

Optimism about the Modern World

John XXIII was not just optimistic about the world in general. His optimism and hopefulness were directed specifically to the *modern* world—meaning the kind of society that had emerged in the Western world as a result of rapid economic growth. Here his tone is notably different from that of Pius XII. He speaks with ringing hope and challenge of this age of the atom and of the conquest of space as "an era in which the human family has already entered on its new advance toward limitless horizons" (*PT* 156, Campion version). He asks whether the modern developments in social relationships will entangle people in a maze of restrictions so that human freedom and responsibility will be eliminated, and his answer is a firm "no" (*MM* 62).[2] The modernization of society can, he believes, have more advantages than disadvantages, if it is properly controlled and directed (*MM* 67).

In a moving passage in *Mater et Magistra* the pope expresses his distress about the plight of poverty-stricken workers of many lands and whole continents. He adds that one of the reasons for this poverty is that these areas are still underdeveloped in terms of modern industrial techniques (*MM* 68).[3] In a later paragraph he says that usually an underdeveloped or primitive state of economic development is the fundamental or enduring cause of poverty and hunger (*MM* 163; cf. *MM* 154, which refers to primitive and obsolete methods of agriculture). Clearly he has no serious doubts about the need for modernization and development as the way in which the world must make progress.

The pope is, of course, aware that this kind of development can create social problems (*MM* 124–25) and even economic difficulties (*MM* 154). He also realizes that the modern situation offers opportunities for a new kind of elitism. So he warns against abuses of power by the new class of managers of large-scale enterprises, and he makes the important point that such abuses can occur both in private business and in public bodies (*MM* 104, 118). Furthermore he notes two causes of poverty that are particularly important in this modern world—the arms race (*MM* 198, 69, 204; *PT* 109) and the squandering of money by governments on prestige projects (*MM* 69). But he would see all of this as an argument

---

[2]Bolté (1964, 1:289) makes the interesting suggestion that the "negandum" of the Latin text should be translated not as "it will not happen" but as "it must be resisted," that is, not allowed to happen. This translation would certainly fit in better with what the pope says in the following two paragraphs, but neither the Italian text nor the letter of the Holy See to the *French Social Week* (the text of which seems to have been the original source for the passage in the encyclical) is open to this interpretation.

[3]See Bolté (1966, 2:376–77) for the nuances of the translation.

for control and balance, not a reason for questioning the whole direction of modern development.

Optimism about Capitalism

Pope John's optimism is not just about the world but about the modern world, including the processes of modernization and development. His optimism extends even further—to the capitalist system that is most conspicuously associated with modernization. (Of course, those nations that rejected capitalism were also dedicated to economic development; but the West, including the Vatican, has tended to assume—and with good reason—that the link between capitalism and development is more natural and more successful.)[4] There are indications that Pope John took an optimistic view of what might be expected from capitalist society in the future. It is not that he ignored its deficiencies and abuses or repudiated the condemnations of capitalism by Leo XIII and Pius XI, but he seemed almost to believe that before too long and without too much trouble the system could be humanized effectively.

In one of the more significant and controversial paragraphs in *Pacem in Terris* the pope drew a distinction between "false philosophical theories" and the "historical movements" that are inspired by these theories (*PT* 159).[5] It is commonly and correctly assumed that Pope John was referring here primarily to those left-wing movements that, historically at least, draw their inspiration from Marx (cf. Utz 1963, 136n47). But the pope would no doubt have also applied the distinction to capitalism: the capitalist ideology or theory remains incompatible with Catholic social teaching, but capitalist society in its actual historical development can be viewed rather more optimistically by Pope John. As Cronin (1964a, 325) says, "It is widely held that they apply to contacts with the Communist world. . . . But the principles as given in the encyclical are general in nature, and we cannot quarrel with those who also see in them reference to anti-clerical movements in Europe and Latin America, or the 'opening to the left' in Italian politics, Spanish fascism or any similar accommodation with historic antagonists."

Already in his 1959 encyclical *Ad Petri Cathedram*, Pope John had

---

[4]See Calvez (1964, 64–66) on development in relation to capitalism and socialism.

[5]The translation of the passage is itself a matter of controversy. I have taken the phrase "false philosophical theories" from the Waterhouse version since it is clearer than the Campion version, which uses the word "teachings" instead of "theories." But I have used the phrase "historical movements" from the Campion version in preference to Waterhouse's vague phrase "practical measures." The translations into other European languages speak of "movements" (see Bolté 1966, 2:613); and the latter part of the paragraph clearly refers to developments within such movements.

remarked that class distinctions were less pronounced than before (§33; cf. *MM* 48). He went on to say, "Anyone who is diligent and capable has the opportunity to rise to higher levels of society" (§33). This statement shows the extent to which he accepted one aspect of the free enterprise ideology, namely, the assumption that it gives most people a reasonably equal chance of "getting on," that is, of moving up in society. The full implication of this belief is that, by and large, the rich and powerful have earned their privileged place in society, whereas the weak and the poor are in some sense responsible for their "failure." Needless to say, the pope did not accept this implication. But his remark suggests that he did not subject the free enterprise ideology to a thorough and critical examination.

A further indication of a certain naïveté is to be found in an important paragraph of *Mater et Magistra* in which Pope John insisted on the need for a wider distribution of property of various kinds (*MM* 115). He maintained that now is a particularly suitable time for countries to adjust their social and economic structures so as to facilitate a wider distribution of ownership—thus overcoming the tendency of capitalism to concentrate wealth in the hands of the few. Why now? Because, said Pope John, this is a time when an increasing number of countries are experiencing rapid economic development. This statement suggests that John accepted the common assumption that rapid economic growth offers the easiest way to overcome the problem of the unequal distribution of wealth. That is not surprising, for, on the face of it, this assumption seems almost self-evidently correct. Instead of having to face the difficult task of taking wealth from the rich to redistribute it to the poor, why not create sufficient new wealth to enable the poor to become reasonably well off? But despite its apparent obviousness, this line of thinking can, in practice, play a part in bringing about the very opposite of what it aims at. This is what, in fact, has happened in large parts of the world. So it will be useful to look more closely at the process.

How best can rapid economic growth be promoted in a society that follows the free enterprise approach? Both the theorists and the real-life capitalists claim that the only effective way is to allow the entrepreneurs and investors an adequate return for their contribution. What this means in practice is that capitalist investors must be allowed a major share of the new wealth in the form of profits and inducements. The argument is that the national "cake" must first be enlarged even at the cost of some delay in redistributing the shares of the "cake." So a higher priority is given to creation of wealth than to its equitable distribution. Once that pattern is established, it becomes exceptionally difficult to change it. There never comes a time that seems right for a more fair distribution.

The belief that the best way to solve social problems is to speed up economic growth was not confined to Western countries. Almost all developing countries accepted the view that their best hope of eliminating poverty lay in rapid growth. And in the heyday of communism, the leaders of the communist countries imposed almost intolerable sacrifices on their people in order to achieve rapid growth. Then with the collapse of communism the new leaders of most of these countries imposed even greater sacrifices on their people in an effort to achieve growth through switching over their economies to free enterprise!

There was an important difference between the communist and the capitalist view of economic growth. In the centrally planned economies of the communist countries, there was no incompatibility in principle between increased growth and equitable distribution. The governments of these countries failed spectacularly to provide genuine human development for their people—and they failed both in terms of growth and of equitable distribution. Their failure was mainly due to bureaucratic mismanagement, corruption, and a pandering to various power elites.

In the capitalist society of the West the relationship between growth and equitable distribution is more complex and is particularly interesting.

- First, capitalism is committed to growth not merely for practical reasons but also ideologically. At a practical level an ever-increasing demand seems to be necessary if the whole system is not to collapse. Hence the need for an ideology of growth. So growth is promoted in various ways, notably by the advertising industry. The belief is fostered that there is no foreseeable limit either to human needs or to the ability of a free enterprise system to meet these ever-expanding "needs."
- Second, the growth that actually takes place tends, as we have seen, to concentrate wealth in the hands of a minority rather than leading to a more equitable distribution.
- But, third, another part of the ideology of capitalism masks this lack of equity. It promotes an image of free enterprise where all have a fair opportunity to use their talents profitably. Hard work and initiative are correlated with success and prosperity. The implication is that poor distribution of wealth is to be explained more in terms of the laziness and lack of ability of some rather than of any lack of opportunity imposed by the system (see Brookfield 1975, 38). Furthermore, the idea is fostered that the new wealth will gradually "trickle down" from the richer to the poorer sectors of society. These beliefs are illusions. They conceal the fact that the normal tendency of the system is to widen the gap between the rich and the poor (see Piketty 2014, 336). One must conclude that these are ideological beliefs that protect the interests of the wealthy.

Needless to say, Pope John did not set out to promote such dangerous illusions. But they must have had some effect on him. This is shown by his statement (quoted above) that anybody who is diligent and careful can rise to higher levels in society. The fact that the pope uncritically accepted this belief suggests that there was a certain blind spot in his outlook. This becomes more evident when one adverts to the gap between the end he was hoping for and the means he proposed to achieve it. The end result he wanted was a wider distribution of property (*MM* 113–14). The means by which he hoped this would come about was a gradual reform of the existing structures and the introduction of controls designed to reverse the tendency of capitalism to concentrate wealth in the hands of a few. But Pope John was unduly optimistic in thinking that this could be brought about fairly easily. He was unrealistic in seeing the current time of rapid growth as the best occasion for a relatively painless reversal of this "normal" pattern (see Klein 2007). Tampering with the system is never easy—and, ironically, it may be especially difficult when the system is working relatively smoothly as it was at the time *Mater et Magistra* was written.

But surely the pope was correct when he supported his case by noting the progress toward wider ownership made in some economically developed countries (*MM* 115). His facts were correct, but it is doubtful whether they should have been used as the basis for a generalization. Undoubtedly the years between 1945 and 1961 saw a considerable growth in prosperity for most workers in Western countries. But this was part of a wider reality—the increased wealth of Western nations as a whole vis-à-vis the poorer counties of other continents. This imbalance was, in turn, related to the extravagant use by industrialized countries of energy and raw materials, much of which came from poorer countries at a very cheap price. So whatever improvement occurred within the Western countries has to be seen in the context of an increasingly lopsided distribution of wealth on the international (or intercontinental) level.

Furthermore, the improvement in the standard of living of workers in Western countries came at a high environmental cost. The most severe damage to the environment came mainly, not in the Western countries themselves, but in the poorer countries that were the source of the raw materials and energy sources used in the West. In the communist countries of Eastern Europe enormous environmental damage was done as a result of their governments' pursuit of rapid growth, and the Chernobyl disaster in 1986 revealed the huge environmental risks that were taken. It is important to realize that the issue of whether or not we care for the environment is a matter of justice. In fact, as I point out in chapter 18, we now have a new term to describe it: intergenerational justice.

Moreover, there is a certain ambiguity in the pope's call, at this point in the encyclical, for a wider distribution of ownership of property. Was he advocating that more people (especially the working class) should become owners of property—a position that would involve the lessening of absolute poverty? Or was he saying that whatever wealth is available should be distributed more equitably—a position that would involve the lessening of relative poverty?

It would seem that he was simply following in the footsteps of Leo XIII by insisting on the importance of more people becoming owners of property, leading to a lessening of absolute poverty—and tacitly assuming that this would involve a lessening of relative poverty by a narrowing of the gap between rich and poor. It is quite likely that John XXIII was not aware that a reduction in absolute poverty can go hand in hand with a widening of the gap between rich and poor.

Statistics show that, in the period between 1980 and 2015 in most of Western society there was an enormous increase in the gap between the very rich and the rest of the population. This took place during a period when there was a small increase in the income of ordinary workers but enough for some to become homeowners. Would Pope John be satisfied with this kind of reduction in absolute poverty combined with an increase in relative poverty? The answer should be "no," because in two earlier paragraphs of the encyclical he had insisted strongly on the central importance of the equitable distribution of wealth (*MM* 73–74). Following Pius XII, he even went so far as to say, "The economic prosperity of any people is to be measured less by the total *amount* of goods and riches they own than by the extent to which these are *distributed* according to the norms of justice" (*MM* 74).[6]

We must conclude that, in terms of his own principles, Pope John was not entitled to present as a "success story" those "nations with developed social and economic systems" where ownership has become more widespread (*MM* 115, Gibbons version). John XXIII was correct when he said that private ownership had increased in some developed countries. But what he said could leave one with a wrong impression, namely, that if the present free enterprise system of the Western world were extended globally, it would bring social justice on a world scale, and that all that is required is a moderate and gradual reform of the system.

The Welfare State

This issue of whether Western countries serve as a model for a humanized version of capitalism is vitally important. It is appropriate to

---

[6]My translation, with emphasis added. The sentence quoted is a summary of an important part of the radio message given by Pius XII in 1941 (D3, 200–201).

say something here about the welfare state approach adopted in several Western European countries in the years after World War II, for it is obvious that Pope John's thinking was very influenced by what he had seen happening in these countries in the late 1940s and the 1950s. These countries expanded their social security services in a major effort to cope with the problems of poverty; to pay for these services they raised their taxation levels far higher than before—to levels that would seem almost unthinkable in the United States.

What was the relationship between economic growth and such high levels of "welfare"? Undoubtedly, the rapid economic growth of those years made it easier for these countries to pay for the welfare services. (And as growth has slowed down in recent years, the social services have come under increasing strain through shortage of funds.) But it is important to note that the determination to alleviate poverty through national social welfare programs came prior to most of the economic growth. It is arguable that the fundamental change in structures and attitudes involved in the welfare state owes more to the chaos at the end of the World War II than to the success of a revived capitalism. Workers were determined never again to face the deprivations of the depression years of the 1930s, and the breaking of the molds that came during and after the war offered the chance to give political expression to this determination. The point is that basic changes in social structures are more likely to be associated with the failure of a growth-oriented free enterprise model of society than with its "success."[7] This suggests that it is illusory to expect raw capitalism to develop naturally, organically, and painlessly into a system characterized by equitable distribution of wealth and effective care for the weaker sectors of society.

It is well to note also the limited aims of the welfare state approach. It did not set out overtly to bridge the gap in ownership between rich and poor by wholesale nationalization or redistribution of capital goods. In other words, it is not to be equated with a full program of socialism. It presupposed the continuance of a free enterprise economy with its inherent tendency toward imbalance and concentration of wealth. Rather than attempting to abandon the capitalist system itself, it sought to cope with some of the evil effects of the system, namely, the poverty and deprivation that it created in some sectors of society. The welfare state was seen by many as

---

[7]Naomi Klein (2007) shows how economists and politicians in many countries acted on Milton Friedman's view that the time when radical changes can most easily be made is when systems have failed. Of course, Friedman and his followers were advocating and implementing changes that involved the adoption of a more raw form of capitalism rather than a more tempered one, but the principle remains the same.

a way of giving "a human face" to a society built on a capitalist economy.

By the early 1960s this approach appeared to be working well. It seemed to offer a direction that could be taken further in the future, not merely in Europe but in the wider world. So the scenario for the future envisaged by many concerned people—including, most probably, Pope John and at least some of the drafters of *Mater et Magistra*—would have been along the following lines: a healthy ever-expanding economy, primarily free enterprise in character but including some degree of state capitalism, combined with expanding public welfare programs (supplemented by the welfare programs of voluntary agencies, especially churches) to mitigate the deficiencies and cope with the casualties of such an economic system.

The intervening years have made this scenario increasingly problematical. First, an indefinite period of rapid economic growth can no longer be presumed: there are severe limits to the amount of cheap energy, raw materials, and accessible water that are available to make this possible. There are several inherent problems of the capitalist system; these include unsustainable ecological exploitation, massive financial speculation, as well as problems of prediction, credibility, cycles, and protectionism. These have proved far more intractable than had been anticipated.

Second, it is now quite evident (to all who have eyes to see it) that the development of the West depended to a large extent on the availability of cheap resources from the poorer countries of other continents; so it cannot be seen as a model that may be repeated all over the world.

Third, the welfare state approach has itself run into serious difficulties in the West. The expansion of the economy has slowed down at the same time as the demands of the stronger groups in society have increased. The result is that there is less left for the poorer segment of society, which in some Western countries now constitutes about a quarter of the population.

Finally, government efforts to stimulate the economy are costing the taxpayer a great deal; the heavy tax burden offers a convenient opportunity for opponents of state welfare to mount ideological attacks on the social services as wasteful and as an encouragement to idleness and parasitism. In such an atmosphere it becomes quite unrealistic to hope that something analogous to the welfare state will emerge at the international level, with the rich nations providing adequate help for the poor ones.

The conclusion that emerges from what has been said is that Pope John, like many of his contemporaries, including notable economists and social scientists, showed a rather uncritical optimism in relation to Western-style democratic capitalist society. Most of the scholars and religious leaders of more recent times are far more cautious; they are slow to assume that national and international social justice can come about through a gradual and relatively painless reform of the capitalist order of society.

International Development Cooperation

We move on now to look at the contribution of John XXIII to the whole question of international cooperation in economic affairs. He pointed out that contemporary problems often "exceed the capacity of individual States" (*MM* 201). So, even from the point of view of their own self-interest, countries must cooperate in promoting the economic development of all (*MM* 202).

He put forward some general principles and guidelines on this issue. Looking back at them with hindsight, we may feel that the naïve and ingenuous quality of what he had to say about the whole capitalist order carried over into his treatment of international economic relations. He seemed to accept uncritically the view that was dominant among Western economists of the period. The core of this view was that the problem of the poor countries was underdevelopment and that the solution was rapid economic growth, which was to be achieved by importing both Western capital and Western skills and technology (see *MM* 163–64).

In line with this view, Pope John came out strongly in favor of international loans to promote development; he even felt he had to "give due praise to this generous activity" (*MM* 165). I note in passing that in later years it became clear that huge loans for unrealistic projects left many poor countries swamped in ever-increasing debt. Pope John was also unquestioning in his support for the sending of "as many youths as possible" from the less developed countries to "study in the great universities of more developed countries" (*MM* 165; cf. *MM* 183). He did not seriously question the whole model of development that was being exported from the West and imposed on the newly emergent nations both through the Western education of their planners and through Western investment and aid programs.

Pope John was not, however, entirely naïve in what he said in *Mater et Magistra* about international economic cooperation. He warned the economically developed countries that they must not seek to dominate poorer countries (*MM* 171); to do so would be, he said, to impose on them a new and disguised form of colonialism (*MM* 172). He also insisted that the rich and powerful countries should respect the culture and way of life of the poorer countries—not least because of the high moral quality of their traditional values (*MM* 170, 176–77).

Two years later, and shortly before he died, Pope John published his other major encyclical, *Pacem in Terris*, which he wanted to leave as a kind of legacy to the Church and the world. On this occasion he addressed himself not only to Christians, but also to all people of goodwill. He devoted one important section of the encyclical to the question of the relationship between nation-states. He laid down two fundamental principles: first, that "all states are by nature equal in dignity" (*PT* 86, 89) and, second, that each state has the right to play the leading part in its own development (*PT* 86, 92, 120).

Pope John called for "active solidarity" (*PT* 98) between the nations—and especially between the rich countries and the poorer ones. He insisted that it would be wrong for more advanced states "to take unjust advantage of their superiority over others" (*PT* 88). The phrasing of this paragraph suggests that the drafter of the encyclical uncritically accepted the assumption current in the wealthy nations that these countries were superior not only in economic development but also in culture and civilization.

A World Authority

According to John XXIII, the urgent need for international cooperation at all levels arises from the fact that "the interdependence of national economies has grown deeper . . . so that they become, as it were, integral parts of the one world economy" (*PT* 130). The effect of this ever-increasing unification of the economies of all the countries of the world is that conferences and international agreements are no longer an adequate means of overcoming economic and political difficulties (*PT* 134). There is, he felt, need for some more effective instrument to ensure cooperation and mutual support. The pope believed that what is required is some form of "world government" or "public authority" (*PT* 137—two different translations use these two different phrases; they may mean the same thing but the overtones are different).

Such a world authority, he said, would have to be accepted by common accord rather than imposed by force since, otherwise, it could be (or could appear to be) "an instrument of one-sided interests" (*PT* 138). The world authority would have to respect the principle of subsidiarity, leaving national governments to exercise their own proper authority and confining its attention to issues that have to do with the common good of all nations (*PT* 140). I note in passing that the encyclical seems unrealistic when it says that a world authority "is not intended to limit the sphere of action" of national governments (*PT* 141), for some degree of limitation is implied in the very acceptance of a world authority.

Pope John went on to speak with approval of the United Nations and the Universal Declaration of Human Rights—though he noted a reservation about some points in the latter. Clearly, he saw the United Nations and the adoption of the declaration as important steps toward the establishment of a governing authority for the whole world (*PT* 142–45). As Charles Curran points out, this encyclical "contains the first full-blown discussion of human rights in Catholic social teaching" (Curran 2002, 218). But Curran adds that the treatment of human rights remains grounded in natural law rather than in the freedom and autonomy of the human person (Curran 2002, 220).

More significant than the details of what Pope John had to say about social justice at the international level is that he located this justice issue within the context of "development." This meant that his teaching on social justice was weakened by his failure to criticize the naïvely optimistic and uncritically Western concept of development that was current at the time. On the positive side, however, he identified two key qualities of genuine international development, namely, solidarity (*PT* 98) and subsidiarity (*PT* 140). Even more important, Pope John was the first pope to move the topic of international development cooperation toward the center of the social justice agenda. In this way he paved the way for the great encyclical *Populorum Progressio* issued by his successor, Paul VI, a few years later.

Option for the Poor?

Pope John's social encyclicals played a major part in bringing the Catholic Church into a more open relationship with modern society. But was this at the cost of an acceptance of the Western status quo, subject only to gradual and relatively minor reforms? Did his openness to existing Western society imply a playing down of the Church's challenge to the world? More specifically, did it involve a failure to make an effective option for the poor? These questions call for a carefully nuanced response.

The first thing to note is that Pope John clearly did not see himself as having to choose between, on the one hand, an option for the poor and, on the other hand, an acceptance of capitalist society. He believed that the latter could be tempered and adapted in such a way as to ensure that the poor really were looked after. His encyclicals appeared at a time when the Western economic model seemed to be working well and seemed to be amenable to the kind of reforms he was looking for. It was not a time when many Church leaders or scholars saw the issue in terms of a clash between capitalism and social justice. To present the issue in terms of such a stark choice is to see it more as it was seen thirty years earlier (at the time of Pius XI's *Quadragesimo Anno*), or as it was seen by a significant number of Church activists in the late 1960s and early 1970s, and as it is seen again today by many ecological activists and by those who, like Pope Francis, are aware of the increasing marginalization of the poor by the way the capitalist system is operating at present.

Richard Camp claimed that Pope John saw capitalism "as a positive good" (Camp 1969, 159). This is an overstatement. We have to remember that John XXIII consistently adopted the "spoonful of honey" approach, avoiding condemnations as far as possible, praising what he could, and inviting people to make improvements. The fact that he is less critical than his predecessors in matters of social injustice is no indication that he had abandoned their concern about the exploitation of the poor. Nor does it prove that he had become an enthusiastic convert to the capitalist system.

Nevertheless, John XXIII differed from the popes who went before him insofar as he seems to have approved of the general direction in which the world was moving. Camp is broadly correct in judging that Pope John "did not want a change of institutions" but instead "frankly admired what was already being done and wished an expansion of its benefits to more people" (Camp 1969, 160). The pope did, however, call for some changes. He thought gradual reforms could make the world a more just and humane community of people and peoples. But in proposing such gradual reform, he was at the same time implicitly giving a considerable measure of endorsement to the existing free enterprise system.

From the point of view of their formal teaching, the social encyclicals of John XXIII show no radical departure from the tradition of social teaching rooted in *Rerum Novarum* of Leo XIII. He did not demand a radical reconstruction of society such as Pius XI had proposed. It is significant that the summary of *Quadragesimo Anno* given in *Mater et Magistra* omitted all reference to Pius XI's account of Italian corporatism (*QA* 91–97). It also preserved a careful vagueness in the way it used such terms as "vocational groups" and "intermediate bodies."[8] But subtle differences in tone and emphasis give Pope John's encyclicals a different effect when seen as interventions by the pope at this particular time. So, despite the continuity with the past from a "doctrinal" point of view, the net effect of the social teaching of Pope John was rather different from that of Pius XI. Its effect was to give a certain approval and legitimation to the Western economic approach, provided this is taken in conjunction with the democratic reformist and socially conscious currents of the thought of that period.

Whether John XXIII's position is considered to be an improvement on that of Pius XI depends of course on the stance of the person making the judgment. A fairly typical contemporary evaluation of *Mater et Magistra* was that of John F. Cronin who was assistant director of the Social Action Department of the Conference of US Bishops. He held that the encyclical was "realistic, moderate, and progressive" (Cronin 1966, 44). Obviously he saw this as high praise. It is a useful exercise to translate his words into more neutral language. In saying that the encyclical was "realistic," Cronin meant that it did not call into question in any radical way the economic order existing in Western society and dominating most of the world. In saying that the encyclical was "moderate," Cronin meant that the reforms it called for would not seriously disrupt this order either in

---

[8] Cf. Bolté (1966, 2:321–25).

their extent or by the speed with which they are to be introduced. When he said that the encyclical was "progressive," Cronin meant that it fitted comfortably into the more "enlightened" and "liberal" strand of Western thinking—not the hard economic liberalism of the nineteenth century but the socially conscious liberal thinking of the year 1966 in which Cronin was writing. Understood in this way, Cronin's words can be applied not only to *Mater et Magistra* but to Pope John's social teaching taken as a whole.

In light of the clarifications just given, it is possible to offer a fairly brief answer to the question of whether the social teaching of John XXIII amounts to a call for an effective option for the poor. He was deeply concerned about the plight of different categories of poor people, and he proposed a variety of measures designed not merely to provide relief but also to prevent imbalances in society (*MM* 124, 150, 154, 157–74, 185; *PT* 88, 95, 96, 101, 103–7, 121–25). Nevertheless, he did not commit the Catholic Church to an option for the poor if one takes that in the very specific sense in which it was articulated by the liberation theologians of Latin America, namely, a radical challenge to the capitalistic structures of the international economic order, structures that for many years have given an unfair advantage to Western countries and to privileged elites in Third World countries, structures that in the 1990s were adopted uncritically in many formerly communist countries whose people hoped to share in the prosperity of the West. On the contrary, the effect of Pope John's interventions in social issues was to give a certain sanction and support to these structures, provided they are supplemented and restrained in ways that limit their harmful social effects.

A CHANGE OF DIRECTION

It would be wrong and misleading to stop at this point in the evaluation of the effect of Pope John's encyclicals, for there is a sense in which his teaching made a major contribution toward putting the Church on the side of the poor. More accurately, one might say that John removed from the rich and the powerful an exceptionally important weapon that they could use to maintain injustice in society. To explain how he did so it is necessary to look closely at his teaching about "socialization."

Probably the single most important passage in *Mater et Magistra* is the following:

> One of the main features which seem to be characteristic of our time is undoubtedly an increase in the number of social relationships. Day by day people become more interdependent and this introduces

into their lives various kinds of associations which are generally recognized in contractual or public law. . . . These developments in social life are both a sign and a cause of an increasing degree of State intervention in matters of considerable importance and risk since they have to do with the intimate life of the person. (*MM* 59–60)[9]

The first English translation of this passage followed the Italian version in using the word "socialization" where the Latin text speaks of an increase in social relationships.[10] But the more widely used English versions avoid this word deliberately,[11] either for the purely linguistic reason that it is not used in the Latin text or on the grounds that its omission from the Latin was a significant correction of an unofficial working text.[12] It was felt by some that to use the word "socialization" in the English translation might give the impression that Pope John had abandoned the papal tradition of being opposed to socialism.

In fact, some sectors of the media did interpret the encyclical as proposing some version of socialism. Consequently, Church spokespersons were kept busy explaining that as used in the working text, "socialization" did not really mean the introduction of socialism—and that it did not mean what Pius XII meant when he used the word. (For Pius it meant, mostly, nationalization—see Pius XII D12, 68–72; D23, 792.) They explained that the word was being used in a technical sense to describe a recent

---

[9]My translation. In order to give some approximation to what the pope had in mind, I have translated *ius privatum* as "contractual law." For the nuances of meaning, see Bolté (1964, 1:231–57); see also the translator's note and publisher's note in Kirwan (1964, 90–93 and (v)); also Calvez (1964, (v)–(vi), 102n13).

[10]"Socialium rationum incrementa"; equivalent Latin phrases are used in each of the paragraphs from 59 to 67 inclusively; in each of these nine cases the Italian text uses "socializzazione." Many translations in other European languages used words equivalent to the Italian word, but one authoritative German version and Bolté's later careful French text gave a more literal translation of the Latin. Mich (2005, endnote 63, 213–15) gives a detailed account of the various translations and the nuances of these translations. He points out that the original version of the encyclical was written in German and that the authors of this German text deliberately used the word *Vergesellschaftung* rather than the word *Sozialisierung* "in order to avoid using the same term that Pius XII had condemned nine years earlier." One of the meanings of the word *Sozialisierung* is "nationalization"; what Pius was condemning was wholesale nationalization rather than what John XXIII meant by using the term "socialization." Mich (2005, 206, endnote 65, 215) points out that the understanding of the word "socialization" as used in the encyclical reflects the thinking of the participants in Semaines Sociales de France who met in France in July 1960 in Grenoble.

[11]The Gibbons version translates the word by the phrase "the multiplication of social relationships"; that of Kirwan (1964) chooses the phrase "the development of the network of social relationships."

[12]Kirwan (1964, 92) sees it as quite significant that the official Latin text "rejected the term"; Bolté (1964, 1:241), however, says that the reason the word was omitted was simply to avoid a Latin neologism.

development in Western industrialized society. I would sum up as follows the main elements in modern society that Pope John had in mind when he used the word "socialization":

> People are now more closely inserted in a web of relationships where the actions of each individual affect many others. Many aspects of daily living which used to be seen as personal or family matters now have to be organized, or at least regulated, on a larger scale. So the individual and the family have to rely more on large institutions. Some of these are, technically, private institutions—trade unions, for instance, or non-state insurance schemes. But many are new organs of the public authorities—ranging from local councils up to national governments and even international agencies.

The originality of John XXIII lies not so much in his noting this fact of modern life as in his response to it. He held that it would be not merely pointless but positively wrong if Christians were just to bemoan and resist this development, pining for the simple life of the past (cf. Cronin 1964a, 44). Of course, the pope admitted the dangers it poses—especially the risk of excessive interference with personal responsibilities (*MM* 62) and an undue degree of bureaucratization. In this he was taking account of the preoccupations of Pius XII. But Pope John evidently considered the positive aspects of the process to be more important: it promotes the personal welfare of individuals in many ways, and it can also enable people to act more as a community in their living, work, and play (*MM* 60). So he believed that the process is not inherently destructive of humanity (*MM* 62). Nevertheless, it is not to be seen as automatically beneficial either. In fact it is not a process whose outcome is predetermined at all (cf. Calvez 1964, 8–9). Everything depends on the people involved; it is they who are responsible for the direction it takes (*MM* 63). As Jean-Yves Calvez (1964, 14) says, "Socialization has no meaning in reality save as . . . a 'should' of personal freedom."

So much for John XXIII's account of "socialization." But what is so significant about his approach? In order to answer this question it is necessary first of all to look closely at the accident of history that makes resistance to "socialization" a policy associated with "traditional conservatism."

The important point to note is that the "socialization" of which Pope John is speaking is a feature of modern Western society, and it can be understood only in the light of *Western* history. One early effect of Western modernization and urbanization was to weaken many traditional social relationships and the obligations attached to them. The result was greater independence for individuals. There was a period when the more fortunate and more ruthless of the new generation seemed to have the best of two worlds. On the one hand, they had a high degree of freedom from social constraints, allowing them a wide scope for initiative—and at times for opportunism and even exploitation. On the other hand, they could still rely on patterns of obedience, respect, and cooperation inherited from the past. The less fortunate people at the bottom of the social ladder had, correspondingly, the worst of two worlds. The decline in social restraints left them open to new forms of oppression. But their efforts to protect themselves were resisted by the rich who justified themselves by invoking a myth they had built around the values of untrammeled freedom and rugged individualism.

Modern society could no longer "free-wheel" on the traditionally ingrained patterns of cooperation. There was an urgent need for new sociopolitical systems to look after security, welfare, public health, education, economic development, the environment, and so on. And these needs expanded as society became less centered on small community units and more concentrated in urban areas.

No wonder then that Pope John felt it was pointless and wrong to resist the expansion of such sociopolitical institutions. He saw that what was required was that they be intelligently planned and controlled. The aim should be to retain as much as possible of the values of personal freedom while protecting the common welfare. But neither was it any wonder that there should be strong resistance to any new restrictions. Precisely because such restraints are needed to prevent the exploitation of the weak by the strong, they are experienced by the powerful as unwarranted limits to their freedom. So they sought to minimize these restraints, claiming that they were defending the "traditional values" of personal initiative and freedom, and old-fashioned rugged independence. A striking example of this approach is the way in which very wealthy people in the United States played a key role in supporting the "Tea Party" (see Mayer 2010).

The Newness of Mater et Magistra

Against this background we can understand the position of John XXIII and the reaction to it. It was a carefully nuanced position. On the one hand, he preserved a clear continuity with his predecessors in his teaching about the values that are to be preserved and the means of doing so. Like them, he stressed the principle of subsidiarity (*MM* 53, 117, 152). Following them, he insisted on the importance of vocational groupings and similar intermediate organizations that are not organs of the state itself (*MM* 65).[13] He maintained that intervention by government or other

---

[13]Kirwan (1964, 93–94) points out that the terms used echo those of *Quadragesimo*

public authorities should be limited to those cases where it is really necessary (*MM* 117, 152).

On the other hand, John XXIII differed from Pius XI and Pius XII in his judgment about where in fact such state intervention is required. It is here that the newness of *Mater et Magistra* becomes evident. Retaining continuity with previous social teaching from a doctrinal point of view, the encyclical was startlingly different in its net effect, for, in fact, it proposed a program of action that might well have been borrowed from the manifesto of a social-democrat political party! The real issue then is not whether the word "socialization" is the correct translation of the Latin text. Rather the issue is whether the pope was moving the Catholic Church away from its long-held suspicion of such "socialistic" notions as that of the welfare state. Those who insisted on a literal translation of the Latin text of the encyclical were not just removing the word "socialization"; they were also trying to rid the encyclical of the overtones of this word, and these overtones might have conveyed more accurately what Pope John was referring to. Conservative Catholics were "up in arms" when they read a translation of the encyclical, which suggested that "socialization" was not necessarily a bad thing. So they preferred the more neutral phrase "an increase in social relationships." But the newness of *Mater et Magistra* could not be removed by providing this more literal translation of the Latin text, for the real novelty comes in the section where Pope John spelled out the practical implications of the process of "socialization." So it is opportune to look at some of these implications as presented in the encyclical.

Pope John developed and extended the teaching of Pius XI (*QA* 65), and bypassed the reservations of Pius XII (D19, 487), when he said that in some circumstances employees may be entitled to a share in the profits of the companies where they work (*MM* 75–77) and to a say in management both at the level of the individual firm (*MM* 92–93, 97) and in determining policy at various levels, even on a national scale (*MM* 97). Again, he said, the state must exercise strict control over managers/directors of large businesses (*MM* 104). He went on to maintain that an increased amount of state ownership is justified by the needs of the common good in the modern situation (*MM* 116–17). It must also be recognized, said the pope, that, in fact, the state and public authorities have taken on a greatly expanded role in coping with social problems (*MM* 120). Indeed, Pope John proposed just such a role for them in dealing with the special difficulties of those working in agriculture (*MM* 128–41), and he went into considerable detail in regard to tax assessment (*MM* 133), credit fa-

---

Anno. For a careful study of the relationship between the words used in the two encyclicals, see Bolté (1964, 1:317–25).

cilities (*MM* 134), insurance, (*MM* 135), social security (*MM* 136), price support (*MM* 137), price regulation (*MM* 140), and even the directing of industry into rural areas (*MM* 141).

The pope saw all this as necessary, because in modern Western life, human interdependence is possible only by going beyond one-to-one relationships and those of the small community; life is lived on a scale that requires the massive apparatus of the state to be actively involved in directing and controlling the economic and social life of the people. Even when a nation keeps this state involvement as low as possible by respecting the principle of subsidiarity (as Pope John called for), still the common good nowadays requires far more state involvement than was needed in the past—an involvement that is seen as interference by those who resist it. *Mater et Magistra* gave a mandate for this extra involvement by the state; and the result began to look like an encouragement to "socialization" in the popular sense of the word.

Now at last we can see why some conservative Catholics, such as William Buckley, editor of the *National Review*, reacted to the encyclical by saying *"Mater si, Magistra no"* (cf. Curran 2002, 113). They were quite correct in understanding Pope John to be approving of welfare state policies, and they were quite unwilling to accept this. Their opposition confirms the fact that there really was a distinct change of emphasis in Pope John's social teaching—even when one makes allowance for exaggerations by some commentators of its socializing tendency. It is true, of course, that there was a considerable degree of continuity between what Pope John was saying and the teaching of Pius XII. But there was also quite a lot of discontinuity. Conservative Catholics had no objection to the social teaching of Pius XII—even though there are echoes of that teaching in even the most "advanced" parts of *Mater et Magistra*.[14] What upset them was the new emphasis on state intervention spelled out in some detail by Pope John. Probably the most important effect of the encyclical, seen as an intervention in the continuing debate about social issues, was that it began the process of breaking the long alliance between Roman Catholicism and socially conservative forces.

With the issuing of Pope John's encyclical in 1961 it began to seem credible, for the first time in the modern era, that Catholicism might have more in common with "the left" than with "the right." There is a certain irony in the fact that *Mater et Magistra* should in this sense be more radical than even *Quadragesimo Anno*, for, as I pointed out above, Pope John was no radical. He was looking for moderate and gradual reforms in the capitalist order, whereas Pius XI was demanding a much more

---

[14]Bolté's discovery of such parallels seems to have led him to play down the difference in approach between Pius XII and John XXIII, for instance, on the question of "socialization" (Bolté 1964, 1:246).

fundamental restructuring of society. But the corporatist ideals of Pius XI were somewhat right-wing, at least in their background and overtones: some strands of corporatism were based on a conservative nostalgia for the guilds of the past; others were drawn from aspects of the fascist model of society. Corporatism was strongly opposed to socialism, and Pius XI rejected even a mitigated form of socialism. Pope John, however, while continuing to insist on the importance of private initiative (*MM* 51, 55), private property (*MM* 109), and intermediate nonstate vocational group-ings (*MM* 65), put forward an ensemble of practical proposals which was far more congenial to "the left" than to "the right."

Misuse of Catholic Social Teaching

Perhaps the most important insight of Pope John was his realization that the Church's traditional defense of private initiative and private property had come to be used in an ideological way. And one of his most important decisions was to put an end to this—even in the face of determined resistance by senior Churchmen within the Vatican itself (cf. Hebblethwaite 1984, 325–40).

Over many years the popes had developed a whole body of social teach-ing as a vindication of the dignity of the individual against a totalitarian type of collectivism or socialism. But this teaching had, in fact, become a support for an individualistic type of free enterprise and for the private interests of individuals or groups over the public interest. It is important to see how this had come about. There was no time at which the Church's social teaching could seriously be accused of giving sanction to capitalism in the form of ruthless big business. But capitalism has another face, a more attractive one. It is what might be called "frontier free enterprise," typified in the small-town entrepreneurs who use local resources and their own initiative and skills to meet local needs and provide employment in the area. Different popes wanted to encourage this kind of initiative and to protect it against bureaucracy. And their defense of this kind of local free enterprise came to be used as giving a measure of support to capital-ism in all its forms.

The idealized image of free enterprise gives a certain respectability to capitalism in its less acceptable forms. Frequently this takes place uncon-sciously, simply because people have not had the opportunity or education to make the necessary distinctions. But it is not at all uncommon to have a deliberate manipulation, a campaign to justify capitalism in its more unacceptable forms through a glamorization of the ideal of free enterprise. One feature of this campaign is the reduction of all the various possible options to just two. People are presented with a stark choice between two alternatives: on the one hand is free enterprise with its respect for personal initiative and responsibility; on the other is a massively bureaucratic state socialism that is centralized, inflexible, and inefficient. The books and television programs of Milton Friedman provided examples of this kind of oversimplification; so too does much of the rhetoric of the Tea Party in the United States.

This background helps one understand what I mean when I say that the Church's social teaching had come to be used in an ideological way to defend sectional interests. In most cases this was not the result of some sinister plot but an unfortunate accident of history. In the political sphere Catholics were among the strongest opponents of socialism. So it is quite understandable that a lot of emphasis was put on those parts of papal teaching most strongly opposed to socialist tendencies. Meanwhile, papal reservations about capitalism were downplayed to some extent— except for the relatively short period when the corporatist proposals of *Quadragesimo Anno* were taken seriously as providing a workable alternative model of society.

In the social sphere there was a similar process. As the typical social patterns of modern living came more and more to replace the traditional patterns, people could no longer rely on the extended family and the local community as their main support systems for the individual and the family. The anonymity of modern urban-style living did not lend itself easily to the development of new voluntary support systems to replace them. So there was a great need for the state or other public authorities to provide the individual and the family with supports in social, cultural, and economic affairs. Without a great increase in public welfare programs of all kinds—and the taxes to pay for them—only the very wealthy could live a dignified human life in this modern world that had emerged. Up to the time of Pope John, Catholic social teaching had not taken sufficient account of this new situation. Church authorities were almost invariably opposed to socialized health care programs. They were also opposed to giving the state a monopoly in the area of education and culture. Traditional papal teaching was that the state should not intrude itself unduly into the economic sphere; therefore, nationalization of industry or of economic services, such as banking, should never go beyond what was proved to be strictly necessary.

The effect of all this was that almost by accident the Church came to be allied with certain sectional interests. It seemed to be more concerned with the defense of the rights of private groups than with the public interest and especially the needs of the poorer classes of society. That was neither its intention nor its ideal; in fact, successive popes had put a strong emphasis on the importance of the common good. The principles proposed in the Church's social teaching were put forward as a defense of people against bureaucracy and totalitarianism. But the way in which they were being applied in practice was now causing the Church to be allied to the opponents of welfare programs badly needed by the poor. Similarly, the Church's defense of private property—intended to protect the dignity of the person—was now invoked to justify resistance to land reform. Furthermore, there was opposition to the payment of the high taxes needed to support social welfare programs for the poor—they were said to be an undue interference in private ownership and a step toward socialism.

The link between sectional interests and Catholic social teaching was further strengthened by the fact that, in most Western countries, dioceses and religious congregations were themselves the private owners of many schools, colleges, hospitals, and other property. They felt themselves threatened by anything that seemed like a move toward nationalization or a state monopoly of such services. This gave them a certain common interest with the privileged groups in society. For instance, the medical profession was jealously guarding its privileged position and resisting the expansion of public health schemes designed to help the poor. Catholic social teaching was often invoked to justify this stance. So the Church found itself allied to a conservative group resisting the kind of changes that would make for a more just society.

In the sphere of education, the situation was rather similar. There were some Catholic schools designed specifically for the wealthy, so it was not surprising that they should find common cause with other elitist institutions. But more interesting is the situation of the great majority of Church-run schools. These had a policy of catering to poorer families by keeping their school fees very low. Nevertheless, it was often middle-class people (or people with middle-class aspirations) who sent their children to such schools. Consequently, these schools were inclined to propagate middle-class values. Many of those who controlled them were opposed to a nationalization of educational institutions, even when the aim of nationalization was to lessen the inequalities in society. Their opposition was felt to be justified by the fact that the policy of nationalization was being put forward by individuals or political parties that were anticlerical or whose aim was to lessen the power of the Catholic Church.

The general image of the Church was therefore that of a socially conservative force giving ideological and quasi-political support to those who were opposed to left-wing changes. All this happened even though the original purpose of the educational and medical institutions of the Church was to serve the poor—and even when most of these institutions continued to be at the service of poor people. It happened even though Catholic social teaching provided the legitimation for the existence of these institutions, for the institutions worked within the existing system. Originally, they had represented a challenge to the current structures of society. But as time went on, they became incorporated as parts of the system. And so the social teaching of the Church seemed, in practice, to be offering support for the status quo rather than calling prophetically for structural changes in the interests of the poor.

What has been outlined so far is an unfortunate but almost accidental process by which Catholic social teaching came to justify conservative social stances, as against efforts to minimize the gap between the different sectors of society. But at times this process was taken further by a deliberate harnessing of the social teaching of the Church to make it serve a political function. This may have taken place in some of the US campaigns against anything that could be labeled "communist" or even "socialist." But the most obvious and blatant example was the way in which right-wing groups in Latin America purported to find in the Catholic faith an ideological support for their attitudes. They resisted land reform and a more equal division of wealth, in the name of the sacrosanct nature of private property. They also invoked Church teaching about obedience to authority and about nonviolence in support of their resistance to the changes demanded by social justice. The social teaching of Pope John was a major step toward the prevention of such an ideological use of Church teaching and toward the recovery of its original purpose.

A Shift to the Left

There are two passages in *Pacem in Terris* that express a key insight of John XXIII's:

> One of the fundamental duties of civil authorities . . . is so to co-ordinate and regulate social relations that the exercise of one person's right does not threaten others in the exercise of their own rights. (*PT* 62, Campion version, adapted)
>
> The common good requires that civil authorities maintain a careful balance between coordinating and protecting the rights of the citizens on the one hand, and promoting them, on the other. It should not happen that certain individuals or social groups derive special advantage from the fact that their rights have received preferential protection. (*PT* 65)[15]

There is, of course, nothing very startling in these as general statements. But the pope obviously had in mind actual situations in which the entrenched rights of some were the main obstacle to the exercise of the

---

[15]The Campion text quoted here is preferable to the Waterhouse version, which fails to bring out the contrast in the first sentence (Latin: "tum . . . tum").

rights of others—especially of the poor. In the modern situation, social justice required the recognition of new rights for the people at the lower end of the social scale. But the recognition and promotion of these rights was being hindered, either deliberately or uncritically, by the invocation of Catholic social teaching about the right to private property and the right to personal initiative. This amounted to an ideological use of this teaching, that is, its use as a cover and legitimation for resistance to the changes needed to promote social justice. So the passages just quoted were intended to prevent such an abuse.

Already in *Mater et Magistra* Pope John had set out to lessen the chances that such things could happen. By means of that encyclical he had publicly and clearly put the weight of the Church on the side of a policy of social reforms in favor of those who are poor and deprived both within each country and at the international level. *Mater et Magistra* advocated a considerable degree of control by public authorities over the activity of individuals and groups. It also recommended certain initiatives to be undertaken by the state to help those who are disadvantaged in society.

In *Mater et Magistra* Pope John was careful to recall the traditional and philosophical basis for such state control and initiative: "Our predecessors have constantly taught that inherent in the right to have private property there lies a social role and responsibility" (*MM* 119).[16] Leo XIII can certainly be cited as insisting on the importance of property owners using their wealth responsibly (*RN* 19). Pius XI insisted that "the right to own private property has been given to people . . . both in order that individuals may be able to provide for their own needs and those of their families, and also that by means of it the goods which the Creator has destined for the whole human race may truly serve this purpose" (*QA* 45). As I have pointed out in chapter 4, Pius XII went further in 1941. He gave priority to the universal purpose of the goods of the Earth and saw the institution of private property as a means for the attainment of this purpose (D3, 198–99). Quite evidently, there is a pattern here: each of these popes in turn lays greater emphasis than his predecessor on the social obligations attaching to private property. In *Mater et Magistra* John XXIII built on the foundation laid down twenty years earlier by Pius XII. John's own contribution consisted mainly in drawing the obvious practical conclusions. He saw clearly that quite often private ownership was not, in fact, serving the purpose for which Pius XII said it had been instituted. So Pope John proposed a variety of measures to ensure that its

---

[16]My translation. The phrase "munus . . . sociale" is very difficult to translate accurately. Kirwan (1964) gives "social function," and the Italian and French texts use a corresponding phrase. But in English this is too vague. The Gibbons text gives "social responsibility"; this is excellent except that it conveys only one of the two aspects of the meaning of "munus." I have added the word "role" to express the second aspect.

social function should be attained. By the very fact of owning property, a person incurs social responsibilities. John XXIII was not content with encouraging property owners to take these responsibilities seriously; he envisaged that they should be compelled by law to do so.

As we have seen, Pope John was not looking for a radical restructuring of the present order of Western society. Given that order, he accepted the need for state intervention in social and economic affairs to an extent well beyond what would have been advocated by Catholic leaders in the past. Perhaps even more important, he eliminated the suspicion of state control and state initiatives that had been a central feature of the Catholic social outlook. In this sense it is not inaccurate to see in *Mater et Magistra* a certain "opening to the left" (*apertura a sinistra*) in the socioeconomic sphere. How closely that was related to an opening toward the left in the political sphere remains open to debate. Certainly, *Pacem in Terris*, issued two years after *Mater et Magistra*, contains a significant passage (*PT* 159), which I referred to earlier in this chapter.[17] In it the pope distinguished between false philosophical theories, on the one hand, and, on the other hand, the historical movements that are inspired by such theories; the latter, says the encyclical, can change profoundly and may contain positive and praiseworthy elements. This statement provided a justification for a significant change of attitude by the Vatican in the political field. It was an irenic gesture directed mainly toward left-wing movements at the national and international level. It left the door open for practical political cooperation between the Catholic Church and communist governments and parties. But it is important not to focus attention on the political question to an extent that plays down the significance of the move toward the left that had already taken place on social and economic matters in *Mater et Magistra*. Perhaps the most accurate way to sum up the effect of that encyclical, and of Pope John's social teaching in general, would be to call it not so much an opening to the left as *a decisive move away from the right*.

This helps one to understand why *Mater et Magistra* contains detailed directives on such specific matters as the two kinds of insurance needed by farmers (*MM* 135). The pope scarcely imagined that his proposals were so original and compelling that governments would immediately adopt them! Rather it must be presumed that John was speaking not to govern-

---

[17]On the issue of the "opening to the left" in Italian politics and the related *Ostpolitik* at the international level, and the hostility and opposition to these policies that the pope encountered from senior Italian churchmen such as Cardinals Siri and Ottaviani, see the helpful treatment by Drew Christiansen (2005, 218–23). Carl Marzani (1982, 14–16) points out that Pope John's political "opening to the left" was actually a belated response of the Vatican to the overtures of the Italian Communist Party, led by Antonio Gramsci and Palmiro Togliatti.

ments or political parties or civil servants as such but to those to whom that encyclical was officially addressed, namely, "the . . . bishops, clergy and faithful of the Catholic world" (*MM*). The pope felt the need to go into specific details, because the approach he was advocating was quite different from the prevailing interpretation of Catholic social teaching, especially concerning its practical applications. One may show, as Bolté does quite effectively (Bolté 1964, 1:245–46), that there is considerable continuity between Pope John's teaching and that of his predecessors. One can conclude quite correctly that he was within a developing tradition. But this continuity applies at the level of doctrine and general principles. In the application of the principles and in the practical implications for the stance of the Christian on social questions, the discontinuity is more obvious. It would be wrong to exaggerate this discontinuity, to speak as though Pope John were advocating socialism. But it must be said that *Mater et Magistra* stands as a turning point in Catholic social teaching.

The extent to which the encyclical was a turning point emerged more clearly in later years. It stands at the source of important developments whose full implications could hardly have been foreseen at the time. The first of these is that the practical and fairly inductive approach of Pope John in *Mater et Magistra* provided support for the "see, judge, and act" methodology that was promoted by Joseph Cardijn and used by the Young Christian Workers movement. In *Pacem in Terris* the inductive approach was carried a stage further by the introduction of the idea of reading "the signs of the times." As Christiansen (2005, 224) points out, this "led to affirmation of the values discerned in the world," including "the claiming of rights by women." This positive assessment of the issue of justice for women and of the rights of women represented a significant change of approach by the Vatican. It is not too much to say that it amounted to an important element in an option for the poor.

From the late 1960s onward the inductive approach was adopted by the Latin American bishops and by all who were influenced by liberation theology. Then in 1971 Pope Paul VI, in his apostolic letter *Octogesima Adveniens*, gave support to a more inductive approach. This, in turn, involved recognizing that the appropriate Catholic response to social, economic, and political problems could vary from one continent to another. Consequently, the idea that Catholic social teaching constituted a single universal body of truth could now be challenged.

A second scarcely foreseen effect of *Mater et Magistra* was that the new approaches that it advocated led to divided opinions and divided loyalties among people, all of whom saw themselves as committed Catholics. The encyclical raised doubts about attitudes that had not been questioned previously, for instance, an attitude of suspicion about state intervention and a conviction that it ought to be kept to a minimum. The fact that the encyclical seemed to favor a welfare state approach opened up the possibility that the Church's social teaching was not as monolithic as had been assumed in the past. Before long there was considerable questioning of many other parts of the traditional Catholic social approach and teaching. Furthermore, since the encyclical was controversial, it was subject to a variety of interpretations. This gave rise to fragmentation at the practical level: there was no longer a clear, universally accepted Catholic "line" on many socioeconomic issues. It was not long before the very concept of a social doctrine was called into question (e.g., Chenu 1979). This is an issue to which I return in a later chapter.

A third consequence of the encyclical was that it led to the establishment of the Pontifical Commission for Justice and Peace. In the following years, under the guidance, inspiration, and energy of its key members, this commission played an important role in influencing Vatican policy on issues of justice. As I point out in a later chapter, members of the commission were the main drafters of the document "Justice in the World" issued by the Synod of Bishops in 1971. The commission adopted an ecumenical approach through its involvement in the work of SODEPAX, the Committee on Society, Development and Peace, which was established in 1968 as a joint venture of the Roman Catholic Church and the World Council of Churches. In its early years SODEPAX was an influential body, but its work was met with increasing suspicion in some Vatican circles. Eventually the Catholic Church withdrew its support, and SODEPAX was disbanded in 1980.

A fourth development was that the encyclical began the process by which the Catholic Church got new allies and new opponents. This was perhaps the most important effect of the encyclical—at least for those who recognize that social teaching arises from, and relates back to, social praxis. The extent of this change and the speed at which it occurred varied from place to place and even from continent to continent. Latin America is the region where the most dramatic changes took place. The option for the poor, which the Church began to make in many parts of that continent toward the end of the 1960s, could never have taken place unless key leaders in the Church had determined that they would no longer allow the institutional Church to be an ally of the rich and powerful. The refusal of these Church leaders to provide a legitimation for the privileges of the elite was a major factor in enabling the Church to opt for solidarity with the poor and oppressed. The Church had, of course, always seen itself as having a message for all of humanity and every sector of society. But many Latin American Church leaders became convinced that they must at times give a specific answer to the following question: "Whose side are you on?" In regard to basic issues of social justice they felt that they could not plead neutrality. So they committed the Church to making what came to be called "a preferential, but not exclusive, option for the poor." The fact that they made such an option was largely due to John XXIII and especially to the social teaching of *Mater et Magistra*.

* * *

SUMMARY

Pope John was optimistic about the world, particularly about the modern world. His two major social encyclicals showed that he was even optimistic about Western capitalist society and did not seek a complete change of the system. He felt it had already been humanized to some degree through various reforms and that it could become more humane in the future through much more intervention by the state to protect the interests of the poor. So he moved Catholic teaching away from its traditional opposition to the welfare state approach. At the international level he also favored a similar approach, with some kind of world governing authority to oversee the process, and he gave a high priority to the issues of international development and social justice at the international level.

In spite of Pope John's moderate position, his encyclical *Mater et Magistra* changed the whole direction of Catholic social teaching. Though he still insisted on the principle of subsidiarity, his proposals for a lot of state intervention amounted to approval of the welfare state—or at least it gave the impression of doing so. In both economic and political affairs Pope John favored an "opening to the left." This meant that left-wing and social-democratic people began to see the Church as a possible ally, and right-wing and conservative sectors of society could no longer presume that the Church would give them religious backing. Pope John's distancing of the Church from right-wing forces was quite deliberate. He realized that the Church's overemphasis on the right to private property and its suspicion of state intervention had allowed Catholic social teaching to become an ideological weapon used by the wealthy and the powerful to resist social change. By breaking decisively with this trend he laid the foundations for an option for the poor by later Church leaders, and he gained for the Church new allies and new enemies.

QUESTIONS FOR REVIEW

1. *What was Pope John's attitude to the modern world and to Western capitalism?*
2. *What is meant by "the welfare state"? And what was Pope John's position in relation to it?*

3. *How did Pope John change the direction of Catholic social teaching?*
4. *Why did he do so?*
5. *What were the effects?*

QUESTIONS FOR REFLECTION

1. *Does it make sense to you to distinguish between a "liberal" and a "radical"? If so, can you pick out examples of each approach among political leaders and among Church leaders?*
2. *Is it possible to have the different countries of the world linked together in an arrangement analogous to "the welfare state"? If so, how could it come about? If not, what alternative ways are there of promoting international justice?*

ISSUES FOR FURTHER STUDY

1. *Examine the different shades of meaning of the word "liberal" from the last century up to today. Is there a close link between an economic liberal and being liberal on moral issues?*
2. *The Catholic understanding of human rights. Read Hollenbach 1979; Curran 2002; Dorr 2013.*

6

Vatican II: Another Agenda

This study of Catholic social teaching is concerned mainly with what the popes had to say. Should I therefore simply omit the teaching of the Second Vatican Council as Richard Camp (1969) does? If not, on what grounds should it be included? I include the teachings of Vatican II, first, because these are official Vatican documents. Second, it would be a mistake to make too sharp a contrast between papal teaching and the teaching of the Council. It is true that the documents of Vatican II represent much more than the views of John XXIII and Paul VI, the two popes who presided over the Council. Indeed, there is little doubt that they contain things that these popes would not have said had there never been a Council. But these two popes played a major part in the genesis of the Council documents. John XXIII set the tone for the Council, and Paul VI generally maintained this tone, though with some reservations. He helped formulate the Council statements, and he signed them, promulgated them, and set up the procedures required to implement them. The documents of the Council represent not merely the consensus of the bishops from all over the world but also the consensus of these bishops with the Vatican, above all with the pope. There can be no doubt of the entire commitment of Pope Paul to the teaching of Vatican II. It is evident, then, that it would be a serious mistake to study papal teaching without making a close examination of the teaching of Vatican II.

THE LIBERAL AGENDA

Just nine days after Vatican II began, the Council Fathers issued a short but significant "Message to Humanity" (Vatican II, *Nuntius*; for background information on this document, see Chenu 1967, 191–93). In it they noted two issues of special urgency that they saw facing them—peace and social justice. However, before long, the bishops and their experts became engrossed in other issues. So there was an interval of more than three years before the Council issued any formal teaching on these two topics that they had singled out in their first message. It is true, of course, that during that interval, work was going ahead on successive drafts of the document that eventually became *Gaudium et Spes*, the Pastoral Constitution on the Church in the Modern World. But until quite near the end of the Council, there was considerable doubt as to whether the document would be issued at all. And when it did eventually come, the parts of it dealing with peace and social justice were comparatively short; in places they showed signs of having been drafted with undue haste.

What happened? Why were these "urgent issues" left until so late in the Council? The standard answer is that the participants in Vatican II had first to work through certain urgent internal theological and pastoral issues such as the sources of faith, the nature of the Church itself, the style of public worship, the nature of the ministry, and the pattern of the Church's authority structure. Only then could they deal satisfactorily with the external issues of the Church's relationship with the world, notably in regard to questions about peace and social justice. This answer is correct as far as it goes, but it is not a complete answer. What has to be added is that at an early stage of the Council, "the liberal agenda" came to dominate both the discussions and the documents of the Council. Among the items on that agenda were the use of the vernacular in the liturgy, the collegiality of bishops, the renewal of religious life, the role of the Bible in revelation, the Church's openness to other Christian churches and to other faiths, and the issue of religious freedom. The main drama of the Council was the struggle between conservatives and liberals on these issues, with the liberals being identified as the progressive group. This polarization applied also in the area of the theology of marriage and sexuality; so it affected one of the major topics dealt with in the second and more practical part of *Gaudium et Spes*.

Interestingly, however, the bishops and theologians of Vatican II did not split along conservative versus liberal lines in regard to the issues of social justice and peace. For instance, one of the champions of the conservative line, Cardinal Ottaviani, spoke out strongly in favor of what was called a progressive stance in regard to war and peace (see Schuijt 1969). However, some of the progressive bishops took a cautious stance when it came to speaking out against the holding of nuclear weapons. This indicates that the usual categories of "liberal" and "conservative" did not apply very well to the views of the bishops and theologians on these political issues. In regard to matters of peace and social justice the issue was to what extent the Council was prepared to take a radical or prophetic stance that would challenge the current values of society. A desire that the Church should take up a prophetic posture is compatible with either conservative or liberal tendencies—though the radical-conservative combination has quite a different character from the radical-liberal one.

Perhaps the most significant thing from our point of view is that at the Council, the struggle between liberals and conservatives on internal Church matters tended to obscure the other issue, namely, the extent to which the Church should mount a radical or prophetic challenge to the world on sociopolitical questions.

But why did the liberal agenda take over in the Council? Because, by and large, it represented the concerns and priorities of the Northern European theologians—and through them of the majority of European and North American bishops—as against those of the Roman establishment. It is important to note that although, on the whole, the bishops from dioceses in Asia, Africa, and Latin America constituted about 40 percent of the bishops at the Council (Aubert et al. 1978, 5:627–28), they were not very involved or very significant in the polarization between liberals and conservatives.

As Vatican II progressed, there came to be a growing realization that the Church is not just Western and Eastern, but also Asian, Latin American, and African—and therefore that the Council documents would have to take serious account of what was called at the time the Third World. But a fully elaborated Third World theology did not emerge at the Council to challenge the liberal and conservative approaches, both of which were quite Western in their concerns. However, at least some of the major questions that were of interest for the Third World came to be given a higher priority than in the past. The drafters of *Gaudium et Spes* tried to take account of these questions. The final result was not altogether satisfactory; a number of the paragraphs of the document read as though statements about the situation in developing countries had been patched in to passages drafted originally with the Western world in mind, for instance, GS 69.2, 70.[1] Some of the drafting committees included people from the Third World, and it is doubtful whether a fuller representation would have led to any great improvement in the text. What was missing was a coherent Third World theology and a body of experts to articulate such a theology. In the absence of these, it is not surprising to find that even Third World problems were looked at to some extent from a First World perspective. This is evident in the treatment of "development" and in the

---

[1] In referring to *Gaudium et Spes* I have used the initials *GS* followed by numbers to designate the paragraph and, where relevant, the subparagraph, as given in the Latin text. In quoting in English from *GS*, I have made use of whichever of the available translations seems most accurate for the particular passage; on some occasions, in the interests of accuracy, I have adapted the translation or given my own translation of the text. For a helpful account of the political and ecclesiastical context of the time, see Hollenbach (2005, 267–69); for an outline of the various stages in the drafting of the document, see Hollenbach (2005, 270–71, 276). For the names of the drafters on the various committees, see Moeller (1969, 21, 39, 40, 49, 63).

chapter on culture (*GS* 53–62, 64–65). Furthermore, there is a rather patronizing tone in *GS* 69.2, which says that customs may be useful if they are brought up to date. Early drafts of the document were criticized as being too Western in outlook by Bishop James Corboy from Zambia (*Acta Synodalia,* vol. 3, paras. 5, 625–26). Despite these shortcomings, *Gaudium et Spes* represents a considerable advance on earlier Church documents—even those of John XXIII—insofar as the Church begins to recognize more clearly that non-Western countries have their own history, traditions, and social structures, as well as their own problems, and that none of these are to be treated as though they were simply adjuncts to those of the West (e.g., *GS* 69.2, 71, 86).

THE CONTRIBUTION OF *GAUDIUM ET SPES*

What contribution does *Gaudium et Spes* make to the Church's social teaching? Before we look at the more significant points in its content it is well to note that the importance of this document lies not only in what it says, but also in the process that produced it. *Gaudium et Spes* expresses the consensus that emerged after three years of private and public dialogue, debate, and even controversy. It crowns a three-year process of thorough and intense exploration by experts in the various matters it deals with as well as a process of education of the bishops and of the millions of people who followed the progress of the Council. So even where it merely repeats the teaching of Pope John or earlier popes, it does so with a greatly increased degree of authority and credibility (see Coste 1969, 368).

Gaudium et Spes repeats important themes from the two social encyclicals of John XXIII. For instance, it follows *Mater et Magistra* in what it says about the process of socialization (*GS* 6, 23.1, 25.2, 75.3). It is interesting to note that the official Latin text of *GS* 75.3 includes the word *socializatio,* in contrast to the Latin text of *Mater et Magistra.* In general, the text of *Gaudium et Spes* tends to temper the extraordinary optimism of Pope John's documents. It does so, not by toning down his Christian hope and his high ideals, but by adopting a more dialectical approach: the ideal is contrasted with reality—a reality marred by social evil (cf. Hollenbach 2005, 272). For instance, *GS* 63.3 notes that economic progress can lead to contempt for the poor. As Hollenbach (2005) points out, the tension noted by the Council Fathers in contemporary culture exists not merely in the outer world but also within the human spirit. People can move in either of two directions—the absolutizing of some limited value in their day-to-day conduct or an authentic belief in God (*GS* 43).

Another important contribution of Vatican II to sociopolitical questions is its attempt to offer a solid theological basis for its practical directives. One of the most significant and controversial examples is the Council's statement on religious liberty, *Dignitatis Humanae*. This document effectively reversed the previous teaching of a succession of popes. It involved the acceptance of the general approach of John Courtney Murray as outlined in the 1950s in a succession of major articles, the final one of which had been withheld from publication at that time (Curran 2002, 244n20). The document bases its acceptance of religious liberty on the dignity and freedom of the human person, which involves the duty to follow one's conscience free from external coercion. Furthermore, it holds that religious acts transcend the limited power of governments. For a helpful extended account of this whole topic see the work of Charles Curran (2002, 222–38).

Other successful instances of the Council's contribution to Catholic social teaching are what it has to say about peace (especially *GS* 78), human work (*GS* 33–39, 67), the nature of human authority and the need for it (*GS* 74), and the relationship of the Church to the world (*GS* 40–44). Rather less successful efforts in this direction are the Council statements on development (*GS* 25–32, 63–72, 85–90) and culture (*GS* 53–62). In presenting a theology of these different realities, a positive effort was made to ensure that a scriptural basis was provided as well as a philosophical component (cf. Hollenbach 2005, 273–74, who refers also to a study by J. Bryan Hehir). In some cases there is quite a good integration of the two (e.g., *GS* 78 on peace; *GS* 34, 37, 39, 57 on work). Elsewhere the integration is not so good (*GS* 57, 72). In those passages of *Gaudium et Spes* that are philosophical in tone the drafters distance themselves somewhat from the neoscholastic approach of earlier documents: the text incorporates what is best in the natural law tradition and integrates it with an existential idiom.

A crucial point about the overall approach of the drafters of the document is what we must call their humanistic theology. This involves three aspects. First, they insist that we must respect the autonomy of the secular world. Second, they hold that we look at this world in terms of our eschatological hope for a new Earth (*GS* 43) that is not the replacement of the present Earth but its transformation and fulfillment. Third, they go further by insisting that the Church "must listen to the many voices of the larger social and cultural domains while it also seeks to shape these values" (Hollenbach 2005, 275). So the approach is one of dialogue with the world (*GS* 40.1), and it is in this dialogue that Christians can "read the signs of the times."

Pope John's determination to issue an encyclical on peace before he died led him to upstage the Council document on this question. While *GS* was being drafted, he issued his encyclical *Pacem in Terris*. This was so comprehensive that those who were writing *GS* found they had little to add to it on the practical aspects of the question of peace and war. They did, however, succeed in making one major contribution on this issue, by offering a conception of peace that provides a philosophical-theological basis for its practical statements, which follow in the same general line as those of Pope John. According to *Gaudium et Spes*, peace is not merely an absence of war. It is an ordering of society; but real peace is built not just on any order but on one that is to be brought into existence by the thirst of people for an ever more perfect justice (*GS* 78.1). There are four important points here.

- First, peace does not just happen. Though in one sense it is a God-given gift to society—"the fruit of that right ordering of things with which the divine founder has invested human society" (Flannery 1977 translation)—nevertheless it has to be brought about by human commitment and effort.
- Second, it is not attained once for all but has to be constantly defended: "the achievement of peace requires . . . unceasing vigilance" (Flannery 1977 translation).
- Third, it has to be constantly renewed and brought nearer to the ideal: "the common good of humankind . . . depends . . . upon circumstances which change as time goes on; consequently, peace will never be achieved once and for all, but must be built up continually" (Flannery 1977 translation, emended).
- Fourth, and most important, peace is firmly linked to justice, and it is the passionate desire ("thirst") for justice that motivates people to work for peace.

The justice of which the document speaks is not simply the putting right of "political" grievances. It extends to the whole economic order. That is why this chapter of the document goes on to treat international cooperation in the economic field (*GS* 83–87). In this way the Council Fathers reacted against the tendency, common among statesmen in the developed countries, to think that a peaceful world can be brought about without too much tampering with the present inequitable economic world order. The Council document helps to make it clear that there are not two distinct international questions, one about peace and one about economics. They are two aspects of one question.

This firm determination to present the problems of the so-called less developed countries in terms of justice marks a subtle but significant development in the social teaching of the Church. It is not entirely original, for Pius XII and John XXIII had both spoken of these problems in terms of the principle that the goods of the world are destined for the people of the world, and the latter had said that it is a matter of justice that the goods of the Earth be better distributed (Pius XII, D3, 200–201; MM 74, 161).[2] As I pointed out in the preceding chapter, Pope John moved the topic of international development cooperation toward the center of the social justice agenda. *Gaudium et Spes* carried this a stage further.

For anybody concerned with the theme of the Church's "option for the poor" the following passage will be seen as one of the most significant statements of the Vatican Council:

> God destined the earth and all that it contains for the use all of people and all peoples. . . . Furthermore, the right to have a share of earthly goods sufficient for oneself and one's family belongs to everyone. . . . If a person is in extreme necessity, that person has the right to take from the riches of others what he or she really needs. Since there are so many people in this world weighed down by hunger, this sacred Council urges all, both individuals and governments, to remember the saying of the Fathers: "Feed the person dying of hunger, because if you have not fed them you have killed them." According to their ability, let all individuals and governments undertake a genuine sharing of their goods. (*GS* 69, Abbott translation, emended)

The train of thought in this passage is particularly interesting. The words "and all peoples" were deliberately added into the first sentence after some discussion, precisely in order to indicate that the Council had in mind the problem of poor countries, not just poor individuals (Calvez 1967a, 502). By going on to speak within the same passage of the person in extreme necessity, the document seems to be suggesting that to be in such extreme need is the plight not just of occasional isolated and desperate individuals but also of whole peoples. This impression is confirmed in the next sentence, which speaks of so many people in the world weighed down by hunger.

In strict logic one might have expected that the document would go on to conclude that the masses of hungry people have the right to take what they need from the rich peoples of the world. Instead, however, the Council Fathers make an earnest appeal to individuals and governments to share what they have with the poor. Why this rather weak conclusion? Could it be that the hungry masses are not considered by the Council Fathers to be in "extreme necessity"? That is most unlikely, since there would then have been no point in referring to the person in extreme

---

[2]For references to two addresses in which Pope John mentions the point, see Bolté (1967, 3:889–90).

necessity. Or could it be that the drafters of the document were drawing back from the obvious conclusion of their statements, namely, that these poor people have the right to take what they need? That is not to be assumed, because, in that case, it is unlikely that they would have written this paragraph in the first place.

The most likely explanation is that the readers are being allowed to draw the conclusion for themselves, precisely because it is so obvious. If the passage is understood in this way, then the exhortation to the rich to share what they have must be seen as a combination of a timely warning and a moral threat. It means if you do not share willingly, then the poorer peoples will in any case take what they need—and they will be justified in doing so. In this way the Council document succeeds in taking a strong stance on the issue of international social justice, without lapsing into fruitless condemnations. The difficulty, of course, is that not everybody will see or accept the full implications of what the Council is saying. But it is doubtful whether harsh words of condemnation would be any more effective than the nuanced approach, adopted in the document, in bringing about the fundamental changes that are called for.

A CHANGE OF INTERNATIONAL ECONOMIC STRUCTURES

Gaudium et Spes insisted that there is need for profound changes in the way international trade is carried out (*GS* 85.2). It called for the establishment of "a truly universal economic order" (*GS* 85.3)—a phrase that seems to anticipate the "New International Economic Order" (NIEO) that was called for, some years later, at the United Nations. *Gaudium et Spes* recognized that a major source of injustice in international trade is the inequality in power between trading partners; to compensate for this, the document called for setting up institutions to promote and regulate international trade (*GS* 86.6). This is precisely the kind of thing that the NIEO was looking for, namely, a major expansion and strengthening of international bodies to regulate the supply and price of the products of developing countries. Such agencies could protect the producers from the exploitation that results from overproduction and erratic supply. If such international agencies really had effective power, and if they were not dominated by the wealthy nations, this in itself would constitute a fundamental change in the existing economic order. If they were gradually extended to cover the whole range of goods and services exchanged in international trade, then the cooperating nations would in effect have built up, piecemeal, the basic elements of an effective world authority in the economic sphere.

The fundamental principle of such an authority, as envisaged by

Gaudium et Spes (*GS* 26.1), would be the common good of all rather than the capitalist "law of supply and demand." To seek to form a community of nations devoted to the common good is an ambitious undertaking. In recent times we see the difficulties and the painful struggle of the nations of the European Community to become a genuine community of nations while respecting the uniqueness of each and the principle of subsidiarity. We see the kind of mechanisms that are required to link the economies of different countries, and we have some idea of the juridical framework and binding commitments that are needed in the social, political, and cultural fields to ensure that the "laws" of capitalist economics are tempered by a concern for such moral values as the welfare of the weak, the young, the old, the vulnerable, and those on the periphery. This gives an indication of what would be required if the nations of the world were to make a serious effort to establish a global economic order devoted to the good of all. So the full implications of the changes proposed in the Council document are quite radical and prophetic—possibly more so than the Council Fathers themselves fully realized.

Gaudium et Spes said explicitly that there is need, not merely for a conversion in the mentality and attitudes of people, but also for "many reforms" in socioeconomic life itself, that is, in its structures (*GS* 63.5).[3] The document did not go into much detail in specifying what these reforms should be; however, L. J. Lebret (1966, 224) (who himself played an important role in helping draft the text) in his commentary on this part of *Gaudium et Spes*, was rather more specific; he maintained that reform of international trade requires reform of the structures of production, the monetary systems, and the economic regimes that actually are in force at present. In one carefully phrased passage the Council said that "in many situations there is urgent need for a reassessment of economic and social structures" (*GS* 86.7, my translation). The choice of the word "reassessment" is noteworthy. Some of the modern language translations speak here of reforming or recasting the structures.[4] But this is to miss the nuance of the Latin version. By choosing the word "reassessment," the Council

---

[3] "Reformationes multae in vita oeconomica-sociali atque mentis et habitudinis conversio ab omnibus requiruntur." The Italian translation brings out the fact that what is in question is structural reform: "si richiedono molte riforme nelle strutture della vita economico-sociale." Chiavacci (1967, 314) understands the Council to be calling for a fundamental reform of the economic system.

[4] The Abbott version speaks of the need for "a reform" of the structures while the Saint Paul version uses the word "revamp"; the Flannery version is more accurate here since it uses the word "reassess" to translate the Latin "recognoscendi." The Italian text has "una revisione." The French text speaks of a "recasting" ("une refonte"); this was probably the working text of the drafting group; but the toning down of the phrase in the Latin text (which is, of course, the official one) was hardly accidental.

Fathers refused to assume glibly that the solution to all social problems was the overthrowing of existing structures. But what is significant is that they did not flinch from calling for a reassessment; they did not start with the presumption that any fundamental restructuring is unnecessary; nor did they rule it out on the grounds that it might be a threat to stability. They did, however, add that there is need for caution lest some of the priceless heritage of non-Western cultures be lost by the hasty imposition of "technical solutions . . . especially ones that offer people material advantages while being inimical to the spiritual character of the human person" (*GS* 86.7, my translation).

It is not sufficient, however, to say *what* changes are called for. Two further questions need to be answered: First, *why* should such changes be made? Second, is it permissible to use *violent means* in the struggle for social justice? I hope to suggest answers to each of these questions in turn.

THE REASONS FOR CHANGE

Gaudium et Spes is not entirely clear in the answers it gives to the first of these questions—why changes are needed. Is it simply to ensure that no significant group of people will be left totally impoverished, meaning in absolute poverty? Or are changes called for also in order to tackle the problem of relative poverty, in other words, to ensure a more even distribution of the goods of the Earth, even in situations where the poorer groups are not in extreme necessity? The Council Fathers seemed to assume that the way to overcome both of these kinds of poverty was by the promotion of development; toward the end of this chapter I spell out what they understood by "development."

As I noted above, the Council document suggests that whole nations may be living in a state of extreme necessity—and it points out that this imposes on rich people and the governments of the wealthier countries a serious and pressing moral obligation to make the changes required to meet their needs (*GS* 69.1). But, clearly, social justice involves something more than the overcoming of such extreme necessity. If the basic principle is that the goods of the Earth are destined for all people of the Earth, this calls for equity in their distribution. But what does equity mean in practice? It can hardly be some utopian attempt to divide the goods of the Earth in exactly equal shares. That would be quite unrealistic, even as an ideal. Indeed, various popes over the previous seventy years had insisted that it is of the nature of human society that its people have a diversity of wealth and status, and Vatican II certainly did not explicitly repudiate this teaching. However, it undoubtedly went much further in the direction of equality than did the papal teaching of the early social encyclicals: "Excessive economic and social inequalities within the one human family, between individuals or between peoples, give rise to scandal, and are contrary to social justice, to equity, and to the dignity of the human person, as well as to peace within society and at the international level" (*GS* 29.3, my translation).

The Council document gave very little by way of guidelines that could enable one to decide at what point the inequalities can be considered so great as to be inequitable or unjust. However, Hollenbach (2005, 281) points out that in condemning any kind of social or cultural discrimination in basic personal rights (*GS* 29), it was rejecting the view of a stratified society espoused by Leo XIII.

One text in the document is significant in regard to structural reform. It is the passage in which the Council declares that in certain circumstances it may be right to expropriate and divide up the *latifundia*, meaning those large estates that are so common in some developing countries and especially in parts of Latin America. What would justify the confiscation of such properties? Is it the mere fact that such huge estates exist in areas where there are so many poor, powerless, and exploited people? The Council does not say so, at least not explicitly. It seems rather to suggest that the key point is precisely the failure of the owners of these estates to make proper use of the land (*GS* 71.6).[5] Presumably, the argument would be that the owner who fails to use the land productively is failing to ensure that the goods of the Earth are used for the benefit of all—and this would justify expropriation of the land. The implication of this line of argument would be that if owners of such enormous estates use the land productively, then it would be wrong to confiscate their lands. But whether following the strict logic of the argument or not, the text seems to recognize that there is a very close connection in practice between the possession of huge landholdings and the blatant exploitation of the local population. This exploitation is at least a contributory factor, if not the primary basis, for the call for expropriation. In theory the exploitation could be remedied in other ways than by confiscation of the land, but, in practice, the two are almost inextricably linked. The Council document remains vague about the precise basis for expropriation. This may well have been deliberate, for many of the bishops would have been reluctant to make any statement that seemed to restrict unduly the right to private property.[6] However, in the Council document the traditional emphasis by the Church on the rights of private property

---

[5]The Latin text is "ut distribuantur fundi non satis exculti."

[6]I note that this vagueness is to be found not merely in the document itself but also in some of the commentaries on it. For instance, the lengthy commentary by Augustino Ferrari Toniolo (1966, 984–85) on this section of *Gaudium et Spes* does little more than repeat the words of the document itself, when treating this delicate issue.

owners had to be balanced against the equally traditional protest of the Church against leaving workers in a totally powerless and vulnerable position, with no property of their own to provide them with a minimum of security. What seems to be original in this statement on expropriation is the willingness of the bishops to accept that in many actual cases the balance tips in favor of the poor and powerless: in the concrete, the right to private property has to yield to the cry of the poor—and, therefore, expropriation becomes justifiable. The Council Fathers would not have made the statement at all unless they believed it had a fairly widespread application. In his commentary on this section of *Gaudium et Spes*, L. J. Lebret raises important questions about the basis on which compensation ought to be calculated in the case of expropriation of land. This issue arises especially, as Lebret (1966, 228–29) notes, in cases where the market value of the land has greatly increased because of such extrinsic factors as the decision to utilize it for housing or for some public purpose. The Council document itself refrains from entering into such detailed questions and is therefore able to retain a certain vagueness about the fundamental moral principles that lie behind its call for social change.

OBLIGATION TO HELP THE POOR

An important light is thrown on the attitude of the Council Fathers by a late addition that they made to one passage in *Gaudium et Spes*. The text is the one in which we are reminded that the fathers and doctors of the Church taught that people are "obliged to come to the relief of the poor *and to do so not merely* out of their superfluous goods" (*GS* 69.1, Abbott translation). The words that I have italicized were added at a fairly late stage in the drafting of the document (cf. Calvez 1967, 503; Lio 1969, col. 1646). Evidently, this involved a major change in the meaning of the statement. It also involved a correction of Leo XIII's statement in *Rerum Novarum* that people are obliged to give to the poor out of what remains over when they have provided for their own needs and for what is appropriate to their station in life (*RN* 19). Pius XI had repeated this teaching in *Quadragesimo Anno* but had added that the use of superfluous wealth to provide work for others is an excellent act of liberality, particularly appropriate to our time (*QA* 50–51). A closer look at the effects of the teaching of these two popes will help to show why a different line was taken at Vatican II.

Pope Leo XIII said that one is obliged to give to the poor out of one's *superflua*. This gave rise to a rather distasteful type of casuistry—an attempt to measure what amount of wealth is appropriate to the status of different classes of people, the remainder of the person's income being seen as "superfluous." This kind of casuistry allowed the rich to calculate that they had no obligation to give to the poor until the normal status symbols of wealthy people had been acquired (e.g., Miller 1947, 91). The basic intention of Pope Leo's statement thus became perverted and even contradicted: instead of imposing a heavy obligation on the rich to help the poor, it offered a kind of justification for turning a deaf ear to the cry of the poor, on the grounds that one has to live up to one's social standing. No wonder then that Vatican II decided to assert a much more urgent obligation to help the poor. The Council was able to do so by appealing to an even more ancient and honorable tradition than that invoked in *Rerum Novarum*. Pope Leo had referred to Saint Thomas Aquinas in support of his position; the Council document by contrast refers to Basil, Lactantius, Augustine, Gregory the Great, Bonaventure, and Albert the Great (*GS* 69.1).

Pius XI introduced a certain modification into the position of his predecessor by trying to take account of the modern economic situation. This is one where wealth cannot be divided simply into that which is used up on consumer goods and that which is hoarded; a third category has to be added, namely, wealth that is invested productively. Given this situation, Pius XI was correct in saying that productive investment can help others by giving employment. The only proviso made by Pius XI in *QA* 51 was that the work should be devoted to the production of really useful goods. Vatican II, like Pius XI, was in favor of investment. *GS* 65.3 insists that the common good is seriously threatened by those who hoard their wealth unproductively. Other statements in favor of investment can be found in *GS* 70 and 85.2. *Gaudium et Spes* does not refer at this point to what had been said by Pius XI. One may surmise that this was because the drafters of the document did not wish to give the impression that the Council Fathers saw capitalist investors as great benefactors of humanity.

When compared with the teaching of Leo XIII and Pius XI, the text of *Gaudium et Spes* represents a notable change of emphasis. There is a shift away from the undue emphasis that had been laid in the past on the rights of property owners. Following the line of Pope John's *Mater et Magistra*, and going even further than him, the Council document relativized the rights of property owners not merely in principle—as Pius XII had already done (D3, 199), but in the practical applications of the principle to the world of the time.

THE PROCESS OF CHANGE: VIOLENT AND NONVIOLENT

The second question posed earlier is whether it is permissible to use violence in struggling for social justice. The key question here is *who* are to be the agents of change—those at the top of society or those at the bottom? If change is to come primarily from the top, then the issue of violence scarcely arises, since whatever changes come will only be ones acceptable to those who hold power. But if those at the bottom of society are the main agents of change, then the issue arises whether, or to what extent, they can use force in their struggle.

Vatican II seems to presume that the required action will have to be taken by the rich and powerful. It directs a strong appeal to them to make changes—both for altruistic or moral reasons (*GS* 69.1, 85.1) and also in their own self-interest—since injustices give rise to discord and war (*GS* 83). The Council does not have anything inspiring or empowering to say specifically to those who are poor and powerless. Indeed, it seems to speak more about the poor than directly to them. Its strongest statement is the one in which it affirms the right of those in extreme need to take what is necessary (*GS* 69.1), and to this statement a cautious footnote was appended pointing out that in applying this principle, all the moral conditions must be fulfilled. The Council did not really address itself to the question of what could be acceptable as a legitimate way of "taking what is necessary." Indeed, it failed to provide any practical guidelines about the use of force by those engaged, on one side or the other, in the liberation struggles taking place at that time in many parts of the world.

At Vatican II the debate about violence and war was dominated by the East–West struggle rather than the North–South issue. A major question was whether modern atomic, bacteriological, and chemical weapons had caused the traditional just war teaching to be no longer applicable to actual situations. The Council forcefully condemned total war (*GS* 80.4) but refused to rule out entirely the possibility of a justified war of defense (*GS* 79.4; cf. Hollenbach 2005, 282–84). Originally it was proposed to insert in the text of *Gaudium et Spes* the passage in Pope John's *Pacem in Terris* (*PT* 127), which states that it is unreasonable to hold that war can any longer be seen as a means to obtain justice for violated rights. But difficulties and objections led to the passage being relegated to a footnote (at *GS* 80.3; see Dubarle 1967, 581n11). This change was obviously significant. So too was the fact that the footnote is appended to a passage in which the Council is condemning total war. In this way the authors of *Gaudium et Spes* imply that Pope John was outlawing only total war, not all kinds of war; and there is some basis for this interpretation, since the relevant passage in *Pacem in Terris* includes a reference to atomic weapons.

It is unfortunate that the text of *Gaudium et Spes* did not deal specifically with the question of war in the form in which it was a very live issue at that time for the inhabitants of most of the countries that had been taken over as colonies by Western powers. For them the issue was whether, or in what circumstances, a war of liberation might be justified.

This omission by the Council reflects the lacuna in theological thinking at that time. Typical of the state of theological reflection and interest of this period is a book titled *International Morality* by the French theologian Alfred de Soras (1963). The author gives a fairly extensive treatment of issues relating to the morality of war between nation-states. But he devotes only a minimum of space to wars of liberation by oppressed peoples. Even more significant is the fact that what he does have to say about such wars is not concerned with whether, or in what circumstances, a people may be entitled to resist colonial or neocolonial oppression; rather, he considers the question from the point of view of the colonial power. He asks such questions as whether it is permissible to engage in psychological warfare against revolutionary forces (de Soras 1963, 87, 95). Undoubtedly this was an urgent issue for French Christians facing the Algerian uprising, but for the indigenous people of Algeria and other colonies, there were far more urgent moral issues that the book makes no effort to deal with.

At one stage in the preparation of drafts for the Council document, a text was proposed recognizing the legitimacy of active resistance to oppression, parallel to the legitimacy of a just war between nation-states. But in the debate many bishops intervened to say that this was too hasty an answer to a delicate question. To nuance the text adequately would require much work, so it was decided to drop the statement entirely (cf. Dubarle 1966, 276–79; Dubarle 1967, 582; Sigmond 1966, 1087–88). However, that the Council omitted the proposed statement does not imply that it rejected the view that it is possible to have a legitimate rebellion or war of liberation (see Dubarle 1966, 581–82). It is better to see it as an indication that the agenda of the people of the colonies was not given a high priority at Vatican II. The failure of the Council to take the time and trouble needed to clarify the issue left something of a gap in the teaching of the Council in relation to war and the use of violence. I note in passing that the World Council of Churches was paying much more attention around this time to Third World issues (see Dorr 1991, 70–71).

High on the agenda for many of the peoples in non-Western countries at this time was the question of nonviolent resistance to oppressive governments. Did the Council have anything to say that would be of help to a people who are the victims of colonial or racialist governments, or of a neocolonial system operating through repressive governments controlled by privileged minorities? In the course of a fine general statement about peace the Council Fathers expressed their admiration for those who renounce the use of violence to vindicate their rights, relying instead on the kinds of defense that are available to those who do not have power, and they added a proviso: "so long as there is no injury to the rights and duties of others or of the community" (*GS* 78.5, my translation). But when it came to saying something more specific on the question of nonviolence, the Council addressed itself to an issue that was mainly of interest to the First World: it spoke of conscientious objection and in a carefully worded passage gave it guarded support. It said, "It seems proper [*aequum videtur*] that the law should make humane provision for those who for reasons of conscience refuse to bear arms" (*GS* 79.3, my translation). This way of expressing the point allowed the Council to bypass the question of the correctness of such a conscientious judgment.

Gaudium et Spes does not examine the kind of issue about nonviolence that would be of particular relevance and urgency to people yearning and perhaps struggling for liberation from an oppressive foreign or indigenous government. The major question for them would be, What does it mean, in practice, to make use of "the kinds of defense that are available to those who do not have power"? (*GS* 78.5). Does such a defense include the use of political strikes, civil disobedience, mass marches (even when such marches are prohibited by the government), sabotage of government property, and so on? The Council did not give an answer, nor did it give any clear guidelines that would enable people suffering gross oppression to work out an answer.

A treatment of such questions, in order to be really helpful, would have to be placed within a wider context. This context is the limits to the right of government to impose its wishes on people who believe they are being treated unjustly. The Council document did not offer any clear teaching on this issue. But it took one important step toward it by giving a clear account of the nature and limits of human authority (*GS* 74). Toward the end of this account the conclusion emerges that people are entitled to defend their own rights and those of their fellow citizens against the abuses of a tyrannical regime. There are, however, two provisos: first, the limits laid down by the natural law and the gospel must be observed; and second, people should not refuse to obey in those matters objectively required by the common good (*GS* 74.5). Each of these two conditions raises more questions than it solves. There is considerable doubt about what limits are laid down by natural law and the gospel—especially on the question of violent resistance or even of any kind of resistance prohibited by law. And the difficulty about the second proviso is that it is so vague as to be practically meaningless. At first sight it seems quite specific: it appears to be saying that people should resist only on the *particular* points where there is an abuse of rights by those in authority. But could it not be that the common good would best be served by an attitude of total noncooperation with an extremely oppressive government? This is what took place during most successful wars of liberation. Such action seems to be compatible with the *Gaudium et Spes* statement, for the text adopts the common good as the criterion. But at that point the meaning of the passage has become so all-embracing that it has little or no content.

SOME INADEQUACIES

There is not much point in combing the text of *Gaudium et Spes* for guidelines about liberation struggles, violent or nonviolent, when, in fact, the Council was working on a different agenda, set mainly by the Western world. As the previous paragraphs should have made clear, one problem about such an agenda is that it does not give a sufficiently high priority to the burning issues of people on other continents, particularly in what were called the colonies. But a further problem is that when co-lonial issues are given consideration, they are looked at mainly from the perspective of the First World. To bring out this point we may note some serious deficiencies in the manner in which the notions of authority and poverty are treated in *Gaudium et Spes*.

Let us look first at the question of authority. At a fairly early stage in the Council document there is a deeply moving passage about the human life of Jesus Christ. It contains one statement that would be unremarkable to a person living in a well-run Western democracy but might pose problems for somebody living under an oppressive colonial regime: "Jesus Christ . . . willingly obeyed the laws of his country" (*GS* 32.2, my translation). This statement seems to foster a spirituality of unquestioning obedience to civil authorities that may be quite inappropriate for millions of Christians who are victims of injustice. Unfortunately, these millions had few bishops or theologians to speak out on their behalf at the Vatican Council. Did nobody think of questioning the accuracy of the statement that Christ willingly obeyed the laws of his country or at least seek to clarify which set of laws was in question? Was there anybody there to point out some of the important things about Christ that the passage fails to say, for in-stance, his challenge to the Jewish authorities of his time and his judicial murder through an alliance between them and the colonial power? To Christians living under a grossly oppressive regime, such facts about Jesus Christ could be just as relevant as his obedience.

The treatment by Vatican II of the question of poverty is also deficient; one reason for this is that the perspective is not that of the masses of the world's poor. In the original "Message to Humanity" from the Council Fathers in the early days of Vatican II, there is deep compassion for the poor but no clear indication of solidarity with them. For instance, the Council Fathers say they "want to fix a steady gaze" on the poor (*Nuntius* 823); this suggests that they are looking at the poor from outside. It is true that in *GS* 1 there is a certain sense of solidarity with the poor: "The joy and hope, the grief and anguish of the people of our time, *especially of those who are poor or afflicted in any way*, are the joy and hope, the grief and anguish of the followers of Christ as well" (Flannery translation, emended slightly and emphasis added). But this sense of solidarity is not evident later in the document. Furthermore, the Council document on the renewal of the religious life, when treating of the vow of poverty, makes only passing reference to people who are poor (*Perfectae Caritatis*, §13). This contrasts sharply with the follow-up apostolic exhortation titled *Evangelica Testificatio*, issued in 1971, in which members of religious communities are exhorted to hear "the cry of the poor" and to see the links between that cry and social injustice (§§17–18). All this indicates that it was only in the few years *after* the Council that the new spirituality of the poor came to the fore.

Perhaps one reason why Vatican II was unable to propose any very rich spirituality of poverty is that, during the years of the Council, bishops and theologians were still in the process of disengaging from an older spirituality. As I noted in a previous chapter, some popes had in the past espoused a rather "escapist" spirituality, where poverty was to be endured in the hope of future reward, and this view had been widely accepted by Christians. The new "worldly" theology associated with the Council—and especially with *Gaudium et Spes*—found little place for such an approach. But changes in spirituality—being changes in the heart as much as in the head—come about rather more slowly than changes in theology. It was too soon to expect a new spirituality of poverty to be available to replace the earlier escapist one. Indeed, one could hardly expect the Council theologians from affluent Europe and North America to forge such a spirituality. So, even in *Gaudium et Spes*, which is perhaps the most radical of the Council documents, poverty was considered mainly from a practical point of view. It was seen as an urgent problem, a problem that is to be overcome mainly by development (*GS* 65–71, 85–88).

At one point in the document Christians are exhorted to have their whole lives "permeated with the spirit of the beatitudes, especially with the spirit of poverty" (*GS* 72.1, my translation). This passage may have been influenced by Paul VI's first encyclical, *Ecclesiam Suam*, which had emphasized the spirit of poverty. In any case, the point was not developed. Indeed, the manner in which the document emphasized full human development left little opening for an integration of a spirit of poverty as a major element in the spirituality it was proposing or presupposing. Various documents of Vatican II refer to the need for Christians to follow Christ who became poor for our sake and came to bring good news to the poor, for example, *Lumen Gentium* §§8, 41; *Apostolicam Actuositatem* §4; *Perfectae Caritatis*, §§1, 13; *Ad Gentes* §§3, 5; *Presbyterorum Ordinis* §17. But none of these documents offers a developed spirituality of poverty that integrates the Christological and evangelical aspects with the economic and social reality.

Within a decade it became evident that a notable lacuna had been left in Christian spirituality. If a fatalistic and escapist spirituality of poverty is to be replaced, there is need for something powerful to take its place. It is not enough to be concerned *for* the poor; one must discover what it means to be *with* the poor. Only then can one experience what it is like to be humanly weak and powerless, but still to be powerful in the awareness that God is on one's side. Out of such an experience can come a spirituality that is not passive and escapist but active and "worldly," although nevertheless open to the transcendent. This will be a spirituality that does not allow itself to be used ideologically by people at either end of the political spectrum: by extreme conservatives, opposed to social change and social justice, or by those revolutionaries whose vision is narrowly materialistic. *Gaudium et Spes* does not propose a fully rounded spirituality of this kind. It was drafted and approved during a period when the leaders of the Catholic Church were so concerned with offering a positive theology of the world that they were as yet unable to discern sufficiently which aspects of the world ought to be challenged. One might say that the document is so taken up with the liberal agenda that it does not deal adequately with the radical agenda.

A STARTING POINT

Despite its shortcomings *Gaudium et Spes* must be judged to be a major achievement. This judgment applies not merely to the document in general, but also to its contribution in the specific area of social justice, for it offers a theology and spirituality of the world that provide a solid foundation for a Christian approach to the question of poverty, an approach that can avoid lapsing into escapism, on the one hand, or secularism, on the other. In the face of issues of social justice, the liberal agenda can lead on naturally to a more radical one. The liberal seeks to be open to the world, accepts the pluralism of modern society, and seeks dialogue with those who have a different outlook—all with the aim of making the world a more human place in which to live. One danger facing the liberal is that openness may come to mean a kind of relativism where one stands for nothing in particular. Related to this is the danger that service of the world may come to mean simply conforming to the existing situation, accepting the dominant values of society. The radical approach offers a corrective for this. It seeks to be of service to the world precisely by challenging some of its dominant values. The world to which the radical is committed is not the present world but the future—or the present insofar as it is open to a different and better future. It is not the world of the rich and the powerful, or, more accurately, not the world as structured to favor this privileged group. It is primarily the world as seen from the perspective of the dominated, the oppressed, the poor—a world in need of liberation.

In regard to the role of the Church in society, *Gaudium et Spes* offers many instances of what I have been calling the liberal agenda. It seeks to make Christians aware that, living in a pluralist world, they must try to understand and engage in dialogue with people of other outlooks, and this applies even in the case of atheists (*GS* 21). The clear acceptance by the Council of the pluralist character of modern society was widely recognized as a significant change (see Joblin 1966).

The theme of understanding and dialogue is evident in the second to last paragraph of the document, which points out the need for dialogue within the Church itself, with other Christians, people of other religious traditions, humanists, and even those who oppose and persecute the Church (*GS* 92). In this passage of the document there are obvious echoes of the passage about dialogue at various levels in Pope Paul's encyclical *Ecclesiam Suam* (1964, 654–59). The basic principle that is being applied is respect for others, a respect that allows them their freedom, and that is what the word "liberal" means. All this is quite central to Christianity. Nevertheless, it is not the only thing that is central to Christianity. There is a danger that having discovered the principle of liberty (or having restored it to its central place), Christians might stop there. If that were to happen, the Church would have become liberal but would have ceased to be prophetic. It would be an exaggeration to suggest that this is what happened during the course of the Vatican Council—and especially in the drafting of *Gaudium et Spes*. But it does not seem unfair to say that on certain matters related to justice, poverty, and development, the liberal dimension of this document is stronger than its prophetic dimension.

Nevertheless, *Gaudium et Spes* provides a solid basis for the step from the liberal to the radical or prophetic agenda. It does so especially in the chapter in which the role of the Church in the modern world is treated formally and explicitly (*GS* 40–45). There the Council Fathers see the role of the Church as making the human family more truly human (*GS* 40.3). Among the ways in which this is to be done are the proclamation and the fostering of human rights (*GS* 41.3), the establishing and building up of the human community, and the initiation of action for the service of all, especially of the poor (*GS* 42.2). This reference to service of the poor is especially significant, but it is weakened by the addition of the phrase "such as works of mercy and similar undertakings." Had these instances been omitted, the text could more easily be taken as referring to a structural reform of society for the benefit of the poor.

It is precisely in its commitment to freedom—to the liberal agenda in the best sense—that the Council took what may well be its most important step toward the adoption of a prophetic role on matters of social justice. In a section of *Gaudium et Spes* titled "The Political Community and the Church" there is a paragraph that can be seen as a new charter or mandate for the relationship between the Church and political authorities (*GS* 76). A key passage states, "The Church . . . does not rest its hopes on privileges offered to it by civil authorities; indeed, it will even give up the exercise of certain legitimately acquired rights in situations where it has been established that their use calls in question the sincerity of its witness or where new circumstances require a different arrangement" (*GS* 76.5, my translation).

In his commentary on this part of *Gaudium et Spes*, Giuseppe Mattai (1969 1049) calls this a truly fundamental proposition, but unfortunately he does little to explain its importance. Oswald von Nell-Breuning (1969, 326–27) sees this relinquishment of privilege as the culmination of this chapter of *Gaudium et Spes* and as a major challenge to the Church—a check that must be honored.

The relinquishing of privilege in order to retain freedom of witness, judgment, and action is central to the liberal outlook. But it is precisely because the Church in Latin America took seriously this liberal principle that it gained the freedom to adopt a prophetic role. So long as Church authorities sought patronage, protection, and privileges from the state, they remained dependent on those who held power in civil society. This dependence inhibited the Church from offering an effective challenge to oppressive governments and unjust social and economic structures. It even allowed the rich and powerful to "use" the Church by giving an aura of religious legitimation to the existing structures of society and a certain approval to those who held power. The passage just quoted from *Gaudium et Spes* was accepted by much of the Church in Latin America as an invitation to adopt a very different posture—to disengage the Church from the embrace of the privileged elites and to challenge structural injustice. In this sense it was *Gaudium et Spes* that provided the foundation on which was built, three years later at Medellín, the Latin American Church's formal commitment to taking "an option for the poor."

HUMAN RIGHTS

Gaudium et Spes has a relatively short but quite important treatment of the topic of human rights. The drafters of this section of the document considered themselves fortunate that already in 1963 Pope John had issued his encyclical *Pacem in Terris*. His approach had involved "a dramatic change of direction," moving the Church leadership "from a position of staunch opposition to modern rights and freedoms to activist engagement in the global struggle for human rights" (Hollenbach 2005, 280). The council document affirms the approach of the encyclical and indicates that because the topic has already been dealt with "at considerable length" (*GS* 23), it can afford to treat it rather briefly. Nevertheless, it develops the Church's approach to human rights further than Pope John had done. It insists that the dignity of persons must be protected by respect for their universal inviolable rights (*GS* 26.2), and it lists a variety of such basic rights. In a later section it affirms the right of women to participate in work outside the home and in cultural life (*GS* 60). The document also makes an effort to provide a scriptural base for its approach to human rights (e.g., *GS* 27, 28).

However, the most significant feature of the Council's treatment of this topic is that it does not simply adopt the current Western conception of human rights. It sees this as unduly individualistic. So the document situates its treatment of rights within the context of the interdependence of people. For the Council Fathers the whole point of protecting human rights is to ensure that humans can live together respectfully in community. As Hollenbach (2005, 281) points out, in the document "protection of human rights and the advancement of the common good are mutually correlative, not opposed to each other" (cf. *GS* 31). *Gaudium et Spes* links rights with responsibilities, insisting that all must contribute to the common good, according to their own abilities and according to the needs of others (*GS* 30). It is a pity that, having refused to adopt a purely individualistic approach to human rights, the Council did not go on to deal with the question of the rights of distinct groups of people, for instance, racial or ethnic minorities. This is a topic that has come to the fore more recently among philosophers, and it is one that theologians and Church authorities need to address.

Gaudium et Spes provides a foundation on which Christians can develop a spirituality centered on human rights. It is important that we do so, because the issue of rights touches a deep chord in the people of today's world. Millions of people find their hearts are moved and their sense of outrage provoked by the gross abuses that they hear of every day. They sense that some rights, such as the right not to be tortured, are so inalienable that they can never be abrogated. However, it is important that we do not allow a focus on individual rights—especially our own—to cause us to become insensitive to the rights of others and to the common good. We must also avoid the danger of emphasizing *human* rights in a manner that would make us insensitive and exploitative in our attitude toward the nonhuman creatures with which we share this world.

A key element in the development of a truly Christian spirituality of human rights is the nourishment in our day-to-day lives of an attitude of deep respect for others. When people speak of "respecting human rights," this is usually taken in a legal sense, where it means not interfering with the rights of others. That is a first step. But an authentic spirituality of human rights requires that we go much further. Instead of just seeing others as people whom we should not hurt or obstruct, our spirituality invites us to empathize with them, to be aware of their fragility and vulnerability. This can lead us to revere them, to love them, and even to treasure them. At its best, our spirituality can inspire us to treat others with great *tenderness*. Ideally, we should find ourselves looking at each person as a sacred being, as a mystery before whom we feel at times like bowing in awe and veneration (cf. Dorr 2008, 124–28). Such spirituality poses a radical challenge to the competitive and exploitative attitude that is fostered by certain aspects of modern Western culture.

We need to nurture our empathetic powers, to be in tune with the feelings of others, and to be sensitive to their needs. This can lead us on to play an active role in educating public opinion on emerging human rights issues. Working with other committed people, we can foster a culture of respect for the fundamental rights of all, both as individuals and as members of local communities, as well as in relation to their ethnic and national identities. If we develop an attitude of empathetic respect and reverence we are equipping ourselves to campaign for, and eventually to negotiate, international treaties and covenants for the protection of all kinds of fundamental human rights.

THE MODEL OF DEVELOPMENT

At this point it is appropriate to look closely at the notion of development that the Council Fathers had in mind when they called for change in the way society was organized. At the time the document was being drafted, the whole idea of development was coming to have a major impact both in secular society and in the Church. As I pointed out in chapter 5, Pope John, in *Mater et Magistra*, had come out strongly in favor of development; he wanted the wealthy countries to assist the poor ones to overcome poverty by helping them to become "developed." But in his encyclicals the notion of development was largely taken for granted. In *Gaudium et Spes*, in contrast, the notion of development is much more central; it functions as an organizing principle for the whole treatment of socioeconomic problems.

A careful examination of the various prescriptions of *Gaudium et Spes* enables one to compile a list of some fundamental values that its authors saw as central to authentic development:

- A more equitable distribution of resources, including land (*GS* 71, 78.1)

- A better sharing of the fruits of economic activity between the nations (*GS* 69.1, 70, 85–87) and within each country, for instance, between the farmers and the rest of the community (*GS* 66)
- The right of workers to share in management and in the whole process of economic planning (*GS* 65, 68.1–2)
- The right of workers to establish trade unions and, as a last resort, to go on strike in defense of their just rights (*GS* 68.2–3)
- The use of improved methods of production (*GS* 66.1, 87.1)
- The importance of investing resources to promote development (*GS* 65.3)
- The need to ensure that workers can live with dignity and have the opportunity to develop their talents, even in their work (*GS* 67)
- The protection of workers against unemployment (*GS* 67.2) and against the effects of automation, relocation, and migration, which are common components of economic development (*GS* 66.2–3)
- The importance of taking account of the needs of future generations (*GS* 70)
- The adoption of more equitable terms of trade between the wealthy nations and the poorer ones (*GS* 85.2) and the establishment of organizations to regulate this trade (*GS* 86.6)

In the 1950s and 1960s, economists, planners, and politicians spoke of development almost exclusively in economic terms. By and large they accepted the view of Walt Rostow (1960) that there were certain fixed stages of development that every country had to go through. The assumption was that if the poorer countries could achieve a certain level of investment, then their economies could "take off" and follow the pattern of Western countries. The Council Fathers were challenging this exclusive focus on the economic aspect of development. They had in mind a notion of balanced development, in which economic values are not the only consideration but are linked to other fundamental human values such as freedom, dignity, and participation. They were concerned not just about material welfare but also about the requirements of "intellectual, moral, spiritual and religious life"; furthermore, they saw development as being at the service of all people, all groups, and every race (*GS* 64). So the process of development should not be controlled by a minority of people or nations; the largest possible number of nations and people should have a share in its direction (*GS* 65.1–2).

The Council document provided important elements for an overall theology of development to underpin the above practical points: (1) it offered a theology of work, seeing it as a way in which humans share in the divine work of creation and the redemptive work of Christ (*GS* 67.2); (2) it provided a theology of the community of humankind (*GS* 33–39);

and (3) it suggested that Christians working for justice and the welfare of humanity should observe the right order of values, in faithfulness to Christ and his gospel, and have their lives permeated with the spirit of the beatitudes, especially the spirit of poverty (*GS* 72).

The authors of *Gaudium et Spes* believed that the main way to overcome global poverty was to ensure that economic development would be made available to all (*GS* 65, 69, 70, 71, 85–87). But they were aware of the dangers. The hasty imposition of "technical solutions" could bring people "material advantages while being inimical to the spiritual character of the human person" (*GS* 86.7, my translation). A too impetuous and ruthless imposition of development could undermine such traditional "worthy customs" as communal modes of ownership (*GS* 69.2). In this way some of the priceless heritage of non-Western cultures could be lost (cf. *GS* 56.2).

However, I think the experts and bishops who took part in the Council gravely underestimated these dangers. They failed to take sufficient account of two important limitations of the concept of development that they were using. First, the kind of development that had been so successful in bringing prosperity to Western countries could not be applied all over the world. The ecological cost would be so high that the Earth's resources could not sustain it. Furthermore, development in the West was at least partly dependent on "underdevelopment" in other parts of the world, for instance, through the availability of low-cost primary products from the poorer countries of the world. This kind of unjust development obviously cannot be extended to all parts of the world (see Dorr 1984, 63–66).

The second limitation of the concept of development used at Vatican II was that this notion was itself a product of Western thinking. Those who drafted *Gaudium et Spes* were no doubt aware of this, but they were themselves too Western in their approach. They underestimated the extent to which the extension of development to other continents would itself be a form of cultural imperialism. I am not, of course, saying that non-Western cultures must remain static, for they too are open to change and development, and they can even borrow elements of that development from Western thinking and practice (cf. Dorr 1990, 168–69; Dorr 1991, 129–34). But the Council Fathers and experts assumed too easily that the basic elements of Western development and its underpinning values are transcultural. In recommending it so enthusiastically, they were unwittingly encouraging an imposition of a product of Western culture that could undermine other cultures.

At the heart of the Western model of development is a certain individualism and competitiveness (a point that is illustrated by the dramatic failure of the communist countries, where competition was limited, to bring about effective development). Competitive individualism is a "value" (or disvalue) that is quite alien to many non-Western cultures; and it is profoundly destructive of these cultures. Western development also presupposes a certain work ethic that is quite foreign, even hostile, to the understanding of work, leisure, and life that lies at the heart of many non-Western cultures. Equally profound differences are to be found in different cultures on a whole range of issues. For instance, various non-Western peoples determine the highest priorities in life in different ways. They have different understandings of the purpose of life. They may have a different conception of time. For example, they may not accept the Western notion that "time is money," and they seldom accept the Western notion that it is important to arrive "on time" for a meeting or to finish "on time." They often have quite a different notion of what gives one person a higher status than others. They may consider it more important to preserve and develop interpersonal and communal relations than to "get the job done." They are likely to have a different conception of the amount of possessions that they consider to be "enough." Finally, they are quite likely to have a different view about what are judged to be the fundamental conditions for living a fulfilled human life.

The Council Fathers wanted to preserve all that was best in non-Western cultures even while they encouraged the extension of Western development to them. They did not appreciate the extent to which these two aims are often incompatible. This failure is related to the way Vatican II treated the question of culture.

CULTURE

One chapter of *Gaudium et Spes* is titled "The Proper Development of Culture" (*GS* 53–62). To devote a whole chapter to the theme of culture is in itself a major achievement, as is the fact that the Council clearly accepted the reality of cultural pluralism. *Gaudium et Spes* rejected the notion of a division of humanity into "civilized" and "uncivilized" peoples. It also pointed out that the Church has used the resources of different cultures not merely in preaching the message of Christ but also in understanding it (theology) and celebrating it (liturgy); so the Church is not tied to any one culture (*GS* 58.2–3). A significant intervention during the Council came from Cardinal Lercaro, who said that the Church must be willing to be culturally poor, that is, to have the courage to renounce, if necessary, the cultural riches of its past in order to open itself to other cultures (see Tucci 1969, 267).

The drafters of *Gaudium et Spes* became almost lyrical when they wrote about "a new age of human history" (*GS* 54) and "the birth of a new humanism" (*GS* 55). They saw this "new humanism" as a more universal form of culture that they believed to be emerging in our time through the interaction of different cultures, the sharing of riches, and the conscious building up of a better world where people take responsibility for each other and for the future (*GS* 54–55).

It is precisely at this point that the Council's treatment of culture was inadequate. It failed to distinguish between the *ideal* unification, which it was describing, and the *actual* unification, which was taking place in the world of that time and is continuing today. The nations of the Earth are becoming increasingly part of one global market, but what is being created is a world where the wealthy nations and classes exploit the others. Again, the world is being linked together ever more closely through the communications media such as television, the great news agencies, and the Internet media, but this unity is one where the cultures and even the languages of the less powerful peoples are being swamped by those of the rich and powerful.

The Council Fathers were concerned about the cultural development of vulnerable groups (*GS* 60.3), but this does not seem to have tempered their enthusiasm for unification. In this part of the document they adverted only very cursorily to the possibility of the traditional wisdom of a whole people being lost (*GS* 56.2). One effect of their failure to take sufficient account of Western cultural domination was that they themselves were unduly Western in their approach; for instance, they assumed that shorter working hours and more leisure are almost universal (*GS* 61.3), whereas this is by no means the reality in many poor countries.

Why did *Gaudium et Spes* fail to take sufficient account of the reality of cultural domination? Mainly because its treatment of culture was left to stand alone, without being integrated with related topics. The strength of the Council's treatment of the issue of international peace was that it was closely linked to its treatment of economics. Culture should have been linked to both of these topics. If that had been done, the Council could have produced a very realistic treatment of the topic. But what we have instead is a somewhat abstract account of culture. The chapter on culture failed to take sufficient account of the economic and political underpinning of a people's culture and of the enormous impact today on the cultures of "the South" of the political-economic dominance of "the North."

Despite these inadequacies the Council document made an important contribution to the Church's teaching on the nature of human development. One of its most significant passages is the following: "Progress begins and develops primarily through the efforts and endowments of the people themselves. Hence, instead of depending solely on outside help, a people should rely chiefly on the full unfolding of their own resources and the cultivation of their own qualities and tradition" (*GS* 86.2, Abbott version emended). This indicates that the authors of the document, while insisting on the importance of foreign aid, were far from accepting a simplistic view of how the problems of poorer countries could be overcome. Development, they realized, is not something that can be imported from outside but is a drawing out of the resources of the people themselves.

Gaudium et Spes also insisted on the importance of "psychological and material adjustments" that must be made by "the developed nations" (*GS* 86.3) in order to meet their obligations to help the rest of the world. The phrase "material adjustments" would include what is called "adjustment aid" designed to make it easier for industries in the North to face increased competition from the South. But economic adjustment of this kind is not sufficient. More important is the "psychological adjustment," that is, a change of mentality. It means that the governments and the people of the North must be prepared to accept the South on terms of equality and partnership. Vatican II, taken as a whole, was an important move toward such a psychological adjustment by the Catholic Church of the West.

I have been suggesting that, when dealing with the topic of development, the authors of *Gaudium et Spes* did not always succeed in practice in avoiding the mistaken attitudes that they were rejecting in principle. A further key point emerges as we look back at the approach of the document to the issue of development: it pays very little attention to the ecological issue. This is quite understandable, since it was only in the very year that the document was promulgated that the environmental issue was coming sharply into focus in public awareness. So it was only in later years that this topic came to be dealt with in Church teaching. What we can say is that the Council document provided a solid basis for the deeper understanding of human development that came just a couple of years later in Pope Paul's great social encyclical *Populorum Progressio*.

CONCLUSION

The Council document *Gaudium et Spes* has proved to be controversial within the Church itself. Many continue to see it as a fundamental mandate for the Church of the future. But an influential body of Church leaders and theologians, including Pope Benedict XVI, have been inclined to question much of its approach. They have seen it not merely as unduly optimistic and downplaying the reality of sin but also as tending to subordinate the values of the transcendent supernatural realm to this-worldly political categories and values. This clash of views is best articulated not in terms of a divergence between liberals, conservatives, and radicals but more as a contrast between an Augustinian outlook and spirituality, on the one hand, and, on the other hand, an outlook that is more in line with Thomistic theology (cf. Hollenbach 2005, 288–89). This tension is a healthy one for the Church—provided that those on both sides remain willing to engage in a serious dialogue with each other.

* * *

SUMMARY

The Second Vatican Council showed considerable concern about the problem of poverty on a global scale. However, the most influential figures in the Council were from the Western world, and they felt it essential to deal with their own liberal agenda before addressing the question of the role of the Church in relation to world poverty. When they did get around to discussing the latter issue, they made an important contribution in *Gaudium et Spes*. This document, while still unduly optimistic about the world, is somewhat more realistic than the encyclicals of Pope John. It presents justice as central both to the issue of poverty and to that of peace. It calls for a change in the international economic structures; it emphasizes the right of the poor to their share of the Earth's goods and insists that this imposes on the rich an obligation that is more than that of giving alms from their superfluous goods. It warns the rich that the poor are entitled to take what they need in order to live. It accepts that some huge landholdings might have to be expropriated and given to the poor. It presents a balanced concept of development. It commits the Church to a relinquishment of its own privileges where that is required to make its witness sincere and effective. This willingness to renounce the patronage of the state sets the Church free to take a prophetic stand against those who hold power, so it was a major step in the progress of the Church toward making an option for the poor.

However, there are some less satisfactory aspects to the document. It offers little by way of a spirituality of poverty. It does not address the moral issues relating to wars of liberation. Above all, it assumes that the main solution to the problem of poverty lies in following the Western model of economic development. It does not take sufficient account of the extent to which this would involve an imposition of Western culture on other peoples. The treatment of culture in the document does not take sufficient account of the links between culture and economics.

QUESTIONS FOR REVIEW

1. *Why was the issue of world poverty not fully addressed until very late in the Council?*
2. *In what ways did Gaudium et Spes add to the Church's social teaching?*

3. Did the Council authorize poor people or peoples to fight for justice and to take what they needed to live a human life?
4. To what extent did the document accept the Western understanding of human rights, and in what ways did it challenge it?

QUESTIONS FOR REFLECTION

1. To what extent can Western-style development really solve the problems of poverty in the poorer countries?
2. In what sense or to what extent does the Church have a privileged position in your country, and what are the effects?
3. On what basis should we develop a spirituality of human rights?

ISSUES FOR FURTHER STUDY

1. Who were the spokespersons for the non-Western Churches at Vatican II? What were their main concerns? What contribution did they make? What did they overlook?
2. The concept of group rights—for instance, the rights of racial or ethnic minorities.

7

Paul VI on the Progress of Peoples

As we have seen, three major documents on social questions were issued by the Catholic Church's highest authorities at two-year intervals in the 1960s—*Mater et Magistra* in 1961, *Pacem in Terris* in 1963, and *Gaudium et Spes* in 1965. One might have expected Pope Paul VI to pause for a while before writing another social encyclical. That he did not do so is an indication of the rapid changes that were taking place at this time in the theology of justice and poverty—and also a sign of the pope's sense of urgency about these issues.

Barely sixteen months after the publication of the Council document, Pope Paul issued *Populorum Progressio* ("On the Development of Peoples"), a major encyclical both in terms of its length and its importance.[1] The teaching in this document was original in two respects. First, it offered a fresh approach to the understanding of development. Second, in its approach to social justice, it shifted the focus from the national to the international scene. I propose to consider each of these points in turn.

AN ORIGINAL APPROACH TO DEVELOPMENT

During the 1950s, the new idea of economic development brought about an enormous change in the thinking of government leaders and their advisers, and this affected the views of industrialists, trade unionists, agriculturalists, and ordinary people. Essentially, this change was the widespread acceptance of the belief that each individual country, and the world as a whole, can grow out of poverty. Prior to this time justice was primarily a matter of ensuring the proper distribution of existing wealth and resources. Now it could be seen in terms of the production of increased resources that could be used to overcome poverty and to ensure that those who had little could catch up with those who had more.

---

[1]Allan Figueroa Deck (2005, 292–96) gives a comprehensive and helpful account of the context of the document in the world and in the Church.

In chapters 5 and 6 I pointed out how this notion of development was adopted by Pope John and how a corrected version of it was given a central place by Vatican II. *Populorum Progressio* also gave a central place to the concept of development, but its approach was sharply different from that of previous Church documents. The difference was a conceptual one. The encyclical was radically new, not so much in its account of the specific details of what development involves, as in the way it seeks to *define* development. At the heart of *Populorum Progressio* lies a notion of integrated development that Paul VI took from Père L. J. Lebret, the Dominican scholar and activist who died some time before the encyclical appeared.[2]

The following analogy may help explain the newness of the approach to development adopted in *Populorum Progressio*. Two people asked to describe their ideal house may respond in two different ways. One may say, "My ideal house would be smaller than my present house; it would have better insulation; it would have solar panels on the roof instead of roof tiles, etc." The other person may say, "My ideal house is one where a family can work, eat, sleep, and relax, with a maximum of ease at a minimum cost to themselves, to the community, and to the environment, etc."

The person giving the first answer starts from a known existing reality (the present house) and lists the differences between it and the ideal. The second answer begins by laying down certain general criteria or standards that the ideal house must live up to.

In regard to human development, the first of these approaches was adopted by the fathers of Vatican II in *Gaudium et Spes* ("The Church in the Modern World"). Their starting point and term of reference was the kind of economic development to which governments all over the world were committed. They set out to correct and expand this conception, to produce an integral and balanced conception of human development. In doing so, they made an important contribution to the Church's body of social teaching. But anybody who starts, as they did, from the current concept of "development" used by economists and planners, is in danger of ending up with a notion of development that is quite inadequate. One great danger is that of assuming, consciously or unconsciously, that economic development is the solid core of any authentic human development. Those who start with this explicit or implicit assumption quickly find themselves trapped into an awkward conceptual framework. They find that they have to engage in a kind of trade-off between the solid

---

[2]It is commonly accepted that the final version of the text of *Populorum Progressio* was edited mainly by Pietro Pavan. But it is clear that much of the early drafting was by Lebret; his inspiration pervades the whole encyclical, and some of its statements are taken almost word for word from his writings. Others who influenced it were Joseph Cardijn and Barbara Ward-Jackson (cf. Malley 1968, 99; Deck 2005, 296–97).

economic core of development and the "soft" elements that surround it. By the "soft" elements I mean those that are not strictly economic, for instance, respect for culture, for the environment, for human rights, for the sense of community, and for the quality of human life. The solid economic core seems to be in competition with the surrounding "soft" elements. Too much insistence on the "soft" elements may seem to put so many restraints on economic growth that planners would fear that the economy would remain stagnant, and there would be no "development" at all.

In sharp contrast to this whole approach, Paul VI in *Populorum Progressio* adopted the kind of approach used in the second of the answers given above to the question about the ideal house. He did not take the current conception of economic development as a starting point and then modify it. Instead, he laid down certain basic standards by which we can measure to what extent any features or changes in society deserve to be called authentic human development. In other words, what *Populorum Progressio* gives is a framework or anticipation of the shape of genuine human development. In technical terms what it offers is a *heuristic* notion of development.

In his account of authentic development the pope quotes from Lebret and follows his humanistic approach, which insists that development "must foster the development of each person and of the whole person" (*PP* 14, my translation). Deck (2005, 298–99) notes that the pope was also deeply influenced by the humanism of Jacques Maritain. He starts from the obligation of each person to attain self-fulfillment (*PP* 15–16). But development is not a purely self-centered affair. Each of us is part of a community and a civilization that has its own history. So we are bound together in solidarity. Just as each of us has benefited from the efforts of others in the community and of those who have gone before us, so each of us has to take account of the welfare of others in the community and of those who will come after us (*PP* 16–17). In a key statement in a later paragraph he said that the development of the individual person involves a simultaneous development of all humanity (*PP* 43).

Populorum Progressio does not give a privileged place to the economic dimension of human development any more than to the cultural, psychological, political, ecological, or religious dimensions. Rather, it challenges Christians to take full account of the noneconomic elements, for instance, to recognize the value of different cultures and of basic human rights. With this approach one is less tempted to take facile shortcuts, to say, for instance, that in the name of development we must sacrifice the environment or give up some treasured cultural tradition or some fundamental human right.

A heuristic concept of development is, of course, of no help unless its structures can be filled in so as to give us some concrete content. Pope

Paul was no doubt aware of this when, following the inspiration of Lebret, he spoke of "a development which is, for each and all, the transition from less human conditions to those which are more human" (*PP* 20). He then went on to indicate those who live in less human conditions. They are people weighed down by material or moral poverty or oppressed by bad social structures created by the abuse of wealth or power, by exploitation of workers, or by unjust business deals. A move to more human conditions would include an escape from destitution, the elimination of social evils, the widening of knowledge, and the acquiring of refinement and culture (*PP* 21).

In the same paragraph of the encyclical Paul VI goes on to include four other important items in the list of what is "more human." They are greater respect for the dignity of others, an orientation toward a spirit of poverty, cooperation for the common good, and a will for peace. By including these items here, he ensures that personal self-fulfillment is not set in sharp contrast to the welfare of others. This links up with his emphasis toward the end of the encyclical on willing self-sacrifice in the interests of peace and unity (*PP* 79).

A dilemma arises for those who measure development only in material terms: the development of one individual or nation appears to be at the expense of others. By widening the concept of development to include spiritual values, the pope succeeds in avoiding this dilemma. He provides a basis for integrating personal development with community development and reconciling national development with global development. His inclusion of self-sacrifice in the definition of development challenges in two ways the assumption of Western economists and development planners that people are motivated mainly by self-interest. First, the pope believes that a human being can be fulfilled personally by a willingness to cooperate with others, even when this imposes a personal cost on the individual; therefore, self-interest is not opposed to concern for others. Second, and equally significantly, the pope sees frugality not as a limitation to personal development but as a positive element within it. This means that development can be reconciled with ecological restraint. It also opens the way to reconciling genuine human development with a relinquishment by the wealthy of waste and excess in order to allow the poor a fair share of the resources of the Earth. In this emphasis on a simple lifestyle *Populorum Progressio* was well ahead of its time.

Having laid down some practical standards for defining genuine human development, the pope uses them to evaluate and correct the changes and so-called development taking place in the modern world. He criticizes liberal capitalism (*PP* 26, 58), technocracy (*PP* 34), a materialistic and atheistic philosophy (*PP* 39), lack of respect for a people's cultural heritage (*PP* 40, 72), and racism (*PP* 63–64).

CAN THE NOTION OF DEVELOPMENT BE RESCUED?

The heuristic approach adopted by Pope Paul to defining the concept of development offers the possibility of finding a middle way between two opposed schools of thought. On the one hand, there are those who are broadly in favor of the plans for economic development adopted by practically all modern governments. They may not agree with every detail, but on the whole they believe that the only effective way to overcome poverty is through increased economic growth. On the other hand, there is a large and growing number of people who are profoundly suspicious of all such development plans. Some of these are people who are influenced by the "small is beautiful" philosophy of E. F. Schumacher and by recent radical ecologists. Others are committed Christians who lived in places like Brazil, various African countries, Tibet, and parts of India, and have witnessed the appalling damage that has been done to people, traditional cultures, and the environment in the name of "development."

Already in the late 1960s many Church people in Latin America saw that the word "development" was being used as a cover for exploitation and the creation of dependency. So they challenged "development" and demanded "liberation" instead. The ecological and liberationist trends converge in Ivan Illich (1988) and his followers (cf. Hoinacki 1991, 53–57; W. Sachs 1991, 59–63). For them the whole notion of development is to be rejected, and the very word "development" is dangerous and un-Christian.

The advantage of the heuristic notion of development put forward in *Populorum Progressio* is that, in principle, it is in no way tainted with the conception of economic development that is so widely and uncritically accepted in our world today. Those who adopt the pope's definition cannot be said to condone the exploitation of people and the Earth that has been carried out under the guise of so-called development, for what it involves is an understanding of development that is not borrowed from Western economics but one whose only content comes from such guidelines as "the flourishing of every person, of all people, and of all peoples." In this way the encyclical represents a serious effort by the pope to rescue the word "development."

The danger, of course, is that those who accept this very general notion may quickly, and perhaps unconsciously, allow it to become tainted with the ideological overtones of meaning that the word "development" carries in everyday speech. This danger is very real—and Pope Paul himself was by no means immune to it. But at least this approach offers the possibility of a genuine dialogue rather than the mutual incomprehension that exists between those who take it for granted that countries should engage in rapid economic development and those who are suspicious of the whole notion of development as it is widely understood and practiced at present.

INTERNATIONAL SOCIAL JUSTICE

At the beginning of this chapter I noted two distinctive features of *Populorum Progressio*: its original approach to development and its shift of focus from the national to the international scene in matters of social justice. Having looked at the first of these points, I now move on to the second. It can be said that *Populorum Progressio* does at the global level what Leo XIII's *Rerum Novarum* did at the level of the nation (cf. Chenu 1979, 75). Its concern is primarily with the relationship between rich and poor nations rather than rich and poor individuals or classes. This is made clear in the first section, in which the pope states baldly, "Today the principal fact we must all recognize is that the social question has become worldwide" (*PP* 3).

In saying this, Pope Paul was taking account of the rapid changes in the world situation that had taken place since the end of World War II. The struggle against colonialism had already reached a peak in the late 1950s and early 1960s. Dozens of new nations were affirming their existence by joining the United Nations. The new prominence of agencies concerned with international trade and finance (e.g., GATT, UNCTAD, the IMF, and the World Bank) showed clearly that justice was no longer something to be worked out only within any given country but was first of all an international matter—even an intercontinental one. Above all, it concerned relations between the industrialized nations and the former colonies in what had come to be called the Third World (which is now more commonly called the South).

INTEREST IN THE CAUSES OF POVERTY

Pope Paul does not rush in with solutions to the problem of poverty at the international level without taking the trouble to seek its basic causes. This is one respect in which *Populorum Progressio* represents a notable advance on earlier Church documents. It analyzes the global situation and sets out to explain why there is such an imbalance between rich and poor countries. Among the causes of poverty and injustice mentioned in the encyclical are the evil effects of the legacy of colonialism, the present neocolonial situation that has largely replaced the older form of colonialism, and the imbalance of power between nations, which gives rise to injustices in trade relations (*PP* 7–9, 52, 56–58).

There is a good case for saying that the encyclical's analysis of the aftereffects of colonialism does not go far enough and that the judgments it makes are too lenient. For instance, the pope seems to suggest that the evils brought by the colonial powers can be balanced against the good they did (*PP* 7). He does not take full account of the extent to which the colonial powers shattered not only the political and economic structures of the colonized peoples, but also the social, cultural, and religious framework that gave order and meaning to their lives.[3] He seems also to overestimate the extent to which Western science, technology, and culture have been of real and lasting benefit to most of the South, for what has to be considered is not the wonderful advantages that *might* have been derived through the interaction of Western learning with the cultures of these other countries, but rather the *actual* effects of the imposition of Western-type schooling in the so-called developing countries. Both Charles Elliott (1975, 228–76) and Michael Todaro (1977, 235–65) show how Western schooling has the effect of reinforcing the gap between the rich and the poor, and has other damaging effects on the economic and social structures of poor countries.

In one paragraph, however, the pope does note the way in which past colonial history has left an enduring bad effect on the economy of many poor countries by leaving them dependent on a single export crop that is subject to price fluctuations (*PP* 7; cf. *PP* 57). For all its caution the encyclical succeeds in ways like this in challenging the view widely held in the West at least at that time—that the former colonies have, in the long run, benefited from their colonial history through being brought into the mainstream of modern civilization.

Pope Paul is equally cautious but firm in the way in which he speaks of neocolonialism. He refers to it more as a suspicion or possibility than as a fact. He leaves it to the readers to judge whether there is justification for such suspicion of "political pressure and economic domination, aimed at maintaining or acquiring control for a few" (*PP* 52). He adverts in different places to the two features that are characteristic of a neocolonial situation: economic domination at the international level and both political and economic domination at the national level. At the national level, he refers to regimes in which small, privileged elites hold a monopoly of wealth and power (*PP* 9). His treatment of the international issue is perhaps the most trenchant part of the whole encyclical: he chal-

---

[3]Cf. Cosmao (1978, 51): "ce que nous appelons le sous-développement s'explique en effet, bien plus fondamentalement, par un *processus de déstructuration des sociétés polarisées par la société dominante en expansion*"; cf. Cosmao (1979a, 44–48). For a historical account of how this process took place over several centuries, see Stavrianos (1981).

lenges the present system of international trading relations (*PP* 57–60), pointing out that they are such that "poor nations become poorer while the rich ones become still richer" (*PP* 57). It is clear that the pope does not simply assume that poverty and underdevelopment arise from purely natural causes or the laziness of the people living in the poorer parts of the world. In *PP* 48, however, he refers to "the gifts that providence has bestowed" on a country. This phrase, coupled with the general tone of the paragraph, could give the impression that the pope accepts the view that the so-called underdeveloped countries have been given a smaller share of such resources. Although this may be true about some individual countries, it cannot be said of the poorer countries as a whole. In fact, it is a myth that people in the West often cling to, perhaps to avoid the implications about past exploitation and present injustice; this myth needs to be challenged.

There is a pressing urgency in the way in which Pope Paul calls for change (*PP* 29). If injustices are to be overcome peacefully, there must, he says, be "bold transformations in which the present order of things will be entirely renewed or rebuilt" (*PP* 32, my translation; the usual English translation, "innovations that go deep," does not do justice to the Latin phrase "rerum forma penitus renovetur"). What he is calling for is evidently a change in the structures. That is shown not merely by the words he uses here but also by the kind of changes he proposes throughout the encyclical and the basic principle that inspires them. This principle is that "the rule of free trade, taken by itself, is no longer able to govern international relations"; therefore, "the fundamental principle of liberalism, as the rule for commercial exchange," is called into question (*PP* 58). The basic reason he gives for this is that international trade is unjust, because there is a gross inequality between the trading partners. So what is called "free trade" must be severely restricted (*PP* 59). Competition should not be entirely eliminated (*PP* 61), but the same kind of support system that is now given within wealthy countries to the weaker sectors of the economy should be introduced, on a global scale between rich and poor countries (*PP* 60–61).

This proposal for a planned approach on a world scale, aimed at the protection of the weaker countries and the stabilization of markets, is very close to the demands made a few years later for a "New International Economic Order" (NIEO). This NIEO, sought by the developing countries in the North–South dialogue, seeks the same goals and proposes the same means as outlined in the encyclical. As Barbara Ward remarked, "Many of the ideas of this New Order have such firm roots in *Populorum Progressio* that the Encyclical might almost have been its founding document" (Ward 1978, 202).

COMPARISON WITH *QUADRAGESIMO ANNO*

In his study of the notion of Catholic social doctrine, written in 1979, Marie-Dominique Chenu (1979, 72), discerned a general pattern. He pointed out that the early social encyclicals tended to be moralistic in tone, whereas the later ones recognized that a change of attitudes is not sufficient—there must be reform of the structures. So he maintained that Paul VI, while still retaining elements of "moralism," was looking for structural change in society. There is a good deal of truth in this view; but the pattern is rather more complex than Chenu suggested. If one compares Leo XIII's *Rerum Novarum* with Pius XI's *Quadragesimo Anno*, one finds that whereas the former is primarily moralistic in tone, the latter calls for both attitudinal and structural change. Each of these encyclicals focuses the reader's attention on the economic situation within the typical industrialized country of the West. The two major social encyclicals of Pope John in the early 1960s represent a shift toward an outlook that is international or global. The solutions put forward by John XXIII for these global problems tend once again to be somewhat moralistic in tone, although he recognizes the need for new institutions or structures. In Pope Paul's *Populorum Progressio*, by contrast, there is a clearer analysis of the problems of the world economic order—and a recognition that they arise largely as a result of the way the existing structures work. Nevertheless, Paul VI remains convinced that attitudinal change is also of major importance; and he does not oppose this to structural change. There is, for instance, a strong moral tone in this passage: "The world is sick. The cause lies less in the lack of resources, or their monopolisation by a small number of people, than in the lack of brotherhood and sisterhood among individuals and peoples" (*PP* 66).

In an earlier passage in the encyclical he had insisted that there is a grave and urgent social duty to ensure that the goods of the Earth are distributed fairly (*PP* 22). Furthermore, in the brief section in which he acknowledged that accelerated population growth causes many difficulties for development, he insisted that parents have a moral obligation to decide on the number of their children, "following the dictates of their own consciences informed by God's law authentically interpreted" (*PP* 37).

We can see that there is a fairly close parallel between *Quadragesimo Anno* and *Populorum Progressio*, with each of them calling for changes both in attitudes and in structures. In particular, there is a similarity between the outspoken rejection in each of the two encyclicals of the liberalism that underlies capitalism. Pope Paul recalls the strictures of Pius XI:

The baseless theory has emerged which considers material gain the key motive for economic progress, competition as the supreme law of economics, and private ownership of the means of production as an absolute right that has no limits. . . . This unchecked liberalism led to dictatorship rightly denounced by Pius XI as producing "the international imperialism of money." One cannot condemn such abuses too strongly, because . . . the economy should be at the service of people. (*PP* 26)

Despite the similarities, there are significant differences in approach between the encyclicals of the two popes. In the first place, as already noted, the international economic order is the principal focus for Paul VI, whereas for Pius XI the individual nation was still central. Second, Pope Paul, while making proposals for major changes in the economic system, does not give the same impression as Pius XI that he is proposing a ready-made alternative to the present capitalist system. This is partly a difference in style: Pope Paul is more concerned with shunning anything that would smack of triumphalism. But the difference is also one of theology: Paul VI is far more reluctant than his predecessor to imply that there is a specific Catholic answer to social and economic problems.

One of the more interesting things that is revealed by a close study of the two encyclicals is that neither of them is quite what it seems. At first sight *Quadragesimo Anno* appears to reject capitalism outright and to propose a corporatist alternative, but what its author actually wanted was a free enterprise system that would be more or less equivalent to capitalism without its abuses and without its ideology. In *Populorum Progressio*, Paul VI's condemnations of capitalism are more subdued, but the changes he proposes in the international order would impose such limitations on international capitalism that if they were properly implemented, they would transform it entirely.

Does this mean that Pope Paul in *Populorum Progressio* is really rejecting capitalism outright? The reply must be, "It depends on what one means by 'capitalism.'" Paul VI, like Pius XI before him, condemns the injustices perpetrated by unchecked capitalistic trading (*PP* 56–59). Like Pius, he insists that a just economic order cannot be built on the principles and ideology of liberal capitalism (*PP* 26). He proposes instead the guiding principles of *solidarity* of rich and poor (*PP* 48–49, 76–77), and of *dialogue* (*PP* 54, 73), leading to *planning* on a global scale (*PP* 50–52, 60–61, 64, 78). However, he does not favor a totally planned international economic order (a kind of world socialism) in which there would be no room for competition and free enterprise. He says explicitly that the competitive market should not be abolished entirely in international trading but that it should be kept within the limits of what is just (*PP* 61).

Pope Paul carefully refrains from going into specific detail about how the international economic order should operate. But it is reasonably clear that he would want to apply on a global level the same kind of guidelines as he lays down for national development:

> It pertains to the public authorities to choose, and even to impose, the objectives to be pursued, the ends to be achieved, and the means by which these are to be achieved; and it is for them to stimulate all the forces required for this common activity. But they should see to it that private initiative and intermediate institutions are involved in this undertaking. In this way they will avoid an absolute community of goods and the danger of arbitrary planning which, by denying liberty, would prevent the exercise of the fundamental rights of the human person. (*PP* 33, translation emended)

This is a remarkably traditional statement, defending the values of subsidiarity and personal initiative with which Catholic social teaching had all along been concerned. But the point I wish to emphasize here is the role that is assigned to "the public authorities" in ensuring that society is organized in this way. If these guidelines were applied on an international scale, there would be need for some kind of world authority to play this role. So one can see why Pope Paul favors a move in this direction (*PP* 78). In fact in his address to the United Nations two years earlier (1965, 880) he had spoken of the need to move progressively toward the establishment of a world authority. Now in this encyclical he insisted that until the time such a world government can emerge, the role of "public authority" at the global level can be played, at least to some extent, by international agencies, by a concerted plan agreed to by the different nations, and by a collaboration on a worldwide scale resulting in a common fund to help all, especially the poorer nations (*PP* 50–55).

One reason why Paul VI stresses the need to move toward a world authority is that he sees the close link that exists between the economic order and the political order. A good deal of the encyclical is concerned with the disparity in power between the rich and the poor (*PP* 9, 58–60). The crucial question is not simply who the owners of wealth and resources are but what individuals or groups or nations have the power to impose their will on others. It is the power of the rich that enables them to become still richer by forcing the weak to make trading agreements that are unjust (*PP* 59). At this point the pope goes on to recall the teaching of *Rerum Novarum* and adds, "What was true of the just wage for the individual is also true of international contracts." Having noted that those who are powerful are also those who are rich, he adds that, conversely, the deprivation of power, of opportunity to determine one's conditions of living and working, is itself a kind of poverty (cf. *PP* 9). In this he was anticipating a key element in the approach of the Nobel prize–winning economist Amartya Sen, who emphasizes the notion of "capability" in relation to what constitutes human flourishing and a decent quality of life (see Nussbaum and Sen 1993).

The encyclical insists that individuals and whole peoples are entitled to become "the agents of their own destiny" and to assume responsibility for their world (*PP* 65). This is one of the central points in Pope Paul's conception of human development—that individuals and peoples should be enabled to have the prime responsibility for their own development (*PP* 77; cf. *PP* 35, 70). In the light of this understanding it is only natural that the encyclical should go on to address the issue of power. But when the question of power is raised, one is led to ask a rather awkward question: Who has the power to bring about the kind of changes the encyclical proposes? From this a further question arises: Is it likely that those who have the power to make effective changes will, in fact, make these changes? Or is the encyclical just another instance of wishful thinking?

COULD A REVOLUTION BE JUSTIFIED?

Quite obviously the pope himself cannot enforce a new international order. He can appeal to statespeople (*PP* 84), scholars (*PP* 85), all people of goodwill (*PP* 83), and especially Christians and other believers (*PP* 82). Above all, he can appeal to the members of his own Church, especially the laity, to bring about the fundamental changes in mentality and structures that are called for (*PP* 81). In addition to a moral appeal made in the name of justice, he can offer strong arguments based on the self-interest of those who could bring about the changes required. He does this by noting that what is at stake is not merely the life of poor nations and civil peace in the developing countries but also world peace (*PP* 55; cf. *PP* 76, 86). It is in this context that he adopts the formula that has become famous: "Development, the New Name for Peace" (heading for *PP* 76–77).

Pope Paul argues that the rich themselves will be the first to benefit if they share their superfluous wealth with the needy. And here his argument is based on a threefold threat facing those who fail to respond to the needs of the poor. First, they place their own highest values in jeopardy by yielding to greed. Second, they call down on themselves the judgment of God. Third, they also call on themselves the wrath of the poor (*PP* 49).This is a very interesting juxtaposition: there are the moral and religious arguments one might expect, but the third point is a clear warning to the rich that if they do not make the necessary changes, then the oppressed may take it into their own hands to bring about change through violent action.

What is the teaching of the pope about such violent action by the poor and oppressed? It is mainly pragmatic rather than moral in character. His attention is not focused principally on whether such violence would be justified but on the fact that it is in everybody's interest not to allow such a desperate situation to develop. He warns the complacent of the risks they run: "When whole populations destitute of necessities live in a state of subjection barring them from all initiative and responsibility, and from all opportunity to advance culturally and to share in social and political life, people are easily led to have recourse to violence as a means to right these wrongs to human dignity" (*PP* 30).

At once, the pope goes on to point out that a revolutionary uprising produces new injustices, imbalances, and disasters (*PP* 31). So he argues that to fight the present evils in this way only produces greater misery. Of course, this does not mean that such evil is to be endured without any resistance. The whole tenor of the pope's teaching is that the situation is to be changed. In the next sentence he does not hesitate to use militant language: injustices are to be fought against and overcome (*PP* 32). What Pope Paul is opposed to is not radical change itself but violent revolution as a means of bringing it about.

Even the rejection of revolution by Pope Paul is not absolute. He inserts a qualifying parenthetical phrase into the passage where he argues against a violent insurrection: "A revolutionary uprising—unless there is question of flagrant and long-standing tyranny which would violate the fundamental rights of the human person and inflict grave injury on the common good of the State—produces new injustices . . . and provokes people to further destructive outrage" (*PP* 31, my translation).

The syntax of this sentence is contorted. The parenthetical comment is clearly meant to suggest that in certain extreme situations, a revolution might be justified (cf. Curran 2002, 163). But it does not say this explicitly, for the sentence does not set out to express a formal moral judgment; instead it points out a fact—that revolution leads to further injustices. We must assume that the element of vagueness in the passage is deliberate. Indeed, there is considerable subtlety in the way the whole sentence is phrased, a subtlety that enables the pope to achieve a number of purposes at the same time. First, and most obviously, the main thrust is to show that violent rebellion is a futile way to seek to overcome injustice, because it tends to bring about the very evils that it sets out to overcome. This already constitutes a strong moral argument against insurrection—as the final sentence of the paragraph points out: "A present evil should not be fought against at the cost of greater misery" (*PP* 31). I note that in this final sentence of the paragraph, the pope is speaking of what ought to be done, as distinct from what happens in fact.

Second, in this passage Paul VI begins to face up to the question of the possibility of a justified revolution, a question that had been shelved by Vatican II. Apparently he recognized that despite the strong arguments against revolution, it would be flying in the face of a strong Catholic tradition to rule it out entirely. His parenthetical comment enabled him to take account of this tradition.

Third, even in this brief parenthetical comment, the pope succeeds in specifying the kind of conditions in which a revolution might be justified: he speaks of flagrant and long-standing violations of human rights and grave injury to the common good of the state. His language here combines a traditional Catholic element (the common good) with a usage more familiar to the modern secular world (violations of human rights).

Fourth, while taking account of the possibility that a revolution might be justified, the pope carefully refrains from saying explicitly that it would be justified in such circumstances. Had he done so, he could have been accused of inciting revolution, by inviting repressed peoples or groups to begin to measure the extent to which their oppressors are violating fundamental rights and injuring the common good. This thought must have weighed heavily on Pope Paul and on those who helped draft the text of the encyclical. Their solution to the difficulty was the parenthetical comment quoted above—a statement that is nuanced to the point of being rather tortuous.

The statement as it stands does not encourage people to use violent means to overcome injustices, even in extreme circumstances. Nevertheless, if the passage were to have any relevance, it had to indicate that the pope was taking some stance or making some judgment, however carefully nuanced, in relation to the possibility of revolution being morally justified. Simply by adverting to violent insurrection and refraining from condemning it absolutely, the encyclical implies that there may well be situations in our world where revolution might be permissible. This point was not lost either on those who looked to the Church for support in maintaining an unjust status quo or on those who wished to enlist the Church on their side in their struggle for liberation. In fact, in an article on the encyclical written shortly after its publication Joblin (1967, 5) remarked about these words that "those who are struggling bravely against injustices will undoubtedly interpret them as approval of their activities." So, despite its brevity and careful phrasing, this passage had, and still has, considerable importance. It serves to clarify the official stance of the Church on an issue that is quite central to the meaning of the notion of an option for the poor.

I am not at all suggesting that the option for the poor necessarily means approval of violent resistance to oppression. However, such an option could involve refusal to make a blanket condemnation of all violent resistance; and that is what we find in *Populorum Progressio*. It is clear that faced with the same ultimate choice as that faced by Leo XIII, Pope Paul refused to take the same position as Leo. As I pointed out in chapter 2, Leo XIII had said that, in the last resort, Christians must endure injustices rather than rebel. Paul VI implies that this is not so.

Although the difference between the positions of the two popes arises in relation to an extreme situation that may arise only rarely, nevertheless the effect extends widely, for the question has to be asked whether the Church is only bluffing when it claims to be on the side of the oppressed. What happens when the bluff is called? Where does the Church stand when flagrant injustice mounts to a point where violent resistance is the only realistic means of bringing about change—as seemed to be the case some years later in the struggles of the people of Nicaragua against the Somoza tyranny and the people of Zimbabwe against the Ian Smith regime?

When there is a struggle against gross injustice and oppression, the Church cannot with any authenticity claim to be totally neutral and uninvolved, on the grounds that it is "above politics." So what stance ought it to take? Obviously, it may not automatically take the side of the "law and order" of the established power. May it, then, condone—at least tacitly—the violent resistance of the freedom fighters? The stance taken in such situations is a test for the credibility of the Church's claim to be committed to social justice. If Church authorities balk at this test under the guise of standing for nonviolence and the rule of law, then one must conclude that social stability has been given a higher priority than social justice. What is at stake is a major issue involving the definition by Church authorities of the nature and values of the Church. Is commitment to justice in the world so central to the mission of the Church that it may never be subordinated to the value of stability without denying or damaging the mission and identity of the Church? As I shall point out in chapter 9, this question was formally answered in a document issued by the Synod of Bishops four years after Pope Paul issued his encyclical. And there can be little doubt that what the pope said in this passage contributed significantly to the strong stand taken by the synod on the indispensability of justice in the Christian message.

We must, of course, remember that even in extreme situations, Church authorities are not usually faced with just a straight choice between two alternatives, namely, that of supporting revolutionary action or of condemning it. People on either side often wish to restrict the choices in this way, but, in fact, a whole range of options is open to those who struggle against injustice. For instance, in most cases a persistent general strike and a refusal to obey orders are likely to be less violent and more effective. Furthermore, Church leaders also have a range of options open to them. It may be that in some situations, the common good and the credibility of the Church may best be served if the Church strongly condemns the oppressive actions of the government but makes no explicit public judgments on whether the freedom fighters are justified in taking up arms.

In fact, when Church leaders make an option for the poor and oppressed, it does not at all follow that they must therefore give unqualified support to those who rebel even against intolerable injustice. A more urgent need may be for them to speak out against atrocities committed by the forces on either side, for it can easily happen in a struggle of this kind that, from the point of view of the means employed, both sides are wrong. However, the crucial point is that a blanket condemnation of all violent resistance to a grossly unjust regime could be interpreted only as tacit support for the status quo. It is precisely this kind of unqualified condemnation that Pope Paul refuses to give in *Populorum Progressio*. His refusal represents an important option by the official Church for the cause of the poor and the oppressed.

MODELS OF CHANGE

As we have seen, Pope Paul calls for radical changes in the structures of society. But he believes that violent revolution is not the way to bring them about. What then are the alternatives? The encyclical makes helpful suggestions about various means that could be used. For instance, it proposes the following measures:

- A world fund to relieve the destitute (*PP* 51)
- More foreign aid in the form of money, goods, and skilled people (*PP* 48–49)
- Limits on international competitive trading, so as to restore some equality between the trading partners (*PP* 61)
- A concerted international plan to promote development (*PP* 50)
- Moves toward establishing an effective world authority (*PP* 78)

However, these are all instrumental means, whereas the issue I wish to raise here is different: If violence is unacceptable, what does Paul VI consider to be a morally acceptable way of inspiring or compelling individuals, groups, and nations to make use of the appropriate instrumental means?

A first step toward answering this question is to find out what model of change the pope has in mind. Two very different models might be used, and it is also possible that elements from both could be combined. On the one hand, there is the confrontation model. In this, the principal means for bringing about change is pressure or threat. It is presumed that those who have wealth or power will yield it up only reluctantly and in the face of some pressure that they dare not ignore. On the other hand, there is a consensus model that lies at the opposite pole from the confrontational approach. Here change is envisaged as coming about by the willing agreement of all parties. The agreement is based on rational argument, emotional appeal, and moral pressure from the various partners in the dialogue. The presupposition in this case is that all the parties are at least willing to negotiate and motivated to make concessions, at best by goodwill and commitment to justice or at a minimum by a realization that it may be necessary to sacrifice their immediate self-interest in order to secure their long-term interests.

There are many indications in *Populorum Progressio* that what Paul VI had mostly in mind was the consensus model of social change. This is quite evident where he expresses the hope that "a more deeply felt need for collaboration and a heightened sense of unity will finally triumph over misunderstandings and selfishness" (*PP* 64). It underlies his commitment to a "dialogue between those who contribute wealth and those who benefit from it" (*PP* 54). Its justification is his conviction that the world, despite all its failures, is, in fact, moving toward greater brotherhood and sisterhood and an increase in humanity (*PP* 79).

At times, however, the pope warns the powerful and even seems to be threatening them to some extent. For instance, he speaks of the danger that the wrath of the poor may be provoked by the greed of the rich (*PP* 49). Again he points out that people may be tempted to seek solutions through violence to problems of injustice (*PP* 30). He also notes that lack of cooperation between rich and poor nations is a threat to the peace of the whole world (*PP* 55). These remarks show that Pope Paul was prepared to strengthen his case for dialogue and collaboration by reminding the rich and powerful that if they do not make concessions willingly, they may eventually be forced to do so—and may in fact lose their wealth and power entirely. But all of this can be understood as part of the rational argumentation involved in using the consensus model. There is very little indication in the encyclical that Paul VI favored a confrontational approach in the effort to overcome injustice and oppression. It is not as though Pope Paul had never adverted to the argument in favor of a confrontational approach. He had in fact invited Saul Alinsky to visit and advise him when he was archbishop of Milan. Alinsky was a famous community organizer who developed various strategies for non-violent confrontation. But Paul opted not to recommend this approach (cf. Deck 2005, 306–7).

There are many campaigners for justice who have come to believe that there is a need, at times, at least, for a confrontation model for social change. In these cases they encourage the poor and oppressed to demand their rights and to organize themselves in such a way that their demands are heard. Such demands (and the organization that underpins them) can take place at two levels: within any given country and at the international level of relationships between rich and poor countries. Conspicuously absent from *Populorum Progressio* is any direct and explicit proposal by the pope to the poorer groups or classes within each country that they should mobilize themselves politically and engage in strong, though non-violent, action in pursuit of justice. Perhaps this was not to be expected in any case, since the main subject of the encyclical is poverty at the global rather than the national level.

What then about confrontation at the international level? What does the pope have to say to the poorer nations? Does he encourage a confrontational approach? Undoubtedly, he supports the concept of regional cooperation among the poorer countries (*PP* 64). But this cooperation is to facilitate planning, investment, distribution, and trade; there is no suggestion that it is for the purpose of confronting the rich countries more effectively. Pope Paul's attitude is summed up in this statement: "The younger or weaker nations ask to assume their active part in the construction of a better world. . . . This is a legitimate appeal; everyone should hear and respond to it" (*PP* 65). Their asking is an appeal rather than a demand. They *ought* to be heard, but if they are not listened to, the pope makes no suggestion about what they might do about it.

AGENTS OF CHANGE

Having considered the question of the model of change envisaged by Pope Paul, the next step in finding out how change may be brought about is to ask, Who are to be the major agents of change? This has to be answered at different levels. In the first place, the encyclical has as a central theme, the idea that every person and all peoples are entitled to be the shapers of their own destinies (e.g., *PP* 15, 20, 65, 70). This is one of the most important contributions of *Populorum Progressio* to the understanding of development: it is not possible to develop people; development is something people have to do for themselves (*PP* 15, 25, 27). It is for this reason that the encyclical stresses the importance of basic education and literacy. These are seen as the key that enables people to assume responsibility for themselves, their lives, and their world: "To be able to read and write, and to get training for a profession, is to regain confidence in oneself" (*PP* 35).

To say that every person and all peoples are called to be agents of change and directors of their own development, though very important, is not enough, for the question arises whether some are called to play a more central role than others. The encyclical seems to give the crucial role to those who hold the top positions in society. Those who are considered to have the most important role in bringing about change are nearly all people or institutions that exercise considerable influence in society as it is at present. This means that the kind of change envisaged by the pope is mainly from the top down. At the international level the pope emphasizes the role of the rich countries and their leaders (*PP* 44, 48, 49, 84) as well as international agencies such as FAO and the UN (*PP* 46, 78, 83). Within wealthy states he puts the emphasis on the roles of statespersons, journalists, educators, and learned people (*PP* 83, 84, 85). With regard to the poorer countries, special mention is made of those elite who are studying in the "more advanced countries" (*PP* 68). Another group that gets special mention is the group of experts and development workers who go from the rich countries to help in the development of the poor ones (*PP* 71–74).

What role is assigned to the Church in transforming the structures of society? The pope asserts that "the Church has never failed to foster the human progress of the nations" (*PP* 12). But in the past, he implies, this was done mainly through "local and individual undertakings," and these "are no longer enough" (*PP* 13). In the new situation, where concerted action on a global scale is required, the role of the Church is to offer "a global vision of the human person and human affairs" (*PP* 13). It is in this context that the pope proposes a conception of integral human development, a development of the whole person and of all persons and all peoples (*PP* 14–21). In addition to this, Church leaders—and especially the pope himself—can make appeals, offer arguments, and issue warnings of the kind noted above. Members of the laity have a role to play: without waiting passively for directives, they should "infuse a Christian spirit into the mentality, customs, laws and structures of the community in which they live," and they should commit themselves to bringing about the basic reforms that are indispensable (*PP* 81). Special reference is made to the role of Catholics in "the more favored nations" in bringing into being "an international morality based on justice and equity" (*PP* 81). Here again it appears that the important agents of change are those who already have wealth, power, and influence.

There is a close connection between the model of change one is using and the kind of agents to whom one assigns a major role in transforming the structures of society. Since Pope Paul envisages change as coming mainly through consensus, it is understandable that he gives special importance to those who now hold economic and political power; for they can easily block the crucial decisions that need to be made. Similarly, another important group comprises those who mold the opinions of society—the educators, journalists, and in general, those who are well educated and privileged.

In sharp contrast to this approach is the view of those who believe that some degree of confrontation will probably be required in order to bring about radical change in society. For them, the major agents of social change are likely to be the people at or near the bottom of society. But if the poor are to exercise real power, they have to become aware of the possibilities open to them, and they need to harness their anger and become organized. In this task they can be greatly facilitated by Church leaders and others who are prepared to forgo their privileged positions and make a real option for, and with, the poor. There is no indication that Pope Paul was thinking along these lines when he wrote *Populorum Progressio*. Such ideas belong to a later stage of Catholic social thought.

LITERACY PROGRAMS

The consensus approach and the confrontational one are not entirely incompatible. They begin to converge once emphasis is placed on literacy and education for people who are poor or oppressed. But this will happen only if the education offered is one that enables people to become aware of their dignity and rights, an education that facilitates them in taking responsibility for changing society. What is the position of the encyclical on this issue? It contains a short but glowing statement on the importance of fundamental education and literacy: "Basic education is the primary object of any plan of development . . . and . . . literacy is . . . 'a privileged instrument of economic progress and of development'" (*PP* 35; the words within single quotation marks are from an earlier message of Pope Paul that he cites here).

In this passage from the encyclical there may well be an echo of the views of the great Brazilian educator, Paulo Freire.[4] But, if so, there is also a significant omission: unlike Freire, the pope does not clearly and explicitly link literacy and basic education with the awakening of a critical and combative political consciousness. The passage from *Populorum Progressio* that I have just quoted could give the impression that the way in which otherwise marginal people are enabled to take control of their lives is simply by learning to read and write, since literacy opens up for them the possibility of being trained for meaningful work in society (*PP*

---

[4]Freire became famous for his literacy work in a national program in Brazil in 1963–64. He was imprisoned by the new military regime in 1964, and while in detention, he began to write his essay "Education as the Practice of Freedom" (first appearing in English in 1973 under the title *The Politics of Education: Culture, Power and Liberation*). His views would have been fairly well known at the time *Populorum Progressio* was being written, even though his better-known works were not written until later. For background on Freire, see Collins (1977).

35). The military regime in Brazil replaced Freire's consciousness-raising literacy program with one that was designed only to insert the participants into an unjust and oppressive society. The purpose of their "education" was to domesticate people rather than to prepare them for real responsibility. Such programs, which claim to be politically neutral, are actually providing support for the status quo.

The encyclical does not bring out in an explicit way that certain political options underlie any adult education program or indeed any kind of education. This omission weakens what it has to say. But it does not deprive it of all value, for it is quite true that in modern society literacy has generally become a sine qua non for anybody who wants to exercise real responsibility. An education program may be designed to domesticate people, but once people have learned to read, it is far more difficult to control what they think and how they act.

That the encyclical does not make a clear link between basic education and the heightening of political awareness is quite significant. It lends support to the view that the pope thought changes in society should be brought about mainly by those at the top. It leaves one with the impression that he was not particularly eager to encourage any great groundswell of pressure for change from below, that is, from the masses of poor and oppressed people. Insofar as the encyclical adverts at all to any such movement, this seems to be thought of as a threat, leading to the danger of violence and perhaps revolution (*PP* 30, 49). There is no indication that the pope sees it as a potentially positive force, which can be harnessed and become a powerful lever for bringing about nonviolent change, something that the Church might therefore encourage and become involved in.

This can be understood in the light of the pope's commitment to a consensus approach. Consensus can be valued so highly that one fears to risk it by encouraging confrontation. So long as the positive value of confrontation is overlooked, it is almost inevitable that there will be a failure to take sufficient account of the role that the poor and marginalized people can play as agents of change for the better. In *Populorum Progressio* there is no indication that such people are seen as specially called by God to transform society. That was a theological insight that had not yet come into prominence.

As noted earlier, *Populorum Progressio* does not offer any strong encouragement to people who are poor and oppressed to organize themselves politically. Perhaps one reason for this is that the pope, like many other Christians, was slow to acknowledge—and perhaps even to recognize—that confrontation may at times be compatible with Christian faith and even demanded by it. It is not uncommon to associate confrontation with angry disagreement, leading easily to violence. That is undoubtedly what happens in many cases, and it is always a risk. But it may be a risk worth taking. For, properly handled, confrontation may provide a firm basis for a healthy consensus; the powerful people may need to be shaken out of their complacency. Furthermore, the act of confronting those in power may give to those who feel powerless a sense of their own dignity and their rights, as well as a belief in their ability to bring about change, with or without the willing cooperation of those whom they are confronting.

The conclusion that emerges from this examination of *Populorum Progressio* is that it contributes significantly toward committing the official Church to a realistic option for the poor. But the contribution of the encyclical is less than it might have been because the pope has shied away from confrontation. Being on the side of the poor in their cry for justice must surely involve encouraging them to find effective ways of ensuring that their voice is really heard. The encyclical places so much emphasis on the value of the collaboration of rich and poor, and on the duty of those at the top to initiate such cooperation, that it does not pay sufficient attention to what can and should be done by the poor themselves.

However, it would be a mistake to make too much of this point. For even though the pope did not explicitly encourage the poor to take the initiative, still the overall effect of the encyclical would be to inspire them to do so. By pointing out the injustices of the world and the obligation of the rich and powerful to remedy them, Paul VI was necessarily making the poor more aware of their rights and in some sense encouraging them to seek these rights actively. The pope may not have set out to stir up the poor, but there is no doubt that, in certain situations, his words could have that effect.

* * *

SUMMARY

In its approach to development *Populorum Progressio* no longer starts from the Western model of economic growth. It seeks to integrate all the dimensions of personal development and also to reconcile personal development with the welfare of other people and peoples. This concept of development should be acceptable even to those who believe that the present style of development is widening the gap between rich and poor, imposing Western values, and destroying the Earth. But the danger remains that one who starts with this ideal notion of development may easily slip back into accepting aspects of the Western model of development.

This encyclical recognizes the massive problem of poverty at the global level and offers some analysis of its root causes. It calls for bold transformations of the structures of the international economic order. Some element of free enterprise would be retained, but the current structures of international capitalism would be replaced, or at least restrained, by a good deal of planning at a global level under the aegis of some kind of world authority.

Paul VI envisaged structural changes coming about through negotiation and consensus rather than through violent revolution. The encyclical comes out strongly against violence, though it implied that in certain extreme circumstances rebellion might be justified. Pope Paul was opposed not merely to violence but to a confrontational approach. He envisaged change as coming from the top down. He did not see the poor as the ones called to play a key role in bringing about change. He did not encourage them to organize themselves politically and demand social change.

QUESTIONS FOR REVIEW

1. *How did Pope Paul's understanding of development differ from that of earlier Church documents?*
2. *What kind of changes did* Populorum Progressio *propose in the international order?*
3. *What was the teaching of the encyclical about revolution?*
4. *How did the pope envisage changes coming about?*

QUESTIONS FOR REFLECTION

1. *Do the benefits of Western-style development outweigh the disadvantages? Are there realistic alternatives?*
2. *What do you see as the most effective ways of working to bring justice to the world?*

ISSUES FOR FURTHER STUDY

1. *An ecological approach to development; study the critiques by Thomas Berry (1988) and Ivan Illich (1978 and 1988) of the Western approach to development.*
2. *Paulo Freire's approach to empowering poor people.*
3. *Amartya Sen's ideas about what constitutes and ensures human well-being.*

8

Medellín and *Octogesima Adveniens*

Many Church leaders and committed Christians in Latin America took very seriously the teaching of Vatican II on the role of the Church in the modern world. They also took to heart and applied to their own situation what Paul VI said in *Populorum Progressio*. This was part of an extraordinary change that was taking place in that continent during the late 1960s. It was something that affected every level of Church life, from the grassroots communities to the bishops and the leaders of religious orders. Of course, many people, and even whole areas, remained largely untouched by the new approach. But the movement for change was sufficiently widespread and influential to find expression in various local conventions of Church leaders—and eventually to become the dominant force at a major gathering of Church leaders from all over Latin America. This meeting took place at Medellín, Colombia, in August 1968. In the first section of this chapter I briefly consider the documents that were issued by the Medellín conference. In the second section I examine at more length the teaching of the apostolic letter *Octogesima Adveniens*, a document that may be understood at least partly as a response by Pope Paul to all that Medellín came to stand for.

THE DOCUMENTS OF MEDELLÍN

It is not my purpose here to study the changes that were taking place in the Latin American Church, in terms of their causes and their effects. But it is necessary to devote some pages to a study of the documents in which the new approach was given classical expression, for otherwise we would be ignoring an event that had a profound influence on Pope Paul VI during the latter half of his pontificate. This event was the second general conference of Latin American bishops that was held at Medellín. For some time before that meeting it had been clear that it would be a most important one. This was recognized by Pope Paul, who traveled to South America to address the gathering. But it is doubtful whether anybody could have guessed beforehand the extent to which Medellín was to be a turning point in the life of the Latin American Church—and indeed of the Catholic Church as a whole. The documents that were issued by the conference have an extraordinary freshness, clarity, and power. They became the charter for those who were working for a radical renewal of the Church in Latin America. But their influence did not stop there. Medellín gave inspiration to committed Christians all over the world. The Vatican itself was deeply affected by Medellín and its aftermath. The major documents concerned with social justice issued by Rome in the following decade have to be understood as being at least partly a reaction to all that is represented by Medellín—a reaction that is at times welcoming and at other times reserved and even worried.

A number of topics are particularly important in the Medellín documents from our point of view. These can be summed up in four main headings: (1) structural injustice, (2) a poor Church, (3) conscientization, and (4) the struggle for liberation. I examine each of these in turn.

Structural Injustice

Time and time again the Medellín documents speak of the Latin American situation as being marked by structural injustice (e.g., Medellín 1.2; 2.16; 10.2; 15.1 [pp. 33, 53, 126, 182]).[1] These unjust structures uphold and foster dependency and poverty. This is carried to a point where the documents say, "In many instances Latin America finds itself faced with a situation of injustice that can be called institutionalized violence" (2.16 [p. 53]). Poverty, then, is not just something that happens; it is caused largely by human action of a kind that does violence to great masses of people. Not just particular actions are being referred to but a pattern of behavior that has over many years created a situation of "internal colonialism" and "external neocolonialism" (2.2–2.9 [pp. 46–49]).

A Poor Church

Church leaders hear the "deafening cry" for liberation (14.2 [p. 172]) that rises from the millions of poor people who are the victims of this situation. What is their response? In the Medellín document on the poverty of

---

[1]Second General Conference of Latin American Bishops, Medellín 1968. *The Church in the Present-Day Transformation of Latin America in the Light of the Council*, II: Conclusions, 3rd ed. (Washington, DC: Secretariat for Latin America, National Conference of Bishops, 1979). There are sixteen main documents, numbered 1 to 16. Each of these is divided into numbered "paragraphs." In referring to the documents I give the number of the document, followed by the number of the "paragraph" within the document, followed by a page reference, within brackets, to the above edition.

the Church, a distinction is made between different meanings of poverty. *Material* poverty is seen as an evil, caused mainly by injustice. *Spiritual* poverty is described as "the attitude of opening up to God." Poverty as a *commitment* is a way in which "one assumes voluntarily and lovingly the condition of the needy of this world in order to bear witness to the evil which it represents and to spiritual liberty" after the example of Christ (14.4 [pp. 173–74]).

The bishops then outline the role they see for "a poor Church." A Church that is poor denounces material poverty caused by injustice and sin; it preaches and lives spiritual poverty; and it is itself bound to material poverty as a commitment (14.5 [p. 174]). The Latin American bishops then go on to recognize that their obligation to evangelize the poor should lead them to redistribute resources and personnel within the Church itself, so as to give effective preference to the poorest and most needy sectors (14.9 [p. 175]).

This preference is one important element in what has come to be called the option for the poor. But such an option cannot be confined to what happens within the organization of the Church itself. Another aspect, equally or more important, is the stance of the Church vis-à-vis society. In the Medellín document the bishops accept that they have a duty of being in solidarity with those who are poor. This solidarity is made concrete through criticism of injustice and oppression. But criticism from the outside is inadequate. The bishops say that solidarity with the poor "means that we make ours their problems and their struggles" (14.10 [p. 176]). It is against this conception of solidarity with the poor and commitment to their struggle against injustice that one must locate the "conscientizing" role of the Church.

Conscientization

The Medellín document on peace points out that people become responsible for injustice by remaining passive, by failing to take courageous and effective action, for fear of the sacrifice and personal risk involved in doing so. So the document favors a process of inspiring and organizing "the ordinary people."[2] It says that justice, and therefore peace, can

---

[2] I cannot find any fully adequate way of conveying in English the meaning of the phrase I have translated here as "the ordinary people." The semiofficial English version translates it as "the popular sectors." But the word "popular," which is widely used in translations of Latin American Church documents, is quite misleading; it does not mean "popular" in the conventional English sense but refers rather to the masses of ordinary people; so "the popular sectors" might be taken as the equivalent of "the masses"—but without the heavy ideological overtones that that phrase carries in English. Similarly, the widely used phrase "popular religion" ought to be translated as "the religion of the ordinary people" or even, at times, as "folk religion."

prevail "by means of a dynamic action of awakening [*concientización*] and organization of 'the ordinary people' who can then put pressure on public officials—for these are often unable to implement social projects without the support of the people" (2.18 [p. 54], my translation; see also 2.7; 7.19; 10.2; 16.2 [pp. 48, 103, 126, 194]).

This statement is especially important because it recognizes the need to stimulate action for justice from the grassroots. What is envisaged is a political campaign: an education of the masses of poor people to understand the causes of their poverty and a process of facilitating their work for improvement by putting pressure on the authorities in order to attain social justice. In the last line of the passage just quoted, the writers tactfully imply that this pressure is a service to the authorities, enabling them to put into practice their plans for reform. The document does not mention that if there had been no pressure from below, the people in authority would often be quite happy to allow such reforms to remain empty promises!

This account of what is involved in conscientization helps one appreciate the significance of the undertaking made by the Latin American bishops at Medellín to commit the Church to the basic education of illiterate and marginal people—and to do so "without counting the cost" (4.16 [p. 76]). The bishops were well aware of what they were taking on and of the possible cost. Their statement makes it clear that the type of basic education they have in mind is one that is not limited to teaching people merely to read and write. Rather the aim is to enable them to become the conscious agents of their own integral development (4.16 [p. 76]). The commitment is undertaken in the knowledge that this kind of basic education will increase the recognition by oppressed people of the fact that they are oppressed, with a consequent increase in tension and a risk to peace (2.7 [pp. 47–48]). It is significant that it is in the document on peace that there is insistence on the awakening of the masses to political consciousness. This indicates that Medellín is committed to the view that there can be no genuine peace that is not based on social justice. So it may happen that an apparent peace, built on oppression, has to be put at risk in the effort to attain true peace and liberty.

Struggle for Liberation

Already in the 1960s many social scientists in Latin America had concluded that the word "development" was being used as a cover for exploitation and the creation of dependency. The Alliance for Progress between the United States and Latin America was to have ensured the development of the latter during the first development decade, the 1960s. But the economic development that took place in countries like Brazil did not solve the problems of poverty. Instead the gap between rich and poor became even wider. So the radical social scientists of Latin America challenged the whole notion of development and demanded liberation instead. For them, "development" became a bad word—a word that could not be rescued. Most of the key Church leaders at Medellín accepted this viewpoint. This helps explain their emphasis on liberation.

The word "development" conjures up the image of a nation harnessing natural forces more effectively and becoming more organized and scientific in agriculture and industry. The word "liberation," in contrast, suggests shaking off an oppression imposed by other people. This oppression might be the obvious political and economic control exercised by the colonial powers in the past. It might be the dependency and poverty created in the South by an unjust international economic order and maintained by the wealthy nations of the North. It might be the domination of a rich and powerful minority within the country. Or it might be a combination of at least two of these elements.

The word "liberation" is used quite frequently in the documents of Medellín (1.3–1.4; 4.2, 4.9; 5.15; 8.6; 10.2, 10.9, 10.13; 14.2, 14.7 [pp. 33–34, 70, 73, 87, 110, 126, 128, 130, 172, 174]). The way it is used does not carry the overtones that would lead it to be seen as a process so dangerous that it should be avoided. In these documents "liberation" has a very positive connotation, and it is closely linked to "humanization" (10.2, 10.9, 10.13 [pp. 126, 128, 130]). The bishops leave no doubt that they want to help the poor and oppressed to attain liberation.

But what does it mean, in practice, for Church leaders to be in solidarity with the victims of injustice and to support them in a struggle for liberty? How far should Church leaders go? Are they to give approval to revolutionary movements using violent means to overthrow unjust structures and oppressive regimes? The Medellín document on peace addresses itself to this question, making use of the statement on this topic in paragraph 31 of *Populorum Progressio.* I have already quoted (in chapter 7) the text of this statement by Pope Paul. There I noted that it contains two elements. The main one is that a revolution is an unacceptable remedy for injustice, because it gives rise to worse evils. The second point is the parenthetical comment in which the pope indicates that there might be certain rare exceptions to this general guideline.

The Medellín document quotes from both parts of Pope Paul's statement—but it does so in reverse order, putting first the point that revolutionary insurrection can sometimes be legitimate and then the point that it generally gives rise to new injustices:

> If it is true that revolutionary insurrection can be legitimate in the case of evident and prolonged "tyranny that seriously works against

fundamental human rights, and which damages the common good of the country," whether it proceeds from one person or from clearly unjust structures, it is also certain that violence or "armed revolution" generally "generates new injustices, introduces new imbalances and causes new disasters; one cannot combat a real evil at the price of a greater evil." (2.19 [pp. 54–55] The passages within double quotation marks are taken from *Populorum Progressio* 31)

The document then goes on to state the judgment of the Medellín conference on the situation in Latin America:

> If we consider then, the totality of the circumstances of our countries, and if we take into account the Christian preference for peace, the enormous difficulty of a civil war, the logic of violence, the atrocities it engenders, the risk of provoking foreign intervention, illegitimate as it may be, the difficulty of building a regime of justice and freedom while participating in a process of violence, we earnestly desire that the dynamism of the awakened and organized community be put to the service of justice and peace. (2.19 [p. 55])

Nobody could claim that this powerful statement of Medellín distorts the meaning of the passage in *Populorum Progressio* to which it refers. In fact the option for nonviolence expressed in it fits in with the reference in an earlier paragraph to "the pacifist position of the Church" (2.17 [p. 54]). Yet there are important nuances to be noted. It is already a significant difference that what was a parenthetical comment for Pope Paul has now been moved to a more central position. This means that the words are given an added weight. They become the basis for a detailed and careful evaluation of the Latin American situation. There is an obvious comprehensiveness and balance in the passage just quoted. It indicates that the bishops at Medellín have carefully weighed the case for and against violent revolution. On balance, because of the convergence of all the factors listed, they "earnestly desire" that Christians should commit themselves to peace rather than violence. The implication must be that if there were to be a change in some of the key circumstances, then the balance might well tip in the other direction.

Indeed, even in regard to the situation depicted in the document, there is a certain reserve in the way in which the bishops express their moral evaluation. What they present is not so much a firm and explicit moral judgment that revolution would be wrong, but rather an exhortation: "we earnestly desire." Once again this is not really contrary to what the pope had said in his encyclical. But it seems to push his words a little further and to draw out implications that he had perhaps deliberately left vague. Confronted with the starkness of poverty and the harshness of oppression in Latin America, and the urgency of the pressure to take a stand on one side or the other, the bishops at Medellín felt they could not take refuge in vagueness. Perhaps more than anything else it is the clarity with which they present the options facing the Church that is most significant in the Medellín documents. They sharpen the issues related to social justice and the option for the poor and thereby pose a serious challenge to the whole Church.

OCTOGESIMA ADVENIENS—A SHIFT TO POLITICS

Less than three years after the Medellín conference, and only four years after *Populorum Progressio*, Pope Paul issued another major document on social issues.[3] This was *Octogesima Adveniens*, published in May 1971 to commemorate the eightieth anniversary of Leo XIII's *Rerum Novarum*. Although this apostolic letter of the pope contains several references to *Populorum Progressio*, nevertheless it has a distinctly different tone and perspective. This difference may be partly expressed by saying that in this new social document, "development" no longer plays such a central role as it did in the earlier one.

When development is taken as the overall integrating concept for the treatment of social issues, there is a tendency to see difficulties such as poverty, apathy, and poor distribution of resources as problems that have not yet been solved. The half-hidden assumption here is that, in general, the world is developing but that in some areas or spheres this process is still at an early stage—and that is why the problems remain as yet unsolved. *Octogesima Adveniens* disengages itself, to a considerable extent, from this almost mythological conception of development, by questioning the notion of "progress" as "an omnipresent ideology" (*OA* 41). Nevertheless, there are indications that Paul VI was still influenced by this concept of development; see, for instance, his references to "stages" in *OA* 2 and *OA* 10.

Even more significant is the fact that when one speaks of development, the emphasis tends to be mainly on economic issues, and this applies even when the word "development" is used in the very broad and rich sense that Pope Paul gives it in *Populorum Progressio*. In contrast, when the word "liberation" is used, it indicates a perspective in which political action is central.

---

[3]Christine Gudorf (2005, 316–17) gives a helpful account of the context in the world and the Church at the time the document was written. She suggests that Pope Paul was influenced by his relationship with Church leaders like Evaristo Arns, the archbishop of São Paulo in Brazil.

Once we advert to the fact that the gap between rich and poor areas is not due simply to the fact that the latter have not yet become developed, it becomes more evident how deceptive it can be to imagine that poor people are the ones at the bottom of a ladder that everybody has the opportunity to climb. The sad truth is that some nations or groups are poor not just because they have so far failed to climb the ladder, but because they have been prevented by others from doing so—or have even been thrown down the ladder! When poverty is seen in this perspective, the solution that comes to mind might be described more properly as "liberation" rather than "development."

As I have already pointed out, the Medellín document, issued in 1968, used the word "liberation" freely and in a positive sense. Ever since that time the more radical committed Christians in Latin America have been inclined to reject utterly the very notion of development. In Africa and other parts of the South, though, Church people were much slower in waking up to the inadequacies of development. They generally saw development as a good thing. As time went on, they became more critical of an unbalanced form of development that widened the gap between the rich and the poor. But they still did not reject the word "development" out of hand. This was the viewpoint adopted by Paul VI, even in *Octogesima Adveniens* where the focus on development is much less than in *Populorum Progressio*.

Octogesima Adveniens does not follow Medellín in more or less replacing "development" with "liberation"; it uses the word "liberation" only rarely and in contexts that do not suggest that it is seen as an alternative to "development" (e.g., *OA* 28, 45). This is scarcely an accident. Presumably the pope was reluctant to use the word "liberation" on the grounds that it might be taken to mean violent revolution and to suggest that other countries should follow the path that Cuba had taken. Nevertheless, the tone and content of this apostolic letter indicate that Pope Paul was concerned about the kind of issues for which liberation is proposed as the solution. Indeed, one significant feature of *Octogesima Adveniens* is that the major issues with which it deals are not purely economic ones. The focus has shifted from economics to politics.

In the few years after *Populorum Progressio* was issued, it began to dawn on more and more people—inside and outside the Church—that underlying most economic difficulties are political problems. This became especially evident in Latin America and led, as I have said, to a cry for liberation rather than development. The problems were political, for even the choice of a particular model of development is itself a political rather than an economic decision. The Latin American bishops and their experts at Medellín were aware of this, so the Medellín documents were notably political in their perspective. No doubt this encouraged Pope Paul to shift his focus of interest to the underlying political questions. Indeed *Octogesima Adveniens* can be seen as a nuanced response by the pope to Medellín—a somewhat qualified approval of at least some aspects of its approach.

Philip Land, a well-known expert on Catholic social teaching, said that Pope Paul was "in notable contrast to papal tradition" when he recognized "that most social problems are at bottom political problems" (Land 1979, 394). This statement is partly true, but it needs to be qualified. Many of the proposals made in earlier social documents of the popes refer to the political sphere. In fact, most of the remedies proposed for socioeconomic problems by various popes are obviously political, ranging from the espousal by Pius XI of a corporative type of system within the state, to Pope Paul's insistence in *Populorum Progressio* on the need for new international institutions leading toward a world government. However, it is one thing to propose political solutions to economic and social problems but quite a different thing to recognize clearly that designing and bringing into effect such solutions brings one into the sphere of political activity. The novelty of *Octogesima Adveniens* lies largely in the extent to which it consciously addresses itself to some of the political problems involved in choosing and implementing an equitable order in society.

At one point in the document, the change of perspective is made quite explicit: the pope says, "The need is felt to pass from economics to politics" (*OA* 46). In order to bring out the full significance of the passage, it is well to quote also some important sentences from the preceding and following paragraphs. This will help show the kind of issues that come to the fore when the focus shifts from economics to politics. It will be noted that certain key words and phrases are prominent—"dependence," "liberation," "model of society," "structures," "politics," and "share in decision making"; in the passages below I am putting these words in italics:

> People today long to be freed from need and *dependence*. But this *liberation* starts with the interior freedom that people must find again with regard to their goods and their powers. . . . Nowadays many are questioning the existing *model of society*. The ambition of many nations . . . blocks the setting up of *structures* which would put some limits on the drive for advancement, in order to ensure greater justice. . . .
>
> Is it not here that there appears a radical limitation to economics? Economic activity is necessary and, if it is at the service of people, it can be "a source of brotherhood and a sign of Providence.". . . Though it is often a field of confrontation and domination, it can

give rise to dialogue and foster cooperation. Yet it runs the risk of unduly absorbing human energies and limiting people's freedom. This is why the need is felt to pass from economics to *politics*. It is true that in the term "*politics*" many confusions are possible and must be clarified, but each person feels that in the social and economic field, both national and international, the ultimate decision rests with political power. . . .

The passing to the political dimension also expresses a demand made by people today for a greater *share* in the exercise of authority and in consultation for *decision making*. (OA 45–47, translation emended)

It is from this political perspective that Pope Paul calls for a revision of the relationships between nations in the economic sphere and questions the models of growth that operate within the rich nations (OA 42). He then goes on to express concern about the growing and uncontrolled power of multinational corporations (OA 44); these too create economic problems that have to be controlled by political action. In an earlier paragraph he had spoken of the power exercised by the mass media and the need for political control to prevent abuses of this power (OA 20).

But how is political control to be exercised in practice over economic activity? *Octogesima Adveniens* calls for devising of new forms of democracy, of a type that will not merely make it possible for all to be informed and to express themselves but will also involve everybody in a shared responsibility (OA 47). Pope Paul sees himself as going beyond John XXIII in this regard: the latter called for a sharing of responsibility in economic life, especially within each company or business, but Paul VI extends the demand to the social and political sphere (OA 47). However, he does not have much to say here about the means by which this can come about. He adverts rather briefly to the role that should be played by trade unions (OA 14) and by the media (OA 20), and he makes some general but important remarks about the role of "cultural and religious groupings" (OA 25), of which, of course, the Church is the one that most concerns him.

Basis and Guidelines for Political Action

As we have seen, it is made quite clear in *Octogesima Adveniens* that economic questions have to be subsumed within the wider sphere of the political. But that has to be balanced against another important point, namely, that politics is not an ultimate either. Political activity has to be based on an adequate concept or model of society. This, in turn, derives from an integral conception of what the human vocation is and an understanding of the wide variety of ways in which that vocation is realized in society.[4] The component elements in this concept of society are convictions about the nature, the origin, and the purpose of the human person and of society. It is not for the state or political parties to impose their views in these matters. If they did so, it would lead to a dictatorship over the human spirit. It is the role of cultural and religious groupings to promote such convictions, and in doing so, they are obliged to respect human freedom and not compel people to accept their views.

Pope Paul suggests that neither Marxist ideology nor liberal ideology is compatible with the Christian understanding of the human person (*OA* 26). He goes on to point out the inadequacies of social ideologies in general, noting especially the danger that an ideology can become "a new idol"—an ultimate justification for action and even for violence. Ideologies, he holds, tend to have a totalitarian character and can impose slavery on people in the name of liberation (*OA* 27–28).

The pope develops this point further by examining in some depth the relationship between socialist or Marxist-inspired movements and Marxist ideology. He begins (*OA* 30) by recalling the important distinction made by Pope John XXIII in 1963 between false philosophies and the historical movements that have sprung from such philosophies (*Pacem in Terris* 159). What follows might be described as a commentary by Paul VI on Pope John's statement insofar as it refers to Marxism. Pope Paul notes certain distinctions that have been made between four different meanings or levels of Marxism. The most "attenuated" of these versions of Marxism is one that would see it merely as a scientific method for analyzing society. He says that it "furnishes some people not only with a working tool but also a certitude preliminary to action: the claim to decipher in a scientific manner the mainsprings of the evolution of society" (*OA* 33).

Gudorf (2005, 325) suggests that Pope Paul is "proposing the possibility that, with careful discernment, Christians might find some Marxist tools, such as social analysis, useful in the work of social justice." This echoes the view of Charles Curran who holds that in this passage of the document "Paul VI cautiously opened the door to Christians who use Marxism as a tool of sociological analysis" (Curran 2002, 203). For myself, I believe that social analysis is essential and that we have much to learn from the work of some more liberal Marxists. But I must admit that I do not find support for this belief in the words of Pope Paul that I have quoted here. I interpret his statement more as an acknowledgment that some Christians do use elements of Marxism and as a warning to those who do so. For he says that "this type of analysis gives a privileged position to certain

---

[4]This sentence and the remainder of this paragraph are my attempt to paraphrase a particularly difficult and obscure passage in *OA* 25.

aspects of reality to the detriment of the rest, and interprets them in the light of its ideology"; so I understand him to be saying that it offers a false objectivity and an unjustified certainty, based on a selective and biased interpretation of the facts (*OA* 33).

Furthermore, in the next paragraph, he goes on to say that it would be "illusory and dangerous" to forget that the various aspects of Marxism are intimately linked and radically bound together. In particular, he notes two dangers. The first danger is that one would accept a Marxist type of analysis of society without adverting to how this is related to ideology. The second danger is that one would become involved in class struggle and the Marxist interpretation of it, without adverting to the totalitarian and violent kind of society to which this activity gradually leads (*OA* 34).

It is clear then that for Paul VI, Marxism as such—at least in any of the versions or aspects he describes—is not compatible with a Christian approach. Furthermore, he is hesitant even in the way in which he speaks about socialist movements. He recognizes in a general and rather reluctant way the possibility that Christians might, in some circumstances, be entitled to play a part within such movements. He does so by making this vague statement: "This insight will enable Christians to see the degree of commitment possible along these lines" (*OA* 31). But he notes that the various forms of the socialist movement drew inspiration from an ideology that is, he says, incompatible with the Christian faith. He stresses the danger that Christians may idealize socialism and be misled in their practical activity by purely abstract and theoretical distinctions between the ideal of a just society, the historical movements that propose to bring about such a society, and the ideology that still influences these movements (*OA* 31).

All this seems to indicate that for Pope Paul the distinction made by his predecessor between movements and philosophies, though valid in theory, ought not to be used in present circumstances as a basis for a rapprochement between Catholicism and socialism—or at least only with extreme caution. Perhaps the pope felt that such caution was the appropriate response from Rome at a time when many Catholics all over the world—and not least in Italy, and even in Rome itself—were attracted by the prospect of "an opening to the left." (At around this time Rome got its first communist mayor—despite the best efforts of many senior Roman Church figures.)

Despite its warnings about the dangers of socialism, one is not entitled to see in *Octogesima Adveniens* an endorsement of Western capitalism. For the pope made a serious effort to balance his misgivings about socialism by making a strong criticism of the liberal ideology (*OA* 35, 26).

An Inductive and Pluralist Approach

Despite the reservations of the pope about a move to the left, *Octogesima Adveniens* still leaves plenty of space for it. This comes not from any enthusiasm of Pope Paul for socialism but rather from the basic approach that he adopts in this document. He takes the view that in the face of "widely varying situations," it is difficult for him "to utter a unified message and to put forward a solution which has universal validity"; and he even adds that it is not his ambition to do so (*OA* 4). He adds later that the Church "does not intervene to authenticate a given structure or to propose a ready-made model" (*OA* 42). This leaves room for a wide measure of pluralism in relation to options about political activity. As Christine Gudorf (2005, 319) puts it, "Because Paul saw the Spirit of the Lord at work in the world, he saw neither the Church nor the papacy as the only source of answers to the social justice problems of the world."

It would appear that there are, in fact, two different but interacting reasons why a certain pluralism of options is accepted in the document. On the one hand, there is the personal (subjective) discernment that each individual Christian has to make, with the likelihood that not everybody will come to the same conclusion (*OA* 49–50); Pope Paul's reference here to *Gaudium et Spes* 43 confirms this understanding of the text. On the other hand, there is also the objective diversity of situations arising from differences of region, culture, and sociopolitical systems (*OA* 3, 4).

The objective differences are of particular interest here, since they raise the possibility that Christians in Latin America might be entitled to, and even obliged to, collaborate far more closely with left-wing movements than would be appropriate in Europe or North America. The paragraph in which the pope issues his warnings about socialism also contains references to "different continents and cultures," to the variety of circumstances that need to be taken into account, and to the need for careful discernment and judgment (*OA* 31). The effect is that, despite a certain similarity between Pope Paul's reservations about socialism and the judgments of Pius XI forty years earlier (*Quadragesimo Anno* 113–26), there is a very great difference between the two.

Philip Land describes the position outlined in *Octogesima Adveniens* as a dramatic departure from the approach of previous papal documents (Land 1979, 394). He sees it as the relinquishment by Rome of the practice of "handing down solutions to specific questions." Marie-Dominique Chenu also believes that at this point the pope has made a truly radical change of approach. Formerly there was a deductive method by which a universally valid "social doctrine" was applied to changing circumstances. But now there is an inductive method in which the different situations are themselves the primary location from which theology springs, through a discernment of "the signs of the times" (Chenu 1979, 80). Furthermore, as Charles Curran (2002, 60) points out, Paul VI adopted "a historically conscious methodology" in contrast to earlier popes such as Pius XI.

One might wonder whether Pope Paul himself would have wished to make such a sharp distinction between what he said here and the approach adopted in earlier papal teaching. But undoubtedly there is a notable difference of emphasis in his approach; and this has implications both for the role of the pope as a moral teacher and for the nature of theological method. It implies that the pope accepts that as a moral teacher he cannot hope to be familiar with situations all over the world; so he must respect the discernment done at the local or regional level. And it indicates that he is far more willing than earlier popes to adopt an inductive theological approach. To accept an inductive method means acknowledging that if one is to discover universal principles about social morality, one must start with, and work upward from, the variety of cultural and geographical situations in which moral issues arise.

The variety in question is not simply a geographical one. The pope also accepts the idea of historical variety, when he says that the Church's social teaching "has been worked out in the course of history" (*OA* 4). This has quite radical implications. It provides an opening for Church leaders who are developing this teaching to make significant changes in it in the light of new situations and new insights. I note in passing that the new insights may be borrowed, wholly or in part, from individuals or movements that are outside the Church and may even be hostile to it. In fact, some of the key elements in present-day Catholic social teaching have come originally or primarily from outside the Church. One thinks, for instance, of the Church's present commitment to democracy, of its emphasis on personal human rights, of its acceptance of the full equality of women with men, and of the right of women to participate fully in public life and work outside the home, and of its strong insistence on ecological responsibility. There is even a good case for claiming that if the *Communist Manifesto* had not been published, then Leo XIII's encyclical *Rerum Novarum* might never have been written.

A discernment of the elements that are new and distinctive in the Latin American region, through a reading of "the signs of the times," is precisely what the Medellín conference had set out to offer, and what its documents claim to represent. These new elements included the imposition in that continent of an unjust and oppressive model of so-called development and the consequent impoverishment of many people. But it also included the emergence among Latin American social scientists of "dependency theory," which held that the effect of so-called development is that poor countries on the periphery are impoverished by rich countries at the center of the world economic system. This theory had a strong influence on key liberation theologians. Another new element in the situation was the armed resistance of people like Fidel Castro, Che Guevara, and Camilo Torres—and the revolutionary ideology they lived by.

Overall, *Octogesima Adveniens* offers solid support to the approach adopted by the Latin American bishops. Pope Paul may not have agreed with the details of their evaluation. But he recognizes their right and duty to make the kind of moral evaluation that they undertook at Medellín. The caution and misgivings that Pope Paul expressed in *Octogesima Adveniens* are to be understood against this background. They ought not to be seen as a rejection of anything in the Medellín conclusions. But they constitute a salutary warning against generalizing the Medellín conclusions and attitudes without going through the same kind of process. The pope is accepting that in each area, the Church must make its own assessment of the social, economic, cultural, political, and religious situation in order to discern what needs to be done. In this evaluation the points made in *Octogesima Adveniens* about the dangers both of socialism and of liberalism ought to be given due weight; they may help local Church people take a more detached and objective view of their situation.

Given the general approach adopted by the pope in this document, there are strict limits to the kind of direction it can give. It must of necessity restrict itself to examining general trends (*OA* 8–21) and promoting key Christian values. The encyclical mentions two in particular: "the aspiration to equality and the aspiration to participation, two forms of man's dignity and freedom" (*OA* 22). As Gudorf (2005, 320–21) points out, in insisting on the value of equality, Pope Paul was abandoning the views of Leo XIII, Pius XI, and Pius XII, who had maintained that social inequality is part of God's will and not an obstacle to unity. However, Pope Paul insisted on the need to balance the value of equality with the value of solidarity: "Without a renewed education in solidarity, an overemphasis of equality can give rise to an individualism in which each one claims his own rights without wishing to be answerable for the common good" (*OA* 23).

Another key value for Pope Paul is participation. He was aware that people are crying out for the right to share in making the decisions that affect their lives. So, as I have already noted, he insisted that they are entitled to a share in decision making, not merely in the economic field as Pope John had maintained, but also in "the social and political sphere" (*OA* 47).

Preferential Respect for the Poor

Pope Paul makes an important contribution to Catholic social teaching by emphasizing that the gospel calls for a "preferential respect" for the poor (*OA* 23). Furthermore, he goes on to insist that "even equality before the law can serve as an alibi for flagrant discrimination, continued exploitation and actual contempt" (*OA* 23). It is obvious that in making these statements, he was responding to and affirming the stance of the Latin American bishops at Medellín. And no doubt he was also influenced by his own experience of seeing the plight of the poor in India and Colombia.

This would have been an ideal opportunity for him to address an important political issue that he had not dealt with in *Populorum Progressio*. As I pointed out in chapter 7, he had left a central issue hanging in his earlier document. This issue is how to help the poor and powerless take responsibility for their lives. Unfortunately, even in *Octogesima Adveniens*, there is a certain incompleteness in the remedy he proposes for the problem. His call for "a renewed education in solidarity" (*OA* 23) is a step in the right direction. But is it enough? It does not seem to take sufficient account of the fact that in some situations, those who hold power have no intention of yielding it to the poor. Indeed, as the pope himself was aware, the temptation to resort to violent revolution arises particularly in those areas where those in power remain unaware of, or insensitive to, the injustices of the present situation and are determined to prolong it (*OA* 3).

Trade Unions and Politics

Octogesima Adveniens does not move to any significant extent beyond the consensus model of social change adopted in *Populorum Progressio*. It does not go as far as Medellín in calling for a conscientization of the masses. In contrast to the Latin American bishops, the pope does not appear to be in favor of encouraging the poorer people of society to demand change (Medellín 2.18 [p. 54]). It is not so much that Pope Paul directly rules it out; it is simply that he does not mention it as a key way in which injustices are to be overcome.

There is one passage in *Octogesima Adveniens* that is quite significant in this regard; it is where the pope speaks about the role of trade unions. Having defined the scope of their activity, he notes the danger that they may abuse their power. One such misuse is in the economic sphere: they may demand more than society can afford, and the demand may be enforced by calling a strike or threatening to do so. The second misuse of power is much more important from our present point of view: "Here and there the temptation can arise . . . to desire to obtain in this way demands of a directly political nature" (*OA* 14). What is notable here is the pope's insistence that unions should not be involved in matters that are "directly political." Apparently Paul VI wanted trade unions to confine their representation of workers to specific economic issues and, presumably, other local grievances. The implication is that unions would be trespassing on the territory of political parties if they were to concern themselves with issues that can be labeled "directly political."

It is difficult to draw a clear distinction between matters that are "directly political" and the more limited issues that are only indirectly political or not political at all. Obviously the pope himself was well aware of this, since a central point in *Octogesima Adveniens* was, as we have seen, the need to "pass from economics to politics" (*OA* 46). Nevertheless, Pope Paul finds himself forced at this point to rely on a distinction between economics and politics. It is not difficult to guess why. Trade unions represent workers against employers. If the unions were to become concerned with issues that are directly political, this could lead to a sharp political polarization of society along class lines. The weapons used by both sides would be mainly economic ones—strikes and lockouts. The end result could be an overt class war. This would go against the whole thrust of Church social teaching since the time of Leo XIII.

It is clear that Pope Paul, like his predecessors, had an ideal of fruitful dialogue and collaboration between all groups in society, particularly across class barriers. So he did not wish to have a political division that reflected and reinforced the existing economic and social divisions of society. And certainly he did not want the strike weapon that was designed to rectify specific economic abuses (mainly local ones) to be employed as a political weapon against governments. Consequently, he insisted that it is an abuse to call a strike for any directly political purpose. This means that he had to maintain the existence of a sphere that is directly political and had to define the role of unions in such a way that they are not concerned with that sphere of activity.

In fact, the pope's account of the role of trade unions is quite vague. The only point at which it becomes rather specific is when it refers to "lawful collaboration in the economic advance of society" (*OA* 14). The encyclical does not spell out any role that trade unions might play in ensuring that workers have adequate participation in decision making in a given factory or in a particular industry. To do so would show just how difficult it is to delineate an area that is directly political, for participation at this level is a political matter in one sense, though not yet political in the fullest sense. The problem becomes much greater when there is an expansion of the traditional role of trade unions so that they come to be accepted as one of "the social partners" in society, with an acknowledged voice in determining the wider pattern of the economic and social life of the nation, for it is clear that such a role is "directly political."

Pope Paul strongly advocates the need for "a greater sharing in responsibility and decision making" both "in economic life" and in "the social and political sphere" (*OA* 47). It is easy for him to make such general proposals for new structures to promote participation in industry and society. But the difficulty for him arises when it comes to moving from this desirable end to the means that might bring it about in practice. It is not easy to overcome the traditional Church suspicions of trade unions of a certain type, suspicions that have their basis in the history of the trade union movement in continental Europe. Furthermore, the pope was aware of the strength of class divisions in our world and was reluctant to approve of anything that might exacerbate them further. No wonder, then, that his treatment of trade unions and of the strike weapon is so limited and cautious. All the indications are that he would be quite reluctant to approve of a general strike designed to put pressure on an unjust regime and perhaps even to bring about its downfall. This would be the clearest instance of the use of an economic weapon in a matter that is "directly political."

One can certainly sympathize with the pope's wish to preserve some kind of distinction between economic affairs and political affairs, for it may be of real benefit to society if political divisions do not follow exactly the economic and social divisions in the country and if economic griev- ances and tensions can be prevented from taking on an overtly political form. However, the main benefits that come from this approach have to do with the stability of society. Stability is a very good thing in a society that happens to be reasonably just. However, stability may not be a good thing in a country that is extremely stratified socially and economically, a society built on flagrant social injustice. In this situation radical change may be a higher priority than stability. And for this to take place it may be necessary for economic and social divisions to be reflected in politics. In practice this means that in such situations of blatant injustice, it is far more difficult for trade unions to avoid playing a political role.

Take a situation where the economic difficulties of workers are due mainly to the grossly unjust structures of the society: if unions are really to promote justice for workers, then they must become involved in wider political issues. To claim that trade unions ought not to concern themselves with matters that are directly political, even in such circumstances, would be to condemn them to impotence and futility. Furthermore, to say that the strike weapon should not be used, even in such situations, for directly political purposes would be to deprive the poor of what may be the most effective means they have of changing society in a not-too-violent way. It is true that in theory, even in a very unjust society, political grievances could be left to political parties. But in practice, a repressive regime will seldom tolerate such overtly political opposition. It is not quite so easy for a repressive government to eliminate or control the activity of trade unions and their use of strikes in a quasi-political way.

It would seem then that Pope Paul, while acknowledging that it was not possible for him "to utter a unified message" of "universal validity" (*OA* 4), did not take this limitation sufficiently seriously in what he said about trade unions and strikes. He was still inclined to generalize from an experience that is too limited, too European.

The significance of this goes beyond the particular issue of the role of trade unions. It throws light on why *Octogesima Adveniens*, for all the important advances it made, still did not face up fully to the major issue left hanging in *Populorum Progressio*—the question of confrontation. The pope has now, in this second document, acknowledged that social and economic progress requires political action. But his ideal of politics is a very high one, perhaps so high as to be unrealistic, except in certain situations. It is one in which there is room for political dialogue and debate and, presumably, even a measure of political confrontation. But this political activity is to remain, in some sense, partitioned off from other spheres of life by being channeled through political parties (or perhaps by other analogous forms of formal political action). Such a version of democracy has worked reasonably well in most of Western society since the end of World War II. It seems to offer North America, Europe, and some countries in Latin America and Asia a greater measure of stability than they had in the past when political activity was less insulated from other spheres of life. So one can see why Pope Paul should favor it.

Unfortunately, the preconditions for such a model of political activity are not always present everywhere in the world. Formal political activity is frequently restricted in places where the gap between rich and poor is very wide. This is because the rich soon find that they have to exert oppressive political power in order to retain their privileged position, and the poor, if they have sufficient spirit left to resist at all, will do so with little regard for the niceties of the political rules. In such circumstances it is no longer realistic to think that political struggles can be confined to a limited sphere where the political game is played out within an agreed-upon understanding in which political activity is differentiated from economic activity. The point is that in such situations there no longer exists the fundamental social consensus that provides the underpinning for a contained measure of disagreement and struggle in the narrowly political sphere. To take account of such situations the Church's social teaching would have to face up to the question of a much more radical kind of confrontation in society than that which takes place between the political parties in a democratic state. *Octogesima Adveniens* does not seem to address itself to situations of that kind.

In my examination of *Populorum Progressio* I noted that Pope Paul seemed in danger of overlooking the positive value of confrontation. In general, the same must be said of his position as presented in *Octogesima Adveniens*: he sets such a high value on consensus that he does not take sufficient account of the fact that genuine dialogue presupposes a degree of equality between the partners; and this equality may be achievable only through a confrontation in which the rich and powerful are compelled to yield some of what they have to the poor. There is, however, one short cryptic statement in *Octogesima Adveniens*, which indicates that the pope was aware of this. In saying that relationships based on force do not lead to a true and lasting kind of justice, he adds the following qualification: "even if at certain times the alternation of positions can often make it possible to find easier conditions for dialogue" (*OA* 43). The English wording here is quite obscure, and the Latin and Italian versions of the text are equally vague. I think the pope is here suggesting that some confrontation may, at times, be helpful. But the statement is so vague that it cannot be taken as representing a significant departure from the pope's commitment to a consensus model of political action, particularly in view of the fact that he does not distinguish here between force and confrontation.

Nevertheless, there is a sense in which *Octogesima Adveniens* goes much further than previous papal teaching on the question of confrontation as on other issues. It does so not primarily because of what it says directly on the question but because of the basic methodological principle that it lays down. This is that solutions to social problems have to be worked out in the light of local cultures and sociopolitical systems (*OA* 3–4). This leaves an opening for a more positive appreciation of the role of confrontation of the rich by the poor. And, in turn, this means that the relatively painless consensus model, which was working fairly well in Western Europe in the time of Pope Paul's papacy, does not have to be taken as the model for the whole world. "For everything there is a season . . . a time to break down and a time to build up . . . a time to embrace, and a time to refrain from embracing" (Eccles. 3:1–5).

CONCLUSION

In some respects *Octogesima Adveniens* marks a high-tide point in the development of Catholic social teaching. In the decades that followed, the tide receded quite a long way. The emphasis of the document on an inductive approach and its acceptance that there is room for a certain pluralism in teaching was soon reversed. One has to agree with the judgment of Christine Gudorf (2005, 330) that "it has had a very limited impact on the way that the official Church acts either internally or externally in the world, and has effectively become a dead letter in the domain of the hierarchy." This was undoubtedly true when she wrote it in the year 2005. Nevertheless, the position adopted by Pope Paul in *Octogesima Adveniens* remained as a vital part of the patrimony of the Church's social teaching—one that could be accepted and acted on by a later pope who had come to believe that Catholic social teaching had become unduly monolithic. As I point out in a later chapter, Pope Francis appears to have adopted this view. He seems to be committed to implementing in practice the more inductive and decentralized approach advocated by Pope Paul, as a more authentic and effective way for the Church to face our diverse and rapidly changing world with faith in the message of Jesus and confidence in the inspiration of the Holy Spirit.

* * *

SUMMARY

At Medellín in 1968 the Latin American bishops took the single most decisive step toward an "option for the poor." While pointing out the massive structural injustice in society in their part of the world, they committed themselves and their Church to giving "effective preference to the poorest and most needy sectors of society." They accepted the obligation to be in solidarity with the poor and marginalized. Most important of all, they came out in favor of a process of consciousness-raising ("conscientization") of the poor, the masses of ordinary people. This is a process that involves educating the poor to an awareness of the basic causes of the marginalization they experience and helping them to organize themselves to overcome injustice and achieve liberation. The Latin American bishops recalled Paul VI's statement that, in extreme circumstances, a revolutionary uprising might be justified, but they proposed that in the Latin American situation, the Christian community should commit itself to using peaceful means in working for justice.

Three years later, in *Octogesima Adveniens*, Pope Paul offered what may be taken as his response to Medellín. It is a remarkable document that integrated a good deal of what the Latin American bishops had said and showed some sympathy for the kind of liberation that they envisaged. Above all, it recognized that economic problems call for political solutions. In this context the pope expressed his misgivings about Marxism, and he also strongly criticized the liberal capitalist ideology. He emphasized the importance of people being allowed to participate in the decision making that shapes society. Another important point in this document was the acceptance by the pope of the need for an inductive approach to social problems and his admission that this would result in a certain pluralism; in different parts of the world, different approaches might be adopted. In this document the pope noted that the gospel calls for a preferential respect for the poor. But he was reluctant to acknowledge that the search for justice may at times call for a measure of confrontation. He did not want trade unions to become involved in issues that are "directly political." He still retained his hope that change could come about through consensus.

QUESTIONS FOR REVIEW

1. *What are the key elements in an option by the Church for the poor?*
2. *What is the link between liberation and conscientization?*
3. *What reservations did Paul VI have about Marxist ideology?*
4. *In what way was Pope Paul's approach more inductive and pluralist than that of earlier popes?*

QUESTIONS FOR REFLECTION

1. *Are there significant differences between development and liberation?*
2. *What are the advantages and disadvantages of trade unions engaging in overt political activities? Are there circumstances in which they would be morally obliged to do so?*

ISSUES FOR FURTHER STUDY

1. *Paulo Freire's approach to empowerment of the poor. Read Freire 1974, 1985.*
2. *How the perspective of an option for the poor affects the assessment of the so-called discovery of America. Read Boff and Elizondo 1991.*

9

The 1971 Synod: "Justice in the World"

Just a few months after Pope Paul VI issued *Octogesima Adveniens* the question of social justice came to the fore once again in Rome. The occasion was the Synod of Bishops that took place there in 1971. Late in that year the Synod of Bishops, having met in Rome, issued a document titled "Justice in the World." Though relatively brief, it is one of the most important statements on social justice ever issued by Rome. The synod brought together bishops from churches all over the world, leaders encouraged by the renewal initiated at Vatican II, people who were ready now to take bold steps in the area of the relationship between Church and world. At the synod, Church leaders from the different continents had the opportunity to engage in formal dialogue with each other and with members of the Vatican curia on the theme of justice. The Latin American bishops and their advisers, who were working hard at that time to implement the directives of Medellín, were a particular source of inspiration at this synod. The synod marked a major step in the effort of the Catholic Church to come to terms with the issue of justice in the modern world. In this chapter I examine the remarkable document that it issued.

Possibly the most important thing about this document is that it was issued by the gathering of the bishops themselves. This was in sharp contrast to what happened at all the later synods. In subsequent synods the bishops left it to the pope to issue sometime later a document based on whatever parts of these deliberations were acceptable to the Vatican. If this had happened in the case of the synod of 1971, the final document might not have included its more radical and controversial aspects; they would probably have been toned down or edited out entirely.

THE PROCESS

The document is important not only for its content but also because of the process used to produce it. Of course, the story of the drafting of every Church document is of interest to historians. But in the case of this document the story of its composition is significant for the future as well as for the past. This is partly because synods, particularly this synod, had been seen by many as a way of putting into practice one of the most important advances made by the Vatican Council of the 1960s, namely, the idea of "collegiality," that is, that authority and leadership in the Church are not vested in the pope alone but are a joint responsibility of the pope and the bishops.

There is a further reason why the process adopted leading up to, and during, this synod is significant. It is that it is a particularly good example of close cooperation between bishops who had formal or institutional authority, theologians and other scholars who had the authority of expertise in their different fields, and people who had the authority that comes from practical experience. The actual text owed much to a few key people working in or with the Pontifical Commission for Justice and Peace. This commission had been established by Paul VI in 1967, and by 1971 it was at the height of its power. It had become the focus in Rome for fresh approaches and deep commitment on social justice questions.[1]

Philip Land was a particularly influential member of the commission at that time. He might be described as an activist working at the institutional level. He had been deeply involved in the work of the Pontifical Commission, including its involvement in dialogue with the World Council of Churches through the work of SODEPAX, which was jointly sponsored by the World Council of Churches and the Catholic Church (see Land 1994, 36–38). Land was the principal drafter of much of the document.

Apart from its full-time staff the commission could draw on the expertise of several highly competent scholars who were members of the commission or consultants to it. Two theologians played a key role in composing and revising the early drafts and even in the rushed finalizing of the document some hours before it was approved. They were Vincent Cosmao, a French Dominican, and Juan Alfaro, SJ, from the Gregorian University in Rome. A little later in this chapter I have more to say about the part played by them in drafting and defending a crucial passage in the document. Another influential consultant was Barbara Ward (Lady Jackson). Five years earlier, she had published a book titled *Spaceship Earth*, and she was a pioneer of the concept of sustainable development. Her study, *The Angry Seventies: The Second Development Decade—A Call to the Church*, had been published by the commission in 1970. She not only drafted background material, but also gave an address to the

---

[1]Himes 2005a (336–38) describes how deeply involved the commission staff and consultants were at each stage of the process, from the drafting of the preliminary paper through to the preparation of the *Lineamenta* and on to the "working paper" (*Instrumentum Laboris*). It is clear that they were also deeply involved, in the background and at times in the foreground, during the synod itself.

bishops, being the first woman to do so. No doubt it was she who convinced them of the linkage between justice and ecology.

One might suspect that those who were not bishops or formal members of the synod were able to carry extra "weight" or authority in the dialogue, because there was some doubt or ambiguity about the precise authority that the synod itself carried. Technically each synod is just an advisory body to the pope—even though when synods were first established, many had hoped that they would be understood to be an exercise of the collegiality of bishops, rather than simply a consultative body for the pope. In view of the fact that the Pontifical Commission for Justice and Peace was, and is, also an advisory body to the pope, its members would probably have been seen by many of the official participants in the synod as having almost as much weight as they themselves had.

The clarity and realism of the document "Justice in the World" is not unlike that found in the Medellín documents. Its overall plan is also clearly influenced by the approach adopted at Medellín. A genuine attempt is made to begin from the real situation in the world, in order to discern there the signs of the times,[2] the specific ways in which God is speaking to today's world and calling people to respond.

STRUCTURAL INJUSTICE AND MISDEVELOPMENT

One of the more significant points in the text is the emphasis on structural injustice. This is described in vivid terms as "a network of domination, oppression, and abuses" (JW 3), and "international systems of domination" (JW 13). The use of these terms indicates that those who drafted the document, and the synod participants who adopted it, had accepted the need for—and the value of—a "structural analysis" of society. The document does not oppose personal conversion to structural reform, nor does it merely juxtapose the two. Instead, it indicates how the former is conditioned by the latter, for it speaks of "the objective obstacles which social structures place in the way of conversion of hearts" (JW 16). Many bishops at the synod spoke out strongly about structural injustice at the international level. The document reflects their views. It does not hesitate to say that the conditions left by the colonial domination of the past may evolve into "a new form of colonialism in which the developing nations will be the victims of the interplay of international economic forces" (JW 16). This outspoken linking of past imperialism with present structural injustices in the international economic order is much stronger than the

---

[2]For background on the use of the phrase "the signs of the times," see Hebblethwaite (1982, 88–89).

position adopted by Paul VI about colonialism and neocolonialism in *Populorum Progressio* (PP 7, 52, 57).

In the same sentence in which the synod document speaks of a new form of colonialism, it insists that this danger can be avoided only by "liberation" (JW 16). The word "liberation" is used in a positive sense, in a way that seems to be a definite advance on the usage of Paul VI in *Octogesima Adveniens*. However, there is a significant difference between the way the word is used here and its use at Medellín. "Justice in the World" speaks of attaining "liberation through development," a usage that does not appear in the Medellín documents. These latter frequently speak of liberation without any mention of development and occasionally put the words "liberation" and "development" side by side. But the more nuanced usage of the synod document does not mean that it is less daring than Medellín. Rather, it had to take account of a variety of different situations. Influenced by "dependency theories," many in Latin America associated the word "development" with an exploitative model of economic growth that widened the gap between rich and poor. However, as I noted in chapter 8, in other parts of the South—above all in the newly independent countries of Africa— "development" was still a positive word. Leaders, including Church leaders, still believed that the way to overcome poverty was through development. The synod phrase "liberation through development" represents an attempt to take account of these different situations and outlooks.

Following the lead of Paul VI in *Populorum Progressio*, the document puts forward a broad heuristic account of the nature of development, and it is significant that it in doing so it uses the language of human rights. "The right to development must be seen as a dynamic interpenetration of all the fundamental human rights on which the aspirations of individuals and nations are based" (JW 15). It is notable also that, in line with the approach of Paul VI in *Octogesima Adveniens*, the document recognizes that "the specific content of the right to development will vary with different social, economic and political contexts" (Hamel 1994, 498). So "a certain responsible nationalism" can give developing peoples "the impetus needed to acquire an identity of their own" (JW 17).

The authors of the document were well aware of the myths and illusions associated with the concept of development. They insisted on the need to get rid of "those myths and false convictions which have up to now gone with a thought-pattern subject to a kind of deterministic and automatic notion of progress" (JW 16). One of the most succinct and striking parts of the document is where the bishops point out that the hope has been in vain that poverty would be overcome through development: "In the last twenty-five years a hope has spread through the human race that economic growth would bring about such a quantity of goods that it would be possible to feed the hungry at least with the crumbs falling from the table, but this has proved a vain hope in underdeveloped areas and in pockets of poverty in wealthier areas" (JW 10).

The document goes on to list several interrelated reasons for this failure: rapid population growth, rural stagnation, lack of land reform, massive migration to the cities, and high technology industry that does not give sufficient employment.

On a first reading, the paragraph could give the impression that a variety of unfortunate circumstances (population growth, migration, and so on) have undermined what would otherwise have been a healthy form of development. But the overall tone indicates support for the view that things have gone wrong not so much in spite of development but more *because* of it. The paragraph concludes with a deeply moving sentence— very Latin American in style—which confirms this impression: "These stifling oppressions constantly give rise to great numbers of 'marginal' persons, ill-fed, inhumanly housed, illiterate and deprived of political power as well as of the suitable means of acquiring responsibility and moral dignity" (JW 10).

Taken as a whole, the paragraph amounts to a radical criticism of the development process that has actually taken place (as distinct from some ideal development that might have occurred). It is not simply that this so-called development has failed to meet the needs of the poor. It is that it has actually *increased* the numbers of the poor by creating a whole category of marginal people. In fact, then, the document makes a far more trenchant criticism of "development" than appears at first sight.

ENVIRONMENT

In the next paragraph the synod puts forward an even more serious criticism of the kind of development that has taken place: the environmental costs of the benefits are so heavy that it is simply not possible for all parts of the world to have the kind of development that has occurred in the wealthy countries:

Furthermore, such is the demand for resources and energy by the richer nations, whether capitalist or socialist, and such are the effects of dumping by them in the atmosphere and the sea, that irreparable damage would be done to the essential elements of life on earth, such as air and water, if their high rates of consumption and pollution, which are constantly on the increase, were extended to the whole of humankind. (JW 11)

This passage, if taken seriously, would on its own completely demolish the myth of development on which rich and poor countries had lived for a generation. Both the wealthy and the deprived had assumed that what had been achieved by some could soon be achieved by others, and eventually by all. This would suggest that the relative poverty of some nations compared with others could be endured by them so long as people thought it was temporary. And the use of the term "developing countries" to describe what were really very poor countries (sometimes growing still poorer) helped to ease the consciences of the well-off in the face of the absolute and abject poverty of millions of people.

To recognize that what had been called "development" is available only to a limited number of countries is, in effect, to accept that it is not true development at all, but rather a kind of exploitation. This is a less obvious type of exploitation than one finds in colonialism or in failure to pay proper prices for products from the "developing" countries. For what is being directly exploited in this case is not other people but the resources of the Earth.

One of the most remarkable and admirable features of the synod document is the emphasis it puts on the environmental issue—long before this had become a major theme for many governments. There is an almost lyrical quality to a phrase used in an early paragraph—"the small delicate biosphere of the whole complex of all life on earth" (JW 8). It is significant also that the seventh of the eight "propositions" that are put forward toward the end of the document to be considered by Catholics is the preoccupation with the environment, which was scheduled to be dealt with at the conference in Stockholm in June 1972. The document goes on to make the following strong statement: "Those who are already rich are bound to accept a less material way of life, with less waste, in order to avoid the destruction of the heritage which they are obliged by absolute justice to share with all other members of the human race" (JW 70). No doubt this keen awareness of "the material limits of the biosphere" (JW 12), and the close link between ecology and justice, owed much to the influence of Barbara Ward-Jackson.

In recent years it has become evident that exploitation of the Earth's resources also involves an indirect exploitation of other people or peoples. The reason is that those countries that were first to get into "development" have taken far more than their fair share of the available resources, leaving much less for others. Until quite recently it was assumed that new technologies, inventions, and discoveries could ensure that shortage of energy or raw materials would not limit growth and that toxic wastes could be dumped and dispersed in the sea or the air. Today, however, as the synod document points out, it is clear that there are severe limits to this destructive type of growth, and this changes the situation entirely. Now that it is recognized that those at the end of the queue for development cannot take as much from the Earth as those who came early, it becomes formally unjust and exploitative for the "developed countries" to refuse to share more fairly the benefits they have received from what was the common heritage of all. I note in passing that this issue came to the top of the agenda, as what came to be called the "equity" issue, in the "COP 17" international negotiations that took place in Durban, South Africa, in December 2011, and again, more strongly, in Lima at COP 20 in December 2014. At that conference the countries that were the first to achieve a high degree of economic development were strongly challenged to make greater reductions in their carbon output in order to allow the late developers to catch up.

In this context it is interesting to see two reasons why the synod document insisted on the importance of "a certain sparingness" by Church people in the use of temporal possessions (JW 47) and of an "examination of conscience" in regard to "life style" (JW 48). It maintains that frugality is important both in order to be in solidarity with the poor and for ecological reasons. The document was ahead of its time in seeing the inseparable link between "an option for the poor" and "an option for the Earth."

That the synod document takes so seriously this issue of the limits to growth shows that in speaking of "liberation through development," the bishops do not imagine that poverty in the world is to be overcome simply by rapid economic growth. What poor countries and poor groups need is a type of development that is not modeled on that of the richer countries and regions. Indeed, a major element in the real development of the poor is that the rich should be stopped from imposing misdevelopment on the world. The notion of "liberation through development" needs then to be complemented by that of "development through liberation." Although the synod document does not use this latter phrase, its teaching about justice amounts to more or less the same thing, though the language is more nuanced and polite.

THE CORE OF THE PROBLEM

According to "Justice in the World," one central issue lies at the heart of the structural injustices of today's world: lack of participation by people in determining their own destiny. The new industrial and technological order "favors the concentration of wealth, power and decision-making in the hands of a small public or private group" (JW 9). The kind of positive action required to reverse this inherent tendency of the system is not being taken, and the result is marginalization of masses of people (JW 9–10). To be in a marginal situation is not simply to be economically deprived but perhaps more basically to be deprived of the political power to change one's situation.[3] The document speaks of "the developing peoples" "taking their future into their own hands" (JW 17). In doing so, it emphasizes not only the more objective aspects of development but also the subjective aspect, namely, the awareness by people of their own dignity and their right to be the principal authors of their own destiny.

The synod document says, "We see in the world a set of injustices which constitute the nucleus of today's problems"; to solve them, concerned people, including Church leaders, must "take on new functions and new duties" (JW 20). It is not clear whether the "we" used in this paragraph is intended to mean "we, the authors of this document," in other words, the synod bishops, or whether it is a more generic "we" meaning people who are reflecting on the world situation and committed to working for justice; but even the more generic "we" would clearly include the bishops and other Church leaders.

The required action is to be "directed above all at those people and nations which because of various forms of oppression and because of the present character of our society are silent, indeed voiceless victims of injustice" (JW 20). This statement implies a definite option in favor of the powerless, the oppressed, and the victims of structural injustice. It goes a step beyond what Paul VI had said in *Octogesima Adveniens* about the need to move from economics to politics (*OA* 46), for it applies this principle to the action of the Church itself in a way that is reminiscent of the commitment undertaken by the Latin American bishops at Medellín (e.g., Medellín 2.7 and 4.16 [pp. 47–48, 76]).

Unfortunately, the document seems to lose its thrust for a while at this point. Instead of spelling out at once what such an option for the voiceless would mean, the following paragraphs go into examples, giving lists of various victims of injustice—migrants, refugees, those persecuted for their faith, people whose rights are restricted, and so on (JW 20–26). No doubt this ensures that the statement does not become too abstract, but it is no longer clear how the various injustices listed spring from a common

---

[3]In a brief but valuable study of the synod document Hollenbach (1979, 86–87) says, "Lack of adequate nourishment, housing, education and political self-determination are seen as a consequence of this lack of participation"; and he maintains that for the synod, the fundamental right to participation "integrates all other rights with each other and provides their operational foundation." Hollenbach is undoubtedly correct in holding that participation is a central issue; but the texts to which he refers are not quite as clear as he is in seeing economic and social deprivations as the consequence of lack of participation; the document seems at times to locate lack of participation alongside other lacks.

root, apart from the general tendency of people to victimize the weak. Furthermore, no effort is made at this stage to clarify what is meant by saying that action is to be directed *at* the victims of injustice. The phrase is ambiguous at best. Does it imply simply working *for* such people, or is it supposed to mean real solidarity *with* them?

The document encourages the poor nations to take their future into their own hands through "a certain responsible nationalism" and by forming "new political groupings" (JW 17). But it does not have anything quite so strong and clear to say to the marginal people within any given society. Instead, it offers two short and rather platitudinous paragraphs under the heading "The Need for Dialogue" (JW 27–28). These contain vague remarks about the need for mediation. As Himes remarks, "Again and again in the document there is a commitment to bring about social change through nonconflictual means" (Himes 2005a, 336–38). When it speaks of "mediation," the document does not indicate what the mediation would involve or who is to do it, or at what level (local, national, or international) it is to take place. Once again, the issue of confrontation, especially between the rich and the poor classes in society, seems to be evaded. That impression is strengthened by the fact that in a later paragraph the issue of how a Christian should act is posed in oversimplified terms; the choice offered is between conflict, on the one hand, and love, right, and nonviolence, on the other hand (JW 39; cf. JW 71, which emphasizes cooperation). This presentation does not pay sufficient attention to the importance of a nonviolent kind of confrontation, one that aims ultimately at establishing more equal conditions for dialogue.

EDUCATING TO JUSTICE

There is, however, one section of "Justice in the World" that goes some distance in the direction that Medellín took when it called for conscientization. The heading is "Educating to Justice." There the synod document speaks of awakening a critical sense and making consciences aware of the actual situation (of injustice) as a step in the process of transforming the world, enabling people to take in hand their own destiny, and bringing about communities that are truly human (JW 51–52). The type of education envisaged by the document is a radical one that was clearly influenced by the Latin Americans who were inspired by what we might call "the spirit of Medellín." It is an "education for justice" that involves "a renewal of the heart"; and its purpose is "to awaken consciences" leading to the beginning of "a transformation of the world" (JW 51). The document makes the point that the liturgy can play an important role in this kind of education (JW 58). The education will help people "to be no longer the object of manipulation by communications media or political forces" (JW 52). It is "a continuing education" that "concerns every person and every age"; and "it comes through action, participation and vital contact with the reality of injustice" (JW 53).

Perhaps it would have been too much to expect that the authors of the document would have gone a step farther, by distinguishing clearly between educating the rich and educating the poor—and by emphasizing particularly the importance of the latter. If Church people devote most of their energy and resources to providing education for the rich—as they did in the past in Latin America—this implies that they assume that change is to come mainly from the top. If, in contrast, they focus mainly on providing the poor with the kind of education that is described in the document, then it is likely that before too long they will have to face up to the question of some measure of confrontation.

The document does not make this distinction or point out the implications of a focus on education of the poor. Consequently it glosses over the crucial point that Church leaders who seek to promote effective change in society can hardly escape the need to make a certain option. They can assume that those at the top of society are the key agents of change, or they can acknowledge that the poor are more likely to bring about the kind of changes that justice requires. Of course, Church leaders will feel called to avoid exacerbating divisions in society, and they must also avoid identifying the Church too closely with the interests of any particular group or class. So they will wish to work with all sectors of society. Nevertheless, a choice, or a series of choices, has to be made on certain issues; and people soon sense where the Church leaders stand in practice, especially in countries where there is gross injustice and oppression.

That the synod of bishops wanted to show special concern for the poor and even to affirm their special role in bringing about a just society is not in doubt. That is made clear once again in the final paragraph of the document that says, "The Church calls on all, *especially the poor, the oppressed and the afflicted*, to cooperate with God to bring about liberation from every sin and to build a world which will reach the fullness of creation" (JW 77, emphasis added). The doubt that remains concerns the means by which all this is to take place. It would appear that the synod, like Pope Paul, hesitated to offer open encouragement to the poorer classes of society to challenge existing structures by demanding change and organizing themselves in support of their demands. One must conclude that the document does not explicitly commit the Church to taking that final step of an option for the poor in the radical sense in which a significant number of Latin American Church people and others understood the term.

JUSTICE WITHIN THE CHURCH

Quite remarkably, the area where the synod of bishops seems to take most seriously the option for the poor is in the organization of the Church itself. "Justice in the World" is strikingly new and encouraging in the way in which it commits its authors to practice justice within the Church. That commitment is given expression in these words: "While the Church is bound to give witness to justice, she recognizes that anyone who ventures to speak to people about justice must first be just in their eyes. Hence we must undertake an examination of the modes of acting and of the possessions and life style found within the Church herself" (JW 40).

This was one area where Philip Land made a key intervention. The idea that the Church needs to examine its conscience in regard to justice in its own life was not welcomed by everybody in the Vatican. When the draft of the statement was being discussed at a preparatory meeting of the Council of the Secretariat of the synod, Cardinal Pericle Felici said, "The Church does not have any injustices." Coming from a cardinal who had been a very influential participant in Vatican II and a major figure in the revision of the Code of Canon Law, this pronouncement carried great weight. Land describes the silence during which nobody dared to disagree with the cardinal. Eventually, Land himself summoned up his courage and said, "Your Eminence, I really believe if we cannot say that the Church has injustices, we should not have a document." This broke the paralysis and led to discussion, after which all the members of the Council except Cardinal Felici voted in favor of the paragraph (cf. Himes 2005a, 360, endnote 54, drawing on Land's *Oral History*).

Having acknowledged the need for the Church to give witness to justice in its own life, the document goes on in the following paragraphs to mention various ways in which the rights of people within the Church have to be respected. These include respect for economic rights (wages), juridical rights, and the right to share responsibility and participate in decision making. The document recommends that laypeople should be given more responsibility in dealing with church property. Of particular significance are two paragraphs in which it addresses the issue of women. JW 42 says, "We . . . urge that women should have their proper share of responsibility and participation in the community life of society and likewise of the Church." In translating this sentence I have translated the Latin words "*propriam partem*" as "their proper share" rather than as "their own share," which is the usual English translation. The point is that the original draft had said that women should have an *equal share* of responsibility and participation with men, but this was changed lest it be interpreted as an endorsement of the ordination of women. Himes suggests that the word *propria* means "due" or "proper." He adds that the phrase "own share" "while not terribly inaccurate is not quite the same" (Himes 2005a, 347–44, and endnote 60).

Even more significant is the next paragraph of the document: "We propose that this matter be subjected to a serious study employing adequate means: for instance, a mixed commission of men and women, religious and lay people, of differing situations and competence" (JW 43). This support for the rights of women, who can be seen as the more vulnerable and voiceless group in the Church itself, gave real weight to the synod in speaking out against the marginalization of people in civil society. Unfortunately, however, the proposal to set up a mixed commission has never been adequately acted on by the Vatican.

The document goes on to recognize "everyone's right to suitable freedom of expression and thought," including "the right to be heard in a spirit of dialogue which preserves a legitimate diversity within the Church" (JW 44). Furthermore, it insists that "the form of judicial procedure should give the accused the right to know his accusers and also the right to a proper defense" and that the procedures should be speedy (JW 45). In putting forward these principles or guidelines the document was issuing a strong challenge to the prevailing practice and views in the Vatican. This is a challenge that is still very relevant today.

In two subsequent paragraphs the bishops address the question of the image of the Church in the world: "If . . . the Church appears to be among the rich and the powerful of this world its credibility is diminished" (JW 47). This leads the bishops to say that the possessions, privileges, and lifestyle of the Church and of its ministers and members must be looked at. They must be judged not simply in terms of efficiency. They must rather be examined to see whether they hinder the Church in its proclamation and witness of the gospel to the poor (JW 47–48). This section of the synod document undoubtedly owes much to the new emphasis of the Latin American Church. Even the crisp simple style in which it is written conveys the same sense of quiet commitment as one finds in the documents of Medellín.

THEOLOGICAL ASPECTS

Only a relatively small part of "Justice in the World" treats strictly theological issues. Nevertheless, the theological contribution of the document is one of its most important aspects. A real attempt is made to sketch out a scriptural theology that links poverty with justice: God is the liberator of the oppressed, and Christ proclaims the intervention of God's justice on behalf of the needy (JW 30–31). This section undoubtedly owes much to the influence and input of the scripture scholar Juan Alfaro.

The authors of the document emphasize that there is a close connection between our relationship to God and our relationship to our neighbor (JW 34). They want to repudiate the dualism that would see Christianity as essentially "spiritual" and otherworldly, so that issues of justice in this world would be of secondary or peripheral importance to it. So they insist that the "present situation of the world, seen in the light of faith, calls us back to the very essence of the Christian message"; and they maintain that the mission of preaching the gospel now calls Christians to dedicate themselves to human liberation even in this world (JW 35). For "the Gospel message . . . contains a . . . demand for justice in the world"; and so the Church, though it does not claim to be the only agency responsible for justice in the world, sees itself as having "a proper and specific role, which is its task of giving witness before the world of the demand contained in the Gospel message, a demand for love and justice" (JW 36).

The passage in which this theology is best summed up comes quite near the beginning of the document. It is the most quoted part of "Justice in the World," a statement that has made this document famous and controversial:

> Action on behalf of justice and participation in the transformation of the world fully appear to us as a constitutive dimension of the preaching of the Gospel, or, in other words, of the Church's mission for the redemption of the human race and its liberation from every oppressive situation. (JW 6)

It was Cosmao who drafted the Introduction that included the crucial and controversial phrase "constitutive dimension."[4] Alfaro was not really happy with the actual word "constitutive," which he considered to be unduly scholastic. But on the basis of his knowledge of both the Old and New Testaments, he held that commitment to justice lies at the heart of the scriptures. It was probably his influence that ensured that the document's strong link between evangelization and justice did not get watered down.

Despite the importance of this passage, I have held over any reference to it until my examination of the document is almost completed. The reason is that the full significance of the statement and its controversial

---

[4]Murphy (1983, 300). Murphy notes that two changes were made to Cosmao's draft of this sentence: Cosmao had used the word "struggle," but this was replaced by the word "action"; and the word "redemption" was added "as a more traditional term to balance the newer term 'liberation' and to avoid the danger of excessive 'horizontalism' " (Murphy 1983, 300).

character emerged clearly only after the synod was over. So a discussion of the passage will lead us on to the debate at the next synod, in 1974, and to Pope Paul's apostolic exhortation *Evangelii Nuntiandi*, which came as a follow-up to that synod.

It appears that the passage just quoted was not considered unusually new or daring when it was presented in draft form to the synod. Perhaps it was accepted rather too easily, because the time available was short and because the bishops and the Vatican officials wanted to avoid the kind of divisive debate and polarization that had characterized the synod during its earlier stages while the priestly ministry was on the agenda.[5]

However, soon after the synod the passage became very controversial, and most of the debate focused on the word "constitutive." By saying that "action on behalf of justice and participation in the transformation of the world" is a constitutive dimension or element (*"ratio constitutiva"*) of the preaching of the gospel, the synod was ensuring that justice work could never be dismissed as being merely incidental to the task of the Church; it would have to be given a central place.

Ever since the document was issued, this passage—and this word "constitutive"—have been cited on innumerable occasions to show that the Church officially rejects the view that action to bring about a more just society takes second place to more "spiritual" or "religious" matters. As David O'Brien and Thomas Shannon (1992, 287) say, "It provides a critical antidote to an exclusively otherworldly Christianity." In fact, the statement has become a kind of manifesto for those who are working for political liberation against oppressive regimes or structures and who want to invoke the Church's support for such activity.

For this very reason the statement came under attack from those Church leaders and theologians who saw the evangelizing mission of the Church as primarily "spiritual" and were afraid of "horizontalism."[6] Their tactic was to replace the word "constitutive" by the word "integral." This latter word refers to something that is not absolutely essential to the life of the Church but pertains rather to its fullness. Those who rejected the word "constitutive" argued that this word should be used only for something that can never be absent without the Church failing to be itself, whereas,

---

[5]I am indebted to Msgr. Charles O'Connor for background information on this controversy. Further background is given in Murphy (1983, 298–311) and in Himes (2005b, 362–65).

[6]One source of confusion was that while the original French text had used the phrase *"une dimension constitutive,"* which is rightly translated in the English text as *"a* constitutive dimension," the Italian translation read *"la dimensione costitutiva"* (Murphy 1983, 301). Since this Italian phrase would mean *"the* constitutive dimension," it would not be unreasonable to see it as "horizontalist," that is, as neglecting the transcendent elements of Christianity.

they claimed, the Church, without ceasing to be Church, may at times find itself so restricted by political authorities that it is totally prevented from undertaking "action on behalf of justice."

This argument about the use of words was the focus for a more fundamental disagreement about how the Church ought to respond when faced with major injustice in society. Should it take an overtly political stand like some of the more "prophetic" leaders of the Latin American Church? Should Church leaders distance the Church from unjust regimes and then encourage active resistance by those who are oppressed? Should Church workers even help organize such resistance? Or, instead, should this kind of activity be seen as an excessive politicization of the Church? In certain influential Church circles there was real distress about the new trends that were emerging, especially in Latin America. It was feared that the new liberation theology was emptying the Christian faith of its deepest transcendent meaning and reducing it to a religious legitimation for revolutionary activity. Those who resisted the use of the word "constitutive" generally wanted to dissociate the Church from liberation struggles of a political kind.

Behind this controversy lie two different spiritualities. On the one hand, there are those who put the main emphasis on what they see as the "spiritual" message of Jesus and the Church and who tend to play down the Church's commitment to transformation of the world. On the other hand, there are those who reject this "dualistic" approach and insist that an essential aspect of living out our faith is to work to overcome injustice and to create a world of justice, peace, reconciliation, and respect for the environment. As I point out in a later chapter, Pope John Paul II, several years after the synod, came down quite firmly on the side of this latter spirituality.

It may be added that many of those who were worried about liberation theology and the politicization of the Church were people who also wished to minimize the importance of synods of bishops. They emphasized the fact that a synod has a merely consultative role. Its function is to advise the pope, and the pope remains free to accept or reject what is said by a synod. The campaign of these people to replace the word "constitutive" with the word "integral" had a further purpose over and above the immediate issue: by implication it brought out the point that the synod document was not fully authoritative or binding but could be superseded by a statement by the pope. So the dispute about this one word became a focus and symbol for different views about the exercise of authority in the Church—about the extent to which the power of the Roman curia should be limited by a synod of bishops. This, in turn, related to a dispute about how much autonomy should be left to Church authorities in a region (e.g., Latin America) and how much control should be exercised by the Church's central administration in Rome.

Our concern here is only peripherally with these questions of Church authority. What is mainly of interest to us is that the controversy about the word "constitutive" brought to the fore two closely related theological issues that arise in relation to the Church's action to promote justice:

1. What is the nature of human salvation, and how is it related to political, economic, and cultural liberation?
2. What should be the role of the Church in working to further these forms of liberation?

Even those who accepted without reservation the teaching of the synod document on these issues would have to admit that there was need for a much deeper and more extensive treatment of both questions. Clearly then there was a very good reason for choosing the topic "evangelization" as the subject for discussion at the following synod, that of 1974. This choice of topic offered an ideal opportunity for the bishops to deal with these two questions. In chapter 10 I examine how these issues were discussed and dealt with in the next synod and in the document that Pope Paul VI issued after that synod.

Even though the document of synod 1971 was produced in great haste and is relatively brief, it is nevertheless both comprehensive and inspiring. "Justice in the World" makes a major contribution to Catholic social teaching, both for its content and for the process through which it was drafted and finalized. For these reasons it remains both relevant and challenging for Christians today.

* * *

SUMMARY

The document "Justice in the World," issued by the 1971 Synod of Bishops, made a major contribution to the development of the social teaching of the Church. Its authors spoke out strongly against structural injustice and against the misdevelopment that is doing so much damage to the poor and to the environment. It questioned the myths of "development"—and especially the assumption that the Western type of economic development could be applied all over the world. The central failure, it maintained, is the lack of participation by people in making the decisions that affect their lives. However, the bishops were reluctant to highlight the class divisions in society.

One of the most important sections of the document is where it says that a Church that presumes to speak to the world about justice must itself practice justice in its own life and structures. It called for justice and greater participation in the life of the Church for laypeople. It went on to insist that women should be allowed their proper share in the Church, and it called for a mixed commission to examine the role of women in society and in the Church.

The document declared that action on behalf of justice is "a constitutive dimension" of preaching the gospel. This phrase became a rallying cry for many engaged in the struggle for justice, but it was played down by those who feared the Church would become too politicized.

QUESTIONS FOR REVIEW

1. *What does the synod document have to say about justice in the Church?*
2. *What is meant by saying that action on behalf of justice is a constitutive dimension of the preaching of the gospel?*

QUESTIONS FOR REFLECTION

1. *Compare the strengths and weaknesses of spiritualities in which commitment to justice is central with those where there is less emphasis on justice. Which do you see as more truly Christian?*
2. *To what extent is justice in the Church an urgent issue for Christians today?*

ISSUE FOR FURTHER STUDY

1. *The relationship between the worldly and transcendent aspects of the Christian faith.*

10

Synod 1974: *Evangelii Nuntiandi* and Liberation

Evangelii Nuntiandi ("Evangelization in the Modern World") is an apostolic exhortation issued by Pope Paul in 1975 as a follow-up to the synod of bishops in 1974, drawing on its discussions and giving his own response to the issues that arose there. In this chapter I briefly discuss the synod and then give an account of the contribution made by *Evangelii Nuntiandi* to Catholic social teaching.

THE SYNOD

The synod of 1974 was an exciting event with a disappointing ending. Some of the excitement in the discussions came from contributions made by participants from Africa and Asia. What they had to say, and their style of saying it, helped the synod to take more seriously the whole question of the Church and non-Western cultures. It became clear that other parts of the South besides Latin America had challenges to issue, and contributions to make, to the wider Church. In the short term all this helped ensure that political and economic liberation were not the only important topics discussed; the agenda was broadened considerably. In the longer term it paved the way for a deeper understanding of evangelization and for a more integral conception of human liberation, one that gives a central role not just to economics and politics but also to culture.

An interesting contribution came from the delegates of the African Church on the issue of "small Christian communities," which was their version of the "basic ecclesial communities" of Latin America. The Asians brought to the synod their particular interest at this time in the issue of dialogue with the great non-Christians religions of Asia. This was already a controversial and divisive issue—and it became much more so in subsequent years. However, the most immediately pressing issue was a key text from the document "Justice in the World," which had been issued by the

1971 synod—the statement that said that action on behalf of justice is "*a constitutive dimension* of the preaching of the Gospel." In the intervening years this had given rise to deep controversy on the question of justice and liberation. As one would have expected, the topic came up for discussion again at the 1974 Synod of Bishops in Rome.

Much of the debate revolved around the use of the word "constitutive." A highly controversial intervention came from Bishop Ramón Torella Cascante, vice president of the Pontifical Commission for Justice and Peace. He maintained "that the 'mind of the synodal fathers' [of 1971] was that 'constitutive dimension' meant 'integral part' " (Murphy 1983, 303). Philip Land, Juan Alfaro, and Vincent Cosmao all disagreed quite strongly with this interpretation (Murphy 1983, 303–7; this is the account of Charles Murphy who, some years later, investigated their views very thoroughly, consulting all three of them, two by way of interview and the third by letter).

This controversy was a major factor in causing the participants in the synod of 1974 to fail to agree on the text of the document that they had hoped to issue. Eventually, two draft texts were put forward, and there was a failure to work out a compromise acceptable to both sides (cf. Land 1979, 394). The result was that both texts were handed over to the pope along with the other synodal materials, in the expectation that he would issue a document on evangelization, making use of this material. So the ending of the synod was quite a disappointment to many of those who took part.

Procedurally, the failure to reach agreement was a major victory for those who wished to play down the importance of synods in the life of the Church. This was especially so since it established a precedent and set a pattern for subsequent synods. It gave the pope a free hand to pick and choose from the materials presented to him and to add new material. It was also used in support of the argument that synods were a rather ineffective invention, an innovation that could be divisive and that needed the strong hand of the pope and the Vatican curia to draw some fruit from them. It was even claimed by some that a relatively small group of more conservative participants in the synod had refused to compromise, in order to ensure that the synod would not be able to issue a formal document that might be as radical as "Justice in the World" from the previous synod. However, this handing over of the synod material to the pope ensured that more time was available for a deeper and more nuanced treatment of the issues raised at the synod.

POPE PAUL'S RESPONSE: *EVANGELII NUNTIANDI*

After an interval of just over a year, Pope Paul VI issued his apostolic exhortation *Evangelii Nuntiandi*, as his response to the request of the synod for a document based on the fruits of its work (cf. *EN* 2 and *EN* 5). It is an exceptionally valuable document, one that explores in depth several vital theological and pastoral issues that had arisen since the time of Vatican II. Needless to say, it builds on the teaching of the Vatican Council, but it does not hesitate to deal with new questions and to offer fresh insights about old questions. One of the most important features of the document is the broad sweep of the vision of evangelization it offers. Precisely because of the comprehensive character of the document, it contains a lot of material that is not of direct concern to us here. It should be noted then that I shall confine my attention to the points directly relevant to our subject, omitting other significant aspects of the document.

Perhaps the best way to begin is to see how the pope deals in *Evangelii Nuntiandi* with the most controversial theological question raised by the document of the 1971 synod—its statement that action on behalf of justice is a *constitutive* dimension of preaching the gospel. Paul VI does not say overtly that he is taking sides in this controversy. But there can be little doubt that what he says in this new document provides a thorough vindication for the statement of the synod. To see how he does so we need to look at what the document has to say about three key concepts—Kingdom, evangelization, and liberation. I shall look at each in turn, the first two briefly and the third more extensively.

What *Evangelii Nuntiandi* has to say about the reign of God, though brief, is vitally important. The central point is summed up in one short passage:

> As the one who proclaims the Gospel, Christ announces above all a kingdom, which is the Kingdom of God; he attributes so much importance to this Kingdom that by comparison with it everything else becomes the "other things that shall be added unto you." Therefore the Kingdom of God must be treated as an absolute, to which everything else must be referred. (*EN* 8)

Since Christ's primary concern was the Kingdom, then even the Church must not be seen as an end in itself. Rather it is a community of believers gathered "in the name of Jesus so that they may together seek the Kingdom, build it up and implement it in their own lives" (*EN* 13). (At a later stage the document sets out to ensure that its teaching does not involve any playing down of the importance of the Church [e.g., *EN* 28].) Building the Kingdom is not confined to what might be called "churchy" activities or even to actions that are religious or spiritual in the usual sense of these terms. It also requires very secular activity, such as working to overcome oppressive or inhuman structures in society. It follows, then, that by refusing to make the Church itself the ultimate term of reference and insisting instead on the Kingdom as the only absolute value of the Christian, Pope Paul has taken a major step toward justifying the claim that action for justice is a constitutive aspect of the work of evangelization.

A second important contribution in this regard is made by the pope in the way in which he clarifies the nature of evangelization and the means by which it takes place. Some key lines are the following:

> The proclamation [of the gospel] must take place above all by witness . . . a witness which requires presence, a sharing of life, and solidarity; in the carrying out of evangelization this witness is an essential part, and often the first one.
>
> However, even the most perfect witness will be of no avail in the end unless there is a clear unambiguous proclamation of the Lord Jesus, to throw light on and justify the witness . . . and to reveal explicitly its true meaning. (*EN* 21–22; cf. *EN* 41–42)

This position represents a notable theological advance on what had been said at Vatican II. For instance, in paragraph 6 of the Vatican II Decree on the Church's Missionary Activity (*Ad Gentes*) the Council says that in situations where there is no possibility of preaching the gospel directly, missionaries ought at least to bear witness to the love and kindness of Christ and thus prepare a way for the Lord and in some way make him present. This indicates that in the Vatican II document, priority had been given to verbal preaching, while witness was relegated to a secondary place. Pope Paul, by contrast, insisted that words and witness are both of fundamental importance—each in a different way. Witness without words may remain ambiguous or opaque; words without witness lack credibility. By refusing to put Christian witness in a secondary place, Paul VI was rejecting an older theology that would tend to see worldly activity as just a preparation for the gospel ("preevangelization") or at best an indirect evangelization. This older theology could not easily show how action for justice is a constitutive element in evangelization in the proper sense.

However, it is not enough to show that Christian living is as important as verbal preaching. A further step is required: one must show why a privileged place should be given to action for justice, over and above many other kinds of secular work. To do this we must go on to look in some detail at the third important word in *Evangelii Nuntiandi*—the word "liberation."

SALVATION AND LIBERATION

"Development," rather than "liberation," was the key word in the Vatican Council's document *Gaudium et Spes* and in Pope Paul's 1967 encyclical *Populorum Progressio*. Medellín gave sanction to the alternative word "liberation" in the Latin American Church. Pope Paul in writing *Octogesima Adveniens* in 1971 was very cautious in his use of the word "liberation." In "Justice in the World," the document issued by the Synod of Bishops in Rome later that same year, the word "liberation" was used more freely alongside the word "development." Three years later at the synod of 1974 there was a lot of debate about "liberation." After that synod Pope Paul and his advisers apparently decided that there was no longer any point in shying away from the word. It would be better to provide a thorough theological analysis of the concept of liberation. In this way he could take what was of value in the word while correcting inadequate or mistaken ideas about its meaning or implications. This is what *Evangelii Nuntiandi* set out to do, and that is why the notion of liberation was given a very central role in the document.

One of the more helpful aspects of the treatment of the theme of liberation in the document is the way in which it is rooted in the gospel. After a few introductory paragraphs explaining the occasion and purpose of the document, the pope plunges at once into an account of the liberating mission of Christ. He says that the two words that provide the key to understanding the evangelization of Christ are "Kingdom" and "Salvation" (*EN* 10). Christ came to bring the Good News of the Kingdom of God, the "good news to the poor" promised in the book of Isaiah (*EN* 6). The content of this Good News is summarized by the pope in a striking passage: "As the main point and the very centre of his Good News, Christ proclaims salvation; this is the great gift of God which is liberation from everything that oppresses people, particularly liberation from sin and the Evil One, together with the joy experienced when one knows God and is known by God, when one sees God and entrusts oneself to God" (*EN* 9).

The most important thing to note here is that the word liberation is given real theological respectability. But this is done in a nuanced way that is typical of Pope Paul. Aware that many people took the word "liberation" to be almost equivalent to "revolution," the pope set out to extricate it from this very restricted meaning. *Evangelii Nuntiandi* speaks of being liberated "from everything that oppresses people, particularly from sin and the Evil One." This clearly extends the meaning of the word far beyond political and economic liberation. Furthermore, the word "liberation" is used in the document in a way that does not allow it to replace the word salvation or even to be seen as entirely equivalent to it. Instead, it is given a more limited role; it becomes one of the explanatory words (such as "gift" and "joy") that are used to spell out what is meant by the more fundamental biblical and theological word "salvation."

Evangelii Nuntiandi makes a notable contribution toward the development of a coherent and comprehensible use of theological language by helping to locate the word "liberation" within a network of other theological concepts. This is a step toward the emergence of a scientific theological vocabulary in which the various concepts are defined in terms of their relationship to each other (cf. Lonergan 1992). But the development of theological language was scarcely the primary purpose of the pope in this pastorally oriented document. No doubt he was more concerned to communicate an overall vision of evangelization, one that transcends any division such as "religious versus secular" or "spiritual versus temporal." The reader of the passage quoted above is offered such a global vision, and it is one in which action for justice can be clearly seen to be a constitutive dimension of evangelization.

Evangelization literally means bringing good news. The passage quoted above says that the Good News of Jesus involves liberation from everything that oppresses people, and economic and political oppression are among the more obvious of such things. So liberation from these forms of oppression is part of the core of the Good News of Jesus—and therefore of evangelization. So too is liberation from cultural oppression, which, though perhaps less obvious, is equally evil. But the passage also makes the point that all this liberation comes as the gift of God. It is part of the subtlety of the passage that this proviso has to be added, although the pope's statement does not put it in the form of a strict condition.

By adding this proviso, the pope is making the point that one is not entitled to claim that any and every overcoming of political oppression is automatically a part of that "salvation," which is the core of Christ's Good News, for salvation is presented as something that is the gift of God. So if it were the case that a particular form of political liberation were contrary to God's will, then it would not be part of salvation. However, one is not entitled to argue that any particular event of political liberation is *not* part of the gift of salvation merely on the grounds that it was brought about by human activity, for human action and divine gift are by no means mutually exclusive.

Pope Paul never says explicitly that he accepts the correctness of the teaching in the document of the 1971 synod that action on behalf of justice is a *constitutive* dimension of the preaching of the gospel. But in *Evangelii Nuntiandi* he provides a key point that clarifies the sense in which that formula is acceptable. The key is his emphasis on salvation as the gift of God. This brings out the point that justice is not just an outcome brought about by human action alone. Justice is rather "conceived in the biblical sense of God's liberating action which demands a necessary human response" (Murphy 1983, 308). No doubt, this way of thinking owes much to the intervention and influence of scripture scholar Juan Alfaro.

To sum up, the pope here offers an integral vision to those who are engaged in what the synod of 1971 called "action on behalf of justice and participation in the transformation of the world." It is a vision that enables them to situate their activity within the total creative-redemptive pattern by which God in Christ brings salvation to the world; their action and their struggles contribute to the saving work of God, God's gift of salvation. In this sense, their activity is part of the Good News, part of evangelization. It is not, of course, the whole reality of evangelization. As noted above, the pope insists that a verbal proclamation is also essential. Indeed, one of the strengths of the concept of evangelization as presented in this document is the insistence that it is a complex reality comprising many elements, no one of which on its own should be taken to be the total reality (*EN* 17; cf. McGregor 1977, 63).

CONCERN ABOUT MISUNDERSTANDINGS

The integral vision of human salvation presented in *Evangelii Nuntiandi* includes, as one would expect, a good deal of synthesizing and balancing of various aspects. Like most theologians, the drafter of the document finds it impossible to satisfy those who ask for a simple, either/or answer to the question, "Is salvation found in this life or in the next?" To this question the answer of the document is that it has its beginning in this life but is fulfilled in eternity (*EN* 27). But what is particularly valuable in the document is that it offers terms in which the relationship between the present and the future can be explored more fruitfully. It speaks of "a hereafter" that is "both in continuity and in discontinuity with the present situation" and of "a hidden dimension" of this world, an aspect that will one day be revealed (*EN* 28).[1]

By using this kind of language, the document is able to avoid any naïve dualism that would equate salvation with spiritual welfare as distinct from merely temporal or material welfare. The contrast offered instead is between, on the one hand, a purely "immanent" salvation (including both material and spiritual elements) and, on the other hand, "a transcendent and eschatological salvation" (*EN* 27). It must be noted at once that this is not a simple contrast between an immanent and a transcendent salvation. Rather the contrast is between one that is *merely* immanent and one that is both immanent and transcendent, in other words, a salvation

---

[1] In translating the Latin in this case I have allowed myself to be influenced by the Italian text because it seems more in harmony with the dynamic quality of the relationship between the present and the future as developed in the rest of the sentence. The Dillon translation (which follows the Latin more literally) speaks of "another life" that is "at once connected with and distinct from" the present state.

that relates to earthly "desires, hopes, affairs, and struggles" but that also "exceeds all these limits" (*EN* 27).

A significant part of the teaching of *Evangelii Nuntiandi* hinges on this vital distinction between a conception of salvation that limits it to this world and one that includes worldly affairs but also transcends them. It provides Pope Paul with a solid basis for using the word "liberation" quite freely and, at the same time, correcting what he considers to be false or inadequate ways of understanding both the word itself and the core of the Christian message. The main worries expressed by him in regard to incorrect ideas about liberation are to be found in *EN* 31–38. His reservations can be grouped under the following five headings: reductionism, politicization, inherent limitations, violence, and attitudinal change. As I examine each in turn, I shall add some comments on the pope's treatment of these different issues.

Reductionism

The first and main concern of Pope Paul is that the liberation heralded by Christ and promoted by the Church might be reduced to a much more limited version of liberation, through a failure to take account of the deepest dimensions of what it means to be human. Speaking of the liberation that is proclaimed and promoted by evangelizing activity, he insists that "it cannot be limited to any restricted sphere whether it be economic, political, social, or cultural. It must rather take account of the totality of the human person in all its aspects and elements, including the openness of the human person to what is absolute, even to the Absolute that is God" (*EN* 33).

There appear to be two slightly different emphases in the way in which the reservations of the pope are expressed. The first is found in the passage just quoted. It is the concern that every aspect of the human person must be taken seriously, including that of a religious openness to God. A somewhat different expression is found in the next paragraph. There the pope says that the Church reaffirms the primacy of its spiritual function (*EN* 34). This statement goes a step further than the previous one: it suggests that the religious aspect is not only indispensable but that it is also the primary concern of the Church. However, this can best be understood as an insistence that the religious dimension of the human person is what is deepest in humanity and is therefore of particular concern to the Church. There are no solid grounds in *Evangelii Nuntiandi* for claiming that social and political concerns are of secondary importance for the Church. It is interesting to note that, in *EN* 32, the pope quotes from an address he gave at the opening of the 1974 synod. He spoke then of the need to reaffirm the specifically religious purpose of evangelization. There is a discernible shift of emphasis in the text of *Evangelii Nuntiandi* itself—an avoidance of the tendency to present the issue in terms of a sharp contrast between the "religious" and the "worldly." The quotation in *EN* 32 from the earlier address may even have been included here precisely in order to ensure that it would be interpreted in the light of the more comprehensive teaching of the later document—and in this way to suggest a continuity between the two.

Politicization

Closely related to the danger of reductionism, and following from it, is the concern of the pope about an excessive politicization of the role of the Church. If a narrowing down of the Christian concept of liberation were to take place, then the Church's function would also be reduced. The Church would lose its deepest meaning, and its activities would be confined to the purely political or social order. That would deprive the liberating message of the Church of its distinctive character. As a result, the message would be liable to be distorted by ideological groups and political parties using it for their own purposes (*EN* 32).

The central point here seems to be that what the Church has to offer is not a specific political or social program, but rather an integral vision of what it means to be human—what the pope calls an anthropology, which includes a theology of redemption (*EN* 33, 31). If the more transcendent aspects of this vision are ignored, then Christians precisely as Christians will have nothing specific to add to what political movements have to offer.[2] In that case the main value of the Church would be simply its ability to animate and mobilize people for social and political action through the invocation of powerful religious symbols and the arousing of religious fervor. It is a great boost for the morale of any political movement if its followers are assured that their political beliefs are endorsed by the Church and by God. Pope Paul wanted to ensure that the Church's commitment to liberation could not be interpreted as support for Marxist ideology. He seemed less aware of the danger that Christianity could be harnessed in support of the right-wing political ideology of "National Security."

Inherent Limitations

"The Church sees the links between human liberation and salvation in Jesus Christ, but does not consider the two to be identical" (*EN* 35).

---

[2]One may recall here what Pope Paul had said in *Octogesima Adveniens* about the Church not having a ready-made model for human society (*OA* 42).

This is an important statement. The pope offers support for it by putting forward a variety of reasons in the remainder of the paragraph. One important point emerges: the achievement of (earthly) liberation and prosperity are not in themselves sufficient to constitute the coming of the Kingdom, because all temporal and political liberation contains within it the seed of failure. This is a point that was developed more fully a few years later, especially by the members of the Ecumenical Association of Third World Theologians (e.g., EATWOT 1980, 129). The achievement of political liberation in a particular area may truly be seen as a salvific event, as the Exodus was for the Jewish people. Nevertheless, this does not mean that salvation has been definitively attained in this liberation. Various inadequacies are there from the beginning, and they tend to grow and to create a widening gap between the ideal salvation that is being reached for and the limited degree of liberation that has been achieved.

Unfortunately, this important point made by the pope tends to become somewhat obscured, because in the passage it is confused with another, slightly different, point. This second point is that even people who invoke the Bible in support of their actions may in fact be operating on the basis of a notion of liberation that is not fully Christian; indeed, some understandings of the word "liberation" are simply incompatible with the Christian view of the human person and of history. No doubt, this warning of the pope was needed, but coming here it tends to distract attention from a major theological issue, namely, how the gift of divine salvation is embodied in human history and in what sense any particular achievement of justice may be called salvific in the proper Christian sense.

Violence

Pope Paul was concerned lest there be any confusion between the Christian conception of liberation and the kind of political liberation sought by revolutionaries. He saw the danger that a certain kind of liberation theology, based largely on the Old Testament, could be invoked to justify violent rebellion against unjust regimes. Of all the objections raised against the word "liberation," this was the most obvious one. It led many rich and powerful groups, including people with power in the mass media, to put considerable pressure on the pope to come out strongly against liberation theology, and this pressure came also from many conservative Church leaders.

Pope Paul, as we have seen, responded not by rejecting the word "liberation" but by clarifying the Christian meaning of the word and then correcting wrong interpretations. Obviously, he felt the need to dissociate the Church unequivocally from violence. He devotes one short paragraph of *Evangelii Nuntiandi* to this question (*EN* 37). What he says is very close to what he had already said in *Populorum Progressio*: violence is uncontrollable; it provokes further violence and gives rise to new forms of oppression, more serious than before. He adds that sudden or violent structural changes are illusory and are of their very nature ineffective; and furthermore, violence is contrary to the Christian spirit. All these points are made in support of his initial stark statement that the Church cannot accept violence—especially armed violence—or the death of anybody as the way to liberation.[3]

The tone of this whole passage is rather more pacifist than that of the corresponding passage in *Populorum Progressio*. In this statement, by contrast to the earlier one, there is no reference to exceptional situations in which violence might be justified, nor is there any footnote reference to the earlier statement. Should one draw the conclusion that Pope Paul had changed his mind in the intervening eight years? It would seem to be more accurate to see this as a change of emphasis rather than a change of mind. The pope was, no doubt, aware that any mention of exceptional circumstances justifying violent action could be used by revolutionary groups to provide a justification for armed resistance. Perhaps he was not entirely happy with the way Medellín had treated his earlier statement, giving rather more prominence to the exceptional situations than he had. It would appear that on this occasion, he decided it would not be appropriate to mention such exceptional situations.

Presumably this decision reflects the pope's assessment of the world situation at the time of writing the document. And indeed in the world of 1975 there did not seem to be any obvious situation where all the various factors required to justify violent rebellion were clearly present. Had the document been written three or four years later, when the struggles in Nicaragua and Zimbabwe had come to a head, it is doubtful whether the pope could have omitted all reference to exceptional situations in which violence might conceivably be justified. The point I am making here is that the passage in *Evangelii Nuntiandi* was not really intended to be a

---

[3]There are two significantly different translations of the first sentence of *EN* 37. The Vatican translation reads, "The Church cannot accept violence . . . and indiscriminate death as the path to liberation." The Dillon translation has: "The church cannot accept any form of violence . . . nor the death of any man as a method of liberation." The Vatican English text may find some basis in the Italian, "*la morte di chicchessia*," while the Dillon text is closer to the Latin "*cuiusvis mortem hominis*." The French text is "*la mort de qui que ce soit*," which still leaves one not quite clear about what is intended. Is the writer saying that the goal of liberation does not justify the death of even one person? Or is it simply that one must not seek liberation through a type of violence that is liable to cause the death of anybody (at random, or indiscriminately)? The former would be a strongly pacifist position, while the latter could be understood as simply a rejection of an arbitrary kind of violence. Perhaps the drafter of the document and the pope himself intended to leave the text somewhat ambiguous.

comprehensive theological statement covering all eventualities; rather it should be understood as a strong pastoral-inspirational exhortation, urging Christians to choose the way of peace, for it is quite unlikely that Pope Paul intended to commit the Church unconditionally to an entirely pacifist position. Furthermore, he would not have wished his words to give any comfort or support to unjust regimes; elsewhere in the document he spoke out strongly against structural injustice (e.g., *EN* 30).

Attitudinal Change

Pope Paul was concerned that a particular notion of liberation could give the impression that a change of structures alone is sufficient to bring about human liberation. So, like his predecessors, he insists that there is need for attitudinal change as well as reform of the structures of society. He speaks of the need for "a conversion of the hearts and minds of those who live under these systems and of those who have control of the systems" (*EN* 36).

This warning was, no doubt, justified, for left-wing reformers have at times been guilty of "dreaming of systems so perfect that no one will need to be good," as T. S. Eliot says. But insistence on the importance of conversion can sometimes be used as a way of playing down the importance of structural change or of suggesting that those who insist constantly on the latter are perhaps a little unbalanced or extremist in their approach. There may be some element of that attitude in this paragraph of the document; certainly the relationship between structural and attitudinal change is not treated very helpfully here. However, another section of the document offers an exceptionally enlightening treatment of this topic, and it is to this question that I now turn.

STRUCTURES AND CULTURE

The topic of structures is dealt with in *EN* 18–20, where Pope Paul explores in some depth what the task of the Church in the world really is. These paragraphs provide some of the most memorable and enlightening passages in the whole document—or indeed in any of the papal writings considered in this study. We begin with the following two statements:

> For the Church, to evangelize is to bring the Good News into all the strata of the human race so that by its power it may permeate the depths of humanity and make it new. (*EN* 18)
>
> The various strata of the human race are to be transformed. This means something more than the Church preaching the gospel in

ever-expanding geographical areas or to ever-increasing numbers.
It also means affecting the standards by which people make judgments, their prevailing values, their interests and thought-patterns,
the things that move them to action, and their models of human
living; in so far as any or all of these are inconsistent with the Word
of God and the plan of salvation they are to be in some sense turned
upside down by the power of the gospel. (*EN* 19, my translation)

Having outlined the task of the Church in this comprehensive way, the
pope then sums up his teaching by saying,

It is necessary to evangelize, and to permeate with the Gospel, human culture and cultures. This has to be done, not superficially, as
though one were adding a decoration or applying a coat of paint,
but in depth—reaching into and out from the core and the roots of
life. . . . The Gospel and the process of evangelization can penetrate
all cultures while being neither subordinate to any of them nor the
monopoly of any. (*EN* 20, my translation)

The pope is here taking the word "culture" in a broad and rich sense.
It refers to the shared understanding and attitudes of any group of people
who together live in their own particular "world." Some of these meanings and values are common to many cultures, while others differ from
culture to culture—for instance, the status given to old people, to women,
to handicapped people, to twins; the value set on cattle, on gold, on cats,
on brevity, on burial sites, and so on. These shared understandings and
values might be called structures or patterns of thinking and feeling. They
become embodied in traditions, and in this way they are passed on from
one generation to the next. The pope is saying that the gospel does not
belong solely to any one such culture and is not embodied exclusively in
any one set of traditions. Rather, it is compatible with all. This does not,
however, mean that it fits comfortably into the different cultures. Quite
the contrary: it poses a challenge to every culture, and it calls for basic
transformations in the traditions, the thought-patterns, and the value
systems of each culture.

The most helpful aspect of this whole account is the way in which
it bridges the gap that is usually presumed to exist between attitudinal
change and structural change. It is commonly assumed that changing
one's attitudes is a matter of personal morality, and this is generally
what people have in mind when they speak of "conversion." Structural
changes, in contrast, are thought of as belonging to the political order,
extrinsic to the person as such, and not a matter of personal morality in

the usual sense. This dichotomy is challenged by the pope's statements quoted above. They suggest that perhaps the most important structures in our world are our patterns of thinking and feeling and valuing. These are deeply personal; yet in many respects they transcend the individual. They are social realities that are often our unexamined presuppositions. They are "within" the person without being private. They are a crucial part of the strata of the human race that are to be evangelized and transformed.

It is against this background that the pope says that the aim of evangelization is to bring about an *interior* change (*EN* 18). To make sure that this is not taken to refer to a purely private and individualistic conversion, he adds at once that, in evangelizing, the Church is "seeking to convert the individual and collective conscience of people, as well as their activities, their lives, and their whole environment" (*EN* 18). To change the collective conscience of a people is to change their value system, and this is linked to changes in the social, political, and economic structures of their society.

People can be oppressed by structures of the mind—by distorted value systems and patterns of action, by misguided expectations, and by inherited prejudices and insensitivities. Indeed, this kind of deformation is especially serious, because it makes a person less human in ways that he or she may be quite unaware of. So there is need for liberation from this oppression of the human spirit. In fact, the question may be asked whether there can be any lasting value in a liberation from political oppression that is not linked to this intimate liberation. For Pope Paul, a change at this level is essential, because "even the best structures and the most wisely planned systems soon become dehumanized if the inhuman tendencies of people's hearts are not healed" (*EN* 36).

POLITICAL AND ECONOMIC STRUCTURES

This account of the need for the transformation of culture and cultures deepens our understanding of the nature of human liberation and is perhaps the most valuable part of *Evangelii Nuntiandi*. Unfortunately, Pope Paul does not provide an equally detailed and careful treatment of the other more visible kinds of oppressive structures. It would have been particularly helpful if he had given an indication of the two-way relationship between economic and political structures, on the one hand, and cultural structures, on the other hand. The document could have pointed out the ways in which oppressive political and economic systems in today's world are shaped by the cultural distortions that are typical of Western society, for instance, excessive competitiveness, consumerism, cultural arrogance, restlessness, and an exploitative attitude toward nature. It could have gone on to show how these cultural evils are, in turn, fostered and intensified by the present social, economic, and political structures.

Such an analysis would have provided the basis for a treatment of human liberation that would be at once profound and comprehensive. But regrettably, there seems to be a certain imbalance and incompleteness in this regard in *Evangelii Nuntiandi*. Having taken the major step of showing the need for the transformation of cultures, the pope did not go on to draw out the implications with regard to changing structures in the economic, social, and political spheres.

Why is it that Pope Paul seems reluctant in this document to examine in any depth the role of the Church in promoting liberation in these public aspects of human living? Perhaps he felt that his treatment of these questions in earlier documents was sufficient and that what was needed now was an analysis of the underlying cultural issue. Probably also he was reluctant to say anything at this time that could contribute to a further heightening of the polarization between rich and poor, powerful and powerless, especially in the Latin American Church. He may have felt it would be less divisive to emphasize the cultural issue, for many of the same cultural distortions may be common to rich and poor in a particular area. It is interesting to note that he does not go into the interesting question of what might be called "the culture of the poor"—a set of thought-patterns and values that contrast sharply at times with those of the rich and powerful. A study of the difference between the thought-and-feeling patterns of the rich and the poor would be essential for a proper understanding of why the Bible presents the poor as privileged and more open to God.

Whatever the reason for the incompleteness in the treatment of the question of liberation, the effect is that the account of the role of the Church remains rather abstract. It does not spell out in any concrete way the commitment of the Church to overcoming of the many forms of injustice in society. When the pope devotes a paragraph to poverty, marginalization, neocolonialism, and the struggle for liberation, he does it in the context of a reminder that these were the concern of many bishops at the synod. He agrees with the bishops in saying that the Church has the duty of proclaiming the liberation of the myriad of the poor and oppressed, as well as helping this liberation come to birth, and witnessing and working to ensure that it comes to completion. Then the pope adds curtly, "All this is in no way foreign to evangelization" (*EN* 30). It would be quite incorrect to suggest that he was half-hearted in his acceptance of these points or reluctant to see such activity as part of evangelization. But it is as though he were using these points as a launchpad for something else, which is his main concern, and that is that the Church must affect the strata of humanity at a deeper level, a level that lies behind the political, social, and economic order.

THE POOR

That *Evangelii Nuntiandi* does not have much to say about the economic and political structures of society means that it does not emphasize the particular importance of the poor and oppressed to the Church in its task of evangelization. An early paragraph, dealing with Christ the evangelizer, mentions that he was sent to bring Good News to the poor (*EN* 6). One might therefore have expected that this theme would be given some prominence in the treatment of the evangelizing role of the Church. There might have been special emphasis on the place of the poor in the chapter titled "The Beneficiaries of Evangelization," or the one called "The Methods of Evangelization." But that kind of mention of the particular role of the poor is not in the document.

Furthermore, when the document deals with the question of "basic communities" (*EN* 58), it does not pay any particular attention to what many of those who advocate them consider to be a central feature of such groups—the fact that they are normally communities of poor people. It would appear that the pope, when dealing with the nature of evangelization, was reluctant to single out the poor and marginalized as a distinct social class. Perhaps he feared that to do so would weaken or compromise his emphasis on universality and unity, two values that should characterize the preaching of the gospel. It may also be that the failure to emphasize the importance of structural change at the political and economic levels was owing to the caution of an aging pope who was inspired by the new approaches to evangelization that had emerged in Latin America, Asia, and Africa, but fearful of liberation movements and liberation theology.

CONCLUSION

Despite the elements of incompleteness in the way in which *Evangelii Nuntiandi* treats the issue of liberation and the role of the Church in promoting it, it must be emphasized once again that the document makes a significant contribution toward a better understanding of this whole question. In fact, an interesting contrast can be seen in this regard between this document and *Rerum Novarum,* the first of the great social encyclicals, issued in 1891 by Leo XIII. As I pointed out in chapter 2, *Rerum Novarum* was particularly important not so much because of its content as because it represented a decisive intervention by the pope on behalf of the poor. *Evangelii Nuntiandi,* in contrast, is important in relation to the poor for precisely the opposite reason. It does not give the impression of being a major protest against the plight of the poor, comparable to Leo's encyclical or to Pope Paul's own *Populorum Progressio*. In fact, if anything, it seems to be urging caution and moderation in the face of the eagerness of the liberation theologians to promote a decisive option for the poor by the Church.

However, some of the *content* of the document is exceptionally important in helping Christians know how the deepest roots of poverty and oppression can be overcome. What the pope says here about the transformation of culture and cultures is central to the question of liberation and the task of the Church in witnessing to it and fostering it. Cultural oppression is just as important as economic and political oppression. Liberation calls not only for the transformation of society structures in the sphere of economics and politics, but also for radical changes in the patterns and structures that mold the way groups of people think and feel and evaluate.

In the years that have passed since *Evangelii Nuntiandi* first appeared, its relevance has in no way diminished. In fact, what it has to say about evangelization is now more important than ever. The Church is faced with the reality that there is a rapid expansion in many parts of the world of escapist types of Pentecostalism and what is called "prosperity Christianity." In response, many Church leaders and committed Catholics are promoting a version of what they call "evangelization." Sadly, it is a quite inadequate version of evangelization, one that emphasizes only the personal aspect of our Christian faith. It is a devotional type of spirituality that neglects or plays down the importance of commitment to the world—especially on the issues of justice and ecology.

As an alternative to this devotionalism, it is essential that our Church leaders and committed Christians—especially the younger generation—should be inspired by an authentic spirituality of evangelization. This must be an evangelization true to the gospel of the Jesus who came to bring Good News to the poor and to bring liberty to captives. The document *Evangelii Nuntiandi* provides a solid foundation for such an authentic and enlightened understanding of what it means to preach the Good News in today's world and for the inspiring spirituality that should flow from it.

* * *

SUMMARY

In 1975 Pope Paul issued the document *Evangelii Nuntiandi* as his response to the synod of 1974. In it he noted that the mission of the Church is to promote the Kingdom or Reign of God and that its "good news" is brought both by witness and by words. He wholeheartedly accepted the word "liberation" and clarified its theological meaning, especially by relating it to the liberating work and word of Christ and by situating it within an integral vision of human life and salvation.

In this document Pope Paul emphasized the cultural aspects of liberation—the need for a change in the structures of thought as well as in economic and political structures. This was not balanced by an equally detailed treatment of oppressive political and economic structures or a strong emphasis on the special role of the poor and oppressed. In this respect the document reflects the caution of an aging pope somewhat fearful of liberation movements and liberation theology.

QUESTIONS FOR REVIEW

1. *Explain the ways in which* Evangelii Nuntiandi *goes further than previous Vatican documents on the issue of liberation.*
2. *What are the different aspects of liberation?*
3. *What is involved in cultural liberation?*

QUESTION FOR REFLECTION

1. *Compare the strengths and weaknesses of the words "redemption," "salvation," and "liberation" as suitable words for describing what is central to the Christian faith.*

ISSUE FOR FURTHER STUDY

1. *Two visions of the Church as seen in the history of the synods in Rome in 1971 and 1974.*

11

John Paul II: An Integral Humanism

Pope Paul VI died in August 1978, and the new pope, John Paul I, died in October 1978, just over a month after he was elected. John Paul II was chosen as the new pope. The deaths of Paul VI and of John Paul I caused a delay in holding a follow-up to the famous Medellín conference of Latin American bishops. The gathering was rescheduled to take place in Puebla, Mexico, in January of 1979, and John Paul announced that he would himself travel to Mexico and address the meeting.

Commentators and journalists revealed, and sometimes exaggerated, the tensions behind the scenes in the preparation for Puebla (see Eagleson and Scharper 1979). There can be little doubt that a determined effort was made by some Church leaders to ensure that both the style and the outcome of Puebla would be quite different from those of Medellín. The preparatory document circulated to participants before the meeting was heavily criticized by progressive elements in the Church in Latin America.

The main body of Brazilian bishops, who had played a key role in implementing the Medellín program, was obviously dissatisfied with this document. But they were also concerned about the serious polarization that was taking place in the Latin American Church. So the Brazilian episcopal conference issued a document of its own as a contribution toward the preparation for Puebla (Bishops of Brazil, *Documento*, 1978). In content and style it followed the pattern set by Medellín. But it also attempted to acknowledge the reservations of those who were afraid that the Church was becoming too political, too identified with the cause of the poor in a sense that turned it against others. For instance, the document accepted that there was also a need for the Church to minister to elite groups and that it must face difficult questions regarding evangelization of the upper classes, military chaplaincies, and so forth.

From a strategic point of view what was most significant in this Brazilian document was its suggestion that Pope Paul VI's *Evangelii Nuntiandi* should be the point of reference or model in regard to style and approach.[1]

---

[1] "*Tome o 'Evangelii Nuntiandi' como documento de referencia no estilo e na forma da elaboração.*"

This offered a middle ground where most of the Latin American bishops could meet. It is not surprising, then, that the final document of Puebla relies heavily on *Evangelii Nuntiandi*. In doing so, it takes a lead from John Paul II, who, in his address to the conference, frequently referred to, or quoted from, Pope Paul's document—especially, as we shall see, on the controversial issue of liberation.

The major issue facing the Puebla conference was not really whether it would say something strikingly new and radical. Rather, it was whether it would reaffirm the basic thrust of Medellín or whether it would allow the commitments of Medellín to die the death of a thousand qualifications. There were two likely ways in which the inspiration and direction of Medellín could be clouded at Puebla. First, the conference would issue conservative statements on the more obviously theological issues. Second, when addressing the pastoral issues, it would put the emphasis on issues related to secularization and culture rather than on economic and political matters.

The final document that emerged from the Puebla conference was one that could give a good deal of satisfaction to those who wanted to reaffirm the direction set by Medellín. Undoubtedly, there were some compromises and disappointments, and the Puebla document is much more uneven than the documents of Medellín. There are sections in which the older style of theology is dominant. In general, these are the more doctrinal parts. It is likely that the more socially committed bishops decided that their best strategy would be to concentrate on pastoral matters, leaving the "high theology" to their opponents. Whatever the reasons, the outcome is, as Jon Sobrino remarked, that "we are faced with the irony that the Christology and, in particular, the ecclesiology underlying the pastoral documents are more inspiring than the doctrinal presentations of Christ and the Church in themselves" (Sobrino 1989, 200).

Despite all this, the Puebla document as a whole reaffirms the direction set by Medellín in regard to the crucial pastoral issues. At first sight, this may seem to be a minor achievement. But, in fact, it was of major importance. For it was one thing to propose a program of engagement in the struggle for justice, as Medellín did, but it was far more difficult to reaffirm a commitment to that program more than a decade later, when the full cost had become apparent—and that is what Puebla did.

OPTION FOR THE POOR

Since the focus of this study is Vatican teaching, I shall examine the Puebla document only in that context. The main success of Puebla, unlike that of Medellín, was not the document produced at the conference.

The Medellín documents had had a profound effect on the life of the Church, not merely in Latin America but far beyond it; and they evoked a significant response both from Paul VI and from the Synod of Bishops in Rome. The Puebla document could hardly have had the same kind of effect. In fact, its main significance is that it shows, despite political and ecclesiastical pressures, that Church leaders were not prepared to compromise on the central elements of the policies adopted at Medellín.

There is, however, one section of the Puebla document that is important in its own right. This is the chapter titled "A Preferential Option for the Poor" (Puebla 1980, 1134–65). The most notable aspect is its title. This bishops' conference was adopting the controversial phrase that had become a powerful summary and symbol of the new approach. The use of this term had evoked strong opposition both inside and outside the Church. Critics maintained that the Church would be abandoning its universal mission if it were to make such an option: it would no longer be preaching the gospel to all people equally.

Some of the more hostile critics went further: they saw an "option for the poor" as more or less equivalent to a Marxist "class option," implying that the Church is taking sides in a "class struggle." In contrast, those who favored the term insisted both before and after the conference that that is not what they meant by it. For instance, Cardinal Paulo Evaristo Arns of São Paulo (1981, 2) wrote, "The option for the poor is not a class option in the Marxist sense" (cf. Baum 1981b, 84).[2]

The concept of an option for the poor has a firm foundation in the Bible, which reveals that God at times deliberately shows a preference for people who are poor or weak or oppressed (see Gutiérrez 1973, 287–306; Tamez 1982; Ferraro 1977, 92–95). For those in favor of the term its main value is that it expresses succinctly and uncompromisingly the practical implication for the Church of committing itself firmly to the promotion of social justice. The presence of the term in the Puebla document is perhaps the clearest indication of the commitment of the conference on this issue.

The Puebla document does not attempt to give a systematic account of what the phrase "option for the poor" does and does not mean. But in a very practical way, it indicates what is involved:

> With renewed hope . . . we are going to take up once again the position of . . . Medellín, which adopted a clear and prophetic option expressing preference for, and solidarity with, the poor. . . . We affirm the need for conversion on the part of the whole Church to

---

[2]For a more extensive account of the difference between a Marxist "class option" and a Christian "option for the poor" see Dorr 2000, 250–53.

a preferential option for the poor, an option aimed at their integral liberation.

This option, demanded by the scandalous reality of economic imbalances in Latin America, should lead us to establish a dignified, fraternal way of life together as human beings and to construct a just and free society.

We will make every effort to understand and denounce the mechanisms that generate this poverty. (Puebla 1134, 1154, 1160)[3]

The document makes it clear that what is required is a change in the structures of society—but it adds that this must be accompanied by a change in people's "personal and collective outlook," a change that "disposes us to undergo conversion" (Puebla 1155). A brief response is given to the objection that an option for the poor would mean an abandonment by the Church of an evangelization of the rich: "The witness of a poor Church can evangelize the rich whose hearts are attached to wealth, thus converting and freeing them from this bondage and their own egotism" (Puebla 1156). In the following year in Colombia, Ricardo Antoncich (1980, 108–15) published a particularly helpful study of the concept of an option for the poor, based on Puebla and on Pope John Paul's addresses in Mexico.

THE POPE AND PUEBLA

What contribution did Pope John Paul II make to the Puebla conference and its document? Endless words were written about the position he adopted in his address to the conference itself and in his other Mexican addresses. Intense efforts were made by journalists and some theologians in both the conservative and progressive camps to convince the public that the pope was on their side—that he had condemned liberation theology out of hand or that he had come down in favor of what the liberation theologians stood for. Not much of this material is of any great value. Even apart from the special pleading that marks such writing, there is the further fact that, if one really wishes to understand the outlook of John Paul II, the Mexican addresses are by no means the best sources to study.

This is not to say that the pope did not express himself clearly or

---

[3]It should be noted that at Puebla, the bishops also committed themselves to a preferential option for young people (Puebla 1166–1205). This had the effect of playing down to some degree the uniqueness of the phrase "option for the poor" and in this way making it less threatening and more widely acceptable.

would not stand behind what he said at Puebla, for, in fact, he contributed significantly to the stance taken by the bishops at the conference. But in many respects the Mexican agenda was already set for the pope. He was not in a position to decide his own terms of reference, so his choices were somewhat limited. He was coming into a highly polarized situation, so it was more or less inevitable that his addresses—especially his talk to the Puebla conference itself—would contain a good deal of "on the one hand . . . and on the other." His opening address to the conference represents a careful balancing exercise in which he warns against dangerous tendencies in regard to the theology of Christ and the Church while encouraging the Latin American Church not to back down on the commitments made at Medellín (cf. Filochowski 1980, 18).

In the first major section of his address the pope spoke out strongly against those who "purport to depict Jesus as a political activist, as a fighter against Roman domination and the authorities, and even as someone involved in the class struggle" (I, §4). He insisted that Jesus "unequivocally rejects recourse to violence" and "opens his message of conversion to all" (I, §4). He went on to speak out against a conception of the building of the Kingdom "merely by structural change and socio-political involvement" without taking sufficient account of the role of the Church (I, §8).

Having issued these warnings, the pope was then in a position to take a strong stand on social and political issues. In the third section of his address he spoke of human dignity and of human rights and their violation. Toward the end of this section he went on to speak of the need for "a correct Christian conception of liberation" (III, §6). The most striking thing about this passage is that it relies almost entirely on *Evangelii Nuntiandi*; Pope Paul's document is quoted from or referred to no less than six times. John Paul ends this section with the following remark: "As you see, the whole set of observations on the theme of liberation that were made by *Evangelii Nuntiandi* retain their full validity." Evidently, he had decided that this was not the opportune time to make any major new statement on the subject. So he offered instead the teaching of his predecessor as a middle ground where bishops of different outlook could come to a measure of agreement.

In one of the more interesting sentences in the Puebla address John Paul paraphrases the controversial passage of the 1971 synod—the one in which the bishops had said that they see action on behalf of justice as "a constitutive dimension of the preaching of the Gospel." In his address the pope said, "The Church has learned that an indispensable part of its evangelizing mission is made up of works on behalf of justice and human promotion" (III, §). It will be noted that he replaced the disputed word "constitutive"—not, however, with the word "integral" as its opponents had wanted, but with the word "indispensable." In his paraphrase the central meaning of the synod statement has not been lost, but a certain verbal concession is made to the opponents, and at the same time the whole idea is presented more clearly and simply. This sentence might be taken as a typical example of what the pope was doing throughout his Mexican visit—trying to bridge the gap between different viewpoints but without compromising on the central issues.

In regard to the question of an option for the poor the pope adopted the same approach. In his address at Puebla he did not use the term. But he found another way of expressing the same idea: he said that the Church "is prompted by an authentically evangelical commitment which, like that of Christ, is primarily a commitment to those most in need" (III, §3). On other occasions in Mexico the pope expressed the same general idea in different words. In a sermon at Guadalupe, he said Medellín was a call of hope showing "preferential yet not exclusive love for the poor" (*AAS* [*Acta Apostolicae Sedis*] 174, 44). And in an address in the Santa Cecilia district of Guadalajara, he said, "I feel solidarity with you because, being poor, you are entitled to my particular concern. I tell you the reason at once: the Pope loves you because you are God's favorites" (*AAS* 220, 113; cf. address in Monterrey *AAS* 243, 149).

Two of the pope's addresses to Mexican audiences are notable for their outspoken character on justice issues. Speaking in the industrial city of Monterrey, he insisted that "the Latin American peoples rightly demand that there should be returned to them their rightful responsibility over the goods that nature has bestowed on them. . . . Bold and renewing innovations are necessary in order to overcome the serious injustices inherited from the past" (*AAS* 242, 148).

His remarks to poor Mexican Indians at Cuilapan were even more explicit. To them he presented himself as one who "wishes to be your voice, the voice of those who cannot speak or who are silenced." Then he insisted on the need for "bold changes, which are deeply innovatory" to be carried out "without waiting any longer." Since he was speaking to very poor peasants, he went straight to what for them would be the crucial change they required: he pointed out that there is "a social mortgage on all private property" so that "if the common good requires it, there should be no hesitation even at expropriation, carried out in due form" (*AAS* 209, 96, translation emended).

In the same speech he then turned to the "leaders of the peoples" and "powerful classes," and he insisted, "It is not just, it is not human, it is not Christian to continue with certain situations that are clearly unjust." He added, "It is clear that those who must collaborate most in this, are those who are in a position to do most" (*AAS* 210, 97). This address shows how keenly the pope was aware of the need for social, political, and economic changes. But it also suggests that he was still convinced that the best way for him to promote such changes was to state the need bluntly and to appeal to the consciences of those who hold wealth and power.

The addresses of John Paul II, both in Puebla itself and in other places in Mexico, were of major importance for the Puebla conference. This is obvious because his words are quoted many times in the document issued by the conference. Quotations from his addresses were used as the basis for reaching consensus on divisive issues, notably the questions of liberation, an option for the poor, and the Church's attitude toward ideologies (Puebla 1980, 489, 1141, 538, 551–52). The Puebla document is a written proof that the pope succeeded in achieving the main purpose of his visit. This was to contribute to the unity of the Latin American bishops and to help them find a direction in which they could go forward together.

SOCIAL DOCTRINE

Toward the end of his opening address to the Puebla conference, Pope John Paul spoke about the "social doctrine" of the Church, using this term four times within the space of a few minutes (III, §7). This usage caused some surprise and unfavorable comment (Chenu 1979, 26; Hebblethwaite 1982, 85–98). Did it signal a return to an approach that had been abandoned? The phrase "social doctrine" as used in the generation prior to Vatican II had suggested a corpus of unchanging teaching on social issues.

One of the more trenchant critics of the term is Marie-Dominique Chenu (1979, 88–89), who associates the term "social doctrine" with an outlook that is no longer acceptable—one that is deductivist and abstract, insensitive to historical and geographical variations, and particularly inappropriate in the Third World, since it imposes Western categories unrelated to local circumstances. Chenu attributes considerable significance to what might have appeared to be minor changes in terminology that had been made in the drafting of *Gaudium et Spes* during Vatican II. In that document the phrases "the social teaching of the Gospel" and "the Christian doctrine about society" were deliberately substituted for the term "social doctrine" (Chenu 1979, 87–88). Chenu notes angrily that the term "social doctrine" was reintroduced into the text of *GS* 76 "by an illegal intervention after its promulgation" (Chenu 1979, 8, 88). For him the gradual abandonment of the older term coincided with a new flexible and inductive approach. He holds that this process reached its culmination in the document *Octogesima Adveniens*, issued by Pope Paul in 1971. So he seems quite shocked that John Paul II, in his address at

Puebla, should have reintroduced the term and insisted on the importance of the Church's "social doctrine" (Chenu 1979, 13).[4]

However, one can interpret the pope's use of the term "social doctrine" in a more sympathetic light than is done by his critics. John Paul was by no means trying to reimpose on the Latin American Church a body of "social doctrine" that was to be seen as universal and timeless. He was well aware that the social teaching of the Church had undergone considerable development since the time of Leo XIII. (Indeed, this became much more evident two and a half years later when he issued the encyclical *Laborem Exercens*; as we shall see, this document combines real continuity with the past with a good deal that is quite new and unusual in Church teaching.)

When John Paul uses the term "social doctrine" he normally understands it in a rather generic sense (cf. Heckel 1980, 23). It seems clear that what he wanted to do was to "rescue" the term. On the one hand, he wanted to rescue it in the sense of bringing it back into use as a theologically respectable term. But in order to do this he had, on the other hand, to rescue it in another sense—to remove the connotations of an unchanging dogmatism. One way in which he does this is by using it as just one term that is interchangeable with a variety of other phrases that refer to the teaching that the Church has developed over the years on social issues. These other phrases included the terms "social morals" and "social thought of the Church."

Furthermore, as Heckel (1980, 21) points out, John Paul's use of the term "social doctrine" is "*discreet* and *relatively rare.*" In the first year of his pontificate he used the term mainly in the context of the Church in Latin America and in Poland. In each case there was a particular reason for doing so. Right-wing governments in South America and left-wing governments in Eastern Europe wanted to restrict the activity of the Church to a private, so-called religious domain. When the pope found himself in confrontation on social issues with such regimes, the use of the term "social doctrine" gave him a certain advantage. The word "doctrine" suggests that what is at stake is something on which the Church will not yield to pressures from an authoritarian government, since it is fundamental to the nature of the Church. The word "doctrine" also carries overtones of something unchanging and timeless, and this strengthens the impression that the Church will not yield on these issues. Another advantage in Latin America was that the word "doctrine" was a suitable one to use when the

---

[4]It may be noted in passing that Chenu's argument is weakened to some degree by the fact that Paul VI had not entirely abandoned the use of the term. He used it in *EN* 38: "Ecclesia . . . praebet . . . doctrinam socialem."

confrontation was with the "doctrines" of national security on the one hand or of a rigid Marxism on the other.

In Latin America, the pope's use of the term "social doctrine" has a further purpose. It represents his rejection of the view of some extreme exponents of liberation that the Church must at this time identify itself fully with the forces of the left. In the years after Medellín, Latin American Christians found themselves increasingly squeezed between ideologies of the right and of the left, each anxious to legitimize itself by enlisting Christian faith in support of its position. One way of escaping this dilemma was to hold that Christianity offered a "third way," neither of the left nor of the right. For some people, this "third way" was to be embodied in the Latin American version of Christian democracy. However, as a realistic political alternative, this option became less and less credible during the 1970s. The result was that a number of influential Latin American Christian thinkers strongly rejected the notion of a "third way" and became highly skeptical of the notion of a Catholic social doctrine on which it relied so heavily. Some of them said openly that committed Christians could no longer afford the luxury of standing on the sidelines; they ought to throw in their lot with the forces of the left while working within these movements to promote Christian values.

By reinstating the term "social doctrine," the pope was undoubtedly putting a large question mark over this line of argument. When he used the term in this context, he was not trying to impose on his opponents an immutable body of social dogma. His aim was rather to encourage them not to submit themselves and the Church entirely and unconditionally to an ideology of the left. He wanted them to continue to believe that the Church has a distinctive contribution to make in working out solutions to social injustices, and to do so, it should maintain a certain distance from all ideologies and all sectional interests.

This is not to say that the pope was himself endorsing the notion of the "third way" in a strictly political sense. But he would be seen as giving some encouragement to those Church leaders who felt that the best course of action was for the Church to distance itself clearly from ideologies of both the right and the left. This was, in fact, the stance adopted at the Puebla conference. The Puebla documents contain strong condemnations of three different ideologies—capitalist liberalism, Marxist collectivism, and the so-called doctrine of national security. Quoting the pope's address, the text goes on to state that the Church chooses to maintain its freedom with regard to the opposing systems. It opts "solely for the human being" and "does not need to have recourse to ideological systems." It finds its inspiration in the tenets of an authentic Christian anthropology (Puebla 542–53). This position was very much what the pope wanted. The "authentic Christian anthropology" from which it derives its inspiration is the basis for—and is indeed more or less equivalent to—Catholic "social doctrine" in Pope John Paul's sense of the term.

In speaking of this authentic Christian anthropology, the Puebla text adds the following significant words: "Christians must commit themselves to the elaboration of historical projects that meet the needs of a given moment and a given culture" (Puebla 553). By inserting this statement, the drafters of the text ensured that there would be no abandonment of the principle laid down by Paul VI in *Octogesima Adveniens*, that the solutions to social problems have to be discerned in each particular time, place, and culture. To accept the term "social doctrine," as Puebla did following John Paul II (Puebla 539), does *not* mean accepting just one universal and timeless model of how society is to be organized (cf. Puebla 472–76). I must add, however, that the drafters of the Puebla document clearly preferred the term "social teaching" to "social doctrine."

The insistence of the Puebla document that Christians must commit themselves to particular "historical projects" is especially significant, because it comes soon after quotations from the pope's opening address to the conference. The crucial quotation is to the effect that the Church opts "solely for the human being" (Puebla 551, quoting John Paul's opening address, III, §3). It would be tempting to conclude from the pope's statement that Christians can somehow opt directly for the human person, without getting involved in awkward political choices. The authors of the Puebla statement make it clear that, in their view, the pope is not to be understood in this way. Rather, the normal way in which Christians, like other people, opt for the human person is through making difficult practical choices between alternative political systems. The Christian cannot remain outside history and therefore cannot normally be "above" the actual politics of each particular time and place.

Here Puebla is adding an important point to what the pope had said. It is not exactly a corrective, since there is no reason to think that the pope would disagree with the point. But it was not the point that the pope chose to make at that time, for his concern was to insist that Christians do not have to limit themselves to the unacceptable ideologies of left or right that are proposed to them. This is one case in which Puebla made a significant contribution to the dialogue in the Church about how Christians can best work for justice. By adding this reference to "historical projects," it tried to ensure that the pope's statement would not be misunderstood or misused.

INTEGRAL HUMANISM: *REDEMPTOR HOMINIS*

A few weeks after his return to Rome from Mexico, Pope John Paul II issued his first encyclical, titled *Redemptor Hominis*, "The Redeemer of

Humankind." This was followed within two years by his second encyclical, *Dives in Misericordia*, "Rich in Mercy." These documents gave him the opportunity to outline a good deal of his vision on his own terms, without the restriction of having to relate it to the demands of a particular local situation.

Redemptor Hominis is a document of major importance, both in its own right and because it provides a background against which one can understand various other statements made by the pope. In this first encyclical he ranges over a wide area, but there is a unifying thread running through it all. The unifying vision of the pope may perhaps be summed up in two phrases from the encyclical: "In Christ and through Christ, human persons have acquired full awareness of their dignity" (*RH* 11; cf. *RH* 10), and "All routes for the Church are directed toward the human person" (*RH* 14 title). These phrases indicate that, although the encyclical is concerned, above all, with the mystery of Christ and the activity of the Church, these concerns in no way take the author into a "spiritual" or "religious" world unrelated to everyday living. Quite the contrary: the pope's concern is directed precisely toward the human person, human society, and the world we live in. He sets out to show that these secular realities are the very things on which Christ and the Church throw light, the thing about which they give hope:

> The human person in the full truth of his or her existence and personal being and also of their community and social being—in the sphere of their own family, in the sphere of society . . . and in the sphere of the whole of humankind—this person is the primary route that the Church must travel in fulfilling her mission: *the human person is the primary and fundamental way for the Church*, the way traced out by Christ himself. (*RH* 14, translation adapted)

The encyclical helps one realize that whenever the pope makes statements emphasizing the primacy of the spiritual—as he did at Puebla (III, §4) and in his address to the United Nations (§4), as well as in the encyclical itself (*RH* 11)—he is *not* reverting to an old-fashioned dualist theology that would justify an "escape" by Christians from social and political involvement. What he envisages is just the opposite: it is an integral humanism embracing all dimensions of life, including the economic, the political, the cultural, and the religious. Within this humanistic vision, "the spiritual" means, for him, those dimensions and aspects of human life that are deepest (cf. Baum 1979, 57). The Christian is called to explore whatever is found to be most profound in human experience and to be particularly concerned about such matters.

It is on the basis of such an approach that John Paul can say, "The

Church considers this concern for humankind, for their humanity, for the future of the human race on earth and therefore also for the direction of the whole of development and progress—to be an *essential* element of the Church's own mission *inextricably* linked to it" (*RH* 15, translation adapted in light of the French and Italian versions; emphasis added).

This statement is a vindication of the position adopted by the bishops at the synod of 1971. By using the words "essential," and "inextricably linked," the pope is really accepting what the synod bishops intended when they used the controversial phrase "constitutive dimension." As we saw in chapter 10, Paul VI in *Evangelii Nuntiandi* provided a sound scriptural and theological basis for the synod statement. In *Redemptor Hominis* John Paul carries this a step further. In fact, he deepens it considerably, because he grounds all action for justice and human progress in a rich integral humanism. It is a humanism that is Christological—and this not in a superficial sense in which Christ is seen as adding something on to humanity or merely rescuing the human race from sin. It is more profound than that: for the pope, it is in Christ that we learn what it really means to be human.

The humanism of John Paul II is comprehensive. He includes the economic and political dimensions, but, like Vatican II and Paul VI, he lays special stress on the cultural dimension. What is significant about his statements on culture is that there is no hint of dualism or escapism in them. One does not have any sense that he is emphasizing culture because it is easier and safer for a Church leader to talk about culture than about the more delicate and dangerous issues of economics and politics. If he speaks out strongly about culture—as indeed he does in Mexico (*AAS* 71, 206 and 208), and in his address to UNESCO (1980, 735–52)—this is because he sees people being injured and exploited in this area of culture as much as in the economic and political spheres. The cultural rights of people can be trampled on just as tragically as can their other rights. It is all part of the same process of marginalization and impoverishment against which the Church is bound to protest.

DEVELOPMENT AND MISDEVELOPMENT

Against the background of his integral humanism one can understand better the fundamental misgivings expressed by John Paul about the present state of society. People, he says, now live "increasingly in fear," afraid of a radical self-destruction (*RH* 15; cf. *DM* 11). The ordinary person lives under the constant threat of atomic warfare, and people also live under the threat of a ruthless oppression and subjugation that can deprive them of their freedom even without resort to military means

(*DM* 11). The fundamental reason for all this is that we have adopted a type of "development" that has got out of control, one that is no longer serving humanity as any genuine development ought to. What has been termed "progress" now has to be called in question. Does it really make us more human? Of course, it does, says the pope, in some respects. But, he asks, "is the human person as such developing and progressing or, on the other hand, regressing and being degraded in humanity?" (*RH* 15).[5] Clearly, the pope's own answer to that question is that in many respects modern development is destroying humanity rather than promoting real progress. He outlines three important ways in which this is happening.

First of all, the world economy is not solving the problems of starvation and malnutrition; in fact, we have in the present international world order the parable of the rich person and Lazarus writ large (*RH* 16). The institutions on which the world economic order rests—the systems that control production, trade, and finance—have proved incapable, says the pope, of "remedying the unjust social situations inherited from the past or of dealing with the urgent challenges and ethical demands of the present" (*RH* 16).

Second, modern so-called development is doing harm not only to the poorer peoples but also to those who live in the better-off countries—the very people who might have been expected to benefit most from it. The "fever of inflation and the plague of unemployment" affect them at the economic and social level while at the cultural and psychological level they experience a sense of alienation (*RH* 15). People can easily be manipulated by political and economic means and also by the communications media. In fact, we are running the risk of being enslaved by the very products we have made (*RH* 16). Furthermore, the massive social injustice that now exists in the world is giving rise to remorse and guilt in those who live in wealth and plenty (*DM* 11).

There is a third major failure of modern development, one that affects the whole world, rich and poor alike. The world economy today depends on activities and systems that are "depleting the earth's resources of raw materials and energy at an ever-increasing rate and putting intolerable pressures on the geo-physical environment" (*RH* 16). Here the pope is adverting to environmental issues—the poisoning of air, water, and land—and to the risk that humans will exhaust the resources of energy and raw materials on which all modern production is based.

The pope's view is that the cumulative effect of all these major inadequacies of modern development is the continual expansion of zones of grinding poverty, accompanied by anguish, frustration, and bitterness.

---

[5]The Vatican translation reads as follows: "Is man, as man, developing and progressing or is he regressing and being degraded in his humanity?"

This is aggravated by the extravagance and wastefulness of the people of the privileged classes and nations that take place before the eyes of the poor. To make matters worse, the poorer nations are being offered armaments to serve nationalistic, imperialistic, or neocolonial purposes rather than being given the food and cultural aid that could be of real benefit to them. The arms race squanders resources that could have been used to overcome poverty (*RH* 16).

These very strong criticisms of the modern process of development are in marked contrast to the optimism displayed by John XXIII and Vatican II. It is clear that John Paul II wants a radical restructuring of our world order. And he is well aware that this will be no easy task:

> There is need for brave and creative initiatives. . . . The task is not impossible. . . . The only way forward is transformation of the structures of economic life. But this road is so difficult that it requires a real conversion of mind, will, and heart. The task calls for the strong commitment of individuals and peoples who are both free and in solidarity with each other. (*RH* 16)

Here the pope is taking it for granted that moral conversion is no substitute for structural reform of society. But at the same time he is insisting that such structural changes cannot be expected to take place without the free cooperation of morally committed people.

By what means can a more genuinely human type of development be brought about? The pope is not specific with regard to details, but his general proposal is clear. Economic progress must be *planned*. The plan or program must be one that takes account of each person and of all people, one that is universal and based on the solidarity of all. It must, above all, ensure that economic growth does not damage society through becoming the highest value; economic growth must rather be at the service of people (*RH* 16). This proposal for a planned global economy follows in the line of Paul VI's *Populorum Progressio* but makes it somewhat more explicit (cf. Cosmao 1979b, 24–25).

The pope goes on to write movingly about human rights. He insists that peace comes down to a respect for the rights of people. The real test of whether justice is present in a given situation is whether human rights are respected in that situation (*RH* 17). He refers here to the United Nations Declaration of Human Rights. A few months later, in his address to the United Nations, he called this document "a milestone on the long and difficult path of the human race . . . the path of the moral progress of humanity" (§7). In this same address he gave a long list of human rights (§13; cf. Mich 2011, 151), and he invoked what he called "the humanistic criterion" as the proper standard for evaluating various systems:

The fundamental criterion for comparing social, economic and political systems . . . must be . . . *the humanistic criterion*, namely the measure in which each system is really capable of reducing, restraining and eliminating as far as possible the various forms of exploitation of man and of ensuring for him, through work, not only the just distribution of the indispensable material goods, but also a participation, in keeping with his dignity, in the whole process of production and in the social life that grows up around that process. (§17)

The humanistic vision that pervades *Redemptor Hominis* and underlies the pope's addresses is filled out and rounded off by some deeply moving passages in *Dives in Misericordia*. There he notes how easily and often it happens that human actions that are "undertaken in the name of justice" can in practice "deviate from justice itself" by becoming distorted through spite, hatred, and cruelty (*DM* 12). He strongly resists the idea that justice and mercy are opposed to each other. Mercy and forgiveness, he maintains, do not "cancel out the obligations of justice"; rather, mercy, when understood properly, is seen to be "the most profound source of justice" (*DM* 14). Furthermore, mercy is not to be seen as something that leaves a distance between the benefactor and the recipient and creates a relationship that is one-sided. On the contrary, mercy includes the reciprocity of justice. Indeed, it even deepens this mutuality, because it brings about an encounter between people that is not confined to external goods but is focused directly on the value of the persons involved; it enables them to meet in reciprocal tenderness and sensitivity (*DM* 14).

This teaching of Pope John Paul about mercy and forgiveness can go a long way toward allaying the fears and reservations experienced by some religious people in relation to an option for the poor. The misgivings of such people arise when they see how this phrase is invoked by certain angry or overenthusiastic activists to justify a strident, combative attitude toward all authorities, toward ordinary "respectable" people—and even at times toward anybody who ventures to disagree with them! The pope's insistence on the importance of mercy, as well as justice, does not, by any means, result in a watering down of the commitment of the Church to an option for the poor. But it does invite us to think about the kind of world we would like to bring about through such an option and also to reflect on what would be the most effective and humane strategy for bringing such a world into existence. If gentleness and human sensitivity are to characterize the world we are working for, then they must also be present in the manner in which we seek to attain it.

THE BRAZIL ADDRESSES

Of the various pastoral visits made by John Paul II to different parts of the world, by far the most significant, from the point of view of an option for the poor, was his first trip to Brazil. It lasted twelve days—from June 30 to July 11, 1980. During that time he gave many addresses, several of which made valuable contributions to the Church's social teaching. But perhaps more important than the content of his talks was the overall impression the pope gave, which was that of being broadly in solidarity with the main body of Brazilian bishops in their commitment to placing the Church on the side of the poor and oppressed.

John Paul was well aware that the government would have liked to use his visit to convey the impression that the Brazilian bishops were being admonished for their outspoken criticism of the regime. So he made his position clear from the start. On the first day of his visit he addressed the president of Brazil. Having outlined his humanistic vision (§4), he went on at once to state that the Church advocates "reforms that aim at a more just society" (§5 and §6), and he insisted on the importance of respect for human rights. That same day, in an address to the diplomatic corps, he took up this theme again. He made an obvious reference to the "doctrine of national security" when he said that while each country has the duty of preserving its internal peace and security, it must "earn" this peace by ensuring the common good of everybody and by respecting human rights. He went on to insist that the Church "will constantly endeavor to recall concern for 'the poor,' for those who are underprivileged in some way" (*AAS* 72, 835).

In a subtle way the pope took issue with another aspect of the national security ideology when he spoke to Brazilian cultural leaders the following day at Rio de Janeiro. Stressing the importance of culture in the process of humanization, he went on to insist that culture must not be imposed on people; there must be respect for their freedom (§1, §2). This was a challenge to the view of those right-wing Latin American ideologues who maintained that culture and, indeed, religion are integral and vital parts of the system to be imposed on all in the interests of the security of the state.

Two of the major addresses given by the pope in Brazil were the talk he gave at Rio (*AAS* 858–73) to 150 members of CELAM (the Latin American Conference of Bishops) and his speech at Fortaleza to the bishops of Brazil (*AAS* 944–60). There are a number of similarities between the two talks. In each case there is generous approval for the general direction taken by the bishops, combined with some expressions of the need to avoid certain dangers. The tone of his CELAM speech is distinctly warmer than that of his opening address at Puebla eighteen months previously. He makes it quite clear that he has given wholehearted approval to the Puebla document, after some modifications had been made to parts of the text in the interests of "accuracy" (III, §1).[6] Referring to Puebla he says, "You rightly called for a preferential option for the poor, not an exclusive nor excluding one" (III, §7). In speaking to the Brazilian bishops he compliments them very warmly on their commitment in matters of poverty; he says it gives him joy to see their witness to poverty and simplicity and their insertion in the midst of their people (§6). A little later he clarifies his understanding of the meaning of the term "option for the poor":

> You know that the preferential option for the poor, forcefully proclaimed at Puebla, is not an invitation to exclusivism, and would not justify a bishop's refusal to proclaim the Word of conversion and salvation to this or that group of persons on the pretext that they are not poor ... because it is his duty to proclaim the *whole* Gospel to *all* people, that *everyone* should be "poor in spirit." But it is a call to a special solidarity with the humble and the weak, with those who are suffering and weeping, who are humiliated and left on the fringes of life and society, in order to help them to realize ever more fully their own dignity as human persons and children of God. (§6.9)

In various addresses—to CELAM (II, §8), to the Brazilian bishops (§6.9), to the shanty dwellers of Vidigal in Rio de Janeiro (§5), and to the workers of São Paulo (§4)—the pope insisted that the Church is completely opposed to class struggle. The aim of the Church is not to exacerbate divisions in society but to heal them; so it refuses to condone violence or to identify itself with the interests and ideology of any one group or class. In his CELAM address he ruled out not merely the Marxist concept of class warfare but also the use of a Marxist analysis; but in doing so he carefully made use of the Puebla text on this question, without adding to it (III, §8). While stressing the need for effective structural reforms, he maintained in several addresses that these must be introduced prudently and peacefully, and therefore in a gradual and progressive way (e.g., to São Paulo workers, §4; to diplomatic corps, *AAS* 835; at Vidigal, §5; to the president, §5).

In his address to workers in the industrial city of São Paulo, Pope John Paul spoke strongly and movingly about the plight of the urban poor and

---

[6]The original Spanish text is "*tras precisar algunos conceptos*." For a list of the modifications that were made to the Puebla text (and an angry reaction to these changes), see *Esperance des pauvres*.

the need to transform the city into a more human place. He referred to overcrowding and the frustration to which it gives rise. He also spoke about the pollution of the environment—a topic that was particularly relevant and urgent in view of the scandalous pollution conditions in that city (§8). Just before he delivered this address, the pope had listened to a trade union activist speak in public about the economic and political repression of workers in Brazil (cf. Kirby 1980, 363). Part of the pope's response to this cry was a firm insistence on the right of workers to form trade unions (§7). This, of course, is a right that had been affirmed by the Church as far back as the time of Leo XIII. But for John Paul to reaffirm it publicly in an address to workers in São Paulo, where in the previous months workers had been harassed, arrested, and even shot for trying to exercise that right, was a clear challenge to the government. It also represented firm support for Cardinal Arns who had helped the workers of São Paulo during the strikes in which they claimed their rights.

In Recife, the city where Helder Camara was archbishop, the pope spoke in an equally challenging way on the question of the ownership and use of land: "The land is a gift of God, a gift that God gives to all human beings, men and women. . . . It is not lawful, therefore . . . to use that gift in such a way that its benefits accrue to only a few, leaving the others, the vast majority, excluded" (§4, my translation).

Once again, the content of the pope's statement was by no means startlingly new; it was the context that made all the difference. He was speaking to exploited rural workers, people who were being impoverished through the loss of their title to the land, which they had considered their own, or people who were being deprived of work or of a living wage. In this situation the pope's address was a forceful protest against current abuses. It was also a strong vindication of the stand taken by Helder Camara, whom the pope pointedly called "brother of the poor and my brother" (*AAS* 924).

THE POOR AND THE "POOR IN SPIRIT"

A very striking witness by the pope to his concern for the poor and marginalized in Brazilian society was his visit to the favela, or shantytown, of Vidigal outside Rio de Janeiro. He told the people there that what he had to say to them was also addressed to all those in Brazil who live in similar conditions (§1, *AAS* 853). And what he offered them was a reflection on the text "Blessed are the poor in spirit." The commentary of the pope on this text is of particular importance for this study of the option for the poor. So I propose to look closely at this address and to relate it to two other talks given by the pope in similar situations and on the same theme; one of the other two talks was given five days later in the favela of Alagados, near Salvador da Bahia in Brazil, and one was given several months later to the shanty dwellers of the Tondo area outside Manila in the Philippines.

In the first of these three addresses the pope notes that the Church in Brazil wishes to be the Church of the poor; so he proposes to clarify what is meant by "the poor in spirit" and to identify who these people are. He says that they are those who are open to God, ready to receive God's gifts, aware that they have received everything from God (§2). The "poor in spirit" are merciful and generous, for to be "poor in spirit" means to be open to others—to God and to one's neighbors. Those who are not poor in spirit are closed to God and to other people; they are merciless (§3). Wealthy people are "poor in spirit," says the pope, when they constantly give themselves and serve others in proportion to their riches (§4).

This last statement, taken on its own, could be used to justify a highly spiritualized notion of poverty of spirit that would have no connection with the presence or absence of wealth or with its use or abuse. The rich could then patronize the poor, for instance, by giving them alms while leaving intact the structures in society that leave the poor trapped in poverty. But the pope makes his statement here in a context where he is trying very hard to show the inadequacy of such an approach. He makes it clear that, for him, being open to God ("poor in spirit") is intimately linked to working for structural change in society.

He does this by pointing out that the first beatitude, while addressed by the Church today to everybody, has, in fact, something different to say to each of three different categories of people. First, to those who live in want, it says that they are very close to God and that they must maintain their human dignity and their openness to others. Second, to those who are somewhat better off it says, "Do not close yourself off in yourselves. Think of those who are more poor . . . share with them . . . in a systematic way." Third, to those who are very wealthy, the Church of the poor says, "Do you not feel remorse of conscience because of your riches and abundance? . . . If you have a lot . . . you must give a lot. And you must think about how to give—how to organize socioeconomic life . . . in such a way that it will tend to bring about equality between people, rather than putting a yawning gap between them" (§4, my translation).

There are two very important points to note in this teaching. First, being "poor in spirit," though it is understood by him in a religious sense, is nevertheless firmly linked to social justice, because it means being open not only to God but also to other people. Second, if one belongs to the very wealthy group in society, then being open to others is not simply a matter of giving alms, however generously; it means transforming the unjust structures of society.

In the next section of his address the pope develops this point more explicitly when he makes a direct appeal on behalf of the Church of the poor to those who make the decisions that affect society and the world:

> Do all you can, especially you who have decision-making powers, you on whom the situation of the world depends, do everything to make the life of every person in your country more human, more worthy of the human person.
>
> Do all you can to ensure the disappearance, at least gradually, of that yawning gap which divides the few "excessively rich" from the great masses of the poor, the people who live in grinding poverty. (§5, my translation)

This eloquent appeal is addressed to the powerful, the decision makers. It is up to them to change the structures of society—a point he also stressed in his address to São Paulo workers: "This is especially the duty of those who hold power, whether economic or political, in society" (*AAS* 890, §4). Although the task is urgent, the pope recognizes that it may take time to bring about the necessary radical changes; so he asks that these decision makers ensure that the wide gap between rich and poor disappears "at least gradually."

What then does the pope have to say about economic poverty? On this point the main thrust of the Vidigal address may be summed up briefly. First, poverty is largely the result of injustice, structural injustice; therefore, there is urgent need for a transformation of the structures that sustain it. In addition, the main responsibility for bringing about these radical changes falls on the rich and powerful, since it is they who are in a position to make the decisions that really matter, they on whom the future depends.

Without playing down the importance of the first of these two points (namely, the need for structural change), I want to look particularly at the second point. According to this address the crucial agents of change are to be those who hold wealth and power in society. What are the implications of this for the poor and for a Church that seeks to be the Church of the poor? If change is to be brought about mainly by the rich, what then does the pope, in the name of the Church, have to say to the poor?

At Vidigal the pope tells the poor (1) that they are close to God; (2) that they must "do everything that is lawful to ensure for themselves and their families all that is required for life and upkeep"; and (3) that they must maintain their human dignity and continue to have that magnanimity, openness of heart, and availability to others that characterize the "poor in spirit" (§4, my translation).

The first and third points here offer some spiritual consolation to the poor, but from a practical point of view the crucial point is the second one. What does it mean to tell the poor to do everything that is lawful to support themselves? Does it, in effect, mean telling them *not* to do anything *unlawful*? Certainly, there is no indication here that the pope is encouraging the poor to organize themselves politically in order to bring about change. It must be admitted that anybody relying on this Vidigal address for guidelines about how to inspire the poor would find a notable gap at this point.

Pope John Paul may have sensed this or even been advised about it by some of the Brazilian bishops. But whatever the reason, he added some important points to what he had to say to the poor when he spoke a few days later to the shanty dwellers at Favela dos Alagados, near Salvador da Bahia. In this address he notes that the poor are actively involved in shaping their own destiny and lives. Then he says, "God grant that there may be many of us to offer you unselfish cooperation in order that you may free yourselves from everything that in a certain way enslaves you, but with full respect for what you are and for your right to be the prime authors of your human advancement" (*L'Osservatore Romano*, July 9, 1980, §2).

The important point here is the pope's emphasis on the fact that the poor themselves are to be the main agents in bringing about their human development. Others are to see themselves not as making the changes in society needed by the poor but simply as cooperating with the poor—with full respect for the right of the poor to take primary responsibility for their own lives. And in a humble and touching way the pope indicates that he himself would like to be one of those who cooperate with the poor.

John Paul goes even further. He encourages the poor to struggle to overcome their poverty: "You must struggle for life, do everything to improve the conditions in which you live; to do so is a sacred duty, because it is also the will of God. Do not say that it is God's will that you remain in a condition of poverty, disease, unhealthy housing, that is contrary in many ways to your dignity as human persons. Do not say, 'It is God who wills it'" (§3, translation emended).

In this passage the pope is addressing himself to the sense of apathy that helps keep the poor in a state of poverty. He is aware that this apathy is given a religious legitimation—poverty is accepted as being the will of God. John Paul challenges this assumption, insisting that what God wants is not that the poor stay poor but that they struggle to escape poverty. He goes on to note that strong action is required not only by the poor themselves but also by others; but he insists that the prime movers have to be the victims of poverty themselves (§3).

It is quite significant that when speaking to the poor, the pope should encourage them to *struggle*. He does not, of course, say they should engage in a class struggle; his phrase is "struggle for life." And he clarifies what he has in mind by giving some examples: "To wish to overcome the poor conditions, to help one another to find—together—better times, not to wait for everything from outside, but to begin to do all that is possible, to try to educate oneself in order to have greater possibilities of improvement: these are some important steps along your way" (§3).

There is a notable difference in emphasis between what the pope had to say to the poor in this address and what he had said at Vidigal. It is as though he had become convinced (perhaps during the Brazilian trip itself) that it is not enough to encourage the rich, the powerful decision makers, to initiate and bring about social change. The Church must also encourage the poor to see themselves as the primary agents of change.

This new approach was reiterated and carried a little further by Pope John Paul in his address to the shanty dwellers of Tondo in the Philippines early the next year. The topic chosen by the pope for his address there was the same as that at Vidigal—the beatitude "Blessed are the poor in spirit." Much of what he had to say was an echo of the earlier talk. But when he speaks to the poor on this occasion about what the beatitude says to them, he includes the fact that "their inviolable human rights must be preserved and protected" (Tondo §5). This is not, of course, the first time the pope had spoken of the rights of the poor. But here he is speaking directly *to* the poor, assuring them that the beatitudes tell them of their rights.

A little later the pope said, "I encourage you, the people of Tondo, and all the People of God in the Philippines, to exercise your individual and corporate responsibility for increasing catechetical instruction as you endeavor to implement fully the social teachings of the Church" (§6).

This is a very subtle passage. Three points may be noted. First, the pope is encouraging the poor themselves to work for social justice—and this is carefully expressed as the implementing of the social teaching of the Church. Second, though addressed specifically to the poor people of Tondo, it is also directed to all the Christians in the Philippines; so there is nothing exclusive in this encouragement to the poor. Third, the pope seems to be encouraging a continuance of the process of consciousness raising, but he expresses this by using the term "catechetical instruction," which is both wider in scope and less radical in tone than the word "conscientization." Since the Philippines was seen as "a Catholic country," the Filipino government could scarcely object to such a traditional Church phrase. Furthermore, much of the work of raising poor people's awareness and encouraging them to work for justice was, in fact, being carried out by catechists—and many of these Church workers had been murdered by supporters of the corrupt regime; so the reference to "catechetical instruction" could be seen as a defense of these committed Christians and perhaps even a warning to the government.

In what it has to say to the poor, the Tondo speech is closer to the second of the Brazilian shantytown addresses (the one at Alagados) than to the one at Vidigal. John Paul tells the Tondo people that "they themselves can achieve much if they pool their skills and talents, and especially their determination to be the artisans of their own progress and development" (§5). Like the address at Alagados, this goes notably further than the vague words of consolation offered at Vidigal. It is an encouragement to the poor to organize themselves, to take charge of their own destiny. They do not have to wait for the rich, "the decision makers," to initiate social change, for they themselves can become decision makers. The pope tells the poor of Tondo and Alagados that they find "strength in human solidarity" (Tondo §5; cf. Alagados §2). One may speculate that some of what the pope said later in his encyclical *Laborem Exercens* came out of what he experienced, and reflected on, in the shantytowns of Brazil and the Philippines. Certainly, the new and more active encouragement to the poor and the reference to their "solidarity" with each other are an anticipation of an important theme of the new social encyclical.

* * *

SUMMARY

In January 1979 John Paul II went to Mexico and faced his first big challenge in the area of social justice. He played a key role in the conference of Latin American bishops at Puebla. The big issue was whether the conference would reaffirm the basic thrust of Medellín. Despite opposition, it eventually did so. The more radical bishops at Puebla had to make some compromises on doctrinal topics, but there was no drawing back from the options taken at Medellín. The final document of Puebla has one section titled "A Preferential Option for the Poor." The Puebla document as a whole is a consensus statement in which Paul VI's *Evangelii Nuntiandi* and the Mexican addresses of John Paul II provided the basis for agreement on the more divisive questions, above all the issue of whether the Church should commit itself to justice, liberation, and the poor.

The pope encouraged the Latin American Church to continue to take a strong prophetic stance on questions of injustice, but he also noted the danger of seeing Christ as a political revolutionary. His strong statements about poverty and oppression showed his special concern for the poor. But it was only in the following year, during his visit to Brazil, that he openly approved and used the controversial phrase "a preferential but not exclusive option for the poor." The pope used the term "social doctrine," not in the sense of a timeless blueprint for society but as a body of beliefs and values that can and should be respected in a variety of different societies.

In his first two encyclicals and his address to the United Nations, John Paul put forward his own vision of what it means to be human, of the place of Christ in this, and of the mission of the Church. It is a vision of integral humanism in which the spiritual is not opposed to the material, in which social justice is of major importance, and in which mercy is essential—but not as a substitute for justice. For the pope, respect for human rights is the test of whether a society is truly just. He challenged and criticized in a radical way the current model of development—seeing it as a cause of injustice, poverty, alienation, destruction of traditional cultures, and ecological disaster.

In Brazil, Mexico, and the Philippines, the pope addressed himself to the issue of the role of the poor in bringing about change in society. He indicated that they are to be the main agents of their own advancement, struggling together to improve their conditions.

QUESTIONS FOR REVIEW

1. *Was Puebla a step forward or a step backward from Medellín?*
2. *Outline the gradual development in the pope's teaching about the poor over the course of his visits to Latin America in 1979 and 1980.*
3. *Examine different understandings of the phrase "social doctrine."*
4. *What does it mean to say that John Paul in his first two encyclicals put forward a vision of integral humanism?*

QUESTION FOR REFLECTION

1. *What have the Vatican and the Latin American Church learned from each other? What do they still have to learn from each other?*

ISSUE FOR FURTHER STUDY

1. *The emergence of Third World theology as something much wider than a liberation theology rooted in Latin America. Read EATWOT 1980; Ellis and Maduro 1989.*

12

An Encyclical on Work and Solidarity

Pope John Paul issued the encyclical *Laborem Exercens*, called in English "On Human Labor" or "On Human Work," to commemorate the ninetieth anniversary of Leo XIII's *Rerum Novarum*.[1] It was to have been issued on May 15, 1981, but its publication was delayed by four months as a result of the attempt on the pope's life. It is a document of major importance, a worthy successor to the encyclical it commemorates, and to the other great social encyclicals. I shall make some general remarks about the approach and contribution of this new encyclical; then I examine two major themes of the encyclical that are especially relevant to the "option for the poor": the concept of the indirect employer and the teaching on the nature of solidarity. I leave to chapter 14 the third important theme of the encyclical—the issue of women and work.

SOCIAL TEACHING

Laborem Exercens represents a new style of social teaching. What John Paul offers us here is a painstaking and profound reflection on the nature of human work and the organization of economic life. This is more than "teaching" in the usual ecclesiastical sense of propounding truths. It is much more like teaching in the ordinary sense of the word, namely, explaining and helping people understand why things are the way they are—and how they might be changed. In adopting this approach, the pope goes a long way toward resolving the doubts that had arisen in relation to the very notion of a "social teaching" of the Church. His approach is "radical" in the literal sense: it goes to the root of the issues rather than

---

[1]Patricia Lamoureux (2005, 390–93) provides a helpful and interesting account of the political and ecclesiastical context in which the encyclical was written and appeared as well as the elements of John Paul's own life experience and philosophical outlook that he brought to its writing.

simply repeating or adapting traditional formulas. Furthermore, he makes a serious effort to integrate the more traditional Catholic approach that emphasizes natural law with a biblical and theological approach (cf. Coleman 2005, 529). For instance, his analysis of the nature of work begins with his reflection on texts from the book of Genesis. He maintains that humans are the image of God partly though the mandate to subdue the Earth (*LE* 4).

John Paul believes that there are some general truths and values that underlie the particular teachings on social issues put forward by the Church over the years. Two of these underlying truths stand out in the encyclical. The first is that "the basis for determining the value of human work is not primarily the kind of work being done but the fact that the one who is doing it is a person" (*LE* 6). Therefore, human labor may not be treated simply as a tool in the process of production and an item to be sold to those who control the means of production (*LE* 7, 8). A second key point is that "capital" is simply an instrument that is to be at the service of the human person, the worker. There is no opposition, in principle, between capital and labor, because what we call "capital" is really the cumulative result of labor (*LE* 12). The present opposition between capital and labor is the result of a wrong direction taken by Western society in the last century (*LE* 13).

By using these key points the pope is able to bring out why the Church insisted on certain things in its social teaching in the past (e.g., *LE* 12, 14, 15, 16). John Paul can rightly claim that his reflections are "in organic connection with the whole tradition" of the Church's social teaching and activity (*LE* 2). This organic unity can be seen despite the fact that the pope does not strive for a purely verbal coherence between what he is saying and what was said by his predecessors. In fact, the continuity with the past is clearer because it is not forced; the pope resists the temptation to repeat verbatim the social teaching of earlier documents. It is remarkable that *Laborem Exercens*, which was issued to commemorate the ninetieth anniversary of *Rerum Novarum*, does not have a single footnote reference to that encyclical, and the references to the other social encyclicals are sparse.

Organic unity allows for notable differences in details and priorities between the social teaching of earlier encyclicals and that of *Laborem Exercens*. It is clear that the attitude of John Paul toward socialism is significantly different from that of his predecessors. The earlier social encyclicals had critical things to say both about capitalism and about socialism, but they almost invariably showed a preference for the Western ideal of "free enterprise." Pope John Paul is more evenhanded in his approach. There is great objectivity—indeed an almost ruthless honesty—in the way in which his philosophical and historical analysis shows up the weaknesses of the socioeconomic models of society of both East and West (e.g., *LE* 7, 8, 11, 14).

Gregory Baum has put forward a strong case for saying that in *Laborem Exercens* John Paul is advocating a modified version of socialism (Baum 1981a, 4; Baum 1982, 55–56, 80–86). That case is more difficult to sustain in the light of the third social encyclical, *Centesimus Annus*, issued by Pope John Paul ten years later. But the pope's criticism of capitalism is trenchant. *Laborem Exercens* contributes notably to a process that has been accurately described in these words by a left-wing writer: "The Catholic Church is consciously, though slowly and deliberately, disassociating itself from capitalism and its institutions as presently structured" (Marzani 1982, 27).

Pope John Paul's reservations about the capitalist order are at least as serious as those of Pius XI in *Quadragesimo Anno*. The overall impression given by his approach is that he does not see it as part of his task to favor one of the existing systems over another, but rather to show where the different systems have gone wrong in relation to the values that ought to be promoted by an adequate socioeconomic order (e.g., *LE* 8, 13–19). He does not do this in a moralizing way but by reference to the structural inadequacies of each system, understood in the light of their historical development.

The presupposition of *Laborem Exercens* is that there may be a variety of quite different ways in which a structurally just society could take shape. The social teaching of the Church, according to this view, provides some basic principles by which any given society could be evaluated, but it does not opt for any particular socioeconomic order as *the* correct one (see *LE* 11, 13, 14). As Jan Schotte (1982b, 31) says, "The pope is cautiously not suggesting any concrete formula," and "he does not propose a 'third way' between liberal capitalism and Marxism. . . . In the debate between capitalism and communism, he offers elements for a critique of both systems" (Schotte 1982b, 27).

THE INDIRECT EMPLOYER

Moving on from these rather general reflections on the contribution of *Laborem Exercens*, we can now look closely at one of the more striking and effective elements in the teaching of the encyclical—the concept of the "indirect employer." The importance of this term lies in the fact that it acts as a bridge, leading the reader from an understanding of injustice in terms of a one-to-one relationship (which is easily grasped) to an understanding of structural injustice (a concept that many people find difficult to comprehend).

If an employer refuses to pay a worker a living wage, that would seem at first sight to be an obvious case of one-to-one injustice. But what if the situation is such that it is economically impossible for the employer to pay a just wage? Many employers are trapped in an economic system that does not enable them to pay their workers properly; if they did so, their products would be priced out of the market. The encyclical notes how this kind of situation arises particularly in the poor countries of "the South":

> The gap between most of the richest countries and the poorest ones ... is increasing more and more, to the detriment, obviously, of the poor countries. Evidently this must have an effect on local labor policy and on the worker's situation in the economically disadvantaged societies. Finding themselves in a system thus conditioned, direct employers fix working conditions below the objective requirements of the workers. (*LE* 17)

The poor countries are not the only places where conditions hinder or prevent the payment of an objectively just wage. There are sectors of the economy in practically all countries where this happens. It is most likely to arise in any situation where workers do not have an opportunity to become highly organized, for instance, where there are migrant workers or part-time women workers doing menial work, or in that rapidly growing sector called "the black economy," where governmental and trade union controls are evaded.

The workers in these situations are undoubtedly the victims of injustice. But the person who is employing them may not be to blame for the evil or may be only partly to blame. Who else may be held responsible for the injustice? To answer that question the pope introduces a distinction between what he calls the "direct" employer, the employer in the usual sense of the word, and the "indirect" employer. The latter term he explains as follows: "We must understand as the indirect employer many different factors, other than the direct employer, that exercise a determining influence on the shaping both of the work contract and, consequently, of just or unjust relationships in the field of human labor" (*LE* 16).

The encyclical goes on to mention some of these determining factors—but only in rather general terms. The state is mentioned, and later on there is reference to those ministries or public departments within the state that make decisions affecting workers or the rights of workers (*LE* 17). The pope also mentions "various social institutions" set up for the purpose of safeguarding workers' rights (*LE* 17). These would presumably include such agencies as trade unions, farmers' organizations, and employers' associations. Voluntary agencies concerned with justice in the economic and social sphere could also be covered, as well as some political parties.

However, the pope insists that his idea of the indirect employer is not adequately understood if it is limited to agencies *within* any particular state. Account must also be taken of the "links between individual States," which, he says, "create mutual dependence," and this dependence "can easily become an occasion for various forms of exploitation or injustice and as a result influence the labor policy of individual States; and finally it can influence the individual worker" (*LE* 17). The pope goes on to spell out what this involves: the policy and practices of the highly industrialized countries and of transnational corporations cause the national income of poor countries to remain low, and this is directly related to the unjust wages paid by employers to individual workers in these countries—because in the poorer parts of the world there is simply not enough money to enable workers to get a just wage (*LE* 17).[2]

To illustrate the kind of situation the pope is referring to, one might cite the international beef trade or the sugar industry. Farming agencies in Western countries put pressure on their governments to protect their interests by restricting the entry of beef from Botswana, Brazil, or Argentina. Similarly, the entry of cane sugar from the Caribbean is limited in some Western countries because of pressures from both industrial and farming agencies. The result, of course, is that the price of these primary products is lowered to an unacceptable level in the rest of the world market. What the pope is saying, in effect, is that Western farmers, factory owners, and workers in the beef and sugar industries are among the "indirect employers" of the cattle herders and sugarcane cutters of the non-Western nations. The Westerners use their protective associations and trade unions to lobby for the restrictive policies that are partly responsible for the unjust wages paid to workers in the South. By using the phrase the "indirect employer," the pope has succeeded in finding a vivid way of expressing the reality of that responsibility—and the fact that it may not be shirked on the plea that such matters are the concern of governments or international bodies.

If the concept of the "indirect employer" is taken seriously, it provides the basis for an answer to the objection that the pope is unrealistic in this encyclical. It is all too easy to accept that it is utopian of the pope to suggest that disabled people have a right to employment (*LE* 22). Again, it is easy to assume that when he speaks (*LE* 19) about the right of workers to a vacation or the right of the old and the sick to social welfare benefits, he could scarcely be taking account of the reality of the poor non-Western countries. But what he says about the "indirect employer" is a clear challenge to all of us—especially to those of us in the North—to create a world

---

[2]Schotte (1982b, 30) makes the point that transnational enterprises should be seen both as direct and indirect employers.

in which such apparently unrealistic ideas can in fact be realized universally. It is not unrealistic to envisage employment for most handicapped people, or a family wage and vacation for workers in the developing countries, or adequate maternity leave for all mothers. All of these things are attainable if a sufficient number of people are prepared to pay the price. One part of the price is indicated—but tactfully understated—by the pope when he says, "These changes . . . will very probably involve a reduction or a less rapid increase in material well-being for the more developed countries" (*LE* 1). There must, of course, be other changes as well—notably a coordinated series of plans and education programs aimed at bringing about a truly just international order (*LE* 1, 17, 18). But the crucial factor remains the willingness of people to submit to the sacrifices required by such programs and their readiness to change their lifestyles accordingly.

To sum up this section: the introduction of the term the "indirect employer" helps one to have a better understanding of what an "option for the poor" implies and of why such an option should be made. What it implies is a dedicated and consistent effort to disentangle oneself from the unjust structures, practices, and traditions that help keep the poor in poverty; it also involves a serious commitment to building alternatives that will be just and truly human. The reason why it should be done is that we cannot evade responsibility for the injustices that mark our world. Almost everybody has some degree of complicity in these injustices—the well-off who protect their own interests at the cost of the poor, and the poor themselves who often remain sunk in apathy.

POVERTY AND IMPOVERISHMENT

The teaching of *Laborem Exercens* about the "indirect employer" helps to bring home an important fact about poverty in today's world: it is generally not just an unfortunate reality, attributable to the lack of the bounty of nature, or even to laziness. It is more likely to be the result of injustice. This point has been emphasized by Third World theologians, who distinguish between poverty and impoverishment (e.g., EATWOT 1980, 127–33). Poverty is a state or condition that can, at times, be the result of misfortune—something that just happens to people. But the word "impoverishment," as used by these theologians, connotes a deliberate action. To impoverish nations or people is to inflict poverty on them.

Studies have helped bring out the fact that the misdevelopment and poverty of many or most of the poorer countries are due less to nature than to human intervention. They are largely the result of unjust actions in the past and present—mainly the actions of people in the wealthier countries—though now, increasingly, a small group of collaborators in the poorer countries must also be held responsible (cf. Stavrianos 1981; Elliott 1975). One must conclude that a crucial element in an option for the poor is a commitment to ensure that one is not guilty of complicity in the impoverishment of vulnerable individuals, groups, or whole countries.

To be a Christian today is to be called to work for justice in society, and an elementary (though difficult) part of this is to stop being unjust, to disentangle oneself from unjust structures for which one is partly responsible. It is true, of course, that wealthy people may become open to God today as in the past. But as the pope pointed out in his address in the Brazilian shantytown of Vidigal, such openness involves a call to dismantle unjust structures. The situation of many rich people and of practically all rich nations today may be compared to that of the wealthy tax collector Zaccheus (Luke 19:1–10). His turning to Jesus involved a call to make recompense for the injustice he had practiced in the past. Today, too, the call to openness to God is at the same time a call to moral conversion, to renunciation of the fruits of injustice. No exegesis of scripture should be allowed to obscure this basic reality.

To introduce a sharp distinction between material poverty and poverty of spirit is to invite a good deal of confusion into the discussion about the appropriate stance for the Church and the Christian in the face of poverty in the world today. Some of those who are reluctant to accept the notion of an option for the poor maintain that a wealthy person may be spiritually poor, in the sense of being open to God. Other people use the same kind of language but with an exactly opposite meaning: they say that the rich are spiritually poor in the sense that they are lacking in spiritual riches; in others words, they are selfish, lonely, alienated from God and from other people. Some Church people use this kind of language to justify the work they are doing. They see themselves as helping the spiritually poor when they educate the children of the rich or provide medical services for the wealthy. This, they argue, is just as important for the Church as service of those who are materially poor. The effect of this use of language is to deprive the notion of an option for the poor of any effective meaning, since everybody can be seen as poor in some respect.

The main problem here is a rather misleading use of language, which may or may not be deliberate. Perhaps it will be helpful at this point if I try to describe the situation of rich and poor in our world in a way that avoids a dualist opposition between material and spiritual poverty. In doing so I shall rely largely on the kind of integral humanistic vision that is expounded so well by Pope John Paul in his first two encyclicals and on the concept of "the indirect employer" found in *Laborem Exercens*, as well as on the list of the qualities of poor people given by the pope in his addresses in the shantytowns of Brazil and the Philippines. Such a description might take this form:

In general the people at the bottom of society are being impoverished by the way in which our world is structured. This impoverishment is both material and spiritual (if one must use these unduly polarized terms): the poor are deprived of adequate food and housing; they are not allowed to participate in decision making that affects them; they are despised because of their language, or accent, or customs; they are deprived of education and of the leisure and opportunity to cultivate the things of the spirit. Nevertheless, their humanity resists this multiple oppression; and to a surprising degree many of the poorest people succeed in finding ways of being deeply human and Christian—in spite of all the handicaps imposed on them.

On the other hand, the interests of the rich and powerful are served by the way in which our world is structured. The system offers them advantages of many kinds, both material and in the area of "higher" or "spiritual" values (e.g., education, leisure for reflection and prayer, access to works of art). In today's world (especially), great wealth and power are very often linked to injustice—either in the way they are acquired or in the refusal to share them with others. This means that very many of the rich and powerful people of our world must be held responsible in some degree for failing to change the unjust order of society. Their failure to change the system corrupts them to a greater or lesser extent—perhaps mainly through their selective and semideliberate blindness to social injustices. Furthermore, the present system has now become so distorted and misdirected—and so much out of human control—that it has become a major cause of alienation; it creates a sense of isolation and of threat even in those who are benefiting from it in economic and political terms. This combination of blindness and alienation in the "privileged" ones of our society entitles one to say that they may be spiritually corrupted or at risk.

On the basis of this kind of description of the present situation of rich and poor, one may come to a better understanding of what is involved in an option for the poor. It implies a commitment to trying to change the unjust structures of society. This includes giving encouragement and hope to those who are being impoverished while challenging the complacency of those who are responsible for this impoverishment or are guilty of complicity in it.

How can this best be done? The answer will vary according to the situation, but some general points may be noted. Clearly, there is a need for many people to work directly with the poor—not just for the poor but in a way that involves sharing their experiences in some degree. Of course, the rich and powerful should not be entirely neglected or ignored.

However, the crucial question is: What should committed Church people be saying to the rich by their words and actions? There are people who believe they can move the rich toward greater social awareness by working closely with and for them, for instance, by providing expensive high-class education for their children. More recently increasing numbers of committed Church people have come to the conclusion that this approach is not sufficiently effective. So they choose to challenge the rich by transferring their energies to working with the poor.

Does an option for the poor mean an option against the rich and powerful? By no means—at least not in John Paul's view. As we shall see in the next section, the pope is firmly opposed to class struggle; so he does not advocate the rejection of rich people. However, an option for the poor does mean the rejection of an evil system and of bad structures in society. The Church has always insisted that people make an "option against sin." Correctly understood, an "option for the poor" is simply one aspect of an "option against sin." For in recent years, theologians and Church leaders have come to realize more clearly that an option against sin must include an option against what is called "social sin" and "structural" injustice. One aspect of social sin is the way in which injustice has become embodied in our world through an unequal distribution of wealth and power. If we opt to resist injustice, we must be opposed to the process of impoverishment and the systems that promote poverty.

SOLIDARITY

I move on now to look at the second key issue in the encyclical, namely, the concept of solidarity. The issue here is one that we were concerned with at the end of chapter 11, namely, what does the Church have to say to the poor? We saw that in two of his addresses to shanty dwellers in Brazil and the Philippines, the pope emphasized the importance of the poor taking responsibility for their own destiny. We saw, too, that John Paul noted that the poor exercise the great virtue of solidarity in the way they help each other. In *Laborem Exercens* he elaborates these points more fully. The points are also situated against a historical background, namely, the struggle of workers in the last century to break out of the degradation that was imposed on them in the industrial revolution (*LE* 8).

Laborem Exercens offers a trenchant criticism of the two major economic systems of the world at the time—that of the West and that of the East (e.g., *LE* 7, 8, 11, 14). It insists on calling for a transformation of the present structures, with the aim of ensuring that the person is respected. But what kind of action does the pope envisage to bring about such radical changes? Not a class struggle. In this encyclical, as elsewhere, the pope rejects the idea that the way to achieve social justice is to struggle "against" others (*LE* 20). He favors a struggle for justice rather than against other people or classes (cf. Naudet 2011, 259).

However, Pope John Paul is quite prepared to approve of resistance to exploitation. He accepts that in the last century industrial workers had to oppose a "system of injustice and harm that cried to heaven for vengeance," in order to protect their human rights and dignity (*LE* 8). There is a certain solemnity—almost a judicial quality—in the way in which the pope states that this reaction of the workers "was justified from the point of view of social morality" (*LE* 8). In the remainder of the same paragraph he goes on to examine the need for similar action to secure social justice in the contemporary world. He notes that there are various sectors where the old injustices persist or other forms of injustice are present—injustices that are "much more extensive" than those of the last century.

The key word used by Pope John Paul in this connection is "solidarity." For him the word "solidarity" seems to play a role analogous to the phrase "class struggle" in Marxist writings. He uses the word nine times in *LE* 8 as well as at least once elsewhere (*LE* 20). His repeated use of the word when he is referring to the reaction of workers against an unjust and exploitative system suggests that the Solidarity union of Lech Walesa of Gdansk and his ten million fellow workers was very much in the mind of this Polish pope.

The fact that a pope from Poland spoke so strongly about solidarity at the very time when the Polish trade union Solidarity was much in the news could give a wrong impression. It might appear that his ideas about worker solidarity were inspired mainly by what was happening in Poland at the time. This would be incorrect—or at least incomplete. In fact, if anything, the position might be the other way round. John Paul's views about solidarity, propounded several years earlier, undoubtedly played some part in creating a climate in Poland favorable to the emergence of the Solidarity trade union—and may well have helped inspire this choice of name for the movement.

Twelve years earlier, when John Paul was still Karol Cardinal Wojtyla, archbishop of Krakow, he published a study titled *Osoba i czyn* (*The Self and the Act*). The English edition was included in an anthology published in 1981 (30–56). In it he put forward a philosophical analysis of the concept of solidarity. This provides an important background for understanding what he wrote twelve years later in *Laborem Exercens*. So it is worthwhile quoting some important passages from this study.

A first passage indicates what the author means by "solidarity," and it shows how it relates to participation by people in the building of community:

The attitude of solidarity is a "natural" consequence of the fact that a human being exists and acts together with others. Solidarity is also the foundation of a community in which the common good conditions and liberates participation, and participation serves the common good, supports it, and implements it. Solidarity means the continuous readiness to accept and perform that part of a task which is imposed due to the participation as member of a specific community. (Wojtyla 1981, 47)

The attitude of solidarity respects the limits imposed by the structures and accepts the duties, that are assigned to each member of the community. (Wojtyla 1981, 48)

The next point is particularly important in our present context. It is that solidarity does not always exclude opposition and confrontation. The following passages throw light on what *Laborem Exercens* has to say about oppressed people asserting their rights—and being entitled to do so:

The attitude of solidarity, however, does not exclude the attitude of opposition. *Opposition is not a fundamental contradiction of solidarity.* One who expresses opposition does not remove himself from participation in the community, does not withdraw his readiness to act for the common good. . . . There are instances . . . when solidarity demands . . . contrariness. In such instances, restricting oneself to the assigned duty only could be tantamount to a lack of solidarity. (Wojtyla 1981, 48)

Opposition is also an expression of the vital need for participation in the community of existence, but especially in the community of action. Such opposition has to be viewed as constructive. (Wojtyla 1981, 49)

It is interesting to notice the link he makes between solidarity and participation. This provides a background to what he later says as pope about the rights of workers to have a sense of participation, in the sense of not feeling themselves "a cog in a huge machine moved from above" but feeling that in some way they are working for themselves (*LE* 15). The right to participate in the process includes the right to dialogue, to question, and to oppose (cf. Lamoureux 2005, 399). In this context, too, we can situate John Paul's strong insistence on the right of workers to have trade unions. He asserts that they have "the right . . . to form associations for the purpose of defending the vital interests of those employed in the various professions" (*LE* 20).

Returning to the study by Cardinal Wojtyla, I note that he goes on to make it clear that it is not sufficient to have an opposition that emerges spontaneously, more or less in spite of the existing structure. The structure itself must facilitate the expression of opposition: "We are concerned with such a structure of community that permits the emergence of opposition based on solidarity. Moreover, the structure must not only *allow the emergence of the opposition, give it the opportunity to express itself, but also must make it possible for the opposition to function for the good of the community*" (Wojtyla 1981, 49).

The final point to note in this important study by the future Pope John Paul is his notion of dialogue. For him, dialogue serves the function of ensuring that opposition is not cut off; it ensures that the structures that seek to promote the common good do not become too restrictive. It is especially important in a situation characterized by militancy, since it can help the participants eliminate purely personal attitudes and preferences, and enable them to agree on what is objectively required. In this way opposition, though it can make it difficult to live and act together, can at the same time contribute to a deepening of human solidarity (Wojtyla 1981, 49–50).

In the light of this account of the meaning of solidarity, one can now see how ideal a word it is for the pope's purposes in the encyclical *Laborem Exercens*. The word "solidarity" is action-oriented. But it does not have the negative connotations of the word "struggle." Instead of evoking an image of divisiveness, it suggests that the primary thrust of the workers' activity is toward unity and community. Their unity may often have to come through their confrontation with those who try to maintain unjust structures. That this is the case is not a necessary part of the order of reality but is due to a perversion of the way things ought to be.

In the section in which the pope examines the concept of "solidarity" in some depth he never once speaks of the "struggle" of the workers for justice. Instead he speaks of a "reaction"—a justified reaction—of the workers to an unjust and exploitative system (*LE* 8). This nuanced use of language suggests that what he sees taking place is not the struggle of two morally equal groups, the employers and the workers. Rather there is "a wide-ranging anomaly," a perversion of right order, which calls forth a justified "reaction." It is only in a much later paragraph, dealing with the role of trade unions, that the pope speaks of the *struggle* of workers; and then it is only with the qualification noted above, namely, that it is always a struggle *for* justice rather than *against* other people or classes (*LE* 20).[3]

---

[3]It is interesting to note the way in which the issue of class warfare was treated by the Pastoral Commission of the Brazilian Bishops. The commission stated that the Church condemns the Marxist postulate of class war, in the sense that to promote such a struggle would be contrary to the gospel and would not provide the solution to the real problems of today. But, it added, the Church recognizes realistically the existence of class conflicts—conflicts that ought to be overcome through the establishment of justice and of a spirit of brotherhood (see Bishops of Brazil 1978, 10).

The pope's choice of the word "solidarity" was also advantageous in that the confrontational aspect of working for justice did not have to be spelled out. Anybody reading the newspapers in the months prior to the publication of the encyclical would be very well aware that action for justice through workers' solidarity is not all sweetness and gentleness; the story of the Polish Solidarity union showed that quite clearly.

In *Laborem Exercens* the pope does not explore the morality of different kinds and levels of confrontation in a variety of different situations. Had he done so, it could have given the wrong impression: it might have been seen as an incitement to workers and others to seek confrontation. In fact, there is no indication either in the encyclical or in his other writings or addresses that John Paul wanted to provoke confrontation. What he has to say about opposition is only a small part of his teaching on solidarity, and this, in turn, is just one part of a balanced and comprehensive social teaching. Indeed, there is a sense in which I may appear to have given an inordinate amount of space to this one issue. But it was necessary to go into the question in some detail because what the pope has to say about opposition is a small but crucial part of the whole edifice of his social teaching. Its significance lies, above all, in the fact that it plugs a gap that had existed in previous papal teaching.

A final advantage of his choice of the word "solidarity" (and one that was probably quite important for the pope personally) is that the repeated use of this word in a papal encyclical undoubtedly had the effect of giving a certain discreet aura of Vatican approval to the Polish workers' move-ment—at least in its overall direction. And why not? If the pope could pronounce a judgment that the reaction of nineteenth-century workers to an oppressive system was justified, why should he not imply that the same is true of the activity of Polish workers in his own time?

Pope John Paul does not claim to have made an exhaustive listing in the encyclical of the kinds of injustice in the present world that call for "new movements of solidarity of the workers and with the workers" (*LE* 8). However he goes quite some distance in that direction. He mentions "various ideological or power systems, and new relationships that have arisen at various levels of society"; these have, he says, "allowed flagrant injustices to persist or have created new ones" (*LE* 8). This general state-ment can be taken to refer to, among other things, power bureaucracies in the East and West, and the ability of rich nations to exercise economic power for their own advantage through such agencies as the Interna-tional Monetary Fund, as well as to the economic abuses of transnational corporations. But the pope's words may apply equally well to structures that give undue power at the local level to politicians or administrators. There is no indication that the pope intended his words to apply also to a clerical power structure in the Church, but they could be applied by others to such a power structure.

The pope also notes that he has in mind not only industrialized countries but also those countries where most workers are engaged in agricultural labor. It can be taken that he is alluding here to the gross injustices associated with land ownership in many countries of the South—and to other abuses in the less industrialized parts of the world. He also makes specific mention of the need for a movement of solidarity among groups of people who may have had a privileged position in the past but now find themselves in the situation of the proletariat; these would include some categories of the working intelligentsia (*LE* 8). The point here is an important one: the proletariat is no longer confined to those who work with their hands. No doubt, the pope derived some satisfaction from pointing out that old-style Marxist descriptions are no longer adequate to describe the present reality.

The introduction of the concept of solidarity provides a perfect solution to a problem that had arisen for Paul VI and even for John Paul himself in earlier teaching. They could point out and condemn injustices in society at the international or national level. They could appeal to those in authority to put things right. But if that was not enough, as clearly it was not, what then? Should a pope invite the poor and oppressed to take matters into their own hands and put things right? Would not this amount to an incitement to open confrontation? Is it not likely that any such statement would be hailed by revolutionary groups as approval of their cause and their activity? All this would seriously weaken the stance of the Church in favor of nonviolence. It could also lessen the effectiveness of the Church from a purely strategic point of view: the explicit identification of the Church with the political struggle of the oppressed could provoke further repression and persecution by those in power.

The word "solidarity" offers a way out of this dilemma. As I have already noted, it is not to be identified with an all-out revolutionary struggle. Nonetheless, it does not exclude whatever degree of confrontation is necessary and prudent. No a priori theory can enable one to predict the risks that are involved or how far the workers would be entitled to go in pressing for justice. It would undoubtedly be necessary to apply traditional Catholic principles about violence, war, and rebellion, to each individual unique situation. But it would not be acceptable to claim that these Catholic principles mean that forceful resistance is *never* justified.

By coming out strongly in favor of "solidarity," Pope John Paul is accepting the need for confrontation. This means he has avoided the false dilemma of having to choose between direct approval for violent action, on the one hand, or, on the other hand, simply issuing warnings about the danger of violence in a way that would look like acquiescence to the status quo. The effect is that the stance of the Church in the struggle for justice is strengthened considerably. It seems, then, that the pope's Polish experience has provided the basis for an important new step in the social teaching of the Church.

DIALOGUE WITH MARXISM?

As I said earlier, the word "solidarity" in the thinking of John Paul seems to play a role analogous to "class struggle" in Marxist writings. "Solidarity" is a master image that does not have the overtly aggressive overtones of the phrase "class struggle." But how different really is the pope's position from Marxism? Is it mainly a matter of words and a different emphasis, or is there a fundamental incompatibility between the two approaches? I shall not attempt here to answer this question fully, but the following remarks may at least help open up the topic for further discussion.

In the past, Catholic thinkers generally followed the Greek tradition of defining the human person as a thinker. In presenting the human person as fundamentally a worker, the pope in *Laborem Exercens* is breaking from this Greek tradition and following in the tradition of Karl Marx. Of course, he does not become a Marxist merely by adopting this approach. Nevertheless, it is evident that his understanding of human life and of society has been profoundly affected by some aspects of Marxist philosophy.

However, it must be added at once that the pope takes a much broader view of what is meant by "work" than is common in the Marxist tradition. A good deal of Marxist writing shows a tendency to use the word "work" mainly to refer to industrial labor (cf. Baum 1982, 13)—or at most to manual labor. For John Paul, in contrast, the meaning of the word "work" is so comprehensive that *everybody* can be called a worker in some sense (cf. Hennelly 1982, 34). Work, for him, includes such intellectual occupations as study, and it also takes in organizational work such as management or the work of caring for a family. What about the unemployed, the disabled, those who are retired, and children? It would appear that the pope intends his teaching on human work to refer to them also, since they can all, in a certain sense, be thought of as potential workers. This may sound rather contrived but only if one is thinking of work in the limited sense of doing a task for which one can be paid. The pope's conception, however, is one of *homo faber*—the human person as a "maker," one who shares in the making of the world.

One of the most important effects of this broadening of the conception of work and the worker is that the notion of "the working class" ceases to have the meaning it had in traditional Marxism. Central to Marxist thinking was the view that the interests of the working class were in conflict with those of owners and managers. What happens when the definition of the worker is extended to cover everybody? The idea of a fundamental clash of interest between "the workers" and others is eliminated. This explains why John Paul can insist that cooperation is fundamental and that solidarity is more basic than opposition (cf. Schotte 1982b, 23).

So much for the basic nature of society as it ideally exists. But John Paul is also prepared to look at the actual situation. He is not so foolish as to think that the problem of class struggle is eliminated by redefining the meaning of the word "worker." He recognizes that there have been major clashes of interest between employers and their employees. In his view, however, it was not predetermined that things should happen in this way; it did not occur because of any "law," as Marxist-Leninist thought maintains. Rather it was because of free decisions made by human beings. Initially, the people mainly responsible were the early capitalists; they were determined to maximize their profits, and they did so by exploiting their workers (*LE* 11). This provoked what the pope calls a justified "reaction" on the part of the workers (*LE* 8).

Having begun in this way, the struggle between the classes has, according to the pope, gone on to develop into an ideological and political struggle between capitalism and Marxism (*LE* 11). John Paul's purpose in *Laborem Exercens* is to unmask the myths and oversimplifications that are part of this struggle. He points out the inadequacy of economic liberalism, the ideology of capitalism. He also rejects the Marxist notion that class struggle is a matter of historical necessity. For him, as we have just seen, it is the result of human decisions, and it is something that can be avoided. As Gregory Baum (1982, 29) says, "Pope John Paul II offers . . . an imaginative rethinking of class conflict. The initiative for the struggle resides in the persons who recognize their common objective situation and freely commit themselves to solidarity in a joint struggle."

Fundamentally, the pope rejects the view of those Marxists who maintain that history is totally determined by economic processes and that human freedom is an illusion. He is opposed to Marxism understood as an ideology. He does not accept that it provides a system that has universal applicability, that gives one a "scientific" understanding of reality (cf. Baum 1982, 85). The view that Marxism is an exact science is linked to the belief that history is determined by economic factors that follow rigid "laws" (cf. Miranda 1980, 69–105).

It should be noted, however, that there are thinkers within the Marxist tradition whose views on these issues are quite close to those of John Paul. Their conception of history is not a determinist one; rather it finds a place for human responsibility (cf. McGovern 1980, 68–80; Miranda

1980 passim). These Marxists agree with the pope in rejecting the kind of doctrinaire approach that would claim to be able to understand the world "scientifically" by means of a ready-made theory (cf. Baum 1982, 85–86).

Even on the question of class struggle, there is by no means as much difference as might appear at first sight between the views of the pope and those of some of the more "critical" Marxists. John Paul would agree with them that a struggle between the working class and the upper classes has actually taken place. They could perhaps agree with him that this was not owing to some necessity of nature but was a matter of history in which humans played a determining part—a history that might well have developed differently in other circumstances and if different key decisions had been made.

These Marxists could even agree that, in the long run, human solidarity is more basic than class struggle. After all, they would say, do we not envisage a classless society in which the divisions between the classes are finally resolved? Is not this, fundamentally, the same goal as the one the pope aspires to when he seeks the elimination of class struggle and the effective solidarity of all? As for the crude accusation that Marxism calls for the elimination of the enemies of the working class, their response would be that what is sought is the ultimate elimination of classes but not of the people who belong to the upper classes.

Another point on which there is room for clarification is the motivation of the poor in struggling to overcome injustice. Pope John Paul frequently warns against any understanding of an option for the poor that would be an incitement to hatred (e.g., his address to CELAM in Haiti in 1983). But does the Marxist conception of class struggle necessarily include a stirring up of the instincts of hatred and revenge? This question calls for a careful answer. Certainly, it is not part of Marxist belief to hold that the poorer classes can be moved to action only by the crudest of motives; if the ultimate aim is the achievement of a classless society, then there is room for higher ideals than those of class interest.[4]

I am not suggesting that there are no real differences between the views of John Paul and those of "critical" Marxists. But there is certainly room for dialogue, and such a dialogue may show that some of the differences are owing to a different use of language. The dialogue might also lead to a discovery, by people on either side, of points that they had not taken sufficiently seriously. By way of example I mention here a question to which I believe those who propound Catholic social teaching have not given enough attention. The question is, "What compromises should

---

[4]On the question of the motivation of the poor in Marx, see Miranda (1980, 1–28). On the question of how, in John Paul's view, the struggle to overcome oppression goes beyond narrow class interest, see Baum (1982, 30–31, 49, 69).

one make in working for justice, and at what point should one be quite uncompromising?" This question arises for me from reflection on situations in which liberation movements, having more or less won a political and military victory over their oppressors, stopped short of dismantling those state structures in which the oppression was embodied. The result was a change of rulers rather than the elimination of injustice. Church leaders frequently call for compromise and reconciliation—and rightly so. But there is need for serious consideration of the need to replace unjust structures as well as unjust rulers. It is also important to face up to the question of restoring equity and balance to society by compensating large numbers of people who have been victims of oppression perhaps for generations.

I have said enough to indicate that there is room and need for a good deal of study, reflection, and dialogue on the relationship between the new current in Vatican social teaching and the more liberal and critical strands in the Marxist tradition. Over many years the Church has been in dialogue with moderate strands in the tradition of liberal political philosophy. As a result of this dialogue, Church leaders now find a wide measure of agreement with moderate Western political theorists and social scientists about fundamental human rights and about the kind of values they would like to see embodied in society. However, the Church's dialogue with Marxism has always been inhibited, largely because of the antireligious bias of communist governments. The tyranny of communism is no longer a major threat. But it would be extremely naïve to assume that because communism collapsed in Eastern Europe and was effectively abandoned in China and Vietnam, therefore, all Marxist thinking is discredited. In fact this may be an appropriate time for Church leaders and thinkers to engage in dialogue with moderate Marxists about issues of social justice (cf. Coleman 2005, 531).

THE ROLE OF THE CHURCH

The final section of the encyclical (*LE* 24–27) has the heading "Elements for a Spirituality of Work." The pope maintains that it is a duty of the Church "*to form a spirituality of work* which will help all people to come closer, through work, to God, the Creator and Redeemer, to participate in his salvific plan for man and the world and to deepen their friendship with Christ" (*LE* 24). Then John Paul returns to the passage from the book of Genesis to which he had referred early in the encyclical. He says that humans share by their work "in the activity of the creator," and humans, like God, must find a place for rest in their lives (*LE* 25). He then goes on to speak of Jesus as "a man of work" and to recall Saint

Paul's insistence on the importance of working for one's living (*LE* 26). Next, since he recognizes that work "is inevitably linked with toil," he turns to the "the cross of Christ and his obedience unto death,"[5] as well as the resurrection, for an answer to the problem that this raises for a spirituality of work (*LE* 27).

A surprising feature of *Laborem Exercens* is how little it has to say about what we might call the active role of the Church in working for justice. Of course, in John Paul's view, the great contribution of the Church lies precisely in the teaching he was proposing in the encyclical—and the long tradition of experience and reflection out of which this teaching came. But the pope says little in this encyclical about the role of the Christian Church in actually implementing the principles and proposals. This is scarcely an accident. Presumably one reason for it is that in this encyclical, as in his first one, John Paul wished to emphasize his "humanistic" perspective (cf. *LE* 13). Christians can stand alongside sincere non-Christians in working for the kind of just society envisaged in *Laborem Exercens*.

What Pope John Paul has to say about the action of the Church in the effort to overcome injustice, though brief, is nevertheless powerful. Significantly, it comes toward the end of the section dealing with the need for new movements of solidarity of and with those who are degraded and exploited. He says, "The Church is firmly committed to this cause, for she considers it her mission, her service, a proof of her fidelity to Christ, so that she can truly be the 'Church of the poor' " (*LE* 8). What more needs to be said? These lines offer a firm commitment to the cause of the poor and the oppressed, together with the fundamental reasons for this engagement. On other occasions the pope elaborated on these points. One has the impression that he preferred to be short and pungent on this point, because it makes clear that what is now called for is action—decisive action by committed Christians in solidarity with the poor of the world.

If this study of Vatican teaching on the option for the poor had been written prior to *Laborem Exercens*, the ending would have had to include a major question about the adequacy of what the Church had to say on this topic. The failure of earlier popes to face up to the question of confrontation was a serious weakness. With the publication of *Laborem Exercens* this weakness has been at least partly overcome. The result is a very rounded body of teaching that offers both inspiration and guidance to Christians concerned about issues of social justice.

It is interesting to reflect that the major advance made by Pope John Paul on the issue of organized opposition by "the poor" to oppressive

---

[5]Lamoureux (2005, 406) notes that some "legitimate criticisms" have been raised to the way John Paul links the toil of work with Christ's suffering and death.

authorities is closely related to the pope's own experience in Poland.

Church leaders in other parts of the world who become fully committed to the promotion of social justice can, like the pope, develop a theology that is rooted in their practical experience. Obviously, the theology that emerges in each region will have its own specific flavor. But there will also be common themes—among them the major themes the pope has taken up in *Laborem Exercens* and in his other writings and addresses. For the Polish experience is now echoed in different ways in many parts of the world: great masses of people are left voiceless or marginalized, the victims of an insensitive ruling group; and their only realistic hope lies in learning how to assert their dignity and going on to organize themselves to claim their basic human rights.

In concluding this chapter, I note that in this encyclical Pope John Paul includes important material on the issue of women and work. His approach to this topic represents a serious attempt to update and develop the Church's social teaching. I am postponing my study of this material to chapter 14 where I examine it in some detail as a significant part of the development of the Church's teaching on the role of women.

* * *

SUMMARY

The encyclical *Laborem Exercens* offers a profound historical and philosophical analysis of the nature of human work and of how society should be organized if workers are to be treated in a way that respects their dignity. The pope's concept of "the indirect employer" is helpful in understanding the causes of the poverty and exploitation endured by workers in the South (and by certain categories of workers in the North). We may not be the direct employer who pays these workers unjustly, but we, and the agencies that serve our interests, can be seen as "indirect employers" insofar as we have some degree of responsibility for poor pay and conditions. This helps to bring home to us that these injustices cannot be simply dismissed as an unavoidable result of "the system" for which nobody is really to blame.

The poverty of most of those who are poor today is not just a fact of nature but is a result of their impoverishment by human actions in the past and present. So those of us who benefit from this exploitation are challenged to take responsibility for our complicity in the system and called to play our part in changing the structures. We must not evade this call by maintaining that those who are materially wealthy may be spiritually poor or by making too sharp a distinction between ordinary poverty and "poverty of spirit."

In this encyclical the pope laid great stress on the solidarity of the poor and oppressed. He encouraged them to struggle to overcome the disadvantages imposed on them, emphasizing especially the importance of trade unions in the struggle for the protection of workers' rights. However, this is a struggle for justice, not a class war. The pope's understanding of solidarity includes an element of opposition or confrontation in the service of the common good. This is an important contribution to Catholic social teaching that had previously been slow to acknowledge the need for confrontation. The pope also commits the Church to solidarity with the poor and oppressed.

The pope, like Marx, defines the human person as a worker. But for the pope work is not just physical labor; all people share in the work of creation. The views of some moderate Marxists are fairly close to those of the pope. There is room and need for further dialogue.

QUESTIONS FOR REVIEW

1. What is the difference between the "direct employer" and the "indirect employer"?
2. Clarify the meanings given to the phrases "spiritual poverty" and "poor in spirit." How do they relate to economic poverty and powerlessness?
3. Why is the concept of solidarity so central to John Paul's teaching?
4. What are the elements in a spirituality of work outlined by Pope John Paul?

QUESTIONS FOR REFLECTION

1. What kind of action by ordinary people in the North would help to improve the working conditions for people in the South?
2. To what extent is it inevitable that society becomes stratified into classes? And what can be done to lessen class tensions?

ISSUE FOR FURTHER STUDY

1. To what extent is John Paul's account of work and society influenced by the work of Marx?

13

Concern and Consolidation

The two terms "concern" and "consolidation" in the title of this chapter sum up the main thrust of John Paul's papacy in the period from 1981 onward. It was a time when the Vatican appeared anxious about many aspects of Church life and made strong efforts to reinforce and consolidate traditional teaching. It is more than a coincidence that "concern" is also the first word in John Paul's second social encyclical (*Sollicitudo Rei Socialis*, translated into English as "On Social Concern") written in late 1987, six years after *Laborem Exercens*. Furthermore, the word "consolidation" may serve as a one-word summary of his third social encyclical *Centesimus Annus*, issued in 1991 to commemorate the hundredth anniversary of *Rerum Novarum*.

MANY CONCERNS

In the area of social justice John Paul's concern ranged widely. He continued his custom of making a number of pastoral visits each year to various parts of the world. On many of these occasions he took the opportunity to speak out strongly against injustices of various kinds. But there seems to be a certain change of tone and emphasis between what he was saying up to 1983 and what he said in later years. In the first period he spoke out very strongly on issues of political oppression, challenging governments quite directly. In the later period his statements on political matters seem rather more muted. This may be related to the ongoing concern in Rome about what were seen as the excesses of liberation theologians and to the Vatican's sustained effort to counteract their influence.

Early in 1983 Pope John Paul II undertook what was probably the most controversial of his missionary journeys: he traveled to Central America and Haiti and gave major addresses in El Salvador, Nicaragua, Guatemala, and Port au Prince. In these addresses there are clear indications of both aspects of the pope's concern: his outrage in the face of regimes that were blatantly oppressive and his fears that the Church's role might be reduced to that of working for political and economic liberation—above all, if this liberation were seen in Marxist terms.

What the pope said in El Salvador and Nicaragua brought out more clearly than ever before his reservations about the Marxist answer to problems of social injustice. He objected to what he saw as an "instrumentalization" of the gospel and to its subjection to an "ideology" (e.g., in Managua; *AAS* [*Acta Apostolicae Sedis*] 75, 720–22). Linked to this is his warning to priests and members of religious communities not to confuse their role with that of political organizers. For instance, he said to priests in San Salvador (*L'Osservatore Romano* [*L'Oss. Rom.*], March 7–8, 1983, 4), "Remember that . . . you are not social directors, political leaders, or officials of a temporal power."[1]

During this same trip, however, the pope made an outspoken demand in Haiti that things must change; he insisted on the crying need for justice and for equitable distribution of goods, as well as for participation by the people in decision making and for freedom of expression of opinions (Port au Prince; *AAS* 75, 768–69).

At this time also he spoke to a group of people who were among the most oppressed in the whole world—the indigenous people (American Indians) of Guatemala. To them he made what is perhaps the strongest and most specific statement he ever made on a burning issue of justice. He assured them that "the Church at this moment knows the marginalization which you suffer, the injustices you endure, the serious difficulties you encounter in defending your lands and your rights." He encouraged them to resist these injustices: "Your brotherly love should express itself in increasing solidarity. Help one another. Organize associations for the defense of your rights and the realization of your own goals" (*AAS* 75, 742–43).

The pope told these oppressed people of the attitude of the Church in the face of the injustices they suffer:

> In fulfilling her task of evangelization, she seeks to be near you and to raise her voice in condemnation when your dignity as human beings and children of God is violated. . . . For this reason, here and now, and in solemn form, in the name of the Church I call on the government to provide an ever more adequate legislation which will protect you effectively against abuses. (*AAS* 75, 742–43, my translation)

---

[1] These were constant themes of the pope (e.g., his Letter to the Religious of Latin America (*L'Oss. Rom.*, July 30, 1990, 4). They were repeated above all during his visits to Latin America—for instance, during his second visit to Mexico (*L'Oss. Rom.*, May 14, 1990, 3) and his second visit to Brazil (*L'Oss. Rom.*, October 28, 1991, 12).

In the same paragraph the pope significantly demanded that the process of authentic evangelization should not be branded as subversion. In other words, he was vindicating the right of the Church to speak and act in the interests of justice even when this was interpreted by authorities, such as those in Guatemala, as a political activity or even as subversive of the state's authority.

Both aspects of the pope's concern found expression in his address to the Council of Latin American Bishops (CELAM) at Port au Prince on March 9, 1983. In the first section of his talk he expressed his concern about poverty and injustice: "A sincere analysis of the situation shows that at its root one finds painful injustices, exploitation of some by others, and a serious lack of equity in the distribution of wealth and the benefits of culture." In the third section of the address he warned against distortions of the gospel and one-sided or partial interpretations of Puebla: "It is necessary to spread and . . . to recover the *wholeness* of the message of Puebla, without deformed interpretations or deformed reductions, and without unwarranted applications of some parts and the eclipse of others" (*AAS* 75, 775–76, my translation).

In the following years the pope continued to emphasize the importance of social justice. But his talks were not perceived as a clarion call in quite the same way as in his earlier years as pope. When he visited southern Africa in 1989, there was considerable disappointment about the reticence and caution of his remarks about the struggle for liberation in South Africa (e.g., *AAS* 81, 331–34). And the addresses of his second visit to Brazil seemed more reserved on issues of justice than those of his earlier visit (such as his addresses in the shantytown of Vitória [*L'Oss. Rom.*, November 4, 1991, 4] and to Amazonian Indians at Cuiabá [*L'Oss. Rom.*, October 28, 1991, 10]).

There is, however, one issue of justice on which the pope focused particular attention—that of the rights of cultural and ethnic minorities. On this question he spoke out strongly on numerous occasions, including to the Indians and Inuit of Canada in 1984 (*AAS* 77, 417–22); in 1984 to Koreans (*AAS* 76, 985, 947); in 1985 to Africans in the Cameroons (*AAS* 78, 52–61); to Amerindian people in Ecuador again in 1985 (*AAS* 77, 859–69); to the Aborigines of Australia in 1986 (*AAS* 79, 973–79); in 1991 to Amazonian Indians in Brazil (*L'Oss. Rom.*, October 28, 1991, 10); and in 1992 in West Africa (*L'Oss. Rom.*, February 26, 1992, 8).

Liberation Theology

From the early 1980s onward the Vatican began appointing many conservative bishops in Latin America and in other sensitive areas. This was a clear indication of the concern felt in Rome about what were perceived to be the dangers of liberation theology. In 1984 this concern took a more obvious form when the Vatican Congregation for the Doctrine of the Faith issued its *Instruction on Certain Aspects of the "Theology of Liberation."* The document was widely understood to be the work of Cardinal Ratzinger, though there was some insistence on the fact that its contents were approved by the pope. It mounted a strong attack on liberation theology (or at least on some versions of it) from several points of view. Among the notable points in the document are (1) its insistence on the priority of personal sin over social sin (IV, 12–15); (2) its emphasis on the incompatibility of Marxist theory with Christian faith (VII, 9) and its assumption that the theologies of liberation have adopted Marxist positions that are incompatible with the Christian vision (VIII, 1); and (3) its accusation that theologies of liberation have radically politicized the faith (IX, 6), have perverted the Christian meaning of "the poor" by confusing "the poor" of scripture with the Marxist proletariat and have then transformed the fight for the rights of the poor into a class struggle (IX, 10), and have rejected with disdain the social doctrine of the Church (X, 4).

There was a very strong reaction to this document, including a comprehensive and sustained attack on it by Juan Luis Segundo, one of the leading liberation theologians. Like other liberation theologians, he claimed that what the document put forward was a gross distortion of the main thrust of liberation theology. But he went much further: he argued that the theology with which the Instruction was imbued was one that located transcendence outside human history (e.g., Segundo 1985, 48, 72, 154), and for him this represented a regression to a pre–Vatican II theology.

The 1984 Instruction had included a promise of a further document on the theme of liberation. As a result of the poor reception given to the Instruction, a consensus soon emerged that it needed to be supplemented, if not superseded, by another Vatican document. The new *Instruction on Christian Freedom and Liberation* was duly issued by the Congregation for the Doctrine of the Faith in 1986. Its teaching was widely seen as representing the views of the pope himself (cf. Hebblethwaite 1987, 85). While stressing the continuity between the two documents, it presented a more balanced account of liberation theology without the harsh judgments and warnings of the earlier document.

This second document approved of many of the themes of liberation theology, such as the special place of the poor (21), the link between earthly liberation and eschatological hope (60), the Church's "special option for the poor" (68), and the need for changes in the structures of society (75). It recognized that armed struggle against oppression could be justified in extreme cases as a last resort, but it suggested that in today's world, passive resistance would be more effective and morally acceptable (79). It warned against "the myth of revolution" (78); it stressed the importance of solidarity, subsidiarity (73, 89), and participation (86), and the need for a cultural transformation of society (81).

This second Instruction could be seen as an acknowledgment by Rome that the main *teachings* of liberation theology were thoroughly Christian. However, neither it nor its predecessor gave any indication of sympathy for liberation theology as a *project*—or indeed any real understanding of it. They showed no enthusiasm for the notion that theology emerges from reflection on the ongoing struggle for justice and liberation, or for the idea that theology should be worked out with and for ordinary grassroots people (cf. Boff 1990, 416). And the Vatican continued its policy of appointing Church leaders who were quite unsympathetic to such an approach.

International Debt

Throughout the 1980s the problem of international debt was becoming ever more serious and urgent, and it had been moving ever higher on the social justice agenda (cf. Potter 1988; Dorr 1991, 11–14). In response to this situation the Vatican Council for Justice and Peace issued in 1986 a document titled "At the Service of the Human Community: An Ethical Approach to the International Debt Question." It explored the problem of debt in some detail, pointing out the burdens imposed on poor nations and especially on poorer people.

The document was by no means radical in its analysis or its proposals. For instance, it did not condone the idea that debtor nations should repudiate their debts unilaterally or that payment defaults should be allowed to happen (13, 25). It did, however, suggest that in the cases of the poorest nations the loans should be converted by the creditors into grants (26). It did not put forward any serious and sustained criticism of the policies of the International Monetary Fund (IMF), on the grounds that "it is not up to the Church to judge the economic and financial theories behind their analyses and the remedies proposed" (28).

Proposals put forward in the document were that international creditors should take immediate action to meet emergency situations (13) and that, as part of a more long-term solution, they should reduce interest rates (19), reschedule debts (25), and eliminate protectionist measures that hinder exports from poorer countries (18). The document went on to suggest that international financial agencies (World Bank, IMF, and so on) should have more representatives from developing countries and should allow these countries a greater share in determining their policies (29). The guiding principle of the authors was that people and their needs should be given priority over financial rectitude (e.g., 22, 31).

Pope John Paul spoke occasionally on the issue of debt, following much the same lines as those of the Council for Justice and Peace, for instance, in an address to the diplomats in 1991 (*L'Oss. Rom.*, January 14, 1991, 3).

A New Social Encyclical

The twentieth anniversary of *Populorum Progressio* was in 1987. To commemorate it John Paul issued his second social encyclical, *Sollicitudo Rei Socialis*, known in English as "On Social Concern."[2] It was dated December 30, 1987, but was not actually issued until February 1988. It gave rise to a certain amount of controversy in the United States where it was criticized by neoconservatives such as Michael Novak for appearing to be as critical of Western capitalism as it was of Eastern Marxism (cf. Walsh 1991, xx). The main contribution of the document lay in its teaching on solidarity, and this was largely ignored not only in the mass media but even in theological and religious reviews.

After some initial observations on the significance of *Populorum Progressio*, the pope goes on to make an extended "Survey of the Contemporary World" (*SRS*, chap. 3). It is quite significant that he chooses this approach. It means that his teaching is not abstract and deductive in style but is rooted in a penetrating sociopolitical and historical analysis of the situation (cf. Land and Henriot 1989, 65–74).

In this survey John Paul does not simply give a value-free account of the situation. He does not hesitate to make moral judgments. For instance, he complains that the gap between "the North" and "the South" has persisted and is often widening. He criticizes, in a strong and even-handed manner, the systems of both "the West" (liberal capitalism) and "the East" (Marxism), maintaining that each of them has a tendency toward imperialism and neocolonialism (*SRS* 22). And he cries out in protest against the arms trade, the plight of refugees, the horror of terrorism (*SRS* 24), and the damaging effects of international debt (*SRS* 19).

Invoking various indicators of genuine human development, the pope has no hesitation in claiming that there has been a failure or delay in fulfilling the hopes of development that were so high when *Populorum Progressio* was written (*SRS* 12, 20). One reason for this, according to the encyclical, is the political, geopolitical, and ideological opposition between the East and the West. The pope strongly condemns the way in which the ideological conflict between East and West has widened the gap between the North and the South. He blames both sides for fostering the formation of ideological blocs, for the arms race, for failing to promote genuine interdependence and solidarity, and for imposing on other

---

[2]For background on the sociopolitical and ecclesiastical situation at the time the encyclical was written, see Curran, Himes, and Shannon (2005, 416–19).

countries two opposed concepts of development, both seriously flawed (*SRS* 20–25; cf. Coleman 1991, 92).

When he uses the terms "the North" and "the South," the pope immediately points out that this terminology is "only indicative, since one cannot ignore the fact that the frontiers of wealth and poverty intersect within the societies themselves" (*SRS* 14). He shows a preference for a different set of terms, namely, the First World, the Second World, the Third World, and the Fourth World. The advantage he sees in this usage is that it brings out the fact that these different worlds are all part of our *one world* (*SRS* 14). In a footnote he clarifies that "the Fourth World" refers especially to "the bands of great or extreme poverty in countries of medium and high income."

Development

The main purpose of *Sollicitudo Rei Socialis* was to meet the need for "a fuller and more nuanced concept of development" in continuity with that of *Populorum Progressio* (*SRS* 4). Like his predecessor, John Paul II understands development to cover all aspects of human life. His emphasis, like that of *Populorum Progressio* (and of Lebret from whom Paul VI borrowed the phrase), is on "being more" rather than "having more" (*SRS* 28; cf. Goulet 1989, 134). In the light of this he speaks out not only against the underdevelopment of the poor countries but also against what he calls "superdevelopment" existing "side-by-side with the miseries of underdevelopment." He explains what he means by this word as "an *excessive* availability of every kind of material goods for the benefit of certain social groups" linked to a civilization of "consumerism" and waste (*SRS* 28).

Development includes an economic and social component. The encyclical refers to a number of ways in which this can be measured, such as the availability of goods and services, of food and drinking water, good working conditions and life expectancy (*SRS* 14), as well as proper housing (*SRS* 17), the extent of unemployment and underemployment (*SRS* 18), and the burden of international debt (*SRS* 19).

However, the pope insists that development cannot be assessed simply in terms of such economic and social indicators. To limit development to its economic aspect, he says, leads to the subordination of the human person to "the demands of economic planning and selfish profit" (*SRS* 33; cf. *SRS* 28). One must also take account of cultural aspects, such as literacy and education, and of political aspects, such as respect for human rights and human initiative, the extent of discrimination, exploitation, and oppression, and also the degree to which people are allowed to be involved in building their own nation or, on the other hand, deprived of initiative and left dependent on a bureaucracy (*SRS* 15; cf. *SRS* 33).

One difficulty about using these indicators of development is that it gives the impression that there is just one pattern of human development that all nations must follow. It is as though there were one "ladder of progress" on which various countries have reached different heights. But the pope does not make this assumption. In fact, he is careful to insist that different groups of people have "*differences of culture* and *value systems* which do not always match the degree of *economic development*" (*SRS* 14).

John Paul sets out to present a theological basis for his teaching on development. He works this out by reflecting first on Old Testament texts such as the Genesis accounts of the relationship of Adam to the Earth, to the animals, and to God (*SRS* 29–30). Then he goes on to reflect on the role of Christ in human history and human progress—and the role of the Church in promoting this vision of the meaning of life (*SRS* 31). Toward the end of the encyclical the pope takes up briefly the topic of liberation. He says, "Recently . . . a new way of confronting the problems of poverty and underdevelopment has spread in some areas of the world, especially in Latin America. This approach makes *liberation* the fundamental category" (*SRS* 46). He refers to the two Vatican documents on the topic of liberation. He also speaks of the intimate connection between development and liberation, and he goes on to say that "the process of *development* and *liberation* takes concrete shape in the exercise of *solidarity*" (*SRS* 46). In this way he attempts to integrate the theology of development elaborated by Paul VI and himself with what might be called a moderate theology of liberation. The integration is not very successful, because the approach and the pattern of thought in the encyclical as a whole have little in common with the "from the ground up" approach of the liberation theologians.

Solidarity

John Paul maintains that genuine development must be understood in terms of solidarity (*SRS* 33). In fact, his notion of solidarity is the very heart of his understanding of development. His treatment of this topic in this encyclical, especially when it is combined with his account of solidarity in *Laborem Exercens*, which I looked at in chapter 12, is a notable contribution to moral theology. Rather than discussing solidarity in abstract philosophical terms, he situates what he has to say in the context of the distinctive contribution of *Populorum Progressio* to our understanding of human development. He sees his treatment as an expansion of the brief reference made by Paul VI in *Populorum Progressio* to "the duty of solidarity" (*PP* 44; cf. *PP* 48).

As I noted in chapter 7, Paul VI's account of development began with self-fulfillment. He then extended it outward by including among the criteria of genuine development an increased concern for others and a desire to cooperate with others for the common good (*PP* 21). John Paul develops this further, offering his teaching on solidarity as a strong bridge to span the gap that might arise between personal fulfillment and concern for others. What he has to say about it can be summarized schematically as follows:

First, he spells out the fact of interdependence. By this he means that we live within a system that determines how we relate to each other in the economic, cultural, political, and religious spheres (*SRS* 38). For instance, the livelihood of coffee farmers in Brazil or Kenya depends on the markets of North America and Europe; and the television soap operas of the United States and Australia now influence the values of people in remote parts of Africa or Asia.

Second, solidarity is a moral response to the fact of interdependence. People are now convinced "of the need for a solidarity that will take up interdependence and transfer it to the moral plane" (*SRS* 26). This is a moral call to overcome distrust of others and to collaborate with them instead (*SRS* 39).

Third, such acts of collaboration spring from the virtue of solidarity (*SRS* 39). As a virtue, solidarity is not just a feeling but "a firm and persevering determination to commit oneself to the common good" (*SRS* 38). It is an attitude of commitment to the good of one's neighbor, coupled with a readiness to sacrifice oneself in the service of the other (*SRS* 38). (I return in the next section to the pope's account of solidarity as a virtue.)

Fourth, the virtue of solidarity transforms the interpersonal relationships of individuals with the people around them. It causes the more powerful people to feel responsible for those who are weak and makes them ready to share what they have with them. It leads those who are weak or poor to reject destructive or passive attitudes. It enables those in an in-between position to respect the interests of others (*SRS* 39).

Fifth, the virtue of solidarity is exercised also by whole nations in their relationships with other nations. Nations, like people, are linked in a system that makes them dependent on each other. Within this international system, the powerful and wealthy nations are morally bound to resist the temptation to "imperialism" and "hegemony"; they must not dominate, oppress, or exploit the others (*SRS* 39). What the pope proposes here is a community of peoples, each with its own unique culture. Solidarity means taking seriously the different value systems of the various cultures (cf. *SRS* 14) rather than the imposition of a Western model of development on other peoples.

Sixth, by transforming the relationships both between individuals and between nations, the virtue of solidarity brings about a radical change in society as a whole. (I develop this point below.)

Seventh, there is a sense in which one might speak not merely of "human solidarity" but even of "ecological solidarity." The pope does not actually use this phrase, but it seems to sum up what he has in mind, for he speaks of "a greater realization of the limits of available resources and of the need to respect the integrity and the cycles of nature" (*SRS* 26). He insists that we are morally obliged to respect "the cosmos," meaning "the beings which constitute the natural world" (*SRS* 34). He goes on to expound at some length on the moral obligations imposed on us by our ecological situation (*SRS* 34). Later, the pope speaks of "the urgent need to change the spiritual attitudes which define each individual's relationship with self, with neighbor, with even the remotest human communities, and with nature itself" (*SRS* 38). This indicates that the moral dimension of genuine human development involves a sense of responsibility for the whole cosmos; such moral responsibility is either a part of the virtue of solidarity itself or else it is a related virtue that has very much in common with it. (Chapter 18 of this book is devoted to the issue of ecology; in that chapter I examine more fully the treatment of ecology in this encyclical.)

Finally, there is the matter of what happens if people refuse the challenge to be in solidarity with others—if they respond with a lack of interest instead of concern, if their attitude is one of "using" others rather than respecting them. If individuals or groups or nations act in this way, they may grow wealthier, but they cannot be said to be truly "developed," for they are ignoring the crucial moral dimension of human development (*SRS* 9). The pope notes that the lack of solidarity between the nations has "disastrous consequences" for the weaker ones, but it also has serious "negative effects even in the rich countries" (*SRS* 17). These include negative economic effects such as inadequate housing and growing unemployment (*SRS* 17, 18). Even more serious are the moral and political effects. For instance, failure of the nations to overcome their distrust of each other leads to continued imperialism and a turning away from the path to peace (*SRS* 39, 22), and the so-called developed nations of East and West become locked into ideological and military opposition (*SRS* 20), wasting on an arms race the resources needed for development (*SRS* 22).

Solidarity as a Virtue

As I pointed out when examining the encyclical *Laborem Exercens*, the pope there employed the term "solidarity," as it is commonly used, to denote the mutual support by which members of an oppressed group strengthen each other to resist injustice. In an earlier work written before he became pope, he gave a more philosophical account of solidarity as a virtue. It is an attitude, a commitment on the part of those who form a community, to participate in the life of that community in a way that promotes the common good.

In the present encyclical the pope puts forward a more theological analysis of the virtue of solidarity. First, it is an enabling power that gives us the capacity to respect others:

> Solidarity helps us to see the "other"—whether a person, people or nation—not just as some kind of instrument with a work capacity and physical strength to be exploited at low cost and then discarded when no longer useful, but as our "neighbor," a "helper" (cf. Gen. 2:18–20), to be made a sharer, on a par with ourselves, in the banquet of life to which all are equally invited by God. (*SRS* 39)

In this way the virtue of solidarity enables us to overcome distrust and to collaborate with others (*SRS* 39). Consequently, the exercise of this virtue is the path to true peace (*SRS* 39). The pope points out that the achievement of peace requires not only justice but also "the practice of the virtues which favor togetherness, and which teach us to live in unity, so as to build in unity, by giving and receiving, a new society and a better world" (*SRS* 39). So solidarity presupposes justice but goes beyond it by including generosity and care for others.

The aspect of generous self-sacrifice is developed more fully by the pope when he goes on to focus attention on the Christian character of the virtue of solidarity. He suggests that "solidarity seeks to go beyond itself, to take on the specifically Christian dimensions of total gratuity, forgiveness, and reconciliation." John Paul finds the basis for this selfless love in the fact that each person is the living image of God (*SRS* 40). He goes on to say that, for the Christian, the ultimate inspiration for solidarity comes from a unity that is even deeper than any unity based on natural and human bonds; this is a communion that is a reflection of the unity of the three Persons in one God (*SRS* 40).

Structures of Sin

The pope's account of solidarity is part of his sustained effort in this encyclical to overcome the individualistic viewpoint that marred moral theology in the past. By emphasizing solidarity, he is saying that virtue is not just a private affair. But just as virtue is not a private matter, neither is sin. So the pope takes up the notion of the social dimension of sin under the title "structures of sin" (*SRS* 36).

He tries to strike a balance between two extremes. On the one hand, he wants to correct the idea that sin is a purely personal action. So he insists that sin becomes embodied in attitudes, traditions, and institutions that endure long after "the actions and the brief lifespan of an individual" (*SRS* 36). On the other hand, he resists the idea that structural evil is the primary reality—a notion linked to the Marxist emphasis on the need for a revolution to overthrow the structures. John Paul insists that structures of sin are "rooted in personal sin, and thus always linked to the *concrete acts* of individuals who introduce these structures, consolidate them and make them difficult to remove" (*SRS* 36). In giving primacy to personal, deliberate sin the pope no doubt saw himself as correcting a dangerous tendency of liberation theology.

John Paul also insisted that structures of sin are to be understood not merely in terms of a social analysis (*SRS* 36) but in theological terms: "Hidden behind certain decisions, apparently inspired only by economics or politics, are real forms of *idolatry*: of money, ideology, class, technology" (*SRS* 37). The essence of this idolatry is an absolutizing of certain human attitudes, for instance, an all-consuming desire for profit and a thirst for power at any price (*SRS* 37). In making this point, the pope was repeating one of the favorite themes of the liberation theologians (e.g., Gutiérrez 1973; Segundo 1985, 55–65; Galilea 1984, 23). However, as Baum notes, his heavy emphasis on the personal roots of social sin means that he pays less attention than Medellín and the liberation theologians to its unconscious aspects, such as the blindness caused by ideology and the dominant culture (Baum 1989, 113–16; cf. Curran, Himes, and Shannon 2005, 427).

If the structures of sin are so pervasive and powerful, how can we hope to bring about genuine development? At the personal level there must be a conversion in the biblical sense, that is, "a change of behavior or mentality or mode of existence" (*SRS* 38). The social dimension of this conversion is the virtue of solidarity. Solidarity brings about a radical change in society because it gives people the ability to oppose diametrically the all-consuming desire for profit and the thirst for power as well as the structures of sin that spring from them (*SRS* 37–38). In this way it provides a foundation of a whole new set of structures, which can be called "*the civilization of love*" (*SRS* 33). So the crucial importance of solidarity in the pope's theology of development is that, for him, it is the only effective response to the misdevelopment and corruption of our world.

Inadequacies

Pope John Paul's account of the virtue of solidarity is a valuable one. He has made a praiseworthy attempt to give solid theological content to a word that is widely used in the world today, a word that describes a feature of modern moral consciousness at its best. There can be no doubt that he has met a real need, since a moral account of human development that is confined to such traditional words as "charity" and "justice" can seem at times to lack the flavor of real life. However, there are some points at which his account of solidarity seems to be insufficiently developed.

The treatment of solidarity in this encyclical fails to put any particular emphasis on the special role that God has given to those who are weak and poor in bringing liberation to all. It is true, and important, that the pope says that the Church feels called by the gospel to take a stand alongside the poor in their public but nonviolent demands for justice (*SRS* 39). He speaks of "the *option* or *love of preference* for the poor" as "a *special form* of primacy in the exercise of Christian charity," and he notes that it applies not only to each individual Christian, but also "to our *social responsibilities* and hence to our manner of living (*LE* 42).

I agree with Charles Curran when he says that preferential love and preferential option "are not exactly the same thing" and when he suggests that the phrasing of John Paul suggests a certain hesitancy about accepting the concept of a preferential option for the poor (Curran 2002, 183). Certainly, the pope does not stress the active role that those who are poor may play in God's plan of salvation. This is a theological issue that can have very practical implications, for if poor and marginalized people are called to be key agents of change, it is unlikely that they can play this role without some confrontation (cf. Baum 1989, 120–21), and if the Church is committed to an option for the poor, then it too must face up to the challenge of serious confrontation.

This points to another inadequacy in the encyclical's treatment of solidarity: the model of social change that the pope envisages here seems to be a consensus model. As I noted in chapter 11, when John Paul spoke to the shanty dwellers of Brazil and the Philippines and to the American Indians of Guatemala, he encouraged them to take responsibility for their lives, to struggle against injustice, and to stand up for their rights. He reaffirmed this approach in *Laborem Exercens*—an approach that, as I noted, was developed more fully in a work he had written in Poland before he became pope.

If one were to rely only on what John Paul wrote and said up to about 1983, in order to assess his attitude on this issue of confrontation, one could conclude that he was willing to break with the tradition established by his predecessors. One could say that he had come to acknowledge that, at least in some circumstances, progress can come only through confrontation. But his statements from that time onward could lead to a revision of that view. It seems to me that the position he adopts in *Sollicitudo Rei Socialis* is a backward step on the issue of confrontation. In this encyclical he does not encourage the poor and powerless to see themselves as key agents of change. Nor does he repeat here what he had said before he became pope about the role of opposition as one aspect of solidarity.

Quite the contrary; his treatment here is distinctly more reserved in this regard (cf. Coleman 1991, 42). It is likely that this reserve is due to his determination to distance himself from the stance of the liberation theologians—not so much in terms of their teaching but with respect to their encouragement to the poor to see themselves, and organize themselves, as the key agents in the struggle for liberation.

Closely related to this is a certain blandness and unreality in the encyclical's treatment of the relationship between different groups or classes in society (*SRS* 39). What is lacking is a social analysis that would take more seriously the causes of the class structure in society and that could then go on to examine ways in which tensions between the different classes can be overcome or lessened.

Another significant point about the treatment of solidarity in *Sollicitudo Rei Socialis* is that it appears to lack an affective dimension. This is surprising since the pope's account of solidarity obviously owes a great deal to the strong affective bonds that have linked him so closely to his own people in their history and their struggles. His treatment of solidarity could have been enriched significantly by a fuller account of the experience of solidarity and the strong feelings that are part of it.

By the "experience" of solidarity I mean the actual sharing of life with a group of people. When one shares the living conditions of a community, one can begin to share their sufferings and joys, their fears and their hopes. Out of this lived solidarity grow the bonds of affection that make one feel part of this people and enable them to accept one as truly part of themselves. These bonds of shared life and feelings evoke and nourish a strong sense of responsibility for the whole community and especially for its weaker members. So the virtue of solidarity should not be defined as purely an attitude of the will in contrast to "mere feelings." The gap between the fact of interdependence and the undertaking of an appropriate moral response is not adequately bridged by academic knowledge, or reasoning, or even by prayer. Study and prayer must be situated within the context of some degree of shared life with people and the bonds of affectivity to which such sharing gives rise.

It is interesting to note that with the collapse of communism in the Soviet bloc, the issue on which the encyclical became controversial—its equal criticism of East and West—has already been overtaken by history. Much more significant is its treatment of solidarity. Despite the incompleteness or weaknesses in what it has to say on this topic, its teaching adds a significant component to the corpus of Catholic social teaching (cf. *SRS* 1, 3, 41), one that should endure and be fully integrated into moral theology.[3]

---

[3]Curran, Himes, and Shannon (2005, 430–33) provide a helpful account of the way

In 1988 the pope issued an important document, *Mulieris Dignitatem*, on the dignity of women. I examine this in some detail in chapter 14, which focuses on the role of women. Two years later came the important "Message for the 1990 World Day of Peace." I shall deal with it in chapter 18 focused on the issue of ecology.

The US Bishops

During the 1980s the bishops of the United States made an important contribution to Catholic social teaching by issuing a number of joint pastoral letters on questions of justice and peace. The most significant aspect of their program was the process they used in preparing these pastorals. They organized many formal and informal consultations on the topics in question. Then they published a series of drafts of each of their pastoral letters. These drafts were discussed and debated in great depth before any definitive document was issued. This consultative process was an effective means of educating both the bishops themselves and the Christian community as a whole.

The first of this series of joint pastoral letters was issued in 1983 under the title *The Challenge of Peace: God's Promise and Our Response*. The second draft of this document had come out quite firmly against nuclear deterrence. There was a strong reaction against this position within the United States. More significantly, there was also resistance to it from the Vatican, mainly, perhaps because at this time Pope John Paul II seemed to be suggesting that deterrence could be considered acceptable if it were a step on the way to progressive disarmament. The bishops bowed to the pressure, and in the final draft of their pastoral letter they did not condemn the idea of deterrence (cf. Geyer 1989, 3).

In 1986 the US bishops issued another joint pastoral, titled *Economic Justice for All: Pastoral Letter on Catholic Social Teaching and the US Economy*. This too went through several drafts, and the final text put forward a fairly strong critique of American capitalist society. As a result, the document was greeted with some hostility by defenders of the system. However, quite a number of socially committed Christians felt dissatisfied with the letter because it seemed to be critical of abuses within the system rather than of the whole capitalist model of development.

The theme chosen for the third joint pastoral letter in this series was

---

the encyclical was received in different parts of the world. It provoked outrage among some right-wing commentators in the United States about what they saw as the manner in which it judged East and West with "moral equivalence," but it was welcomed in Latin America and the Philippines. However, some commentators saw it as backtracking from the more inductive methodology that had come into favor and that had been affirmed by Paul VI in *Octogesima Adveniens*.

the role and situation of women. This proved to be an exceptionally difficult topic. One reason for this was that many feminist theologians (and others) were resistant to the very idea that a group of men should attempt to define the place of women (cf. Price 1991, 125). Another reason was the disappointment and anger of many Christians about the unwillingness of Rome to make any concession on the question of the ordination of women and related issues.

The focus of attention in this book is on Vatican teaching rather than on the teaching of any regional grouping of bishops, so I am not concerned here with the detail of the contents of these documents of the US bishops. However, there are two points about these pastoral letters that are of particular interest from my present point of view. The first is that the Vatican kept a keen eye on their proposed contents and did not hesitate to subject the US bishops to considerable pressure to ensure that what they said would conform to the current Roman line. This does not fit in well with the teaching of Paul VI in *Octogesima Adveniens* that, given the variety of situations in which the Church finds itself, it cannot propose a detailed unified message of universal validity on social issues (*OA* 4). It would appear that the Vatican took a very restricted interpretation of Pope Paul's words.

The second significant point is that the participative process used in the preparation of these US documents contrasts sharply with the secretive approach used in the Vatican during the preparation of documents of all kinds, including those on social justice issues. The adoption of a consultative process in the United States led many Christians to ask why Rome does not use a similar process. In this way, then, the US bishops issued a strong challenge to Rome, whether or not they intended to do so.

An Encyclical on Mission

At the end of 1990 Pope John Paul issued an encyclical about missionary activity, titled *Redemptoris Missio*. It is a document of major importance, but only a few points of it are relevant to the issue of justice, poverty, and liberation. In general, this encyclical gives a rounded and valuable account of the evangelizing role of the Church. But the vision that permeates it seems to lack some of the spirit of universality and integral humanism that are typical of John Paul. There is a tendency at times to define the work of the Church as "spiritual" in contrast to what is "temporal" or secular, with a consequent playing down of the centrality of a commitment to justice.

Toward the end of the encyclical there is a passage that reads as follows:

It is not right to give an incomplete picture of missionary activity as if it consisted principally in helping the poor, contributing to the liberation of the oppressed, promoting human development, or defending human rights. The missionary Church is certainly involved on these fronts but her primary task lies elsewhere: the poor are hungry for God, not just for bread and freedom. (*RM* 83)

It is unfortunate that, in rejecting an incomplete and inaccurate picture of missionary work, the encyclical seems to make an unduly sharp contrast between the hunger for God and the hunger for bread and freedom. When it speaks of "the Church's primary task," it could give the impression that everything else is only secondary. This somewhat dualistic tone is perhaps owing to the fact that at least parts of the encyclical may not have been drafted by the pope himself or his inner circle of advisers.

Referring to non-Christians who live according to gospel values and are open to the Spirit, the encyclical refers to this as the "temporal dimension of the Kingdom" (*RM* 20). It would have been more accurate to acknowledge that such non-Christians may be in touch not just with the temporal aspect of the Kingdom or Reign of God, but with its transcendent and eschatological aspect as well.

THE CENTENARY ENCYCLICAL

Unlike many other encyclicals that were not anticipated, Pope John Paul's third social encyclical was long awaited. Various efforts had been made to prepare for it, partly in response to the request of the Pontifical Council for Justice and Peace that the centenary of *Rerum Novarum* be celebrated all over the world by conferences. A number of people had asked or hoped that the encyclical would be preceded by a fuller consultative process than that envisaged by the Council for Justice and Peace; they would have liked to see a public sifting of suggestions from Christians in different parts of the world about the content and style of this centenary document. This expectation had been aroused by the elaborate consultation process used by the bishops of the United States in the preparation of their pastoral letters on peace, economic justice, and the situation of women—as well as by the somewhat similar process used by the Australian bishops and by the fact that the Irish bishops had set up a series of consultations with representatives from different sectors of society in preparation for a new pastoral letter on justice.

Furthermore, just about the time that the new encyclical was being drafted, the World Council of Churches was engaged in a complex process of consultation and revision of the draft document for its 1991 General Assembly in Canberra. Pope John Paul undoubtedly engaged in some consultation prior to writing the encyclical. But when he published

Centesimus Annus in May 1991, both its contents and its style indicated that this new encyclical was very much his own document.[4]

The contents of the encyclical caused a good deal of surprise. It was not the wide-ranging document that many had expected on this occasion. Nor was it, as the more ecologically minded had hoped, a profound critique of the expansionist model of economic development on which most governments were resting their hopes. The heart of the document consisted rather of the personal reflections of a man who had played a key role in the transformation of Europe. In this encyclical the pope looked back on his own struggle and that of his people, and he shared the lessons of this experience with his worldwide audience; he also extended his reflections back over a hundred years of European history and adverted occasionally to the situation of the wider world.

A striking feature of *Centesimus Annus* is the extent to which it reaffirms the teaching of *Rerum Novarum*. The first chapter is devoted to a lengthy examination of Leo's encyclical. But John Paul does not read this hundred-year-old document in the manner of an academic historian. Rather, his reading is unashamedly selective, because it was done with a pastoral intent. He is concerned, above all, with the many ways in which its teaching can be seen as still relevant a hundred years later. He points out various ways in which it pioneered a new approach and has enduring value:

1. Leo insisted that the Church has a corpus of "social doctrine" the teaching of which "is an essential part of the Christian message" (*CA* 5).
2. *Rerum Novarum* insisted on the dignity of work and of the worker (*CA* 6).
3. It also upheld certain fundamental human rights—the right to own private property (*CA* 6), the right to form professional associations or trade unions (*CA* 7), the right to proper working conditions (*CA* 7) and to a just wage (*CA* 8), the right to discharge one's religious duties, which John Paul sees as "a springboard for the principle of the right to religious freedom" (*CA* 9).
4. Over against socialism and liberalism, *Rerum Novarum* defended the principle of solidarity, even though Leo did not

---

[4]Daniel Finn (2005, 437–42) gives a particularly interesting account of the political and ecclesiastical context in which the encyclical was written and of the process of its formulation. He notes three developments in the Church which were significant background influences on it—liberation theology, the rise of a neoconservative defense of what Michael Novak called "democratic capitalism," and the pastoral letters on economic issues that had been issued by conferences of Catholic bishops in various parts of the world.

employ this term but instead used the word "friendship" as a technical term (*CA* 10).

5. John Paul sees *Rerum Novarum* as "an excellent testimony to the continuity within the Church of the so-called 'preferential option for the poor'" (*CA* 11).

6. Finally, the pope sums up by noting how these themes that he has highlighted in Leo's encyclical are all situated within a coherent Church teaching that deals with private property, work, the economic process, the role of the state, and the nature of the human person (*CA* 11).

John Paul's rereading of *Rerum Novarum* in *Centesimus Annus* verges on the anachronistic; he sees in it a depth of insight that the secular historian would never find. At times, too, his praise for Leo's encyclical has a tinge of triumphalism. He does not refer at all to the inadequacies of *Rerum Novarum*, for instance, its overemphasis on the right to private property, its ambivalence on the question of a family wage (see Molony 1991, 85–87), or its very limited conception of what a trade union should be. Clearly John Paul's purpose is to nourish the faith of his readers by writing a kind of "salvation history" of the document, one that emphasizes its positive points, that develops points that were not at all clear in the document itself, and that bypasses negative aspects.

The Events of 1989

Using the concept of salvation history as a key category for understanding the style and tone of *Centesimus Annus* can throw light on not only the first chapter of the encyclical but also on the following two chapters in which the pope examines the "new things" of today and particularly the great events of 1989. Salvation history is always written in the light of a particular experience of God's saving power. The Jews wrote their history largely in the light of the Exodus experience. It would seem that in the writing of *Centesimus Annus*, the key experience for Pope John Paul is the collapse of communism in Eastern Europe.

The pope was no detached observer of this process. No less an authority than the former Soviet president, Mikhail Gorbachev, testifies to the major political role played by the pope in the collapse of communism: "Everything that happened in eastern Europe during these last few years would not have been possible without the presence of this pope, without the leading role—the political role—that he was able to play on the world scene" (Gorbachev 1992, 9). And John Paul himself indicated a qualified acceptance of this assessment. So John Paul's view of the events of the years 1989 and 1990 is that of a committed activist with his own perspective and particular interests. He says openly that his analysis of the events of recent history "is not meant to pass definitive judgments since this does not fall *per se* within the *Magisterium*'s specific domain" (*CA* 3).

Most people who look back on the extraordinary months of late 1989 and early 1990 are left with two dominant images. The first is the dismantlement of the Berlin wall, and the second is Nelson Mandela walking with extraordinary dignity out of the prison where he had been "buried" for twenty-seven years. If the pope had been an African, he might well have been inclined to see the second of these events as even more important than the first—and he might have chosen it as the key development on which to base his reflections on the centenary of *Rerum Novarum*. The result could have been an extremely interesting encyclical, for the pope might then have insisted that the basic split in our world is not between East and West but between the North and the South. In that perspective the East and the West would be seen as just two variants of the North. The collapse of communist economics and ideology in Eastern Europe might then be seen as an early stage of the mortal illness of the whole Northern approach to development and to the world.

But John Paul wrote his encyclical out of a Polish experience, not out of an African one. What he offers in much of the encyclical are pastoral reflections (cf. *CA* 3) arising largely from his own deep involvement in the struggle against an oppressive tyranny. The result is that what he writes has the feel of life. That is its strength. But it also accounts for its limitations.

It has been suggested that in this encyclical, the pope's vision is unduly Eurocentric. Perhaps it would be more accurate to suggest that he has a global view but one that is deeply anchored in a long and exciting Eastern European experience. This is undoubtedly a healthy corrective to the excessive weight given by many of his predecessors to Italian or Western European experience. But it may mean that at times the East European experience unduly colors his interpretation of situations in other parts of the world.

Was John Paul Accepting Capitalism?

Two crucial issues arise in relation to the teaching of this encyclical. The first is whether the pope is accepting capitalism, and the second is whether he is rejecting the notion of "the welfare state."

Concerning capitalism, John Paul's position is very much in line with the tradition of social teaching laid down by the Church over the previous hundred years: he favors a good deal of free enterprise but is not satisfied with the ideology of liberal capitalism. Daniel Finn helpfully sums up his approach: "The interplay of the two principles of subsidiarity and solidarity sets the stage for John Paul's careful moral assessment of capitalism. Where subsidiarity argues for respectful recognition of individual economic initiative, solidarity calls for strong communal action to prevent abuses and ensure the common good" (Finn 2005, 449).

John Paul distinguishes two meanings of the word "capitalism" and accepts one of them—though he prefers to use such terms as "business economy," "market economy," or "free economy" (*CA* 42; cf. Finn 2005, 452–53). He maintains that the free market is "the most efficient instrument for utilizing resources and effectively responding to needs" (*CA* 34). He notes that the mechanisms of the market "help to utilize resources better; they promote the exchange of products; above all they give central place to the person's desires and preferences, which, in a contract, meet the desires and preferences of another person" (*CA* 40). He also acknowledges "the legitimate role of profit as an indication that a business is functioning well" (*CA* 35).

On the other hand, he spells out clearly that there is an unacceptable conception of capitalism—one where there is an "absolute predominance of capital" (*CA* 35), where the economic sector is not controlled by "a strong juridical framework which places it at the service of human freedom" (*CA* 42). He insists that the market must be "appropriately controlled by the forces of society and by the State, so as to guarantee that the basic needs of the whole of society are satisfied" (*CA* 35). This position is almost exactly what had been demanded by Leo XIII a hundred years earlier.

Despite his acceptance of "the market economy," John Paul does not back away from the strong stance taken by Paul VI in *Octogesima Adveniens* that the Church has no ready-made universal model for society (*CA* 42; cf. *CA* 4). Immediately following his acceptance of one meaning of the word "capitalism," John Paul goes on to insist: "The Church has no models to present; models that are real and truly effective can only arise within the framework of different historical situations" (*CA* 43), and at this point he refers to *Octogesima Adveniens*. We must conclude, then, that in opting for a "market economy," John Paul is not really giving approval to capitalism as *the* correct system. He is simply laying down certain minimum conditions for any acceptable model of society, namely, that the right to own, buy, and sell goods, and the right to take other economic initiatives, while they may need to be controlled, must not be entirely abolished. Having asserted the need to respect certain basic rights, the encyclical goes on to insist that the Church "is not entitled to express preferences for this or that institutional or constitutional solution" (*CA* 47).

In line with the tradition of his predecessors, and especially the encyclicals of Leo XIII and Pius XI, John Paul concludes that neither liberal capitalism nor communism fulfills the minimum conditions required in order that an economic system should be morally acceptable. The former subordinates people to profit; it gives rise to alienation in workers, since it is not concerned about whether they grow through their work or are swamped in a maze of destructive, competitive, and estranging relationships (*CA* 41). Communism, on the other hand, turns out to be state capitalism, or what the encyclical (rather oddly) calls "Real Socialism" (*CA* 35, 56). I note in passing that the term "Real Socialism" used in the English translation is rather misleading. Perhaps a better translation would have been "*actual* socialism," that is, the version of socialism that actually developed in Eastern Europe as distinct from some ideal socialism of which philosophers or politicians might speak.

John Paul maintains that this collectivist system actually increases alienation rather than doing away with it (*CA* 41). In various parts of the encyclical he puts forward a philosophical critique of Marxism and Marxist-Leninism (e.g., *CA* 44–45). Furthermore, he maintains that the deepest cause of the collapse of communism in Eastern Europe was "the spiritual void brought about by atheism" (*CA* 24).

The Welfare State

One section of the encyclical caused disappointment, if not dismay, among many committed Catholics who had been struggling to care for the casualties of the Western capitalist system (see, e.g., Fitzgerald 1991, 11). It is the section in which the pope speaks out strongly against the welfare state, which has, he says, been dubbed "the Social Assistance State" (*CA* 48). He maintains that "the Social Assistance State" has failed to respect the principle of subsidiarity. By intervening directly and unnecessarily it has, he says, given rise to bureaucratic ways of thinking and has deprived people of responsibility and caused a loss of human energies. He goes on to suggest that various categories of people in need, ranging from refugees to drug abusers, can be helped effectively not by the state but only by people close to them who offer them personal care and support (*CA* 48).

This is undoubtedly a strong attack on the Western model of state welfare, one that is reminiscent of the Catholic social teaching of forty or fifty years earlier. Indeed, John Paul's concern about the effects of bureaucracy seems to be an echo of the views of Pius XII. No wonder, then, that the encyclical gave rise to some gloating by neoconservatives, who hailed it as an indication that the pope had at last come to his senses and returned Catholic social teaching to its original and true position.[5]

---

[5]For an interesting account of the reaction of American neoconservatives such as Michael Novak and Richard John Neuhaus and for critical responses to their interpretation of the encyclical, see Finn (2005, 458–62).

The question has to be faced whether John Paul moved backward in this encyclical on this aspect of the social question, reinstating an old-style Catholic approach to social issues and reversing the remarkable advances made by John XXIII, Paul VI, and Vatican II. At first sight, it would undoubtedly appear that he did. Some of his remarks about the welfare state sound quite like the kind of things that were said in the 1980s by Margaret Thatcher and her followers, and that are frequently said by many politicians and others in the United States.

However, it is possible to read *Centesimus Annus* in a different light. There is a strong case for saying that, instead of moving backward from the welfare state, what John Paul is suggesting is that we move *onward* toward a more effective and respectful approach. He clearly believes that one aspect of this is that the principle of subsidiarity should be applied. This implies that welfare should not be left entirely to the national government (cf. Finn 2005, 452). Charles Curran sums up the situation well: "The papal criticism of the social assistance state is based on John Paul II's emphasis on a participatory community. The state has an important role to play in bringing about such a participatory community, but its assistance should not be in the form of impersonal bureaucracies that foster passive dependence" (Curran 2002, 209). The pope's criticism of bureaucracy is a valid one, but, in the context of modern society, it is not at all easy to see how welfare can be safely and effectively left entirely in the hands of local authorities and voluntary agencies.

A second aspect of the approach favored by John Paul is that people who are poor or disadvantaged should not be treated as objects to be assisted but as subjects in their own right. They are not just to be helped but to be empowered. One important passage lends support to such a reading of the encyclical. Having reaffirmed the Church's preferential option for the poor (*CA* 57), the pope points out that love for the poor has to be made concrete through the promotion of justice. Justice is not fully attained, he says, so long as the poor are seen as a burden. Then he goes on to say:

> It is not merely a matter of "giving from one's surplus," but of helping entire peoples which are presently excluded or marginalized to enter into the sphere of economic and human development. . . . [This] . . . requires above all a change of . . . the established structures of power which today govern societies. Nor is it a matter of eliminating instruments of social organization which have proved useful, but rather of orienting them according to an adequate notion of the common good. (*CA* 58)

The pope seems to be thinking here mainly of poor nations, but there is no doubt that he would also want his words to apply to poor or marginalized groups within any given country. He wants deprived nations and groups to be allowed and enabled to become self-sufficient economically and so to be no longer a "burden" to be supported reluctantly by others. So his criticism of what he calls the "Social Assistance State" is an invitation to committed people to devise ways in which poor people can be empowered economically and can in this way get out from under the dead hand of bureaucracy.

The pope himself lived for years at the mercy of the *nomenclatura*— the awful Polish bureaucracy. So he had direct experience of how such bureaucracies can smother people while claiming to be looking after them. And the experience of some groups of marginal people in most Western countries is similar to that in Poland. Many of those who are dependent on some kind of unemployment benefit from the state feel themselves disempowered and marginalized by the way in which this "assistance" is provided.

The real test of a social security system is whether it creates unnecessary dependency or whether it goes some way toward empowering people, making them aware of their own dignity and supporting them in taking initiatives on their own behalf. It may be argued that *Centesimus Annus* does not put forward any practical proposals for how such an empowerment can take place. That is true. But the pope may respond that it is not his task to get into such concrete detail. It is up to committed citizens (both Christians and non-Christians) to find a way forward.

My conclusion is that the pope is not suggesting that Western social security systems be disbanded and that we go back to old-style private charity toward the poor. What he is calling for is, first of all, that governments should respect the principle of subsidiarity. Second, we should modify the existing welfare systems so that they become a more humane and empowering way of exercising our solidarity with the victims of our society. It is regrettable that this is not immediately evident to those who read the encyclical superficially. It is even more regrettable that the pope's harsh criticism of the "Social Assistance State" provides convenient ammunition for those who want to play down their obligation to help the poor, leaving it to be a matter of voluntary and private charity. But even though there is a danger that the pope's words will be misunderstood or deliberately misinterpreted, nevertheless they are valuable; they stand as a strong and necessary challenge to committed people to go beyond the welfare approach and seek a radical and effective response to the problems of poverty in today's world.

Property and Work

The second half of the encyclical puts forward a philosophical account of the economic and cultural aspects of human society. Much of the writing in the later part of the encyclical is dense, and the direction of the argument is not always clear. However, some important points emerge. One is John Paul's firm insistence on the universal destination of the goods of the Earth. In reference to the first sentence in *CA* 30, Daniel Finn (2005, 446) points out that the pope shifts the issue "from the right *of* private property to the right *to* private property."

The pope also addresses the issue of employment. It is clear that he is critical of the situation that has emerged in countries of the North where large numbers of workers are made redundant, or laid off—either because of new technology or as a result of the "outsourcing" of work to countries where wages are very low—purely in order to enhance the profits of employers:

> A society in which this right [to employment] is systematically denied, in which economic policies do not allow workers to reach satisfactory levels of employment, cannot be justified from an ethical point of view, nor can that society attain social peace. . . . Ownership morally justifies itself in the creation, at the proper time and in the proper way, of opportunities for work and human growth for all. (*CA* 43)

John Paul outlines the general principle guiding his views on such matters by saying that the state "has the task of determining the juridical framework within which economic affairs are to be conducted, and thus of safeguarding the prerequisites of a free economy, which presumes a certain equality between the parties, such that one party would not be so powerful as practically to reduce the other to subservience" (*LE* 15).

In a later section he spells out more fully the competence of the state and the limits to the extent to which it should be directly involved. At this point he is making an important distinction between the state and society as well is applying his understanding of the principle of subsidiarity. He says that

> primary responsibility in this [economic] area belongs not to the State but to individuals and to the various groups and associations which make up society. . . . This does not mean, however, that the State has no competence in this domain. . . . Rather, the State has a duty to sustain business activities by creating conditions which will ensure job opportunities, by stimulating those activities where they are lacking or by supporting them in moments of crisis. (*CA* 48)

He goes on immediately to add the following:

> The State has the further right to intervene when particular monopolies create delays or obstacles to development. In . . . exceptional

circumstances the State can also exercise *a substitute function,* when social sectors or business systems are too weak or are just getting under way, and are not equal to the task at hand. Such supplementary interventions, which are justified by urgent reasons touching the common good, must be as brief as possible, so as to avoid removing permanently from society and business systems the functions which are properly theirs, and so as to avoid enlarging excessively the sphere of State intervention to the detriment of both economic and civil freedom. (*CA* 48)

In all this, it is evident that John Paul's approach is in line with the tradition of the earlier social encyclicals. However, he is not just repeating what was said by his predecessors about the limits to the role of the state and the principle of subsidiarity; he is attempting to apply the traditional principles and guidelines to the contemporary situation.

One interesting and controversial point that emerges in this encyclical is the extent to which the pope's approach is anthropocentric when he is dealing with the ecological issue. This is a topic I examine in some detail in chapter 18.

I conclude my commentary on the centenary encyclical by noting an important point made by the pope toward the end of the document. He points out that the social message of the Church will gain credibility not so much from its internal logic and consistency as "from the witness of actions" (*CA* 57). In other words he is saying that, in matters of social justice, actions speak louder than words.

* * *

SUMMARY

From 1983 onward Pope John Paul continued to express his concern about injustice in society; he focused particular attention on the right of people to maintain their own culture. The pope took up some of the key themes of the liberation theologians. But he and Vatican officials were greatly concerned about liberation theology, fearing that the Christian faith would be reduced to the service of a Marxist political ideology.

The encyclical *Sollicitudo Rei Socialis* adopts and extends the approach to development put forward by Paul VI in *Populorum Progressio*. At the heart of the encyclical John Paul develops an elaborate and valuable teaching on the virtue of solidarity, but this does not take much account of the role of confrontation. The encyclical also gives an account of the structures of sin, one in which he emphasizes the priority of personal sin.

The consultative process used by the bishops of the United States in preparing joint pastoral letters on social issues is an important contribution to the tradition of Catholic social teaching.

The pope's encyclical on mission is valuable, but in some respects it does not reflect the breadth of vision of his earlier encyclicals.

The centenary encyclical *Centesimus Annus* highlights and reaffirms many of the traditional elements of Catholic social teaching, emphasizing the continuity of that teaching over the previous hundred years. The pope distinguishes two meanings of the word "capitalism," rejecting capitalism insofar as it means economic liberalism and accepting it insofar as it means allowing people to take economic initiative. The encyclical is critical of the welfare state. But this should not be seen as approval by the pope for the liberal capitalist approach. It can rather be understood as a challenge to people to develop caring societies in which the state protects the weaker sectors but does not cripple their initiative or make them dependent on the state.

The encyclical criticizes any economic system in which workers can lose their employment simply in order to increase the profits of employers. He insists on the need for the state to provide a juridical framework that ensures a reasonable degree of equality in society. However, in line with traditional Catholic teaching, he also insists that the state should not take over responsibilities that should rest with civil society.

QUESTIONS FOR REVIEW

1. *What aspects of the social justice agenda did John Paul highlight in his overseas journeys from 1982 onward?*
2. *What are the differences between the two Vatican documents on liberation?*
3. *Why is the notion of solidarity so central to the encyclical* Sollicitudo Rei Socialis?
4. *In what sense does the centenary encyclical accept capitalism and in what sense does it reject it?*
5. *What is the attitude of the encyclical toward "the welfare state"?*

QUESTIONS FOR REFLECTION

1. *Why does John Paul's teaching on solidarity in* Sollicitudo Rei Socialis *have a different emphasis from some of his earlier views on the subject?*

2. *Can you see any acceptable alternative to the welfare state?*
3. *Does the practice of the Church live up to its official teaching on justice in society?*

ISSUES FOR FURTHER STUDY

1. *The effect of the collapse of communism in Eastern Europe and central Asia on the countries of the South.*
2. *The policies of the wealthy nations in negotiations about world trade and how they affect the poorer countries.*
3. *The teaching and action of the World Council of Churches (and its member churches) on "Justice, Peace and the Integrity of Creation."*

14

Women: Justice, Equality, and Complementarity

The older traditional Catholic teaching on women is found in Leo XIII's *Rerum Novarum*. It says, "A woman is by nature fitted for home-work, and it is that which is best adapted at once to preserve her modesty and to promote the good of bringing up children and the well-being of the family" (*RN* 42). Pius XI's 1930 encyclical *Casti Connubi* spells out more fully the official Church's view of women in his time. It insists on "the primacy of the husband with regard to the wife and children, the ready subjection of the wife and her willing obedience" (26). Assuming that the role of women is a purely domestic one, it also insists that the husband, as head of the family, should be paid sufficient to support the whole family (117).

Things began to change from 1963 onward with John XXIII's encyclical *Pacem in Terris*. It openly acknowledged the obvious fact that a large number of women were going out to work rather than just engaging in domestic work at home. Taking account of this, Pope John wrote, "Women must be accorded such conditions of work as are consistent with their needs and responsibilities as wives and mothers" (*PT* 19). This represented an early stage in the quite radical changes in the Church teaching about women that have taken place since then.

The Pastoral Constitution *Gaudium et Spes*, issued by Vatican II in 1965, affirmed clearly that all humans are equal and that any discrimination on the basis of sex is contrary to God's will and is to be overcome (*GS* 29). The document went on to make an extended attempt to take account of the reality that women are a significant part of the workforce outside the home. It said, "Women now work in almost all spheres" (*GS* 60). However, it also said that their "domestic role . . . must be safely preserved, though the legitimate social progress of women should not be underrated on that account" (*GS* 52). So when dealing with women's work outside the home, the document struck a rather uneasy balance by saying, "It is fitting that they are able to assume their proper role in accordance with their own nature" (*GS* 60). It was only in later documents that what the official Church sees as characteristic of this specific "nature" of women was spelled out.

In his closing address to the Vatican Council on December 8, 1965, Pope Paul VI issued a special call to women:

> You women have always had as your lot the protection of the home, the love of beginnings and an understanding of cradles. . . . Our technology runs the risk of becoming inhuman. Reconcile men with life and above all, we beseech you, watch carefully over the future of our race. Hold back the hand of man who, in a moment of folly, might attempt to destroy human civilization. . . .
> Women of the entire universe, whether Christian or non-believing, you to whom life is entrusted at this grave moment in history, it is for you to save the peace of the world.

Commenting on this call, Ivy Helman (2011, 26) remarks, "The church is placing a heavy and difficult burden on the backs of all women." She adds, "The idea that women are naturally better at teaching, conveying the truth, helping men focus their minds toward life, creating peace, and saving humanity from itself all seem to be new additions to the official theology of womanhood" (Helman 2011, 28). She follows this up by referring to an address of Paul VI in reference to the 1975 International Year of the Woman, in which he invokes the "perseverance, generosity, and humility" of women to preserve the future of society (Hellman 2011, 46). Meanwhile, the document "Justice in the World" issued by the 1971 Roman Synod of Bishops included one brief but important statement: "We . . . urge that women should have their proper share of responsibility and participation in the community life of society and likewise of the Church" (JW 42). This indicates that the authors of the document had abandoned the traditional Church teaching that "the woman's place is in the home," insofar as that phrase is understood to mean that women should not work in the public sphere. As I have noted in chapter 9, the synod document went on to propose that a mixed commission of men and women, religious and laypeople, of differing situations and competence, should be set up to examine women's role in church and society (JW 43). This proposal has not (yet) been adequately acted on.

INTER INSIGNIORES (1976)

In 1976 the Congregation for the Doctrine of the Faith issued a document called *Inter Insigniores*; and it was approved and confirmed by Pope Paul VI. Acknowledging that the issue of women's ordination has become a difficult ecumenical issue, this document nevertheless firmly rejects the idea that women could become priests. The document examines the issue in some detail from a biblical and historical point of view, and it offers answers to the various current arguments in favor of a change of practice.

The basic position is put forward as follows:

> The Catholic Church has never felt that priestly or episcopal ordination can be validly conferred on women. . . . By calling only men to the priestly Order and ministry in its true sense, the Church intends to remain faithful to the type of ordained ministry willed by the Lord Jesus Christ and carefully maintained by the Apostles. . . . The Church's tradition in the matter has . . . been so firm in the course of the centuries that the Magisterium has not felt the need to intervene in order to formulate a principle which was not attacked, or to defend a law which was not challenged. (1)

The document goes on to offer two biblical arguments in favor of its position. The first is that Jesus "did not call any women to become part of the Twelve," and this was not just in order "to conform to the customs of his time" (2). The second is that in forbidding women to speak in the assemblies, the apostle Paul was referring not to the right to prophesy there but rather to "the official function of teaching in the Christian assembly" (4).

Perhaps aware that these arguments from the Bible do not convince everyone, the document goes on to affirm, "In the final analysis it is the Church through the voice of the *Magisterium*, that, in these various domains, decides what can change and what must remain immutable." It adds that "it is a question of unbroken tradition throughout the history of the Church, universal in the East and in the West" (4).

It then puts forward what it says is not "a demonstrative argument" but one that has the aim of "clarifying this teaching by the analogy of faith." It says, "The bishop or the priest in the exercise of his ministry, does not act in his own name, *in persona propria*: he represents Christ," and "there would not be this 'natural resemblance' which must exist between Christ and his minister if the role of Christ were not taken by a man: in such a case it would be difficult to see in the minister the image of Christ" (5). The final key point made in the document is that "the priesthood does not form part of the rights of the individual" (6).

LABOREM EXERCENS (1981)

On September 14, 1981, a very significant development in Catholic social teaching came in paragraph 19 of Pope John Paul's first social encyclical, *Laborem Exercens*. What the pope wrote there can be seen as a major advance in the Church's thinking and teaching on the topic of women and work.

Three subparagraphs (all in *LE* 19) deal with three distinct but related topics: family, mothers, and women. In the first subparagraph the pope writes about the family, insisting on the need for an adequate income and that it should not be necessary for both spouses to be employed outside the home. The really significant point is the language used here. In referring to "the head of the family" the Latin text uses the word "homo" rather than "vir"—and the Italian text is "*persona adulta*." Furthermore, the word "spouse" is used rather than the word "wife." It seems likely that these gender-neutral words were deliberately chosen to take account of situations where the woman who goes out to work is the main wage earner—and of situations where a woman is the head of the family. This suggests that John Paul had taken account of the reality of work in the present-day world and had moved on—at least in principle—from the notion that "the woman's place is in the home."

In the next subparagraph the pope addresses himself to the role of mothers. He insists that society should recognize that the mother who cares lovingly for children in the home is doing real and valuable work. He suggests that it should be possible for a mother to take care of her children without penalizing her or discriminating against her for doing so. Mothers should not be forced to abandon the care of their children and take up paid work outside the home. In a crucially important parenthetical comment he says this should be done "without inhibiting her freedom." By inserting these words he is affirming a point made by many in the women's movement: a woman should have the economic freedom to devote time to her young children if she chooses to do so. However, some of the words here suggest that the pope is still holding on to a traditional view: he speaks of the "primary goals of the mission of a mother" as "taking care of her children and educating them in accordance with their needs" (cf. Hinze 2009, 79–80).

The third subparagraph is devoted to women, so it applies in principle even to those who are not wives or mothers—although there are indications that John Paul is not making a clear distinction between the position of women and the role of motherhood. He insists that work in the public sphere should be organized in such a way that "women do not have to pay for their advancement by abandoning what is specific to them and at the expense of the family." This can be seen as reaffirming traditional ideas about the role of woman as wife and mother. However, it may be understood as an acceptance of a major demand of the women's movement: that women should not be forced to fit into the present male-oriented economic system—a system that causes a woman to lose out on her career prospects if she takes a break in her career in order to spend time with her young children.

There seems, then, to be a real ambivalence in the message of *Laborem Exercens*. Its wording seems to have been carefully chosen to avoid the accusation that it is reaffirming the traditional teaching that a woman's place is in the home. Nonetheless, it does not clearly dissociate itself from that older view of the nature and role of women. It seems likely that the ambivalence is owing to the fact that John Paul was determined to take account of the real world where huge numbers of women work outside the home, while he was still inclined to think of "the women" mainly in terms of some ideal of the woman as mother. Later in this chapter I look at some feminist criticisms of John Paul's position.

The failure of the pope and other Church leaders to highlight the quite radical new elements in the encyclical's teaching about women meant that the media and ordinary readers of the encyclical saw it simply as reaffirming the Church's traditional teaching on women. Furthermore, later official Vatican statements did little or nothing to correct this view. What seems to have happened instead is that Church spokespersons have been reluctant to step into this minefield and so have largely gone silent on this whole issue. It is quite significant that the bishops of the United States, having issued important joint pastoral letters about peace in 1983 and about the economy in 1986, were unable to get agreement in their endeavor to issue one about women. All this has led to disappointment and anger among those who believe that the Church should take a lead in promoting justice for women. And, of course, the disappointment and anger have increased greatly as a result of later Church statements and actions in relation to the ordination of women.

FAMILIARIS CONSORTIO (1981)

The 1980 Synod of Bishops in Rome considered the topic of marriage and the family. At the end of the synod they handed over to Pope John Paul a series of "propositions" addressing various issues on which they had come to some measure of consensus. In his closing homily, the pope gave an initial response to some of these propositions, putting forward his own views on the topics—including his view that "a mother should devote herself fully to her family (not to any outside profession)" (Cahill 2005, 368). In November 1981, just two months after the publication of *Laborem Exercens*, the pope issued his apostolic exhortation *Familiaris Consortio*. In it he spelled out his views on the family in much greater detail. This document "reflects convictions expressed in the closing homily, but it also indicates that further reflection, nuancing, and balancing of concerns had occurred" (Cahill 2005, 368).

Perhaps the most important statement in this document is the affirmation, "Above all it is important to underline the equal dignity and responsibility of women with men" (*FC* 22). Furthermore, John Paul insists that "there is no doubt that the equal dignity and responsibility of men and women fully justifies women's access to public functions." However, he immediately adds: "On the other hand the true advancement of women requires that clear recognition be given to the value of their maternal and family role, by comparison with all other public roles and all other professions." Furthermore, he insists that "the work of women in the home be recognized and respected by all in its irreplaceable value" (*FC* 23). He goes on to say, "While it must be recognized that women have the same right as men to perform various public functions, society must be structured in such a way that wives and mothers are not in practice compelled to work outside the home" (*FC* 23).

A little later he focuses on the role of men. He emphasizes the importance of their family role and says that "efforts must be made to restore socially the conviction that the place and task of the father in and for the family is of unique and irreplaceable importance" (*FC* 25). This statement is weaker than the corresponding statement about women that I have quoted: there he seems to be suggesting that the maternal and family role is more important than their public functions. It is this imbalance that dismays and distresses many women and men who are concerned about justice for women. Their dissatisfaction is not with the fact that the pope should emphasize the importance of the role of women in the family. It is rather that he seems to lay this family responsibility more heavily on women than on men.

MULIERIS DIGNITATEM (1988)

Seven years later, Pope John Paul issued his apostolic letter *Mulieris Dignitatem*, an important document on the dignity of women. One can look at it from two points of view. On the one hand, there is a strong assertion that women must not be "dominated" by men—and this is linked to a repeated emphasis on the equality and equal dignity of women and men. On the other hand, there is also a strong and quite controversial emphasis on a particular conception of the complementarity of women and men, with implications for the issue of the ordination of women.

Let us consider first the issue of equality. The pope is quite explicit in his insistence on this point. He refers to the Genesis account of the creation of Adam and Eve, pointing out that humans were "created as man and woman" "in the image of God," and insisting that just as Eve is the helpmate of Adam, so also he is her helpmate (*MD* 7). He also notes feminine images of God in the Old Testament and says, "We find in these passages an indirect confirmation of the truth that both man and woman were created in the image and likeness of God" (*MD* 8).

John Paul then goes on to look in some detail at certain key texts from the New Testament: "Christ's attitude to women confirms and clarifies, in the Holy Spirit, the truth about the equality of man and woman. One must speak of an essential 'equality,' since both of them—the woman as much as the man—are created in the image and likeness of God" (*MD* 16).

Closely related to this is the question of the domination of women by men and whether, or in what sense, women are called to be "subject to" their husbands. On this issue Pope John Paul takes quite a radical position. He refers to "the rightful opposition of women to what is expressed in the biblical words 'He shall rule over you' (Gen. 3:16)" (*MD* 10). He insists that "*The woman cannot become the 'object' of 'domination' and male 'possession'*" (*MD* 10). He goes so far as to offer what one might call a "creative" understanding of the text in the Bible where the first woman is said to be a helpmate for the first man. His conclusion is that the wife is a helpmate to the husband and is "subject to" him only in the same sense as the husband is a helpmate and "subject to" her; each is called to be at the service of the other. "On this fundamental level—it is a question of *a 'help' on the part of both, and at the same time a mutual 'help'*" (*MD* 7).

Later in the document the pope puts forward his interpretation of the passage in the Letter to the Ephesians that reads, "Wives, be subject to your husbands, as to the Lord. For the husband is the head of the wife" (Eph. 5:22–23). He recalls the previous verse (v. 21) in which the writer says, "Be subject to one another out of reverence for Christ." This provides him with the basis for saying that the injunction that wives are to be subject to their husbands is "profoundly rooted in the customs and religious tradition of the time" and "is to be understood and carried out in a new way . . . the 'subjection' is not one-sided but mutual" (*MD* 24). "All the reasons in favor of the 'subjection' of woman to man in marriage must be understood in the sense of a 'mutual subjection' of both 'out of reverence for Christ'" (*MD* 24).

If this interpretation of the biblical teaching were widely preached and accepted by Christians, it could make a major contribution toward moving them on from the older tradition in which wives were expected to obey their husbands without any suggestion that this was to be reciprocated. Unfortunately, this radical change of direction by the pope went almost unnoticed. It was effectively eclipsed by other elements in the document—the ones we now go on to consider.

These further elements are more controversial. They concern the pope's account of the specific nature of woman and the complementarity between women and men. The view expressed by John Paul in this document can perhaps be summed up by saying that women and men are "equal but different and each is complementary to the other."

The controversial aspect comes when the pope spells out his understanding of this complementarity. Using the word "ontological" on three occasions in the document, he expounds on the fundamental nature of humanity—and more specifically of women. For him the complementarity of men and women is grounded on an invariant element that transcends all social and cultural conditioning. In one passage the pope insists strongly on this point:

> When we say that the woman is the one who receives love in order to love in return, this . . . [is] based on the very fact of her being a woman. . . . This concerns each and every woman, independently of the cultural context in which she lives, and independently of her spiritual, psychological and physical characteristics, as for example, age, education, health, work, and whether she is married or single. (MD 29).

Using a wealth of biblical references, images, and arguments, he spells out in great detail what he sees as specific to the nature of woman that makes her different from man and complementary to man. He is insistent that from the beginning, women have been given "personal resources of femininity" that "are certainly no less than the resources of masculinity: they are merely different." He maintains that the "fulfillment" of the woman as a person and "her dignity and vocation" must be "on the basis of these resources, according to the richness of the femininity that she received on the day of creation and that she inherits as an expression of the 'image and likeness of God' that is specifically hers" (MD 10). Elsewhere in the document he says, "Christ emphasized the originality which distinguishes women from men, all the richness lavished upon women in the mystery of creation" (MD 25).

The writing in this document is quite dense, so it is not easy to discover what it is in practice that John Paul sees as the specific essential element that makes a woman different from a man. I shall quote three passages that give an indication of what he has in mind. Toward the end of the document the pope says:

> The moral and spiritual strength of a woman is joined to her awareness that *God entrusts the human being to her in a special way.* . . . This entrusting concerns women in a special way precisely by reason of their femininity—and this in a particular way determines their vocation . . . that which constitutes women's dignity and vocation,

as well as that which is unchangeable and ever relevant in them, because it has its "ultimate foundation in Christ, who is the same yesterday and today, yes and forever." (*MD* 30)

In an earlier section devoted to motherhood he writes, "Motherhood implies from the beginning a special openness to the new person: and this is precisely the woman's 'part.' In this openness, in conceiving and giving birth to a child, the woman 'discovers herself through a sincere gift of self' " (*MD* 18). Later in the same section he says.

Motherhood involves a special communion with the mystery of life, as it develops in the woman's womb. . . . In the light of the "beginning," the mother accepts and loves as a person the child she is carrying in her womb. This unique contact with the new human being developing within her gives rise to an attitude toward human beings—not only toward her own child, but every human being—which profoundly marks the woman's personality. It is commonly thought that *women* are more capable than men of paying attention *to another person*, and that motherhood develops this predisposition even more. (*MD* 18)

John Paul also emphasizes "a woman's sensitivity" and the fact that "she often succeeds in resisting suffering better than a man" (*MD* 19). Ivy Helman sums up John Paul's attitude by saying that for him,

The world needs to make sure women are properly cared for and treated with the respect and dignity equal to that which men are accorded. . . . At the same time, women must also work to make the world a better place through the use of their feminine qualities. Women should teach men how to be better fathers, better listeners, better people, and in that way help the world become a more just, equitable, and fair place. Women need to show the world how to love. (Helman 2012, 108)

Convinced that he knows and can explain what he calls the specifically feminine "resources," the pope maintains that "in the name of liberation from male 'domination,' women must not appropriate to themselves male characteristics contrary to their own feminine 'originality.' " He says: "There is a well-founded fear that if they take this path, women will not 'reach fulfillment,' but instead will *deform and lose what constitutes their essential richness*" (*MD* 10).

On the basis of his account of the specific nature of woman, the pope insists that women cannot be ordained. Following up on the 1976 document *Inter Insigniores* from the Congregation for the Doctrine of the Faith, he rejects the argument that it was only because of the culture of his time that Christ chose only men as his apostles:

> *In calling only men as his Apostles*, Christ acted *in a completely free and sovereign manner*. In doing so, he exercised the same freedom with which, in all his behavior, he emphasized the dignity and the vocation of women, without conforming to the prevailing customs and to the traditions sanctioned by the legislation of the time. Consequently, the assumption that he called men to be apostles in order to conform with the widespread mentality of his times, does not at all correspond to Christ's way of acting. (*MD* 26)

Again following the 1976 document, the pope notes what he sees as a fundamental reason why women cannot be ordained: "It is *the Eucharist* above all that expresses *the redemptive act of Christ the Bridegroom toward the Church the Bride*. This is clear and unambiguous when the sacramental ministry of the Eucharist, in which the priest acts 'in *persona Christi*,' is performed by a man" (*MD* 26).

ORDINATIO SACERDOTALIS (1994)

In the apostolic letter *Ordinatio Sacerdotalis* issued in 1994 by Pope John Paul, he made this solemn declaration: "In order that all doubt may be removed regarding a matter of great importance, a matter which pertains to the Church's divine constitution itself, in virtue of my ministry of confirming the brethren (cf. Luke 22:32) I declare that the Church has no authority whatsoever to confer priestly ordination on women and that this judgment is to be definitively held by all the Church's faithful" (4). The significant point here is that the main emphasis is not on theological arguments about whether or not the nature of women makes them suitable to be priests. It is rather on two aspects of what the pope sees as the limits and the extent of the authority of the Church. First, he insists that the Church does *not* have the authority to admit women to the priesthood. Second, he is, in fact, exercising his own authority to make such a statement authoritatively (cf. Helman 2012, 168).

EVANGELIUM VITAE (1995)

In March 1995 John Paul issued his encyclical *Evangelium Vitae*. It contains the following passage:

In transforming culture so that it supports life, women occupy a place, in thought and action, which is unique and decisive. It depends on them to promote a "new feminism" which rejects the temptation of imitating models of "male domination," in order to acknowledge and affirm the true genius of women in every aspect of the life of society, and overcome all discrimination, violence and exploitation. . . . I address to women this urgent appeal: "Reconcile people with life." You are called to bear witness to the meaning of genuine love, of that gift of self and of that acceptance of others which are present in a special way in the relationship of husband and wife, but which ought also to be at the heart of every other interpersonal relationship. The experience of motherhood makes you acutely aware of the other person and, at the same time, confers on you a particular task. . . . Women first learn and then teach others that human relations are authentic if they are open to accepting the other person. (99)

In response to this call of the pope for a "new feminism" a number of women have developed an alternative form of feminism that accepts John Paul's understanding of the complementarity of women and men (cf. Beattie 2006, 23–26; Hinze 2009, 83–84; Helman 2012, 249–52).

"LETTER TO WOMEN" (1995)

Later that year John Paul wrote a "Letter to Women" prior to the Fourth World Conference on Women that was held in Beijing later that year. He thanks women for being present "in every area of life—social, economic, cultural, artistic and political" (2). In an interesting passage he acknowledges that historical conditioning "has been an obstacle to the progress of women." The result is that "women's dignity has often been unacknowledged and their prerogatives misrepresented; they have often been relegated to the margins of society and even reduced to servitude" (3). He then makes what might be called a conditional apology, saying, "If objective blame . . . has belonged to not just a few members of the Church, for this I am truly sorry." Furthermore, he notes that women have contributed as much as men to human history, even though they often did so in much more difficult conditions (3).

The pope goes on to say, "The time has come to condemn vigorously the types of *sexual violence* which frequently have women for their object and to pass laws which effectively defend them from such violence" (5). He writes,

I cannot fail to express my admiration for those women of good will who have devoted their lives to defending the dignity of womanhood by fighting for their basic social, economic and political rights, demonstrating courageous initiative at a time when this was considered extremely inappropriate, the sign of a lack of femininity, a manifestation of exhibitionism, and even a sin! (6)

He does not go so far as to acknowledge explicitly that these harsh judgments about the struggle of women were made by some of his own papal predecessors! He does, however, affirm that the process of women's liberation has been "substantially a positive one," and he adds, "This journey must go on!" (6).

Next the pope repeats in a more succinct and clear way the ideas about equality and complementarity that he had already written in *Mulieris Dignitatem*:

> The creation of woman is . . . marked from the outset by *the principle of help*: a help which is not one-sided but mutual. Woman complements man, just as man complements woman: men and women are *complementary*. Womanhood expresses the "human" as much as manhood does, but in a different and complementary way. (7)

He holds that the contribution of women "is primarily spiritual and cultural in nature" and in the "*social and ethical*" spheres, though he adds that it is also in the "socio-political and economic" spheres (8–9). He invites women to reflect on the "*genius of women*" (10). And he maintains that "in giving themselves to others each day women fulfill their deepest vocation" (10). The pope also repeats his insistence that only men can be ordained to the ministerial priesthood but that "this in no way detracts from the role of women" (11).

On December 8, 1995, the Pontifical Council for the Family issued a document titled *The Truth and Meaning of Human Sexuality: Guidelines for Education within the Family*. The interesting element in it is that it suggests that there is empirical evidence to support John Paul's conception of the complementarity of women and men. It does so by contrasting the psychosexual development of girls with that of boys, noting that as children "girls will generally be developing a maternal interest in babies, motherhood and homemaking" (81).

INFALLIBLE?

In October 1995, just two months before that document from the Pontifical Council for the Family was issued, the Congregation for the Doctrine of the Faith issued a statement (*Responsum ad Dubium*), signed by its prefect, Cardinal Ratzinger, stating that "the teaching that the Church has no authority whatsoever to confer priestly ordination on women, which is presented in the Apostolic Letter *Ordinatio Sacerdotalis* to be held definitively, is to be understood as belonging to the deposit of faith" and that it "requires definitive assent, since, founded on the written Word of God, and from the beginning constantly preserved and applied in the Tradition of the Church, it has been set forth infallibly by the ordinary and universal Magisterium."

In June 1998, three years later, Pope John Paul issued a *motu proprio* titled *Ad Tuendam Fidem*, in which he added an extra paragraph to Canon 750 in the Church's Canon Law. This referred to what were called "the second category of truths" that are to be definitively believed by Catholics. The Congregation for the Doctrine of the Faith, under its Prefect, Cardinal Ratzinger, issued a *"Doctrinal Commentary"* *"coincident with the promulgation of Ad tuendam fidem by Pope John Paul II."* The kernel of this commentary was the following: "Regarding the doctrine that priestly ordination is reserved only to men. The Supreme Pontiff . . . intended to reaffirm that this doctrine is to be held definitively, since, founded on the written Word of God, constantly preserved and applied in the Tradition of the Church, it has been set forth infallibly by the ordinary and universal Magisterium."

These statements in 1995 and 1998 from the Congregation for the Doctrine of the Faith caused consternation among those who believed that the issue of the ordination of women was still an open question. However, the controversy continued, though perhaps in a more muted fashion. It was argued by some that the issue was still not definitively resolved, since the statements by the Congregation could not themselves be seen as infallible statements (cf. Helman 2012, 247–48).

OBJECTIONS

Although welcoming the advances made by the popes and senior Church authorities on the issue of equality and justice for women, feminist theologians and many others are unwilling to accept Pope John Paul's account of the fundamental nature of woman.[1] This study of Vatican teaching is not the place to go into a full account of the views of those who object to it. However, it seems appropriate to give some indication of the main problems that various theologians have raised in relation to the pope's position.

One key figure in the Catholic challenge to patriarchy in the Church

---

[1] I wish to acknowledge the advice of Dr. Mary T. Malone on this topic.

is Elisabeth Schüssler Fiorenza. In 1983 she published her study of the early Church titled *In Memory of Her*. Her conclusion was: "As long as women Christians are excluded from breaking the bread . . . *ekklesia* as the discipleship of equals is not realized and the power of the Gospel is greatly diminished" (Schüssler Fiorenza 1983, 345–46). Other writers take up the story. They hold that Pope John Paul's understanding of the complementarity between women and men—and the conclusions that he draws from it—undermine, in practice, his commitment to equality and justice for women (cf. Cosgrave 2010b, 28–35; Helman 2012, 253–54).

In an interesting study of *Laborem Exercens*, Christine Firer Hinze (2009, 63) acknowledges that "by highlighting the importance and value of work performed in the household, *LE* offers a powerful critique of neoliberal capitalist political economies, where care-work continues to be under-valued and under-supported." But she goes on to speak of John Paul's "gender-keyed interpretation that sees women as especially suited to and needed in the work of home and family, and also having a distinct, feminine contribution to make to culture and society." She maintains that he offers an "asymmetrical picture of women's work" by his "affirmation that women's nature . . . makes them preeminently needed in the work of domesticity and mothering." This "legitimates, or at least fails to challenge, the persistence of a problematically gendered division between public and domestic economies" (Hinze 2009, 80).

In the concluding section of her article Hinze maintains that one is entitled to disagree with the so-called new feminists who adopt and defend John Paul's concept of complementarity. She does so on the grounds that his account of "feminine genius" is firmly joined to "an even more fundamental insistence on the common and full humanity of men and women" (Hinze 2009, 91). I take this to mean that since the pope's acceptance of the common humanity of women and men is more fundamental, it can be presented as an effective challenge to his conception of a distinct "ontological" nature of women.

THE "NATURE" OF WOMEN

The objection to the position put forward in the various documents I have cited is twofold. First, it is seen as a priori rather than an approach that begins from a study of "the facts on the ground." Second, it is claimed that, despite his insistence on equality, the pope's approach is still shaped by a patriarchal and androcentric mentality.

Those who are dissatisfied with the pope's approach hold that the issue of complementarity should be approached not in an a priori way with an assumption that one already knows what the "ontological nature" of women is. It should rather be addressed in an a posteriori way by taking account of both what anthropology and sociology tell us about gender roles in different human cultures and what modern neuroscience has revealed about the development of sexual and gender differentiation.

Anthropological study has shown that in all, or practically all, cultures, there is a complementarity in the roles played by women and men. In most cultures—though not in all—men and boys are considered to be superior to women. The differences in roles are generally accompanied by some significant differences in the typical qualities, attitudes, and styles exhibited by most women and most men in these different cultures. However, there is also a wide variation in personal differences within any particular culture. It seems likely that some of the more common or typical differences between women and men are determined mainly by the social conditions, traditions, and expectations in the various cultures.

It is only in the light of recent advances in neuroscience that one can begin to determine which aspects of sexual and gender differentiation are truly universal, transcending cultural differences. Fairly recent research has shown the vital role played by the mother in infant development. "Mothers shape their children in long-lasting and measurable ways, bestowing on them some of the emotional attributes they will possess and rely on, to their benefit or detriment, for the rest of their lives" (Lewis, Amini, and Lannon 2001, 75). And scientists have come to see that the surge in the level of oxytocin in mothers at the time of giving birth is crucial to ensuring a close bond between mother and child (Lewis, Amini, and Lannon 2001, 97). This means that at first sight, modern neurobiology seems to provide solid backing for the notion that women are "ontologically" different from men. But if one decides to make use of such knowledge from the field of neurobiology, then one is not entitled to be selective. As I shall indicate, it is important to take account also of new knowledge that calls in question the whole notion of a fixed one-size-fits-all "ontological" nature in women or men. Consequently, it would be quite naïve to use the facts revealed by neurobiology as a basis for suggesting that women cannot be ordained because they are "ontologically" different from men.

Neuroscientists are unlikely to speak of the "ontological" nature of women or men. But they have made major advances in showing that sexual and gender differentiation occurs as part of the neurobiological development of the fetus and infant. What is particularly significant is that they have discovered that there are two distinct biochemical agents involved. One of these is called DHT, and it affects the body of some fetuses and causes them to develop male sexual characteristics. The other is estrogen—its effect is on the brain and therefore more directly on the mind of the fetus. This latter is the agent that leads to gender differentiation as distinct from sexual differentiation. Its effect is that it causes some fetuses to develop in such a way that they eventually come to experience themselves as male rather than female.

The usual or typical situation is that "the underlying hormonal control mechanisms" lead to a clear differentiation between, on the one hand, those who are sexually male and who feel themselves to be male and, on the other hand, those who are sexually female and who feel themselves to be female (Panksepp 1998, 234). However, this is not always the case. It sometimes happens that there is a divergence between sexual differentiation and gender differentiation. Neuroscientist Jaak Panksepp explains why: "The fact that individuals who look like men on the outside can come to feel like women on the inside, and individuals who look like women on the outside can come to feel like men on the inside arises from a simple biological fact. The signals that trigger babies' brains and bodies to take various possible gender and sex paths are separable" (Panksepp 1998, 232).

This means that some women may feel themselves to be male and act in a typically masculine manner, and some men may feel themselves to be female and may act in a typically female fashion. This occurs only in a small minority of cases. But the fact that it is unusual does not mean that it should be called "unnatural"; it is simply a result of the way that the biological hormonal process works in these cases.

Gender differentiation is not determined entirely by what happens in the womb before birth. The environment in which the infant lives for the first two years of its life also plays a major role in the process. A particularly significant point revealed in recent studies is that this "shaping" of the gender of the young child is not simply a matter of social-cultural influences operating within already established neurobiological structures. What happens is rather that social-cultural influences play a key role in actually establishing the neurobiological structures. As Allan N. Schore (1994, 246) remarks, "It is therefore misleading to ask whether behavioral sex differences . . . are due to social-cultural *or* biological-genetic factors." On the same page Schore says, "The critical variable in determining gender identity is known to be postnatal learning experience, specifically the sex in which the infant is raised in the first two years."

A crucially important point in all this is that these prebirth and postbirth processes do not work in an "all-or-nothing" manner. In some cases there is a close correlation between sexual differentiation and gender differentiation, whereas in other cases the correlation is much less close. In fact, there are a whole series of possibilities, all within the range of what can be called natural. This indicates that to speak of the "ontological nature" of women simply does not take into account the complexity of reality. We live in a world that is not composed of realities that have fixed and static natures but one where gradation is of the very nature of things; so the psychological differences between women and men can be measured only in statistical terms. Consequently, we are not entitled to assume that it is "unnatural" or "disordered" if some women have qualities or attributes that are more typical of men in any particular culture and vice versa. Taking account of this background, many people would wish to question the validity or cogency of the claim that the "ontological nature" of women is such that they cannot be ordained as priests.

PATRIARCHAL

The second major objection put forward to the pope's conception of complementarity is that he unconsciously accepts as universally normative some of the traditional patriarchal Western attitudes and beliefs about women and, furthermore, that he interprets the scriptures in the light of these beliefs. The argument is that it is these unquestioned assumptions that lead him to his conclusions about the distinctive ontological nature of women and their "moral and spiritual strength," their "dignity and vocation, as well as that which is unchangeable and ever relevant in them" (*MD* 30). A particular difficulty arises when the pope moves from the "is" to the "ought," that is, when he maintains that women must live out of, and act on the basis of, what he holds to be their unchangeable nature.

Those who object to the pope's view would have no difficulty in agreeing with him that women should be caring, compassionate, and nurturing. They would even acknowledge that the pope wants men, too, to have these qualities. But they maintain that his approach is inequitable because it puts on women the main responsibility and burden of displaying these "feminine" qualities. In other words, he does not make it sufficiently clear that these are fundamental *human* qualities that should characterize men as well as women.

If one insists that these qualities are *human* rather than specifically *feminine*, then one can interpret key scripture passages in a way that is different from the way the pope does—and draw quite opposite conclusions. For example, there is a passage in Second Isaiah that says that God's care for us surpasses even the concern of a woman for the child at her breast (Isa. 49:15). One reading of this text is that the scripture assumes, and more or less affirms, that women are "naturally" more compassionate than men. But a different conclusion can be drawn from the text. One may start from the fact that both men and women are created "in the image of God" (Gen. 1:27). This means that all humans should mirror in human terms the qualities of God. Consequently, men as well as women should embody and display the compassion of God that is even greater than that of a woman for her baby.

LETTER ON THE COLLABORATION
OF MEN AND WOMEN (2004)

Toward the end of John Paul's long pontificate the Congregation for the Doctrine of the Faith, under the leadership of Cardinal Ratzinger, issued a "Letter to the Bishops of the Church on the Collaboration of Men and Women in the Church and in the World." This document was approved by the pope. It is an impressive and moving document, written in a style that is far clearer than that of John Paul himself. It is of particular interest because it includes a response to those who maintain that the values and attitudes that are named as *feminine* are in fact *human* values and attitudes that should also characterize men.

The document follows the general line on complementarity laid down in previous Church documents, particularly *Mulieris Dignitatem*. Its main concern is to show that there should not be a power struggle between women and men, and that in order to avoid the domination of women by men, the differences between them should not be denied, played down, or be seen as simply due to cultural conditioning (2). It insists that between men and women, there is a "physical, psychological and ontological complementarity" (8).

This document goes on to maintain that "women's physical capacity to give life" is "a reality that structures the female personality in a profound way." It gives them "a singular capacity to persevere in adversity, to keep life going even in extreme situations, to hold tenaciously to the future, and finally to remember with tears the value of every human life." This, it says, is "what John Paul II has termed *the genius of women*." It goes on immediately to say that this "implies first of all that women be significantly and actively present in the family." However, it adds, "It means also that women should be present in the world of work and in the organization of society, and that women should have access to positions of responsibility which allow them to inspire the policies of nations and to promote innovative solutions to economic and social problems" (13).

The final section of the document addresses the question of the role of women in the Church. It highlights key dispositions of Mary, the mother of Jesus—her "listening, welcoming, humility, faithfulness, praise and waiting." These dispositions, it says, "should be characteristic of every baptized person," but "women in fact live them with particular intensity and naturalness." By doing so, "women play a role of maximum importance in the Church's life by recalling these dispositions to all the baptized." It then adds a key statement: "In this perspective one understands how the reservation of priestly ordination solely to men does not hamper in any way women's access to the heart of Christian life" (16).

An important clarification is made in the document. It points out that "the feminine values mentioned here are above all human values." Then it makes this significant addition: "It is only because women are more immediately attuned to these values that they are the reminder and the privileged sign of such values. . . . Therefore, the promotion of women within society must be understood and desired as a humanization accomplished through those values, rediscovered thanks to women" (14). Later on, the document insists that men must respect and appreciate the witness of women's lives "as revealing those values without which humanity would be closed in self-sufficiency." Side by side with this, women "need to follow the path of conversion and recognize the unique values and great capacity for loving others which their femininity bears" (17).

Feminists and others hold that the clarification made by the Congregation's document does not provide an adequate response to their objections. They note the statement that "women are more immediately attuned to these values" and so are a "reminder and the privileged sign of such values" (14). In their view, even the more nuanced position put forward in this document still puts a one-sided onus on women to be a "reminder" to men of the importance of these values. So they see this as just a more subtle way of reaffirming the pope's conception of complementarity. And so the debate continues.

Those who see the issue of ordination as a fundamental issue of justice for women believe that the intransigence of the Church authorities shows that the thinking and attitudes of the Roman authorities are still fundamentally patriarchal. They point out that no woman has yet been appointed to any position of senior management in the Vatican—a change that, they say, could have taken place even if women were not ordained. Such a change would require a modification of Canon 129 of the Code of Canon Law, which states that governance in the Church is reserved to those who are ordained. As of mid-2015 when I am writing this, there has as yet been no indication that the Vatican intends to change this canon. It is not surprising then that those who are dissatisfied with the present position should suggest that the various scriptural, historical, and theological arguments against women's ordination—as well as the whole concept of "ontological complementarity"—are simply ideological justifications put forward to provide "cover" for a deeply ingrained unwillingness to allow women genuine equality in the Catholic Church.

Tina Beattie (2004) wrote a very insightful and helpful article in *The Tablet* about this document. She pointed out that the majority of feminists would agree with its view that women are more relational than men. She also said that the document represents "a significant breakthrough in terms of anthropology and sociology." But she criticized it for its failure to acknowledge that in this regard, it is deeply indebted to feminist thinking. She went on to suggest that "on the level of theology it represents a devastating catastrophe." This is because the idea that there is an *essential* difference between the sexes is not part of the Catholic tradition. So she maintained that "the theology underlying this new sexual essentialism is potentially disastrous."

The controversy about the infallibility issue took a new turn in May 2011, when Pope Benedict XVI removed Australian Bishop William Morris from office. Bishop Morris reported that, in a letter written to him by Benedict, the pope stated that Pope John Paul "decided infallibly and irrevocably that the church has not the right to ordain women to the priesthood" (Filteau 2011).[2] The fact that Benedict repeated as pope the position he had already taken in 1995 and 1998, when head of the Congregation for the Doctrine of the Faith, adds a new seriousness to this issue.

In November 2013, Pope Francis in *Evangelii Gaudium* said: "Demands that the legitimate rights of women be respected, based on the firm conviction that men and women are equal in dignity, present the Church with profound and challenging questions which cannot be lightly evaded." This could have given people hope that he was prepared to adopt a more open position in regard to the possibility of women being ordained as priests. But he immediately went on to add that this "is not a question open to discussion." To justify this position he distinguished between "sacramental power" and "power in general" (*EG* 104; Francis was referring here to John Paul's 1988 apostolic exhortation *Christifideles Laici*). This is not an argument which everybody finds convincing, and the optimists still hope that this is not the end of the story. In this they may perhaps be encouraged by the pope's acknowledgment toward the end of that paragraph that "pastors and theologians" have to face "a great challenge with regard to the possible role of women in decision-making in different areas of the church's life."

CONCLUSION

Without playing down the crucial significance of the issue of women's ordination, it must be said that the fact that it has assumed such prominence has had an unfortunate effect. It means that in the public perception this issue has largely eclipsed the other important developments in the Church's teaching. The effect is that many Church people and others have little awareness of the major advances that have taken place since Vatican II in the Church's teaching on justice for women.

---

[2]See also John Allen's column in the NCR website of May 9, 2011.

Among these advances one may note particularly the Church's insistence on the equality and equal dignity of women and men, its strong condemnation of injustices inflicted on women, its recognition that women have an important contribution to make in the public sphere as well as in the home, and that by being true to their distinctive gifts and qualities, women can help both society and the Church to live up to the highest human values of trust, respect, and openness to the fullness of life, in accordance with God's will. What has emerged in the Church's social teaching about the role of women is a position that, in some respects, is very liberal but that, in other ways, can be seen as quite conservative and controversial.

The greatest weakness of the Church's teaching about women lies not so much in the *content* of what it holds but in the *process* by which it has been developed: it is a body of teaching about women and for women that has been worked out and proclaimed almost entirely by men. One must hope that in the next stage of the development of this teaching the experience of women will be taken more seriously. It will be very helpful if women are allowed and encouraged to play a more active role in exploring and reflecting on their experience and in articulating Catholic social teaching.

* * *

SUMMARY

Catholic social teaching on the issue of the role of women has made major advances since the time Pope John XXIII became pope. It now insists firmly on the equality of women and men, although it continues to emphasize the difference between them. It speaks out strongly against the exploitation of women and against situations where they are treated as second-class citizens. It no longer holds that "the woman's place is in the home" if that phrase is understood to mean that women should not work in the public sphere. It fully accepts their right to go out to work or to engage in political activity if they choose to do so. In fact, it holds that the distinctive qualities and gifts of women can help promote peace and better understanding in the wider political and social world. However, it continues to insist that the role of women in the home is of particular importance. So it maintains that the public sphere should be organized in a way that ensures that women are not discriminated against if they choose to take time out to rear their family.

The Vatican has put forward a quite controversial understanding of the complementarity of women and men, one which has been contested by some theologians. Various documents of the popes and the Vatican curia have insisted that women are ontologically different from men. This has, in turn, been put forward as a major reason why women cannot be ordained to the priesthood. The other major reasons put forward in favor of this position are the fact that Jesus did not choose any women as apostles and the fact that the Church has never ordained women and never believed that it had the authority to do so.

QUESTIONS FOR REVIEW

1. *Does the Church still teach that "the woman's place is in the home"?*
2. *What new elements did the encyclical* Laborem Exercens *bring to the Church's teaching on women and work?*
3. *What arguments does the Vatican put forward to justify its insistence that women may not be ordained?*
4. *According to John Paul, what are the distinctive gifts of women that make them complementary to men?*

QUESTIONS FOR REFLECTION

1. *Are the psychological and spiritual qualities of most women different from those of most men? If so, in what ways?*
2. *Does the word "ontological" apply to the nature of women and men?*

ISSUES FOR FURTHER STUDY

1. *The different versions or strands of feminism.*
2. *The psychosexual development of infants before and after birth. Read Panksepp 1998; Schore 1994.*

15

Deus Caritas Est
and Catholic Charitable
and Development Agencies

Cardinal Ratzinger became pope in April 2005 and took the name Benedict XVI. His first encyclical, *Deus Caritas Est*, is dated December 25, 2005, but was not actually promulgated until a month later on January 25, 2006. It is an important document mainly because it throws a lot of light on how he believes the Catholic Church should respond to the problems of poverty in today's world. It focuses quite specifically on Catholic agencies that have played a major role in responding to world poverty. Most of these agencies are linked to each other through the umbrella organization Caritas Internationalis, a confederation of 165 national or regional Catholic agencies spread over five continents. The central office of Caritas Internationalis is in Rome. Since 1951 it has played a vital role in coordinating the work of its members that operate in the different countries. Many of the national agencies go under the generic name Caritas, while others use their own distinctive names; these latter include Catholic Relief Services (CRS) in the United States, "Development and Peace" in Canada, CAFOD in England and Wales, SCIAF in Scotland, and Trócaire in Ireland.

Over the years the focus of most of the Caritas-linked agencies—and of Caritas Internationalis itself—has changed. Many of them were first concerned mainly with providing and coordinating charitable relief. By the 1970s most began to move into the area of long-term human development. This, in turn, led them to pay more attention to justice issues. And in more recent years two further areas of major concern of some of these agencies have been the promotion of ecological awareness and reconciliation in war-ravaged countries and in the wider world.

Deus Caritas Est deals with two crucial issues regarding the work of these Catholic agencies: first, their nature and purpose and, second, the type of personnel who should staff them. In this chapter I first look closely at the text of the encyclical in order to see what it reveals of Benedict's views on the role of the Church in relation to justice and charity. This will lead to an account of what he believes should be the proper role of the Catholic agencies and the kind of people who should staff them. Later in the chapter, I look at the context in which the encyclical came to be written. Finally, I note recent Vatican actions that may perhaps be seen as a result of the line taken by the pope in the encyclical.

A NEW EMPHASIS

A full understanding of Benedict's distinctive approach to Catholic social teaching requires one to take account of what he says both in *Deus Caritas Est* and in *Caritas in Veritate* (2009), since the main content of each is quite different. The teaching in the two taken together gives the impression that what he had in mind was to provide a more solid theological basis for the Church's social teaching and to ensure that it does not become imbalanced or distorted. Needless to say, he aimed to take account of and integrate the key contributions made to this teaching over the previous century. But the effect of his approach in the two encyclicals might have been to shift the main focus of Catholic social teaching away from the orientation that it had taken since the time of Pope John XXIII. However, as I indicate in chapter 19 of this book, such a change of focus has become much less likely as a result of the teaching of Pope Francis.

Leaving to the next two chapters (chapters 16 and 17) a study of *Caritas in Veritate*, I focus in this chapter on *Deus Caritas Est*. This first encyclical includes three key elements. The first is his account of divine and human love. The second is the distinction he makes between the role of the Church in relation to charitable activity and its role in regard to promoting justice in society. The third element is his stance in relation to the personnel who should staff Catholic charitable agencies such as CRS or CAFOD and similar Caritas-linked agencies in other countries.

"LOVE" IN PART 1 OF THE ENCYCLICAL

The first part of *Deus Caritas Est* (DCE 1–18) is a fine presentation of Pope Benedict's theology of love. He makes it clear that he sees this as providing the background for the second part where he teases out the relationship between justice and love/charity, and clarifies the role of the Church in the sphere of politics. His meditation on love as *eros* and *agape* is a rich biblical and philosophical study of the different shades of meaning of the word love. One notable point in this section is his insistence that one must not make too sharp a contrast between *eros* and *agape*. For instance, *DCE* 7 notes that the element of *agape* enters into *eros*, since otherwise *eros* would be impoverished and would lose its own nature; in other words, it would no longer be real love.[1] In *DCE* 9 he goes so far as to say that God's love is both *eros* and *agape*. In *DCE* 10 he says that in the Logos, *eros* is so purified that it becomes one with *agape*. In all this, he brings out the point that the real meaning of "charity" is far richer and deeper than just "charity" in the sense of providing relief to the poor.

A significant point comes in *DCE* 18 where he says "seeing with the eyes of Christ, I can give to others much more than their outward necessities; I can give them the look of love which they crave." This statement provides the theological background for the position put forward by Benedict much later in the encyclical when he considers the qualities of the personnel who should staff Catholic charitable agencies.

PART 2 OF THE ENCYCLICAL

On January 23, 2006, two days before the encyclical was promulgated, Pope Benedict gave a short address to the participants in a meeting in the Vatican organized by the Pontifical Council Cor Unum. There he spoke about the encyclical and said,

> A first reading of the Encyclical could possibly give the impression that it is divided into two parts that are not very connected: a first part, theoretical, which speaks about the essence of love, and a second, which speaks of ecclesial charity and charitable organizations. I was particularly interested, however, in the unity of the two themes that are well understood only if seen as a whole.

In these words he set out to preempt a criticism that the first part of the encyclical was just a prologue written by him personally to a document that had originally been drafted for Pope John Paul. However, I hope to show that some doubt remains about how well the two parts are integrated.

In the second part, the pope insists that charity is part of the deepest nature of the Church (*DCE* 25). He maintains that while there is "some truth" in the Marxist claim that what the poor need is justice not charity,

---

[1]Stephen J. Pope (2008, 273) suggests that "Benedict's description of agape as 'descending' love and of eros as 'ascending' love . . . obscures the natural moral capacity of human love, healed by grace." Pope goes on to say, "through grace human love moves towards mutuality, friendship and communion." Cf. Dorr (2002, 209–10): "The values of respect, caring, sensitivity, and creativity . . . bridge the gap between *agape* and *eros*."

there is also "much that is mistaken" (*DCE* 25). For Benedict, both are essential. In a moving passage he says,

> Love—*caritas*—will always prove necessary, even in the most just society. There is no ordering of the State so just that it can eliminate the need for a service of love. . . . There will always be suffering which cries out for consolation and help. There will always be loneliness. There will always be situations of material need where help in the form of concrete love of neighbor is indispensable. (*DCE* 28b)

As I point out in chapter 16, Benedict emphasizes this point again and develops it more fully three years later in *Caritas in Veritate*.

Benedict points out that the "just ordering of society and the State is a central responsibility of politics." So he follows Vatican II in recognizing "the autonomy of the temporal sphere" (*DCE* 28). However, he also insists that the Church has a part to play in promoting justice. It "cannot and must not remain on the sidelines in the fight for justice." He mentions two ways in which this takes place. First, the Church "has to play her part through rational argument." It can do this most effectively because "faith liberates reason from its blind spots and therefore helps it to be ever more fully itself." A second contribution of the Church is "to reawaken the spiritual energy without which justice, which always demands sacrifice, cannot prevail and prosper" (*DCE* 28).

There cannot be any serious doubt about Pope Benedict's commitment to having the Church play a major role in the establishment of justice in society. Just as his predecessor Pope John Paul made many strong interventions on issues of justice, so too Benedict has not hesitated to speak out on issues of justice and politics. Furthermore, in a letter that he wrote to introduce the encyclical he said that "the Church participates passionately in the battle for justice." This insistence by Benedict on the importance of justice and of the duty of the Church to play its part in the promotion of justice is very important. It gives the lie to those who suggest that he is playing down the importance of justice or of the Church's commitment to working for justice. A particular concern of Benedict in this encyclical is to clarify that role and to explain how it differs from the Church's charitable role.

There is a strong case for saying that Pope Benedict's emphasis differs to some extent from significant aspects of the Church's position on social issues as it had developed under his predecessor. One difference of emphasis concerns the means by which the Church promotes justice. As David L. Schindler points out, "The issue . . . concerns the manner in which the commitment is to be executed" (Schindler 2006, 360). He focuses particularly strongly on the role of the laity in working for a just society.

This is a point on which he insists in *Deus Caritas Est*, and in his next social encyclical, *Caritas in Veritate*, he spells out in considerable detail what it should involve. Nevertheless, as I point out later, he also maintains that there is a vital role to be played by the (institutional) Church: it is one of purifying reason and "reawakening . . . moral forces" (*DCE* 29).

The second area in which Pope Benedict seems to have a different emphasis is not precisely an area of formal teaching but more of the Church's practice. During the forty years after Vatican II the Church had developed a large network of relief and development agencies, and these agencies had come to focus much of their energy on justice issues. As I point out later, the encyclical *Deus Caritas Est* gives a clear impression that Benedict would prefer that Church agencies should focus more on charitable relief and perhaps less on issues of structural injustice. As Drew Christiansen says, the second part of the encyclical seems "to put love and justice in tension in a way that is foreign to the modern tradition of social teaching beginning with John XXIII, placing emphasis on direct service rather than on transformation of structures" (Christiansen 2010, 6). The key point to note is not that Benedict holds that there should be less emphasis on justice in society as a whole; it is rather that he wants Church agencies, precisely because they are part of the institutional Church, to focus more on charitable relief.

THE AMBIGUOUS WORD "CHARITY"

Perhaps the most significant point in the second part of the encyclical is that the pope generally gives a more restricted meaning to the word "charity" than the word has in the first part of the encyclical. Nobody could disagree with Benedict's statement that charity is part of the Church's deepest nature (*DCE* 22, 23, 29). However, a major difficulty arises here. It springs from the ambiguity in the meaning of the word "charity." On the one hand, this word refers to the virtue of love, a central element in the life of the Church. On the other hand, the word "charity" means the giving of alms and relief to those in want. In the first part of the encyclical there is no doubt that the pope is speaking primarily of the virtue of love. In the second part of the encyclical, however, there can be little doubt that the word "charity" refers mainly to actions by individuals and by the Church that are designed to relieve the distress of the poor. The encyclical says,

> Following the example given in the parable of the Good Samaritan, Christian charity is first of all the simple response to immediate needs and specific situations: feeding the hungry, clothing the naked, caring for and healing the sick, visiting those in prison, etc. The Church's

charitable organizations, beginning with those of *Caritas* (at diocesan, national and international levels), ought to do everything in their power to provide the resources and above all the personnel needed for this work. (*DCE* 31)

It is clear from this passage that for the pope, the word "charity" covers not just almsgiving on a one-to-one basis but is extended to include the whole apparatus with which the Church offers relief to people in need.

CONTRAST BETWEEN CHARITY AND JUSTICE

Benedict makes a clear distinction between the role of the Church in regard to charity and its role in regard to the promotion of justice. A key passage comes in *DCE* 25: "The Church's deepest nature is expressed in her three-fold responsibility: of proclaiming the word of God (*kerygma-martyria*), celebrating the sacraments (*leitourgia*), and exercising the ministry of charity (*diakonia*). For the Church, charity . . . is a part of her nature, an indispensable expression of her very being" (cf. *DCE* 22). In *DCE* 23 he says, "Charitable activity on behalf of the poor and suffering was naturally an essential part of the Church of Rome from the very beginning." And in *DCE* 29 the encyclical says: "The Church's charitable organizations . . . constitute an *opus proprium*, a task agreeable to her, in which she does not cooperate collaterally, but acts as a subject with direct responsibility, doing what corresponds to her nature."

In sharp contrast to the direct duty that the Church exercises through its charitable activity, the encyclical says that the Church has only "an indirect duty" to be involved in "the formation of just structures" in society; this "is not directly the duty of the Church" (*DCE* 29). Benedict spells out how he sees the Church carrying out this indirect duty: it "is called to contribute to the purification of reason and to the reawakening of those moral forces without which just structures are neither established nor prove effective in the long run" (*DCE* 29). He goes on immediately to contrast this indirect duty of "the Church" with the direct duty of "the lay faithful": "The direct duty to work for a just ordering of society, on the other hand, is proper to the lay faithful. As citizens of the State, they are called to take part in public life in a personal capacity." In this same paragraph the pope for once adverts to the fact that the word "charity" has both a wider and a narrower meaning. He contrasts "the specific expressions of ecclesial charity" with the "charity [that] must animate the entire lives of the lay faithful and therefore also their political activity, lived as 'social charity.'"

IS JUSTICE WORK ESSENTIAL FOR THE CHURCH?

In this encyclical Benedict is making a clear contrast between works of charity as an "*opus proprium*" of the Church and the Church's action to promote justice, which, he implies, is not an "*opus proprium*." It would be wrong and quite tendentious to suggest that he sees the Church's work for justice as an "*opus improprium*" or an "*opus alienum*." But this leaves us with a question: What is the other term of the comparison? For him, it is clear that the contrast or comparison is between an "*opus proprium*" and an indirect duty of the Church.

This use of language raises an important issue. Does it mean that he believes that the Church's action to promote justice is not a "constitutive dimension of the preaching of the Gospel" as was affirmed by the 1971 Synod of Bishops? In answer we must say that it would be a mistake to conclude that Benedict was effectively agreeing with those who held that justice work is an integral rather than an essential aspect of the mission of the Church. As I have suggested earlier, he was not playing down the crucial importance of the work for justice. Rather his focus was on which component in the Church—the Church authorities or the lay Christians—is primarily and directly responsible for promoting justice; for him it is the laity. He was also concerned about the means which the official Church should use. As I noted above, the appropriate means for him are "the purification of reason and the reawakening of . . . moral forces" (*DCE* 29).

APPROPRIATE LANGUAGE

Having defended Benedict against the accusation that he is playing down the importance of the promotion of justice, I must now add that the language used in this part of the encyclical in contrasting works of charity as an "*opus proprium*" and "an indirect duty" is rather confusing and liable to give a wrong impression. It would certainly have been helpful if the encyclical had said clearly that work on behalf of justice is an essential duty of the Church, a duty that falls particularly on the lay Christian community.

Is it accurate and appropriate to say that the Church has only an indirect duty to promote justice? Benedict is obviously correct in saying that the Church must not usurp the role of the state in establishing structures of justice in society. But this applies to the institutional Church. The difficulty here with the encyclical's use of language lies in the ambiguity of meaning of the word "Church." What is Benedict referring to when he speaks of "the Church" as having only an indirect role in working for justice? Is he thinking of "the Church" in a restricted sense as the institutional Church acting through its official leaders, the pope and the bishops? In what sense, if any, is he referring to the Christian community? Referring to Benedict's distinction between "the Church" and "the lay faithful" in *DCE* 29, Lisa Sowle Cahill (2010, 297) goes so far as to say, "The unavoidable connotation is that the Church's 'real' identity inheres in the ordained and in ecclesial structures supervised by the episcopacy."

Benedict's position is that the task of making society more just is one that falls directly and primarily on lay Christians, working "in a personal capacity." Take the case of a Christian community, all of whom, inspired by their Christian faith, engage seriously in promoting justice in their local society and in the wider world. Is it not the case that this activity by the Christian community is one that is truly proper to the Church? It is hard to believe that Benedict would see such justice work by the lay Christian community as less "proper" or less "agreeable" to the Church than the work of its strictly charitable agencies. Would it not then have been less confusing and more accurate if the encyclical had made clear that in speaking of an indirect duty of "the Church," it is referring to the official leadership of the Church?

I must add that a further difficulty arises even if the word "Church" is taken to refer to the institutional aspect of the Church, meaning the actions by its official leaders and agencies. I shall suggest a little later that there are various ways in which Church leaders and Church agencies can and do play a quite direct role in promoting justice in society and in the world, even though they are not passing laws or enforcing justice in the way the state does.

Before that, however, I want to point out that another language issue arises. It concerns the ambiguity of the word "charity" and the sense in which the Church's *diakonia* is a service of charity. The Church's *diakonia* is undoubtedly manifested in works of charity in the restricted sense of almsgiving and emergency relief, but its *diakonia* is broader than this. It is also realized in other actions of charity or love where "charity" is understood in a wider sense—the sense in which charity is "the form of all the virtues," including justice. *Diakonia*, in this more ample and integral sense, covers the Church's prophetic challenge to injustice in the world and its promotion of human development, reconciliation, and respect for the environment. If one accepts this less restricted and more integral understanding of the Church's *diakonia*, should one not say that action by the Church on behalf of justice is truly "proper" to the Church—an "*opus proprium*"? In the light of an integral concept of *diakonia*, can one any longer maintain that there is a valid basis for distinguishing between a direct duty to provide relief to the needy and a merely indirect duty to be involved in working for justice in society?

Stephen J. Pope (2008, 271) expresses the same general idea in a slightly different way. He is uneasy about the way in which the encyclical places charity "above" justice, maintaining that this obscures the value of justice "as a necessary condition" of charity. Later in the same article (Pope 2008, 274) he says, "The assumption that the church's central moral concern ought to be charity rather than justice is troubling . . . [because] charity for the needy requires us to work for their rights and to address the causes of their suffering and therefore to struggle for justice in a collective, concerned way."[2]

HOW IS THE *DIAKONIA* EXERCISED?

Yet another difficulty arises in relation to the encyclical's use of the rather vague term, "the formation of just structures" (*DCE* 29). I have already acknowledged that if this phrase is taken to mean supporting one political party rather than another in the context of a truly democratic society, then the official Church should normally refrain from taking sides. But apart from such an overt taking of one side in a truly democratic society, there are other ways of fostering justice in which Church authorities have been involved down through the ages and right up to the present.

The way the encyclical spells out the role of the Church in promoting justice in society is by saying that it "is called to contribute to the purification of reason and to the reawakening of those moral forces without which just structures are neither established nor prove effective in the long run" (*DCE* 29). At first sight, at least, this statement suggests an educational or catechetical program for laypeople—a program that would include a strong emphasis on justice as part of an overall formation in the Christian faith. Undoubtedly, this is one crucially important way in which the Church promotes justice in society.

But surely Archbishop Oscar Romero went much further than a catechetical program when he called on his government's soldiers to refuse to obey the order to shoot their own people? The same applies to the action of Cardinal Evaristo Arns of São Paulo in inviting those who protested against the oppression of the Brazilian military government to meet in

---

[2]Pope (2008, 275) goes on to say, "The encyclical's high praise for the superiority of charity can also create the impression that the church transcends justice and so need not be focused on it. Yet the concrete practice of the church, from local to the universal contexts, is different than the lofty theology with which it is sometimes described."

Catholic churches when they could not meet elsewhere. No doubt these challenges to tyrannical governments contributed to "the purification of reason" and "the reawakening of moral forces." But these phrases in the encyclical seem to be a rather weak and inadequate description of such openly political challenges by outspoken Church authorities to government injustice and oppression. Do they not count as direct rather than indirect actions in support of justice in society?

Of course it might be claimed by some that these were the actions of maverick Church leaders. But we can respond by recalling the uncompromising criticism that Pope John Paul II directed against the repressive government of Guatemala and his encouragement to the indigenous peoples of that country to organize associations for the defense of their rights (*AAS* [*Acta Apostolicae Sedis*] 75, 742–43). Was this not a directly political intervention? Is it not the case that when the Christian community finds itself living under a government that is outrageously unjust and oppressive, then the norms that apply under a democratic regime are no longer adequate? In such situations it may sometimes be necessary and appropriate for Church authorities to engage in outspoken criticism, and even to encourage and support movements of empowerment and resistance—actions that must be seen as directly political. As Stephen J. Pope (2008, 275) says, "At times we contribute to a better world by promoting justice via partisan strategies that concretely advance the rights of the poor."

A SPECTRUM OF APPROACHES

The encyclical says that political activity is to be left to lay Christians who "are called to take part in public life *in a personal capacity*" (*DCE* 29, emphasis added). This raises a major issue. A key part of the Christian commitment to the promotion of justice and integral human development is the exercising of direct or indirect influence on governments and intergovernmental agencies. There are different conceptions of how this should be done. In the 1930s the French Catholic philosopher Jacques Maritain rejected the ideology of right-wing Catholics and movements like Action Française, which wanted Catholicism to be the state religion. Maritain put forward a pluralist alternative in which Christians would engage in political activity in a personal capacity. The position outlined by Benedict in *Deus Caritas Est* seems to fit in with this approach.

The Maritain analysis and conclusion was an important contribution to Catholic social theology. In its time, it helped clarify the relationship between church and state, particularly in the modern pluralist world. However, the approach is incomplete insofar as it fails to take adequate account of the quasi-political activities engaged in by Church leaders of recent times—Church people who are not demanding that Catholicism become the official religion of the state but who want the voice of the Church to be heard on issues of justice in a pluralist society.

In practice, there is a wide variety of ways in which the Catholic Church in its official capacity and as an institution exercises an influence on political issues in the interest of justice. Several of these are illustrated in the following diagram:

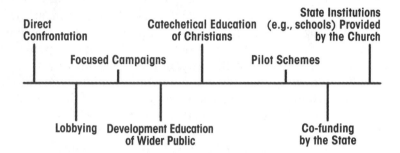

In the middle of this spectrum I have located what we might call the catechetical education by the Church of its own members on issues of social justice. A little further along the scale we can locate the general development education programs through which official Church relief and development agencies seek to educate the wider public, including non-Christians. Further along to the left come what I am calling the "focused campaigns," for instance, the Lenten campaigns that focus on raising awareness on specific issues such as child labor or human trafficking; the aim here is rather more overtly political. Further to the left is the direct lobbying of government by Church agencies seeking changes in official policy on specific issues, for instance, on such issues as the dumping of agricultural products.

At the furthest left point on the spectrum comes the kind of direct confrontation that takes place when repressive governments are openly challenged by liberation-minded Church authorities. One thinks of Archbishop Denis Hurley of Durban, who took part in street protests against the forced removal of African people by the apartheid government in South Africa, or of the leading role played by Cardinal Jaime Sin of Manila in the People's Power Movement that forced President Marcos to flee the country.[3] It is clear that when these Church leaders engaged

---

[3]Two books that provide helpful analysis and practical examples on the whole issue of different models of Church engagement, especially in relation to confrontational approaches, are José Casanova (1994) and William T. Cavanaugh (1998).

in such acts of confrontation, they were not acting in a purely personal capacity. They were putting the Church on the side of the citizens who were engaged in confronting the government. So it is not surprising that the political leaders should have believed that these Church leaders were inciting people to rebel against the government.

On the right-hand side of the spectrum one can locate situations where the Church adopts a cooperative approach with the state. In one example a Church agency sets up a pilot scheme or program of development, either with the intention of handing it over to government when it has got off the ground or in the hope that it will be a model that governments will follow. Where cooperation is taken a stage further there is an ongoing partnership with the civil authorities, through which Church-sponsored projects, such as schools or health programs, are cofunded by government. Finally, furthest to the right-hand side there are situations where Church-owned schools or hospitals in some countries are fully funded by government and have become an integral part of the national educational or health systems.

One should not adopt a doctrinaire position that would claim that one of these approaches is always the correct one. Church-run development and justice agencies have to make strategic decisions about where best to locate themselves on this spectrum at any particular time. It is interesting to note that, in practice, at a particular moment, two different agencies of the Church may be located on different points on the spectrum. For instance, one Church agency may be strongly challenging the government by a lobbying program on, say, the treatment of prisoners, while the Church is happily cooperating with the government in, say, the provision of schooling. This is quite acceptable, provided that the challenging dimension of one program is not being played down in order to ensure cofunding for another program. It is particularly important that the agencies reevaluate their decisions on a regular basis, in order to ensure that partnership and cofunding have not led to their being tamed and acquiescent on key issues of justice.

I hope that what I have been saying here indicates that it is hardly an adequate account of the role of the Church in relation to justice in society to say, as the encyclical says, that "The direct duty to work for a just ordering of society . . . is proper to the lay faithful. As citizens of the State, they are called to take part in public life in a personal capacity" (*DCE* 29).

There is no mention here of the need for Church leaders to challenge governments—and even on rare occasions to confront them openly in the name of the Church—in certain situations of gross injustice or oppression. This omission could, perhaps unintentionally, leave people with the impression that the pope is excluding or playing down the importance of such prophetic challenges made by Church leaders in their official capacity.

THE STATUS OF CHURCH AGENCIES

As I have pointed out above, Benedict makes a very clear contrast between, on the one hand, charity as a direct duty of the Church and, on the other hand, justice as an indirect duty; the latter, he says, is to be carried out by laypeople in a personal capacity—rather than formally in the name of the Church. This contrast seems to bypass a whole variety of activities engaged in by organizations that were established by the Church authorities and that are clearly intended to represent the Church. These Church agencies are involved in working for justice through quasi-political activities. For instance, CRS in the United States is an official Church organization that engages in development education programs under the titles "Global Solidarity Partnership" and "Operation Rice Bowl." Similarly, the extensive development education programs of the official Church organizations CAFOD (in England and Wales), SCIAF (in Scotland), and Trócaire (in Ireland) must surely be seen as an action of "the Church." Furthermore, in many developing countries Church leaders have established agencies that engage in even more obviously political activities, for instance, Church agencies that work for the defense of human rights or to promote reconciliation between warring countries or factions. These too must be seen as part of the action of "the Church."

In this encyclical the term the pope consistently uses in referring to these agencies is "the Church's charitable organizations." This is hardly accidental, since Vatican officials involved in preparing the first draft of the second part of the encyclical argued that, from a theological point of view, there can be no true charity without justice, and so they insisted that Church agencies whose declared purpose is working for development and justice should nevertheless call themselves "charitable organizations"!

The encyclical does not advert to the promotion of development and justice, which in recent years has become so central to the work of many Catholic agencies. It is true that the pope does not rule out the very positive action for justice undertaken by "the Church" through these official Church agencies. It is always risky to draw conclusions on the basis of an argument from silence. But in this case the fact that he fails to mention these quasi-political activities seems quite significant. It is hard to avoid the impression that this more political approach is being played down, perhaps even being frowned upon.

The question arises whether Pope Benedict was suggesting that such activities should no longer be taken by "the Church," as such, but should be left to lay Christians acting in what he refers to as "a personal capacity." Was the pope suggesting that the Caritas network of agencies should step back from their strong focus on issues of justice and long-term human development, on the grounds that such political work is not the direct duty of the Church? Did he want them to confine themselves mainly to charitable relief, which he sees as an *opus proprium* of the Church?

Lisa Sowle Cahill lists ways in which Church agencies such as CRS and Catholic Charities USA do, in fact, participate in social and political collaboration with government; and she adds, quite correctly, that "the specific mission of many Catholic agencies . . . is to advocate for justice . . . and to participate directly in advocacy efforts." She suggests that Benedict has this in mind when he writes in *DCE* 30b that Church agencies will work with other religious organizations and with civil agencies to achieve "solutions to the social and political problems of the day" (Cahill 2010, 308–10).

The difficulty here is that it is Cahill rather than Benedict who is naming various ways in which official and unofficial Church agencies work directly for justice. It seems significant that Benedict does not mention this promotion of justice by Church agencies. There is no indication that Benedict, in the quoted words or elsewhere in the encyclical, is giving his approval for Church agencies to engage directly in justice promotion. In fact, when he refers in *DCE* 30b to "coordination" between Church agencies and state agencies, he specifically relates it to "the effectiveness of *charitable* service" (emphasis added). The whole thrust of the encyclical suggests that there is a wide gap between what Church agencies are actually doing at present and what Benedict believed they should be doing.[4]

THE STAFF OF CATHOLIC AGENCIES

One of Pope Benedict's concerns in this encyclical is what he refers to as "activism and the growing secularism of many Christians engaged in charitable work" (*DCE* 37). This explains why he devotes quite a lot of space to writing about the staff of Catholic agencies. In *DCE* 31 he writes about "those who work for the Church's charitable organizations." He maintains that "while professional competence is a primary, fundamental requirement, it is not of itself sufficient." Writing about those who care for people in need, he says that they "need a 'formation of the heart': they need to be led to that encounter with God in Christ which awakens

---

[4]If, however, Benedict was really accepting that what he repeatedly called "Church charitable agencies" should indeed be promoting justice directly, then this implies that there is an inconsistency in the encyclical; no wonder then that Cahill (2010, 310) would refer to "the encyclical's internal tensions regarding Catholic agencies." Personally, I do not think that Benedict and his advisers would have allowed the encyclical to have such an obvious inconsistency. In chapter 16 I suggest that there is no significant inconsistency between the positions he has adopted in *Deus Caritas Est* and in *Caritas in Veritate*.

their love and opens their spirits to others." He points out that charity "cannot be used as a means of engaging in what is nowadays considered proselytism." However, he adds, "But this does not mean that charitable activity must somehow leave God and Christ aside." And he says,

> A Christian knows when it is time to speak of God and when it is better to say nothing and to let love alone speak. . . . It is the responsibility of the Church's charitable organizations to reinforce this awareness in their members, so that by their activity—as well as their words, their silence, their example—they may be credible witnesses to Christ. (*DCE* 31)

In an interesting commentary on the encyclical, David Schindler expands on what he believes all this involves in practice. He holds that it is not sufficient that the love of those who work for Catholic agencies should affect only their intention, leaving their actions to be just the same as those who have "conventional professional-secular training." He holds that what the encyclical calls for is "rather more substantial than this." Drawing on what Benedict said in his homily in Saint Peter's Basilica on March 18, 2005, just a month before he was elected pope, Schindler insists that it involves putting Catholic teaching into practice on such issues as placing orphaned children "inside monogamous marriages between a man and a woman" and "exclusion of contraceptive devices from insurance benefits" (Schindler 2006, 365–66).

In the encyclical, the pope does not go into this kind of detail. In *DCE* 33, he simply says,

> With regard to the personnel who carry out the Church's charitable activity on the practical level, the essential has already been said: they . . . should . . . be guided by the faith which works through love (cf. Gal. 5:6). Consequently, more than anything, they must be persons moved by Christ's love, persons whose hearts Christ has conquered with his love, awakening within them a love of neighbor.

Taken together, and linked to the words that I quoted earlier from *DCE* 18 about "seeing with the eyes of Christ," these statements give the clear impression that the pope assumes—and presumably expects—that those who work for Catholic agencies should be deeply committed practicing Catholics. However, on November 11, 2012, Pope Benedict issued the *motu proprio: Intima Ecclesiae Natura*. A passage in Art. 7 §1 of this document allows a greater degree of flexibility than was evident in *Deus Caritas Est*. It says that Catholic agencies should "select their personnel from among persons who share, or at least respect, the Catholic identity of these works." This very reasonable requirement indicates that such employees need not be Catholic, provided that they respect the Catholic identity of the agency.

During the final years of John Paul's papacy an influential body of Vatican officials, particularly those associated with the Pontifical Council Cor Unum, became critical of the focus on justice by Caritas Internationalis and by many of the national and regional Caritas agencies. The Vatican people seemed also to resent the relative independence of these Church agencies, many of which were effectively led by laypeople. Pope Benedict's insistence in *Deus Caritas Est* on the priority of charity seemed to provide a theological basis for these criticisms and concerns. Furthermore, the pope apparently shared the concern of Cor Unum that Caritas agencies were in danger of no longer being sufficiently Christian.

In his encyclical Benedict made specific reference to the role of Cor Unum as "orienting and coordinating the organizations and charitable activities of the Catholic Church" (*DCE* 32). This was taken as a mandate by the Cor Unum officials to exercise such tight control over Caritas Internationalis that some saw it as effectively "a takeover bid." Cor Unum also proceeded to give strict directions to the various national Caritas agencies about their direction and their staffing policies. These interventions caused great difficulties and were widely resented and resisted.[5] It seems likely that the strong and repeated emphasis by Pope Francis on de-clericalization and decentralization will lead to a change of policy by the Vatican on these issues.

It will be clear from what I have written here that, in the encyclical *Deus Caritas Est*, Benedict expressed serious reservations about the policies and overall approach that the main Catholic "charitable agencies" had come to adopt since the time of Vatican II and of *Populorum Progressio*. There was some uncertainty about the practical implications of the encyclical. No doubt, the pope was calling the Caritas agencies to be less secular, and to act less independently of the Church authorities. But was he also asking that they should abandon their specific function of promoting development in order to focus instead on charitable relief? If so, the question arose whether, or to what extent, the bishops' conferences in the different countries would be entitled to authorize the agencies under their control to tacitly resist any such major change of direction? Should local bishops'conferences perhaps go so far as to argue with the Vatican, pointing out that the direct involvement in development and justice issues by Church organizations had been approved by Church authorities over many years and should not be abandoned lightly?

---

[5]In the 2012 edition of this book I devoted several pages to a detailed account of this controversy; I have omitted this account in the present edition, hoping that the whole affair will be reduced to a footnote of history,.

* * *

SUMMARY

In the first part of *Deus Caritas Est*, his first encyclical, Pope Benedict offers a rich theology of the nature of charity or love. In the second part he focuses not on love in its broadest sense where it is "the form of all the virtues" but mainly on charity as offering assistance to those in need. He suggests that this should be the main purpose of the Caritas agencies, because charity in this sense is part of the proper nature of the Church. It is the responsibility of laypeople, in their personal capacity, to work for justice in the world. Benedict holds that the promotion of justice is only an indirect duty of the Church; it is done by educating the consciences of laypeople (including non-Catholics) and awakening in them the spiritual energy required for action.

There is an ambiguity in the way Benedict uses the words "Church" and "charity" in this encyclical. It is not clear why Church agencies should focus mainly on charitable relief and play down their present involvement in work for human development and the promotion of justice, especially in developing countries. Furthermore, there seems to be some doubt about whether Benedict approves of the more direct political challenge offered by some brave Church leaders in situations of extreme political oppression.

Benedict insisted that the staff of Catholic agencies should not only be professionally qualified, but should also be animated by Christian charity. They should not proselytize, but their love should be evident to the recipients. Following the encyclical, influential figures associated with the Vatican agency Cor Unum moved to take more control over Caritas Internationalis, and also over the Catholic agencies in different countries and regions.

QUESTIONS FOR REVIEW

1. *What is the originality of Pope Benedict's account of the nature of love in part 1 of the encyclical?*
2. *According to the encyclical, does the Church have a direct obligation to promote justice?*
3. *Is the promotion of justice part of the* diakonia *of the Church?*
4. *What is the role of the Caritas agencies, according to the encyclical? Do you agree?*
5. *Name various ways in which the official Church influences political society.*
6. *What qualities should the staff of Catholic agencies have?*

QUESTIONS FOR REFLECTION

1. *How can Church agencies in countries in the North best promote justice, respect for the Earth, and authentic human development in countries in the South?*
2. *How can Church agencies be a model of respectful participative communities?*

ISSUE FOR FURTHER STUDY

1. *The whole issue of the empowerment of people. Read Paulo Freire 1974, 1985.*

16

Caritas in Veritate and an "Economy of Communion"

On July 7, 2009, Pope Benedict XVI issued a major social encyclical titled *Caritas in Veritate*.[1] Coming forty years after Paul VI's *Populorum Progressio*, it provided Benedict with an opportunity to celebrate the virtues of that ground-breaking document and to update it by addressing the major insights and issues that had emerged in the intervening period (*CiV* 8). The overall theme of *Caritas in Veritate*, like that of Pope Paul's encyclical, is "integral human development." There had been a number of delays in the publication of the encyclical, the most recent of which was to allow the pope time to take account of the financial and economic crisis that had erupted around this time. However, the encyclical was much more than a response to the problems of the day. It is a remarkably insightful and comprehensive presentation of the Christian and Catholic approach to economic activity, to business, and to social justice at the national and international levels.

In this chapter I examine the encyclical in some detail, leaving over to chapter 17 most of the reactions to it and the follow-up from it. I focus first on four guiding principles that run through the encyclical: (1) the relationship of justice to love; (2) the close linkage of justice-love with truth; (3) the nature of integral human development; and (4) the crucial importance of the experience of "gift" in the whole area of social justice, development, and ecology. Then I consider the practical ways in which the encyclical addresses important issues of the world of the present and the foreseeable future. Next I consider the issue of whether *Caritas in Veritate* represents a revision of the views that Benedict espoused in *Deus Caritas Est*. Finally, I attempt to answer two questions: (1) In what sense was Pope Benedict committed to the belief that individual Christians and the Church as a whole should make an option for the poor? and (2) Was

---

[1] Although the encyclical is dated June 29, 2009, it was not actually issued until eight days later.

Benedict seeking to give a new direction or a new emphasis to Catholic social teaching?

THE RELATIONSHIP OF JUSTICE TO LOVE

A particularly valuable feature of this new encyclical is that it makes a significant advance on *Populorum Progressio* in offering a richer and more satisfying theology of human development and of social justice. The distinctively new element is that it explicitly grounds the Christian's commitment to build a more just world in the love that God, through the Holy Spirit, has poured into our hearts.

Here we have a theology that is not only profound but also realistic— one that rings true to the experience of those who have worked "on the ground" to promote justice and human development. It reminds Christian activists that the commitment to justice is rooted not just in that vague sense of guilt that we feel when we hear of people living in grinding poverty and not merely in the compassion and anger we feel when we hear of abuses and oppression. Behind these immediate responses, and underpinning them, lies some degree of awareness of the gratuitous outpouring of God's love that floats quietly in the background of our consciousness as Christians and that occasionally bubbles up, warming us with a sense of being loved and accepted. It is this awareness of being accepted and loved by God that enables the Christian activist to persevere in reaching out to others in respect and love, even when there seems to be little hope of success. The encyclical reminds us that this love is pure grace and that it is both creative and redemptive (*CiV* 5; cf. *CiV* 34).

This is the background that underpins a central guiding principle of the encyclical, namely, its strong emphasis on the complementarity of justice and love. Earlier social encyclicals rightly emphasized the fact that our response to issues of poverty and oppression is an obligation of justice and not merely a matter of charity. But now that there is no longer any doubt about that, Benedict sees it as essential to insist that love must animate and permeate all our efforts to create a more just world:[2]

Justice is inseparable from charity, and intrinsic to it. Justice is the primary way of charity. . . . On the one hand, charity demands justice: recognition and respect for the legitimate rights of individuals and peoples. It strives to build the *earthly city* according to law and

---

[2]In the passage that I am quoting here, and in various other parts of the encyclical it would have been better if the translation had used the word "love" instead of the word "charity."

justice. On the other hand, charity transcends justice and completes it in the logic of giving and forgiving. (*CiV* 6)[3]

Benedict believes strongly that in order to build a better world, we undoubtedly must respect the rights of others. But that is not enough; it is even more important that our relationships with others be ones of gratuitousness, mercy, and communion (*CiV* 6; cf. *CiV* 38).

The focus on gratuitousness is the most significant element in the encyclical. Benedict's insistence on the need for gratuitousness and mercy does not at all soften the call to justice or introduce an element of sentimentality into it. Quite the contrary: it makes our commitment to justice more realistic. For we know by bitter experience how easily progress gets blocked when the various groups and individuals in society focus mainly on their own rights. The impasse can only be broken when we, as individuals and in groups, begin to reach out to each other with the kind of generosity that loosens up our demands, that makes us willing to play down the faults and mistakes of others, and that, in this way, creates a real sense of community where all are respected, forgiven, and loved. This generosity of ours is itself a gift of God's grace and a way in which we live as images of God in our daily interactions. For Benedict there is an inseparable connection between justice, love, and grace. As he had already said eighteen months earlier in his second encyclical *Spe Salvi* 42: "A world which has to create its own justice is a world without hope."

THE ROLE OF TRUTH

A second fundamental principle in Benedict's encyclical is his linking of justice-love with truth. An insistence on the importance of truth has been a feature of all of Benedict's work, going back to a time long before he became pope. In the present encyclical this is given a new richness. The pope points out that charity/love without truth degenerates into sentimentality and emotionalism. He reminds us that the God of the Bible is "charity and Truth, Love and Word" (*CiV* 3).

Benedict's vision is a fully integral one where it is unthinkable for a Christian to make any sharp distinction between being a follower of Christ and engaging in economic activity in the world. On the date the encyclical was issued, a senior churchman with an insider's knowledge of Vatican affairs remarked that an early draft of Pope John Paul's encycli-

---

[3]Benedict's account of the relationship between justice and love is quite similar to what John Paul had written in his second encyclical, *Dives in Misericordia*, to which I referred in chapter 11.

cal *Sollicitudo Rei Socialis*, issued in 1987, included a chapter on Jesus Christ. However, in the final version John Paul omitted this because his advisers told him it would lessen the impact of the encyclical among non-Christians. Benedict XVI had no such inhibitions. So in the very first paragraph of the encyclical he says that our search for love and truth is purified and liberated by Jesus and that Jesus reveals "the plan for true life that God has prepared for us." The truth revealed by Jesus and the truth that is known by reason are the two pillars on which authentic human development is grounded (cf. *CiV* 29, 52, 78; cf. Schindler 2010, 567).

Benedict goes on to spell out the implications of this in more detail (*CiV* 4). Perhaps his thinking could be expressed in popular language by saying that it is not enough to have good intentions and to mean well; we need also to know what is good both for individuals and also for society as a whole. At a later point in the encyclical Benedict says, "Deeds without knowledge are blind, and knowledge without love is sterile . . . *love is rich in intelligence and intelligence is full of love*" (*CiV* 30). Earlier he had devoted a long and quite dense paragraph (*CiV* 7) to spelling out what he means by "the common good."

INTEGRAL HUMAN DEVELOPMENT

The third guiding principle that permeates the encyclical is the pope's broad understanding of the phrase "integral human development"—a phrase that was central to Paul VI's encyclical *Populorum Progressio*. Benedict extends the scope of the phrase so that it covers not only sociopolitical-economic issues but also issues related to sexual ethics and bioethics. For the pope, Christian teaching on each of these spheres of life is part of one "seamless robe," so he refuses to accept the traditional distinction that was made between them. This means that he has no hesitation in bringing right-to-life, abortion, and euthanasia, as well as the cloning of embryos and other biotechnology issues, into this "social encyclical" (see especially *CiV* 28, 75).

This idea of a "seamless robe" that includes sexual ethics and bioethics is one that makes sense. As David Cloutier (2010, 618) points out, Benedict wants to move beyond a "humanocentric" interpretation of natural law to a more holistic cosmological one. Cloutier suggests that Benedict is seeking in this way "to draw modern secular societies back to the natural law through their concern for the environment." However, the approach of Benedict in this encyclical is not very satisfactory. In sharp contrast to the encyclical's detailed treatment of economic issues, the sexual and bioethical issues are mentioned rather infrequently and in no great detail. This could leave one with the impression that the pope, by linking them with the more traditional social justice agenda, assumes that there will be unquestioned acceptance of the teaching of *Humanae Vitae* and other Vatican documents on sexual and bioethical issues (cf. Ryan 2010, 345).

As part of his integral view of authentic human living the pope insists strongly and in some detail on the duty of humans to respect the environment (see *CiV* 48–51; cf. *CiV* 67, 69). As he puts it, "The book of nature is one and indivisible: it takes in not only the environment but also life, sexuality, marriage, the family, social relations: in a word, integral human development" (*CiV* 51). In chapter 18 I undertake a more extended examination of Benedict's teaching on ecology.

As one would expect, Benedict insists that integral human development "must include not just material growth but also spiritual growth" (*CiV* 76). He spells this out in a moving way in his two final paragraphs. In (*CiV* 78) he says, "*God's love calls us to move beyond the limited and the ephemeral, it gives us the courage to continue seeking and working for the benefit of all.*" Even more striking is the following passage:

> Development requires attention to the spiritual life, a serious consideration of the experiences of trust in God, spiritual fellowship in Christ, reliance upon God's providence and mercy, love and forgiveness, self-denial, acceptance of others, justice and peace. All this is essential if "hearts of stone" are to be transformed into "hearts of flesh" (Ezek. 36:26). (*CiV* 79)

THE EXPERIENCE OF "GIFT"

In a key passage at the beginning of chapter 3 of the encyclical, Pope Benedict writes, "*Charity in truth* places man before the astonishing experience of gift. Gratuitousness is present in our lives in many different forms, which often go unrecognized because of a purely consumerist and utilitarian view of life" (*CiV* 34). He offers this succinct explanation of what he means by gift: it is an experience that "by its nature goes beyond merit, its rule is that of superabundance." Benedict goes so far as to say, "The human being is made for gift" (*CiV* 34); later in the encyclical he writes, "The environment is God's gift to everyone" (*CiV* 48). For Benedict the crucial point about the experience of gift is that it is "a sign of God's presence in us"; it "expresses and makes present" the human person's "transcendent dimension" (*CiV* 34).

Benedict goes on at once to recall that humans are sinful, and this leads them to imagine that they can eliminate evil by their own efforts. Furthermore, the assumption that economic theory and economic development are to be worked out independently of ethics has led to the emergence of "economic, social and political systems that trample upon personal and social freedom, and are therefore unable to deliver the justice that they promise." Challenging this assumption, Benedict insists that the transcending of barriers and the creation of genuine human community can only come as a gift from God. This gift is what Benedict calls "charity in truth" (*CiV* 34). He also links this with justice: "The logic of gift does not exclude justice, nor does it merely sit alongside it as a second element added from without; on the other hand, economic, social and political development, if it is to be authentically human, needs to make room for the *principle of gratuitousness* as an expression of fraternity" (*CiV* 34).

Benedict goes on to insist that the need for ethical norms applies to the whole sphere of economics. He writes, "The economic sphere is neither ethically neutral, nor inherently inhuman and opposed to society. It is part and parcel of human activity and precisely because it is human, it must be structured and governed in an ethical manner" (*CiV* 36). But ethics alone is not sufficient. Over and above that, it is essential that an element of gratuitousness be brought into economic affairs:

> The Church's social doctrine holds that authentically human social relationships of friendship, solidarity and reciprocity can also be conducted within economic activity, and not only outside it or "after" it . . . in *commercial relationships* the *principle of gratuitousness* and the logic of gift as an expression of fraternity can and must *find their place within normal economic activity.* (*CiV* 36)

Coming to apply this "logic of gift" to practical economics, Benedict makes what is perhaps the most original proposal in the whole encyclical:

> Space . . . needs to be created within the market for economic activity carried out by subjects who freely choose to act according to principles other than those of pure profit, without sacrificing the production of economic value in the process. The many economic entities that draw their origin from religious and lay initiatives demonstrate that this is concretely possible. (*CiV* 37)

What Benedict has in mind is a different kind of business enterprise—one in which the aspect of gratuitousness is evident. Before going into the detail of what this would look like, it is important to look briefly at Benedict's view of the ethical requirements of any authentic economic system and then at the inadequacies that he sees in the present dominant crude capitalist model, on the one hand, and the socialist model, on the other.

Benedict insists that business activities of all kinds have to be reinserted into a wider network of social relationships where business managers must take account not just of how much money they make for their share-holders but also of how their decisions affect all the other stakeholders. Those who own and manage companies have a serious responsibility for the health and welfare both of the workers in their own companies and for the workers in poor countries to which their production has been outsourced as well as for the effects of their products on those who buy them. They are also responsible for the good of the wider society and for the damage that may be done to the environment (*CiV* 40).

Looking at the present scene, the pope concludes that the way the present market economy is working does not measure up to this high ideal, because it gives almost absolute priority to making profits for the shareholders and high salaries for "a new cosmopolitan class of managers" (*CiV* 40). But he is equally convinced that it would be no solution to the problem to move toward a socialist system where the state takes an ever-larger share of the economic activity in society. The problem here is that this "socialist" model (which, in effect, is just "state capitalism") fails to respect the principle of subsidiarity (cf. *CiV* 57). On this point Benedict is in line particularly with the early social encyclicals that emphasized the dangers of an excessively controlling and bureaucratic state.

Nowadays most social democrats and most moderate capitalists would probably agree that what is needed is a balanced division of the economy. On the one hand, there would be a large number of private enterprises mo-tivated largely by the profit motive but subject to various legal restrictions designed to protect the common good. On the other hand, there would be a fairly small number of state enterprises committed to protecting the common good in areas of the economy where there would be too much risk in handing them over to private capitalists. Benedict refuses to settle for such a two-way division of the economy. He says, "The exclusively binary model of market-plus-State is corrosive of society" (*CiV* 39). So he maintains that: "Today's international economic scene . . . requires a *profoundly new way of understanding business enterprise*" (*CiV* 40).

A WAY FORWARD

Benedict goes on to say, "Old models are disappearing, but promising new ones are taking shape on the horizon" (*CiV* 40). He does not make the mistake of imagining that he or the Church has a blueprint that can solve all the economic problems of today's world. He does, however, have an ideal in mind. It is that the whole financial and economic enterprise be situated within the context of human interactions characterized by such fundamental virtues as social and distributive justice, respect, solidarity, trust, participation, transparency, generosity, love, and concern for the common good and for the environment. If people's desire to make money were tempered and balanced by a commitment to these virtues, then the major economic and social problems of the world would be avoided or at least minimized.

In addition to an ideal, Benedict also puts forward a practical proposal that he believes can be a step in the right direction and can act as a model for a way forward. So he proposes an initiative that is both radical and quite simple to understand. It is for the development of "an economy of communion."

Here we come to what is distinctly new in Benedict's position. He calls for the establishment of new types of business enterprise that will be located in "a broad intermediate area" that has emerged "between profit-based companies and non-profit organizations." He has in mind the kind of company that "does not exclude profit, but instead considers it a means for achieving human and social ends"; this is a company willing to "view profit as a means of achieving the goal of a more humane market and society" (*CiV* 46). Earlier he had stressed the need for "those types of economic initiative which, without rejecting profit, aim at a higher goal than the mere logic of the exchange of equivalents, of profit as an end in itself" (*CiV* 38). The pope believes that "the logic of gift" would be a fundamental feature of such business enterprises.

The passage that I quoted above from *CiV* 37 includes this key sentence: "The many economic entities that draw their origin from religious and lay initiatives demonstrate that this [i.e., enterprises that 'act according to principles other than those of pure profit'] is concretely possible." Vatican insiders say that what the pope has in mind is an initiative taken by members of the Focolare movement in recent years. Inspired by the call of their founder, Chiara Lubich, for "an economy of communion," the movement "has brought together 754 companies worldwide that are committed to pursuing higher goals than just profit."[4] The call by Benedict for such an "economy of communion" is a striking example of the extent to which the outlook and spirituality of the Focolare movement permeates much of the encyclical. There are also indications that Benedict's concept of an "economy of communion" was influenced by the economists Luigino Bruni and Stefano Zamagni of the Bologna school of economics and by Franciscan economic theory, going back to Saint Bonaventure, the subject of Benedict's dissertation (Thomas 2010, 25; Small 2011, 8–10; Healy 2010, 582).

In fact, several years before Pope Benedict issued his call for this "new" form of economy, Bruni had published his lecture titled "Economy of

---

[4]See Mark Zwick and Louise Zwick, "Pope Benedict XVI Cites Focolare's Economy of Communion as Economic Model," *Houston Catholic Worker* 29 no. 4 (September–October 2009). http://www.cjd.org; cf. Christiansen (2010, 21); cf. Gold 2010.

Communion: Between Market and Solidarity," in which he gave an account of the Focolare initiative. He concluded,

> If we look at the history of economic and social life in a short-sighted way . . . we must admit that an economic life based on individualistic self-interest is the rule and "communion" the exception. But if we lengthen our perspective and look at history through centuries . . . we must say that "communion is the rule" of organizing economic and social life, and self-interest the exception. (Bruni 2000, 247)

In the same collection in which Bruni's lecture was published, Zamagni also insisted strongly on "the principle of reciprocity." He said that "economic phenomena have a primary interpersonal dimension" because there is "a pre-existing network of social relations which cannot be thought of as a mere constraint, as mainstream economists continue to believe" (Zamagni 2000, 167–68).

In 2010, Zamagni spelled out his position more fully. He criticized "a twofold error"—one that assumes that, on the one hand, "the sphere of the market coincides with egoism," where everybody pursues individual self-interest and that, on the other hand, "the sphere of the State coincides with solidarity, the pursuit of collective interests" (Zamagni 2010, 82). For him it is essential to realize that the maintenance of solidarity cannot be left entirely to be enforced by the state. Humans have what he calls "a sense of fraternity" that leads each of us to feel responsible for other humans. "A society without the principle of fraternity has no future" (Zamagni 2010, 84). If society is to survive, we must not see "interpersonal ties" as irrelevant but must find room for "fraternity, reciprocity, and gift" (Zamagni 2010, 85).

The term "economy of communion" may be relatively new, but it is well to remember that the idea is by no means new. The notion of integrating economic and social goals has been around for a long time. An outstanding example is the Mondragón Cooperative Corporation in the Basque region of Spain. Its origins go back to the 1940s and the inspiration of a Catholic priest. It is composed of more than 160 employee-owned companies involving 23,000 owner-members; estimates of the number of its employees vary from 73,000 to more than 100,000 (cf. Pabst 2010, 596).[5] One thinks also of various business enterprises founded by Quaker families in the nineteenth century.[6] One should also recall the seventeenth- and

---

[5] I venture to add that in the western Irish village where I was born, a factory was founded and managed by the Catholic nun, Sister Mary Arsenius Morrogh-Bernard, for similar social reasons; it was founded in 1892 and is still functioning today. See http://www.museumsofmayo.com.

[6] See, for instance, http://www.cadburyindia.com and http://www.catholicireland.net.

eighteenth-century "Reductions" that the Jesuits established in Paraguay, and even earlier, the craft-guild system that, at its best, represented a successful integration of social and economic values.[7]

Benedict is not at all proposing that the dual-purpose enterprises that he advocates should replace the regular business enterprise. It is clear, however, that he believes they can not only compete successfully with the profit-oriented companies but can also provide a challenge to them to take more seriously their social obligations. In this way they can play a key role in "civilizing the economy" (*CiV* 38). They do this by showing that "authentically human social relationships of friendship, solidarity and reciprocity can also be conducted within economic activity, and not only outside it or 'after' it" (*CiV* 36).

IS IT REALISTIC?

A key question is whether Benedict's advocacy of dual-purpose or multipurpose business enterprises is realistic. Is his proposal destined to meet the same fate as that of the "vocational" corporatist "third way," neither capitalist not socialist, favored by Pius XI in his 1931 encyclical *Quadragesimo Anno*? That was a corporatist model partly borrowed from, or inspired by, the fascist system being imposed in Italy at that time by Mussolini. (See *QA* 79, 82, 83, 85, 92–94; see my account of the position of Pius XI in chapter 3.) From the 1930s to the 1950s many Catholic theologians and activists believed that Pius XI's vocational proposal could resolve the economic crisis following the Great Depression and ensure social justice in the future. Despite the pressure that they put on governments to adopt this "third way," their hopes proved in vain. In Ireland, for instance, the government set up a Commission on Vocational Organization. It was chaired by a bishop who worked with the commission from 1939 to 1943 and produced an enormous report. It is said that when the commission's report eventually came before the government, the key cabinet minister, Sean Lemass, promptly consigned it to the wastepaper basket!

Seventy-five years later, Pope Benedict's encyclical again put forward an ideal vision for society and a proposal for moving toward it. Is it any

---

[7]In relatively recent years the university departments that focus on the development of leadership skills in the business world have turned some of their attention to leadership in what they call "social enterprises," which are in fact instances of "the economy of communion." On the basis of their studies of a variety of such enterprises, the academics have come up with some helpful guidelines for the development of appropriate leadership skills. See, for instance, Tian and Smith 2014, 42–45, and McDougall and McDavid 2014, 46–51.

more likely to be acted on than that of Pius XI? Can we really expect a significant number of people to take seriously the proposal to establish business enterprises that aim to provide employment, to respect the environment, to give the workers a sense of active involvement in the project, and even of shared ownership—and to maintain all these values while still being commercially viable? Is the pope engaged in just the kind of moralizing that is so easily dismissed by hard-nosed economists and politicians?

This calls for a nuanced answer. On the one hand, Benedict's proposal is far more realistic than that of his predecessor because it does not involve an immediate radical restructuring of the whole economic order as did that of Pius XI. It can be implemented piecemeal on an incremental basis. Those who opt to establish dual-purpose business enterprises can do so while continuing to live within the present free-enterprise system. As mentioned, Benedict is not asking that dual-purpose business enterprises replace the usual profit-oriented companies but that they exist alongside them—as a challenge and an invitation to them to adopt a more ethical approach to business. Furthermore, Benedict's proposal is more likely to be ecumenically acceptable. As I have already pointed out, the concept of a dual-purpose business enterprise is by no means confined to Catholics; in fact, some Quakers and others adopted it many years ago.

On the other hand, however, Benedict's proposal faces serious obstacles. First, we need to consider the practical challenge that makes it hard for the kind of ethical business advocated by Benedict to flourish. The enterprise will have to compete in our globalized world where other companies outsource as much work as possible to areas where workers are poorly paid and are frequently exploited. If any ethical business is to survive, it must find ways to be even more efficient than the competing companies whose sole or primary purpose is the generation of profit.

Second, an equally challenging difficulty arises at what we may call the cultural level. This is the extent to which the prevailing class structure of society has affected the attitudes of almost all who are involved in the world of business. It is taken for granted that the interests of workers are directly opposed to those of entrepreneurs. It is no easy task to change this "culture" to a trusting one that promotes a "win-win" approach. It is, I think, significant that the cooperative movement that flourished for decades in various countries has recently come under increasing pressure. The members of many cooperative businesses abandoned their ideals and settled for the quick gain that came from selling out to entrepreneurs who turned the cooperatives into regular commercial companies.

Furthermore, the present-day culture of the business world makes it difficult to maintain a good balance between the entrepreneurial spirit and an idealistic commitment to noble social values. It is all too easy to tip over into a hard-nosed realism that neglects or sacrifices ideals—or, in contrast, to focus so much on high ideals that one fails to take account of real-life difficulties. In order to find a good balance, it is necessary to have the kind of support and challenge that can be provided by a committed community. That is why it makes sense to attempt to establish ethical business enterprises within the countercultural atmosphere that is generated in communities of like-minded people such as the Focolare, the Sant'Egidio community, or other preexisting or ad hoc groups.

If the dual-purpose model is to succeed on any significant scale, I think it will be necessary for the owners, managers, employees, and other stakeholders to take time out from their regular work to engage in some joint workshops to share their ideals with each other and to come to understand the pressures that each group experiences. Such workshops can offer the participants an opportunity to reflect on their experiences as individuals, as members of working teams, as stakeholders in a joint business enterprise, and as members of the wider human community where they have to face up to such global issues as structural injustice at an international and national level, racial and gender discrimination, and urgent ecological issues. In the course of these workshops they will have an opportunity to share their fears and their hopes, and to experience the challenge of listening, in an atmosphere of safety and respect, to the difficulties that arise for people whose situation in life is quite different from their own.

OTHER HELPFUL INITIATIVES

The dual-purpose business enterprise proposed by Benedict is not the only way in which "an economy of communion" can be fostered. There are various other significant features of the present situation that indicate that the radical change of direction the encyclical calls for is possible. One can already find what might be called actual or potential pilot schemes or instances of the new approach. The pope refers to "fair trade" initiatives that ensure that producers of tea, coffee, and other primary products are paid fairly (*CiV* 66). He notes with approval the development of "ethical investment" initiatives (*CiV* 45), while insisting on proper criteria for deciding what counts as ethical. He reminds us how important it is that local grassroots people be involved in the implementation of development programs and the distribution of international aid (*CiV* 47, 58). He notes the value of consumer cooperatives and of the availability of micro-credit, as well as the role that credit unions are playing and can play in genuine human development (*CiV* 66). All these are ways in which economic affairs are, at present, infused with elements of gratuitousness.

Benedict also points out how important it is that trade unions in the more prosperous countries should ensure that workers in poorer countries are not exploited: "The global context in which work takes place also demands that national labour unions, which tend to limit themselves to defending the interests of their registered members, should turn their attention to those outside their membership, and in particular to workers in developing countries where social rights are often violated" (*CiV* 64).

In this regard he might have gone further and offered encouragement to the development of international and intercontinental trade union federations. Such federations would promote global solidarity among workers (cf. Pennings 2010, 73). They would pay a lot of attention to areas where workers everywhere can make common cause against exploitative styles of outsourcing and other abusive practices. This would mean that the safeguarding of the interests of workers in poor countries would not be dependent solely on the altruism of trade unionists in prosperous countries.

If we focus only on the instances that I have mentioned already of the element of gift in economic enterprises, there is a danger that we would miss out on the importance and the relevance of what Benedict is saying in this encyclical. It is best to see the instances mentioned as striking examples and reminders that a large element of gratuitousness should permeate all economic relationships. Not only should this be the case but, to a large extent, it is what actually does happen quite commonly in our everyday world, even though mainstream economic theory seldom takes account of it.

In an important passage in *CiV* 38 Benedict writes of "an *economy of gratuitousness* and fraternity" and goes on immediately to insist that "the aspect of fraternal reciprocity must be present" at every level of economic life. It is important to note that Benedict is here equating "gratuitousness" with "fraternity" and "fraternal reciprocity." This has the effect of bringing the idealistic concept of "gratuitousness" down to earth, making it realistic and practical. In chapter 17 I refer to some commentaries on the encyclical which spell out in more detail how an element of gratuitousness can be brought into everyday economic relationships.

CURRENT ISSUES

I come now to the practical aspects of Benedict's encyclical and what it has to say about a range of specific issues that are particularly relevant in the current situation. A key to understanding the pope's approach is this sentence: "I express my conviction that *Populorum Progressio* deserves to be considered 'the *Rerum Novarum* of the present age' " (*CiV* 8).

Let me explain what this implies. The first of the modern social encyclicals, *Rerum Novarum*, was issued by Leo XIII in 1891. Forty years later, Pius XI issued the second social encyclical. In *Quadragesimo Anno* he set out to apply the principles of that first encyclical to the new situation of economic crisis in 1931 and "to give it teeth" by making various practical proposals. Being documents of their time, these two encyclicals focused on justice at the national level. In 1967 Paul VI issued *Populorum Progressio*, which addressed the issue of international social justice. Now, just over forty years later, Benedict has looked back at *Populorum Progressio* and has set out to do for it what Pius XI's *Quadragesimo Anno* did for Leo's encyclical—applying its principles to the present globalized situation and giving it some practical "teeth."

Benedict's encyclical sets out to address the many new issues that have arisen as a result of "the *explosion of worldwide interdependence*, commonly known as globalization" and notes that "the ferocious pace at which it has evolved could not have been anticipated" (*CiV* 33). Globalization is not only "a socio-economic process . . . [but] also a cultural event both in its causes and its effects" (*CiV* 42). In seeing it as a cultural event, Benedict is saying that it is not something that happened automatically in a predetermined way; it is a result of human decisions, and the implication is that we humans have both the power and the responsibility to control and direct it. As the encyclical says, "globalization, *a priori*, is neither good nor bad. It will be what people make of it. We should not be its victims, but rather its protagonists" (*CiV* 42).

The encyclical addresses a whole variety of the practical justice issues in the world today—problems that arise mainly as a result of the form globalization has taken. It refers to "new forms of colonialism" (*CiV* 33). Later, it warns against "presumed cultural superiority" by technologically advanced societies (*CiV* 59). I add that one result of this arrogance is the way officials of international institutions, such as the International Monetary Fund, have imposed harsh conditions on the inhabitants of poor countries as part of what they call "structural adjustment programs" (cf. *CiV* 25; also Stiglitz 2002, 98–120, 135–65; Dorr 2007, 257–58).

In two places in the encyclical (*CiV* 25, 40) Benedict refers to the "outsourcing of production" to poor countries where labor is cheap, and he is very aware of the problems that are associated with this practice. He notes how ever-increasing competition results in "the downsizing of social security systems . . . with consequent grave danger for the rights of workers" (*CiV* 25). He points to the serious effects of "the systemic increase of social inequality, both within a single country and between the populations of different countries (i.e., the massive increase in relative poverty)." This, he says, leads to a damaging of "social cohesion . . . placing democracy at risk." Furthermore, it damages "the economy, through the progressive erosion of 'social capital': the network of relationships of trust, dependability, and respect for rules, all of which are indispensable for any form of civil coexistence" (*CiV* 32).

The encyclical notes the problems associated with the hoarding of "non-renewable energy sources" by wealthy countries (*CiV* 49). It also points out the problems associated with international tourism (including sex tourism) (*CiV* 61). Elsewhere it refers to the "rigid assertion of the right to intellectual property" (*CiV* 22). Here Benedict is obviously referring to the patenting laws that so disadvantage poorer countries, and he may well be thinking especially of the patenting of life-forms. Later on he refers (*CiV* 65; cf. *CiV* 40) to the abuse of "sophisticated [financial] instruments" and, in doing so, obviously has in mind the hedge funds and other devices used by bankers and financiers to generate vast amounts of what is being called "virtual money," which has now turned out very largely to be "mythical money"!

He is also aware of the danger of protectionist policies adopted by technologically advanced countries against poorer countries, especially in regard to the importation of agricultural products (*CiV* 58).

In this encyclical the pope also shows his concern about problems related to the environment, a topic I take up in chapter 18.

SOLIDARITY AND SUBSIDIARITY

The word "solidarity" is used in twenty-seven paragraphs of the encyclical, sometimes more than once in the same paragraph. This frequent emphasis on solidarity is closely related to Benedict's insistence of the centrality of gift in our experience and our responses. That is because the practice of solidarity—by one person with another or with a community, and by communities of all kinds with other communities, ranging from the local to the global—is perhaps the most obvious way of bringing gratuitousness into human relationships and human experience. This shows that Benedict's emphasis on the notion of gift is not just a pious idea brought in early in the encyclical before the pope gets down to the central issues; it is rather a central integrating theme that runs right through the encyclical. It is true that in this encyclical Benedict does not offer any sustained account of the nature of solidarity such as John Paul did in *Sollicitudo Rei Socialis*. However, we may assume that he accepts and relies on his predecessor's account, without feeling the need to repeat it or expand it.

In the first sentence of *CiV* 58 Benedict makes a statement that is both important and quite dense: "*The principle of subsidiarity must remain closely linked to the principle of solidarity and vice versa,* since the former without the latter gives way to social privatism, while the latter without the former gives way to paternalist social assistance that is demeaning to those in need."

The term "social privatism" is quite unusual in English, and the corresponding phrase used in the text of the encyclical in various other languages throws no further light on its meaning. Benedict is here rejecting the view that one can invoke the principle of subsidiarity without reference to solidarity. In this context I take "social privatism" to refer to the view that there is no need for humans to be organized at an international or even national level. Benedict is rejecting that view because he is keenly aware of the need for institutions at the state or international level as well as at the local and regional levels.

The whole point of the principle of subsidiarity is that affairs should be dealt with by the lowest or least centralized competent authority. It is difficult to have a personal experience of solidarity with a very large, distant, and anonymous institution such as a national Department of Health. So it is best that most of the institutional relationships of individuals should, as far as possible, be mediated through intermediate groups or bodies such as local and regional communities. Only those tasks that cannot be performed effectively at an immediate or local level should be left to the higher or more central authority. Pope Benedict is very aware of both aspects of the principle of subsidiarity.

Undoubtedly, he maintains that "subsidiarity is the most effective antidote against any form of all-encompassing welfare state" (*CiV* 57). He favors a "more devolved and organic system of social security" that would be "less bureaucratic" and, perhaps, linked to "fiscal subsidiarity" and "welfare solidarity from below" (*CiV* 60). In adopting this position, Benedict is following a long tradition in Catholic social teaching, going back to *Quadragesimo Anno* and beyond. So he would prefer that as much as possible of social welfare should be handled at a level lower than that of the national state. One might speculate that in adopting this position, Benedict was influenced by his German background, a country where many governmental functions are carried out at the level of the various regional *Länder* rather than at the national level.

It would be a serious mistake to assume that because Benedict insists on subsidiarity, he is calling for an abolition of a universal social security system, leaving social protection to non-state agencies, such as churches, or to insurance policies that individuals could take out on a voluntary basis. In fact, he points out that "the market has prompted new forms of competition between States [that] . . . have led to a *downsizing of social security systems* as the price to be paid for seeking greater competitive advantage in the global market, with consequent grave danger for the rights of workers, for fundamental human rights and for the solidarity associated with the traditional forms of the social State" (*CiV* 25). Johan Verstraeten sees Benedict's position as "undeniably a correction of the un-nuanced rejection . . . of the social assistance state by Pope John Paul II in *Centesimus Annus*" (Verstraeten 2011, 325).

SOLIDARITY AT THE INTERNATIONAL LEVEL

It is clear, then, that Benedict knows that in the modern world there are many tasks that do require involvement of the state; in acknowledging this, Benedict is being true to the position adopted by John XXIII in *Mater et Magistra*. Furthermore, Benedict clearly agrees with the view espoused by Paul VI in *Populorum Progressio* that there are now many issues that can only be tackled effectively at the international level—and not merely through bilateral agreements but at the level of some kind of international authority. Benedict is very aware that in the forty-year interval between the encyclical of Paul VI and his own *Caritas in Veritate* there has emerged a greater need for some kind of international authority—and not merely in regard to political issues, but even more obviously and urgently in relation to economic issues.

In proposing some such authority, Benedict is simply applying both the principle of solidarity and the principle of subsidiarity to the present globalized world. So he is being fully consistent with his overall theme of gratuitousness in calling for reform of international institutions, both political and financial. For him, the aim of such a reform would be to give the poorer nations an effective voice in them and to ensure that there is genuine "shared decision-making." This throws light on the final part of the statement from *CiV* 58 that I quoted above: "The latter [the principle of solidarity] without the former [the principle of subsidiarity] gives way to paternalist social assistance that is demeaning to those in need." The point here is made clear in the two sentences that follow the one I have quoted: "This general rule must also be taken broadly into consideration when addressing issues concerning *international development aid*. Such aid, whatever the donors' intentions, can sometimes lock people into a state of dependence and even foster situations of localized oppression and exploitation in the receiving country" (*CiV* 58). Benedict is saying that the principle of subsidiarity requires that international development agencies or governments that genuinely wish to help local communities in poor countries must be willing to allow the people of these communities to decide the kind of help they want.

In line with these general guidelines, the pope goes on in a later paragraph to spell out the practical implications in some detail:

In the face of the unrelenting growth of global interdependence, there is a strongly felt need, even in the midst of a global recession, for a reform of the *United Nations Organization*, and likewise of *economic institutions and international finance*, so that the concept of the family of nations can acquire real teeth. . . . This seems necessary in order to arrive at a political, juridical and economic order which can increase and give direction to international cooperation for the development of all peoples in solidarity. To manage the global economy; to revive economies hit by the crisis; to avoid any deterioration of the present crisis and the greater imbalances that would result; to bring about integral and timely disarmament, food security and peace; to guarantee the protection of the environment and to regulate migration: for all this, there is urgent need of a true world political authority, as my predecessor Blessed John XXIII indicated some years ago [in *Pacem in Terris*]. Such an authority would need to be regulated by law, to observe consistently the principles of subsidiarity and solidarity, to seek to establish the common good. . . . Furthermore, such an authority would need to be universally recognized and to be vested with the effective power to ensure security for all, regard for justice, and respect for rights. (*CiV* 67)

In chapter 17 I look at the reactions of some commentators to this strong statement of the pope.

A REVISION OF *DEUS CARITAS EST?*

In a wide-ranging article, Lisa Sowle Cahill suggests that "*Caritas in Veritate* could be seen as a revision of *Deus Caritas Est*"; and Johan Verstraeten adopts a similar view. Cahill points out that *Caritas in Veritate* "prioritizes 'integral human development and authentic development' " and "names work for structural change as intrinsic to Christian love as such, not only for the laity" (Cahill 2010, 304–5; cf. Verstraeten 2011, 316, 328). Noting Benedict's involvement in the preparation for the African synod at the time of the publication of *Caritas in Veritate*, Cahill holds:

The sociopolitical awareness of Benedict XVI at the turn of the decade seems quite different from that of Joseph Ratzinger and the new pope of 2005. The commensurate adjustment of his vision of the Church's social mission—as global rather than Eurocentric, as politically engaged as well as evangelistic—reflects his new global responsibilities. (Cahill 2010, 311)

In the light of the broadening of Benedict's vision in the years between the two encyclicals, and in view of "the encyclical's internal tensions regarding Catholic agencies," she holds that it would be "premature" and "untenable" to conclude that in *Deus Caritas Est*, Benedict is "sending signals to rein in political activity" (Cahill 2010, 310).

I fully agree that in *Deus Caritas Est*, Benedict is not reining in political activity. But the key issue is what kind of political activity does he approve of? My study of both encyclicals convinces me that there is no major inconsistency in his approach between the two encyclicals. His position in *Deus Caritas Est* is that politics, as such, is the domain of the laity. The Church in its teaching role can and must make a vital but indirect contribution to political life. It "liberates reason from its blind spots," and it reawakens "the spiritual energy without which justice, which always demands sacrifice, cannot prevail and prosper" (*DCE* 28). I see no indication in *Caritas in Veritate* that Benedict has moved beyond that position. What he has done is to spell out, in some detail, various things that need to be changed in the political world and to invite lay Catholics, along with other committed people, to model "an economy of communion" that will serve the common good by not focusing exclusively on making profits. The significant point to note is that of its nature this "economy of communion" is one that has to be developed by laypeople rather than by the institutional Church. For Benedict, in both encyclicals the direct responsibility for making society more just falls on the laity. So the proposal in *Caritas in Veritate* to establish enterprises that combine the meeting of social needs with making profit fits quite well with the stance spelled out by Benedict in *Deus Caritas Est* on the respective roles of the laity and the official Church.

It is interesting to note that in *Caritas in Veritate* Benedict makes no mention of a role for the Caritas agencies or other official Church agencies in promoting justice and protection of human rights. Furthermore, he does not mention the work done by so many religious congregations and their individual members in working for justice by their actions and their whole way of life, especially in making a clear option for the poor. One should not read too much into any such omissions in the encyclical. But they may perhaps be an indication that, in this sphere of the promotion of justice in the world, Benedict looks more to the present and future contributions of the relatively new Catholic movements in which laypeople play a major role such as Focolare, Comunione e Liberazione, Opus Dei, and Sant'Egidio.

The main difference between the two encyclicals is that in *Caritas in Veritate*, Benedict is addressing a different part of his very broad agenda. In it he is not dealing with the issue of what Catholic charitable or development agencies should be doing. But there is no indication that he has changed his belief that their main role should be that of providing charitable relief and their staff should not acquiesce in secular views but should be animated by Christian faith.

I think it is quite true, as Cahill says, that Benedict's vision has become more global during the years of his papacy. No doubt, the ecclesiastical and political situation in Africa has moved up alongside Benedict's previous and ongoing concern about secularism in Europe, about religious relativism and syncretism in Asia, and about liberation theology in Latin America. He is, of course, interested in the contribution that Church leaders and the Christian faithful can make to genuine political and social development in Africa. But presumably this will come only through "the liberation of reason" and "the reawakening of spiritual energy" that *Deus Caritas Est* describes. It is significant that in an address to the participants at the end of the synod for Africa on October 24, 2009, Benedict said that "the temptation could have been to politicize the theme, to talk less about pastors and more about politicians, thus with a competence that is not ours." He followed this up in his postsynodal exhortation to African Bishops, *Africae Munus*, issued on November 19, 2011, in which he insisted that "the Church's mission is not political in nature" (§23); he said, "There is no doubt that the building of a just social order is part of the competence of the political sphere. Yet one of the tasks of the Church in Africa consists in forming upright consciences receptive to the demands of justice" (§22).

Late in his papacy, on December 5, 2009, Benedict reminded bishops from Brazil about the *Instruction on Certain Aspects of the "Theology of Liberation"* published by the Congregation for the Doctrine of the Faith twenty-five years earlier when he himself was the prefect of that Congregation. Warning the Brazilian bishops again of the dangers of "an a-critical acceptance on the part of certain theologians of theses and methodologies that derive from Marxism," he said,

> Its more or less visible consequences consisting of rebellion, division, dissent, offence, and anarchy make themselves felt, creating in your diocesan communities great suffering and a serious loss of vitality. I implore all those who in some way have felt attracted, involved and deeply touched by certain deceptive principles of Liberation Theology to consider once again the above-mentioned Instruction, perceiving the kind light with which it is proffered.

This uncompromising statement suggests that Benedict is as opposed as ever to any overt or "direct" political involvement by Church leaders or official Church agencies in political affairs. I have not seen any indication in *Caritas in Veritate* or elsewhere that he had changed the view that emerges from *Deus Caritas Est*—that the primary focus of Church agencies should be on providing charitable relief—or that he had come to approve of the kind of direct intervention in political struggles engaged in by Oscar Romero, Denis Hurley, and other politically activist Church leaders.

OPTION FOR THE POOR?

Now that I have examined most of the main works of Pope Benedict since he became pope, a fundamental question arises: Where does he stand in relation to the option for the poor, the primary theme of this book? This question requires a nuanced answer. On the one hand, in *Deus Caritas Est* Benedict maintains that care for the poor is part of the very essence of being Church and is therefore an immediate and direct obligation not only for individual Christians but for the Church as such. Furthermore, there can be no doubt that Benedict, like his predecessors, is deeply concerned about the issue of justice in the world. This comes through again and again—above all in *Caritas in Veritate* where the central theme is a call to create a more just world. Quite obviously, to work for justice is to be concerned for the poor and oppressed who are victims of injustice (cf. O'Boyle 2010, 10–11). On the other hand, the passage that I have just quoted from Benedict's address to Brazilian bishops in 2009 is a clear indication that he still retained what one can only describe as a visceral rejection of liberation theology, which is the original source of the phrase "option for the poor."

It is true that Benedict accepts the term "preferential option for the poor." For instance, in his Address to the Inaugural Session of the Fifth General Conference of the Bishops of Latin America and the Caribbean, at Aparecida, May 13, 2007, he said, "The preferential option for the poor is implicit in the Christological faith in the God who became poor for us, so as to enrich us with his poverty." However, in accepting even the toned-down term "preferential option for the poor," he is committed to setting it apart from any association with liberation theology. He does not link it to a clear choice to be on the side of those who resist oppression and who are willing not only to struggle for justice but to do so by engaging in sharp contestation with those who oppress them. There is no indication that Benedict himself experienced such contestation and struggle as intrinsic to his own spirituality—or that he encouraged others to adopt and develop such a spirituality. It is particularly significant that in his 2009 Message for World Day of Peace he wrote of the "preferential *love* for the poor" (my emphasis; cf. Verstraeten 2011, 327). On this occasion Benedict gave a reference to John Paul's *Centesimus Annus* that uses the term "preferential *option* for the poor" (*CA* 57, my emphasis); he also gave a reference to John Paul's *Sollicitudo Rei Socialis*, which uses the phrase "the *option* or *love of preference* for the poor" and which immediately stresses that it "is an option" (*SRS* 42).

I am inclined to think that the notion of "an option for the poor" retains its full meaning, its implications, and its challenge only as part of a spirituality that values and emphasizes the concept of liberation, with its background of social analysis and its overtones of contestation and struggle. This is a passionate spirituality that finds much of its spiritual nourishment precisely in the passion and the struggle. Furthermore, it involves the adoption of a sharply countercultural focus for one's activities, one's interests, and one's energy, and it is usually linked to a significant change in one's lifestyle.

That overall pattern is not the kind of spirituality that seems to be promoted in either the official or less formal writings of Benedict before and after he became pope, even though some of the elements that I have listed are to be found there. The spirituality that is reflected in his writings and speeches is one that, in some respects, is rational, even cerebral, but is, at the same time, profoundly spiritual and, on occasion, emotional and deeply moving. The passion and the spiritual nourishment aspects of the spirituality he espouses seem to be found mainly in the sphere of one's personal relationship with God, and possibly also in interpersonal relationships, leaving the public sphere of economics and politics to be experienced and dealt with in a committed but rather more rational manner. In this sense his is rather a more traditional type of spirituality. For this reason my tentative conclusion is that a better way to describe the stance of Benedict is to say that it involves not so much an *option* for the poor in the sense in which that term is properly understood; for him it is more a matter of having a preferential *concern* for the poor, linked to a deep and well-grounded commitment to justice in the world (cf. Renouard 2010, "Concluding Remarks").

BENEDICT: A NEW DIRECTION OR A NEW EMPHASIS?

At the beginning of chapter 15 I raised the question of whether Pope Benedict was aiming "to shift the main focus of Catholic social teaching away from the orientation that it had taken since the time of John XXIII." It would appear that Benedict himself considers that such a question should not even be raised, for he maintains that "there is *a single teaching, consistent and at the same time ever new*" and that one must not "lose sight of the coherence of the overall doctrinal *corpus*" (*CiV* 12). But I suggested in chapter 5 that Pope John XXIII, while maintaining continuity with his predecessors from a doctrinal point of view, made a radical shift of emphasis or direction in regard to the way he applied the basic principles and values of the tradition. I believe that it is a valid question to ask whether Benedict also maintained a certain continuity with the past but, at the same time, wished to turn Catholic social teaching in a new direction or at least to switch its focus or change its main emphasis.

I feel I can now give a nuanced answer to this question. It seems clear that Benedict has made a positive and valuable contribution by emphasizing the role that lay Christians can play in challenging the present unjust structures of our world. For him, their challenge is to come not just by what they say or write, but above all by restoring an experience of communion and fraternity/sorority to everyday economic relationships. His *Caritas in Veritate* proposes that this can and should be done first of all by the development of many enterprises that model an "economy of communion."

These enterprises will be models of gratuitousness by deliberately combining two aims: (1) making a modest profit; and (2) serving the common good and various social functions, such as providing employment, enabling employees to have a share in management and profits, promoting teamwork and a spirit of cooperation and friendship in the workplace, and protecting the environment. Furthermore, his proposal is that the economy should be rehumanized by reinserting an element of what he repeatedly calls "gratuitousness and fraternity" into all economic relationships and not just into the special mixed-aims enterprises I have just mentioned. In all of this the pope has undoubtedly given a new and very valuable emphasis to Catholic social teaching.

It seems clear that Pope Benedict was fully committed to having the Church work to promote justice in the world. However, he had a strong, and controversial, view about the way in which this should be done. It appears that he feels that the balance has swung too much in the direction of having Church leaders and Church agencies directly involved in the struggle for justice. He holds that the official Church and Church leaders should not be directly involved in promoting justice. Their role should rather be one of educating consciences and evoking the spiritual energy of laypeople to engage—in a personal capacity—in the work of justice. So he does seem to be shifting the focus away from the direction that had been taken by significant sectors of the Church, particularly since the emergence of liberation theology and its widespread—though attenuated—influence. This change of focus has more to do with Catholic social practice than with its formal teaching.

Benedict's writings leave me with the impression that he did not really approve of open confrontation. I suspect that he saw it as springing from, and evoking, a type of anger that is rather destructive and un-Christian—and that may also, in fact, be quite ineffective. Furthermore, he seemed to find a connection between this kind of contestation and an unduly secular approach—one that takes little account of gratuitousness and the free gifts and grace of God. If this is true, then one can see why he was particularly opposed to the official Church or its clergy becoming involved in this style of struggle for justice.

It is important to emphasize that Benedict's stance was not simply one of questioning or rejecting this kind of overt struggle for liberation. He was putting forward a positive alternative approach—one in which Christians open themselves to the gifts of God and work conscientiously to bring that gratuitousness into their everyday human relationships. And this is to take place not just at the interpersonal level but also in the sphere of economics and politics. In all this, Benedict has brought a valuable new emphasis to Catholic social teaching and practice.

However, I do not think this should be put forward as a substitute for a more overt struggle for justice and liberation. It would be better—and at times necessary—that both approaches should be used. In chapter 15 I suggested that Benedict had not taken sufficient account of two situations. The first of these is where a government is blatantly corrupt and oppressive and where one or more Church leaders may feel it necessary, for the sake of the credibility of the Church, to support the repressed people by openly challenging the government and even providing some public support to those who are engaging in peaceful protest. The second situation is where official Church agencies—both those within the Caritas network and those outside it—are in a position to provide support, particularly in developing countries, to people who are working for authentic human development, justice, and environmental protection. Commitment to support poor and oppressed people in their struggle to survive, to develop, and to establish a society that is just and humane can go hand in hand with, and be greatly enriched by, a conscious commitment to Benedict's ideal of an economy of communion.

They are two aspects of the Church's mission. There is every reason why Church agencies should include both as part of their integral view of inserting the Good News of Jesus in the world—and especially among those who are poor or oppressed. What we can hope for—in developing countries and in the West—is that the Church should play an active role in the establishment of genuinely democratic and participative societies and in the emergence, with official Church support, of many initiatives of a cooperative nature, rather like that of Mondragón in Spain. This involvement should be evident not only in the community aspect of the Church but also in its institutional aspect and through its official and unofficial organizations. This would involve not an entirely new direction but a new and important emphasis in Catholic social teaching and practice.

* * *

SUMMARY

Pope Benedict's 2009 encyclical *Caritas in Veritate* makes an important contribution to Catholic social teaching. Emphasizing that love is a free gift of God, the pope insists that while love presupposes and includes the obligation to be just, it also transcends justice. Benedict also stresses the role of truth, saying, "Deeds without knowledge are blind." He puts forward an integral view of human development, including even sexual and bioethical issues that are usually treated separately from sociopolitical issues.

As a way forward, the pope proposes that a number of entrepreneurs would set up enterprises that would be models of an "economy of communion" where social purposes, such as providing employment, would be combined with making profit. He also insisted that an element of gratuitousness should be present, not just in these initiatives, but also in all economic activities.

He went on to address a variety of challenges that face the world today, mainly as a result of the tremendous growth of globalization. He called for global solidarity through the development of international political and economic institutions, including a reform of the United Nations, respecting the principle of subsidiarity. There is no indication that Benedict had changed his position as outlined in *Deus Caritas Est* that all this political work should be carried out by laypeople. Benedict has a deep concern for justice and for the poor, but his position does not seem to amount to an "option for the poor" in the sense in which that term has been understood. His emphasis on gratuitousness and an economy of communion gives Catholic social teaching a rather different emphasis than that of previous popes.

QUESTIONS FOR REVIEW

1. *What does Benedict see as the relationship between justice and love?*
2. *Why is truth so important for Benedict?*
3. *What is included in his integral view of human development?*
4. *What is distinctive about the "economy of communion?"*
5. *What are the two key principles on which Benedict insists?*

QUESTIONS FOR REFLECTION

1. *Why has so much of the modern economy become dehumanized?*
2. *Name some instances where gratuitousness is part of economic relationships.*

ISSUES FOR FURTHER STUDY

1. *The nature of globalization.*
2. *The background to the emergence of the notion of an option for the poor.*

17

Reactions and Follow-up
to *Caritas in Veritate*

In the first part of this chapter I examine the views of some of the many commentators who reacted or responded to *Caritas in Veritate*. In the second part I examine an important document by the Pontifical Council for Justice and Peace issued two years after the encyclical—a document that spells out in specific detail some of the topics dealt with in a more general way in the encyclical.

REACTIONS AND RESPONSES TO THE ENCYCLICAL

When the encyclical *Caritas in Veritate* first came out, it was not given much prominence in the mainstream media. Journalists picked out a few items that they thought might be newsworthy and then moved on to other issues. However, it did generate considerable interest among a fairly small number of commentators. But here the key issue was how they interpreted it. In recent years ideologues of all kinds have become very aware of how important it is to put their own "spin" on papal documents. The encyclical *Centesimus Annus*, issued by Pope John Paul II eighteen years earlier, was densely written, and key parts of it were open to different interpretations. Right-wing Catholics, mainly in the United States, were quite successful in having it seen primarily as approval by the pope of the capitalist system, even though it took quite a strong stand against the economic liberalism that has been characteristic of the capitalism of recent decades.

Early Negative Reactions

It was more difficult to "spin" the present encyclical in the same direction, though this has not prevented some writers from trying to do so. For instance, Robert Sirico (2009) of the Acton Institute said that it "doesn't attack capitalism," but he failed to mention that it condemns the way capitalism has been operating in our world.

The most glaring example of selective reading of the encyclical came from George Weigel, whose reaction to major elements in Benedict's encyclical was decidedly negative. So Weigel drew what he called a "red marker" over all the passages he did not like, claiming that they were written not by the pope but by members of the Pontifical Council for Justice and Peace. Among the parts that Weigel maintained do not represent Benedict's own thinking is its treatment of gratuitousness as well as its emphasis on the importance of the redistribution of wealth and on the need for a world political authority. He maintained that these "clotted and muddled" ideas, marked by "confused sentimentality," had been previously rejected by John Paul II. Weigel went on to suggest that "Benedict XVI, a truly gentle soul, may have thought it necessary to include in his encyclical these multiple off-notes, in order to maintain the peace within his curial household" (Weigel 2009). This quite outlandish interpretation of the encyclical strains credibility beyond the breaking point.

Michael Novak (2009) damned the encyclical with faint praise—praising the fact that it starts with *caritas* but going on to criticize Benedict's writing as "uncharacteristically waffly and opaque," and complaining about his "bureaucratic jargon."

As one would have expected, Benedict's call for some kind of world authority in both the political and economic spheres was dismissed by right-wing Catholics, particularly in the United States, as utterly misguided. Whether inadvertently or deliberately, many of these critics failed to take account of Benedict's careful insistence that any such authority would have to respect the principle of subsidiarity: "In order not to produce a dangerous universal power of a tyrannical nature, *the governance of globalization must be marked by subsidiarity*, articulated into several layers and involving different levels that can work together" (*CiV* 57).

In his rejection of any kind of world governance in the present situation, Douglas Farrow went so far as to say, "What would a world political authority be but a secularist—or perhaps some day an Islamist—competitor to the Church, intent on imposing on her its own very different concepts of security, justice, and rights?" (Farrow 2010, 746). A gathering of Protestant evangelicals in the United States also expressed widespread rejection of what they saw as Benedict's "explicit endorsement of a world political authority" (P. S. Williams 2010, 68).

More Serious Evaluations

A serious and rather critical evaluation of the encyclical comes from Agbonkhianmeghe Orobator. Having grown up in Nigeria, Orobator was, at the time of writing his article, the provincial of the East African Province of the Jesuits and in a position to have extensive knowledge of the African situation. He criticizes the encyclical for not taking adequate account of the extent to which Africa has been, and still is, exploited and impoverished by external powers: "In presuming the demise of ideologically opposing blocs, *Caritas in Veritate*'s analysis of geopolitical and economic history may placate Western conscience, but not victims of regnant ideologies of exploitation and extraction of the mineral and natural wealth of African countries" (Orobator 2010, 325). Later, he detects "a noticeable irony" in the fact that "Africa is often labelled as corrupt precisely for practicing what *Caritas in Veritate* extols as the economics of communion and affection"; he says there is need for nuances in the encyclical's ideas of gratuitousness and solidarity (Orobator 2010, 327).

Orobator goes on to describe how underdevelopment doubly affects women, notably in regard to HIV/AIDS and in situations of forced displacement. Then he points out that, apart from "a passing comment in no. 28 on women, abortion, and sterilization," the encyclical "maintains a deafening silence on the situation of women in the context of development" (Orobator 2010, 330). Moving on to the issue of the relationship between religion and development, he notes that "the ideological sparring partner of Benedict XVI is secularism in its various forms, especially atheism and relativism." Orobator insists that in Africa this is not an issue. What is, however, of concern is the proliferation of "the gospel of prosperity" that equates faith with prosperity. Religion of this kind "is a double-edged sword capable of inflicting permanent damage on the development of peoples." In this context there is need to focus on "the principles of Catholic social teaching on the structural causes of poverty" (Orobator 2010, 331–32).

Perhaps the most challenging element in Orobator's analysis is his insistence that the criteria on the basis of which the encyclical "criticizes and excoriates social, political, and economic systems" should be applied to the Church itself. In this regard he mentions "the exercise of authority, equality in mission, and attentiveness to the needs of the marginalized, impoverished, and vulnerable" (Orobator 2010, 329–30).

It is reassuring to find that, despite his critical comments, Orobator's final judgment on the encyclical is positive. He maintains that, when "taken as a whole," it "outlines the kind of development suited for Africa . . . founded on the principles and virtues of human dignity, justice, global solidarity and shared gratuitousness" (Orobator 2010, 334).

A quite critical Catholic response to the encyclical comes from Drew Christiansen. While noting key points in the encyclical, he suggests that it represents "a return to an earlier deductive model of teaching on social questions" (Christiansen 2010, 7). A rather similar view is expressed by Johan Verstraeten, who says,

> We can understand the genuine concern of Pope Benedict to value the distinctiveness of the Christian contribution to the humaniza-tion of the world, but it does not follow that this should become a matter of top-down doctrinal truth propositions. A more dynamic approach is proposed by "*Gaudium et Spes*": scrutinizing the signs of the times "in the light of the Gospel." (Verstraeten 2011, 318)

David Hollenbach focuses his criticism on one key point in the encycli-cal—its treatment of the relationship between love and justice. He writes, "The precedence granted to charity over justice risks downplaying the work of justice to a lower spiritual plane than the love-as-gift that the encyclical strongly and repeatedly stresses" (Hollenbach 2011, 174). He holds that "the encyclical . . . downplays those aspects of love that are most important in the quest for structural change" (Hollenbach 2011, 175).

On this issue I venture to suggest that when Benedict maintains that love transcends justice, he is not opposing one to the other and not at all suggesting that love is an alternative to justice. He accepts, and even takes for granted, that love demands that we be just, that we treat everybody equitably (e.g., *CiV* 6: "charity demands justice"). But he is adding that love demands that we go beyond what justice requires of us. My love does not entitle me to ignore structural injustices in society, but rather to work with great generosity to overcome these injustices.

Bernard Laurent is critical of the encyclical on the grounds that it "focuses solely on individual responsibility" (Laurent 2010, 537). He criticizes Benedict for "his refusal to deliver any form of analysis of the structures, accusing individual responsibility alone. . . . No mention is made of the idea of social sin which cannot be reduced to individual sin. . . . Benedict calls more for conversion of hearts than for action against structures" (Laurent 2010, 538).

Johan Verstraeten (2011, 318) also maintains that the encyclical "lacks analysis and, in particular, references to social, economic and political analyses conducted by prominent scholars." But he feels that Laurent's view "should be nuanced, since the encyclical contains at least some hints as to the structural dimensions of problems. On the other hand, it cannot be denied that the focus is mainly on either individual conversion or the changing of personal relations and 'fraternity' " (Verstraeten 2011, 318).

Verstraeten is quite critical of the encyclical on the grounds that Benedict "implicitly suggests that non-Christians . . . have an inadequate understanding of what is good and just; that without the truth proposi-tions offered by the Church, a 'correct' understanding of charity, justice and development is impossible" (Verstraeten 2011, 315). Benedict does, indeed, lay great emphasis on the importance of the truths of the Catholic faith for a true understanding of human development. But I do not think that he would go so far as to maintain that all non-Christians have a quite inadequate understanding of what is good and just.

Nonetheless, I agree entirely with Verstraeten's criticism (Verstraeten 2011, 322–23) that the encyclical fails to include any reference to the various documents issued by the bishops' conferences in various parts of the world. This is a serious lack not only in this encyclical, but in many other Vatican documents, including the 2004 *Compendium of the Social Doctrine of the Catholic Church*. Verstraeten is rightly highly critical of what he calls a "unilateral view on communication" in the *Compendium*, which limits the role of bishops to "*promoting* the teaching and *diffusion* of the Church's social *doctrine*" (Verstraeten 2011, 323; he is quoting from §539 of the *Compendium*, and he has added the emphasis).

Positive Developments

Among the positive responses to Benedict's encyclical are those that set out to show that his proposal for an "economy of communion" is not unrealistic and that, in fact, elements of such an economy already exist to a much wider extent than is generally recognized. In a very enlightening article James Franklin (2011, 1–9) writes:

> A cynical view of business would dismiss Benedict's hopes of an economy informed by love as naïve, in the belief that the profit motive driving business is incompatible with genuinely giving away anything free. But a closer look at business practice in real economies, especially those well-regulated Western ones dominated by the service sector, will show that developments of the kind the Pope describes are well under way. The encyclical calls attention to economic and personal realities not often spoken about in the context of social justice or political economy, but which are crucial to understanding the direction of current economic progress.

Franklin notes that the main economic activities in the Western world are now a wide variety of service industries. He points out that in the way these industries actually operate at present, there is a certain warmth in the interpersonal relationships between the parties engaged in the transactions. The most obvious example is the relationship between a counselor or psychotherapist and a client. This is an economic relationship, but in order for it to work effectively, it is essential that it be characterized by a close interpersonal bond between the parties involved. Franklin mentions a whole variety of other economic relationships, where a human relationship of friendliness and kindness is vitally important. He notes that economists take little account of this relationship. But he points out that management and marketing consultants set a high value on it—under the headings of "communication skills" and "teamwork" (Franklin 2011, 7). He goes on to note that many private schools and care facilities where old people are looked after are not, in fact, run primarily on a profit-making basis. And, of course, numerous charities of all kinds are prime examples of gratuitousness (Franklin 2011, 8).

Early in 2010 the Pontifical Council for Justice and Peace sponsored a major conference in Rome under the title "The Logic of Gift and the Meaning of Business: An Experiential, Scholarly and Pedagogical Examination of Business in light of *Caritas in Veritate*." A paper presented there by Jean Staune and Christopher Wasserman followed a rather similar line to that of Franklin. An important point in their presentation is that "solidarity and reciprocity can . . . be experienced within the actual business life and not only outside it or 'after' it. The challenge currently facing the market economy is to integrate such values within the very heart of its operations" (Staune and Wasserman 2010, §1). They give instances of a variety of ways in which an "economy of gift" is in operation successfully in the business world at present. For them, "fair trade is a new sustainable economic form which creates . . . solidarity among manufacturers" (Staune and Wasserman 2010, §3.1).

They cite Wikipedia as "a true example of economy of gift" (Staune and Wasserman 2010, §3.4). They also mention the Grameen Bank and quote an inspirational statement of its founder, Nobel Peace Prize winner, Muhammad Yunus:

> The core problem of "unidimensional" capitalism is that it only allows for one way of doing things: achieving immediate profits. Why not integrate the social dimension within economic theory? Why not build businesses with a vision to decently pay their employees and improve their social situation rather than looking for managers and shareholders to achieve profits? (Staune and Wasserman 2010, §3.2)

Another important speaker at that Rome conference was Luigino Bruni, who presented a paper under the title "Reciprocity and Gratuitousness in the Market: A Challenge for the Economic Theory." Bruni is himself one of the economists who had, for some time, been promoting the idea of an "economy of communion" and whose views are said to have influenced Pope Benedict in the writing of the encyclical; thus, Bruni's view carries some extra weight. In the introduction to his paper he insisted that "reciprocity and gratuitousness are founding principles, even for the ordinary economy and market—and not only for the non-profit market" (Bruni 2010). He went on to deepen the concept of an "economy of communion" in the following profound statement:

> The gift that we find again in the encyclical . . . is mostly a "giving of oneself," a "self-dedication" of the person, which is applied first in one's being and then in his acting. It is an action that can take on various forms . . . a "how" one acts rather than a "what" one does. This is the more real and deep meaning of gratuitousness-gift, and we can and should find gratuitousness in the unfolding of every kind of action, even in our duties, contracts, the market and in business. (Bruni 2010, §2)

Some years prior to the encyclical, Bruno Frey, a professor of economics at the University of Zurich, wrote an interesting study of the personal motivation people have when they engage in economic transactions. His book is titled *Not Just for the Money*. In this book he refers to a wealth of empirical psychological studies to show that, regardless of abstract economic theory, in actual practice people are influenced not merely by narrowly economic considerations such as price but also by what he calls "intrinsic motivation" (such as friendship, interest, or environmental concern); he goes on to give a fascinating account of the delicate interaction between extrinsic and intrinsic motivation (Frey 1998, passim).

Benedetto Gui, of the Department of Economics in Padua, adopted a rather similar approach. His study emphasizes the importance of what he calls "relational goods," such as good relationships in the workplace. He maintains that high-quality relationships in the workplace "have an economic dimension" (Gui 2000, 139–70).

Economic Relationships in the Street Market

The most difficult challenge to be faced by those who find the modern Western business world inhuman and grossly immoral is the apparent impregnability and inevitability of the present business ethos. So it can be both enlightening and encouraging to realize that there is an alternative style of doing business—one that continues to exist in the narrow spaces where the dominant model has not yet taken over. In what follows, I am reflecting on my own experience of shopping in the open-air markets of Africa, Asia, and Latin America.

When engaging in this kind of economic activity, one soon becomes aware that buying and selling there are governed by rather different norms from those of the Western business world. It is important not to romanticize this alternative system. There is no doubt that a central feature of this market world is the need and desire to buy or sell the goods at "a good price." It has this in common with mainstream business. But alongside this strictly economic value, other values seem to be equally important.

Respect is a value that must be taken very seriously when one comes to buy something at the market stall. If the seller sees that my only concern as a potential buyer is to beat her down to the last cent, or if she feels insulted by my arrogance or brusqueness, then the whole transaction may fall through. If, however, I show some respect and delicacy in the way I approach the whole transaction, if I take time to talk to the seller and admire the goods, then the other values that are normal in this situation begin to come into play.

Sellers in these public markets are generally interested in establishing a personal relationship with the customer. If the buyer's response is positive, seller and buyer can go on to engage in the subtle game of bargaining. Playing that game successfully cannot be defined simply in purely economic terms. Buyer and seller must end up not only agreeing on the price, but also respecting each other, perhaps even liking each other—or at least open to the possibility of engaging in further transactions. I know from my own experience that if I, as a potential buyer, develop a liking for the seller, it is quite likely that I will pay more than I would be willing to pay the next-door seller for the same item.

If my mentality as a buyer is entirely mercenary and calculating, I may interpret the special offers and all the other nuances of the bargaining in narrowly economic terms. In that case I have missed much of the point. I am like a golfer whose only interest is in winning the game and who scarcely adverts to the physical joy of playing and the pleasure of conversation with the other players. If, however, I am able to enter willingly into this bargaining game, I will know that "success" has a much broader definition. It includes the exhilaration of wrestling with the seller, making use of various acceptable ploys, but never insulting the seller or trying to manipulate or exploit him or her. All this means that we have established some degree of genuine interpersonal relationship, characterized by an element of gratuitousness. At best, we have become good friends. And this friendship is quite compatible with a high degree of shrewd worldly wisdom. Neither of us is naïve enough to imagine that the other is just a generous benefactor; each of us knows that the other is looking for the best available price.

In the world of the street-market both the buyer and the seller operate on the basis of a whole variety of mixed motives. This means that the buyer-seller relationship is quite similar to most other interpersonal relationships of daily life. That is the key point: that the business world has not been hived off from the rest of our everyday world. There is no assumption that the activity of buying and selling is governed by different norms and operated on the basis of entirely different values. Precisely because it has such a central role in everyday life, it is considered vital that it be permeated by those values that are the mark of the human person and of civilized society.

What emerges clearly from all this is that gratuitousness in economic relationships is not an all-or-nothing affair. There are various kinds and degrees of it. A high level of gift or gratuitousness is the mark of charities that are both well run and totally respectful. A more limited degree of graciousness and gratuitousness is possible and appropriate when a medical specialist visits his or her patient during hospital rounds. And at least a minimum degree of cordiality and warmth should characterize any economic interaction. A central point is that not only is it wrong to cut off economic relationships from the wider human context in which they occur, but also that it does not even make economic sense to do so. This is most obviously the case in the service industries. But it extends to the whole range of economic activities, once the seller and buyer take account of the importance of the development of long-term relationships of mutual respect and trust.

A DOCUMENT FROM THE PONTIFICAL COUNCIL FOR JUSTICE AND PEACE

On October 24, 2011, the Pontifical Council for Justice and Peace issued an important document titled "Towards Reforming the International Financial and Monetary Systems in the Context of Global Public Authority." This document takes up some of the issues dealt with rather briefly in *Caritas in Veritate*. It supplements *Caritas in Veritate* by spelling out some key aspects of it—though not the more theological and spiritual aspects, such as the experience of "gift," or even the more idealistic parts, such as the "economy of communion."

It focuses rather on two crucial points. First, it offers a sharp analysis of how the following of extremely liberal policies in the globalized situation of the world has led to the present crisis and the huge problems we currently have. I note in passing that these "liberal" policies correspond generally to the policies that would be called "neoconservative" in the United States. Second, it puts forward some practical proposals on the actions that need to be taken to overcome these problems. The document is much more specific than the encyclical. The detail it offers provides a response to those who felt that the approach adopted by the pope in the encyclical was too "broad brush" in character, trying to cover too much without sufficient nuance (e.g., Orobator 2010, 324).

The first section of the document traces how the economic crisis of

2008 developed. A key point is the clear contrast the document makes between markets for material goods and monetary and financial markets. In the case of the former there are limits based on "natural factors and productive capacity as well as labor." In the latter, by contrast, this does not apply; the banks "extended credit which generated money, which in turn sought a further expansion of credit." This led to "an inflationary spiral" and eventually the institutions that gave credit "faced the ultimate danger of bankruptcy, with negative consequences for the entire economic and financial system" (Pontifical Council for Justice and Peace 2011, §1).

The document goes on to pose a crucial question and to answer it in uncompromising terms:

> What has driven the world in such a problematic direction for its economy and also for peace? First and foremost, an economic liberalism that spurns rules and controls. . . . The inequalities and distortions of capitalist development are often an expression not only of economic liberalism but also of utilitarian thinking: that is, theoretical and practical approaches according to which what is useful for the individual leads to the good of the community. This saying has a core of truth, but it cannot be ignored that individual utility—even where it is legitimate—does not always favour the common good. In many cases a spirit of solidarity is called for that transcends personal utility for the good of the community. (§1)

In a later section the document expands on the calls of John XXIII in *Pacem in Terris* and Benedict XVI in *Caritas in Veritate* for an effective world authority. It says that such a supranational authority

> should have a realistic structure and be set up gradually. It should be favorable to the existence of efficient and effective monetary and financial systems. . . . The establishment of a world political Authority should be preceded by a preliminary phase of consultation from which a legitimated institution will emerge that is in a position to be an effective guide and, at the same time, can allow each country to express and pursue its own particular good. (§3)

It envisages that the principle of subsidiarity should apply not only at every level from local communities up to the supranational level, but also "between public and private institutions"; all this should apply not just in the strictly political sphere but also in relation to "the monetary and financial institutions." It insists that it is only by putting into operation the principle of subsidiarity that a supranational authority can ensure its "democratic legitimacy" and avoid a "bureaucratic isolation" that "would risk its being delegitimized by an excessive distance from the realities which underlie its existence, and easily falling prey to paternalistic, technocratic or hegemonic temptations" (§3).

The document is realistic in recognizing that "a long road still needs to be travelled before arriving at the creation of a public Authority with universal jurisdiction." But it is clear in maintaining that the obvious starting point is the United Nations: "It would seem logical for the reform process to proceed with the United Nations as its reference because of the worldwide scope of the UN's responsibilities, its ability to bring together the nations of the world, and the diversity of its tasks and those of its specialized Agencies" (§3).

The next section of the document notes "the gradual decline in efficacy of the Bretton Woods institutions beginning in the early 1970s," focusing on the way the International Monetary Fund lost its ability to regulate the supply of money and amount of credit risk taken on by the system. It points to the "abrogation of controls on capital movements and the tendency to deregulate banking and financial activities." It also notes a further key factor that played a major role in the crisis, namely, "advances in financial technology, due largely to information technology" (§4).

Next it proposes a way forward—not by a one-time major replacement of existing institutions, but by a "gradual adaptation of the existing instruments." It sees the need for "a body that will carry out the functions of a kind of 'central world bank' that regulates the flow and system of monetary exchanges, as do the national central banks." But it recognizes that this cannot happen all at once, and it insists that the process of "gradual adaptation of the existing instruments" must involve "the emerging and developing countries." It suggests that, as a first step at "the regional level, this process could begin by strengthening the existing institutions, such as the European Central Bank." This will be "a first stage in a longer effort by the global community to steer its institutions toward achieving the common good" (§4).

The purpose in this whole process must be the restoration of "the primacy of the spiritual and of ethics." Significantly and realistically, the document immediately adds there must be the restoration of "the primacy of politics—which is responsible for the common good—over the economy and finance" (§4). The point is that humans must take moral responsibility for taking the firm political action that is required to ensure that economic and financial activities are not fenced off into a zone where morality does not apply but are compelled by law to take account of "their obvious responsibilities to society."

Finally, the document makes three concrete and practical proposals that it says should be reflected on. These refer to changes that can be made in the immediate future. The first is the introduction of a financial transaction tax. This involves putting a small tax on "financial transactions . . . especially those made on the 'secondary' market." In line with similar proposals made elsewhere, the document says, "This taxation would be very useful in promoting global development and sustainability according to the principles of social justice and solidarity. It could also contribute to the creation of a world reserve fund to support the economies of the countries hit by crisis as well as the recovery of their monetary and financial systems" (§4).

The second proposal is the "recapitalization of banks with public funds, making the support conditional on 'virtuous' behaviors aimed at developing the 'real economy' " (§4). In other words, banks would be compelled to use these funds, and perhaps their other funds, in truly productive ways rather than in using them in the kind of complex financial instruments, such as hedge funds, which have caused an inflationary spiral.

The third proposal is again one that has been widely called for. It is that there should be a clear separation of the two main aspects of the banking industry—investment banking, on the one hand, and, on the other hand, the kind of everyday banking where people at times lodge money and at other times seek credit in the form of a loan from the bank (§4).

Near the end of the document the authors return again to the need for "a gradual, balanced transfer of a part of each nation's powers to a world Authority and to regional Authorities." The authors maintain: "In a world on its way to rapid globalization, orientation toward a world Authority becomes the only horizon compatible with the new realities of our time and the needs of humankind" (§4).

Reactions to the Pontifical Council's Document

Predictably, there were immediate negative reactions to the document from conservatives in the United States. Bill Donohue wrote, "Today's statement uses terms like 'supranational Authority' and 'supranational Institution.' These neologisms are purely the creation of the authors, Cardinal Peter Turkson and Mario Toso. They are not found in the pope's encyclical" (Donohue 2011).

Donald McClarey wrote that the document is "a waste of paper," with "no new ideas," "a confusion of religion and politics"; he maintained that "using the United Nations as a starting point dooms this from the start" (McClarey 2011). Amy Sullivan, acknowledging that the document "can be seen as a practical extension of Pope Benedict XVI's 2009 encyclical *Caritas in Veritate*," wrote that it is "calling into question the entire foundation of neo-liberal economics and proposing one world financial order." Then she added, "you never know what those radicals over at the Pontifical Council for Justice and Peace will come up with next" (Sullivan 2011).

George Weigel went into more detail. He played down the significance of the document, calling it a "brief document from the lower echelons of the Roman Curia." He insisted that

> The document's specific recommendations do not necessarily reflect the settled views of the senior authorities of the Holy See. . . . The document doesn't speak for the Pope, it doesn't speak for "the Vatican," and it doesn't speak for the Catholic Church. (Weigel 2011)

In response to these strongly negative rejections of the document, Vincent Miller invited people to stop and ask the following: "Is the idea of some sort of global government really that radical?" He suggested that it is not surprising that "people feel they have no option but to take to the streets" when "a moderate proposal such as this would be received as controversial." Defending the proposal in the document for a "decidedly gradualist" movement toward some kind of global governance, he pointed out that "the thrust of the entire document is that private financial organizations and the global system of voluntary governance have failed and thus require intervention." He asserted that the vision in the document is underpinned by the Catholic principle of subsidiarity. The document, he insisted, applied the fundamental understanding of subsidiarity as "no bigger than necessary, no smaller than appropriate" (V. Miller 2011).

There can be no doubt that both the encyclical *Caritas in Veritate* and the document from the Pontifical Council make important contributions to Catholic social teaching. But there remains a troubling question: Will they make any practical difference to what is happening in the world? That depends on how they are received, how they are interpreted, and how people respond to them. It would be a great loss if they were left to the mercy of ideologues of the right or left who would quarry them for sentences to bolster their own opinions. In order to avoid such a situation it is important that mainstream committed Christians, together with other people of goodwill, should make a serious effort to make them known and their vision implemented. There is little or no evidence that this has taken place.

The biggest single difficulty is that relatively few people—and even few Catholic clergy—have taken the time to read and study them. It is doubtful whether either document got much attention in Church preaching and teaching. One may wonder how many actual or potential entrepreneurs have really heard Benedict's invitation to change the way business is conducted in our world. And one may doubt whether many Catholics—not to mention non-Catholics—have any real awareness of the careful analysis of the Pontifical Council's document. The key elements of the two documents need to be presented in an inspiring and easily digestible way through preaching, lectures, conferences, and workshops. The encyclical and the Council's document are extremely relevant not only to the economic crisis in which the world finds itself but also to the fundamental issue of how society is organized. If a sufficient number of Christians and others were to take them seriously and act on them, this could change the world.

* * *

SUMMARY

A number of right-wing commentators reacted strongly against aspects of *Deus Caritas Est* that they disagreed with—particularly its support for international institutions, including the United Nations. More serious commentators also disagreed with particular aspects of the encyclical. One writer noted its failure to note that in Africa, the problem is not so much secularization as "the gospel of prosperity." Others saw its approach as unduly deductive rather than inductive. Another felt that it downgrades the emphasis on justice in comparison with love. Some felt it focuses unduly on individual responsibility, not taking sufficient account of structural injustice. A further criticism of this and other Vatican documents is that they fail to refer to the important contributions made to Catholic social teaching by bishops' conferences in various parts of the world.

Positive assessments came from commentators who stressed the importance of Benedict's concept of an "economy of communion." It was noted that this is not an all-or-nothing matter: in many present-day economic relationships—especially in the service industries—an element of gratuitousness and "fraternity" is necessary and is actually present. One commentator noted that gratuitousness and self-giving are more a matter of what a person is than of what the person does.

In October 2011 the Pontifical Council for Justice and Peace issued an important document about the reform of international economic and financial systems. This spells out in concrete detail elements that are touched on in more general terms in Benedict's encyclical. The document comes out very strongly on the need for such international institutions, starting with the United Nations. But, like the encyclical, it stresses the need to balance the principle of international solidarity with the principle of subsidiarity. This document was angrily rejected, and its authority downplayed, by the same critics who were unhappy about aspects of Benedict's encyclical. It is important that both the encyclical and the document be studied and taken seriously by Catholics and others. Together they make an important contribution to Catholic social teaching.

QUESTIONS FOR REVIEW

1. *Name some of the main objections that have been put forward to the encyclical.*
2. *Does the encyclical play down justice issues, particularly the issue of structural injustice?*
3. *Name some economic transactions that have an element of gratuitousness in them.*
4. *What is the main proposal of the 2009 document from the Pontifical Council for Justice and Peace?*

QUESTIONS FOR REFLECTION

1. *How would you convince a businessperson that it makes both moral and economic sense to bring an element of gratuitousness and humanity into business?*
2. *How can powerful nations be persuaded to cede more authority to the United Nations—and how can that organization be made more effective?*

ISSUE FOR FURTHER STUDY

1. *The history of the United Nations and its precursor, the League of Nations: their successes and their failures.*

18

Anthropocentric Ecology

For many decades, or even centuries up to the early 1960s, one of the main courses in what was called "Dogmatic Theology" was "The Theology of Creation." During the 1960s this course was widely replaced by a course called "Theological Anthropology." In many respects this was a valuable development; it was part of what has been called "the turn to the Subject," and it led to a far deeper understanding of what it means to be human in the world. However, in more recent decades Christians came slowly to realize that theological anthropology has to be situated within the much wider context of a theology of creation as a whole. A true understanding of ourselves as human can take place only within an Earth-centered or creation-centered approach. In tracing this development, I shall be offering an extended treatment of points that I may have mentioned briefly in previous chapters, and in most cases I shall look at material that I have not previously touched on at all.

INTEGRAL HUMANISM

In the development of Catholic social teaching a humanistic theme began to take shape—or at least to be prefigured or prepared for—by the two social encyclicals of John XXIII, *Mater et Magistra* and *Pacem in Terris*. A big breakthrough came with the Pastoral Constitution *Gaudium et Spes* of Vatican II. Already the four key words "joys, hopes, grief and anguish" in its opening line indicate that it represents a quite dramatic openness to the reality of human life in the world. The whole document is humanistic in its content and style; in fact, looking back, many theologians suggest that it was unduly optimistic in its account of the relationship of the Church to the world.

Paul VI continued this humanistic approach. Charles Curran (2002, 130) says that in *Populorum Progressio* the pope "develops the concept of a new humanism—an integral or transcendent humanism that recognizes all aspects of anthropology." In *Evangelii Nuntiandi* (1975) Pope Paul embraced the word "liberation" and put forward a rich and comprehensive account of the whole concept of human liberation in all its dimensions.

Probably the two high points of John Paul's teaching on Catholic social teaching came in his very first encyclical *Redemptor Hominis* (1979) and in his first social encyclical *Laborem Exercens* (1981). The former is particularly important in terms of the present topic. In it the pope put forward a radical theological basis for a humanistic approach. He wrote, "The human person is the primary and fundamental way for the Church" (*RH* 14). In his address to the United Nations in 1979, John Paul insisted on the importance of what he called "the humanistic criterion" as the basis for assessing various systems (*AAS* [*Acta Apostolicae Sedis*] 71, 1156, §17).

The second high point in John Paul's contribution to Catholic social teaching came two years later with his encyclical *Laborem Exercens*. Here he broke from the long tradition of defining the human person as a thinker. Instead, he took the radical step of defining the person as a worker. In this he was not only adopting an integral humanist position, but grounding it in a realistic account of human life in its economic and political reality.

ECOLOGY

I want now to explore whether there are links between the integral humanistic perspective that had developed in Catholic social teaching and its teaching on ecological issues. The first step is to trace the development of that teaching in the post–Vatican II period.

The Vatican II document *Gaudium et Spes* gives the human person so central a role that, as Charles Curran (2002, 132) says, it treats other created realities "only as instrumental with regard to the human person." In 1971 in *Octogesima Adveniens* Pope Paul VI mentions the risk associated with "an ill-considered exploitation of nature" (*OA* 21). Later that year the document "Justice in the World," issued by the Synod of Bishops, is far more specific—influenced no doubt by Barbara Ward-Jackson, who was a consultant before and during the synod. As I have noted in my treatment of that document in chapter 9, it points out that it is not possible for all parts of the world to have the kind of "development" that has occurred in the wealthy countries (JW 11). So it calls on the rich "to accept a less material way of life, with less waste, in order to avoid the destruction of the heritage which they are obliged by absolute justice to share with all other members of the human race" (JW 70). I have also noted that this document was one of the first to emphasize the close link between ecology and justice. Using more recent language, one could say that it brought out the connection between an option for the poor and an option for the Earth—although it did not use these phrases.

A few years later, in *Redemptor Hominis*, Pope John Paul II writes of "the visible world which God created for man." He says that it is through Jesus that the created world, which had been "subjected to futility" (Rom. 8:20) through human sin, "recovers again its original link with the divine source of Wisdom and Love" (*RH* 8). Already in this his first encyclical he is providing a basis for what Celia Deane-Drummond (2012n15) calls "cosmic christology" or "deep incarnation" (cf. Deane-Drummond 2009; Edwards 2006, 58–60).

John Paul goes on to refer to "the threat of pollution of the natural environment" (*RH* 8) and the fact that humans frequently look on the natural environment only insofar as it serves them "for immediate use and consumption" (*RH* 15). He insists that "man should communicate with nature as an intelligent and noble 'master' and 'guardian,' and not as a heedless 'exploiter' and 'destroyer'" (*RH* 15). It is significant that he used the word "master" in this context. Perhaps even more significant is his use of the word "exploitation" in a favorable sense: "The exploitation of the earth, the planet on which we are living, demands rational and honest planning" (*RH* 15). Of course, one should not read too much into his use of the word "exploitation," since it was only some time later that most people became aware of how inappropriate it is to use this word to describe our relationship with the Earth. But even a more benign interpretation of the word suggests that John Paul had a quite anthropocentric conception of the relationship between humans and the rest of nature.

In *Sollicitudo Rei Socialis* John Paul returned to the issue of ecology in a passage in which he referred to "the limits of available resources" (*SRS* 26), and in a later passage he again noted that "natural resources are limited" (*SRS* 34). In the first of these passages he referred to "the integrity and cycles of nature" (*SRS* 26). His use of the word "integrity" echoes the phrase "integrity of creation" that had already been accepted by the World Council of Churches (cf. Dorr 1991, 73–74). Without using this exact term, John Paul gave a brief account of what is meant by "the integrity of creation" by pointing out that each being is connected to other beings, where there is "mutual connection in an ordered system, which is precisely the 'cosmos.'" He went on to say that in making use of other creatures, humans must take account not only of the nature of each creature but also of "its mutual connection" as part of the wider whole that is the cosmos (*SRS* 34).

It is significant that in *SRS* 29, as Deane-Drummond (2012, 199) says, "The image of humanity as the gardener is used as a way of reflecting what true development should be like." The basis for this image is, of course, the story of Adam and Eve in the Book of Genesis. The encyclical explains that the task of men and women is to cultivate the garden in accordance with divine law. It says that humans are "superior to the other creatures," and the other creatures have been placed by God under human dominion. But God imposes limits on this dominion and on the use that humans may make of other creatures. When humans go beyond these limits, they are failing to obey God's law, because they are failing to respect their own nature as images of God. The result of this disobedience of God is that "nature rebels" and no longer recognizes humans as its "master" (*SRS* 29). This use of the word "master" is reinforced in the address that John Paul gave to the 35th General Assembly of the World Medical Association in 1983. In it he said, "God willed that man should be the king of creation" (§6).

On several of his foreign visits Pope John Paul stressed the vital relationship that exists between indigenous peoples and their land. He did so during his addresses to the peoples of the Amazon region of Brazil in 1980, to indigenous peoples of Guatemala in 1983 (§4), to indigenous peoples of Canada in 1984 (§4), and to indigenous peoples of Ecuador in 1985 (§3), as well as in his homily to indigenous people in the Peruvian Amazon in 1985 (§7), in his address to peoples of Australia in 1986 (§4), and again in his address to Native Americans in 1987 (§4). In doing so, he was bringing out again, as the document of the 1971 Roman synod had already done, the close link between an option for the poor and an option for the Earth.

Pope John Paul made an important point in his Address to Session XXV of the Conference of the Food and Agricultural Organization in November 1989. In that address he spelled out the need for nations and enterprises of all kinds to build the cost of ecological protection into the financial estimates of every development project. He said,

> Such expenses must not be accounted as an incidental surcharge, but rather as an essential element of the actual cost of economic activity. The result will be a more limited profit than was possible in the past, as well as the acknowledgment of new costs deriving from environmental protection. (§8)

1990 WORLD DAY OF PEACE MESSAGE

The brief points that I noted above in *Sollicitudo Rei Socialis*, taken in conjunction with the various addresses to which I have referred, amount to a sophisticated scriptural and theological underpinning for ecological concern. Nevertheless, the Vatican was slower than the World Council of Churches in giving a prominent place to the ecological question as a whole. So Catholics and other Christians welcomed the first major Vatican statement devoted specifically to environmental issues. This was

Pope John Paul's "Message for the World Day of Peace" for January 1, 1990. It is a significant document, particularly in its emphasis on the importance of respect for creation. It speaks movingly of "the plundering of natural resources and . . . a progressive decline in the quality of life," "the widespread destruction of the environment" (§1), the way in which the sin of Adam and Eve resulted in the "rebellion" of the Earth, and how "creation became subject to futility" (§3).

Spelling out the chief ecological issues as they were seen in 1990, the Message says,

> The gradual depletion of the ozone layer and the related "greenhouse effect" has now reached crisis proportions as a consequence of industrial growth, massive urban concentrations and vastly increased energy needs. Industrial waste, the burning of fossil fuels, unrestricted deforestation, the use of certain types of herbicides, coolants and propellants: all of these are known to harm the atmosphere and environment. (§6)

It goes on to insist that *"no peaceful society can afford to neglect either respect for life or the fact that there is an integrity to creation"* (§7, emphasis in the original).

When it comes to consider the solution to these problems, the Message insists strongly that "the concepts of an ordered universe and a common heritage both point to the necessity of a *more internationally coordinated approach to the management of the earth's goods*" (§9). It goes on to say, "The ecological crisis reveals the *urgent moral need for a new solidarity*, especially in relations between the developing nations and those that are highly industrialized" (§10). Furthermore, the Message points out that the ecological problem cannot be solved unless modern society "*takes a serious look at its life style.*" It insists that "simplicity, moderation and discipline, as well as a spirit of sacrifice, must become a part of everyday life" (§13).

Having recognized that there is integrity in creation, the Message puts forward three reasons why we should respect this integrity. The first of these is simply that humans are called to respect the plan of God. "When man turns his back on the Creator's plan, he provokes a disorder which has inevitable repercussions on the rest of the created order" (§5).

The second reason why humans should respect the integrity of creation is the one to which most of the Message is devoted. It is that respect for the environment is necessary for the present and future welfare of humanity. The Message points out that environmental changes result in "damage to health"—and in doing so, it is obviously referring to the health of humans (§6). It goes on to say that when "delicate ecological balances are upset by the uncontrolled destruction of animal and plant life or by a reckless exploitation of natural resources," this "is ultimately to mankind's disadvantage."

Then it warns of the danger of "indiscriminate genetic manipulation and . . . unscrupulous development of new forms of plant and animal life . . . and unacceptable experimentation regarding the origins of human life itself." The Message says that "in any area as delicate as this, indifference to fundamental ethical norms, or their rejection, would lead mankind to the very threshold of self-destruction" (§7). Citing the Vatican II document *Gaudium et Spes*, the Message insists that "the earth is ultimately *a common heritage, the fruits of which are for the benefit of all*" (§8). It is quite clear that in this context the "all" who are to benefit are all humans. While this statement does not exclude the survival and welfare of other species, it simply does not advert to this issue.

There is also a rather brief mention of a third reason why we should respect the integrity of creation. The Message says that "*the aesthetic value of creation cannot be overlooked*." Then it adds, "Our very contact with nature has a deep restorative power; contemplation of its magnificence imparts peace and serenity. The Bible speaks again and again of the goodness and beauty of creation, which is called to glorify God (cf. Gen. 1:4ff.; Pss. 8:2; 104:1ff.; Wis. 13:3–5; Sir. 39:16, 33; 43:1, 9)" (§14).

This is both true and important, but it seems to suggest that the value of the nonhuman parts of nature springs mainly from the fact that contemplation of them can bring peace and serenity to humans. The pope seems reluctant to say that they have an intrinsic value in themselves. The focus is on the role and responsibility of humans.

In the final paragraph of the "Message for the World Day of Peace" the pope goes some way toward suggesting that the nonhuman parts of nature have a value in their own right: "Respect for life and for the dignity of the human person extends also to the rest of creation, which is called to join man in praising God (cf. Ps. 148:96)." He goes on to say, "It is my hope that the inspiration of Saint Francis will help us to keep ever alive a sense of 'fraternity' with all those good and beautiful things which Almighty God has created. . . . And may he remind us of our serious obligation to respect and watch over them with care."

Having referred to human "fraternity" with other parts of nature and our duty to care for them, however, the pope immediately adds that this is to be done "in light of that greater and higher fraternity that exists within the human family" (§16). Once again, we are left with the impression of a reluctance to acknowledge the inherent value of the nonhuman world, without immediately insisting on the higher value of humanity. All this suggests that the approach of the pope is still fundamentally anthropocentric, even in the way he understands the phrase "the integrity of creation." In the case of Pope John Paul this can be partly explained as "the flip side" of the valuable humanistic approach that he brought to Catholic social teaching and indeed to his understanding of evangelization.

CENTESIMUS ANNUS

On the hundredth anniversary of *Rerum Novarum* in 1991 John Paul issued his new social encyclical, *Centesimus Annus*. Here again, his approach can be termed integrally humanistic. For instance, the heading of §6 of the encyclical is "Man Is the Way of the Church"—a clear echo of what he had said twelve years earlier in his first encyclical, *Redemptor Hominis*. In this case, too, his humanistic approach is linked to a treatment of environmental issues that is unapologetically anthropocentric. Referring back to Vatican II's *Gaudium et Spes,* he says that "man . . . is the only creature on earth which God has willed for its own sake" (*CA* 53).

The following passage of the encyclical is quite significant: "The earth . . . is God's first gift. . . . But the earth does not yield its fruits without a particular human response to God's gift, that is to say, without work. It is through work that man . . . succeeds in *dominating* the earth" (*CA* 31, emphasis added).

This idea of the Earth as a gift is valuable, and it prefigures a similar statement in Pope Benedict's encyclical *Deus Caritas Est*. However, the emphasis here is on the fact that the Earth is given as a gift *to humans*, whose task is to shape and *dominate* it. In the case of the phrase "dominating the earth," as in the case of his earlier use of the word "exploitation," even a benign interpretation of the phrase suggests that John Paul had an anthropocentric conception of the relationship between humans and the rest of nature.

The encyclical makes some linkage between human development, economics, and ecology. For instance, it says that "the state and all of society have the duty of defending those collective goods which, among others, constitute the essential framework for the legitimate pursuit of personal goals on the part of each individual" (*CA* 40).

Air, earth, water are here seen as the "collective goods" which are the underpinning for human development—but the focus remains on humans. Even from within that perspective, the encyclical does not spell out the extent to which, in our present-day world, the continued existence of human society depends on finding a better balance between human development and ecological sensitivity.

The encyclical does indeed advert to the integrity of creation. It accounts for this in terms of "the God-given purpose" of the Earth, a purpose "which man can indeed develop but must not betray." So humans are not entitled to set themselves up "in place of God" and "make arbitrary use of the earth" (*CA* 37). A significant point here is that the pope sees the human duty to respect the integrity of creation in terms of obedience to God's plan, with no explicit reference to the order and value that is inherent in the created world. He has little or nothing to say about the value of nonhuman creatures or how important it is that humans should live in partnership with the rest of creation. Insofar as he locates human-ity within the much wider context of creation as a whole, he does it in a manner which emphasizes human superiority and responsibility.

Pope John Paul rejects the arrogance that assumes that humans are entitled to mold and control nature in any way they wish. He holds that those who have such an attitude are failing to respect the "prior God-given purpose" of the Earth and are attempting to take on the role of God (*CA* 37). However, he does not wholeheartedly adopt an approach that locates humanity firmly within the wide context of creation as a whole, called to live in partnership with other creatures. There is no indication that he has changed the view he espoused in *Sollicitudo Rei Socialis* that humans are "superior to the other creatures," with "dominion" over them, and responsible for them as their "master" (*SRS* 29).

In this encyclical, the pope's strong anthropocentric stance is par-ticularly evident in the way in which he contrasts natural ecology with "human ecology." He acknowledges that the destruction of the "natural environment" is a "worrying" question. But almost immediately he puts it in second place when compared with "the more serious destruction of the human environment." He goes on at once to say that "too little effort is made to safeguard the moral conditions of an authentic 'human ecology'" (*CA* 38).

The difficulty here is the unduly sharp contrast he makes between "human ecology" and "natural" ecology. The term "human ecology" is one that has been used in the social sciences since the early 1920s. It is a global term that refers to the relationship between humans and their natural, social, and cultural environments. So it includes our relationship to nature. For this reason it seems inappropriate to contrast it with "natu-ral ecology," except when the latter term is wrongly taken in a restricted sense that fails to include humans in the natural order.[1]

Statements by John Paul on ecology or references to it in the last sixteen years of his pontificate indicate that he continued to draw attention to the ecological question. But there is not much sign that he changed his approach to the topic in any significant way. For instance, in his 1995 encyclical *Evangelium Vitae*, he returns again to the theme of the human

---

[1]Celia Deane-Drummond (2012, 202, 205) reads this and similar passages in a more benign way, seeing the pope's account of "human ecology" as particularly valuable.

cultivation of "the garden of the world" and to a focus on "human ecology" in contrast to "natural ecology." He emphasizes that the dominion given to humans by the Creator is "not an absolute power," not a freedom to dispose of things as they please. Humans are "subject not only to biological laws but also to moral ones" (*EV* 42).

In March 1997, John Paul spoke to the Conference on Environment and Health. In the course of his address he used a striking phrase: "The environment as 'resource' risks threatening the environment as 'home'" (§2). He went on to insist on the need for an "open and comprehensive solidarity with all men and all peoples" (§5). It is perhaps significant that his reference to solidarity was confined to humans, with no reference to anything approximating to a sense of solidarity that humans might have with animals or with the rest of creation.

In a General Audience address on January 17, 2001, John Paul spoke again about the sheer magnitude of the ecological issue and the need for an "ecological conversion." This concept of an ecological conversion is an important contribution to the development of Catholic social teaching.

In his postsynodal apostolic exhortation *Pastores Gregis*, dated October 2003, John Paul has a brief section on ecology. In it he emphasizes again the "need for an *ecological conversion*." He goes on to say that bishops can contribute to this conversion "by their teaching about the correct relationship of human beings with nature. . . . This relationship is one of 'stewardship': human beings are set at the center of creation as stewards of the Creator" (*PG* 70).

In *Pastores Gregis* John Paul makes a contrast between "a physical ecology, concerned with protecting the habitat of the various living beings" and "a human ecology capable of protecting the radical good of life in all its manifestations and of leaving behind for future generations an environment which conforms as closely as possible to the Creator's plan" (*PG* 70). In this case it is clear that he is using the term "human ecology" in its fully inclusive meaning. But he contrasts it with what he calls "a physical ecology," which, as he describes it, involves only concern for the physical "habitat of various living beings."

It is important to note a significant phrase in the passage that I have just quoted. It is the pope's reference to "future generations." Here he is adverting to the importance of the concept of "intergenerational justice," which was spelled out more fully seven years later by Pope Benedict XVI in his World Day of Peace Message of 2010.

One particularly moving occasion was the "Common Declaration 2004 of Pope John Paul II and Ecumenical Patriarch Bartholomew I" in which they committed themselves to "collaborate so that our earth may not be disfigured and that Creation may preserve the beauty with which it has been endowed by God." They also said that "we must first regain our humility and recognize the limits of our powers, and most importantly, the limits of our knowledge and judgment."

The overall conclusion one has to come to from a study of the many documents and addresses of Pope John Paul is that he made a valuable contribution to Catholic social teaching both by adopting an integrally humanist approach and by putting a new emphasis on ecological issues. But he failed to move on from this to adopt the kind of Earth-centered or creation-centered approach that many theologians have now come to recognize as the way forward for Christian theology today.

POPE BENEDICT

It is generally recognized that Pope Benedict was concerned about environmental issues and was deeply committed to raising awareness about the urgency of finding solutions to ecological problems and promoting an ecologically respectful lifestyle. He even had solar panels installed as a step toward making the Vatican "carbon-neutral."

In general, however, Benedict's approach to ecological issues continued in the anthropocentric line adopted by John Paul. One may note one slight change. As noted above, John Paul downplayed the ecological issue by contrasting it with what he saw as the "more serious" issue of "the human environment." Benedict's approach was generally more subtle: he insists on the inseparable link between the two. In his Message for the World Day of Peace of 2007, titled "The Human Person, The Heart of Peace," he wrote,

> Humanity, if it truly desires peace, must be increasingly conscious of the links between natural ecology, or respect for nature, and human ecology. Experience shows that *disregard for the environment always harms human coexistence*, and vice versa. It becomes more and more evident that there is an inseparable link between peace with creation and peace among men. (§8)

This linkage was repeated in the final paragraph of Benedict's "Address to the Diplomatic Corps" on January 11, 2010: "May the light and strength of Jesus help us to respect human ecology, in the knowledge that natural ecology will likewise benefit, since the book of nature is one and indivisible." In his "Message for the 2008 Fraternity Campaign" of the Brazilian bishops, Benedict followed John Paul in insisting that "human ecology" takes priority: "The human being will be capable of respecting other creatures only if he keeps the full meaning of life in his own heart. . . . For this reason, the first ecology to be defended is 'human ecology.'"

On June 9, 2011, in an address to ambassadors from six African countries, the pope said that "a change in mentality" is necessary in order to "quickly arrive at a global lifestyle that respects the covenant between humanity and nature, without which the human family risks disappearing." In the same address he said that "human ecology is an imperative."

On July 24, 2007, in responding to questions submitted by members of a gathering of diocesan priests in Italy, Pope Benedict XVI had already stressed the moral dimension of our relationship with the Earth. He said,

> Everyone can see today that humanity could destroy the foundation of its own existence, its earth. Therefore we can no longer simply do whatever we want with this earth that has been entrusted to us, or what seems to us in a given moment useful or promising. On the contrary, we have to respect the inner laws of creation, of this earth; we have to learn these laws and obey them if we want to survive." (Response to first question, my translation)

CARITAS IN VERITATE

As I pointed out in chapter 17, Pope Benedict's *Caritas in Veritate* (2009) adopts an extended understanding of the phrase "integral human development." Pope Benedict sees it as "a seamless robe." Having looked in chapter 16 at the economic and social aspects of Benedict's teaching in the encyclical, I am focusing here on his strong insistence on our duty to respect the environment. He makes it clear that what he has to say about ecology is part of his integral view of authentic human living (see *CiV* 48–51; cf. *CiV* 67, 69).

Here again Benedict emphasizes the notion of gift. For him the environment is "God's gift to everyone" (*CiV* 48). He insists that "nature is at our disposal not as 'a heap of scattered refuse,' but as a gift of the Creator who has given it an inbuilt order, enabling man to draw from it the principles needed in order 'to till it and keep it'" (Gen. 2:15) (*CiV* 48).

In his postsynodal apostolic exhortation, *Sacramentum Caritatis*, on February 22, 2007, Benedict made an important point: "The world is not something indifferent, raw material to be utilized simply as we see fit. Rather, it is part of God's good plan" (§92). In *Caritas in Veritate* he developed this point further by pointing out two contrasting false understandings of nature that must be rejected:

> But it should also be stressed that it is contrary to authentic development to view nature as something more important than the human person. This position leads to attitudes of neo-paganism or a

new pantheism—human salvation cannot come from nature alone, understood in a purely naturalistic sense. This having been said, it is also necessary to reject the opposite position, which aims at total technical dominion over nature, because the natural environment is more than raw material to be manipulated at our pleasure. (*CiV* 48)

The next words are significant because they indicate that Benedict has a clear understanding of the unity and coherence of the patterns of nature. He says that nature "is a wondrous work of the Creator containing a 'grammar' which sets forth ends and criteria for its wise use, not its reckless exploitation." The image of "grammar" is particularly helpful. It would only be a short step for him to go from this grammar of nature to affirming that each of the elements of nature has its own inherent value, but he does not take this final step. Near the end of this chapter I examine the reasons why he does not do so.

In the next paragraph Benedict refers, in some detail, to various ecological issues—to "the energy problem," to competition for natural resources and the exploitation of them (*CiV* 49), and to the need to ensure that "the economic and social costs of using up shared environmental resources are recognized with transparency and fully borne by those who incur them" (*CiV* 50). He maintains that humans are entitled to exercise "a *responsible stewardship over nature*, in order to protect it, to enjoy its fruits and to cultivate it in new ways."[2] He points out the need for "an effective shift in mentality which can lead to the adoption of *new lifestyles*" (*CiV* 50). He also reminds us "how many natural resources are squandered by wars" (*CiV* 51).

In the final sentence of *CiV* 48, he went a stage further by referring to "*inter-generational justice*." This is a point that had already been touched on by John Paul in his encyclical *Pastores Gregis* (70), although John Paul did not use that term.[3] Benedict took it up again in his "Message for World Day of Peace 2010" titled "If You Want to Cultivate Peace, Protect Creation." A key passage in this Message is "*A greater sense of intergenerational solidarity* is urgently needed. Future generations cannot

---

[2]This concern of Pope Benedict was provided with strong scientific backing by the document *Fate of Mountain Glaciers in the Anthropocene: A Report by the Working Group Commissioned by the Pontifical Academy of Sciences*, issued on May 11, 2011. This document strongly challenged the claim that global warming is a natural event: "Human-induced changes in carbon dioxide, other greenhouse gases, and soot concentrations are taking place . . . at least a hundred times as fast" as "natural events."

[3]The *Compendium of the Social Doctrine of the Church* (2004, §467, p. 236) suggests that Paul VI had already referred to this idea in *Populorum Progressio*. The passage to which it refers is not dealing specifically with ecology but can apply to it. It reads, "We cannot disregard the welfare of those who will come after us. . . . The reality of human solidarity brings us not only benefits but also obligations" (*PP* 17).

be saddled with the cost of our use of common environmental resources" (§8). Linking this intergenerational solidarity with the need for solidarity between "developing countries and highly industrialized countries," he called for "*a solidarity which embraces time and space*" (§8).

Caritas in Veritate and various statements of Pope Benedict contain a lot of valuable material about environmental issues and about our relationships with the natural world. Nevertheless, I am inclined to feel that they do not emphasize sufficiently the sheer urgency of the need for a model of human development which respects the environment and repairs the damage already done to it.

BIOTECHNOLOGY

A major concern of those who devote themselves to ecological issues is the use of biotechnology to modify crops or animals. This is not a topic on which there have been many statements by the popes. John Paul spoke about it in an Address to the Pontifical Academy of Sciences in October 1981. There he said that he appreciated "the benefits that can be derived ... from the study and application of molecular biology, supplemented by other disciplines such as genetic technology and its application to agriculture." He went on to say that he had "confidence in the global scientific community" that they would carry out this research "with full respect for moral standards" (§3, my translation).

A year later, in October 1982, John Paul spoke again to the Pontifical Academy of Sciences. In this second address he said, "I have no reason to be apprehensive for those *experiments in biology* that are performed by scientists who, like you, have a profound respect for the human person, since I am sure that they will contribute to the *integral well-being of man*" (§4).

Referring to experimentation on animals he said, "It is certain that animals are at the service of man and can hence be the object of experimentation." But he added that "the diminution of experimentation on animals, which has progressively been made ever less necessary, corresponds to the plan and well-being of all creation" (§4).

Unfortunately the pope's confidence in the scientists who carry out research into genetic modification of plants and animals has not been justified. The reality is that most of this kind of research is funded, directly or indirectly, by a small number of powerful transnational corporations—especially pharmaceutical companies and companies involved in agribusiness. It is closely linked to the fact that since 1980, genetically engineered materials can be patented (cf. S. McDonagh 2004b, 33; S. McDonagh 2009).

This privately funded research is by no means disinterested. Its ultimate purpose is to enable the companies who fund it to make greater profits. So questions arise about its objectivity or at least its selectivity. One can no longer be sure that the reported results accurately reflect the outcome of the research. Time after time we hear of situations where reports on research have been doctored to play down or eliminate results that would cast doubt on the value of new products and on the benefits that they are supposed to bring. Harmful side effects or long-term consequences are concealed, or there is a failure to take account of the effects that the applications of the research may have in the wider society (see S. McDonagh and Dorr 2008, 18). Furthermore, conscientious scientists are likely to lose their jobs if they dare to express doubts about the value of the research or about ways in which it may be used. They may even find themselves pilloried in scientific journals that are funded, in whole or in part, by the companies that are sponsoring the research (see S. McDonagh and Dorr 2008, 10–11).

A particularly significant instance of genetic modification of the seeds of major food crops is what has come to be called "terminator technology." This involves modifying the seeds of crops such as rice or maize or wheat. What is "created" is a type of seed that produces a crop that cannot be carried over as seed for planting in the following year. The effect is that farmers are trapped into buying seeds each year anew from a company that gains increasing monopolistic control of the seeds. What this means, in practice, is that farmers and consumers are left at the mercy of the corporation. The result is that both farmers and consumers become disempowered. The rich and powerful become richer and more powerful, while the poor become poorer and more disadvantaged. Ordinary people have far less control over their environment. Furthermore, biodiversity is greatly diminished—and this leaves millions of people open to famine or food shortage, since the few remaining strains of rice or maize or wheat could be wiped out by some virulent disease (cf. McDonagh and Dorr 2008, 14; McLoughlin 2004, 192).

The *Compendium of the Social Doctrine of the Church* issued by the Pontifical Council for Justice and Peace in 2004 devotes one section of its treatment of ecology to the issue of biotechnology (§§472–80, pp. 239–42). As one would expect, it refers to the above addresses of the pope. Oddly, and perhaps significantly, it fails to refer to a passage that I have referred to above in the 1990 Message for World Day of Peace—a passage in which Pope John Paul warns about the danger of "indiscriminate genetic manipulation and . . . unscrupulous development of new forms of plant and animal life" (§7).

Overall, the *Compendium* gives a highly favorable account of biotechnology. It says that "nature is not a sacred or divine reality that man must leave alone." It maintains that "the Christian vision of creation makes a positive judgment on the acceptability of human intervention in nature." So it concludes that it is not wrong for humans to intervene in other living beings "by modifying some of their characteristics or properties." It does, however, call for responsibility, saying that it is "necessary to evaluate accurately the real benefits as well as the possible consequences in terms of risks" (§473, p. 240). Referring to the role of politicians and legislators in evaluating the benefits and possible risks, it says, "It is not desirable for their decisions, at the national or international level, to be dictated by special interest groups" (§479, p. 242).

The treatment of this topic in the *Compendium* remains at a high level of generality. It makes no real attempt to address the reality that I have described, where research and implementation of genetic modification remain largely in the hands of a few transnational corporations. The effect is that the *Compendium* gives the impression of being in favor of genetic modification, with the proviso that it be carried out responsibly. This favorable attitude has been challenged by some experts on ecological issues. Serious questions have also been raised about the fact that some of the studies and conferences sponsored by the Vatican on this topic have been funded by the government of the United States, whose policies are heavily influenced by the corporations engaged in genetic modification (cf. S. McDonagh 2004b, 8–21).

EVALUATION

In the light of the overall approach adopted in the many documents to which I have referred in this chapter, it is, I believe, reasonable to say that Catholic social teaching, as articulated in official Vatican documents on ecological issues prior to 2013, was basically anthropocentric in outlook. By this I mean that it consistently put humans at the center, that the value judgments it made were generally made in terms of what will be of benefit to humans, and that it showed a marked reluctance to put any emphasis on what we might call the intrinsic value of animals, plants, forests, scenery, and all the other myriad nonhuman aspects of creation.

I hasten to add two important qualifications or clarifications. The first is that this is a nuanced anthropocentricity. It differs quite radically from the view that is a common assumption in our world today—one that takes it for granted that there are few or no limits to the extent to which we humans are entitled to exploit nature for our own benefit. This latter view may not always be overtly expressed, but it seems to be widely operative in the worlds of business and politics. I say that the anthropocentric approach of Vatican teaching was nuanced, because it was balanced by, and strictly limited by, a strong emphasis on the idea that God demands that we humans should respect the order or pattern that is evident in nature and in the whole of creation. The popes insisted that creation has its own integrity, because it is a cosmos, an ordered unity. They asserted repeatedly that it is God's will that we should be aware of and respect that pattern. They themselves, and those who followed their teaching, were committed campaigners for ecological sensitivity.

The second clarification follows from the first. It is that this Vatican teaching cannot be reasonably accused of providing a scriptural or theological justification for the exploitation of the Earth. Over the past generation, various authors have suggested that the Genesis text "have dominion over ... every living creature" (Gen. 1:28) (as well, perhaps, as Genesis 2:19–20 where Adam names the animals) has been understood—especially in Western Christianity—as a mandate to humans to exercise unrestricted control over all the nonhuman elements in nature. As Elizabeth Johnson aptly points out, God's mandate to the original human couple to have "dominion" over the other creatures (Gen. 1:26) was interpreted in the West in recent centuries to mean having *domination* over nature (Johnson 2015, 102).

There may be a basis for this accusation in some strands of Christianity. But this does not apply to the teaching of Pope John Paul or Pope Benedict, both of whom insist repeatedly that God demands that humans respect the pattern of nature, which Benedict so aptly describes as its "grammar" (*CiV* 48). Precisely because John Paul and Benedict are good theologians, their anthropocentric approach is located within a God-centered vision. If committed Christians and other people of goodwill take seriously the teaching of these popes on environmental issues, they can help bring about the "ecological conversion" that the popes call for and they can play their part in solving the environmental problems that our world now faces. Elizabeth Johnson offers an inspiring account of what this involves: "Ecological conversion means falling in love with the Earth as an inherently valuable, living community in which we participate, and bending every effort to be creatively faithful to its wellbeing, in tune with the living God who brought it into being and who cherishes it with unconditional love" (Johnson 2014, 257).

Having insisted that the popes are not guilty of justifying the kind of gross exploitation of the Earth that has led to our problems, I must nevertheless say that I agree with the many Christian theologians who were dissatisfied with the Vatican position up to the coming of Pope Francis. My major regret about the teaching of Pope Benedict on the issue of ecology is that he, who was so committed on environmental issues, did not locate everything he had to say about human responsibility and business activity in this time of economic crisis within the broader context of the ecological crisis of our time. His teaching emerged from an older anthropocentric paradigm where ecological issues are treated almost entirely in terms of present-day human concerns. What is needed today, however, is a kind of Copernican revolution leading to a major paradigm shift. We need to locate all our human concerns—and especially our approach to economics—within the far wider context of an ecological and cosmic vision. Nothing would have been lost and much would have been gained if what the pope wrote in *Caritas in Veritate* and elsewhere about economics and ecology were framed within this wider vision.

I noted above two occasions on which Pope John Paul called for "an ecological conversion." While fully accepting the urgency of such a conversion in terms of national and international economic policies and personal lifestyle, it has become clear that there is need for a corresponding conversion in theology and in spirituality, namely, a rethinking of Catholic social teaching in the light of an ecological paradigm.[4] The call for such a change of outlook was expressed as early as 1988, by Thomas Berry when he wrote these words in his book *The Dream of the Earth*:

> The time has come for the most significant change that Christian spirituality has yet experienced, but this change is itself part of a much more comprehensive change in human consciousness brought about by the discovery of the evolutionary process. . . .
>
> The industrial-commercial mode of consciousness in our society has coexisted with . . . Western classical spirituality. These two patterns cause little trouble to each other because neither . . . is concerned with the integral functioning of the earth community. Indeed, both modes of consciousness experience the human as Olympian ruler of the planet. (Berry 1988, 117, 119)

Some of the practical ethical implications were expressed in *The Universe Story*, which Berry coauthored with Brian Swimme: "All the more substantive words in the language are undergoing a transformation, words such as *society, good* and *evil, freedom, justice, literacy, progress.* All these words need to be extended to include the various beings of the natural world, their freedoms, their rights, their share in the functioning of the Earth" (Swimme and Berry 1992, 258).

Christian theologians who adopt a geocentric, or Earth-centered, ap-

---

[4]In chapter 20 we shall see that the encyclical *Laudato Si'* of Pope Francis represents just such an ecological conversion of theology and spirituality.

proach are unwilling to describe the relationship of humans to the other parts of creation in terms of "dominating" (*CA* 31) or "exploitation" (*RH* 15) or of being the "master" (*RH* 15; *SRS* 29) or "king of creation" (John Paul's Address to World Medical Association in 1983, §6), or "the only creature on earth which God has willed for its own sake" (*CA* 53).[5] Some of them are even rather hesitant about using the term "stewardship"—not because they deny our duty to treat the Earth responsibly but because it might suggest that we humans can take control of every aspect of the processes of nature. Denis Edwards writes,

> I prefer the biblical language of "cultivating and caring for" to the language of "stewardship." . . . Of course, the language of steward-ship can be used meaningfully to point to human responsibility for creation before God. But when stewardship is used to characterize the human stance before other creatures, it can run the risk of sug-gesting an inflated view of the human as a necessary intermediary between God and other creatures. It can seem to suggest that other creatures do not have their own relationship with the living God or their own integrity. (Edwards 2006, 25)

Those who hold a geocentric position agree with the popes in reject-ing the kind of ruthless and mindless exploitation of nature which has occurred over the past century and still continues today in many parts of the world. For them, as for the popes, a primary virtue is respect, ac-companied by a high degree of modesty, even humility, in the way we relate to nature. It is interesting to see that such a profound and deeply committed ecotheologian as Denis Edwards argues in favor of "a bibli-cal theocentric vision" (Edwards 2006, 19). In this respect he has much in common with Pope John Paul and Pope Benedict, whose vision, as I pointed out earlier, is fundamentally God-centered.

The ecotheologians accept that God calls us to respect the pattern of nature. But they do not believe that one has to rely on an explicit reference to this call from God. They are aware that agnostics and atheists may be committed on ecological issues and that they have a sound moral basis for this commitment. Christians, Muslims, Buddhists, Hindus, agnostics, and atheists can all apprehend and respond to the "law" that is, so to speak, built into the reality we see all around us. They see and respond with awe to animals, forests, flowers, and scenery, to the marvels and majesty of the distant galaxies and to the organic wonders that are revealed only

---

[5]John Feehan refers to "the argument of Thomas Aquinas that created nature is not intended primarily for us: it is for God's own pleasure" (Feehan 2012, 74).

under the microscope. They are responding not just to brute facts but to the value of each of these aspects of creation.

Christian ecotheologians locate humans firmly within the whole process of evolution, while recognizing the important distinction between humans and other life forms.[6] With John Feehan they point to the "incontrovertible demonstration by modern science of the extent to which all life is one family." With him they maintain that "the ripples of consanguinity must extend to all creatures, and with those expanding ripples the ethical imperative that is grounded in relationship" (Feehan 2012, 93).

Denis Edwards provides some biblical references in support of what he calls a "kinship within a community of God's creation" (Edwards 2006, 22), and he goes on to refer to the work of Rosemary Radford Ruether and Elizabeth Johnson in support of the notion of a "community of creation" (Edwards 2006, 24). Johnson herself points out that "the paradigm of the community of creation" is more common in the Bible than "the paradigm of dominion" (Johnson 2014, 261).

Why have the popes, at least up to the time of Pope Francis, been reluctant to take the small extra step of moving from a nuanced anthropocentric approach to one that is rather more geocentric? Why is it that as late as his Message for World Day of Peace of 2010, Pope Benedict expressed "grave misgivings about notions of the environment inspired by ecocentrism and biocentrism"? An answer to this question is given in the *Compendium of the Social Doctrine of the Church* (2004). It says,

> The Magisterium finds the motivation for its opposition to a concept of the environment based on ecocentrism and on biocentrism in the fact that "it is being proposed that . . . man's superior responsibility can be eliminated in favor of an egalitarian consideration of the 'dignity' of all living beings." (*Compendium*, §463, p. 234; the quotation within this passage is taken from §5 of an Address of John Paul to participants in a convention on the Environment and Health, March 24, 1997)

There is no doubt that there are some who have adopted an extreme position. Outraged about factory farming, overfishing, irresponsible genetic modification of animals and plants, and other instances of human exploitation of other species, they adopt a position of ecological egalitarianism and maintain that other species have just the same rights as

---

[6]Ilia Delio complains about the ambivalence of official Church teaching about evolution: "The church recognizes evolution as a possible scientific explanation of biological life but does not accept it as *the* explanation of all life" (Delio 2013, 119).

humans (cf. Edwards 2006, 21–22). Indeed, some of them seem, at times, to be more concerned about cats or dogs or lions than about humans. In insisting on the priority of human ecology, John Paul and Benedict were reacting against this view that would reject or downplay the distinctiveness of humans, claiming that the "rights" of animals and plants are equal to those of humans—if not in fact superior to them.

It is true, too, that some ecology campaigners have adopted an extreme version of James Lovelock's concept of *Gaia* (Lovelock 1988). They hold that the Earth is the divine "Earth Mother." In their view the Earth has a certain transcendent quality, but they do not see any need for a transcendent God in the Judeo-Christian sense. Their conception of the divine is effectively a pantheistic one. It is not surprising, then, that the *Compendium*, recalling a document about New Age ideas that was issued by the Pontifical Council for Culture and the Pontifical Council for Interreligious Dialogue, says that "one can go so far as to divinize nature or the earth, as can readily be seen in certain ecological movements" (§463, p. 234). Similarly, Marjorie Keenan wrote of "a type of new paganism, fostering a form of nature worship" (Keenan 2000, 25). Some years later Pope Benedict showed the same concern about "attitudes of neopaganism or a new pantheism" (*CiV* 48).

It seems, then, that the Vatican has had two interrelated objections to the adoption of a geocentric position: first, a concern that it denies or downplays the transcendence of God and, second, a concern that it denies the uniqueness of humans. One can respond quite briefly to the first of these concerns. An authentic Christian faith recognizes that God is not only transcendent but also immanent in our world. Western Christianity has tended to put an unbalanced emphasis on the transcendence of God, playing down the immanent presence. Christian ecotheologians are helping us return to a more authentic understanding of God by putting renewed emphasis on the presence of God in nature. But this does not, by any means, involve the denial or neglect of the transcendence of God.

It is unfair to assume that ecotheologians agree with those who divinize nature or adopt a pantheistic position. Some, but not all, of them opt for what is called panentheism. The emphasis of the ecotheologians on God's immanence in the world provides a healthy balance to the insistence of the popes on the transcendence of God. The popes and the ecotheologians agree on the particular responsibility of humans to care for creation.

In regard to the issue of the uniqueness of humans, a way forward can be found in Bernard Lonergan's writings. In *Insight* ([1957] 1992) he put forward a detailed account of the different levels of reality, with increasing degrees of complexity. There is a qualitative shift as one moves from the chemical to the level of living organisms, another qualitative shift as one moves to the level of animal psychology, and yet another in the move to the human level of consciousness. Reality at each of these successive levels is good and has value.[7]

In *Method in Theology* and in various other writings Lonergan spells out his understanding of the human response to value. The distinctive feature of humans is that we not only have value, but that we are "originating values" (Lonergan [1972] 1990, 51, 53). We can apprehend value, and we can create value. We apprehend value by responding affectively to the beauty, the intelligibility, and the mystery of the cosmos as a whole and to its individual components, as well as to the whole process of evolution that gives rise to this complexity and beauty. Our response is not just a cerebral one, grasping the intelligibility of objects. It is also a response of the heart—an affective response, in which we are moved by empathy with various other beings. All are integral parts of this wondrous cosmos, and we can, at times, sense our oneness with the whole and with each of its parts.

We not only apprehend value, but we also have the privilege of creating value. Indeed, this is a fundamental way in which we are created in the image of God—that we have the power to co-create with God. This power of co-creation carries with it a responsibility to use it wisely. That does not mean that we have a moral right to use the rest of creation purely for our own benefit. Our call is to use both our intelligence and also our affective-empathetic links with other creatures to find ways to live responsibly as humans. This involves, first, living respectfully and contemplatively in the world of which we are an integral part and that comes to us as a gift from God. Second, it involves the reshaping of some parts of our inanimate and animate environment in ways that benefit us and that respect the gift we have been given.

The detail of what this reshaping may involve and the limits to our intervention have to be worked out in dialogue with other humans. In engaging in this dialogue, we must pay particular attention both to those who put forward creative plans for changing the environment and also to those who experience such strong empathetic links with animals, trees, plants, and the other wonders of nature that they advocate a more contemplative style of living with minimum intervention by humans in the way things are at present.

But how is one to reconcile the tension that often exists between the desire to change the world and the desire to contemplate it? On the one hand, we must avoid naïve romanticism about nature and, on the other hand, a utilitarian technocratic capitalist mentality interested only in

---

[7]David C. Schindler (2010, 355) helpfully points out the inadequacy of a view in which "goodness has its meaning *posterior* to the meaning of things in themselves"; it is important to see goodness as an aspect of the very nature of things.

exploiting nature. What is important is to understand and appreciate the pattern of nature and to work with it.[8]

In the light of all this we can ask the following: What words are appropriate to describe the relationship of humans to the rest of creation? Certainly not words such as "exploitation" or "domination." But what about the controversial word "stewardship"? My own opinion is that it remains an acceptable term—but only on condition that it is always used in conjunction with the word "partnership." We have the privilege of caring for the parts and aspects of creation that come under our control, but we also have the privilege of allowing our bodies and our spirits to be nourished by the world we share with the rest of creation. We are an integral part of the world, and our relationship with the other parts of it is one of partnership and stewardship.

* * *

SUMMARY

From the time of Pope John XXIII onward—and particularly with John Paul II—the social teaching of the Catholic Church came to have an integrally humanistic approach. It could be argued that its flip side was that its teaching on ecology has tended to be unduly anthropocentric. Nevertheless, the Church gradually developed an impressive body of valuable ecological teaching. As far back as 1971 the Synod of Bishops called on the rich nations to accept a less wasteful way of life in order to protect our common heritage that they are bound in justice to share with others. Pope John Paul's Message for the 1990 World Day of Peace is a major contribution to the Church's teaching. It stresses that it is in the interests of humankind to protect the environment and adopt a simpler, less wasteful lifestyle. It, and later documents of John Paul and Benedict, emphasize our duty to respect the pattern that God has given to the order of nature—a pattern that Pope Benedict calls its "grammar." Benedict also emphasizes the importance of intergenerational justice—not using up resources needed by our descendants in the future.

The issue of the proper limits to biotechnology is a crucial one. It is suggested that the *Compendium of the Social Doctrine of the Church* has failed to take a sufficiently strong stance on the dangers of the issue of genetic modification.

There seem to be two main reasons why the official teaching of the

---

[8] This notion of working with the pattern of nature is central to the thinking and practice of Wendell Berry (cf. Cloutier 2010, 619).

Church was slow to move beyond an anthropocentric viewpoint. One is a fear of pantheism or a neopagan worship of nature; the other is a fear of a kind of egalitarianism where the uniqueness of humans and human responsibility will be played down. These are real dangers, but they can be avoided while still recognizing that nonhuman species should be respected as having an intrinsic value in their own right. One is entitled to describe the responsibility of humans to care for creation as "stewardship," provided one links this word with the word "partnership."

QUESTIONS FOR REVIEW

1. *What was involved in the shift toward "integral humanism" in Catholic social teaching?*
2. *Name key points about ecology in the 1971 Synod of Bishops document.*
3. *Is it acceptable to use the term "exploitation of nature?"*
4. *What reasons does the 1990 World Day of Peace Message offer for respecting nature?*
5. *Why would Pope Benedict use the term "grammar" in referring to nature?*
6. *Why was the Vatican reluctant to move beyond an anthropocentric stance in relation to ecology?*

QUESTION FOR REFLECTION

1. *How does an ecological perspective enrich Catholic social teaching?*

ISSUES FOR FURTHER STUDY

1. *Ecological theology. Read Denis Edwards 2006; Elizabeth Johnson 2014; Ilia Delio 2013.*
2. *Biotechnology and genetic modification.*

19

Pope Francis: A Radical Option for the Poor

The preceding chapters should have made clear that, although there has been considerable continuity in Catholic social teaching over the years since Leo XIII's great encyclical *Rerum Novarum* of 1891, different popes have at times shifted the emphasis in significant ways. Perhaps the most dramatic of these changes came in 1961, when John XXIII effectively proposed the kind of welfare state which his predecessors had considered quite unacceptable. The Vatican Council made a radical change in the Church's approach to the relationship between the Church and the state as well as in its abandonment of the idea that "error has no rights" and its teaching about respect for conscience. I have suggested that Benedict XVI made a determined effort to shift the emphasis of Catholic social teaching away from the influence of the theology of liberation and to put it instead on his teaching about the importance of an "economy of communion."

With Pope Francis has come yet another shift of emphasis. Indeed, there is a strong case for saying that his approach represents a significant break with the past. As Leonardo Boff says, "He inaugurates another style of being pope and of being church." And Boff adds: "There are no better words to describe this than the terms *break* and *beginning anew*" (Boff 2014, 7). Leaving to the next chapter a treatment of the teaching of Francis on ecology, I outline in this chapter the other main elements in his teaching and approach. In doing so, I draw on a great variety of papal and Vatican documents, especially on the text of Pope Francis's apostolic exhortation *Evangelii Gaudium*, issued on November 24, 2013, and on an address he gave on October 28, 2014, to representatives of a variety of movements which in the English language are rather misleadingly called "Popular Movements."[1] In *Evangelii Gaudium*, hereafter referred to as

---

[1]In the interests of brevity, in references to this speech I shall call it *Movements*. It is important to note that in this mainly Latin American context the word "popular" does not mean "widely liked" or "widely accepted" as in English. Perhaps the nearest one could get to

"*EG,*" he presents Christians with what he calls his "dream" (*EG* 27). In fact this document can be seen as a kind of manifesto by Francis of what he stands for—the vision that he aims to see lived out in the Church and in the lives of Christians. The pope's address of October 28 comes across as a quite passionate cry of outrage about the present unjust situation and of positive encouragement by Francis to his friends in these movements to continue their crucial work of empowering poor and marginalized people in their struggle to bring about a more just world.

MERCY AND JOY

For previous popes the key word in Catholic social teaching was "solidarity." Francis, too, sees this concept as crucial. But for him, in everything he says and writes, the words which take pride of place are "mercy" and "joy." The word "joy" is in the very title of *Evangelii Gaudium* and is a fundamental theme of the document (e.g., *EG* 2–8), and Francis again put the emphasis on joy in his Message for Mission Sunday 2014 (2–3). This emphasis on mercy is linked to his frequent emphasis on the importance of tenderness. For instance, in Cuba, during his homily at the shrine of Our Lady of Charity in El Cobre, Santiago, on September 22, 2015, he spoke of a call to live a "revolution of tenderness." Francis stressed the importance of mercy again and again, culminating in his proclamation of a Jubilee Year of Mercy scheduled to begin on December 8, 2015. His insistence on the importance of mercy does not mean that he sees mercy as replacing justice and law. But in his statements, his responses to difficult questions, and above all in his spontaneous actions, he makes it clear that it is not enough for Church leaders or for any Christian to insist on laying down laws or principles. For him there is a delicate balance to be preserved: on the one hand, Christians are called to hold onto, and proclaim, the basic principles of Catholic social teaching, but, on the other hand, they must not apply these principles in a rigid "take-it-or-leave-it" manner. He holds that, in seeking to implement Catholic social teaching as well as all other aspects of church teaching, it is essential that Christian leaders do so with sensitivity and respect, taking account of the real-life situations of those with whom they are dealing and always keeping in mind the fundamental Christian belief in the compassion and mercy of God.

Perhaps the most striking instance of the belief and teaching of Pope

---

an accurate English translation of the term "movimientos populares" would be "movements of the common people or ordinary people." See my footnote 2 to chapter 8 above.

Francis on this issue of compassion and flexibility comes in the address he gave on October 24, 2015, at the conclusion of the Synod on the Family. While acknowledging that dogmatic questions are clearly defined by the magisterium, he pointed out that cultures are quite diverse and that "every general principle needs to be inculturated, if it is to be respected and applied." He said that the experience of the synod "made us better realize that the true defenders of doctrine are not those who uphold its letter, but its spirit." In a quite sharp rebuke to those who are unduly rigid upholders of the law, he said that the synod "was about bearing witness to everyone that, for the Church, the Gospel continues to be a vital source of eternal newness, against all those who would 'indoctrinate' it in dead stones to be hurled at others." He insisted:

> It was also about laying bare the closed hearts which frequently hide even behind the Church's teachings or good intentions, in order to sit in the chair of Moses and judge, sometimes with superiority and superficiality, difficult cases and wounded families. . . . It was about trying to open up broader horizons, rising above conspiracy theories and blinkered viewpoints, so as to defend and spread the freedom of the children of God, and to transmit the beauty of Christian Newness, at times encrusted in a language which is archaic or simply incomprehensible.

Pope Francis himself is a good model of how to combine strong condemnation of social evils with a nonjudgmental attitude in relation to the individual person. In his interview for the Jesuit magazines he said: "During the return flight from Rio de Janeiro I said that if a homosexual person is of good will and is in search of God, I am no one to judge." He then went on to say: "A person once asked me, in a provocative manner, if I approved of homosexuality. I replied with another question: 'Tell me: when God looks at a gay person, does he endorse the existence of this person with love, or reject and condemn this person?' We must always consider the person" (interview with Spadaro 2013).

In a moving passage toward the end of *Evangelii Gaudium* Francis invites his readers to follow Jesus by entering "fully into the fabric of society, sharing the lives of all, listening to their concerns, helping them materially and spiritually in their needs, rejoicing with those who rejoice, weeping with those who weep." He adds that as we go "arm in arm with others, we are committed to building a new world," and "we do so not from a sense of obligation, not as a burdensome duty, but as the result of a personal decision which brings us joy and gives meaning to our lives" (*EG* 269).

CAPITALISM AND THE POOR

In the social and political sphere the most controversial element in the new approach of Pope Francis is his extraordinarily blunt condemnation of the present world order, where there is an ever-widening gap between rich and poor: "While the earnings of a minority are growing exponentially, so too is the gap separating the majority from the prosperity enjoyed by those happy few" (*EG* 56). He goes on immediately to point out that this is no accident: "This imbalance is the result of ideologies which defend the absolute autonomy of the marketplace and financial speculation. . . . A new tyranny is thus born, invisible and often virtual, which unilaterally and relentlessly imposes its own laws and rules" (*EG* 56).

Of course, the condemnation of an unregulated capitalist system has been a basic part of Catholic social teaching over the past 130 years. But what is new is the freshness and harshness of Francis's words and the vividness with which he spells out the consequences of this ideology. In the first paragraph of his "Message for World Day of Peace 2014," he says: "New ideologies, characterized by rampant individualism, egocentrism and materialistic consumerism, weaken social bonds, fuelling that 'throw away' mentality which leads to contempt for, and the abandonment of, the weakest and those considered 'useless.' " In *Evangelii Gaudium* he uses even stronger words: "Human beings are themselves considered consumer goods to be used and then discarded. We have created a 'disposable' culture which is now spreading. It is no longer simply about exploitation and oppression, but something new. . . . The excluded are not the 'exploited' but the outcast, the 'leftovers' " (*EG* 53). In his October 2014 address to activists he spells this out more fully: "The excluded are discarded, as 'leftovers.'. . . This is what takes place when the god of money is at the center of an economic system. . . . Children are disposed of . . . because . . . neither children nor the elderly are producers" (*Movements*).

In the light of this outspoken condemnation of the capitalist system as it is practiced at present, it is no wonder that the conservative radio host Rush Limbaugh should say about *Evangelii Gaudium*: "This is just pure Marxism coming out of the mouth of the pope."[2] Apparently the direct and uncompromising quality of Francis's words are more effective than the measured statements of previous popes in making it clear that the present political-economic system is quite incompatible with Catholic social teaching.

---

[2] See Rush Limbaugh's website.

CHANGE IN THE STRUCTURES

Francis is not content just to condemn the evils of the system or to appeal to those in power to change their attitudes and approach. Nor is he content merely to advocate welfare programs to help the poor survive. Instead, he calls loudly for governments and society to bring about changes in the political-economic structures: "Welfare projects, which meet certain urgent needs, should be considered merely temporary responses" (*EG* 202).

Francis goes to the root of the problem when he says: "As long as the problems of the poor are not radically resolved by rejecting the absolute autonomy of markets and financial speculation and by attacking the structural causes of inequality, no solution will be found for the world's problems or, for that matter, to any problems" (*EG* 202). He even goes so far as to say that "the socioeconomic system is unjust at its root" (*EG* 59). That is why he calls for a radical change in the very structure of the economic system.

In his insistence on the need for structural change, Francis is adopting one of the main themes of liberation theology. This means that his response to this theology is significantly different from that of Benedict XVI, whose suspicion of it led him to adopt what would be called a "moralizing" approach—that is, an emphasis more on personal conversion than on structural transformation. Of course, Francis is not so naïve as to believe that structural changes can be a substitute for radical personal change. In fact, he insists on the need for an attitudinal and cultural transformation alongside a change in political and economic structures: "Changing structures without generating new convictions and attitudes will only ensure that those same structures will become, sooner or later, corrupt, oppressive and ineffectual" (*EG* 189).

This change of convictions and attitudes must lead to a change in lifestyle by those of us who are relatively well-off. So Francis stresses the fundamental need for "the detachment of those who choose to live a sober and essential lifestyle, of those who, by sharing their own wealth, thus manage to experience fraternal communion with others" (Peace Message 2014 §5).

THE CRY OF THE POOR

One of the most frequent challenges posed by Francis to Christians everywhere, and to their pastors, is to "hear the cry of the poor" (*EG* 191). He insists that his dream is of something much more than simply providing them with what he calls a "dignified sustenance." Those who are poor need "education, access to health care, and above all employment, for it is through free, creative, participatory and mutually supportive labor that human beings express and enhance the dignity of their lives." And he goes on at once to emphasize the importance of a just wage, for it is only in this way that they can have "adequate access to all the other goods which are destined for our common use" (*EG* 192).

Francis was realistic enough to know that in some of the wealthier countries there are politicians, economists, and commentators who deny or play down the need for radical change of structures on behalf of those who are poor or excluded. He knew also that a significant number of those who hold this view are Catholics, and that some of them are church leaders and commentators who claim that their position is fully in line with Catholic social teaching. So one must assume that he has these people in mind when he says: "This message is so clear and direct, so simple and eloquent, that no ecclesial interpretation has the right to relativize it" (*EG* 194).

In his lengthy dialogue with the leaders of the religious congregations of men, Pope Francis adopted a position that is in line with the conferences of Medellín, Puebla, and Aparecida, and the stance of the liberation theologians on an important issue. As reported by Father Antonio Spadaro, the pope referred to a letter that had been written years ago by Father Pedro Arrupe, former General of the Jesuits, a letter in which Arrupe had referred to the necessity for some real contact with the poor. According to Spadaro's account, the pope then said: "This is really important to me: the need to become acquainted with reality by experience, to spend time walking on the periphery in order to really become acquainted with the reality and life experience of people" (Dialogue with leaders of USG).

In his address to the representatives of the movements, Francis says: "You have your feet in the mud, you . . . carry the smell of your neighbourhood, your people, your struggle! We want your voices to be heard—voices that are rarely heard. No doubt this is because . . . your cries are bothersome, no doubt because people are afraid of the change that you seek" (*Movements*). His use, with obvious approval, of the word "struggle" is quite striking; it represents a sharp departure from the almost invariant stance of previous popes.

Another insight of the liberation theologians that Francis wholeheartedly adopts and expresses can be found in a moving passage in *Evangelii Gaudium*. It is that making an option for the poor is not a one-way process. Francis maintains that we Christians "need to let ourselves be evangelized by them." He spells this out, insisting that we are invited "to acknowledge the saving power at work in their lives . . . to find Christ in them, to lend our voice to their causes, but also to be their friends, to listen to them, to speak for them and to embrace the mysterious wisdom which God wishes to share with us through them" (*EG* 198). Earlier in that document he maintains that the various examples of "popular piety" of poor people are the work of the Holy Spirit and a *locus theologicus*—the means used by God to share with us that divine "mysterious wisdom" (*EG* 126).

It had been suggested that Francis is "softer" than previous popes on the issue of abortion. So it brought some relief to those who campaigned on this issue to see his statement: "Among the vulnerable for whom the Church wishes to care with particular love and concern are unborn children, the most defenseless and innocent among us. . . . This defense of unborn life is closely linked to the defense of each and every other human right. It involves the conviction that a human being is always sacred and inviolable, in any situation and at every stage of development. Human beings are ends in themselves and never a means of resolving other problems" (*EG* 213).

Although Pope Francis adopted in *Evangelii Gaudium* several key elements in liberation theology, he did not explicitly emphasize the need for empowered poor people to challenge the rich and the powerful. However, eleven months later, his address to the representatives of the movements left no room for doubt on that point. The whole tone of his words on that occasion is that of a person who identifies with these activists as his colleagues and friends. He begins by saying that their presence is a sign or witness to a reality that is often silenced, namely, that "the poor do not only suffer injustice; they also struggle against it!" Speaking directly to these activists, he said: "You are not satisfied with empty promises, with alibis or excuses. Nor do you wait with arms crossed for NGOs to help, for welfare schemes or paternalistic solutions that never arrive; or if they do, then it is with a tendency to anaesthetize or to domesticate . . . and this is rather perilous. One senses that the poor are no longer waiting. You want to be protagonists. You get organized, study, work, issue demands and, above all, practice that very special solidarity that exists among those who suffer, among the poor, and that our civilization seems to have forgotten or would strongly prefer to forget" (*Movements*).

Some of his words could well have been spoken by any of the pioneers of liberation theology: "The scandal of poverty cannot be addressed by promoting strategies of containment that only tranquilize the poor and render them tame and inoffensive. How sad it is when we find, behind allegedly altruistic works, the other being reduced to passivity or being negated; or worse still, we find hidden personal agendas or commercial interests." Francis makes it clear that he fully identifies with the ministry of these activists:

How marvellous it is . . . when we see peoples moving forward [*cuando vemos en movimiento a Pueblos*], especially their young and their poorest members. Then one feels a promising breeze that revives hope for a better world. May this breeze become a cyclone of hope. This is my wish. (*Movements*)

These words suggest that Francis as pope was prepared to give effective support to on-the-ground activists and Church leaders who remain close to poor people in a committed and risky but nonviolent struggle for justice. This would represent a distinct break from the attitude of Pope John Paul II during most of his papacy, that is, once the Polish activists had succeeded in toppling the communist regime. Some of John Paul's warnings and most of the practical policies of the Vatican during this period gave the clear impression that the more liberation-minded activists and Church leaders had gone too far and that Rome actively disapproved of them.

In his passionate address to these activists, Francis delivered what one might almost call a diatribe against a whole list of abuses, which for him are an intrinsic aspect of the present unjust order. He mentioned the hoarding of land, deforestation, privatization of the water supply, and the use of dangerous pesticides. Then he pointed out that millions of people die when the price of food is determined by financial speculation while tons of food are thrown away: "Hunger is criminal, food is an inalienable human right." He spoke out strongly against homelessness and against the euphemisms that are employed to disguise the crimes committed in the whole area of housing. He expressed his outrage about the manner in which settlements of poor people are marginalized or even wiped out, as bulldozers are brought in to flatten the shacks of the poor. The proper alternative, he insisted, is a genuine and respectful urban integration where every neighborhood is a real community in which the people have security of tenure and the area has adequate facilities such as schools, health centers, and sports clubs.

Next, Pope Francis spoke with equal passion about abuses in relation to work, insisting that the worst form of poverty and indignity is the creation of a situation where people cannot find work. It is by no means inevitable that young people should suffer unemployment, he noted. It is not necessary that people be forced to work in what is euphemistically called "the informal sector," and there is no need for people to be deprived of basic labor rights. These injustices, he insisted, are the result of the deliberate prior decision by those in power to opt for a system that gives priority to profit rather than to human beings and of a throwaway culture that treats humans as "a consumer good, which can be used and then thrown away." Later in his address he spoke of "the balance sheets of economies that sacrifice people at the feet of the idol of money."

Alongside his sharp condemnation, Pope Francis made clear his support both for those who are victims of abuses and for the activists who are working to change the system. He warmly praised those "excluded workers, the discards of this system" who have succeeded in inventing work, using "materials that seemed to be devoid of further productive value" in a people's economy through their solidarity and their community work. Waxing quite lyrical, Francis said that this is not just work, "this is poetry!" Then he spoke of the rights of "every worker, within the formal system of salaried employment or outside it," including the waste collectors, recyclers, peddlers, seamstresses and tailors, street traders, fishermen, farmworkers, builders, miners, workers in previously abandoned enterprises, members of cooperatives, all kinds of workers in grassroots jobs who are not allowed to have workers' rights, who are denied the opportunity to join trade unions, and who do not have a steady or adequate income. He insisted that all of these have the right to decent remuneration for their work and also to social security and to a retirement pension. He said: "I want today to join my voice to yours and to support you in your struggle."[3]

He told the activists to whom he was speaking that the movements that they represent are expressions of "the urgent need to revitalize our democracies." For him it is a matter of "active participation of great majorities as protagonists." This kind of "proactive participation overflows the logical procedures of formal democracy." "Moving towards a world of lasting peace and justice calls us to go beyond paternalistic forms of assistance; it calls us to create new forms of participation that include popular movements and invigorate local, national and international governing structures with that torrent of moral energy that springs from including the excluded in the building of a common destiny. And all this with a constructive spirit, without resentment, with love." It involves the establishment of genuine solidarity: "Solidarity . . . means fighting against the structural causes of poverty and inequality, of the lack of work, land and housing; and of the denial of social and labour rights. . . . Solidarity, understood in its deepest sense, is a way of making history." This, he said, is what the people's movements are doing.

In the light of his quite radical remarks we can see why Francis said to these activists: "It is strange but, if I talk about this, some say that the Pope is communist." Rejecting this accusation strongly, he insisted that love for the poor is a central element of the gospel, that the things the activists

---

[3] Gerry O'Hanlon rightly reminds us that "not everything that the pope says is to be taken as carrying equal weight" (O'Hanlon 2015, 29). So the words of Francis in this speech do not have the same formal authority as the words of an encyclical. Nevertheless, this address was not just an informal and spontaneous set of remarks but was clearly part of the pope's formal teaching and was treated as such on the Vatican website. The address must be seen as a clear indication of the pope's strongly held belief in the need for radical initiatives and struggle by social activists.

are struggling for—land, housing, and work—are sacred rights, and that there is nothing unusual about making this claim, since it is simply part of the social teaching of the church (*Movements*).[4]

Many people wondered whether Francis would repeat his outspoken condemnation of the abuses of capitalism in the course of his visit to the United States. In fact, in his address to the joint session of the Congress on September 24, 2015, the tone of his remarks was quite different, and his overall approach was carefully calculated to appeal to his audience. Nevertheless, he succeeded in getting across the key points of his position. He shrewdly quoted a passage about business from his own encyclical in which he had pointed out that business must serve the common good:

> Business is a noble vocation, directed to producing wealth and improving the world. It can be a fruitful source of prosperity for the area in which it operates, especially if it sees the creation of jobs as an essential part of its service to the common good. (*Laudato Si'* 129)

Pope Francis did not hesitate to use the controversial phrase "unjust structures," pointing out, "Even in the developed world, the effects of unjust structures and actions are all too apparent." He quoted from the Declaration of Independence, adding at once, "If politics must truly be at the service of the human person, it follows that it cannot be a slave to the economy and finance." Politics, he said, must serve the common good "of a community which sacrifices particular interests in order to share, in justice and peace, its goods, its interests, its social life." In this way he made it clear that he was not backing down from his condemnation of a type of unregulated capitalism that exploits people and the environment and thus fails to serve the common good. In a carefully nuanced passage he said: "I would encourage you to keep in mind all those people around us who are trapped in a cycle of poverty. They too need to be given hope. The fight against poverty and hunger must be fought constantly and on many fronts, especially in its causes." By emphasizing the causes of poverty, he was diplomatically reminding the audience of his strong condemnation in his encyclical of "the deified market" (*LS* 56).

INEQUALITY IN SOCIETY AND RELATIVE POVERTY

Francis shows that he is well aware that Western politicians often defend the present economic order on the grounds that at least it has led to a

---

[4]For my account of an important follow-up address which Francis gave in Bolivia on July 9, 2015, to this group of activists see the final pages of the following chapter.

reduction in the level of absolute poverty in most of the poorer countries. His response is unequivocal: "If on the one hand we are seeing a reduction in absolute poverty, on the other hand we cannot fail to recognize that there is a serious rise in relative poverty, that is, instances of inequality between people and groups who live together in particular regions or in a determined historical-cultural context" (Peace Message 2014 §5). It is clear that he is calling for the elimination or major reduction in relative poverty as well as absolute poverty, for he says, "Inequality is the root of social ills" (*EG* 202).

As I pointed out in chapter 4, there is scientific research that provides solid support for this statement of Pope Francis (see Wilkinson and Pickett 2010 passim; cf. Dorling 2014 passim). Furthermore, recent groundbreaking research by Thomas Piketty has shown the relevance of the pope's concern about the growth in relative poverty. Piketty's historical study puts forward a convincing case in favor of the view that down through history the capitalist system has tended to widen the gap between the rich and the poor,[5] except when this economic pattern has been broken by a political policy of having progressive taxes or by such exceptional events as major revolutions or wars. His detailed study documents the remarkable extent to which, particularly in the United States and Britain, there has been a major reduction in progressive tax rates in the period between 1980 and the present (e.g., Piketty 2014, 499, figure 14.1; 508–12). This has given rise to an alarming widening of the gap between the very rich and the rest of the population.

I venture to add that Piketty's explanation of the widening gap between the rich and the poor was focused almost entirely on economic patterns. But one should also take account of the political reasons for the widening gap: those who have economic power generally use their wealth both to influence politicians through lobbyists and to gain control of the media. In this way they ensure that political policies favor their interests and that large sections of the popular media fail to expose the close links between politicians and wealthy individuals or corporations.

Piketty holds that the only effective ways in which the widening gap between rich and poor can be bridged is by the introduction of seriously progressive taxation on income and a global tax on capital or wealth (Piketty 2014, 512–13; 515–30; 572; 640n51). He says that "without a global tax on capital or some similar policy, there is a substantial risk that the top centile's share of global wealth will continue to grow indefinitely—and this should worry everyone" (519).[6] Far more detailed proposals for reduc-

---

[5]The basic reason for this, according to Piketty, is that, apart from exceptional situations, the share of income generated by capital has always tended to be greater than that which is earned by labor.

[6]As one might have expected, Piketty's study stirred up a lot of controversy. Quite a

ing inequality are spelled out by Anthony Atkinson, whose study focuses mainly on the situation in the United States and Britain. If implemented, his fifteen key proposals would have the effect of bringing about a radical reduction in the gap between the rich and the poor (Atkinson 2015 passim; summarized on pp. 303–4). They include a statutory minimum wage set at the level of a living wage, guaranteed public employment at the minimum wage for those who seek it, a progressive rate of income tax up to a top rate of 65 percent, and substantial child benefits. However, Piketty expresses his regret that in Atkinson's study "the space devoted to international matters is relatively limited" (Piketty 2015, 28).

The proposals put forward by Piketty and Atkinson could be implemented without seriously disrupting the effective economic working of society at the national and international levels; in fact, they would greatly lessen the looming danger of a spiral that may lead to another major economic collapse. From the point of view of Catholic social teaching, perhaps the most valuable aspect of Piketty's and Atkinson's proposals are that they represent ways of realistically "putting flesh on" demands by Pope Francis and other concerned people for structural change. In the absence of grounded studies such as those of Atkinson and Piketty, one might easily have assumed that the call for structural change in the political-economic structures of society was equivalent to a call to establish some kind of socialist system. What these authors offer is a realistic way of restructuring the present free-market system without overthrowing it entirely. So it may appeal to those who fear that Pope Francis's outspoken criticism of the present world order means that he is in favor of a socialist system.

However, immensely powerful forces resist the kind of changes proposed by Piketty and many others: very rich individuals and corporations have enormous power in both the political field and in the media. Furthermore, the present level of international cooperation in regard to taxes and the elimination of tax havens is grossly inadequate. It is for this reason that Piketty acknowledges: "A global tax on capital is a utopian idea" (Piketty 2014, 515). Nevertheless, he goes on to say that "it is perfectly possible to move toward this ideal solution step by step" (515). This provides an incentive for Catholics to cooperate closely with other Christians, people of other religions, and all who are committed to working for justice in society to build a strong coalition that will campaign effectively for the necessary changes. In this, as on several other apparently "unrealistic"

---

number of conservative economists and commentators attacked his findings on various grounds, while many others rallied to his defense. Having examined a representative sample of this material, I have come to believe that, although the critics have located some relatively minor inadequacies in his study, on the whole Piketty's conclusions and proposals remain valid.

aspects of Catholic social teaching, we must "hope against hope," holding on to our belief that sustained human commitment, fortified by divine grace, can bring about what had seemed virtually impossible.

TRAFFICKING: MODERN SLAVERY

One of the ways in which Pope Francis's teaching has addressed current justice issues in our present-day world is the prominence he has given to the issue of trafficking of persons. In two places in *Evangelii Gaudium* he put this modern version of slavery at the top of the list of social evils which he mentioned (*EG* 75, 211). One has the sense that he was speaking in the light of his own experience of personal contact with the victims of trafficking when he made an impassioned plea and challenge: "Where is your brother or sister who is enslaved? . . . Let us not look the other way. There is greater complicity than we think. The issue involves everyone! This infamous network of crime is now well established in our cities, and many people have blood on their hands as a result of their comfortable and silent complicity" (*EG* 211).

Francis devoted almost the whole of his address to foreign diplomats on December 12, 2013, to the issue of trafficking. He said:

> There is one area I would like to consider with you which concerns me deeply and which currently threatens the dignity of persons, namely, human trafficking. Such trafficking is a true form of slavery, unfortunately more and more widespread, which concerns every country, even the most developed. It is a reality which affects the most vulnerable in society: women of all ages, children, the handicapped, the poorest, and those who come from broken families and from difficult situations in society.

He returned to this topic in his Peace Message 2014. In the first paragraph of that message he referred to "the tragic phenomenon of human trafficking, in which the unscrupulous prey on the lives and the desperation of others;" and in paragraph 8 he referred to "the abomination of human trafficking."

In August 2013 he asked the Pontifical Academies of Sciences and of the Social Sciences to convene a workshop to examine human trafficking and modern slavery. We may assume that one reason why he did this was that he knew the problem quite directly, having worked closely with those fighting human trafficking when he was archbishop in Buenos Aires. This gathering took place in the Vatican on November 2–3, 2013. It had originally been intended that it would include only scholars who had studied and written about this topic. But at the request of activists "on the ground," the invitation was extended to sixty "observers"—people who had practical experience of ministering to victims of trafficking. These observers were allowed to participate actively, and it was acknowledged that this provided an enriching experience for all the participants. The pope was particularly interested in what was going on at the conference, and afterward he engaged in dialogue with the activists. One of the participants was Detective Inspector Kevin Hyland of the London Metropolitan Police. He described a new and more effective program which had been put in place at Scotland Yard, one that enables the victims of trafficking to testify in court against the traffickers.

Two further developments on the trafficking issue took place within less than a month of each other in 2014. The first of these came on March 17 at the Vatican, when representatives from several of the great world religions signed what was called a "revolutionary and unprecedented" agreement called *"The Global Freedom Network."* They said: "Modern slavery and human trafficking are crimes against humanity," and they committed themselves to working together to eradicate modern forms of slavery and human trafficking by 2020.

The second development was a conference at the Vatican on April 9–10. This one brought together police and law enforcement officers from various parts of the world as well as social workers dealing with the victims of trafficking. They agreed to advance their international cooperation to combat the scourge of trafficking. In his address to the participants Pope Francis said:

> Human trafficking is an open wound on the body of contemporary society, a scourge upon the body of Christ. It is a crime against humanity. The very fact of our being here to combine our efforts means that we want our strategies and areas of expertise to be accompanied and reinforced by the mercy of the Gospel, by closeness to the men and women who are victims of this crime.

Just before his address to the participants, the pope held a private meeting with four rescued victims of human trafficking, two from Eastern Europe and two from South America. Following on from that gathering the Vatican has hosted further conferences on trafficking.

Francis returned to the issue of trafficking in his "Message for World Day of Migrants and Refugees 2016," issued on September 12, 2015. And at two points of his address to the General Assembly of the United Nations on September 25, 2015, Francis spoke out strongly against the evil of trafficking in persons.

JUSTICE AND CHARITY

Popes are invariably too diplomatic to reject overtly a teaching espoused by an immediate predecessor. However, it appears that on one major issue Pope Francis has adopted a position that is quite distinctly different, at least in emphasis, from that of Benedict XVI. That issue is the Church's stance in relation to charity and justice—an issue that has important practical implications.

As I pointed out in an earlier chapter, Pope Benedict had insisted that the official church has only an indirect involvement in the promotion of justice in the world but that charity is a direct and essential element in the life of the church. He seemed to be proposing that official Catholic relief and development agencies should concentrate particularly on giving immediate charitable relief in emergency situations rather than supporting people's struggles for justice and long-term human development. Furthermore, he mandated the Vatican agency Cor Unum to exercise effective control over Caritas Internationalis, which is a network of 164 Caritas agencies in practically every country in the world. This downgrading of Caritas Internationalis would mean that this decentralized and participatory network would now be under the direct control of a highly conservative agency in the Roman curia. This would seriously undermine the ethos and daily practice of the on-the-ground Catholic development agencies all over the world.

Pope Francis did not explicitly repudiate this initiative of his predecessor. But it is significant that Cardinal Oscar Andrés Rodríguez Maradiaga, who was at that time the president of Caritas Internationalis, was the person Francis chose as the chair of his body of eight cardinal advisers. And it was hardly a coincidence that the pope himself, in a video on December 10, 2013, gave his strong explicit support to the launch of a major appeal by Caritas Internationalis: "I give all my support to the Caritas Internationalis campaign against world hunger. . . .We are facing a global scandal where nearly a billion people go hungry. We cannot turn the other way and pretend it does not exist." What is particularly notable is that the appeal to which the pope was giving his support included the following words of Cardinal Maradiaga:

The work of Caritas organizations on hunger ranges from providing food aid in times of crisis to longer-term programs improving small-scale agriculture, livestock breeding, infrastructure, agro-forestry and reforestation. Caritas also promotes civic participation on social and economic issues such as access to markets, nutrition, water and sanitation for vulnerable communities.

This means that Pope Francis was giving his strong support to Caritas programs concerned not just with emergency aid but with long-term human development.

The whole approach of Francis indicated that he had reverted to the traditional theology so well expressed by Saint Thomas Aquinas when he said that "charity [or love] is the form of all the virtues." What this means in practice is that it is a mistake to oppose charity to justice, since action in support of justice is itself a form of charity, taking the word "charity" in its broad sense. Providing charitable relief is, of course, one way in which individual Christians and the official church respond to the call to put their love into action; but so too are action on behalf of justice and long-term human development, defense of human rights, work to promote reconciliation, and action to care for the environment. The statements and documents of Francis give no indication that he believes that charitable relief is more central or important than any of these other activities in the life of the Church and of Christians.

JUSTICE IN THE CHURCH

From the point of view of everyday Church life, the biggest change of emphasis by Pope Francis is the generous spirit in which he maintained that Catholic social teaching, as well as other Catholic teaching, should be applied in everyday living. But there is also a change in emphasis in regard to the actual content of this teaching. In this regard the overarching contribution of Francis is his renewed emphasis on all that Vatican II stood for. In the years between 1985 and 2013 the Roman authorities had frequently invoked Vatican II but had in fact engaged in a consistent attempt to play down its originality. Indeed, in some respects they had acted quite contrary to the direction proposed by the Council; one thinks particularly of the ever-increasing centralization of power in the Roman curia with the consequent undermining of the concept of episcopal collegiality. From the moment when he became pope, Francis repeatedly affirmed his commitment to the vision of Vatican II.

When historians look back on the pontificate of Francis they may well conclude that the area in which his contribution to Catholic social teaching on justice was most effective in practice was in his commitment to applying that teaching to the Church itself. From the beginning of his papacy he was evidently determined to make an option for those who could be seen as the poor in relation to the institutional Church—that is, those who had been left in a disadvantaged or marginal position, ranging from laypeople vis-à-vis clergy, up to bishops' conferences and diocesan bishops vis-à-vis Vatican curia officials. He began to put into practice the fundamental principle of subsidiarity by implementing the Council's teaching on collegiality.

It is significant that Francis quotes from the important document *Octogesima Adveniens* (*OA*), which Paul VI had issued in 1971. The passage that Francis quotes is one in which Pope Paul pointed to the variety of different situations faced by the church in different parts of the world and said: "In the face of such widely varying situations, it is difficult for us to utter a unified message and to put forward a solution which has universal validity. . . . It is up to the Christian communities to analyze with objectivity the situation which is proper to their own country" (*OA* no. 4, quoted by Francis in *EG* 184). The commitment of Paul VI to govern the Church in a collegial manner had been largely ignored by Pope John Paul II and by Pope Benedict, and perhaps more particularly by the Vatican curia in the intervening years. Francis was now pledging to put collegiality into practice. One of the most important ways in which Francis proposed to take seriously the emphasis of Vatican II on collegiality was by enabling the Synod of Bishops to play the major role envisaged by the Council. This was shown by his calling of a two-phase synod, held in the autumn of 2014 and of 2015, and by his insistence on the importance of genuine dialogue and even disagreement among the synod participants (e.g., his "introductory remarks" to the Synod Fathers on October 5, 2015).

Before Pope Francis, when people wished to invoke the principle of subsidiarity, they were told bluntly by the Roman authorities that the principle applied in civil and political society but not in the Church. Francis, on the other hand, says in *Evangelii Gaudium*: "I am conscious of the need to promote a sound 'decentralization'" (*EG* 16). Later in this manifesto document he goes on to say, "In the dialogue with our Orthodox brothers and sisters, we Catholics have the opportunity to learn more about the meaning of episcopal collegiality and their experience of synodality" (*EG* 246). He even goes so far as to make statements that must have seemed quite shocking to many in the Vatican: "Since I am called to put into practice what I ask of others, I too must think about a conversion of the papacy. . . . The papacy and the central structures of the universal Church also need to hear the call to pastoral conversion. . . . Excessive centralization, rather than proving helpful, complicates the Church's life and her missionary outreach" (*EG* 26). In this context he proposes that episcopal conferences should have a juridical status so that they can have "genuine doctrinal authority" (*EG* 26). Francis made it clear that he wanted to undo the severe limitations that had been imposed on the effective authority of episcopal conferences by the 1998 *motu proprio Apostolos Suos* of Pope John Paul.

On October 17, 2015, Francis gave an important and radical address at a ceremony commemorating the fiftieth anniversary of the institution of the Synod of Bishops. In it he put forward the image of the Church as "an inverted pyramid, [where] the top is located beneath the base." He went on to say:

> The first level of the exercise of *synodality* is had in the particular Churches . . . the presbyteral council, the college of consultors, chapters of canons and the pastoral council. Only to the extent that these organizations keep connected to the "base" and start from people and their daily problems, can a synodal Church begin to take shape.

He went on at once to emphasize the importance of developing what he called "intermediary instances of *collegiality*" at the level of ecclesiastical provinces, regions, and conferences of bishops, "perhaps by integrating and updating certain aspects of the ancient ecclesiastical organization." He said that the hope of the Vatican Council "that such bodies would help to increase the spirit of episcopal *collegiality* has not yet been fully realized." And he repeated the call he had already made in *Evangelii Gaudium* for "a sound 'decentralization.'" He followed this by saying:

> I am persuaded that in a synodal Church, greater light can be shed on the exercise of the Petrine primacy. The Pope is not, by himself, above the Church; but within it as one of the baptized, and within the College of Bishops as a Bishop among Bishops, called at the same time—as Successor of Peter—to lead the Church of Rome which presides in charity over all the Churches.

In these statements, and in a variety of widely quoted *obiter dicta* in which he overtly or tacitly acknowledged that some Vatican curia officials had overstepped the mark, Francis was clearly recognizing that Catholic social teaching must apply not just to civil and political society but also to the church itself. In this regard it is hard to avoid the conclusion that he was deliberately reaffirming the strong stance on issues of justice within the church taken at the 1971 Synod of Bishops—a synod whose teaching Vatican officials had ignored for forty years.

This firm commitment to the principles of subsidiarity and collegiality is closely linked to the frequently repeated condemnation by Francis of clericalism.[7] Francis rehabilitated the Vatican II term "people of God" which had fallen out of favor among Vatican people in the previous twenty years; and he committed himself to giving "the people of God" an effec-

---

[7]See, for instance, his letter of January 12, 2014, to the new cardinals and his uncompromising speech to the members of the Roman curia on December 22, 2014.

tive role in decision making and to working with others to bring about changes in Church structures and practices that will reflect this equality.

RADICAL

Paul Vallely, whose *Untying the Knots* is an insightful book about Pope Francis, wrote an interesting article[8] in which he outlined the stance of Pope Francis on three distinct issues where there are sharp differences of opinion within the Catholic Church. On the left-right division about whether or to what extent one accepts capitalism, Vallely sees Francis as being quite far to the left. On the issue of centralization versus decentralization and subsidiarity, he sees Francis as being quite radical. And on the progressive-conservative division on doctrinal questions, he notes the nuanced pastoral approach of Francis. Needless to say, it is not possible to sum up all the nuances of Francis's views in just a few lines. But Vallely's summary is quite perceptive, and the various quotations and references given above provide solid support for his view. I would venture to add that the teaching of Pope Francis on solidarity with the poor and option for the poor has a truly prophetic quality and represents a major contribution to Catholic social teaching.

* * *

SUMMARY

Pope Francis bluntly condemns the present inadequately regulated capitalist system, accusing it of treating poor people as if they are of no importance. Aware that the system creates a widening gap between rich and poor, he has spoken out not just against absolute poverty but also against relative poverty, saying that "inequality is the root of social evils." He calls both for structural change and for personal conversion. He has adopted the type of spirituality advocated by liberation theologians, insisting that religious leaders and pastors must be in close touch with those on the margins; they need to be acquainted with the experience of the marginalized and allow themselves to be evangelized by poor people. Pope Francis welcomed warmly the social activists who are working to empower poor and marginalized people to struggle for justice. He has spoken out strongly against the evil of human trafficking and has played a key role in action against it. He has been supportive of the develop-

---

[8] *Irish Times*, February 4, 2014.

ment and justice work of the Caritas agencies. One of the most important contributions which Francis has made to Catholic teaching on justice is his commitment to structural justice in the Church itself, above all in the manner in which the papacy exercises authority. He has initiated a process of greater collegiality in line with the intention of Vatican II.

QUESTIONS FOR REVIEW

1. *Is Pope Francis's condemnation of unregulated capitalism different in any significant way from that of previous popes?*
2. *In his address to the US Congress, did Francis give a different message about capitalism?*
3. *What is the difference between absolute poverty and relative poverty?*
4. *Where does Pope Francis stand in relation to liberation theology?*
5. *What actions has Pope Francis taken to combat human trafficking?*
6. *What is the relationship between justice and charity?*
7. *What significant changes has Pope Francis implemented in the way the Church is governed?*

QUESTION FOR REFLECTION

1. *Does the present understanding of "absolute poverty" take sufficient account of the widely different situations in which people live?*

ISSUES FOR FURTHER STUDY

1. *The understanding of synodality in the Eastern Churches.*
2. *The radical ministry of Jesus as described in Pagola 2009.*

20

Ecology in the Teaching of Pope Francis

There are four sections in this chapter. In the first section I give an account of the main elements in the teaching of Pope Francis prior to the publication of his encyclical on ecology. In the second section I pick out what I see as the key points in the encyclical itself. In the third section I offer a commentary and evaluation of the encyclical. The final section is a rather brief follow-up in which I take account of some important statements made by Francis in the four months after his encyclical was published.

NEW EMPHASIS ON ECOLOGY

From the very beginning of his papacy Francis showed a particular concern for the environment. On March 16, 2013, just three days after he had been elected, he told journalists that he had chosen the name of Francis of Assisi, because "Francis was a man of poverty, who loved and protected creation." Three days later, he linked protection of people with protection of the environment, pointing out that being a protector "means protecting all creation, the beauty of the created world"; and he added: "Everything has been entrusted to our protection, and all of us are responsible for it." His linking of concern for the exploited Earth with concern for victims and for marginalized and exploited people has been a consistent theme. It is clear, then, that for Francis, the word "solidarity" has an expanded range of meaning. He invites us not merely to be in solidarity with excluded and fragile humans, but also with nonhuman creatures and the whole of the fragile ecosystem.

On June 5, 2013, UN World Environment Day, Francis devoted his General Audience message to this topic. Condemning "consumerism" and a "culture of waste," he called for "a spirit of solidarity grounded in our common responsibility for the earth and for all our brothers and sisters in the human family." He spoke of the importance of holding on to an attitude of wonder, contemplation, and listening to creation. Then, as on previous occasions, he called for people "to respect and care for creation, to be attentive to every person, to oppose the culture of wastefulness and waste, and to promote a culture of solidarity and encounter." In his *Urbi et Orbi* message on Easter Sunday 2013, he said, "Let us be . . . channels through which God can water the earth, protect all creation and make justice and peace flourish." Fifteen months later, on September 21, 2014, during his address to civil authorities in Tirana, Albania, he again linked human solidarity with respect for creation: "Alongside the globalization of the markets there must also be a corresponding globalization of solidarity; together with economic growth there must be a greater respect for creation."

In his address to the bishops of Brazil in July 2013, Francis recalled the gathering of the Latin American and Caribbean bishops in Aparecida which drew up the CELAM 2007 document, of which he was a major architect and which underscored the dangers facing the Amazon environment and the indigenous people living there. In this context he called for "respect and protection of the entire creation which God has entrusted to humanity." He went on to say that creation should not be "indiscriminately exploited but rather made into a garden." His address gave encouragement to indigenous people from the Amazon region, whom he met and who have been resisting the encroachment on the forest by ranchers, farmers, and agribusiness enterprises.

It may seem surprising that Francis devoted only a small section of *Evangelii Gaudium* to the topic of ecology. This was perhaps partly because that document was a response to what had emerged in the 2012 Synod of Bishops on the new evangelization, where the environment had not been a major issue. It may also be that the pope was holding back on this topic because of his intention to treat it much more comprehensively in an encyclical.

In *Evangelii Gaudium*, the pope's first reference to the topic of ecology comes when he says, "Whatever is fragile, like the environment, is defenseless before the interests of a deified market" (*EG* 56). Later in the document he says:

There are other weak and defenseless beings who are frequently at the mercy of economic interests or indiscriminate exploitation. I am speaking of creation as a whole. We human beings are not only the beneficiaries but also the stewards of other creatures. Thanks to our bodies, God has joined us so closely to the world around us that we can feel the desertification of the soil almost as a physical ailment, and the extinction of a species as a painful disfigurement.

Let us not leave in our wake a swathe of destruction and death which will affect our own lives and those of future generations. (*EG* 215)

He then says: "Small yet strong in the love of God, like Saint Francis of Assisi, all of us, as Christians, are called to watch over and protect the fragile world in which we live, and all its peoples" (*EG* 216).

Francis took up the topic, again rather briefly, in his "Peace Message 2014." He referred to "the devastation of natural resources and ongoing pollution" (§8). He then went on to repeat the emphasis of Benedict XVI, in his encyclical *Caritas in Veritate*, on nature as gift and his use of the phrase "the grammar of nature":

> The human family has received from the Creator a common gift: nature. The Christian view of creation includes a positive judgment about the legitimacy of interventions on nature if these are meant to be beneficial and are performed responsibly, that is to say, by acknowledging the "grammar" inscribed in nature and by wisely using resources for the benefit of all, with respect for the beauty, finality and usefulness of every living being and its place in the ecosystem. Nature, in a word, is at our disposition and we are called to exercise a responsible stewardship over it.

Francis pointed out that we are failing in the task of stewardship: "So often we are driven by greed and by the arrogance of dominion, possession, manipulation and exploitation; we do not preserve nature; nor do we respect it or consider it a gracious gift which we must care for and set at the service of our brothers and sisters, including future generations" (Peace Message 2014, §9).

In an address at the University of Molise on July 5, 2014, Pope Francis insisted that "one of the greatest challenges of our time [is] changing to a form of development which seeks to respect creation." He added: "This is our sin: exploiting the land and not allowing it to give us what it has within it, with our help through cultivation."

Francis came back to the issue of care for the Earth in the address he gave to the representatives of the people's movements at their gathering in Rome on October 28, 2014. The theme of that meeting was "Land, Housing [literally, *techo*, "a roof"], and Work." The pope said to them:

> There cannot be land, there cannot be housing, there cannot be work if we do not have peace and if we destroy the planet. These are such important topics that the peoples of the world and their popular organizations cannot fail to debate them. This cannot just remain in the hands of political leaders. All peoples of the earth, all men and

women of good will—all of us must raise our voices in defence of these two precious gifts: peace and nature or "Sister Mother Earth" as Saint Francis of Assisi called her.[1]

He pointed out that an economic system which has at its center the god of money makes it necessary also to plunder nature, in order to sustain the frenetic pattern of consumption which is an intrinsic aspect of the system.[2]

He continued: "Climate change, loss of biodiversity, and deforestation are already having the catastrophic effects which we are seeing; and it is you, the poor people who live in precarious dwellings near coasts, or who are so economically vulnerable, you are the ones who lose everything when a disaster strikes" (*Movements,* my translation). He went on to insist that creation is not an item of property that we can dispose of as we wish, still less a property owned or controlled by just a few people. On the contrary, it is a wonderful gift from God, entrusted to us to take care of and to use for the benefit of all. He concluded by promising his listeners that he would take account of their concerns about these issues in his forthcoming encyclical.

On May 6 and 7, 2015, Pope Francis and the Vatican endorsed a petition of the Global Catholic Climate Movement calling on world leaders to "keep the global temperature rise below the dangerous threshold of 1.5°C, and to aid the world's poorest in coping with climate change impacts."

In his homily at the Mass for the opening of the Caritas Internationalis General Assembly, May 12, 2015, Pope Francis said, "We must . . . remind the powerful of the earth that God will call them to judgment one day, and it will be seen if they truly tried to provide food for him in every person, and if they worked so that the environment would not be destroyed, but could produce this food."

In an address to the participants of the meeting of the Food and Agri-

---

[1] Address to the Participants in the World Meeting of Popular Movements, October 28, 2014, hereafter referred to as *Movements.*

[2] When Francis calls for a change in the present model of development, he is taking up once again his critique of the present dominant system that does so much damage to poor and fragile people and to the fragile environment. His outspoken protest against this type of so-called development—and of the unrestrained capitalism on which it is based—finds strong support in the powerful polemic of Naomi Klein's book *This Changes Everything: Capitalism vs. the Climate,* and the extensive research and documentation that she cites. She maintains that "there is a close correlation between low wages and high emissions" (Klein 2014, 81). She points out that "we have not done the things that are necessary to lower emissions because these things fundamentally conflict with unregulated capitalism . . . [and] are extremely threatening to an elite minority that has a stranglehold over our economy, our political process, and most of our major media outlets" (Klein 2014, 18). Robert Manne (2015) shrewdly notes that Francis's position has much in common with that of Naomi Klein, but "while the revolution Klein looks for is political and economic . . . the revolution that Francis's vision requires is cultural and spiritual."

culture Organization (FAO) on June 11, 2015, Francis pointed to a serious imbalance or injustice that has emerged in recent times in the use of many agricultural products. Instead of being used to meet the basic need of poor people for food, they are instead being used to produce biofuels or to feed animals.

In various statements and comments in the period leading up to the promulgation of his encyclical on the ecology, Francis suggested that his understanding of the term "human ecology" is subtly but significantly different from that of John Paul and Benedict. Rather than making a sharp contrast between "human ecology" and "natural ecology," he made a very close link on several occasions between exploited people and the exploited environment, describing both of them as "fragile" or "defenseless" (see, for instance, *EG* 56 and 215). He did not set humans over against the rest of the natural environment. Instead, he interprets the term "human ecology" as one that focuses mainly on the responsibility of humans to protect creation in all its manifestations. This would involve giving the term "human ecology" a wide meaning similar to what it has in the social sciences. So it would mean that the pope would be situating us humans and our relationships within the context of our diverse social and cultural environments and, more especially, of our situation as an integral part of the whole evolving natural order.

The increased emphasis of Francis on respect for the environment was reflected in various Vatican-based agencies. For instance, on May 2–6, 2014, an important joint workshop of the Pontifical Academy of Sciences and the Pontifical Academy of Social Sciences was held in the Vatican, under the title "Sustainable Humanity, Sustainable Nature: Our Responsibility." In his opening address to this conference Cardinal Maradiaga said: "Only through universal unitedness between men, animals, plants, and things will we be able to push aside the conceit of our race—which has come to think of itself as the despotic ruler of Creation—and turn it into the elder brother of all of its fellow creatures." The Final Statement of the Conference included this sentence: "Today we need a relationship of mutual benefit: true values should permeate the economy and respect for Creation should promote human dignity and well-being."

On September 21, 2014, the Interfaith Climate Summit held in New York issued a strong statement that was signed by representatives of a wide range of representatives from the religions of the world, including Cardinal Maradiaga (representing Caritas Internationalis) and Father Michael Czerny, SJ (representing the Pontifical Council for Justice and Peace). The statement included the following words:

> As representatives from different faith and religious traditions, we
> . . . acknowledge the overwhelming scientific evidence that climate

change is human-induced. . . . When those who have done the least to cause climate change are the ones hardest hit, it becomes an issue of injustice. . . . We recognize that climate change stands today as a major obstacle to the eradication of poverty.

The signatories went on to insist that the burden of limiting global warming to well below 2 degrees Celsius should be distributed "in an equitable way."

Pope Francis met with UN Secretary General Ban Ki-moon before a summit conference of religious, political, and business leaders, scientists, and development practitioners held in the Vatican on April 28, 2015, under the title "Protect the Earth, Dignify Humanity: The Moral Dimensions of Climate Change and Sustainable Development." The aim was to "build a consensus that the values of sustainable development cohere with values of the leading religious traditions, with a special focus on the most vulnerable." Opening the conference, Ban Ki-moon said: "The reason I am coming to the pope is that now I need moral support." The final declaration said:

Human-induced climate change is a scientific reality, and its decisive mitigation is a moral and religious imperative for humanity. In this core moral space, the world's religions play a very vital role. These traditions all affirm . . . the beauty, wonder, and inherent goodness of the natural world, and appreciate that it is a precious gift entrusted to our common care, making it our moral duty to respect rather than ravage the garden that is our home. The poor and excluded face dire threats from climate disruptions, including the increased frequency of droughts, extreme storms, heat waves, and rising sea levels.

THE ECOLOGY ENCYCLICAL *LAUDATO SI'* ON THE CARE OF OUR COMMON HOME

Laudato Si', the encyclical of Pope Francis on ecology, is the first fully comprehensive treatment of environmental issues issued by the Vatican. The encyclical locates humans as an integral part of nature and calls for what Francis calls "an integral ecology." The document is original both in content and in style. In it Francis enters into dialogue with other Christians, with people of other religions, with humanists, scientists, and politicians—inviting and challenging people everywhere to share his broad perspective on the role of humans in care for the Earth and all its inhabitants. The encyclical shows that he has the courage to be controversial and challenging while maintaining a respectful and irenic posture.

His Sources

I begin by noting a point that was overlooked in much of the original spate of comments on the encyclical. It concerns the *sources* that Francis has drawn on. He quotes from the ecological reflections published by Conferences of Bishops from Bolivia, Brazil, Paraguay, Mexico, Argentina, Dominican Republic, the United States, Canada, South Africa, Australia, New Zealand, Japan, Germany, and Portugal. In doing this he shows that he has not forgotten his commitment to exercising a collegial style of government and teaching in the Church, rather than having everything handed down from the Vatican. He takes account particularly of the documents issued by Church leaders who have been addressing real-life justice and ecological problems "on the ground" in their particular regions.

In the opening section Francis quotes five different passages from a variety of statements of the Orthodox Patriarch Bartholomew (*LS* 8, 9). This is highly unusual in a Vatican document and is a clear indication both of Francis's commitment to church unity and his conviction that the pope and the Catholic Church have much to learn from others. Even more unusual and radical is that Francis quotes the words of a Sufi mystic, the ninth-century Muslim poet Ali al-Khawas (*LS* n159). In this way Francis underlines his respect for other religions and his belief that religious people of all persuasions need to work together on issues of ecology and justice (cf. *LS* 201). Furthermore, in sharp contrast to previous Vatican statements, he praises the work of the worldwide ecological movement (*LS* 14), in which leading roles are played by people who have little or no time for formal religion. Later in the encyclical he quotes from what he calls "the courageous challenge" of the Earth Charter (*LS* 207).

Mistreatment of "Our Common Home"

It is fairly widely known that in the first draft of the encyclical, which was prepared by a team under the direction of Cardinal Peter Turkson of Ghana, the first chapter was devoted to a scriptural theology of creation. But Francis has changed the order of the material; he follows the pattern of the Spiritual Exercises of the Jesuit founder Saint Ignatius, which starts with meditations on our sinfulness. So, before describing a biblical ecological spirituality, and before spelling out what is involved in an ecological conversion, he invites us first to reflect on the sinful way we are despoiling and neglecting our world.

Already in the introductory paragraphs of the encyclical Francis reminds us of "the violence in our hearts, wounded by sin," which has led us to harm "our Sister, Mother Earth" "by our irresponsible use and abuse of the goods with which God has endowed her" (*LS* 1, 2). Then, in the first full chapter he puts forward a detailed account of the damage we are doing to what the subtitle of the encyclical calls "our common home." (Perhaps a better English translation would have been "our *shared* home"—a home that we share with the other creatures of this world.) Francis outlines the different environmental problems that we face. His account is solidly based on the consensus view of the great majority of reputable scientists. And, as Fritjof Capra notes, "throughout the document, Pope Francis uses contemporary scientific language with complete ease" (Capra 2015).[3] While acknowledging that some environmental changes are caused naturally, he does not hesitate to challenge the climate-change deniers and skeptics, insisting that human activity is the main cause of the problems.

Francis spells out the problems caused by climate change due to global warming. These include melting glaciers, rising sea levels, acidification of the oceans, and extreme weather events such as droughts and floods (*LS* 23–28). He points out that it is the poorest people who suffer most from these problems (*LS* 48) even though they are the ones who have done the least to cause the problems.

There is also a lengthy account of a second major environmental issue, namely, pollution of indoor and outdoor air, of the land, fresh water, and the oceans (*LS* 20–42). Francis says: "Each year hundreds of millions of tons of waste are generated, much of it non-biodegradable, highly toxic and radioactive, from homes and businesses, from construction and de-molition sites, from clinical, electronic and industrial sources. The earth, our home, is beginning to look more and more like an immense pile of filth" (*LS* 21).

Closely related to the issue of pollution is the problem of waste. This is an ecological problem not only because of the pollution it causes but also because we are using up the precious resources of the Earth at an unsustainable rate. Francis says: "The pace of consumption, waste and environmental change has so stretched the planet's capacity that our contemporary lifestyle, unsustainable as it is, can only precipitate catastrophes, such as those which even now periodically occur in different areas of the world" (*LS* 161). He contrasts the kind of recycling that is part of natural ecosystems with the failure of our industrial system, which "has not developed the capacity to absorb and reuse waste and by-products. We have not yet managed to adopt a circular model of production capable of preserving resources for present and future generations" (*LS* 22). Francis is particularly concerned about the generation of waste by rich

---

[3]Capra (2015) suggests that the success of Francis in accurately reflecting the consensus of scientists on climate change is probably due to the fact that Hans Joachim Schellnhuber, one of the world's leading climate scientists "was a key scientific adviser to the Pope for many months during the drafting of *Laudato Si'*."

countries and rich people. He points out that "approximately a third of all food produced is discarded, and 'whenever food is thrown out it is as if it were stolen from the table of the poor'" (*LS* 50). So he protests against the consumerist "use and throw away," which now generates so much waste (*LS* 123).

Another topic that is treated extensively in the encyclical is the loss of biodiversity (*LS* 24, 32–42, 167, 169, 190, 195). Francis maintains that a major cause of this loss is the modern mentality that sees the animals and the plants simply as resources, there to be exploited (*LS* 33).

Francis maintains that concern for the environment and concern for the poorest in our world are intimately linked. He insists repeatedly that the damage we are doing to the environment affects poor people most severely. He calls on us to "hear both the cry of the earth and the cry of the poor" (*LS* 49). So he takes a strong stand alongside the many campaigners for eco-justice, insisting that we must integrate justice into environmental discussions.

A Contemplative Spirituality

In a particularly important paragraph toward the end of the encyclical, Francis says that the ecological crisis is a summons to "profound interior conversion." He goes on at once to add:

> It must be said that some committed and prayerful Christians, with the excuse of realism and pragmatism, tend to ridicule expressions of concern for the environment. Others are passive; they choose not to change their habits and thus become inconsistent. So what they all need is an "*ecological conversion*," whereby the effects of their encounter with Jesus Christ become evident in their relationship with the world around them. (LS 217, emphasis added)[4]

At the heart of the new "ecological spirituality" (*LS* 216), which is the fruit of an ecological conversion, is a contemplative nature-based quasi mysticism (cf. Michaelson 2015)—a quite radical alternative to the activism that is so characteristic of most Western Christian spirituality. We are invited to be fully present to nature, to the scenery and the seasons, to the lilies of the field and the birds of the air (*LS* 226). A contemplative approach enables us to "be serenely present to each reality" (*LS* 222)—including, of course, each person with whom we come into contact.

---

[4]We should note, however, that this order may be reversed: an ecological conversion may be precipitated by a person's contemplative encounter with the natural world and this may lead on to a turning (or returning) to Jesus.

In the introductory section of the encyclical Francis reminds us that he took Saint Francis of Assisi as his "guide and inspiration" when he was elected Bishop of Rome (*LS* 10). In describing the relationship that Saint Francis had with nature, he says that it is just like "when we fall in love with someone" (*LS* 11). He is inviting us to have an intimate loving and tender relationship with the creatures and the world around us. He wants us not to approach them in a confrontational way, trying to squeeze them dry (*LS* 106). We should rather see them as gifts: "Creation can only be understood as a gift from the outstretched hand of the Father of all" (*LS* 76; cf. *LS* 5, 71, 146, 155, 159, 220, 226, 227).

A key phrase for Francis is "everything is connected" (*LS* 91, 117; cf. "everything is interconnected," *LS* 70). Ecological activists express this idea by referring to "the web of life" and the wider "web of the cosmos." The point of this image of a web is that when one touches any part of a web, the movement extends to every part of the web. Francis does not use this image, but it conveys what he has in mind. It is not surprising, then, that he says, "We do not look at the world from without but from within" (*LS* 220). We are an integral part of the web of life and of the cosmos; our bodies are composed of molecules that are billions of years old; and when we die these are "recycled" into other parts of the web. Francis speaks of "a loving awareness that we are not disconnected from the rest of creatures, but joined in a splendid universal communion" (*LS* 220). The word "splendid" is particularly appropriate since it suggests that the communion is not merely superlative but also has the quality of being marvellous and even mysterious, more than we can fully comprehend.

Since we are in communion with the rest of nature, Francis draws a parallel between how we treat nature and how we treat humans: "A sense of deep communion with the rest of nature cannot be real if our hearts lack tenderness, compassion and concern for our fellow human beings" (*LS* 91). Later in the encyclical he says: "We are speaking of an attitude of the heart, one which approaches life with serene attentiveness, which is capable of being fully present to someone without thinking of what comes next" (*LS* 226).

The attitude of being in love with every aspect of the natural world lies at the very heart of the quasi-mystical kind of ecological spirituality that Francis is advocating. It is clear that he realizes that it is love that will inspire and impel us to change our ecological behavior, whereas guilt is a poor motivator—it often causes us to bury our heads in the sand.

The distinctive type of nature-mysticism favored by Francis involves two levels of transcendence. In the first level of transcendence we recover "a capacity for wonder which takes us to a deeper understanding of life" (*LS* 225). Our spirituality is deepened and transformed:

This conversion calls for a number of attitudes which together foster a spirit of generous care, full of tenderness. First, it entails gratitude and gratuitousness, a recognition that the world is God's loving gift, and that we are called quietly to imitate his generosity in self-sacrifice and good works. . . . It also entails a loving awareness that we are not disconnected from the rest of creatures, but joined in a splendid universal communion. As believers, we do not look at the world from without but from within, conscious of the bonds with which the Father has linked us to all beings. (*LS 220*)

So we experience "a serene harmony with creation," where we are no longer clogged up by "frenetic activity" (*LS 225*), by busyness and the "constant flood of new consumer goods [which] can baffle the heart and prevent us from cherishing each thing and each moment" (*LS 222*; cf. *LS 113*). This brings about a liberation from worries and calculations about the future or the past. It is an attitude which is beautifully expressed by Jesus in his advice: "Do not worry, saying, 'What shall we eat?' or 'What shall we drink?' or 'What shall we wear?' " (Matt. 6: 31). Francis points out that it is related to a mentality adopted by those who "take up an ancient lesson, found in different religious traditions and also in the Bible, . . . the conviction that 'less is more' " (*LS 222*).

This mystical spirituality can also lead to a further, deeper, level of transcendence. It comes when we experience not only the gifts of God but also *experience God in the gifts.* So our contact with the people and the nonhuman creatures around us can be a means or channel for coming in touch with God. Pope Francis says: "The ideal is not only to pass from the exterior to the interior to discover the action of God in the soul, but also to discover God in all things" (*LS 233*). We experience each creature as an occasion for raising our voices with Saint Francis of Assisi in praise both of the gift of the other and of God, the ultimate Other whom we dimly experience *in* and *through* these gifts of nature.

Praised be you, my Lord, with all your creatures, . . .
    through Sister Moon and the stars,
    and *through* the air, cloudy and serene, and every kind of weather.
(LS 87 emphasis added)

Pope Francis reminds us that we humans are not the only ones who praise God. Other parts of nature are so close to us, so similar to us, that they too can be seen as praising God in their own way. He says: "The Psalms . . . also invite other creatures to join us in this praise: 'Praise him, sun and moon, praise him, all you shining stars! Praise him, you highest heavens, and you waters above the heavens! Let them praise the name of the Lord' " (*LS* 72).

An Ecological Conversion in Theology

Francis insists that concern for the environment is central to the Christian faith—"not an optional or a secondary aspect of our Christian experience" (*LS* 217). This is the fundamental basis for an ecological conversion.

Following from this, Francis puts forward his concept of "an integral ecology" and develops a whole theology centered on this term. Both John Paul and Benedict were inclined at times to put the emphasis on the *difference* between humans and other creatures, setting "human ecology" over against a so-called "physical ecology" or "natural ecology" (e.g., *Centesimus Annus* 38). Francis, by contrast, highlights all that we humans have in common with the rest of creation. He says, for instance, "A good part of our genetic code is shared by many living beings. . . . Nature cannot be regarded as something separate from ourselves or as a mere setting in which we live. We are part of nature, included in it" (*LS* 138–39).

Francis uses the term "integral ecology" eight times in the course of the encyclical (*LS* 10, 11, 62, 124, 137, 159, 225, 230). One important aspect of his understanding of this term is that it represents a move away from the anthropocentric thrust of Catholic social teaching during the period from Vatican II up to the coming of Pope Francis in 2013. As I pointed out in chapter 18, nonhuman creatures were generally seen as valuable primarily in terms of their use for humans.[5] A crucial aspect of the theological change represented by *Laudato Si'* is the insistence by Francis that nonhuman creatures have value in their own right, intrinsic value (*LS* 33; cf. *LS* 69, 115, 118, 140, 190). Francis quotes Saint Thomas Aquinas, who wrote that God's goodness "could not be represented fittingly by any one creature" so God created many creatures in order that "what was wanting to one in the representation of the divine goodness might be supplied by another" (*LS* 86).

Use of the term "integral ecology" offers Francis a creative way of avoiding an explicit disagreement with the previous popes. Like them, he uses the term "human ecology," but for him it has a different connotation—one could almost say a different meaning—because it is situated within the wider context of an integral ecology. It refers to our responsibility for all

---

[5]In an exception to this, we should note a passage from the *Catechism* which Francis quotes in endnote 43: "Each of the various creatures, willed in its own being, reflects in its own way a ray of God's infinite wisdom and goodness."

aspects of our lives—political, social, economic, and cultural—and with particular reference to how our actions and whole way of life affects the Earth. It is not surprising then that Fritjof Capra says that "integral ecology" as used by the pope is equivalent to "systems thinking" (Capra 2015).

The term "integral ecology" has the advantage that it is broad enough to cover within its wide ambit the protection of the unborn, which was a major concern of Pope Benedict when he used the term "human ecology." Francis expresses this eloquently:

> Since everything is interrelated, concern for the protection of nature is also incompatible with the justification of abortion. How can we genuinely teach the importance of concern for other vulnerable beings, however troublesome or inconvenient they may be, if we fail to protect a human embryo, even when its presence is uncomfortable and creates difficulties? (*LS* 120; cf. *LS* 117)

A further advantage of the term "integral ecology" is that it enables one to appreciate the ecological dimension of Catholic sacramental theology: "The Sacraments are a privileged way in which nature is taken up by God to become a means of mediating supernatural life. . . . Water, oil, fire and colors are taken up in all their symbolic power and incorporated in our act of praise. . . . It is in the Eucharist that all that has been created finds its greatest exaltation" (*LS* 235–36).

Not content with just a generic theology of ecology, Francis provides us with a theological underpinning for the particular contemplative nature-mystical spirituality which he is advocating. He quotes Saint Bonaventure, a privileged follower of Francis of Assisi, who invites us to "encounter God in creatures outside ourselves" (*LS* 233). Invoking the Sufi mystic Ali al-Khawas, Francis also says: "The universe unfolds in God, who fills it completely" (*LS* 233). And to remind us even in this contemplative moment of the inseparable link between the fragile Earth and fragile people, he immediately goes on to maintain that "there is a mystical meaning to be found [not only] in a leaf, in a mountain trail, in a dewdrop, [but also] in a poor person's face" (*LS* 233).

In a section with the significant title "The Mystery of the Universe," Francis is careful to point out that he is not a pantheist. He says: "Judaeo-Christian thought demythologized nature. While continuing to admire its grandeur and immensity, it no longer saw nature as divine" (*LS* 78; cf. *LS* 90). However, while insisting that creation is not God, Francis goes on to say that we can think of the whole of our universe "as open to God's transcendence, within which it develops" (*LS* 79). These words should be taken in conjunction with the following two sentences in the next paragraph:

God is intimately present to each being, without impinging on the autonomy of his creature, and this gives rise to the rightful autonomy of earthly affairs. His divine presence, which ensures the subsistence and growth of each being, "continues the work of creation." (*LS* 80. Each of these two sentences is backed by an endnote reference to the works of Thomas Aquinas.)

Francis goes on to quote with approval the statement of the bishops of Brazil that "nature as a whole not only manifests God but is also a locus of his presence. The Spirit of life dwells in every living creature" (*LS* 88).

The technical term *panentheism* is not used in the encyclical. But when taken together, several short passages from paragraphs 79, 80, and 88 add up to a position that is effectively panentheistic. This is the belief that God is present in every aspect of the creation, while not being identical with it. As a theological belief, it provides solid underpinning for the special kind of nature-mysticism to which Francis is inviting us as a crucial aspect of an ecological conversion. I pointed out in chapter 18 that, prior to the coming of Francis, the Vatican was critical of "certain ecological movements" on the grounds that they divinized the Earth. Francis has not allowed this kind of suspicion to inhibit him from offering us a spirituality and theology that fully respects both the transcendence of God and, at the same time, God's immanence in our universe.

THE ACTIVE ASPECT OF AN ECOLOGICAL CONVERSION

So far I have been describing the contemplative dimension of an ecological spirituality. But this spirituality also has a more active dimension. This too is the fruit of the ecological conversion that Pope Francis is calling for.

Francis provides the biblical basis for this active aspect of the conversion by looking at key texts in the Book of Genesis (*LS* 67). He responds to "the charge that Judaeo-Christian thinking, on the basis of the Genesis account which grants man 'dominion' over the earth (cf. Gen. 1:28), has encouraged the unbridled exploitation of nature." He says bluntly: "This is not a correct interpretation of the Bible as understood by the Church." He immediately goes on to add: "Although it is true that we Christians have at times incorrectly interpreted the Scriptures, nowadays we must forcefully reject the notion that our being created in God's image and given dominion over the earth justifies absolute domination over other creatures." A little later he says: "It would also be mistaken to view other living beings as mere objects subjected to arbitrary human domination" (*LS* 82). In a later chapter of the encyclical he says: "Modernity has been marked by an excessive anthropocentrism," and he acknowledges that "an inadequate presentation of Christian anthropology gave rise to a wrong understanding of the relationship between human beings and the world. Often, what was handed on was a Promethean vision of mastery over the world" (*LS* 116).

Determined to correct this mistaken notion, Francis puts forward what he sees as the biblical basis for humans to have a correct relationship with the rest of nature:

> They tell us to "till and keep" the garden of the world (cf. Gen. 2:15). "Tilling" refers to cultivating, ploughing, or working, while "keeping" means caring, protecting, overseeing and preserving.[6] This implies a relationship of mutual responsibility between human beings and nature. Each community can take from the bounty of the earth whatever it needs for subsistence, but it also has the duty to protect the earth and to ensure its fruitfulness for coming generations. (*LS* 67)

The encyclical goes on to point out that the Sabbath is a key element in an authentic biblical ecology. It says, "Rest on the seventh day is meant not only for human beings, but also so 'that your ox and your donkey may have rest' (Exod. 23:12)" (*LS* 68). Francis strongly rejects what he calls a "tyrannical anthropocentrism unconcerned for other creatures" (*LS* 68). He cites biblical passages that insist that humans should allow animals and land to have a Sabbath rest and even to protect a bird that is caring for its chicks. He insists that the weekly Sabbath, the sabbatical year, and the Jubilee year have a twofold objective. Their purpose is, on the one hand, to ensure balance and fairness in the relationships between the human inhabitants and the land on which they lived and worked, and, on the other hand, to acknowledge that "the gift of the earth with its fruits belongs to everyone; those who tilled and kept the land were obliged to share its fruits, especially with the poor, with widows, orphans and foreigners in their midst" (*LS* 71).

Moving on to the New Testament, Francis says:

> Jesus lived in full harmony with creation, and others were amazed: "What sort of man is this, that even the winds and the sea obey him?" (Matt. 8:27). . . . He was far removed from philosophies which despised the body, matter and the things of the world. Such

---

[6]It is interesting to note the similarity between this passage in the encyclical and some lines from a poem called "Tragic Error" written many years earlier by Denise Levertov: "*subdue* was the false, the misplaced word in the story. . . . Surely our task was to have been to love the earth, to *dress and keep it* like Eden's garden."

unhealthy dualisms, nonetheless, left a mark on certain Christian thinkers in the course of history and disfigured the Gospel. Jesus worked with his hands, in daily contact with the matter created by God, to which he gave form by his craftsmanship. (*LS* 98)

Then Francis reminds us that, according to the Christian faith, "The destiny of all creation is bound up with the mystery of Christ, present from the beginning: 'All things have been created though him and for him' (Col. 1:16)" (*LS* 99).

Call for a Cultural Transformation

Building on this solid theological base, Francis spells out the practical implications of the ecological conversion that can lead to a truly integral ecology. For Francis an ecological conversion is primarily a personal spiritual change in people "whereby the effects of their encounter with Jesus Christ become evident in their relationship with the world around them" (*LS* 217). But he goes on to say, "The ecological conversion needed to bring about lasting change is also a community conversion" (*LS* 219). A large part of the encyclical is devoted to describing how the community dimension of an ecological conversion should be given expression or embodied in the economic, political, social, and cultural institutions of our world. I propose first to focus on the cultural aspect because it underpins the other aspects of the transformation involved in an integral and comprehensive ecological conversion.

Francis reminds us that "culture is . . . a living, dynamic and participatory present reality, which cannot be excluded as we rethink the relationship between human beings and the environment" (*LS* 143). He acknowledges the various ways in which technology has not only enabled humans to live more comfortably but has also contributed to human artistic achievements (*LS* 103). But he goes on to speak out strongly against the "tendency to believe that every increase in power means 'an increase of progress' " (*LS* 105). Behind this tendency, he says, is "an undifferentiated and one-dimensional paradigm," which gives rise to a technocratic mentality where humans seek to "extract everything possible" from the natural world. This involves manipulating nature rather than respecting it and being in tune with it. This, in turn, has made it easy for people "to accept the idea of infinite or unlimited growth . . . based on the lie that there is an infinite supply of the earth's goods, and this leads to the planet being squeezed dry beyond every limit" (*LS* 106).

The technocratic mind-set "ends up conditioning lifestyles and shaping social possibilities along the lines dictated by the interests of certain powerful groups" (*LS* 107). Toward the end of the encyclical Francis returns to this issue. He says:

> Since the market tends to promote extreme consumerism in an effort to sell its products, people can easily get caught up in a whirlwind of needless buying and spending. Compulsive consumerism is one example of how the techno-economic paradigm affects individuals. (LS 203)

The kernel of the problem is that "the economy accepts every advance in technology with a view to profit, without concern for its potentially negative impact on human beings. Finance overwhelms the real economy." This happens because groups whose only interest is in maximizing profits have no concern for "better distribution of wealth, concern for the environment and the rights of future generations" (*LS* 109). Later in the encyclical Francis puts forward an even stronger criticism of this mind-set: "Where profits alone count, there can be no thinking about . . . the complexity of ecosystems which may be gravely upset by human intervention. Moreover, biodiversity is considered at most a deposit of economic resources available for exploitation" (*LS* 190).

According to Francis, if we are to create an ecological culture we need to adopt an alternative "distinctive way of looking at things, a way of thinking, policies, an educational programme, a lifestyle and a spirituality which together generate resistance to the assault of the technocratic paradigm" (*LS* 111). He even goes so far as to borrow a notorious phrase from Mao Zedong when he writes that there is an "urgent need for us to move forward in a bold cultural revolution" (*LS* 114). A cultural transformation of this kind is the only way to counter "the mindset of those who say: 'Let us allow the invisible forces of the market to regulate the economy, and consider their impact on society and nature as collateral damage'" (*LS* 123).

Alongside our efforts to bring about a shift from the technocratic mindset, we need to work for the protection of non-Western cultures, which have managed to preserve a healthier, ecologically oriented culture. Francis insists that "it is essential to show special care for indigenous communities and their cultural traditions" (*LS* 146; cf. *LS* 179).

The whole question of employment and unemployment is, of course, a crucial economic issue. So Francis devotes several paragraphs to this topic, insisting strongly on the importance of safeguarding people's employment (*LS* 124–29). However, it is important to note that Francis also sees work as a fundamental cultural issue. He maintains that a proper appreciation of the role and value of human work is an important element in the cultural change that he is calling for. This is because, "Work is a necessity, part of the meaning of life on this earth, a path to growth, human development and personal fulfilment" (*LS* 128). Toward the end of the encyclical Francis notes a further important dimension to his understanding of work: "Christian spirituality incorporates the value of relaxation and festivity. . . . We are called to include in our work a dimension of receptivity and gratuity, which is quite different from mere inactivity" (*LS* 237).

It is clear that, for Francis, the crucial element in an ecological conversion is a willingness to resist the present-day consumer culture. Referring to those who adopt a simple lifestyle, he says, "Even living on little, they can live a lot, above all when they cultivate other pleasures and find satisfaction in fraternal encounters, in service, in developing their gifts, in music and art, in contact with nature, in prayer" (*LS* 223).

Furthermore, he emphasizes the importance of the "historic, artistic and cultural patrimony which is . . . a part of the shared identity of each place and a foundation upon which to build a habitable city" (*LS* 143). He maintains that this patrimony is under threat from the technocratic mind-set. So an important aspect of the ecological conversion that he calls for is a serious commitment to preserve and develop people's rich cultural heritage:

> If architecture reflects the spirit of an age, our megastructures and drab apartment blocks express the spirit of globalized technology, where a constant flood of new products coexists with a tedious monotony. Let us refuse to resign ourselves to this. (*LS* 113)

We are being invited not just to change our mentality and mind-sets but to find ways of embodying a new way of thinking, feeling, and valuing in our buildings and our cities. Francis quotes from his apostolic exhortation *Evangelii Gaudium*: "How attractive are those cities which, even in their architectural design, are full of spaces which connect, relate and favour the recognition of others!" (*LS* 152).

As though to ensure that his concern about the design of cities could not be dismissed as elitist, Francis goes on immediately to address the very practical issue of the transport systems in modern cities. He agrees with those who insist on "the need to give priority to public transportation." But he also points out that this will not be widely acceptable if people have to "put up with undignified conditions due to crowding, inconvenience, infrequent service and lack of safety" (*LS* 153).

Culture is largely shaped by formal education in schools, colleges, and church-run programs, as well as by informal education through the media. Not surprisingly, then, Francis has a lot to say about the "educational challenge" which is required if we are to avoid environmental disaster (*LS* 202, 209). In a particularly valuable passage he says:

> Environmental education has broadened its goals. Whereas in the beginning it was mainly centered on scientific information, consciousness-raising and the prevention of environmental risks, it tends now to include a critique of the "myths" of a modernity grounded in a utilitarian mindset (individualism, unlimited progress, competition, consumerism, the unregulated market). It seeks also to restore the various levels of ecological equilibrium, establishing harmony within ourselves, with others, with nature and other living creatures, and with God. Environmental education should facilitate making the leap towards the transcendent which gives ecological ethics its deepest meaning. (*LS* 210)

An important component in a genuine ecological education is helping people appreciate literature, poetry, art, and the beauty of nature. Francis says, "By learning to see and appreciate beauty, we learn to reject self-interested pragmatism" (*LS* 215). He also insists that the aim of education must be not merely to provide information but also to instill good habits, to cultivate sound virtues (*LS* 211). An ecologically oriented education is integral: it seeks to shape more enlightened and responsible ways of thinking, of feeling, and of behaving.

Francis lays particular emphasis on the educative role of the family in shaping young people's awareness of their relationship with the rest of the natural world, and inculcating the virtue of respect for the environment.

Ecological Economics

If individuals, communities, and whole societies adopt the transformed culture described by Pope Francis, then it becomes realistic to believe that the present-day market-dominated economics can be replaced by a truly ecological economics or what Francis calls an "economic ecology" (*LS* 141). This involves a rejection of the "deified market" (*LS* 56), a term which he later explains by referring to "a magical conception of the market, which would suggest that problems can be solved simply by an increase in the profits of companies or individuals." In the same paragraph he points out that, "Where profits alone count, there can be no thinking about . . . the complexity of ecosystems which may be gravely upset by human intervention." In that situation, he adds, "Biodiversity is considered at most a deposit of economic resources available for exploitation" (*LS* 190).

An important account of what Francis sees as essential to an ecological economics comes in this passage:

Environmental impact assessment should not come after the drawing up of a business proposition or the proposal of a particular policy, plan or program. It should be part of the process from the beginning, and be carried out in a way which is interdisciplinary, transparent and free of all economic or political pressure. It should be linked to a study of working conditions and possible effects on people's physical and mental health, on the local economy and on public safety. Economic returns can thus be forecast more realistically, taking into account potential scenarios and the eventual need for further investment to correct possible undesired effects. (*LS* 183)

Another crucial aspect of the converted economics that Francis calls for is that it puts a high value on employment—ensuring that people are not put out of work (*LS* 129; cf. *LS* 51, 127, 189, 192). He says, "In order to continue providing employment, it is imperative to promote an economy which favors productive diversity and business creativity." He points out that most of the peoples of the world are engaged in "a great variety of small-scale food production systems . . . using a modest amount of land and producing less waste, be it in small agricultural parcels, in orchards and gardens, hunting and wild harvesting or local fishing." This type of economy provides adequate employment, whereas modern systems which seek economies of scale "end up forcing smallholders to sell their land or to abandon their traditional crops" (*LS* 129).

A crucially important aspect of a renewed economics is the adoption of more ecologically respectful methods of production and consumption (*LS* 23; cf. *LS* 5, 138, 191). So too is a great reduction in the amount of waste we generate and the way we deal with it (see *LS* 44, 50, 51, 90, 129, 161). For instance, the encyclical refers to the possibility of "developing an economy of waste disposal and recycling" (*LS* 180).

Francis makes three very strong statements that are probably the most challenging in the encyclical. The first is this passage:

Given the insatiable and irresponsible growth produced over many decades, we need . . . to think of containing growth by setting some reasonable limits and even retracing our steps before it is too late. We know how unsustainable is the behaviour of those who constantly consume and destroy, while others are not yet able to live in a way worthy of their human dignity. That is why *the time has come to accept decreased growth in some parts of the world*, in order to provide resources for other places to experience healthy growth. (*LS* 193, emphasis added)

The second blunt statement is:

We know that technology based on the use of highly polluting fossil fuels—especially coal, but also oil and, to a lesser degree, gas—needs to be progressively replaced without delay. (*LS* 165)

These two issues are emphasized time after time, not merely by ecological campaigners but also by the majority of responsible scientists who have studied these issues. And they are, of course, issues that politicians in both the developed and the developing world are very slow and reluctant to face up to and act upon.

A third strong statement of Francis poses an enormous challenge that the leaders of the developed countries have been most reluctant to accept:

Inequity affects not only individuals but entire countries; it compels us to consider an ethics of international relations. A true "ecological debt" exists, particularly between the global north and south, connected to commercial imbalances with effects on the environment, and the disproportionate use of natural resources by certain countries over long periods of time. (*LS* 51)

Francis goes into some detail on this issue of ecological debt. He refers to the loss of valuable raw materials exported from South to North, to deforestation, and to the environmental damage done to poor countries by mining of gold and copper, dumping of toxic wastes, and lack of adequate controls on pollution by companies operating in the South; and he also mentions the global warming caused by the excessive consumption in rich countries, which causes particular problems in the South, especially in Africa (*LS* 51). By way of driving home his challenge to the leaders of the rich countries, Francis goes on to say: "The foreign debt of poor countries has become a way of controlling them, yet this is not the case where ecological debt is concerned" (*LS* 52).

Francis leaves us in no doubt that his concept of a truly ecological economics is one that takes full account of the impact of present-day economic decisions on the future generations of people and other inhabitants of our world. He insists that "the notion of the common good also extends to future generations" (*LS* 159); and his concern for future generations is expressed in no less than eight other paragraphs of the encyclical (see *LS* 22, 95, 109, 160, 162, 169, 190, 195).

The encyclical has words of praise for "cooperatives of small producers" who adopt less polluting means of production (*LS* 112). Similarly, there are places where "cooperatives are being developed to exploit renewable sources of energy which ensure local self-sufficiency and even the sale of surplus energy" (*LS* 179). Francis sees these cooperatives as models of an alternative economics—an economics that does not follow the dominant ideology of subordinating ecological concerns to the making of short-term profit.

The encyclical includes a significant treatment of the issue of genetic modification (*LS* 131–35), including a strong but carefully nuanced warning about its dangers. A key passage is the following:

> In various countries, we see an expansion of oligopolies for the production of cereals and other products needed for their cultivation. This dependency would be aggravated were the production of infertile seeds to be considered; the effect would be to force farmers to purchase them from larger producers. (*LS* 134)

On the question of alternative forms of energy, Francis says, "How could we not acknowledge the work of many scientists and engineers who have provided alternatives to make development sustainable?" (*LS* 102). He also maintains that "poor countries . . . are . . . bound to develop less polluting forms of energy production." He points out that this "will require the establishment of mechanisms and subsidies which allow developing countries access to technology transfer, technical assistance and financial resources"—and he adds, "To do so they require the help of countries which have experienced great growth at the cost of the ongoing pollution of the planet" (*LS* 172). However, he has chosen not to give detailed references to different alternative energy sources. Having noted how developing countries can take advantage of "abundant solar energy," he does not mention wind power, tidal power, or thermal energy from deep within the Earth (*LS* 172).

The encyclical offers no support at all to those who maintain that nuclear energy is the solution to the issue of global warming. Furthermore, Francis does not even bother to mention the more bizarre technological "solutions" that are sometimes proposed—for instance, shooting billions of reflectors into or above the atmosphere in order to lessen global warming, or sucking huge amounts of carbon out of the atmosphere.[7]

Political Aspects of an Ecological Conversion

Small-scale alternatives undertaken on a voluntary basis cannot, on their own, constitute the economic conversion that is required to safeguard

---

[7]Perhaps Francis or somebody who helped him draft the encyclical had been reading Naomi Klein's recent book, in which she argues quite convincingly that reliance on this kind of "geoengineering" is not merely futile but is part of the problem rather than a solution (Klein 2014, 256–68). So it is not so surprising that she was invited to take part in the Vatican conference about the encyclical in early July 2015.

the Earth and its more vulnerable inhabitants, and Francis is well aware of this. He sees an urgent need for decisive political action to eliminate abuses or "freeloading" by individuals or companies. So he says:

> Civil authorities have the right and duty to adopt clear and firm measures in support of small producers and differentiated production. To ensure economic freedom from which all can effectively benefit, restraints occasionally have to be imposed on those possessing greater resources and financial power. (*LS* 129)

This applies at both the national and the international levels. Focusing first on the national level, he insists that when any policy, plan, program, or business proposition is being drawn up it is important that all the different stakeholders should be involved and should reach consensus. He insists that "the local population should have a special place at the table; they are concerned about their own future and that of their children, and can consider goals transcending immediate economic interest" (*LS* 183).

However, adequate protection of the environment is an issue that goes beyond individual countries. There is urgent need for international binding agreements, since otherwise there will be a continuation of the present situation where countries compete with each other in regard to which of them can get away with doing the least to prevent further global warming and more pollution. Francis insists that "it is essential to devise stronger and more efficiently organized international institutions, with functionaries who are appointed fairly by agreement among national governments, and empowered to impose sanctions" (*LS* 175).

He harshly criticizes political leaders who fail to respond adequately to ecological problems; he maintains that this happens because "there are too many special interests, and economic interests easily end up trumping the common good and manipulating information so that their own plans will not be affected" (*LS* 54). He points out that the UN Conference on Sustainable Development in Rio in 2012 "issued a wide-ranging but ineffectual outcome document" (*LS* 169).

Perhaps the pope saw himself as contributing to the agenda of the COP 21 Paris conference scheduled for December 2015 when he wrote the following passage:

> A global consensus is essential for confronting the deeper problems, which cannot be resolved by unilateral actions on the part of individual countries. Such a consensus could lead, for example, to planning a sustainable and diversified agriculture, developing renewable and less polluting forms of energy, encouraging a more efficient

use of energy, promoting a better management of marine and forest resources, and ensuring universal access to drinking water. (*LS* 164)

From his experience in Latin America the pope knew how the poorest people suffer when the water supply is privatized. So his emphasis in the above quotation on the right to universal access to drinking water is particularly significant. Earlier in the encyclical he had said: "Fresh drinking water is an issue of primary importance, since it is indispensable for human life" (*LS* 28). A little later he said: "*Access to safe drinkable water is a basic and universal human right, since it is essential to human survival and, as such, is a condition for the exercise of other human rights. Our world has a grave social debt towards the poor who lack access to drinking water, because they are denied the right to a life consistent with their inalienable dignity*"[8] (*LS* 30, emphasis in the original; cf. *LS* 185).

By insisting on the universal right to clean water, Francis shows how aware he is of the need to protect "the global commons," a term that refers to resources such as the oceans and the air, as distinct from local commonages of land or forest. He says, "What is needed, in effect, is an agreement on systems of governance for the whole range of so-called 'global commons' " (*LS* 174). The argument against the privatization of commons is put forward very effectively by David Bollier (2014) who also emphasizes the significance of new kinds of commons, such as Wikipedia and Linux open-source software.

Francis adopts a controversial position when he puts forward a strong criticism of the system of "carbon credits," which is widely used at present. He maintains that this arrangement, which appears at first sight to be an easy way for rich countries to avoid having to reduce their carbon emissions, is really a way of refusing to face the difficulty. It can give rise to speculation and actually enable rich countries and sectors of society to increase their carbon emissions (*LS* 171)

Responding to those who maintain that part of the solution to the environmental crisis is a reduction in the birth rate, Francis says bluntly: "To blame population growth instead of extreme and selective consumerism on the part of some, is one way of refusing to face the issues. It is an attempt to legitimize the present model of distribution, where a minority believes that it has the right to consume in a way which can never be universalized, since the planet could not even contain the waste products

---

[8]We may presume that Francis is not suggesting that the water supply must always be provided entirely free; it is more likely that what he is condemning here is a type of privatization of the water supply that has occurred recently in some parts of Latin America— one where poor communities were left short of water because they were deprived of access to traditional sources of water, or because their area was not provided with an adequate water supply, or because the price was set at a level they could not afford.

of such consumption." He does, however, qualify his statement by adding the rather vague comment that "attention needs to be paid to imbalances in population density" (*LS* 50).

Ecological Conversion at the Social and Community Level

Francis is keenly aware that we dare not leave everything to the initiative (or lack of it) of our political leaders. He holds that "while the existing world order proves powerless to assume its responsibilities, local individuals and groups can make a real difference." So he insists that "society, through non-governmental organizations and intermediate groups, must put pressure on governments to develop more rigorous regulations, procedures and controls" (*LS* 179). One of these nongovernmental organizations is, of course, the Church. Francis says that all Christian communities have an important role to play in ecological education (*LS* 214). This education can take place not only through words but also through a wide variety of committed actions.

Pressure has to be put not only on governments but also more directly on business interests. Francis spells out one way in which this can be done. He points out that consumer movements bring healthy pressure to bear on those who wield political, economic, and social power by using the tactic of boycotting certain products. In this way, "They prove successful in changing the way businesses operate, forcing them to consider their environmental footprint and their patterns of production" (*LS* 206).

As I have already pointed out, he praises the cooperatives of small producers that model an alternative model of business that uses renewable sources of energy and fosters local self-sufficiency (*LS* 112, 179). He also recommends a whole series of practical actions that each of us can take: "avoiding the use of plastic and paper, reducing water consumption, separating refuse, cooking only what can reasonably be consumed, showing care for other living beings, using public transport or car-pooling, planting trees, turning off unnecessary lights" (*LS* 211).

Two Concluding Prayers

Drawing the encyclical to a close, Francis offers us two prayers that sum up the key themes of his encyclical. In the one which "we can share with all who believe in a God who is the all-powerful Creator," he asks "that we may protect the world and not prey on it" and that we may "discover the worth of each thing, to be filled with awe and contemplation." In the second prayer he addresses God as revealed to Christians: "Triune Lord, wondrous community of infinite love, teach us to contemplate you in the beauty of the universe" (*LS* 246).

Ecological Spirituality

The whole of the encyclical can be described as a call by Francis for us to adopt an ecological spirituality. I have already spelled out in some detail the contemplative aspect and the active aspect of this spirituality. I have also noted the fairly brief treatment of the sacramental and liturgical dimension of the ecological spirituality that Francis is proposing (see *LS* 235–37). The main characteristics of the ecological spirituality in *Laudato Si'* are contemplative wonder, peace, joy, and hope combined with an active, passionate commitment to protect the whole of creation, of which we are an integral part.

AN EVALUATION OF *LAUDATO SI'*

The encyclical *Laudato Si'* is an exceptionally important document, which will surely rank with the Vatican II Pastoral Constitution on the Church in the Modern World (*Gaudium et Spes*). I make this comparison because each of these documents represents a major development in Catholic social teaching. Like *Gaudium et Spes*, this encyclical of Pope Francis makes a major contribution not just to the body of formal Catholic social teaching but also to Catholic spirituality. In *Laudato Si'* one does not find the suspicion with which the Vatican had tended in the past to view the ecological spirituality that had been emerging over the previous generation within the churches, in other religions, and beyond the borders of all formal religion. It offers strong support for a *contemplative* and quasi-mystical spirituality, which emphasizes the experience of God *in* creation while not neglecting the transcendence of God.

A More Comprehensive and Challenging Spirituality and Theology

The encyclical also contributes greatly to the active dimension of spirituality and to the enriched theology that underpins it. Francis's account of an integral ecology represents a major breakthrough in Catholic social teaching. His teaching moves beyond the anthropocentric approach of most previous official Vatican teaching. He recognizes, first, that we humans are an intrinsic part of the cosmos and are close kin to other species and, second, that the other parts of creation have an intrinsic worth—their value does not depend solely on how they can serve human needs. In this way Francis provides a solid theological basis both for a greatly enriched, actively committed Christian spirituality that is both personal and communal, including a crucially important political dimension.

At a practical level the encyclical includes many important developments in Catholic social teaching:

1. It puts forward a rich Bible-based theology of ecology, which firmly rejects an interpretation of biblical texts that would be used to justify an exploitation of the resources of the Earth.

2. It offers a comprehensive account of the major environmental issues facing our world in the present and near future, an account that is solidly based on the consensus of responsible scientists, and presented in a manner that is readable by and understandable to the ordinary reader.

3. It maintains quite clearly that most of our environmental problems are the result of human actions and behavior. It poses a stern challenge to climate-change deniers and skeptics, refusing to soften its stance on this issue despite serious pressure from some US think tanks, politicians, and prominent Catholics.

4. In this encyclical Pope Francis insists even more strongly than previously on the close linkage between concern for the fragile Earth and for the most fragile people. He points out clearly and repeatedly that it is the poorest and most marginal people who suffer first and most seriously from environmental problems. It is in the light of this inseparable link that Francis calls on us to "hear both the cry of the earth and the cry of the poor" (*LS* 49).

5. Francis maintains that most of our ecological problems are largely caused by what he calls the "technocratic paradigm" that is dominant in our world today (*LS* 101). He suggests that this mentality gives rise to the short-sighted, unsustainable, and exploitative style of so-called development, which has increasingly been adopted in almost every country of the world. He makes it quite clear that he is not simply repeating the traditional Catholic social teaching that criticizes unregulated capitalism; he is referring to the type of business economics practiced almost universally today and supported by most governments. So his position is quite close to that of moderate versions of liberation theology. This raises a serious challenge not just for the owners and managers of companies but also for politicians and for us the citizens who elect our politicians.

6. Francis issues a strong call for a search for an alternative economics—one that is based not on short-term profits but on concern for the common good of present and future generations of humans and of the other species with whom we share this world.

7. The encyclical does not include the term "restorative justice." However, what Francis has to say about "ecological debt" (*LS* 51)

amounts to a quite compelling case in favor of this kind of justice. He recognizes that the better-off countries, mainly Western ones, have built their wealth to a large extent on their profligate use of the limited resources of the Earth over the past two centuries. Consequently, they are morally obliged to provide adequate support to poor countries in adopting a sustainable and ecologically respectful model of development through which they can overcome poverty. Francis's statement poses a serious challenge to the leaders and citizens of wealthy countries who are reluctant to acknowledge this kind of obligation.

8. Francis has words of praise for local cooperatives and indigenous communities that are using environmentally friendly practices.

9. He encourages initiatives by individuals and communities to adopt environmentally friendly practices. He challenges us to realize that quite radical changes are called for in our lifestyles: changes in our eating habits, transportation, generation of energy, and energy conservation.

10. Nevertheless, he recognizes that such small-scale efforts are not sufficient. So he insists on the need for enforcement measures at the national and international levels. This is the only way in which "free-riding" industries or countries can be prevented from gaining unfair advantage over others.

11. He supports the notion that politicians should be pressured to take the radical enforcement actions that are required. This pressure can come from nongovernmental organizations and from Christian communities. Francis goes further than previous popes in mentioning with approval the way consumer groups have succeeded in putting pressure on business interests by organizing boycotts of certain products.

Some Room for Improvement?

There is so much that is truly valuable in the encyclical that I feel reluctant to offer even any mild criticism of it. However, since I am attempting to provide a critical assessment of this encyclical as I have done for previous ones, I shall suggest some areas where I believe it might have been improved.

Francis says: "When media and the digital world become omnipresent, their influence can stop people from learning how to live wisely, to think deeply and to love generously" (*LS* 47). However, it would have been helpful if he had gone on to mention that the media in very many countries are owned or controlled by a small number of extremely rich individuals or companies. These are generally a key part of the powerful establishment whose interests would be threatened if the readers and viewers were educated by the media to "live wisely and love generously."

Francis makes one oblique reference to the role of the advertising industry in creating a throwaway, wasteful, and ecologically damaging culture when he says that "the market tends to promote extreme consumerism in an effort to sell its products" (*LS* 203). But it would have been helpful if he had spelled out explicitly and bluntly the extraordinary power of the advertising industry, the huge sums of money that are spent on advertising, and the shocking extent to which it contributes to creating a consumerist and wasteful culture.

The Population Issue

Pope Francis and his advisers were doubtless acutely aware that, if the encyclical had contained anything new or significant on the issue of population control, the mass media were likely to focus on this; so the main message of the encyclical could be missed. Furthermore, Francis might have wished to leave the topic of responsible parenthood—and the morally acceptable means to achieve it—to the synod of bishops in Rome scheduled to take place in October 2015. These considerations may help explain why he mentions the issue of population control only briefly, suggesting that extreme consumerism by wealthy people is the real problem (cf. R. Williams 2015).

However, it would have been helpful if he had repeated in polite and measured terms the remarks he had made during his journey back to Rome from the Philippines on January 19, 2015. On that occasion he rejected the idea that "in order to be good Catholics, we should be like rabbits," and used the phrase "responsible parenthood" twice. He could have strengthened his case for linking the issue of poverty with that of protecting the environment by pointing out why it is economically necessary and socially acceptable for poor people in developing countries to have large families. They have a high level of infant mortality and no public social security system. The children who survive are expected to support members of the immediate and extended family, especially their parents and relatives in their old age. The conclusion is obvious: the only effective way to avoid a population explosion in poor countries and at the same time to protect the environment is to develop an ecologically sustainable model of development that gives priority to the elimination of poverty and that provides people with some adequate level of social security.[9]

---

[9]I shall deal with this issue more extensively in chapter 21.

The Cosmic Christ

Francis quotes the Canadian bishops as saying that "nature is . . . a continuing revelation of the divine" (*LS* 85).[10] The phrase "continuing revelation" can be understood as equivalent to the phrase "primary revelation," which is now widely used in theology.[11] What this means is that the revelation of the Jewish scriptures and of the New Testament follows on from, and in some sense presupposes, the revelation of God in creation, starting with the Big Bang of 13.8 billion years ago.

One way of expressing this is to speak of the "Cosmic Christ." This is a phrase that remains obscure and misleading for many people. The main reason for the confusion is that people fail to realize that the word "Christ" is not a name but a title. Those who use the phrase the "Cosmic Christ" are referring to a reality much wider than the person Jesus. Rather, they are emphasizing the point that billions of years before "the Word was made flesh" in the person of Jesus, the Word of God had already become "embodied," in a different way, in the natural world. Ilia Delio writes, "The whole cosmos is incarnational" (Delio 2011, 50); and Richard Rohr (2011) says, "The Christ is born the moment God decides to show himself. . . . The Big Bang is the birth of the Christ. . . . That's the Cosmic Christ."

This primary revelation of God in creation finds its high point and fulfillment with the coming of Jesus, who as human is fully embedded in the history of our cosmos, which began 13.8 billion years ago. The more immediate connection to the human Jesus comes through his resurrection, in which "Jesus of Nazareth becomes the Cosmic Christ" (Edwards 1999, 122). Key passages in the Epistles of Saint Paul (Col. 1:12–20; Eph. 1:3–10) indicate that the resurrection of Jesus can be seen as the transforming restoration of the entire creation. In the encyclical Francis says, "The ultimate destiny of the universe is in the fullness of God, which has already been attained by the risen Christ" (*LS* 83); and at that point he adds a rather vague and cautious reference to the contribution of Pierre Teilhard de Chardin, SJ (n. 53). It might have been helpful if Francis had included, at least in that endnote, a mention of the phrase the "Cosmic Christ," in order to endorse it and give it some measure of wider acceptability.

---

[10]However, in his comment on the Canadian bishops' words, and again later in this paragraph, Francis himself uses the traditional word "manifestation" rather than "revelation."

[11]In this context I understand the word "primary" as equivalent to "first" rather than as "more important."

The "New Story"

When he uses the phrase "*continuing* revelation" in his encyclical (*LS* 85), Francis may perhaps also have had in mind the fact that our universe is *continuing to evolve* and that the Spirit of God is continuing to preside over the ongoing process of evolution (cf. *LS* 79: "things evolving positively"; *LS* 80: "God . . . 'continues the work of creation' "). Francis insists that humans are an intrinsic part of the reality that has evolved over millennia through the ongoing immanent and creative power of the Spirit. He reminds us that science has shown the extent to which we share much of our DNA with other creatures, even those that might have seemed quite different from us. He insists repeatedly that we live as part of a complex web of relationships with the rest of creation, which sustains our very existence.

Modern scientific advances have enabled us to look back in time to the instant of the primordial explosion 13.8 billion years ago when our universe began. We are beginning to understand how from that starting point there has emerged a universe of ever-increasing complexity.[12] The nature and functioning of each new level of reality cannot be understood or predicted on the basis of our knowledge of the lower-level constituent parts.[13] Our growing understanding of this process of evolution has enabled theologians, following the inspiration of Teilhard de Chardin, to develop what the pioneering Passionist priest and self-styled "ecologian" Thomas Berry called "The New Story."

This New Story of creation supplements and enriches the biblical "Genesis Story" of creation and the elaborate Bible-based theology on which Christians have relied until recent times. It does so by taking seriously the story of the evolutionary process as revealed by the scientists, seeing the world as "a continuing process of emergence in which there is an inner organic bond of descent of each reality from an earlier reality" (Berry 1978, 6). However, one must then go on to appreciate the fact that "the universe carries within it a psychic as well as a physical dimension." "Each new level

---

[12]Ilia Delio, drawing on the work of Niels Henrik Gregersen, points out that "nature is a nested hierarchy of ontological levels" where higher-level realities emerge, composed of lower-level components but where something quite new has emerged, so that "the whole is greater than the sum of its parts"(Delio 2011, 54–55).

[13]This evolutionary emergence did not, and does not, take place in any deterministic fashion. Apparently random interactions and statistical probabilities are central to the process. Nevertheless, one can discern in these interactions a certain upward-directed intentionality that Bernard Lonergan has helpfully described as "emergent probability" (Lonergan 1992, 145–46). For an insightful account of how this differs from deterministic versions of Darwinism, and how it expands and corrects Darwin's own work, see Byrne 2009, 13–57, especially 36 and 51–53.

of being emerges through the urgency of self-transcendence," and if this were absent, human consciousness would emerge "out of nowhere" and would find "no real place in the story" (8). The *spirituality* that emerges from this understanding has two key aspects. The first is that we can have "confidence in the *continuing revelation* that takes place in and through the earth" (13; I have emphasized the words "*continuing revelation*" to recall that the encyclical uses this phrase in *LS* 85). The second is that we now have "a new paradigm of what it is to be human"—an awareness that humans, having emerged through the earth process, are now largely responsible for how that process develops (9).

In the English text of the encyclical, there is one phrase that seems rather odd: "even if we postulate a process of evolution" (*LS* 81).[14] This wording seems to suggest that there is real doubt about the reality of evolution—and it is very unlikely that this was the intention of Francis. The context suggests that in using these words he is referring not to evolution in general but to the specific issue of the evolution of *humans*. In regard to the emergence of humanity Francis repeats the traditional Catholic insistence that this required "a direct action by God." I venture to suggest that this is an unnecessary and outdated way of expressing a vital truth. The kernel of the Catholic view is that humans are qualitatively different from their nonhuman ancestors. As Christians, we believe that God is the primary cause of the whole process of evolution, including the emergence of humans. God's action is transcendent in its nature. But to make a distinction between "direct action" by God and indirect action is to apply inappropriately to God's transcendent causal action categories that are applicable *within* our universe but not to God. We do not need to speak of a direct action by God in relation to humanity in general or to each human person. It suffices to say that humans in general are unique in our world, and that each human person is unique—and that all this is part of the creative plan of God, which unfolds in the process of evolution.

Some Church leaders and theologians (including some ecologically minded ones) have reservations about the term "The New Story." This is mainly because some enthusiasts for this approach have suggested that it replaces the traditional theology of Christ and redemption. Another mistake is the assumption by some that the adoption of "the New Story" dispenses one from the need to engage in serious dialogue with scientists on the nature of the whole evolutionary process—a process that the scientists themselves are only gradually coming to understand. Needless to say, Thomas Berry himself cannot be held responsible for these unfortu-

---

[14] I think a better phrasing would have been "even *though* we accept that there is a process of evolution."

nate distortions. And it would be a pity to dismiss his rich insights simply because of the mistakes of some his would-be "disciples."

Although Francis refers in one endnote to Teilhard de Chardin, he does not refer to Berry and does not make any explicit reference to "The New Story." I think that perhaps the only serious lack in the encyclical is its failure to give an account of this new theology and spirituality. Francis may have felt it was wiser not to use the term "The New Story" because the Vatican under previous popes had been quite mistrustful of ecological theology and the spirituality associated with this term. But there is no doubt that the theology and spirituality that Francis advocates coincide to a considerable extent with that of the New Story. I think it would have added greatly to the comprehensiveness of the encyclical if it had referred more extensively to how our theology and spirituality can be enriched by taking more account of the reality of evolution as revealed by modern science. I think especially that the contemplative quasi-mystical spirituality that Francis puts forward would be greatly enhanced if people were encouraged to experience wonder and awe in the face of the complexity and beauty not just of the multiform creatures in our world but also of the process of evolution through which they have emerged. The New Story approach could inspire people to think poetically of our universe as a cosmic symphony, which began with the extraordinary drumbeat of the Big Bang, which develops though many "movements," and which is evolving toward a culmination that for us remains shrouded in mystery, but which our faith assures us is already anticipated in the resurrection of Jesus.

FOLLOW-UP TO THE ENCYCLICAL

Just a few weeks after the publication of the encyclical Pope Francis embarked on a visit to three Latin American countries, during which he made some important speeches that reinforced the message of his encyclical and located it within a wider context. Particularly important was his very radical address on July 9, 2015, in the city of Santa Cruz de la Sierra in Bolivia, to a gathering of social activists from several countries.

Speaking to this group, he recalled his previous meeting with them several months earlier in Rome, and at this second meeting he was even more explicit in condemning exploitation and encouraging those who struggle against it. Being fully aware that many of the more conservative bishops in Latin America offer little support to these church activists, Francis tactfully said:

I am pleased to see the Church opening her doors to all of you, embracing you, accompanying you and establishing in each diocese, in every justice and peace commission, a genuine, ongoing and serious cooperation with popular movements. I ask everyone, bishops, priests and laity, as well as the social organizations of the urban and rural peripheries, to deepen this encounter.

He then said: "I wish to join my voice to yours in calling for the three 'L's' for all our brothers and sisters: land, lodging and labor. I said it and I repeat it: these are sacred rights. It is important, it is well worth fighting for them." Having mentioned some of the problems confronted by these people, he said: "Let us not be afraid to say it: we want change, real change, structural change. This system is by now intolerable: farmworkers find it intolerable, laborers find it intolerable, communities find it intolerable, peoples find it intolerable. . . . The earth itself—our sister, Mother Earth, as Saint Francis would say—also finds it intolerable."

Francis then went on to offer hope to these activists who are struggling to bring about change. He spoke of a change that is redemptive, and said that in his many meetings and travels he has "sensed an expectation, a longing, a yearning for change, in people throughout the world." Speaking from the heart, he said: "You, the lowly, the exploited, the poor and underprivileged, can do, and are doing, a lot. I would even say that the future of humanity is in great measure in your own hands, through your ability to organize and carry out creative alternatives." He insisted that the seeds of hope are "patiently sown in the forgotten fringes of our planet." Later in his address he said: "People and their movements are called to cry out, to mobilize and to demand—peacefully, but firmly—that appropriate and urgently needed measures be taken. I ask you, in the name of God, to defend Mother Earth. . . . The future of humanity does not lie solely in the hands of great leaders, the great powers and the elites. It is fundamentally in the hands of peoples and in their ability to organize."

Speaking of the importance of constructing "a humane alternative to a globalization which excludes," he said, "The Church cannot and must not remain aloof from this process in her proclamation of the Gospel." But then he went on to say:

> Don't expect a recipe from this Pope. Neither the Pope nor the Church has a monopoly on the interpretation of social reality or the proposal of solutions to contemporary issues. I dare say that no recipe exists. History is made by each generation as it follows in the footsteps of those preceding it, as it seeks its own path and respects the values which God has placed in the human heart.

Having insisted that the pope or the Church does not have a formula for a perfect society, Francis pointed out some relevant guiding principles:

A just economy must create the conditions for everyone to be able to enjoy a childhood without want, to develop their talents when young, to work with full rights during their active years and to enjoy a dignified retirement as they grow older. It is an economy where human beings, in harmony with nature, structure the entire system of production and distribution in such a way that the abilities and needs of each individual find suitable expression in social life. You, and other peoples as well, sum up this desire in a simple and beautiful expression: "to live well," which is not the same as "to have a good time." Such an economy is not only desirable and necessary, but also possible. It is no utopia or chimera. It is an extremely realistic prospect. We can achieve it.

Repeating a point made by Pope John Paul in his encyclical *Centesimus Annus* and which was misinterpreted by some as a rejection of any form of "welfare state," Francis said: "Welfare programs geared to certain emergencies can only be considered temporary and incidental responses. They could never replace true inclusion, an inclusion which provides worthy, free, creative, participatory and solidary work."

Francis went on to appeal to "my brothers and sisters of the popular movements" to work for unity between the different Latin American countries. He sees this as a way of resisting

the new colonialism [which] takes on different faces. At times it appears as . . . certain "free trade" treaties, and the imposition of measures of "austerity" which always tighten the belt of workers and the poor. . . . Similarly, the monopolizing of the communications media, which would impose alienating examples of consumerism and a certain cultural uniformity, is another one of the forms taken by the new colonialism. It is ideological colonialism. . . .

Colonialism, both old and new, which reduces poor countries to mere providers of raw material and cheap labor, engenders violence, poverty, forced migrations and all the evils which go hand in hand with these, precisely because, by placing the periphery at the service of the center, it denies those countries the right to an integral development.

Toward the end of his address Francis said, "Some may rightly say, 'When the Pope speaks of colonialism, he overlooks certain actions of the Church.' I say this to you with regret: many grave sins were committed against the native peoples of America in the name of God. . . . I humbly ask forgiveness, not only for the offenses of the Church herself, but also for crimes committed against the native peoples during the so-called conquest of America."

Showing his sensitivity to nonbelievers among his audience, Francis concluded his address by saying, "I ask you, please, to pray for me. If some of you are unable to pray, with all respect, I ask you to send me your good thoughts and energy."

This address of Pope Francis is a striking example of the unity of his vision: his concern for the environment and his concern for people who are poor and exploited are inextricably connected. Together, they are the basis for his passionate demand for a transformation of the present dominant mentality and policies—a radical conversion at the economic, political, cultural, and spiritual levels.

On July 18, 2015, after his return to Rome, Francis sent a strong message to participants in a conference in Rome organized by the Pontifical Council for Justice and Peace about the effects of mining in their countries. In this message he spelled out eloquently and in some detail the very damaging environmental and human costs of the manner in which mining takes place in many countries at present. He listed six "cries" that are heard, including a cry of sadness and impotence for the contamination of water, air, and land, and a cry of indignation and for help for violations of human rights. He insisted that "the entire mining sector is undoubtedly required to effect a radical paradigm change to improve the situation in many countries."

Pope Francis to the US Congress and at the United Nations

One of the more significant speeches that Francis gave during his visit to the United States was his address to the Joint Congress on September 24, 2015. In the course of this wide-ranging speech he devoted an important paragraph to recalling and quoting his appeal in *Laudato Si'* "for a courageous and responsible effort to . . . avert the most serious effects of the environmental deterioration caused by human activity." Stressing the "important role" that the United States and Congress can play, and, as always, linking care for the environment with care for vulnerable people, he said: "Now is the time for courageous actions and strategies, aimed at implementing a 'culture of care' (*LS* 231) and 'an integrated approach to combating poverty, restoring dignity to the excluded, and at the same time protecting nature'" (*LS* 139).

On September 25, 2015, Francis gave a major address to the members of the General Assembly of the United Nations. It offered a comprehensive take on a variety of topics such as sustainable development, the importance of peacemaking, the damage done by drugs, respect for religious freedom, and the whole issue of human rights. Interestingly, one part of his speech was a close echo of a key part of his address to social activists in Bolivia on July 9, 2015; this was where he said that everybody has a right to the "absolute minimum . . . lodging, labor, and land."

The most original and striking element in his address was his stark statement: "It must be stated that a true 'right of the environment' does exist" (*"existe un verdadero 'derecho del ambiente' "*). No doubt, theologians and philosophers will devote much energy to exploring and explaining what it means for Francis to claim that the environment has rights. They will explore how this statement can be interpreted in terms of the human rights tradition, or the natural law tradition, or an ethics based on virtue or value. It seems, however, that Francis was not concerned with any such philosophical exploration. He simply went on immediately to give two reasons to justify his claim that "a true 'right of the environment' does exist":

> First, because we human beings are part of the environment. We live in communion with it, since the environment itself entails ethical limits which human activity must acknowledge and respect. . . . Any harm done to the environment, therefore, is harm done to humanity. Second, because every creature, particularly a living creature, has an intrinsic value, in its existence, its life, its beauty and its interdependence with other creatures. . . . In all religions, the environment is a fundamental good.

In this way Francis finds the basis for his statement at the UN in what he had already said in *Laudato Si'* that "everything is connected" (*LS* 91, 117) and in his call to us to hear "the cry of the earth" (*LS* 49). It may be best to accept that he is using both the word "cry" and the word "right" in a real but analogical sense when they are applied to the environment; he is saying that we have a responsibility to respect the environment.[15]

It is quite likely that Francis will continue to make statements and issue documents that will add further important material to the body of Catholic social teaching. However, I have no hesitation in saying that, even if he were to become silent at this time in late October 2015 when the final text of the present book is being sent to the publisher, he has

---

[15]It is also helpful to remember that Francis is not saying that each member of every species has an absolute right to exist; not all rights are absolute. In this regard it might be better to say that the nonhuman parts of creation have *inherent* value rather than *intrinsic* value, since the use of the word "intrinsic" may be understood as being equivalent to "absolute," as when Church leaders and some moral theologians say that certain actions are "intrinsically evil." The challenge facing all of us—and particularly our scientists and politicians—is to determine the extent to which it is right and appropriate to use the resources of the earth respectfully and modify our environment.

already made the most important contribution to the body of social teaching since Vatican II.

***

SUMMARY

Pope Francis is strongly committed to putting ecology at the very heart of Catholic social teaching, and doing this in a way that emphasizes the inseparable link between justice and ecology. He links concern for the fragile Earth with concern for fragile people. His concept of an "integral ecology," in which he avoids making an unduly sharp distinction between "human ecology" and "natural ecology," is a valuable contribution to Catholic social teaching. In his encyclical *Laudato Si'* he accepts the consensus view of responsible scientists that our present ecological problems are caused mainly by human activity. He provides us with a comprehensive account of the many threats to the environment. Building on a solid biblical foundation, he offers us a rich ecological theology and spirituality. Inspired by Francis of Assisi, his ecological spirituality is both contemplative and action-oriented. He strongly rejects what he calls a "technocratic paradigm" and calls for an *ecological conversion*. He puts forward a series of important practical proposals for ways in which this conversion can be lived out in the spheres of economics, politics, community action, and culture. All through his encyclical he draws heavily on documents issued by conferences of bishops on all the continents of the world. He also quotes from the works of the Orthodox Patriarch Bartholomew, from a Sufi mystic, and from the Earth Charter. Shortly after the publication of the encyclical he addressed a group of social activists in Latin America, strongly supporting their struggle and suggesting that the future of our world is largely in the hands of committed and loving people like them. In his address to the United Nations he maintained that " a true right to the environment does exist."

QUESTIONS FOR REVIEW

1. *What are the major contributions that Pope Francis has made to Catholic teaching on ecology?*
2. *In what ways might his teaching be further expanded?*
3. *What is the biblical basis for a theology and spirituality of ecology?*
4. *What grounds does Francis offer for his statement that the environment has a right to exist?*

QUESTIONS FOR REFLECTION

1. *Why is it that there is an ever-increasing convergence between concern for poor people and for fragile nature?*
2. *What is the basis in Catholic teaching for respect for animals, for plants, for beautiful landscapes?*

ISSUES FOR FURTHER STUDY

1. *The pattern of evolution and the role of God in it.*
2. *The relationship between the ideas of Teilhard de Chardin and Thomas Berry.*

21

Drawing the Threads Together

There are three sections in this concluding chapter. In the first I look at the overall flow of Vatican teaching on justice and ecology issues, focusing on the elements of continuity and discontinuity in it. This will lead to an examination of whether, or in what sense, there is a coherent and organic tradition of social teaching in the Catholic Church, stretching over the period of a hundred years. In the second section I outline some of the strengths of Catholic social teaching and some of the areas where it needs further development. In the third section I offer a fairly extended account of the various aspects of the concept of an option for the poor and for the Earth, as it has developed in Catholic social teaching up to and including the encyclical of Pope Francis on the ecology, *Laudato Si'*, in 2015.

AN ORGANIC TRADITION? THE FIRST SEVENTY YEARS

During the period between 1891 and 1961, Catholic social teaching developed into a fairly coherent body of doctrine. Two central themes lay at the heart of this teaching: (1) a particular concern for the poor and powerless, together with a criticism of the systems that leave them vulnerable; and (2) a defense of certain personal rights (above all, the right to private property) against collectivist tendencies.

Throughout these seventy years the popes were consistently critical of both liberal capitalism and of socialism. And they put forward certain fundamental principles about human nature and the nature of human society in its economic, political, social, cultural, and religious aspects. I have given an extended account of these principles elsewhere (Dorr 1991, 83–102), so here I shall merely list a few of the more central ones:

- The right of the individual to own property
- The right of workers to join trade unions
- The right of the head of a family to be paid a family wage for work done

- The obligation of mothers to care for their children in the home
- The duty of the citizen to obey lawful authorities
- The duty of governments to work for the common good
- The right of citizens to resist oppression by lawful means
- The obligation of governments and of the rich and powerful to help the poor
- The duty of governments and larger agencies to respect the principle of subsidiarity
- The right of believers to freedom of worship
- The right of the Church to carry out its functions and to speak out on issues of public morality

As we look back on the Catholic social teaching of that period, it is clear that these principles were so general that they were compatible with a variety of social, economic, and political systems. However, at the time this was not at all so clear. In fact, many committed Catholics would have considered that the Church's teaching represented "a third way" that was neither capitalist nor socialist. The truth is, however, that it was only for a few years after *Quadragesimo Anno* was issued in 1931 that the Vatican was really suggesting such a "third way," namely, the "corporatist" or vocational system. For the rest of the time the popes did not try to spell out how Catholic social principles should be applied in practice.

Nevertheless, there was a pervasive "Catholic ethos" that determined the limits of what would be considered a proper implementation of the general principles. For instance, it came to be accepted that governments could, and should, pay modest old-age pensions and that there should be free universal primary education. However, it was not considered acceptable that the government should provide free health care for everybody or that it should provide post-primary education. These would have been seen as instances of a failure to respect the principle of subsidiarity and as giving undue power to the state. This Catholic ethos was a strongly conservative cultural force in society. It was hostile to anything that smacked of socialism or even social democracy, and of any political movements that seemed to be "left-wing" in approach.

In practice, then, the Church gave a certain religious legitimation to the "free enterprise" model that was dominant in Western society. Its protests against the excesses of capitalism—protests that reached a peak in the early 1930s—became muted during the later years of the papacy of Pius XII. The Church still challenged the ideology of liberal capitalism, but its hostility to all forms of socialism was more total, explicit, systematic, and effective. The Church reacted less quickly and strongly against right-wing excesses than against those of the left wing.

During the late 1920s and early 1930s, the Vatican worked out a rather uneasy modus vivendi with fascist leaders in Europe, and Pope Pius XI expressed a highly qualified measure of approval of the fascist-corporatist model of society. Many local Church leaders and lay Catholics followed suit. The accommodation with the fascists in Italy and the Nazis in Germany did not last long. But in Spain, Portugal, and much of Latin America the alliance with "the right" lasted for decades and caused the Church to be perceived as a right-wing force in society.

The effect of the prevailing Catholic ethos was that the Church became (or continued to be) one of the key agencies opposed to those political movements that were working for the kind of changes that would have redistributed wealth and power and brought greater equity into society. It remained true that Catholic social teaching was marked by genuine concern for the plight of the poor, and the Church was deeply and sincerely involved in providing a whole range of services needed by the poor. Nevertheless, Catholic teaching, and its associated ethos, had come to represent, in practice, almost the exact opposite of what is now meant by an "*option* for the poor"; it provided support and legitimation for those who resisted the efforts of the champions of poor people to gain a fair share of power in society and of its resources.

I have been looking at the elements of continuity in Catholic social teaching and in the Catholic ethos in the period 1891 to 1961. But there was also some discontinuity, and it is important to acknowledge these discontinuities (cf. Curran 2002, 117) rather than insisting that what we have is a single fully coherent body of teaching. As I have noted, there was a period, mainly in the first half of the 1930s, when Vatican teaching seemed to favor a corporatist model of society as an alternative to the capitalist order.

As time went on, the context changed, and there was a readjustment of emphasis in the interpretation of the papal teaching. However, there was little or no formal recognition that this kind of "revision" was taking place. The teaching of Pius XI simply came to be understood in a less specific way, more typical of the general tradition of "social doctrine." In chapter 4 on Pius XII, I mentioned how he presented his predecessor's view as an ideal that was not realizable until some indefinite future time. This was one of the few occasions when there was even an implicit acknowledgment that there was some incompatibility between the teachings of the two popes.

A Change of Direction

A much more significant element of discontinuity came with the teaching of John XXIII. His encyclical *Mater et Magistra* in 1961 shifted the focus of Catholic social teaching by coming out in favor of what amounted to a "welfare state" model of society. Furthermore, Pope John no longer gave the right to private property a uniquely privileged place in Catholic social teaching. For about twenty years after the time of Pope John, the Catholic Church was no longer the natural ally of the forces in society that were most opposed to structural change.

I have suggested that Pope John XXIII's two major encyclicals can best be understood not precisely as "an opening to the left" but more as a decisive move away from the right in regard to economic affairs. Further light may be thrown on the contribution of Pope John by seeing it not as a change in the main content of Catholic social teaching, but rather as a shift of emphasis from the second to the first of the two main themes in Catholic social teaching—from concern about the right to private ownership to concern about poverty. Pope John and the Church leaders who came after him saw more clearly and insisted more forcefully that the right to private property is not an end in itself; it is simply a means of ensuring that people are not left at the mercy of powerful people or, especially, of an all-powerful state.

This change of emphasis had profound practical repercussions on the spirituality of Catholics and on the life of the Church. It led to a change in "the Catholic ethos." Most Catholics became willing to accept more intervention by the state in economic and social life. Furthermore, a sizable number of Catholics (including some priests and an occasional bishop) began to demand more intervention by the state. With the fervor of new converts, they called for a radical restructuring of society of the kind socialism stood for. In support of this stance they could invoke the strand in traditional Catholic social teaching that expressed concern for the poor and criticized the systems that create poverty and marginalization.

However, it was not to be expected that the traditional Catholic ethos would be replaced in a short time by such a radical outlook. After the time of John XXIII, many Catholics wanted changes of a more modest kind. Others remained largely untouched by the new ideas. They held on to the traditional understanding of Catholic social teaching and continued to be allied with, or supportive of, the conservative forces in society. In many cases the reaction of traditional Catholics was one of real incomprehension in the face of the call for what they saw as socialism if not anarchy. When they saw that Church leaders seemed to share some of the more radical new attitudes, the incomprehension of some traditionalists gave way to a sense of betrayal and even a suspicion that left-wing theorists had managed to delude the bishops or even the pope.

The effect of all this was that the old monolithic Catholic ethos began to crumble rapidly and was replaced by a new pluralism in Catholic thinking about social, economic, and political affairs. This pluralism was welcomed by many not just as an unfortunate fact but as a positive value.

The Vatican Council contributed greatly to the dissolution of the traditional Catholic ethos. It did so mainly by coming out firmly in support of the new "liberal Catholicism" of the time. Its contribution to *"radical Catholicism"* was more limited. But in declaring the Church's willingness to relinquish privilege and patronage in the interests of its mission, it was adopting a position that was not merely liberal but also radical, for it was distancing the Church from the rich and the powerful.

On the Side of the Poor

I suggested in chapter 5 that Pope John's encyclical *Mater et Magistra* stands as a turning point in Catholic social teaching—the beginning of a process in which the Church came to have new allies and new opponents. This led to a change over the next generation that may well be judged to be as profound as that which took place at the time when the Emperor Constantine made Christianity the religion of the Roman Empire. Since Constantine, the Christian Church had generally been part of "the establishment" in most of the Western world. There were, of course, occasions when governments harassed or persecuted the Church. However, almost invariably this was not because Church leaders did not want to be part of the establishment but was simply the result of a struggle for power between alternative power blocs. The crucial point is that it was taken for granted that, in normal circumstances, the Church should be part of the establishment—and *wanted* to be part of it. Furthermore, when the West became dominant at a global level, the Christian religion was seen as going hand in hand with Western "civilization," offering little effective challenge to Western imperialism (again allowing for some few exceptions).

The new Catholic ethos which developed as a result of the work of John XXIII and Vatican II prepared the ground for a truly remarkable shift in the relationship between the Church and the dominant powers in society, the beginnings of a break from the Constantinian conception of the role of the Church. This shift is summed up in the term "option for the poor." The first full-fledged commitment to such an option came in 1968 at Medellín, when Latin American Church leaders pledged themselves to side with the poor in the struggle for justice.

Before long, the stance of the Church began to change in other parts of the world where resistance to gross oppression was coming to a head, for instance, in the Philippines, Zimbabwe, Korea, and South Africa. In these crisis situations the Church as a whole, or (more commonly) key sectors of it, came to be seen—both by defenders of the status quo and by those seeking liberation—as one of the most effective opponents of oppressive governments. Far from offering religious legitimation to unjust regimes, it became a powerful "voice for the voiceless," as Pope John Paul said to the Mexican indigenous peoples; frequently it set out not just to speak on their behalf but to help them find their own voices.

Though it is mainly on the frontiers of the Western world that the strong prophetic voice of the Church emerged, the repercussions gradually began to be felt nearer the center. All the churches—and the Catholic Church especially—are international movements of solidarity. When Christians are persecuted for standing up for justice and human rights in one area, the sense of outrage tends to spread to fellow Christians elsewhere. This process speeds up enormously on those occasions when martyrs in the non-Western countries happen to be citizens of North America or Europe. For instance, the 1980 murder of four women missionaries from the United States in El Salvador (Ursuline Sister Dorothy Kazel, lay missionary Jean Donovan, and Maryknoll Sisters Maura Clarke and Ita Ford) helped Christians in the West realize what had been going on in Central America.

It has also become ever clearer that the West can no longer disclaim responsibility for the poverty and exploitation that characterize many countries in "the South." Committed Christians in the West began to challenge the international economic policies of their own governments in the name of the gospel. Meanwhile, financial and banking crises and other economic difficulties have hit the poorer sections of the population of the Western countries, giving rise to increasing unemployment and a scaling down of welfare benefits. As a result, large numbers of jobless people have been excluded from the benefits of the Western way of life. Some of the areas where they live have become centers of alienation and of crime. This has posed a threat to the existing system.

The increasing global inequity allied to the rise of various fanatical fundamentalisms has led to a growing terrorist threat. A number of "failed states" and other countries in the South whose governments lack effective authority have become locations where terrorists from all parts of the world are trained. The terrorist threat has been met by an increasing tendency in the West to adopt a national security mentality and ideology, which in the past had been more typical of countries in the South.

For all these reasons many committed Christians and a large number of religious congregations have distanced themselves from the establishment and set out to be with, and on the side of, the poor and the powerless. A significant number of these have effectively made an option for the poor in the full sense. What this means in practice is that these individuals and groups have, as I suggested toward the end of chapter 16, adopted "a spirituality that values and emphasizes the concept of liberation, with its background of social analysis, and its overtones of contestation and struggle."

Furthermore, an increasing number of Church leaders, including Pope Paul VI and Pope John Paul II, expanded and made more explicit the prophetic stance that had been present in Catholic social teaching since the time of Leo XIII. John Paul traveled to parts of the world where oppression of the poor was rampant, and speaking directly to marginalized and exploited people, he bluntly condemned the systems that were creating so much suffering, alienation, and powerlessness. These actions of the pope amounted to what one might term an option for the poor in a far more limited or qualified sense. I say it is qualified because the Vatican in the time of Pope John Paul, especially after his very early years as pope, practiced a policy of strong disapproval of church people who favored liberation theology; and over the years the bishops who favored this approach were replaced by conservative bishops. A further reason for suggesting that in this period an option for the poor applied only in a qualified sense to the top leadership of the Church is that the liberationist spirituality that is an integral aspect of this option was by no means evident in the lives of most senior Church leaders.

A Different Emphasis

Pope Benedict never repudiated the approach of his two predecessors, but his priorities seemed rather different. At the heart of his teaching on economic and political affairs was his strong insistence that active commitment and direct action in these spheres is the mission and role of *lay* Christians rather than of those who represent the official Church. He spelled this out in a very helpful way by his emphasis on the "economy of communion." This can take two forms. The most obvious instances are the kind of enterprises set up by the Focolare movement and others—industries or other business ventures that have the specific aim of meeting social needs as well as making enough profit to be able to continue trading (see chapter 16). Less obvious or more attenuated instances are the whole variety of everyday economic activities that are not coldly impersonal but in which a warm interpersonal relationship is a central part of the interaction (see chapter 17 above).

In Benedict's view, the official Church and its leaders should hold back from being directly involved in working for change in the political and economic structures of society. This does not at all mean that the official Church is not concerned about justice issues or is retreating from seeking to influence the secular world. Benedict held that the Church has a vital but *indirect* role to play. This indirect role consists of using "rational argument" and "awakening the spiritual energy" that is required if people are to make the kind of sacrifices that justice requires (*Deus Caritas Est* 28).

As I pointed out in chapter 15, this leaves one with a number of unanswered questions, both about the occasional challenging actions of such Church leaders as El Salvador's Oscar Romero and South Africa's Denis

Hurley and also about the work of official Church agencies, many of which are part of the Caritas network. It is clear that it is quite inappropriate for official Church leaders or agencies to become directly identified with particular political parties. At the other end of the spectrum, it is clear that "indirectly political" is a correct way to describe a general education program making use of rational argument in relation to issues of justice. But what about a situation where official Church individuals or agencies get involved in *advocacy* of the kind involved in the Lenten campaigns of several of the Caritas agencies on specific justice or ecological issues? Does this count as indirectly political in Benedict's sense?

What about the work of agencies like Franciscans International, which have full-time representatives accredited to the United Nations to campaign on justice and ecology issues? They use rational argument, but some of them at least describe their work as lobbying—even though they try hard not to be seen as lobbyists in the same sense as the highly paid lobbyists of the tobacco or coal industries. Should their work be described as directly or indirectly political? Finally, there are the very exceptional but vitally significant cases where Church leaders have felt morally obliged to oppose a repressive regime quite directly. They did so by engaging in acts of civil disobedience, as Archbishop Hurley did when he led an anti-apartheid march that had been banned by the government. Surely this must be seen as being directly political, even though not in the party-political sense?

Benedict's first encyclical, *Deus Caritas Est*, seemed to suggest that official Catholic agencies should draw back from direct action on justice issues, concentrating instead on charitable relief. There was a fairly wide-spread sense that, during the papacy of Benedict, the Vatican was making a deliberate effort to change the emphasis of Catholic social *teaching*, and more particularly, of the appropriate *actions* of the official Church in working to promote justice. If this is an accurate reading of the situation during that period, it would mean that there was quite a significant shift away from the focus that Church teaching and action had been taking since the time of Vatican II. It would undoubtedly have involved a step back from all that is involved in an option for the poor in the strict sense. As I suggested toward the end of chapter 16, Benedict's position might more accurately be described not as an *option* for the poor but as a preferential *concern* for the poor.

The stance of Pope Francis, in contrast, goes beyond concern for the poor. If one is to judge by his official documents and statements, and particularly his explicit support for, and encouragement of, campaigning social activists, Francis stands solidly behind those who are making, and calling for, a radical option for the poor. Most striking are his blunt condemnations of the present political-economic order of society and his insistent call for a fundamental change of these structures. Coupled to this is the convincing manner in which he has linked an option for poor and marginalized people with an option for the Earth along with a sharp condemnation of ecological exploitation.

However, as pope, Francis inherited a set of traditions, practices, expectations, and restrictions that set severe limits to his freedom of action. He has had to exercise prudence and considerable caution in following the call of his heart to take radical action. Otherwise, he may fail to get the cooperation he needs from the people around him in the Vatican. Perhaps even more important from his point of view is the danger that he may not get the kind of enthusiastic support he desires and needs from the bishops all over the world—almost all of whom were chosen by John Paul and Benedict on the basis of a quite different set of criteria.

Despite these difficulties Francis did not hesitate to break with tradition in the various ways that I noted in chapter 20. His choice of where to live, how to dress, the type of transportation he uses, and his obvious reaching out to people on the margins—all have enormous symbolic significance; they are clear indications of his adoption of a spirituality of liberation. Furthermore, he has taken two strategic actions that have shifted the balance of power between the Vatican curia and the local leadership of the global church: his establishment of a small but powerful advisory group of cardinals from the different continents and his new emphasis on the importance of the Synod of Bishops.

Facing the Future

Nobody can predict in which direction the Church will go in the future. It is possible that the new-style papacy of Francis will gradually become toned down and may perhaps be just a flash in the pan. It is possible that most Church leaders will suffer a failure of nerve and will continue to remain establishment figures who occasionally make ineffectual sounds of disquiet. If this happens, then many prophetically minded Christians may well become more and more alienated from the Church leadership. However, it is possible that many Church leaders, inspired by Pope Francis, will take a prophetic stance and will be willing to suffer the consequences. Even if most bishops and other Church leaders take up a challenging position, it is unlikely that they will succeed in carrying the whole Church membership with them. Some divisions and polarization are almost inevitable, but their extent will depend on the degree of moral authority the leaders can exert.

The position of the pope will be of crucial importance. It is clear that recent popes have played a key role in setting the direction of Catholic social teaching and giving a lead in social action. They have done so both directly through their own moral authority and charisma, and indirectly through their appointment of bishops and their influence on national hierarchies. Needless to say, some local bishops or hierarchies may still remain quite far to the left or to the right of the pope. But what the pope says and does is usually taken very seriously. National and regional episcopal conferences and individual bishops almost invariably give verbal assent to what the pope says. In actual practice, however, there may be significant differences in the extent to which Church leaders in different regions, and even in different dioceses, follow the prevailing Vatican line.

The tradition of social teaching in the Catholic Church might be compared to a large flotilla of ships, sailing in the wake of one leading ship. For years they were moving forward in one direction, with some relatively minor diversions due largely to the surrounding tides and currents. When Pope John took the helm, he began to turn the leading ship in a different direction. At first there was some pitching and rolling of the ship, and some observers thought it was sinking. But eventually the new direction became fairly well established, due to skillful steering and courageous leadership by Paul VI and by John Paul II in the first four years of his papacy.

In the later years of John Paul's papacy some doubts crept in. On the one hand, John Paul played an exceptionally prominent part of the struggle against tyranny in Eastern Europe. But, on the other hand, the pope and the Vatican sent mixed messages to Christians struggling for justice in other frontier situations. There was a reaffirmation of the Church's commitment to liberation, justice, human rights, and the poor. But at the same time there was a determined effort to distance the Church from the individuals and the movements that were in the forefront of the struggle for liberation. This caused some confusion. To some it suggested that the Vatican was weakening in its commitment to justice, while others saw it mainly as concern that the Church should not become politicized and should not become tainted with Marxist ideology. During the papacy of Pope Benedict the doubts and questions grew stronger and more explicit. Then he resigned, and Francis became pope. Francis immediately began a program that involved not merely an unambiguous return to the direction set by Vatican II but also one that is fully in line with the more radical commitments of the Latin American bishops among whom he played a key role when he was archbishop of Buenos Aires.

Precisely because of the great weight given to papal teaching there have been many attempts by ideologues to harness this teaching in support of their own political views. The result is that Catholic social teaching has become a battleground on which the ideological struggle between the right and the left is fought. It is commonly assumed by the ideologues on both sides that the teaching of John XXIII, Paul VI, and Pope Francis represents a shift of the official Church to the left while John Paul and Benedict represent a reaffirmation of the more traditional conservative position. Quentin Quade, for instance, claimed that Paul VI's *Populorum Progressio* and the documents of the synods of 1971 and 1974 represent a drift away from the mainstream of Catholic social teaching—a drift that was sharply corrected by John Paul II (Quade 1982, 6–10). To sustain such an argument requires a very selective reading of the pope's documents and statements.

The truth is more complex. Where John Paul and Benedict took a conservative line was primarily in the area of Church discipline, and their actions in this area had only an indirect impact on social teaching (e.g., action against liberation theologians). In fact, during his early years as pope, John Paul took much stronger stands against injustice in society and in defense of human rights than were ever taken by his predecessors. As regards the content of social teaching during the later years of John Paul's papacy and that of Benedict, there was no overt backtracking from the positions adopted by Paul VI or John XXIII. John Paul in his later years as pope and Benedict were conservative in the sense that they refused to take the kind of stances that liberation-minded Catholics would have liked them to take. For instance, John Paul did not give outright support to the liberation movement in South Africa or to activists in the land agitation movement in Brazil. He was unwilling to move the Church to the left side of the political spectrum, preferring to hold the moral high ground where he spoke out against oppression in general terms.

John Paul occasionally used the term "Catholic social doctrine," a term that seemed to have been abandoned by Paul VI because of its overtones of a timeless, monolithic body of principles. But, as I pointed out in chapter 11, John Paul's reinstatement of this term was a highly nuanced one, which effectively purged it of the overtones of monolithic dogmatism.

The unwillingness of John Paul and Benedict to move the Church to the left on economic issues caused disappointment and even dismay among the people in one ideological camp, and it gave rise to some gloating by those in the opposite camp. This refusal tempted the enthusiasts on both sides to claim that these two popes had returned Catholic social teaching to a traditional or conservative position. But to make such a claim is to misunderstand both what John Paul and Benedict were trying to do and why they were doing it. They were both determined not to get drawn into what they saw as political issues. John Paul was willing to accept the view of Mikhail Gorbachev that he had a major political impact on Eastern Europe; but he was very careful to clarify it in this way:

> I do not believe that one can talk about a political role in the strict sense, replied the Pope, because the Pope has as his mission to preach

the Gospel. But in the Gospel there is man, respect for man, and, therefore, human rights, freedom of conscience and everything that belongs to man. If this has a political significance, then, yes, it applies also to the Pope. (Gorbachev 1992)

Obviously there is a very thin line between taking "a political role in the strict sense" (to use John Paul's own words) and taking stances that have "a political significance." Critics may disagree with the judgments made by John Paul and Benedict about particular situations such as those in Poland, Nicaragua, Brazil, South Africa, and Turkey. They may have questions about whether the Church can always remain above politics. But it is a gross misunderstanding (or misinterpretation) of the popes' position to assume that these two popes returned to old-style Catholic social doctrine.

There are "new right" or neoconservative political theorists who try to use Catholic social teaching as an ideological support not merely for Western democracy but for liberal capitalism. They would like to have John Paul and Benedict as allies. But the social teaching of these popes, taken as a whole, cannot be used in this way; it is far too critical of the inadequately regulated capitalist system as it currently operates in our world. So the ideologues pick out passages from the popes' statements that, taken out of context, can be used as weapons in their ideological struggle. Some years ago the theorists of the left were engaged in a similar project—making their selections from papal statements to be used as ideological weapons, but the later John Paul and Benedict gave them very little material which can be used in this way!

The words and actions of Pope Francis have given a new twist to this contest between ideologically inclined commentators. There can be little doubt that he has provided comfort to those on the left and has discomfited those on the right. But clearly his aim was not to take sides in this kind of ideological quasi-political contest. His intention was simply to be true to the gospel, to the direction set by Vatican II, and to the Spirit-inspired insights of Medellín, Puebla, and Aparecida. The task facing theologians today is to help people understand the main direction of Catholic social teaching and to avoid being manipulated by the ideologues of the left or the right.

A Struggle within the Church

It is easy to see why the notion of an option for the poor is divisive in society, but why should it be even more controversial and divisive in the Church itself? One reason is the traditional hesitancy of Church leaders about anything which may cause major disruption in society. A second reason is the inclination of many Church leaders to work out a modus vivendi with those who are politically powerful and those who are wealthy.

However, there is something more: the whole idea of an option for the poor may be perceived by some Church leaders as a threat not just to the wealthy and powerful in civil society but also to these Church leaders themselves. In chapter 1 of this book I pointed out that the option for the poor is closely associated with liberation theology. Those who make such an option are committing themselves not just to helping the poor resist exploitation and oppression; they are also undertaking to be an empowering presence with ordinary poor people, helping them explore and articulate the meaning of the gospel in their daily lives and struggles. That is a further reason why some Church leaders find it so hard to accept or even to understand. They experience it, perhaps only half consciously, as a challenge to their exclusive authority to interpret the Word of God and the message of Jesus for today. They see it as a threat because they have not fully accepted the insight so well articulated by Pope Francis that Church leaders must allow themselves to be evangelized by those who are poor, embracing "the mysterious wisdom which God wishes to share with us through them" (*Evangelii Gaudium* 198).

This helps explain why until recently there has been strong resistance to liberation theology and the spirituality that accompanies it within much of the Church leadership, particularly in the Vatican curia. The issue of an option for the poor has at times been almost as divisive as the issue that split the Church at the time of the Reformation. But this time the Roman authorities have been somewhat more flexible—or at least rather more subtle—and most of the new reformers have not allowed themselves to be pushed out of the Church. There has been an ongoing encounter between the two sides. At its best this has been a dialogue and at its worst it has been a painful conflict. The encounter has taken place in three spheres—the theological, the political, and the ecclesiastical.

By and large, liberationists seem to have won the *theological* debate. In 1975 Pope Paul VI, in the document *Evangelii Nuntiandi*, gave the word "liberation" a high measure of theological respectability. Pope John Paul II came more and more to use the language of liberation theology. The 1986 Vatican document on liberation represented an important backing down by Rome from the hard line adopted only two years previously. In October 2011, Cardinal Müller, prefect of the Vatican Congregation for the Doctrine of the Faith, speaking of Gustavo Gutiérrez, who is regarded as the father of liberation theology, assured Catholics that his theology is orthodox. And in an interview in October 2014, he said that as far as pastoral work is concerned, Pope Francis has close ties with liberation theology's concerns. Furthermore, both Gutiérrez and Leonard Boff were invited by Francis to make suggestions about the content of the ecology encyclical.

However, the movement has not been entirely on one side. The number of theologians who explicitly identify themselves as liberation theologians has dwindled, and those who remain have distanced themselves more and more from Marxism, except insofar as they still speak of a global imperialism of Western capitalism and still emphasize the need for a structural analysis of society and for changes at the structural level. Two major factors in the growing acceptance of liberation theology have been its new emphasis on respect for indigenous cultures and the convergence between it and feminist theology. This has led to a broadening of both the agenda and the approach of the liberation theologians.

At the *political* level the liberationists won a spectacular early victory. In 1979 the Somoza regime in Nicaragua was overthrown by an alliance of freedom fighters, of whom a significant segment were committed Catholics inspired by the theology of liberation. But there was bitter disappointment for those who expected that these first fruits would be followed quickly by others. Oppressive governments in Guatemala and El Salvador, strongly supported by the US government of that period, succeeded for quite some time in holding the line against those who were struggling for liberation. However, over the following decade, democracy was restored as a result of nonviolent struggles in Brazil, Argentina, Chile, and several other parts of the world; and Catholics fired by the ideal of liberation contributed a great deal to the winning of these victories. Somewhat more recently, in Venezuela and in some other Latin American countries the Church has remained divided; most of the Church leaders are quite hostile to populist left-wing governments, but a significant number of grassroots Christians are in favor of the government policies.

At the *ecclesiastical* level, those who favored the liberationist approach were, by and large, defeated. Their early achievements were mainly on the ground at the local level. Many thousands of lay leaders, trained and formed in basic communities, provided a very effective ministry and helped many Christians come to a deeper understanding of their faith and play a far more active and effective part in the life of the Church. There were also significant efforts in some dioceses to adopt a participative model of planning; where this succeeded, it led to a real empowerment of lay-people. But, sadly, the development of a collaborative model of Church organization was blocked or even reversed in many places as a result of the Vatican policy of appointing bishops who were unsympathetic to such an approach. And Church authorities often attempted to silence or mar-ginalize theologians who were considered to be liberationist in outlook. There are indications that Pope Francis has begun to reverse this process.

Disturbed by the rapid growth of Pentecostalism in Latin America, Africa, and Asia, and by the number of Catholics who joined these churches or sects, the Catholic Church authorities responded with a new emphasis on "evangelization." But in many situations the chosen model of evangelization was an inward-looking and devotional one that does not give a high priority to issues of justice or ecology.

The understanding of evangelization espoused by Pope Francis is clearly much broader and richer than the one that was put forward earlier. It obviously includes a devotional element, but it also includes a strong commitment to justice and ecology. Francis repeatedly called Christians and the wider human community to work on behalf of fragile people and the fragile Earth, insisting that there is an inseparable link between an option for the poor and an option for the Earth.

Continuity with Shifting Emphases

I have maintained that there was notable continuity in Catholic social teaching over the seventy years between 1891 and 1961, and that since then there has been a shift in emphasis and even, to some extent, in direction. I suggested that Pope Benedict aimed to give Catholic social teaching another change in emphasis if not in direction. Finally, I examined the words and actions of Pope Francis and concluded that his aim has been to shift the emphasis back to the direction opened up by Vatican II and then to take mainstream Catholic social teaching further along the lines adopted by the Latin American bishops, under the influence of liberation theology.

Is there any sense in which we can speak of a consistent tradition of social teaching spanning the whole period of about 130 years? Not in the sense of repeating today the very specific principles that I listed earlier as characteristic of the first 70 years and not in the sense of having the same Catholic ethos that I described as typical of that period. The principles have been adapted significantly in ways that I have spelled out elsewhere (Dorr 1991, 83–102). In addition, the Catholic ethos has changed enormously both in regard to the attitudes held by typical Catholics and in being far less monolithic than in the past.

It is, however, possible to speak of an organic tradition in a general sense—a sense that is, nevertheless, authentic. Pope John Paul presented his teaching on sociopolitical and economic issues as part of an organic tradition. Pope Benedict was particularly insistent that there is a single coherent tradition. In *Caritas in Veritate* he said: "It is not a case of two typologies of social doctrine, one pre-conciliar and one post-conciliar, differing from one another: on the contrary, there is *a single teaching, consistent and at the same time ever new*" (*CiV* 12). And Pope Francis quite evidently sees his teaching and actions as situated within a coherent tradition, even though he has spelled out in some detail what it means in practice for the Church to be on the side of those who are poor or marginalized and has made a major contribution to Catholic teaching on the environment.

The popes do not have in mind a rigid system made up of a body of immutable truths, but rather a pattern of teaching that has been consistent over the years, while allowing for development and even, perhaps, changes of emphasis. In this view the coherence or consistent character of the teaching is based on an enduring commitment of the Church to certain basic values such as human dignity, the value of the person as a worker, the right of everybody to the conditions required to be free and responsible, the importance of human community and solidarity, the importance of subsidiary levels of organization, the notion of the common good as meaning the welfare of all, and, most recently, the extension of the understanding of the common good to include nonhuman creatures as well as humans.

These values, in turn, are based on certain fundamental truths about the human person, the nature of society, and the role of the Church. These truths include the following:

1. Every person is called by God to share in the divine creative work, the redemption of the world, and the promotion of the Reign of God.
2. Human cooperation in creation, redemption, and the furthering of God's Reign is brought about through an integral development that has social, economic, environmental, political, cultural, and religious aspects.
3. An integral development is one where the spiritual and the temporal are not sharply opposed to each other and where the mission of the Church is not limited to purely religious matters.

Already in 1891, Leo XIII was defending the fundamental truths and values that lie at the heart of the Church's social teaching today. Furthermore, this continuity is not just nominal but is the basis for continuity in practical implications. For instance, John Paul, when defending the right of Brazilian workers to form trade unions, could present his teaching as part of a tradition stretching back to Leo XIII. Again, there is a real continuity in the misgivings of all the popes from Leo XIII up to the present about both liberal capitalist ideology and Marxist ideology.

The conclusion that emerges is that there is a certain organic unity in Catholic social teaching, even though there has been considerable development and significant shifts of focus and emphasis over the years. It would be foolish to imagine that the Church can provide clear practical guidelines to politicians, economists, or planners. But the vision of life derived from the gospel and developed in the Church over centuries does provide Christians and all people of goodwill with important criteria that can be of great help in their ongoing search for ways of living in society that are truly just and humane.

However, the body of Catholic social teaching is not a single indissoluble whole. It is composed of many different strands, and some of these are more developed and more valuable than others. I now move on to explore some of the strengths and weakness of this tradition of social teaching.

STRENGTHS AND WEAKNESSES OF CATHOLIC SOCIAL TEACHING

The first and greatest strength of the tradition of Catholic social teaching is that, with the issuing of *Laudato Si'*, Pope Francis's encyclical on the environment, it has become truly *integral*: it combines a strong *humanistic* aspect with an equally strong *ecological* aspect. It is not, of course humanist in the sense of excluding faith or the supernatural. In saying it is humanistic I am referring to the deeply human aspect which Pope John Paul constantly emphasized, for instance, in his first encyclical (*Redemptor Hominis* 14–15), in the centenary encyclical (*Centesimus Annus* 53–55), and when he was acknowledging that his gospel message could have political effects in Eastern Europe, as noted above. In the past this humanistic aspect of Catholic social teaching was expressed mainly by saying that it is based on natural law. After Vatican II, this aspect was not played down, but there was a new emphasis on human rights and, with Pope John Paul, on a Christian anthropology.

A particular advantage of having a social teaching that is humanistic is that it aims to appeal not merely to Christians but to all people of goodwill. Furthermore, it means that there is room for a constant dialogue with other traditions—not merely a desire to teach others but also a willingness to learn from others. Perhaps the most obvious example of this is the way in which over the past generation the popes have taken up and used the language of human rights, which was originally articulated not in the Catholic tradition but in the humanistic traditions of Enlightenment France and the newly independent United States. More recently the Church has begun to make its own the moral wisdom that is emerging through the ecological movement and the feminist movement, neither of which was distinctively Catholic at first.

When Pope Benedict introduced the helpful image of "a grammar of nature" (*CiV* 48), he wanted to integrate traditional Catholic sexual teaching with Catholic social teaching on ecology. But his ecology was still marked by a certain anthropocentric character. The *integral ecology* put forward by Pope Francis is no longer anthropocentric but remains fully humanistic. In fact, I am inclined to say that what he offers us is not just an integral ecology but a framework for an *integral Catholic social teaching*, which includes not just the items that Francis emphasizes but also all the other significant elements in the Catholic social tradition. His account of "our common home" has taken seriously the full meaning of the word "ecology" which is based on the Greek word *oikos*, meaning "home." The word "ecology" as commonly used refers to nature as distinct from what is human. But the integral ecology of Francis is not confined to nonhuman nature. It includes also the whole range of what is involved for humans in being "at home"—including culture, politics, and economics. (The word *oikos* is also the basis for the word "economics.") Furthermore, the ecological teaching of Francis provides a solid biblical-theological basis for a prophetic ecological spirituality, which is a profound and uncompromising challenge to the present dominant model of the unsustainable development that exploits both the Earth and its poorest people.

A second strength of Catholic social teaching is that it has a rich *contemplative* dimension. Prior to the coming of Francis the contemplative aspect of social teaching was more or less implicit. But in *Laudato Si'* Francis insists strongly and eloquently that the Christian understanding of our close relationship with the rest of the natural world nourishes our spirits and can lead us into a contemplative quasi-mystical experience of solidarity, sisterhood/brotherhood, and even oneness.

A third strength of Catholic social teaching is its strong affirmation of personal human rights. Because the fundamental basis of Catholic teaching is respect for human dignity, it puts the focus not merely on political and civil rights but equally on social, economic, and cultural rights, such as adequate housing, secure, employment, and respect for cultural differences (see Connolly 2014, 3–9, for the corresponding developments in the political world).[1]

A fourth strong point of Catholic social teaching as it is understood today is that it is focuses particular attention on participation. This value is crucial because it puts limits on the arbitrary exercise of power by those in authority. In any society or organization where the value of participation is respected, people themselves can claim their own rights and shape their own destiny. So participation is a value that opens the way to a whole wide range of other values. It serves to give content to Catholic social teaching in a variety of different situations, and it provides criteria that

---

[1] I have put forward the view elsewhere that the natural law tradition and the human rights tradition can fit together very well and that each can enrich the other and compensate for the weaknesses of the other tradition—see Dorr 2013, 33–42.

can be applied in practice. Furthermore, those who participate in decision making are energized, feel respected, and have a sense of involvement and ownership in the whole project.

A fifth strength of Catholic social teaching is its strong emphasis on solidarity. When people take solidarity seriously it rescues them from selfish individualism and enables them to avoid the danger of an unduly individualistic conception of personal human rights (cf. Dorr 2013, 36–37). A sense of solidarity gives people an awareness that they are responsible for each other and for the welfare of the community. Solidarity is a virtue that gives people the will, the energy, and even the passion not to be content with theory and words but to act justly in their personal lives and to work and struggle for justice and ecological respect both in the wider society and in any organization or movement, including the Church, in which they are involved (cf. Dorr 2015, 32–39). In more recent years, there has been a further development in relation to solidarity, namely a stronger insistence on the importance of intergenerational solidarity. Pope Benedict and Pope Francis have emphasized that we have a responsibility for future generations, so solidarity is to be extended in time as well as in space.

Furthermore, there is a strong and growing awareness that we humans may not confine our sense of solidarity to other humans. We are called to have a sense of solidarity with other living beings and with the whole of creation. So the Catholic concern for ecological issues is now firmly rooted in this wider understanding of solidarity. The ecological dimension of solidarity is particularly prominent in the teaching of Pope Francis.

A sense of solidarity with all of humanity and with the other creatures with whom we share this world provides a solid basis for people to act responsibly in the sphere of sexuality. Being liberated from a narrow and selfish individualism, each person can freely choose how best to engage in loving sexual relationships. Couples who are biologically infertile may choose to extend their love for their partners to the wider local and global community. Being aware of the problem of overpopulation, fertile couples may choose responsibly to be loving with each other in ways that limit the number of their children. The motivation of those who freely choose to be celibate may include a desire to exercise their love in a manner that does not burden our overstretched world with a larger human population than it can sustain.

A sixth strength of the Church's teaching on justice and ecology is the way in which it refuses to treat these as two separate topics but instead links them very closely together. This linkage was already present in the document "Justice in the World," issued by the 1971 Synod of Bishops in Rome. Pope Francis took up this theme and made it perhaps the most central aspect of his social teaching. His position is encapsulated in his insistence that at the heart of the Christian faith is a commitment to protect fragile people and the fragile Earth.

The seventh strong point of the Church's social teaching is that it is not too detailed or specific but is compatible with a certain pluralism. It is open to a variety of applications on different continents and in different circumstances. Very closely related to this is the fact that, while touching on the political sphere in a general way, Catholic social teaching seeks to avoid being identified with the policies of any particular political party or movement. It claims rather to offer criteria by which such specific policies may be evaluated.

The official Church has learned how important it is to keep at a certain distance from the popular trends or preferred options of any particular era, even those which seemed very admirable to Christian leaders at the time. Around the time of Leo XIII it seemed to many that the true Christian option was a revival of the guild system. In the 1930s it seemed that a vocational or corporative organization of society was the only correct Christian answer to social problems. After World War I and again after World War II there was a strong move to identify Church teaching with the policies of Christian Democracy parties in many countries. In the aftermath of John XXIII's encyclicals many Christians opted for a "welfare state" model. In the late 1960s and early 1970s Christians for Socialism and other New Left movements seemed to many to be the only authentic way forward. From the mid-1980s onward some sectors of the Church, especially in the United States, came to believe that the solution is to identify authentic Catholic social teaching with a close linkage between democracy and capitalism.

There have been occasions when various popes have flirted to some extent with one or other of these trends—but never to the extent to which the enthusiasts would have wished. On the whole the pope and bishops have tried to keep the official Church above politics; they have maintained a certain distance from specific applications of the general principles, leaving it to lay Christians as citizens to opt for one policy or another. However, they have not hesitated to suggest that some of the proposed policies—particularly outright socialism and unrestricted capitalism—are incompatible with the basic principles of Catholic social teaching.

An eighth strength of Catholic social teaching is that it is based on some degree of social analysis, on a serious attempt to identify the historical, economic, and cultural root causes of global poverty and inequity. Consequently, it is not content with speaking out against unjust actions or people but condemns the sinful structures that are both the effect and the cause of acts and attitudes of social injustice.

A ninth important strength of Catholic social teaching is that it insists that it is essential to tackle not just absolute poverty but also relative poverty. This point was already made by Pius XII as long ago as 1941 (see chapter 4). Much more recently it was put in very stark terms by Pope Francis in his statement: "Inequality is the root of social ills" (*EG* 202).

A tenth strength of Catholic social teaching is the emphasis on what Pope Benedict calls an "economy of communion." The initiatives of the Focolare and others in establishing what Benedict called dual purpose enterprises are important. Possibly even more significant is the fact that a minority of economists and others have pointed out the many unrecognized ways in which even the regular economic interactions in our world are characterized by, and dependent on, a significant degree of interpersonal respect and trust. If mainstream Catholic social teaching takes up and develops this point, it may make a major contribution to the emergence of a more humane model of economics. However, such an emphasis on "an economy of communion" should not be seen as an alternative to an overt struggle for justice and liberation; both approaches are required.

The eleventh strong point about the Church's social teaching, especially as it has developed in recent years, is that it is biblical, at least in the sense that it can find a solid basis in the Bible. One of the most helpful parts of *Laudato Si'*, Pope Francis's encyclical on the environment, is the section on the biblical basis for a theological ecology. That Catholic social teaching on justice and ecology is soundly biblical means that there is ample room for ecumenical dialogue on social issues with other Christian churches, most of which tend to rely more on the Bible than on a natural law or humanistic basis.

A twelfth strength of Catholic social teaching is that it is prophetic in the sense that it is radically challenging and inspirational. It calls on settled people to open their hearts and their countries to refugees. It is uncompromising in its condemnation of the oppression and trafficking of people, the exploitation of the Earth, and the consumerism and alienation linked to these abuses. It is in direct continuity with the words of the Old Testament prophets in denouncing injustice and announcing new hope for all, above all for the poor and oppressed, as well as in its insistence on respect for the land. At its best it can be experienced as a sharing in the liberating task of Jesus. It calls on Christians and all people of goodwill to work for a fundamental reshaping of society both at the global and the local levels. Over the past fifty years Catholic social teaching has come to a deeper understanding of the Church's call to side with the poor and the powerless in working for justice and for respect for the environment; and it has found in the term "preferential option for the poor and for the Earth" a striking and effective way of expressing this call. For these reasons Catholic social teaching is inspiring and evangelical, a teaching which lies at the heart of the Christian faith.

Weaknesses in the Social Teaching Tradition

Nonetheless, Catholic social teaching is somewhat weak or at least insufficiently developed in some areas.

The first and most obvious inadequacy in the social teaching of the Catholic Church is its failure to provide an adequate treatment of the issue of justice for women. It is a matter of astonishment that in a world where women exercise top leadership roles in various governments, the business world, and the media, they are precluded from holding significant authority in the institutional (hierarchical) structures of the Catholic Church. This was understandable—though of course inexcusable—in the past when Catholic theology held that women were inferior to men and that "the woman's place was in the home." However, recent scriptural studies have emphasized the radical character of the ministry of Jesus. They have shown how he clearly challenged the patriarchal structure of his society—even scandalizing the religious authorities by inviting women to be an integral part of the community he formed around himself (cf. Pagola 2009, passim). They have also noted how, before very long, the young Christian communities slipped back into a patriarchal style of governance. Church authorities have also been influenced—sometimes reluctantly and occasionally gratefully—by the challenge to patriarchy posed by the women's movement in recent years. In attempting to be truer to the message and spirit of Jesus, official Catholic teaching has insisted time and time again over the past fifty years that women are equal in dignity and status to men and has condemned in the strongest terms the many injustices suffered by women. Furthermore, Church leaders have affirmed clearly that women have a critically important role to play in public life.

In the light of these developments it is a cause of serious disquiet, even of scandal, that Church authorities have not yet been prepared to allow women to hold leadership roles equivalent to those held by men. The question concerning the ordination of women is a separate issue, but it is often used as an excuse for not facing up to the choice of appointing women to top leadership roles in the Vatican. So long as this anomaly remains in the practice of the Catholic Church, it remains as a fault line that seriously lessens the credibility of its teaching over the whole range of Catholic social teaching. Pope Francis insists repeatedly that "everything is connected" in our world and our cosmos. That women are not allowed to play their full part in the interconnected web of life must be seen as a serious flaw in the web, one that mars its beauty and damages its effectiveness.

Quite some time ago Amata Miller wrote a striking study, the title of which sums up her main point: "Catholic Social Teaching—What Might

Have Been If Women Were Not Invisible in a Patriarchal Society" (A. Miller 1991a). She emphasized the "fundamental congruence" between the basic values undergirding Catholic social teaching and the values of the women's movements of the past hundred years. But she spelled out a major blind spot in those who articulated Catholic teaching during that period: they did not take account of the real situation of women in the workplace during that time.

Miller documented the exploitation of women in the economic life of the nation. This is the basis for what is perhaps the most valuable aspect of her study, namely, the way in which she inserted the victimization of women into the mainstream of social injustice, rather than allowing women's issues to remain in a separate category. She brought out how, in the past, the commitment of Church leaders to the ideal of "woman in the home" prevented them acknowledging (or perhaps even seeing) the numbers of women who were going out to work and how this caused them to overlook the gross exploitation of women's labor. Miller pointed out that the blindness in relation to women at work persisted for very many years after the time of Leo XIII. She held that even John Paul II maintained an unrealistic approach on this issue. She went on to bring out very effectively the gap that was left in Catholic social teaching. She speculated shrewdly about the advances that might have been made "if church leaders had been able to see and hear the women of their times, and if women struggling for justice had found consistent support in the official teaching of the church." For her, what was in question was a serious sin of omission that weakened the impact of the "exhortations to justice in the workplace" issued by Church leaders like Pope John Paul and made "their calls for respect of life hollow and partial to many."

I suggested in chapter 14 that *Laborem Exercens* may be understood as a significant break with previous Church teaching about women and work. But even if the official teaching on women and work has changed, the change has been so surreptitious and unheralded that it may well have been counterproductive in its effect. I suspect that it has left Church spokespersons with no clear sense of where Catholic social teaching now stands on this issue. The result is that they seldom or never speak out strongly on the various kinds of exploitation of women that commonly occur in the workplace. This spares women from hearing the old-fashioned and patronizing defense of women that they often heard from Church leaders in the past. But the resulting silence may well be even more damaging, because it makes women at work more invisible than ever—which means that Catholic social teaching still suffers from the blind spot identified by Miller so many years ago.

Also in chapter 14 I noted that the way in which Pope John Paul described the complementarity of women and men remains a highly controversial topic. The real difficulty here is his insistence on using the word "ontological." It would be better to avoid the use of this word and instead rely on the relatively recent findings of neurobiology. Scientific studies show clearly the extraordinary bonding that occurs between infants and their mothers during the first couple of years of the infant's life—and the importance of this for the proper development of the child. This is about *mothers* rather than about women as such. It raises important and challenging issues about how our society is organized at present—issues that are high on the agenda of many feminists and others. Would it not be wonderful if Church leaders were to join their voices with enlightened feminists and all who have come to see how important it is that mothers who choose to spend significant periods of time with their infant children should be supported morally, socially, and financially in doing so, rather than being pressured to return as quickly as possible to full-time work outside the home?

The issue of the complementarity of women and men is linked to the even more controversial issue of the insistence by the popes that the Church does not have the authority to ordain women to the priesthood. As Mary T. Malone remarks: "The question of the ordination of women has remained a kind of permanent battleground in the Catholic Church" (Malone 2014, 160). The controversy has become one of the most high-profile issues on the Church's agenda in relation to women and has led to a serious alienation from the Church of many women and men. One of the results of the time and energy devoted to such hot-button issues is that Catholic social teaching until very recently has failed to give as much prominence as it should to certain key areas of the exploitation of women, such as the extraordinary increase in pornography, especially through the internet and the trafficking of women for sexual exploitation. So the strong emphasis of Pope Francis on the issue of trafficking is to be greatly welcomed.

Probably the most impressive statement by the official Church on justice from the point of view of women is a short passage in the document issued in 1971 by the Synod of Bishops in Rome. In it the bishops urged that women should have their proper share of responsibility and participation both in society and in the Church (JW 42). It is time that the official Church took up this theme once again. The controversy surrounding the efforts of the bishops of the United States a generation ago to prepare a document about women is a clear indication of how difficult it will be to find a way forward so long as the main articulators of Catholic social teaching are male clerics. The Church must find a means of enabling women to play a central role in formulating the social teaching and policies of the Church, especially those that concern women. An important step in the right direction would be that the Vatican should at last act more effectively than in the past on the recommendation of the 1971 synod that a mixed commission be set up to explore the issue of the role of women in society and in the Church.

A second issue is that it is only with the coming of Pope Francis that the Church's social teaching is becoming sufficiently ecological in its scope. The relative weakness of the approach to ecology adopted by Pope John Paul and Pope Benedict was that their ecological teaching was too anthropocentric. These two popes were inclined to make an unduly sharp contrast between "natural ecology" and "human ecology." In one way it was a step forward when Church leaders after Vatican II began to switch their emphasis from natural law to "the defense of the human." In a similar way it was a kind of progress when, at about the same time, theologians began to replace their courses and books on "The Theology of Creation" with "Theological Anthropology." But what tended to become lost as a result of these changes was a sufficiently profound awareness of the unity of creation as a whole. In the vision of Pope Francis there is a very close link between fragile people and the fragile Earth. His teaching on the environment represents an important step toward the development of a theological anthropology that is firmly located within the context of a renewed theological cosmology or theology of creation, which recognizes the intrinsic value of every level of being in creation. This now provides a solid theological basis for a Catholic social teaching on economic issues situated within the wider and more fundamental context of the environmental crisis that the world is facing.

However, as I pointed out toward the end of the previous chapter, the relative absence of an explicit emphasis on the "New Story" is a significant lacuna in official teaching. The "New Story" provides the basis for a rich and comprehensive spirituality that appeals both to the head and to the heart. Catholic teaching on the environment would be greatly enriched if it took more account of the work of ecological theologians over the past generation. Their emphasis on how an awareness of the whole evolutionary process contributes a valuable and even essential focus to theology and spirituality is insufficiently adverted to in the social teaching of the popes; and this is a serious gap in Catholic social teaching.

A third weakness of Catholic social teaching is that it does not yet provide us with practical criteria for discerning the limits of human interference with nature. Pope Francis has made a major contribution to social teaching on the environment. In doing so he has built on the strong emphasis of Pope Benedict on respect for the environment and on Pope John Paul's teaching on the integrity of creation. But Catholic teaching has not succeeded in giving us clear guidelines for knowing how to respect this integrity. There is need for serious work to be done on the right to continued existence of various species of living beings and even of individual animals, as well as on the duty of humans to protect places of natural beauty.

Up until very recently Catholic social teaching presented the duty of respecting the environment mainly in terms of its effect on *humans*. This was supplemented by reference to the ultimate criterion of the "prior God-given purpose" of the Earth (*CA* 37) or the God-given "grammar" of nature (*CiV* 48). The problem, of course, is how we humans are to discern this grammar. An urgent task for Church leaders today is to be aware of the ways in which scientists are exploring the "grammar of nature," that is, the pattern of evolution and the ways in which the myriad strands in the web of life and the web of the wider cosmos all hold together. "New Story" thinking would provide a context in which these difficult issues could be addressed.

A fourth weakness of Catholic social teaching is that the human values that it embodies may not be as fully transcultural as they have been assumed to be. These values were articulated almost entirely in a Western context. Rome has been unduly reluctant to allow the local Churches of different continents to develop their own articulations of social teaching. The present body of teaching, for all its merits, needs to be supplemented, and partially corrected, by the values that have been or will be articulated in situations where Christianity is incarnated in, say, Asian, African, Oceanic, or Latin American cultures, as well as in the many subcultures in various parts of the world. An example may bring out the point. At present, Catholic social teaching seems generally to presuppose that the word "family" refers to the nuclear family. Consequently, it tends to neglect or ignore the rich values embodied in the extended family, although this is an institution that plays a central role in the lives of most African peoples and many of the peoples of Asia and elsewhere.

Another example raises even more far-reaching questions. Catholic social teaching now places a lot of emphasis on the right to development. But, as I pointed out toward the end of chapter 6, it is essential to distinguish between development and *Western-style* development. Many Church leaders and theologians have not succeeded in holding on to this distinction, despite the helpful approach adopted by Paul VI in *Populorum Progressio*. Consequently, there was a real danger that the promotion of Catholic social teaching, as articulated up to the papacy of Pope Francis, would contribute to the imposition of Western values on people of other cultures. It could also lead to the neglect, in Catholic social teaching, of some of the most fundamental values of non-Western cultures, for instance, serenity, respect, gentleness, harmony, cooperation, rootedness, contemplation, and a sense of oneness with nature or with "the All." If the contemplative ecological spirituality put forward in *Laudato Si'* is fully accepted, it will provide a vital safeguard against this danger.

There are indications that when Western-style "development" is promoted in non-Western cultures it brings with it an exploitative attitude, competition, and consumerism. After John Paul became pope and during the period prior to the collapse of communism the pope and some other Church leaders seemed to think that these problems were characteristic not of Western culture as such but only of the "decadent West"—and that they could be remedied by an influx of renewed faith coming from the resurgent Catholics of Eastern Europe. But what happened in Eastern Europe in the 1990s showed that this was wishful thinking. When countries of the former Soviet bloc embraced capitalism, there was quite a shocking increase in consumerism, exploitation, and a gross widening of the gap between the rich and the poor.

Over the past two hundred years insensitivity to the Earth and lack of respect for people became features of large sectors of Western civilization and culture, in North America, Western Europe, and Australia, as well as in communist countries. If Catholic social teaching and practice is to challenge this effectively, it needs to be far more open than in the past to the values of non-Western cultures and of other religious visions of life. As Charles Curran (2002, 92) points out, the great diversity in our world means that "there are no easy, ready-made solutions to the manifold problems facing the world." So the only way forward is to return to the approach outlined by Paul VI in *Octogesima Adveniens*, in which he recognized that in the face of widely varying situations he does not aim "to put forward a solution which has universal validity" (*OA* 4). Pope Francis is clearly committed in principle to adopting this approach. But we must wait and see how well and how widely this will be acted on in practice in future teaching and practice.

A fifth area in which Catholic social teaching is somewhat weak or undeveloped concerns the issue of alternatives to the present model of development. This is closely related to the topic I have just been discussing. It is understandable—though inexcusable—that politicians should play down the problems associated with a reliance on rapid economic Western-style development as a solution to problems of poverty, inequity, and unemployment. But it is more difficult to understand why so few Church leaders at the local level have taken seriously the sharp criticism by recent popes of the present model of development. The world needs to be forcefully reminded how futile and foolish it is to imagine that more economic growth can solve the major economic problems that face all of us. Furthermore, the popes and other Church leaders need to go beyond their call for a change of lifestyle and for frugality by those who are well-off. They need to spell out practical ways in which people can live more simply, less exploitatively, and more in partnership with nature. Pope Francis, in his ecology encyclical has taken an important step in this direction by radically challenging the present model of development, praising small-scale alternative approaches, and indicating various ways in which people should live more simply.

However, there is need for something more—for influential groups of scientists, politicians, and theologians to work together in proposing realistic alternatives to the present dominant model of development. The Church need not claim to have a Catholic blueprint for society; but it could certainly point out some of the criteria, for example, reliance on renewable energy, technology that does not lead to mass unemployment, policies that favor public transport systems rather than private vehicles, production units that are not so big and so specialized that the workers are alienated from the products that are produced, and reliance as far as possible on local food products and raw materials. Some of these criteria are already implicit in the Church's traditional emphasis on the principle of subsidiarity; but the implications need to be spelled out.[2] Church leaders in all corners of the world must follow the lead of Pope Francis in insisting on the urgent need of a search for alternative styles of living and of organizing society.

It is particularly important that Church leaders should offer moral and practical support to those committed Christians and others who are already modeling such an alternative lifestyle. Perhaps it is not too much to expect that Church leaders should find ways in which they themselves can model a pattern of living that is ecologically sustainable and that does not require more than an equitable share of the limited resources of the Earth. This may be dismissed as unrealistic. But since the Church is called to be prophetic it has to be somewhat unrealistic. It cannot allow the prevailing situation to be the sole determinant of what is considered realistic.

The sixth area in which Catholic social teaching needs further development and clarification has to do with the role of the Church in politics. The Church has developed some general guidelines over the past 100 years. Central to the accepted approach is a practical distinction between the area of politics and that of religion—even though the two overlap to some extent. Within the terms of this distinction, the Church's main concern is with religion, but by its nature this includes some involvement in the social and political spheres of life. It is accepted that Church lead-

---

[2]It is also important to take account of a point noted as early as the 1970s by Ivan Illich in his essay "Energy and Equity." He pointed out that an increased use of energy goes hand in hand with an increase in the gap between the rich and the poor; this brings out the close links between the ecological issue and the justice issue (Illich 1978, 110–43) and the urgent need for an alternative to the present-day unsustainable and exploitative pattern of so-called development.

ers are not entitled to claim any special competence in purely political matters. Lay Christians, in their capacity as citizens, are encouraged to take part in politics, even party politics. The Church discourages priests and members of religious communities from becoming actively involved in overtly political activity, or party politics; the aim is to ensure that the Church does not compromise its basic function by becoming too closely identified with any particular party.

These guidelines have served the Church well and are not to be discarded lightly. But they still leave some awkward questions—particularly since Church leaders have committed the Church to the defense of poor and oppressed people and of the Earth. When Church leaders speak out on justice issues they enter the political area. The distinction between politics in a broad sense and party politics is very helpful where a number of different democratic parties, sharing the same fundamental moral values, differ in regard to priorities and programs; the Church can then maintain its neutrality in relation to all of them. But what happens if there are two major parties and the policy of one of them is to maintain an unjust and totally undemocratic social order while the other party is committed to social justice? What if a tyrannical government outlaws democratic opposition and the only effective resistance is through movements that the oppressive government labels subversive? If Church leaders speak out clearly and specifically on issues of justice in such situations, they will be understood to be taking sides on political issues, and they will in effect be no longer keeping aloof from party politics.

It would be helpful if Catholic social teaching were to acknowledge more clearly the difference between this kind of situation and one where the differences between political parties are concerned not with fundamental issues of social justice but only with the practical means of attaining it. Furthermore, there is a lack of clarity in Church teaching about whether or to what degree official Church people should be involved in advocacy or lobbying in relation to specific justice or ecology issues.

The seventh area in which Catholic social teaching needs to be developed more fully concerns the matter of social analysis. In listing the strengths of the tradition I noted that present social teaching is based on a good deal of social analysis. But this analysis is incomplete. There is some attempt to explore the historical roots of international injustice. But there seems to be a reluctance to engage in an analysis of the root causes of social injustice at the national and local levels. In *Laborem Exercens*, Pope John Paul went some way toward closing this gap. But even his account remained rather generic and put the focus more on the past than on the present. Pope Francis has been blunt in his condemnation of the exploitative model of capitalism that is dominant at present and of how it damages developing countries. But there is need for an even more explicit condemnation of the ways in which present-day neocolonialism is perpetuating and in some respects exacerbating the exploitation and injustice of the colonialism of the past.

It seems that the reason why Catholic social teaching is reticent on the issue of social analysis is that it reveals and highlights the extent to which most modern societies are divided into different social classes. For well over a century Church authorities have tended to shy away from the question of the class structure of society. This springs from an understandable desire not to foment class struggle. But the consequence is that Church leaders often fail to take full account of the conflicting interests of the rich and the poor.

Critics would say that Church leaders are unwilling to acknowledge the extent to which the official Church is itself unduly tied to the interests of the more powerful classes in society. There was truth in this accusation at least in the past; so it is not surprising that Church people tended to dismiss social analysis as a Marxist idea. When Church leaders in Latin America and elsewhere made an option for the poor, they were setting out to correct this imbalance. The sectors of the Christian community who favor such an option are also committed to serious social and structural analysis. They believe that it is only in this way that they can discover who the poor really are and what the fundamental causes of their poverty are. But commitment to social analysis was not welcomed by Vatican authorities, and, up to the present, it has not had a major impact on the main Church documents on social justice issues. The new emphasis of Pope Francis on the structural causes of poverty may lead to a more welcoming attitude to social analysis by the Church's highest authorities.

An eighth point on which the teaching of the Church remains insufficiently developed is related to the previous one; it concerns the question of confrontation and conflict. I have touched on aspects of this in various parts of this book and have discussed the topic of confrontation at some length in chapter 13 in which I examined John Paul's teaching on solidarity in *Sollicitudo Rei Socialis*. It suffices to say here that the traditional social teaching put so much emphasis on harmony and consensus that it played down the fact that confrontation can at times be an essential aspect of working for social justice. The early teaching of John Paul on solidarity provided a partial corrective for this oversight. But even after that insufficient attention has been paid to this issue. Vatican authorities seemed reluctant to say anything that might be taken as an incitement to the poor or the powerless to demand their rights. Furthermore, priests or members of religious communities who help the poor in organizing themselves to press for their rights have often been frowned on or condemned as being too political or as being involved in a suspect form of liberation theology.

Charles Curran (2002, 85–89) has a helpful treatment of the issue of conflict and power. He suggests that the organic and hierarchical approach to society found in Catholic social teaching (especially in the earlier years) leads to a downplaying of conflict. Furthermore, Catholic social teaching up to very recently has focused mainly on general principles rather than on the specific situations where conflicts generally occur. Curran (2002, 90) suggests that conflict is often seen as the consequence of sin, bringing division, and therefore as something to be avoided. He holds that it is important to appreciate that conflict can also have a positive aspect and that power includes not only domination but also empowerment.

The fact is that most modern societies are made up of groups with conflicting interests. This means that Christians often find themselves in situations where society is created as much through conflict as through consensus and harmony. So there is need for Catholic social teaching to offer realistic guidelines to help those who are struggling for social justice in such situations; they need support and guidance in finding ways to struggle for their own basic values and rights while respecting the views of those whose vision of life is quite different.

As I pointed out in chapters 19 and 20, Pope Francis has adopted a far more supportive role toward Church activists who engage in contestation in a responsible nonviolent manner. He complimented social activists for having "the smell of the struggle," and gave examples of various spheres of life where he saw their nonviolent struggle as justified. This represents a quite radical change of emphasis in Catholic social teaching. If it is widely accepted by Church leaders on the ground, it will lead to a situation where the official Church will adopt a far more confrontational and controversial posture vis-à-vis governments. It will be offering solid support to activists who are campaigning for justice and respect for the environment, not only against governments that are notoriously tyrannical, but also against Western governments that are at present reluctant to face up to the ways in which their policies amount in practice to an exploitation of poor countries and of the Earth.

A ninth issue on which there is need for development in Catholic social teaching is where Church teaching on personal sexual morality intersects with wider social issues—the issue of the population explosion. The immediate issue that needs to be addressed is not mainly the sheer size of the global population, which is now in excess of seven billion. There are two more pressing issues. The first of these is the vicious circle in which the population of very poor countries find themselves. Huge numbers of poor people are living in a situation in which they do not have reliable health services or government-provided social services. Consequently, many children die in infancy, and those who survive and prosper are expected to support their younger siblings and relatives, as well as their aged parents. The resulting rapid growth in population undermines governmental development plans and leads to intolerable pressure on environmental resources. The second pressing issue that needs to be addressed is the rapid growth in the numbers of people in many developing countries who are now living a more Western lifestyle and thereby putting a greatly increased demand on the limited resources of planet Earth. The ecology encyclical of Pope Francis has gone quite some way toward stressing the urgency of this latter issue.

Governments faced with population growth that seems almost out of control have the challenge of finding ethically acceptable ways of encouraging people to have smaller families. Clearly, a key way forward is to develop an ecologically sustainable model of development that gives priority to the elimination of poverty and that provides people with some adequate level of social security. But alongside this, there is the other key issue of whether particular forms of contraception are morally acceptable. The Vatican's consistent refusal to rethink the strong stance against contraception in *Humanae Vitae* has meant that Church authorities are reluctant to make a serious examination of the problems arising from rapid population growth in many developing countries.

Another challenging topic related to personal sexual morality is the protection of uninfected people (mainly women) from infection by sexual partners who are carrying the HIV/AIDS virus. This is a particularly serious issue in poor countries. Many of these countries have lost a high proportion of their badly needed professional people (healthcare workers, teachers, etc.). Furthermore, the rapid growth in the number of AIDS orphans has overwhelmed the ability of the traditional extended family support system to cope. The Catholic Church has responded magnificently in providing health services, health education programs, and care for orphans. But in this area, too, the strong stand of the official Church against contraception leads to a reluctance to examine the whole issue from a wider perspective.

A tenth issue on which the social teaching of the Church is in need of further development concerns the question of justice within the Church itself. Prior to the coming of Pope Francis, the only major document in which this issue was taken up courageously was the document "Justice in the World," which was issued by the Synod of Bishops of 1971. It recognized that if the Church's social teaching about society is to be credible and effective, then the Church must be a living witness to this teaching. The crucial test is whether Church leaders are prepared to take seriously the commitments made in that synod and ensure that the institutional Church gives more effective witness to justice in its structures and style of operation. Many observers of the Church accuse it of authoritarianism at every level. They say that the Vatican curia reduced the bishops to the role of line managers, that most diocesan bishops do not share authority adequately with their priests, and that many local pastors do not allow lay Christians, especially women, effective participation in decision making. The radically new approach of Pope Francis has given hope that all this can change. From the beginning he made it quite clear that he wanted to share decision making at the highest level with the bishops. And his repeated sharp condemnation of clericalism shows his determination to do all he can to ensure that this kind of participatory decision making will operate at every level of church life. Particularly striking is his statement in *Evangelii Gaudium*: "Since I am called to put into practice what I ask of others, I too must think about a conversion of the papacy" (*EG* 32).

A further issue in relation to justice in the Church concerns the use of sexist language in most of its official documents and especially in the texts of the liturgy. Many people, above all in the English-speaking world, are quite shocked at the reluctance of the Vatican to use more inclusive language, especially in liturgical texts, as well as at other instances of what they see as sexism in the Church. Some go much further and accuse the official Church of being grossly patriarchal in its organization and mode of acting.

The eleventh and final lacuna in the social teaching of the Catholic Church has to do not with its content but rather with the process through which the teaching is worked out and articulated. In recent years the Vatican has begun to consult lay experts more frequently. But private consultation with specialists is not sufficient. The US Catholic bishops and the World Council of Churches have shown that it is possible to have a much more widespread and public type of consultation. The Roman authorities must find more effective ways of listening to the *sensus fidei* (cf. Coleman 2005, 535). People expect to be consulted about matters that touch their own lives. Many Catholics would like to be actively involved in the formulation of the Church's social teaching. They have much to contribute. Church leaders should make special efforts to find ways of listening more effectively to the voices of people who are poor, of young people, and of women.

Charles Curran offers some helpful ideas on this topic:

> The hierarchical Magisterium is not only an authoritative teacher . . . it is also a learner. This hierarchical office does not simply possess the necessary moral truths in its "sacred patrimony." It is searching continually for the moral truth . . . and testing this truth in broader dialogue with all human sources of moral wisdom and knowledge and all people of good will. (Curran 2002, 116)

Since this is the case, Church leaders should acknowledge that the Holy Spirit speaks through many voices and should welcome the new light which comes from a wide variety of sources, from inside and outside the Church. As Curran points out, "A more open and consultative process would ensure the truly authoritative nature of the teaching" (2002, 118).

Pope Francis has made it clear that he favors a participatory or consultative approach. A very significant move toward such an approach was his insistence that part of the preparation for the Synods of Bishops in 2014 and 2015 should be the preparation of a questionnaire to be sent to bishops all over the world with the request that it would be used to ascertain the views of Christians on the ground. It is true that the actual content of the questionnaires left much to be desired. And in some dioceses the consultation was very inadequate. But the questionnaires were a first step that signaled the possibility—even the likelihood—of much more effective participation and consultation at every level of the Church.

OPTION FOR THE POOR AND FOR THE EARTH

In this final section I propose to give a rather more comprehensive account than I have given previously of what is involved in an option for the poor and for the Earth. My description of the various aspects of this option is based on Catholic teaching as it has developed since the 1960s and on my own reflections on what this teaching includes explicitly and implies implicitly.

The first key point to note about the Christian understanding of such an option is that it is based on the Bible. There is solid scriptural evidence that God is outraged by social injustice and inspires prophetic figures to challenge oppression and work to establish a just society. In the Hebrew Bible we have the call of Moses to rescue his people from slavery; and he was followed by a long line of Spirit-inspired men and women who led their people in resisting oppression. This struggle against injustice is complemented by the Jubilee and Sabbath regulations that are designed to restore justice, protect the land, and provide a time of leisure for humans and animals.

Jesus goes further: he "emptied himself" (Phil. 2:7) to live as one of the poor; he condemned the exploitation of the poor that flourished under the rule of the Roman Empire; he challenged and rejected the oppressive version of Jewish religion that was dominant at that time in his country—one that taught that God did not look with favor on the poor, the sick, and those who did not abide by a multitude of petty regulations; and he proclaimed and witnessed to the Reign of God where the poor are blessed (Luke 6:20), "on earth as in heaven" (Matt. 6:10).

Saint Paul spells out what all this involves. He invites us to recognize how the option of God and of Jesus to be on the side of the poor overturns our everyday experience of the exercise of power. He insists that God "has chosen the weak to confound the strong" (cf. 1 Cor. 1:27.) So those who make an option for and with the poor are surrendering themselves to the power and the justice and the mercy of God rather than relying on some purely human hope of success.

This special role given by God to those who are weak is the basis for the conviction of liberation theologians that poor and marginalized people have a special insight into the mystery of God and human salvation; they can read "the signs of the times" more accurately than those who live a more privileged life (cf. Dorr 2007, 247–57). Pope Francis is fully in line with this position when he maintains that we are called not only to be on the side of the poor but to listen to their insights about God, about Jesus, about the Church, and to allow ourselves to be evangelized by them (*EG* 198).

Another point that has emerged more recently and is strongly confirmed in the teaching of Pope Francis is that the option for the poor and the option for the Earth are not two different realities. The two are intrinsically and inseparably linked together; and both aspects are solidly based on the Bible.

Before I go on to spell out in some detail the many different elements in this option, it is well to note that there are difficulties about the wording of the phrase "option for the poor." First, the use of the words "*for* the poor" could suggest that the poor are passive and that more privileged people who make a choice to help them are the significant ones in the process. So it would be better to speak about an option *with* the poor to be made by people who are not themselves poor. This should be linked to an option *by* the poor made by poor people who decide not to lie passively under their fate but to act together to change the structures that are making and keeping them poor.

A second difficulty about the phrase "option for the poor" is one which I already pointed out in chapter 1 of this book. It is that many people who work respectfully with poor people, as well as quite a lot of poor people themselves, object to the phrase "the poor"; they prefer to speak of "people who are poor." In this way they put the emphasis on the fact that these people are to be defined by their humanity rather than by their poverty. My reasons for continuing to use the phrase "option for the poor" are because it has by now become an accepted standard phrase and also because it links nicely with the phrase "option for the Earth."

Solidarity with the Poor

There are many aspects to an option for the poor and for the Earth as it has emerged and developed in Catholic social teaching. The central practical element in such an option is one of political or quasi-political engagement in an ongoing effort to challenge and overcome structural injustice, by and with people who have been impoverished, oppressed, or marginalized or are suffering the more serious effects of damage to the environment.

Before spelling out the various elements or stages in such a political or quasi-political commitment, I want to devote four paragraphs to exploring what is in some respects a prior aspect of option for the poor. This is the notion of solidarity with the poor. People who come from a rather more privileged background and wish to be authentic in making such an option need to have an experience of real solidarity with those with whom they have chosen to work. I believe that in order to experience this kind of solidarity they need to have some degree of immersion for a significant time in the world and everyday experience of people who are living on the margins of society or are vulnerable as a result of poverty, oppression, or ecological problems. They need to share in some degree in these people's experience of being mistreated, bypassed, or left helpless. This choice of a different life experience springs from compassion—a word that means, literally, suffering with others. By entering the world of deprived people, one extends and deepens one's experience of suffering with those on the margins; and by doing so one comes to share not only their pain and struggle but also their hopes and their joys.

It is only in this way that privileged people can come not merely to understand what people are suffering but also to identify with them at a feeling level. Without this experiential solidarity they are almost certain to retain a degree of what might be called cultural or class insensitivity and even arrogance. This insensitivity will quickly be noticed by those on whose behalf they wish to work, and they will not be fully accepted and trusted by those on the margins.

Solidarity is a gift that those who are poor or marginalized may freely offer to the person who opts to share their life in some degree. It is a gift that cannot be presumed or demanded from them. They give it in their own time and in their own degree, and only to one who comes to them with no air of superiority or paternalism. Despite differences of skin color, or accent, or background, the group may choose to accept this person as "one of us"—or at least "one *with* us"—a person who shares their interests, in both senses of that word.

Pope Francis obviously had this kind of immersion in mind when, very shortly after he became pope, preaching at the Chrism Mass of Holy Thursday (March 28, 2013) he insisted that priests should be living with "the smell of the sheep." In his letter of March 10, 2015, he maintained that this also applies to good theologians. And in his October 28, 2014, address to activists he went so far as to commend them for carrying "the smell of your neighborhood, your people, your *struggle*" (emphasis added). An option for the poor is a commitment that emerges from the praxis of immersion on the ground with poor and marginalized people.[3]

Elements or Stages

I return now to the political or quasi-political aspect of an option for the poor. It involves several elements that are logically, but not necessarily chronologically, distinct from each other. The first of these is a social/structural analysis of the situation that exposes in a fairly comprehensive and systematic manner the oppressive or dysfunctional structures which are root causes of the problem. This leads on to a realization that treating the effects of the wrong structures is not sufficient; the only effective way to change the situation is by changing the structures that cause poverty and oppression.

A further crucial realization is that the main agents in working for liberation and bringing about structural change must be the poor, the oppressed, and the marginalized people and groups themselves. Linked to this is an awareness by those who live in a privileged situation that they can play an important role in overcoming structural injustice by supporting those who are poor in challenging injustice, by helping to empower them in various ways, for example, by awareness-raising and educational and training programs, and by standing in solidarity with them when they take action. This applies especially to those in leading roles in various agencies such as trade unions, educational establishments, and church agencies of all kinds.

All this leads on to a commitment by poor and marginalized people to take action to challenge structural injustice and to confront those who are

---

[3]In his detailed study of the ministry of Pope Francis in Argentina during the many years before he became pope, Austin Ivereigh provides ample evidence that Father Bergoglio was deeply committed to the ministry of solidarity with the poor. Ivereigh suggests that much of the opposition which Bergoglio had to face as provincial and in subsequent years was fomented by a small number of Jesuits in Argentina, who espoused an idealogical version of liberation theology, strongly influenced by Marxisim. Ivereigh maintains that those who held this view made little or no attempt to immerse themselves in the day-to-day life of poor people and were quite opposed to Bergoglio's on-the-ground ministry to and with the poor (e.g. Ivereigh 2015, 171–197). I leave it to later historians to judge whether Ivereigh's account of the position of the anti-Bergoglio faction is unduly one-sided. What is clear is that the teaching of Pope Francis *as pope* continues to stress the importance of solidarity with the poor—as seen, for instance, in his insistence on priests and theologians having "the smell of sheep" on them. But it is also clear that he fully supports activists in the political or quasi-political pursuit of justice—as seen, for instance, in his commendation of them in Rome in October 2014 for carrying "the smell of your neighborhood, your people, your struggle" and his explicit encouragement of their actions in Bolivia in July 2015.

resisting the necessary change of structures. Alongside this option *by* the poor is the option *with and for* the poor, which is to be taken by more privileged people and sectors of society. This involves a concrete on-the-ground commitment to give this kind of support. Such a commitment almost always requires that they act against the short-term interests of the more privileged class or group to which they belong, and therefore against the unfair advantages that they themselves have had.

I think it is helpful to spell out in some detail a series of different stages in this option or commitment. A crucial first stage is to ensure that one is not unconsciously colluding in the impoverishment or marginalization of poorer people. When people from a fairly privileged background have opted to work with a group of marginalized people they may have a blind spot about ways in which they are still colluding with structural injustice. It may take a sharp challenge from other members of the group to make these privileged people aware of their unconscious collusion.

Obviously it is not sufficient to stop colluding in injustice. It is necessary to undertake positive joint action to challenge the unjust structures and those who defend them. A crucial point here is that it is not enough that privileged people make a protest on behalf of those who have been marginalized; the challenge must come primarily from the disadvantaged group. This means that those who have opted to be in solidarity with the oppressed or marginalized often have to hold back. They must not assume that they have the clearest understanding of the issues and how best to tackle them—or even that they are the ones who should set the agenda. And when they do intervene, it should be to encourage or facilitate the disadvantaged people themselves in articulating their own experience and in planning realistic action. The people who have been marginalized should be empowered to speak and act on their own behalf, so as to overcome their sense of helplessness. Marginalized groups that begin to stand up for themselves are profoundly changed by their action. This inner change is probably more important than any changes in behavior and attitude in those who are being challenged.

In addition to the solidarity aspect and the political or quasi-political aspect of an option for the poor there are three other important aspects. The first of these is a visionary aspect: political action to challenge structural injustice must be undertaken with a view to the installation of an alternative society to be built around structures that ensure and promote justice and respect for the environment. It is not necessary—and generally not advisable—to have a rigid detailed alternative system in mind. But it is important that those who are challenging unjust structures have a broad measure of agreement about the kind of political values and structures that are to replace the old system. The effort to design and establish just structures may involve a lifetime of work with no guarantee of short-term success. What spurs one on is not a naïve optimism but a hope based on trust in the power and promises of God. This becomes evident when we advert to the biblical and theological dimension of an option for the poor and for the Earth, which is the most notable way in which this option differs from a Marxist-inspired class option.

Another aspect of an option for the poor concerns lifestyle. This refers to the personal choices each person and each family or community makes about living more simply, in terms of the food they eat, the kind of housing they live in, and whether they use bicycles and public transportation or drive privately owned cars. In themselves such choices, unless they are made by millions of people, will not go very far in changing the structures of society that exploit poor people and the Earth. But choosing to live more simply ensures that there is consistency between what we stand for and how we live. Furthermore, the pattern of our lifestyle plays an important symbolic role for ourselves and for others—as we see very clearly in the lifestyle of Pope Francis. He refused to live in the elegant and isolated papal apartments; he traveled in a bus with others or in a small automobile, he rejected the ornate and costly papal vestments that were offered to him. These actions are reminders first of all to himself and second to all of us, that he does not see himself as superior to others and that he really believes in what he says when he calls better-off people all over the world to live far more simply in order to protect the Earth and leave sufficient resources for the billions of people who are truly poor.

The final important aspect of an option for the poor is conversion. This permeates the whole process and may be particularly operative and evident at key points, which may vary from one person to another. The point is that at one or more crucial stages in one's awakening to the reality of the society and the world in which we live, the scales drop from the eyes of the person and the light dawns about the reality of injustice and exploitation that is built into the system and about the need for—and the very possibility of—courageous, decisive, and cooperative action to challenge the system. Like any other conversional experience, this event or process involves a quite mysterious cooperation between the divine and the human—an initiative of God's grace to which the person freely responds.

Many Christians and many Church leaders now acknowledge that in preaching the gospel and working for justice they must make a clear option both for the Earth and for the poor. They believe that they must be in effective solidarity with those who are powerless and voiceless and must seek to empower them and give them back their voice. Furthermore, they accept that the Church as a whole must listen to the voices of those who live on the margins of society and allow itself to be evangelized by them.

Prior to the coming of Pope Francis, the position of the popes and the Vatican was reserved on the issue of option for the poor. It could best be described in terms of having a "preferential *concern* for the poor." With Francis, that has changed significantly; there is a strong case for saying that as pope he is committed to a full *option* for the poor, as well as for the *Earth*—and that for him they amount to a single integral option. Furthermore, there are indications that, granted the limitations imposed on him by his position, he has actually already made such an option in practice. It remains to be seen whether his example and influence will persuade Church leaders and the great majority of Christians all over the world to make a similar option in their own diverse situations. In any case, Catholic social teaching recognizes that the poor and the powerless are "God's favorites" (to use the words of Pope John Paul). They can no longer be seen as just the ones who are to be helped by others. They are called by God to be key agents, under God, in bringing justice, liberation, and respect for the environment to our world; and the Church is called to be with them and on their side in this task.

***

SUMMARY

In the seventy years between 1891 and 1961 Catholic social teaching had a high level of consistency. A Catholic ethos led the Church to give religious backing to conservative political groups. An important change of direction in social teaching and in the Catholic ethos began with Pope John and came to fruition at Medellín. This led to a struggle within the Church between those who favored liberation theology and those who opposed it. The word "liberation" came gradually to be accepted and used by the popes. But up to the time of Pope Francis, liberation theology was treated with great suspicion by the Roman authorities. For some years it had a big impact on the life of some local churches, especially in Latin America. But the appointment of unsympathetic bishops caused its influence to be greatly reduced.

There is an organic unity in the tradition of papal social teaching since the time of Leo XIII. However, this has been compatible with a significant change of direction in the time of John XXIII. During the papacy of Pope Benedict there seemed to be a further change of emphasis, if not of direction. Pope Francis is clearly committed to bringing social teaching back to the characteristic positions and tone of the decade after Vatican II—and to pushing it forward in radical directions in relation to ecology and to issues of structural injustice both in society and in the Church itself.

Among the strong points of Catholic social teaching are its humanistic and ecological character, and its practical emphasis on participation, subsidiarity, and solidarity between humans and the rest of creation. Also important are its refusal to become identified with any political party, the fact that it identifies structures of sin, its biblical aspect, and the fact that it is radical in its commitment to the poor and is therefore evangelical and inspirational.

Among the less well-developed aspects of Catholic social teaching, the most obvious is an inadequate treatment of justice for women. Prior to the papacy of Pope Francis the teaching on ecology was unduly anthropocentric and had an excessive emphasis on Western cultural values. There is a lack of emphasis on alternative models of development, an unduly simple distinction between politics in the broad sense and party politics, an insufficient use of social analysis to reveal the class structures of society, a playing down of the importance of confrontation in the struggle for justice, a reluctance to face up to rapid growth in population, a failure to focus on issues of justice in the Church, and a lack of adequate consultation processes that would enable many Christians to play a full role in articulating the teaching. Despite these inadequacies Catholic social teaching provides support and inspiration for Christians in their efforts to bring justice to the world.

An option for the poor and for the Earth has many aspects—biblical, political or quasi-political, experiential, and theological. An option for the poor and for the Earth affects one's lifestyle and requires solidarity and a real conversion.

QUESTIONS FOR REVIEW

1. Describe the Catholic ethos dominant around 1950.
2. What were the stages in the breakup of this outlook?
3. In what sense is there continuity in Catholic social teaching over the past hundred years?
4. What are the strong points of the Catholic social teaching tradition?
5. In what areas does it need further development?
6. Name the key aspects of an option for the poor and for the Earth.

QUESTIONS FOR REFLECTION

1. What kind of process would be most helpful in enabling many Christians of all kinds to play an active role in exploring and articulating Catholic social teaching?
2. Why is the Church's teaching on justice for women so underdeveloped and so controversial? What ways forward would you suggest?

3. *Is Catholic social teaching unduly Western in its underlying values and assumptions? How can there be more effective dialogue on justice and ecology issues with the Orthodox Churches, Muslims, adherents of Eastern religions, those who practice primal-traditional religions, and people who reject formal religion?*

ISSUES FOR FURTHER STUDY

1. *The meaning of respect for creation, and its practical implications.*
2. *The concept and reality of patriarchy.*
3. *The "New Story."*

Bibliography of Primary Sources

In cases where no reference is given to an English translation the translation used is the one given on the Vatican website.

Leo XIII

Actes de Léon XIII, Encycliques, Moto Proprio, Brefs, Allocutions, Actes de Dicastrères etc. Paris: Bonne Presse, n.d. This seven-volume collection gives the text of the documents in Latin together with a French translation. I have used this Bonne Presse Latin–French collection as the main source for references to the writings of Leo XIII, since it is more complete and accessible than the *Acta Sanctae Sedis (ASS)*; in referring to it, I have cited the volume and page number, preceded by the initials BP (for Bonne Presse).

The Great Encyclical Letters of Pope Leo XIII (with a preface by John J. Wynn). 1903. New York: Benziger Brothers. This collection is referred to as *Great Ency.*

The Church Speaks to the Modern World: The Social Teachings of Leo XIII. Edited by Étienne Gilson. 1954. Garden City, NY: Doubleday Image. This collection is referred to as *Gilson.*

Encyclical *Rerum Novarum*, May 15, 1891, *Acta Sanctae Sedis* 23 (189–91): 641–70; also available in Latin (together with a French translation) in BP III, 18–70. In neither of these texts are the "paragraphs" numbered. The numbering of the "paragraphs" was added by the Vatican in a revised edition, issued in 1931. For the text of various drafts, see Antonazzi 1957. The official Vatican translation into English is available in Fremantle 1963, 20–56, and in *Great Ency.*, 207–48. A revised version of this translation was published by the Catholic Truth Society and reprinted many times under the title *The Workers' Charter: On the Condition of the Working Classes* (London: CTS, 1960). In these two texts the "paragraphs" are numbered in accordance with the 1931 Vatican edition. An entirely new translation by John Molony is available in Molony 1991, 165–203. Unfortunately the "paragraphs" are not numbered in this version. Partly for this reason and partly because the older version is so widely used I have quoted from the Catholic Truth Society version and have occasionally adapted it. References to the encyclical are given by citing the "paragraph" number, preceded by the initials *RN.*

Encyclical *Inscrutabili*, April 2, 1878, BP I, 8–25; *Great Ency.*, 9–21.

Encyclical *Quod Apostolici Muneris,* December 28, 1878, BP I, 26–41; *Great Ency.,* 22–33.

Encyclical *Humanum Genus,* April 20, 1884, BP I, 242–77; *Great Ency.,* 83–106.

"C'est avec une particulière satisfaction," February 24, 1885, translated as "Working-Men's Clubs and Associations," in *The Pope and the People: Select Letters and Addresses on Social Questions by Pope Leo XIII, Pope Pius X, Pope Benedict XV and Pope Pius XI.* 1929. London: CTS, 1937.

Encyclical *Libertas Praestantissimum,* June 20, 1888, BP II, 172–213; *Great Ency.,* 135–63.

Encyclical *Exeunte Jam Anno,* December 25, 1888, BP II, 226–49; *Great Ency.,* 164–79.

Encyclical *Sapientiae Christianae,* January 10, 1890, BP II, 262–97; *Great Ency.,* 180–207.

Apostolic Letter *Ad Extremas,* June 14, 1893, BP III, 204–13.

Encyclical *Laetitiae Sanctae,* September 8, 1893, BP III, 242–55.

Encyclical *Praeclara Gratulationis Publicae,* June 20, 1894, BP IV, 82–107; *Great Ency.,* 303–19.

Letter to Bishops of the United States *Longinqua Oceani,* January 6, 1895, BP IV, 158–79; *Great Ency.,* 320–35.

Encyclical *Graves de Communi,* January 18, 1901, BP VI, 204–27; *Great Ency.,* 479–94.

Antonazzi, Giovanni, ed. 1957. *L'enciclica Rerum Novarum: testo autentico e redazioni preparatorie dai documenti originali.* Roma: Edizioni de Storia e Letteratura.

Pius X

Motu proprio, *Fin Dalla Prima,* December 18, 1903, *ASS (Acta Sanctae Sedis)* 36 (1903–4): 339–45.

Letter on *Le Sillon,* August 25, 1910, *AAS (Acta Apostolicae Sedis)* 2 (1910): 613–33.

Benedict XV

Encyclical *Ad Beatissimi, AAS* 6 (1914): 565–81.

Letter to the Bishop of Bergamo, *AAS* 12 (1920): 109–12.

Encyclical *Maximum Illud,* November 13, 1919, *AAS* 11 (1919): 440–55.

Pius XI

Encyclical *Rerum Ecclesiae,* February 28, 1926, *AAS* 18 (1926): 65–83.

Message to the Bishops of China, August 1, 1928, *AAS* 20 (1928): 245–46.

Encyclical *Casti Connubi.* 1930. http://www.vatican.va.

Encyclical *Quadragesimo Anno,* May 15, 1931, *AAS* 23 (1931): 177–228; English translation: *The Social Order.* London: Catholic Truth Society; Oxford: Catholic Social Guild. A second English translation is incorporated in Miller 1947; another English translation is to be found in Nell-Breuning

1936, 401–42. The "paragraphs" are not numbered in the original Latin text, but they are numbered in each of the above three translations. Unless otherwise stated, all quotations in English are taken from the first of the three translations mentioned above. References are given by citing the number of the "paragraph" preceded by the initials *QA*.

Address of May 31, 1931, *AAS* 23 (1931): 229–32.

Encyclical *Nova Impendat, AAS* 23 (1931): 393–97.

Encyclical *Caritate Christi Compulsi, AAS* 24 (1932): 179–94.

Encyclical *Divini Redemptoris, AAS* 29 (1937): 65–106 (Latin text) and 107–38 (Italian text); English translation in *Twelve Encyclicals of Pius XI (with a foreword by Msgr. P. E. Hallett)*. 1943. London: Catholic Truth Society. The original Latin text does not have the "paragraphs" numbered, but the "paragraphs" are numbered in the Italian and English texts. References are given by citing the number of the "paragraph" preceded by the initials *DR*.

Encyclical *Firmissimum, AAS* 29 (1937): 189–99 (Latin text), 200–211 (Spanish text). This encyclical is also known as *No es muy*. English translation in *Twelve Encyclicals of Pius XI (with a foreword by Msgr. P. E. Hallett)*. 1943. London: Catholic Truth Society. The "paragraphs" are numbered in the English text.

Encyclical *Mit brennender Sorge, AAS* 29 (1937): 143–67; English translation in *Twelve Encyclicals of Pius XI (with a foreword by Msgr. P. E. Hallett)*. 1943. London: Catholic Truth Society. The "paragraphs" are numbered in the English text.

Twelve Encyclicals of Pius XI (with a foreword by Msgr. P. E. Hallett). 1943. London: Catholic Truth Society.

Action Populaire. 1931. *L'Encyclique sur la Restauration de le l'Ordre Social: Texte français complet, table analytique, étude doctrinal*, 81–108. Paris: Editions Spes.

Pius XII

(In order to avoid long and cumbersome references to the many writings and addresses of Pius XII, I have numbered the following thirty-two documents as D1 to D32 in chronological order; in referring to them in this book I identify them as D1, D2, etc.)

D1 = Encyclical *Sertum Laetitiae, AAS* 31 (1939): 635–44.

D2 = Christmas 1939 Address, *AAS* 32 (1940): 6–13.

D3 = Radio Message *La sollenità della Pentecoste*, June 1, 1941, *AAS* 33 (1941): 195–205 (Italian text), 216–27 (English text).

D4 = Christmas 1941 Radio Message, *AAS* 34 (1942): 10–21.

D5 = Christmas 1942 Radio Message, *AAS* 35 (1943): 9–24.

D6 = Address of June 13, 1943, *AAS* 35 (1943): 175.

D7 = Christmas 1943 Radio Message, *AAS* 36 (1944): 11–24.

D8 = Radio Message of July 1, 1944, *AAS* 36 (1944): 252–53.

D9 = Radio Message of September 1, 1944, *AAS* 36 (1944): 252–53.

D10 = Christmas 1944 Radio Message, *AAS* 37 (1945): 10–23. An English translation is available in Pius XII, *Selected Letters and Addresses*, 299–318.

D11 = Address to the Nobles of Rome January 1945, Savignat II, 1586.

D12 = Address of March 11, 1945, *AAS* 37 (1945): 68–72.

D13 = Address of June 2, 1945, *Documentation Catholique* 24, June 1945.

D14 = Address of October 2, 1945, *AAS* 37 (1945): 256–62.

D15 = Address to the Nobles of Rome, January 1946, Savignat II, 1595–96.

D16 = Address of November 15, 1946, *AAS* 38 (1946): 435–36.

D17 = Address to the Nobles of Rome, January 1947, Savignat II, 1603.

D18 = Address of November 1, 1947, Savignat II, 1774.

D19 = Address of May 7, 1949, *AAS* 41 (1949): 283–86.

D20 = Address of June 3, 1950, *AAS* 42 (1950): 485–88.

D21 = Christmas 1950 Message, *AAS* 43 (1951): 49–59.

D22 = Address to the Nobles of Rome, January 1952, Savignat II, 1605.

D23 = Address of January 31, 1952, Savignat II, 1670.

D24 = Radio Message of September 14, 1952, *AAS* 44 (1952): 789–93.

D25 = Christmas 1952 Radio Message, *AAS* 45 (1953): 33–46.

D26 = Letter to Charles Flory July 14, 1954, Savignat II, 1748.

D27 = Christmas 1954 Message, *AAS* 47 (1955): 15–28.

D28 = Address to FAO, November 10, 1955, *Documentation Catholique* 52 (1955): 1488–91.

D29= Christmas 1955 Message, *AAS* 48 (1956): 26–41.

D30 = Address of February 17, 1956, *L'Osservatore Romano*, February 18, 1956.

D31 = Encyclical *Fidei Donum*, April 21, 1957, *AAS* 49 (1957): 223–48.

D32 = Address of April 13, 1958, *Documentation Catholique* 55 (1958): 543–46.

Pius XII: *Selected Letters and Addresses of Pius XII*. 1949. London: Catholic Truth Society.

Savignat, Alain, ed.1956. *Relations humaines et société contemporaine: Synthèse. Chrétienne directives de S.S. Pie XII*. Fribourg, Switzerland: St Paul. (Savignat's compilation is an expanded version of an earlier compilation by Utz and Groner.)

John XXIII

Encyclical *Ad Petri Cathedram*, June 29, 1959, *AAS* 51 (1959): 497–531. English text in John XXIII, *The Encyclicals and Other Messages*.

Encyclical *Mater et Magistra*, dated March 15, 1961, but actually issued two months later. *AAS* 53 (1961): 401–64. There are at least five English versions, of which the most widely used at present seems to be that of W. J. Gibbons (Paulist Press). This text is available in Gremillion, 141–200; also in O'Brien and Shannon, 50–123. J. R. Kirwan made an interesting translation that often succeeds in expressing the underlying meaning of the text much better than the other versions but is occasionally unacceptable. It can be found together with some helpful comments in Kirwan. A very careful French translation is to be found in Bolté. As a companion to his translation, Bolté has produced a four-volume commentary on the text (see bibliography of secondary sources). References to the text of *Mater et Magistra* are given by citing the "paragraph" number preceded by the initials *MM*.

Encyclical *Pacem in Terris*, dated April 11, 1963, *AAS* 55 (1963): 257–304. There are a number of English versions, some of which differ from each other only in minor respects. The easiest to read is that of Henry O. Waterhouse, available in *The Social Thought of John XXIII*, but it seems rather less accurate in some important places than the version of Donald R. Campion available in Gremillion, 201–41. References to the text of *Pacem in Terris* are given by citing the "paragraph" number preceded by the initials *PT.*

The Encyclicals and Other Messages of John XXIII. 1964. Washington, DC: T.P.S. Press.

The Social Thought of John XXIII. 1964. Oxford: Catholic Social Guild.

Vatican II

(In this bibliography I have listed separately the various documents of the Council to which I have referred specifically).

Nuntius ad Universos Homines Summo Pontifice Assentiente a Patribus Missus ineunte Concilio Oecumenico Vaticano II, *AAS* 54 (1962): 823–24; English translation in Gremillion, 351–54.

Gaudium et Spes, *AAS* 58 (1966): 1025–1115. There are three English translations in common circulation. They are to be found in Abbott 1966, 199–308; Gonzalez, 513–624; and Flannery, 903–1001. The second of these almost always follows the sub-paragraphing of the Latin text; the third does so in most cases; the first does not do so.

Dignitatis Humanae, *AAS* 58 (1966): 929–41.

Perfectae Caritatis, *AAS* 58 (1966): 702–12.

Lumen Gentium, *AAS* 57 (1965): 7–71.

Apostolicam Actuositatem, *AAS* 58 (1966): 837–64.

Ad Gentes, *AAS* 58 (1966): 947–90.

Presbyterorum Ordinis, *AAS* 58 (1966): 991–1024.

Sacrosancti Concilii Oecumenici Vaticani II. 1975. Rome: Vatican Press. This collection contains all the official documents of the Council.

Abbott, Walter M., ed. 1966. *The Documents of Vatican II*. New York: America Press; also London: Chapman, 1967.

Flannery, Austin, ed. 1975, 1977. *Vatican Council II: The Conciliar and Post-Conciliar Documents*. Northport, NY: Costello.

Gonzalez, J. L., and the Daughters of St. Paul. n.d. *The Sixteen Documents of Vatican II*. Boston: St. Paul Editions.

Acta Synodalia Sacrosancti Concilii Oecumenici Vaticani II. 1970–1999. Vatican City: Typis Polyglottis Vaticanis.

Paul VI

Encyclical *Ecclesiam Suam*, August 6, 1964, *AAS* 56 (1964): 609–59.

Address to Women at the Closing of the Vatican Council, December 8, 1965; http://www.vatican.va.

Address to the United Nations, *AAS* 57 (1965): 877–85.

Encyclical *Populorum Progressio*, March 26, 1967, *AAS* 59 (1967): 257–99; English translation of Vatican Polyglot Press in Gremillion, 387–415, and in O'Brien and Shannon, 313–51. A slightly different (and better) version of this translation is in *Encyclical Letter of His Holiness Pope Paul VI: On the Development of Peoples (with Commentary by Barbara Ward)*. 1967. New York: Paulist Press. Quotations from the encyclical in English are taken from this last text except in cases where I considered it necessary to adapt it or to give my own translation from the Latin.

Apostolic Letter *Octogesima Adveniens*, May 14, 1971, *AAS* 63 (1971): 401–41. English translation from the Vatican Press in Gremillion, 485–512, and in O'Brien and Shannon, 352–83. A slightly emended version of this text is given in the booklet *Social Problems: Apostolic Letter of Pope Paul VI: "Octogesima Adveniens"* (No. S 288). n.d. London: Catholic Truth Society. Quotations in English are taken from this booklet, unless otherwise stated. References are given by using the initials *OA*, followed by the number of the "paragraph."

Apostolic Exhortation *Evangelica Testificatio*, June 29, 1971, *AAS* 63 (1971): 497–526.

Message to the United Nations International Conference on the Environment, June 1, 1972, *AAS* 64 (1972): 443–46.

Apostolic Exhortation, *Evangelii Nuntiandi*, *AAS* 68 (1976): 5–76. There are two easily available English translations: one is published by the Vatican Press and distributed by the Catholic Truth Society, London; the other is by Dom Matthew Dillon and is published in a special issue of *Doctrine and Life* 27 (1977): 3–52. The latter is based on the Latin text, whereas the former appears to follow the Italian text. Neither translation is wholly satisfactory, so in most cases I give my own translation of the official Latin text. References to the document are given by using the initials *EN* followed by the number of the "paragraph."

John Paul II

Encyclical *Redemptor Hominis*, *AAS* 71 (1979): 257–324; English translation issued by Libreria Editrice Vaticana. References to the encyclical are given by citing the number of the "paragraph" preceded by the initials *RH*. In quoting from the document I have adapted the Vatican translation and have at times used my own translation.

Encyclical *Dives in Misericordia*, *AAS* 72 (1980): 1177–1232; English translation issued by the Vatican Press. References to the encyclical are given by citing the number of the "paragraph," preceded by the initials *DM*. Quotations in English are from the Vatican text.

Encyclical *Laborem Exercens, AAS* 73 (1981): 577–647; English translation issued by Vatican Press. References to the encyclical are given by citing the number of the "paragraph," preceded by the initials *LE*. Quotations in English are from the Vatican text.

Encyclical *Sollicitudo Rei Socialis*, December 30, 1987, English translation, Vatican City: Libreria Editrice Vaticana, 1998. The text is divided into numbered "paragraphs." References are given by citing the "paragraph" number, preceded by the initials *SRS*.

Encyclical *Redemptoris Missio*, December 7, 1990, *L'Osservatore Romano* (English edition), January 28, 1991, 5–20. References are given by citing the "paragraph" number, preceded by the initials *RM*.

Encyclical *Centesimus Annus*, May 1, 1991, Vatican City: Libreria Editrice Vaticana, 1991. References are given by citing the "paragraph" number, preceded by the initials *CA*.

Encyclical *Evangelium Vitae* (1995); http://www.vatican.va.

Addresses of John Paul II's Mexican visit of 1979. The official texts of the pope's addresses, in the original languages, are given in *AAS* 71 (1979): 164–246. The best available translation of the opening address of the pope to the conference is contained in the two English editions of the Puebla document. I have used this translation and given references by citing the numbered sections and "paragraphs." In the case of all of the other addresses I have used the English text from *John Paul II in Mexico: His Collected Speeches*. 1979. London and New York: Collins; this is the Vatican translation of *L'Osservatore Romano*. References to these addresses are given citing the page number in *AAS* 71, followed by (in square brackets) the page number of the above English version.

Address to the Pontifical Commission, "Justice and Peace." *L'Osservatore Romano* (English edition), November 30, 1978, p. 4.

Address to the United Nations, *AAS* 71 (1979): 1153–54.

Address to UNESCO, *AAS* 72 (1980): 735–52.

Addresses of John Paul II's Brazil visit of 1980. The text of the major addresses given by the pope in Brazil is available (in the original languages, Portuguese, Spanish, and French) in *AAS* 72 (1980): 825–961, but not all of his addresses are given there. The full texts of all of his addresses are given in the various issues of *L'Osservatore Romano* from July 2 to 13, 1980 (inclusive), which also contain an Italian translation in a series of supplements to these issues. An English translation of all the addresses is given in the English language weekly edition of *L'Osservatore Romano* of July 7, 14, 21, and 28, and August 4, 11, and 25, 1980. The longer addresses are divided into numbered "paragraphs." References are given by citing the "paragraph" number (where available) and the page reference to the original text as given in *AAS* (or, where the text is not given in *AAS*, to the original text as given in the [daily] *L'Osservatore Romano*). Quotations in English are from the translation referred to above unless otherwise stated.

Addresses of John Paul II's Philippines visit of 1981. The text of the pope's addresses on this visit to the Far East is given in *AAS* 73 (1981): 304–429. The address at Tondo is also available in the English edition of *L'Osservatore Romano*, February 23, 1981, 13–14.

Familiaris Consortio, Apostolic Exhortation on the Role of the Christian Family in the Modern World, November 22, 1981; http://www.vatican.va.

Address in Managua, Nicaragua, March 4, 1983, *AAS* 75 (1983): 718–23.

Address to Priests in San Salvador, March 6, 1983, *L'Osservatore Romano* (daily edition), March 7–8, 1983, 4.

Address to American Indians at Quetzaltenango, Guatemala, March 7, 1983, *AAS* 75 (1983): 740–44.

Address at Port au Prince, March 9, 1983, *AAS* 75 (1983): 765–71.

Address to Council of Latin American Bishops (CELAM) at Port au Prince, Haiti, March 9, 1983, *AAS* 75 (1983): 771–79.

Address to the 35th General Assembly of the World Medical Association, October 29, 1983; http://www.vatican.va.

Address to Educators and Scientists in Seoul, Korea, May 5, 1984, *AAS* 76 (1984): 984–88.

Address to Pastoral Conference, Korea, May 6, 1984, *AAS* 76 (1984): 994–99.

Address to Indigenous Peoples of Canada, September 15, 1984; http://www.vatican.va.

Address to Indians and Inuit of Canada, September 18, 1984, *AAS* 77 (1985): 417–22.

Address to Indigenous Peoples of Ecuador at Latacunga, Ecuador, January 31, 1985, *AAS* 77 (1985): 859–69.

Homily to Peruvian Indigenous Peoples, February 5, 1985; http://www.vatican.va.

Address at University of Yaoundé, Cameroon, August 13, 1985, *AAS* 78 (1986): 52–61.

Address to Aborigines of Australia at Alice Springs, November 29, 1986, *AAS* 79 (1987): 973–79.

Address to Peoples of Australia, November 30, 1986; http://www.vatican.va.

Address to Native Americans, September 14, 1987; http://www.vatican.va.

Apostolic Letter *Mulieris Dignitatem*, On the Dignity and Vocation of Women, August 15, 1988; http://www.vatican.va.

Address to Scientists and Cultural Leaders in Assuncion, Paraguay, May 17, 1988, *AAS* 80 (1988): 1612–18.

Apostolic Letter *Dignitate Mulieris*, On the Dignity of Women, August 15, 1988, *AAS* 80 (1988): 1653–729.

Address to Bishops of Southern Africa, September 2, 1989, *AAS* 81 (1989): 322–34.

Address to the XXV Session of the Conference of FAO, November 16, 1989; http://conservation.catholic.org.

Address to Priests, Religious and Laity in Mexico City, May 12, 1990, *L'Osservatore Romano* (English ed.), May 14, 1990, 3–4.

Address to Mexican Business Leaders, in Durango, Mexico, May 1990, *L'Osservatore Romano* (English ed.), May 28, 1990, 6–7.

Address to Participants in Study Week on the Environment, Vatican City, May 18, 1990, *L'Osservatore Romano* (English ed.), May 28, 1990, 5.

Letter to the Religious of Latin America, June 29, 1990, *L'Osservatore Romano* (English ed.), July 30, 1990, 1–7.

Address to People of Comacchio (Northern Italy), September 22, 1990, *L'Osservatore Romano* (English ed.), October 8, 1990, 4–5.

Message for the World Day of Peace 1990: "Peace with God the Creator: Peace with All of Creation," Vatican City, December 8, 1989, *AAS* 82 (1990): 147–56. (References given are to the numbered "paragraphs.")

Address to the Diplomatic Corps January 12, 1991, *L'Osservatore Romano* (English ed.), January 14, 1991, 1–3.

Address to Factory Workers at Matelica: "Working Woman's Dignity," *L'Osservatore Romano* (English ed.), March 25, 1991, 6–7.

Meditation: "Experts Contribute to Social Doctrine," on April 21, 1991, *L'Osservatore Romano* (English ed.), April 29, 1991, 2.

Address to Amazonian Indians at Cuiabá, Brazil, October 16, 1991, *L'Osservatore Romano* (English ed.), October 28, 1991, 10.

Address to Laity at Campo Grande, Brazil, October 17, 1991, *L'Osservatore Romano* (English ed.), October 28, 1991, 12–13.

Address to the Shanty-Dwellers of Vitória, Brazil, October 19, 1991, *L'Osservatore Romano* (English ed.), November 4, 1991, 4.

Address to the Diplomatic Corps in Dakar, Senegal, February 22, 1992, *L'Osservatore Romano* (English ed.), February 28, 1992, 8.

Apostolic Letter *Ordinatio Sacerdotalis*, "On Reserving Priestly Ordination to Men Alone," May 22, 1994; http://www.vatican.va.

"Letter to Women," June 29, 1995; http://www.vatican.va.

Address to the Conference on Environment and Health, 1997; http://www.vatican.va.

Motu proprio, *Ad Tuendam Fidem,* May 28, 1998; http://www.ewtn.com.

General Audience Address, January 17, 2001; http://conservation.catholic.org.

Post-Synodal Apostolic Exhortation *Ecclesia in Europa*, June 28, 2003; http://www.vatican.va.

Post-Synodal Apostolic Exhortation *Pastores Gregis*, 2003; http://www.vatican.va.

John Paul II and Ecumenical Patriarch Bartholomew I
Common Declaration 2004; http://www.ewtn.com.

Benedict XVI
Encyclical *Deus Caritas Est*, December 25, 2005; http://www.vatican.va. Abbreviated *DCE*.

Encyclical *Spe Salvi*, November 30, 2007; http://www.vatican.va.

Encyclical *Caritas in Veritate*, June 29, 2009; http://www.vatican.va. Abbreviated *CiV*.

Address to Participants at Meeting Promoted by the Pontifical Council *Cor Unum*, January 23, 2006; http://www.vatican.va.

Message for the World Day of Peace 2007, "The Human Person, the Heart of Peace"; http://www.vatican.va.

Post-Synodal Apostolic Exhortation, *Sacramentum Caritatis*, February 22, 2007; http://www.vatican.va.

Address to Inaugural Session of the Fifth General Conference of the Bishops of Latin America and the Caribbean, at Aparecida, May 13, 2007; http://www.vatican.va.

Speech to Priests of the Dioceses of Belluno-Feltre and Treviso, July 24, 2007; http://www.vatican.va.

Message for the 2008 Fraternity Campaign of the Brazilian Bishops; http://tisk.cirkev.cz.

Address to the Participants at the End of the Synod for Africa on October 24, 2009; http://www.vatican.va.

Address to Bishops of the Episcopal Conference of Brazil (South Regions 3 and 4) on their *ad limina* visit, December 5, 2009; http://www.vatican.va.

Message for World Day of Peace 2010: "If You Want to Cultivate Peace, Protect Creation"; http://www.vatican.va.

Address to the Diplomatic Corps on January 11, 2010; http://www.vatican.

Address to Ambassadors from Six African Countries, June 9, 2011; http://www.theafricanews.com.

Address to The Bundestag in Berlin on September 22, 2011; http://www.vatican.va.

Post-Synodal Apostolic Exhortation *Africae Munus*, November 19, 2011; http://www.vatican.va.

Motu Proprio: Intima Ecclesiae Natura ("On the Service of Charity"), November 11, 2012; http://www.vatican.va.

Pope Francis

Address to Journalists, March 16, 2013; http://w2.vatican.va.

Homily of Pope Francis at his inaugural Mass, March 19, 2013; http://w2.vatican.va.

Address to Diplomats, March 22, 2013; http://w2.vatican.va.

Homily of Pope Francis at Chrism Mass on Holy Thursday, March 28, 2013; http://www.news.va.

Urbi et Orbi Message, Easter Sunday, March 31, 2013; http://w2.vatican.va.

General Audience, June 5, 2013; http://w2.vatican.va.

Meeting with Brazil Bishops, July 28, 2013; http://w2.vatican.va.

Interview with Antonio Spadaro, SJ, September 30, 2013; http://www.americamagazine.org.

Apostolic Exhortation *Evangelii Gaudium*, November 24, 2013; http://w2.vatican.va.

Dialogue with Leaders of USG. The dialogue took place on November 29, 2013. Original text of Fr. Spadaro's account of the dialogue published in Italian in *La Civiltá Cattolica 2014, I, 3-17; English translation by Fr. Donal Mardari, SJ, revised January 6, 2014, http://www.laciviltacattolica.it.*

Address to Diplomats, December 12, 2013; http://w2.vatican.va.

Message for World Day of Peace 2014; http://w2.vatican.va.

Letter of January 12, 2014: To Those Who Will Be Created Cardinals at the Upcoming Consistory of February 22; http://w2.vatican.va.

Agreement re Trafficking March 17, 2014; http://www.zenit.org.

Letter to Cardinal Lorenzo Baldisseri April 1, 2014; http://w2.vatican.va.

Address to Conference on Combatting Human Trafficking, April 9–10, 2014; http://www.news.va.

Message for World Mission Day, June 8, 2014; http://w2.vatican.va.

Address to Archbishop Justin Welby, June 16, 2014; http://w2.vatican.va.

Address in University of Molise, July 5, 2014; http://w2.vatican.va.

Dialogue with journalists on flight back to Rome from Korea, August 18, 2014; http://www.news.va.

Address to civil leaders in Albania, September 21, 2014; http://w2.vatican.va/.

Address to the Participants of the World Meeting of Popular Movements, October 28, 2014; http://w2.vatican.va. In the text this address is referred to as *Movements.*

Message to the President of the 20th Conference of States Party to the United Nations Framework Agreement on Climate Change, held in Lima, Peru, December 2014; http://www.news.va.

Address to members of the Vatican curia, December 22, 2014; http://w2.vatican.va.

Message for World Day of Peace, January 1, 2015; http://w2.vatican.va.

Dialogue with Journalists on journey to Rome from Philippines, February, 19, 2015; http://w2.vatican.va.

Letter of Pope Francis to Catholic University of Argentina, March 10, 2015; http://www.zenit.org.

Bull of Indiction of the Jubilee Year of Mercy: *Misericordiae vultus*, April 11, 2015; http://w2.vatican.va.

Endorsement by Pope Francis of petition of the Global Catholic Climate Movement, May 6, 2015; http://ncronline.org.

Homily at the Mass for the opening of the Caritas Internationalis General Assembly, May 12, 2015, http://ncronline.org.

Encyclical *Laudato Si'*, May 24, 2015; http://w2.vatican.va.

Address to Participants in 39th session of FAO, June 11, 2015; http://w2.vatican.va.

Address to Participants in the Second World Meeting of Popular Movements, in Santa Cruz de la Sierra (Bolivia), July 9, 2015; http://w2.vatican.va.

Message to Participants in Conference in Rome on Mining, July 18, 2015; http://w2.vatican.va.

Message for World Day of Migrants and Refugees 2016, September 12, 2015; http://w2.vatican.va.

Homily at Shrine of Our Lady of Crity of Cobre, Santiago, Cuba, on September 22, 2015; http://w2.vatican.va.

Address to US Congress, Washington DC, on September 24, 2015; http://w2.vatican.va.

Address to the General Assembly of the United Nations, New York, September 25, 2015; http://w2.vatican.va.

Introductory Remarks to Synod Fathers, October 5, 2015; http://w2.vatican.va.

Address to Commemorate the 50th Anniversary of the Institution of the Synod of Bishops, October 17, 2015; http://w2.vatican.va.

Address at the Conclusion of the Synod, October 24, 2015; http://w2.vatican.va.

Synod of Bishops

De Justitia in Mundo, AAS 63 (1971): 923–42. English translation: "Justice in the World." 1971. Rome: Vatican Press; this translation is also given in Gremillion, 513–29 and in O'Brien and Shannon, 390–408. The "paragraphing" in each of these three English texts is the same; but that of the Latin text is slightly different. Only the Gremillion text actually numbers the "paragraphs." References to this document are given by using the initials JW followed by the number of the "paragraph," as in Gremillion. Quotations in English are from this text unless otherwise stated; in cases where the "paragraphing" in the Latin text, as given in *AAS*, is different, a reference is also given to the number of the "paragraph" in the Latin text.

Sacred Congregation for the Doctrine of the Faith

Inter Insigniores: Declaration on the Question of Admission of Women to the Ministerial Priesthood, October 15, 1976; http://www.papalencyclicals. net.

Instruction on Certain Aspects of the "Theology of Liberation," Vatican City (1984), *AAS* 76 (1984): 876–909. (References are given according to section and "paragraph" numbers.)

Instruction on Christian Freedom and Liberation, Vatican City (1986), *AAS* 79 (1987): 554–99. (References are given according to the "paragraph" numbers.)

"Concerning the Teaching contained in *Ordinatio Sacerdotalis*: Responsum ad Dubium," October 28, 1995; http://www.ewtn.com.

Doctrinal Commentary on the Concluding Formula of the *Professio Fidei*, June 29, 1998; http://www.ewtn.com.

"Declaration on Priestly Ordination of Catholic Women," July 10, 2002; http://www.ourladyswarriors.org.

"Letter to the Bishops of the Catholic Church on the Collaboration of Men and Women in the Church and in the World," May 31, 2004; http://www. vatican.va.

Pontifical Commission for Justice and Peace (name changed later to Pontifical Council for Justice and Peace)

Ways of Peace: Papal Messages for the World Days of Peace (1968–1986). n.d. Vatican City.

"At the Service of the Human Community: An Ethical Approach to the International Debt Question." 1986. Vatican City. (References are given according to the "paragraph" numbers.)

"The Church and Racism: Towards a More Fraternal Society." 1988. Vatican City.

The Holy See at the Service of Peace: Pope John Paul II to the Diplomatic Corps (1978–1988). 1988. Vatican City.

Human Rights and the Church: Historical and Theological Reflections. 1990. Vatican City.

Compendium of the Social Doctrine of the Church. 2004. Vatican City: Libreria Editrice Vaticana; London and New York: Burns & Oates.

"Towards Reforming the International Financial and Monetary Systems in the Context of Global Public Authority," October 24, 2011; http://www.vatican.va.

Pontifical Council for the Family
The Truth and Meaning of Human Sexuality: Guidelines for Education within the Family, December 8, 1995; http://www.vatican.va.

Pontifical Academy of Sciences
Fate of Mountain Glaciers in the Anthropocene: A Report by the Working Group, May 11, 2011; http://www.vatican.va.

Conference on Trafficking, November 2–3, 2013; http://www.catholicnewsagency.com.

Conference of PAS/PASS on Sustainable Humanity: Sustainable Nature: Our Responsibility, May 2–3, 2014: Final Statement from the Conference; http://www.casinapioiv.va. Opening Statement of Cardinal Madariaga to the Conference, May 2, 2014; http://catholicclimatecovenant.org.

Final Statement of Leaders at Interfaith Climate Summit, New York, September 21, 2014; http://interfaithclimate.org.

Pontifical Academy of Sciences: Workshop on April 28, 2015, "Protect the Earth, Dignify Humanity: The Moral Dimensions of Climate Change"; http://www.casinapioiv.va; http://www.news.va.

Pontifical Council for Culture and Pontifical Council for Interreligious Dialogue
Jesus Christ the Bearer of the Water of Life: A Christian Reflection on the "New Age." 2003. Vatican City: Libreria Editrice Vaticana.

Medellín: Second General Conference of Latin American Bishops, Medellín, 1968.
The Church in the Present-Day Transformation of Latin America in the Light of the Council, II: Conclusions (3rd ed.). 1979. Washington, DC: Secretariat for Latin America, National Conference of Bishops. There are sixteen main documents, numbered 1 to 16. Each of these is divided into numbered "paragraphs." In referring to the documents I give the number of the document, followed by the number of the "paragraph" within the document, followed by a page reference, within brackets, to the above edition.

Puebla: Third General Conference of Latin American Bishops, Puebla, 1980.
Evangelization at Present and in the Future of Latin America: Conclusions (Official English Edition). Middlegreen and London: St Paul Publications and CIIR. The "paragraphs" of the text are numbered. References are given by citing the "paragraph" numbers. The text is also available in John Eagleson and Philip Scharper, eds. 1979. *Puebla and Beyond: Documentation and Commentary*. Maryknoll, NY: Orbis Books.

Aparecida: Fifth General Conference of Latin American Bishops, Aparecida, 2007.
Aparecida: Documento Conclusivo. 2010. Consejo Episcopal Latinoamericano (CELAM).

Bishops of Brazil
"Fraternidade no Mundo do Trabalho." 1978. In *Trabalho e Justiça para Todos, Campanha da Fraternidade* 1978, Rio de Janeiro: CNBB.
"*Documento: As Reflexões da Assembleia Geral Extraordinaria realizada em Itaici, de 18 a 25 de abril [1978]*." *O São Paulo*, April 29—May 5, 1978.

National Conference of Catholic Bishops [of the United States]
The Challenge of Peace: God's Promise and Our Response: Pastoral Letter on War and Peace in the Nuclear Age. 1983. Washington, DC, and London: USCCB/CTS/SPCK.
Economic Justice for All: Pastoral Letter on Catholic Social Teaching and the U.S. Economy. 1986. Washington, DC: USCCB.
Justice in the Marketplace: Collected Statements of the Vatican and the U.S. Catholic Bishops on Economic Policy, 1891–1984. Edited by David M. Byers. 1985. Washington, DC: United States Catholic Conference.

Conference of Irish Catholic Bishops
The Cry of the Earth: A Pastoral Reflection on Climate Change. 2009; http://www.trocaire.org.
The Cry of the Earth: A Call to Action for Climate Justice. 2014. Maynooth: Irish Catholic Bishops' Conference.

Conference of European Churches

Peace with Justice: The Official Documentation of the European Ecumenical Assembly, Basel, Switzerland. May 15–21, 1989. 1989. Geneva: Conference of European Churches. (References are given according to the "paragraph" numbers.)

Collections of Texts

Carlen, Claudia, ed. 1991. *Papal Pronouncements, A Guide: 1740–1978.* Ann Arbor, MI: Perien Press.

De "Rerum Novarum" à "Centesimus Annus": Textes intégraux des deux Encycliques avec deux études de Roger Aubert et Michel Schooyans. Vatican City. 1991.

Giovanni Paolo II alla Chiesa che é in Messico: Discorsi del primo viaggio apostolio. 1979. Alba. Figlie di San Paolo.

Gremillion, Joseph, ed. 1976. *The Gospel of Peace and Justice: Catholic Social Teaching since Pope John.* Maryknoll, NY: Orbis Books.

Hickey, Raymond, ed. 1982. *Modern Missionary Documents.* Dublin: Dominican Publications.

John Paul II in Mexico: His Collected Speeches. 1978. Glasgow: William Collins.

O'Brien, David J. and Thomas A. Shannon, eds. 1977. *Renewing the Earth: Catholic Documents on Peace, Justice and Liberation.* Garden City, NY: Doubleday Image.

The Pope and the People: Select Letters and Addresses on Social Questions by Pope Leo XIII, Pope Pius X, Pope Benedict XV and Pope Pius XI. 1929. London: CTS, reprinted 1937. Abbreviated in the text as *Pope and People.*

Walsh, Michael J., and Brian Davies, eds. 1991. *Proclaiming Justice and Peace: Documents from John XXIII to John Paul II* (new exp. ed.). London: CAFOD/Collins.

Bibliography of Secondary Sources

Alfaro, Juan. 1973. *Theology of Justice in the World*. Vatican City: Pontifical Commission for Justice and Peace.

Alix, Christine. 1967. "Le Vatican et la decolonisation." In *Les Églises chrétiennes et la décolonisation*, edited by Marcel Merle, 17–113. Paris: Armand Colin.

Antonazzi, Giovanni, ed. 1957. *L'enciclica Rerum Novarum: Testo autentico e redazioni preparatorie dai documenti originali*. Rome: Edizioni de Storia e Letteratura.

Antoncich, Ricardo. 1980. *Los Cristianos ante la Injusticia: Hacia un lectura latinamericano de la doctrina social de la Iglsia*. Bogotá: Ediciones Grupo Social.

Arns, Paulo Evaristo Cardinal. 1981. "The Church of the Poor: A Persecuted Church." *Center Focus: News from the Center of Concern*, July 1981.

Atkinson, Anthony. 2015. *Inequality: What Can be Done?*. Cambridge MA: Harvard University Press.

Aubert, Roger. 1963. *Le pontificat de Pie IX* (vol. 21 of *Historie de l'Église*), 2nd ed. Paris: A. Fliche et V. Martin.

Aubert, Roger, et al. 1978. *The Church in a Secularized Society*. Vol. 5 of *The Christian Centuries*. London: Darton, Longman and Todd; New York: Paulist.

———. 1991. "L'Encyclique *Rerum Novarum*, point d'aboutissement d'une lente maturation." In *De "Rerum Novarum" à "Centesimus Annus,"* edited by Pontifical Council for Justice and Peace, 5–26. Rome: Pontifical Council for Justice and Peace.

Baum, Gregory. 1979. "The First Papal Encyclical." *The Ecumenist: A Journal for Promoting Christian Unity* 17:55–59.

———. 1981a. "John Paul II's Encyclical on Labor." *The Ecumenist: A Journal for Promoting Christian Unity* 20:1–4.

———. 1981b. "Liberation Theology and 'The Supernatural.' " *The Ecumenist: A Journal for Promoting Christian Unity* 19:81–87.

———. 1982. *The Priority of Labor: A Commentary on Laborem Exercens, Encyclical Letter of Pope John Paul II*. New York/Ramsey: Paulist Press.

———. 1989. "Structures of Sin." In *The Logic of Solidarity: Commentaries on Pope John Paul II's Encyclical "On Social Concern,"* edited by Gregory Baum and Robert Ellsberg, 110–26. Maryknoll, NY: Orbis Books.

Baum, Gregory, and Robert Ellsberg, eds. 1989. *The Logic of Solidarity: Commentaries on Pope John Paul II's Encyclical "On Social Concern."* Maryknoll, NY: Orbis Books.

Beattie, Tina. 2004. "Feminism, Vatican Style." *Tablet*, August 7, 2004.

————. 2006. *New Catholic Feminism: Theology and Theory*. London and New York: Routledge.

Berry, Thomas. 1978. *The New Story* (Teilhard Studies, no 1, Winter 1978). Chambersburg PA: Anima Books.

————. 1988. *The Dream of the Earth*. San Francisco: Sierra Club Books.

Bloch, Alfred, and George T. Czuczka, eds. 1981. *Karol Wojtyla (Pope John Paul II): An Anthology*. New York: Crossroad.

Boff, Leonardo. 1989. "The Originality of the Theology of Liberation." In *The Future of Liberation Theology: Essays in Honor of Gustavo Gutiérrez*, edited by Marc H. Ellis and Otto Maduro, 38–48. Maryknoll, NY: Orbis Books.

————. 1990. "Vatican Instruction Reflects European Mind-Set." In *Liberation Theology: A Documentary History*, edited by Alfred T. Hennelly, 415–18. Maryknoll, NY: Orbis Books.

————. 2014. *Francis of Rome and Francis of Assisi: A New Springtime for the Church*. Maryknoll, NY: Orbis Books.

Boff, Leonardo, and Virgil Elizondo. 1991. *1492–1992: The Voice of the Victims (Concilium* Special) London: SCM (book edition of *Concilium*, December 1990).

Bollier, David. 2014. *Think Like a Commoner: A Short Introduction to the Life of the Commons*. Gabriola Island, BC: New Society Publishers.

Bolté, Paul-Emile. 1964. *Mater et Magistra, commentaire*, vol. 1. Montreal: University de Montreal.

————. 1966. *Mater et Magistra, commentaire*, vol. 2. Montreal: University de Montreal.

————. 1967. *Mater et Magistra, commentaire*, vol. 3. Montreal: University de Montreal.

————. 1968a. *Mater et Magistra, commentaire*, vol. 4. Montreal: University de Montreal.

————. 1968b. *Mater et Magistra: Texte latin, nouvelle traduction, index analytique*. Montréal: University de Montreal.

Bonino, José Miguez. 1984. *Toward a Christian Political Ethics*. London: SCM and Philadelphia: Fortress Press.

Boswell, J. S., E. P. McHugh, and J. Verstraeten, eds. 2000. *Catholic Social Thought: Twilight of Renaissance?* Leuven, Belgium: Peeters/Leuven University Press.

Bride, A. "Tyranni," and "Tyrannicide." In *Dictionnaire de théologie catholique* XV, cols. 1969–71 and 1987.

Brookfield, Harold. 1975. *Interdependent Development*. London: Methuen.

Brouard, Susy. 2011. "Reconstructing the Body: Bringing Catholic Social Teaching to Life." Unpublished paper (July), quoted with permission of the author.

Bruni, Luigino. 2000. "Economy of Communion: Between Market and Solidarity." In *Catholic Social Thought: Twilight of Renaissance?* edited by J. S. Boswell, E. P. McHugh, and J. Verstraeten, 239–48. Leuven, Belgium: Peeters/Leuven University Press.

———. 2010. "Reciprocity and Gratuitousness in the Market: A Challenge for Economic Theory," paper at Rome Conference sponsored by Pontifical Council for Justice and Peace, February; http://www.stthomas. edu.

Burke, Joseph Anthony. 2009. "Pope Benedict on Capitalism, Marxism, and Globalization." *Catholic Social Science Review* 14:167–91.

Byrne, Patrick H. 2009. "What Is an Evolutionary Explanation? Darwin and Lonergan." In *Lonergan Workshop,* vol. 23, edited by Fred Lawrence, 13–57. Boston College.

Cahill, Lisa Sowle. 2005. "Commentary on *Familiaris consortio* (Apostolic Exhortation on the Family)." In *Modern Catholic Social Teaching: Commentaries and Interpretations,* edited by Kenneth B. Himes, 361–88. Washington, DC: Georgetown University Press.

———. 2010. "*Caritas in Veritate*: Benedict's Global Reorientation." *Theological Studies* 71:291–319.

Calvez, Jean-Yves. 1964. *The Social Thought of John XXIII Mater et Magistra.* London: Burns and Oates.

———. 1967. "Commentary on *Gaudium et Spes.*" In *L'Église dans le monde de ce temps: Constitution pastorale "Gaudium et Spes": Tome II, Commentaires* (Unam Sanctam 65–62), edited by Yves M. J. Congar and M. Peuchmaurd. Paris: Cerf.

Calvez, Jean-Yves, and Jacques Perrin. 1961. *The Church and Social Justice: The Social Teaching of the Popes from Leo XIII to Pius XII (1878–1958).* Chicago: Regnery.

Camp, Richard L. 1969. *The Papal Ideology of Social Reform: A Study in Historical Development 1878–1967.* Leiden: E. J. Brill.

Campaign for Human Development and the Office of Domestic Social Development. 1982. *On Human Work: A Resource Book for the Study of Pope John Paul II's Third Encyclical.* Washington, DC: United States Catholic Conference. (Contains the text of *LE* as well as background articles and a condensed paraphrase of the text by James R. Jennings.)

Capra, Fritjof. 2015. "*Laudato Si*': The Ecological Ethics and Systemic Thought of Pope Francis." June 22, 2015; http://www.fritjofcapra.net.

Carr, Anne E. 1990. *Transforming Grace: Christian Tradition and Women's Experience.* San Francisco: Harper and Row.

Carrier, Hervé. 1990. *The Social Doctrine of the Church Revisited: A Guide for Study.* Vatican City: Pontifical Council for Justice and Peace.

Casanova, José. 1994. *Public Religions in the Modern World.* Chicago: University of Chicago Press.

Cavanaugh, William T. 1998. *Torture and Eucharist: Theology, Politics and the Body of Christ.* Malden, MA: Blackwell.

Charles, Rodger. 1982. *The Social Teaching of Vatican II, Its Origin and Development: Catholic Social Ethics, An Historical and Comparative Study.* Oxford: Plater Publications; San Francisco: Ignatius Press.

———. 1991. "General Introduction." In *Catholic Social Teaching: A Textbook of Christian Insights,* edited by Theodor Herr, 7–27. London: New City.

Chenu, Marie-Dominique. 1967. "Le Message au monde des Pères conciliaires (octobre 1962)." In *L'Église dans le monde de ce temps: Constitution pastorale "Gaudium et Spes": Tome II, Commentaires* (Unam Sanctam 65–2), edited by Yves M. J. Congar and M. Peuchmaurd. 191–93. Paris: Cerf.

———. 1979. *La "doctrine sociale" de l'Église comme idéologie.* Paris: Cerf.

Chiavacci, Enrico. 1967. *La costituzione pastorale sulla Chiesa nel mondo contemporaneo: Gaudium et Spes.* Rome: Studium.

Christiansen, Drew. 2005. "Commentary on *Pacem in terris (Peace on Earth).*" In *Modern Catholic Social Teaching: Commentaries and Interpretations,* edited by Kenneth B. Himes, 217–43. Washington, DC: Georgetown University Press.

———. 2010. "Metaphysics and Society: A Commentary on *Caritas in Veritate.*" *Theological Studies* 71 (1): 3–28.

Cloutier, David. 2010. "Working with the Grammar of Creation: Benedict XVI, Wendell Berry, and the Unity of the Catholic Moral Vision." *Communio: International Catholic Review* 37 (4): 606–33.

Cohen, Nick. 2010. "The Book That Has the Tories Running Scared: A Polemic That Blames Inequality for Most Troubles in Our Society Has Energised Labour." *Observer,* August 8.

Coleman, John A. 1989. "The Culture of Death." In *The Logic of Solidarity: Commentaries on Pope John Paul II's Encyclical "On Social Concern,"* edited by Gregory Baum and Robert Ellsberg, 90–109. Maryknoll, NY: Orbis Books.

———, ed. 1991. *One Hundred Years of Catholic Social Thought: Celebration and Challenge.* Maryknoll, NY: Orbis Books. As well as editing this compilation, Coleman contributed two of the articles in it—the introduction (1–10) and "Neither Liberal nor Socialist" (25–42).

———. 2005. "The Future of Catholic Social Thought." In *Modern Catholic Social Teaching: Commentaries and Interpretations,* edited by Kenneth B. Himes, 522–44. Washington, DC: Georgetown University Press.

Collins, Denis. 1977. *Paulo Freire: His Life, Works, and Thought.* New York: Paulist Press.

Congar, Yves M. J., and M. Peuchmaurd, eds. 1967a. *L'Église dans le monde de ce temps: Constitution pastorale "Gaudium et Spes": Tome II, Commentaires* (Unam Sanctam 65–2). Paris: Cerf.

———, eds. 1967b. *L'Église dans le monde de ce temps: Constitution pastoral "Gaudium et Spes": Tome III, Reflections et perspectives* (Unam Sanctam 65–3). Paris: Cerf.

Connolly, Jerome. 2014. *Unfinished Business: The Case for Housing, Health and Other Social Rights in the Irish Constitution.* Dublin: privately published.

Cosgrave, Bill. 2010a. "From Patriarchy towards Equality." *Doctrine and Life* 60 (November): 40–54.

———. 2010b. "Are Men and Women Complementary? 2: An Egalitarian Understanding." *Doctrine and Life* 60 (December): 28–35.

Cosmao, Vincent. 1978. *Dossier: Nouvel ordre mondial; les chrétiens provoqués par le développement.* Paris: Chalet.

———. 1979a. *Changer le monde: Une tâche pour l'Église.* Paris: Cerf.

———. 1979b. *Le Rédempteur de l'homme: Lettre encyclique de Jean-Paul II: Un guide de lecture.* Paris: Cerf.

Coste, René. 1963. "Le problème de la légitimité de principe de la guerre révolutionnaire." In *Guerre révolutionnaire et conscience chrétienne,* edited by Pierre Marie Theas et al. 200–201. Paris: Pax Christi.

———. 1969. "Commentary on *Gaudium et spes.*" In *Commentary on the Documents of Vatican II,* vol. 5, edited by Herbert Vorgrimmler. London: Burns and Oates; New York: Herder and Herder.

Cronin, John F. 1964a. "A Commentary on *Mater et Magistra.*" In *The Encyclicals and Other Messages of John XXIII,* edited by the staff of *The Pope Speaks.* Washington, DC: T.P.S. Press.

———. 1964b. "A Commentary on *Pacem in Terris.*" In *The Encyclicals and Other Messages of John XXIII,* edited by the staff of *The Pope Speaks.* Washington, DC: T.P.S. Press.

Curran, Charles. 1985. *Directions in Catholic Social Ethics.* Notre Dame, IN: University of Notre Dame Press.

———. 2002. *Catholic Social Teaching 1891–Present: A Historical, Theological, and Ethical Analysis.* Washington, DC: Georgetown University Press.

Curran, Charles, Kenneth R. Himes, and Thomas Shannon. 2005. "Commentary on *Sollicitudo rei socialis (On Social Concern).*" In *Modern Catholic Social Teaching: Commentaries and Interpretations,* edited by Kenneth B. Himes, 415–35. Washington, DC: Georgetown University Press.

Curran, Charles, and Richard McCormick. 1986. *Readings in Moral Theology No. 5: Official Catholic Social Teaching.* New York: Paulist Press.

de Riedmatten, H. et al. 1966. *La Chiesa nel mondo contemporaneo: Commento alla costituzione pastorale: "Gaudium et Spes."* Brescia, Italy: Queriniana.

de Soras, Alfred. 1963. *International Morality (Faith and Fact Books No. 58).* London: Burns and Oates.

Deane-Drummond, Celia. 2008. *Eco-Theology.* London: Darton, Longman and Todd.

———. 2009. *Christ and Evolution: Wonder and Wisdom.* Minneapolis: Fortress Press.

———. 2012. "Joining the Dance: Catholic Social Teaching and Ecology." *New Blackfriars* 93, no. 1044 (March): 193-212.

Deck, Allan Figueroa. 2005. "Commentary on *Populorum progressio (On the Development of Peoples)*." In *Modern Catholic Social Teaching: Commentaries and Interpretations*, edited by Kenneth B. Himes, 292–314. Washington, DC: Georgetown University Press.

Delio, Ilia. 2011. *The Emergent Christ: Exploring the Meaning of Catholic in an Evolutionary Universe*. Maryknoll, NY: Orbis Books.

———. 2013. *The Unbearable Wholeness of Being: God, Evolution, and the Power of Love*. Maryknoll, NY: Orbis Books.

Donohue, Bill. 2011. "Vatican Council Calls for Financial Reform." *Catholic League for Religious and Civil Rights* (online), October 24; http://www.catholicleague.org.

Dorling, Danny. 2014. *Inequality and the 1 Percent*. London: Verso Books.

Dorr, Donal. 1984. *Spirituality and Justice*. Dublin: Gill and Macmillan; Maryknoll, NY: Orbis Books.

———. 1990. *Integral Spirituality: Resources for Community, Justice, Peace and the Earth*. Dublin: Gill and Macmillan; Maryknoll, NY: Orbis Books.

———. 1991. *The Social Justice Agenda: Justice, Ecology, Power and the Church*. Dublin: Gill and Macmillan; Maryknoll, NY: Orbis Books.

———. 2000. "Option for the Poor Revisited." In *Catholic Social Thought: Twilight or Renaissance?* edited by J. S. Boswell, E. P. McHugh, and J. Verstraeten, 249–62. Leuven, Belgium: Peeters/Leuven University Press.

———. 2002. "Bringing Ethics and Spirituality into Business." In *Work as Key to the Social Question: The Great Social and Economic Transformations and the Subjective Dimension of Work*, edited by Pontifical Council for Justice and Peace, 195–213. Rome: Libreria Editrice Vaticana.

———. 2007. "The Perspective of the Poor: What We Can Learn from Liberation Theology about the 'Signs of the Times.'" In *Scrutinizing the Signs of the Times in the Light of the Gospel*, edited by Johan Verstraeten, 247–72. Leuven, Belgium: Peeters/Leuven University Press.

———. 2008. *Spirituality: Our Deepest Heart's Desire*. Dublin: Columba Press.

———. 2013. "A Spirituality of Human Rights." *Doctrine and Life* 63, no. 8 (October) 33–42.

———. 2014. "Waardengericht en Spiritueel Leiderschap." In *Mensgericht Sociaal Ondernehmen*, edited by Dominiek Lootens 125–34. Antwerpen-Apeldoorn: Garant.

———. 2015. "Morality, Empathy, and Grass-roots Movements." *Doctrine and Life* 65, no. 3 (March): 28–39.

Dubarle, D. 1966. "Commentary on *Gaudium et spes*." In *La Chiesa nel mondo contemporaneo: commento alla costituzione pastorale: "Gaudium et Spes,"* edited by H. de Riedmatten et al. Brescia, Italy: Queriniana.

———. 1967. "Commentary on *Gaudium et spes*." In *L'Église dans le monde de ce temps: Constitution pastorale "Gaudium et Spes": Tome II, Commentaires* (Unam Sanctam 65–2), edited by Yves M. J. Congar and M. Peuchmaurd. Paris: Cerf.

Duncan, Bruce. 1991. *The Church's Social Teaching: From Rerum Novarum to 1931*. Melbourne: Collins Dove.

Dwyer, Judith, ed. 1994. *The New Dictionary of Catholic Social Thought*. Collegeville, MN: Liturgical Press.

Eagleson, John, and Philip Scharper, eds. 1979. *Puebla and Beyond: Documentation and Commentary*. Maryknoll, NY: Orbis Books.

EATWOT. 1980. "Final Document: International Ecumenical Congress of Theology, February 20–March 2, 1980, São Paulo, Brazil" (EATWOT Conference). In *Occasional Bulletin of Missionary Research*, July, 127–33. This document is also available in Sergio Torres and John Eagleson, eds. 1981. *The Challenge of Basic Christian Communities*. Maryknoll, NY: Orbis Books.

Edwards, Denis. 1999. *The God of Evolution: A Trinitarian Theology*. New York: Paulist Press.

———. 2006. *Ecology at the Heart of Faith: The Change of Heart That Leads to a New Way of Living on Earth*. Maryknoll, NY: Orbis Books.

Elliott, Charles 1975. *Patterns of Poverty in the Third World: A Study of Social and Economic Stratification*. New York: Praeger.

Ellis, Marc H., and Otto Maduro, eds. 1989. *The Future of Liberation Theology: Essays in Honor of Gustavo Gutiérrez*. Maryknoll, NY: Orbis Books.

Espérance des Pauvres. 1979. *Revue de presse*, no. 183 (September).

Farley, Margaret. 2006. *A Framework for Christian Social Ethics*. New York: Continuum.

Farrow, Douglas. 2010. "Baking Bricks for Babel?" In *Nova et Vetera*, English ed. 8 (4): 745–62.

Feehan, John. 2012. *The Singing Heart of the World: Creation, Evolution and Faith*. Maryknoll, NY: Orbis Books.

Ferraro, Benedito. 1977. *A significação politica e teologica da morte de Jesus à luz do Novo Testamento*. Petropolis, Brazil: Vozes.

Filochowski, Julian. 1980. "Medellín to Puebla." In *Reflections on Puebla*, Pope John Paul II and others. London: CIIR.

Filteau, Jerry. 2011. Article in online edition of the *National Catholic Reporter* of May 25; http://ncronline.org.

Finn, Daniel. 2005. "Commentary on *Centesimus annus* (*On the Hundredth Anniversary of* Rerum novarum)." In *Modern Catholic Social Teaching: Commentaries and Interpretations*, edited by Kenneth B. Himes, 436–66. Washington, DC: Georgetown University Press.

———, ed. 2010. *The True Wealth of Nations: Catholic Social Thought and Economic Life*. New York: Oxford University Press.

Fitzgerald, Garret. 1991. "Encyclical Is Impressive but Insensitive on Some Issues." *Sunday Press*, May 5, 11.

Flannery, Harry W., ed. 1962. *Pattern for Peace: Catholic Statements on International Order*. Westminster, MD.: Newman Press.

Franklin, James. 2011. "*Caritas in Veritate*: Economic Activity as Personal Encounter and the Economy of Gratuitousness." *Solidarity: The Journal of Catholic Social Thought and Secular Ethics* 1 (1): 1–9.

Freire, Paulo. 1974. *Education for Critical Consciousness*. New York: Continuum/Seabury; also rev. ed. 1985. London: Sheed and Ward.

———. 1985. *The Politics of Education: Culture, Power and Liberation.* South Hadley, MA.: Bergin and Garvey; Basingstoke/London: Macmillan.

Fremantle, Anne, ed. 1963. *The Social Teachings of the Church.* New York: Mentor-Omega.

Frey, Bruno. 1998. *Not Just for the Money: An Economic Theory of Personal Motivation.* Cheltenham, UK, and Northampton, MA: Edward Elgar.

Galilea, Segundo. 1984. "The Theology of Liberation: A General Survey." In *Liberation Theology and the Vatican Document*, vol. 1, edited by Sonia R. Perdiguerra, 1–51. Quezon City, Philippines: Claretian Publications.

Garofalo, Salvatore, ed. 1969. *Dizionario del Concilio Ecumenico Vaticano Secondo.* Rome: Vatican Press.

Geyer, Alan. 1989. "Two Peace Pastorals Compared." In *The Ecumenist: A Journal for Promoting Christian Unity*, no. 28.

Gilson, Etienne, ed. 1954. *The Church Speaks to the Modern World: The Social Teachings of Leo XIII.* Garden City, NY: Doubleday Image.

Gold, Lorna. 2010. *New Financial Horizons: The Emergence of an Economy of Communion.* Hyde Park, NY: New City Press.

Gorbachev, Mikhail. 1992. "Pope John Paul." *La Stampa*, English version. *Irish Times*, March 4, 9.

Goulet, Denis. 1989. "The Search for Authentic Development." In *The Logic of Solidarity: Commentaries on Pope John Paul II's Encyclical "On Social Concern,"* edited by Gregory Baum and Robert Ellsberg, 127–42. Maryknoll, NY: Orbis Books.

Gremillion, Joseph, ed. 1976. *The Gospel of Peace and Justice: Catholic Social Teaching since Pope John.* Maryknoll, NY: Orbis Books.

Guano, E., et al. 1966. *La costituzione pastorale sulla Chiesa nel mondo contemporaneo: Introduzione storico-dottrinale; testo latino e traduzione italiano; esposizione e commento.* Turin, Italy: Elle di Ci.

Gudorf, Christine E. 1980. *Catholic Social Teaching on Liberation Themes.* Lanham, MD: University Press of America.

———. 2005. "Commentary on *Octogesima adveniens (A Call to Action on the Eightieth Anniversary of* Rerum novarum*)*." In *Modern Catholic Social Teaching: Commentaries and Interpretations*, edited by Kenneth B. Himes, 315–32. Washington, DC: Georgetown University Press.

Gui, Benedetto. 2000. "Beyond Transactions: On the Interpersonal Dimension of Economic Reality." *Annals of Public and Cooperative Economics* 71 (2): 139–70.

Gutiérrez, Gustavo. 1973. *A Theology of Liberation: History, Politics and Salvation.* Maryknoll, NY: Orbis Books.

Hamel, Ronald. 1994. "Justice in the World." In *The New Dictionary of Catholic Social Thought*, edited by Judith Dwyer, 495–501. Collegeville, MN: Liturgical Press.

Hauerwas, Stanley. 1982. "Work as 'Co-Creation'—A Remarkably Bad Idea." *This World* 3 (Fall): 89–102.

Healy, Nicholas J. 2010. "*Caritas in veritate* and Economic Theory." *Communio: International Catholic Review* 37 (4): 580–91.

Hebblethwaite, Peter. 1982. "The Popes and Politics: Shifting Patterns in 'Catholic Social Doctrine.'" *Daedalus: Journal of the American Academy of Arts and Sciences.* 111 (1): 85–99.

———. 1984. *John XXIII: Pope of the Council.* London: Geoffrey Chapman.

———. 1987. "Spiritual Points in Liberation Themes Basic to the Document: An Analysis." In *Liberation Theology and the Vatican Documents,* vol. 3: *Perspectives from the Third World,* edited by Claretian Team, 85–95. Quezon City, Philippines: Claretian Publications.

Heckel, Roger. 1980. *The Social Teaching of John Paul II, Booklet I, General Aspects of the Social Catechesis of John Paul II; the Use of the Expression "Social Doctrine" of the Church.* Vatican City: Pontifical Commission for Justice and Peace.

Hehir, J. Bryan. 1990. "The Church in the World: Where Social and Pastoral Ministry Meet." *Church* (Winter): 17–22.

Helman, Ivy. 2012. *Women and the Vatican: An Exploration of Official Documents.* Maryknoll, NY: Orbis Books.

Hennelly, Alfred T. 1982. "A Spirituality of Work." *On Human Work: A Resource Book for the Study of Pope John Paul II's Third Encyclical,* edited by Campaign for Human Development and the Office of Domestic Social Development. Washington, DC: United States Catholic Conference.

———, ed. 1990. *Liberation Theology: A Documentary History.* Maryknoll, NY: Orbis Books.

Henriot, Peter. 2011. "Remembering 'Justice,' Retrieving a Forgotten Proclamation." *America,* November 14.

Herr, Theodor. 1991. *Catholic Social Teaching: A Textbook of Christian Insights.* London: New City.

Hickey, Raymond, ed. 1982. *Modern Missionary Documents.* Dublin: Dominican Publications.

Himes, Kenneth B. 2005a. "Commentary on *Justitia in mundo (Justice in the World)*." In *Modern Catholic Social Teaching: Commentaries and Interpretations,* edited by Kenneth B. Himes, 333–62. Washington, DC: Georgetown University Press.

———, ed. 2005b. *Modern Catholic Social Teaching: Commentaries and Interpretations.* Washington, DC: Georgetown University Press.

Hinze, Christine Firer. 2005. "Commentary on *Quadragesimo anno (After Forty Years)*." In *Modern Catholic Social Teaching: Commentaries and Interpretations,* edited by Kenneth B. Himes, 151–74. Washington, DC: Georgetown University Press.

———. 2009. "Women, Families, and the Legacy of *Laborem Exercens*: An Unfinished Agenda." *Journal of Catholic Social Thought* 6 (1): 63–92.

Hogan, Linda. 2000. "Trocaire: A Catholic Development Agency Working to Support Communities in the Efforts to Overcome Poverty and Oppression." In *Catholic Social Thought: Twilight or Renaissance?* edited by J. S. Boswell, E. P. McHugh, and J. Verstraeten, 183–90. Leuven, Belgium: Peeters/Leuven University Press.

Hoinacki, Lee. 1991. "Development and John Paul II." *Aisling Magazine* 3:53–57.

Holland, Joe, and Peter Henriot. 1983. *Social Analysis: Linking Faith and Justice*. Rev. exp. ed. Maryknoll, NY: Orbis Books.

Hollenbach, David. 1979. *Claims in Conflict: Retrieving and Renewing the Catholic Human Rights Tradition*. New York: Paulist Press.

———. 2005. "Commentary on *Gaudium et spes (Pastoral Constitution on the Church in the Modern World)*." In *Modern Catholic Social Teaching: Commentaries and Interpretations*, edited by Kenneth B. Himes, 266–91. Washington, DC: Georgetown University Press.

———. 2011. "*Caritas in Veritate*: The Meaning of Love and Urgent Challenges of Justice." *Journal of Catholic Social Thought* 8 (1): 171–82.

Illich, Ivan D. 1978. *Toward a History of Needs*. Berkeley, CA: Heyday Book.

———. 1988. *Tools for Conviviality*. Berkeley, CA: Heyday Books; London: Marion Boyars.

Ivereigh, Austin. 2015. *The Great Reformer: Francis and the Making of a Radical Pope* (with new epilogue). London: Allen and Unwin.

Jedin, Hubert, ed. 1981. *The Church in the Industrial Age (History of the Church, vol. 9)*. New York: Crossroad.

Joblin, Joseph. 1966. "'The Church in the World': A Contribution to Pluralism." *International Labour Review* 93 (5): 459–76.

———. 1967. *Towards Complete Development*.Booklet reprint from the *International Labour Review* 96 (September) Geneva.

Johnson, Elizabeth A. 2006. *Truly Our Sister: A Theology of Mary in the Communion of Saints*. New York: Continuum.

———. 2014. *Ask the Beasts: Darwin and the God of Love*. London: Bloomsbury.

———. 2015. *Abounding in Kindness: Writings for the People of God*. Maryknoll, NY: Orbis Books.

Juniper, Tony. 2013. *What Has Nature Ever Done for Us?: How Money Really Does Grow on Trees*. London: Profile Books.

Kairos Theologians. 1986. *The Kairos Document: A Theological Comment on the Political Crisis in South Africa*. Rev. ed. Braamfontein, South Africa: Skotaville Publishers; Grand Rapids, MI: Eerdmans; London: C.I.I.R.

Keenan, Marjorie. 2000. *Care for Creation: Human Activity and the Environment*. Vatican City: Pontifical Council for Justice and Peace/Libreria Vaticana.

———. 2002. *From Stockholm to Johannesburg: An Historical Overview of the Concern of the Holy See for the Environment, 1972–2002*. Vatican City: Pontifical Council for Justice and Peace/Libreria Vaticana.

Kertzer, David L. 2014. *The Pope and Mussolini: The Secret History of Pius XI and the Rise of Fascism in Europe*. Oxford: Oxford University Press.

Kirby, Peadar. 1980. "The Pope in Brazil." *Doctrine and Life* 30:363.

Kirwan, J. R. 1964. *Mater et Magistra* in *The Social Thought of John XXIII*. Oxford: Catholic Social Guild.

Klein, Naomi. 2007. *The Shock Doctrine: The Rise of Disaster Capitalism*. New York: Metropolitan Books.

———. 2014. *This Changes Everything: Capitalism vs. the Climate*. New York: Simon and Schuster; London: Allen Lane.

La Stampa. 1992. Interview with Pope John Paul II about article by Mikhail Gorbachev; English version in *Irish Times*, March 4, 9.

Lamoureux, Patricia A. 2005. "Commentary on *Laborem exercens (On Human Work)*." In *Modern Catholic Social Teaching: Commentaries and Interpretations*, edited by Kenneth B. Himes, 389–414. Washington, DC: Georgetown University Press.

Land, Philip S. 1979. "The Social Theology of Pope Paul VI." *America* , May 12, 394.

———. 1994. *Catholic Social Teaching: As I Have Lived, Loathed, and Loved It*. Chicago: Loyola Press.

Land, Philip S., and Peter J. Henriot. 1989. "Toward a New Methodology in Catholic Social Teaching." In *The Logic of Solidarity: Commentaries on Pope John Paul II's Encyclical "On Social Concern,"* edited by Gregory Baum and Robert Ellsberg, 65–74. Maryknoll, NY: Orbis Books.

Langan, John P. 2005. "The Christmas Messages of Pius XII (1939–1948): Catholic Social Teaching in a Time of Extreme Crisis." In *Modern Catholic Social Teaching: Commentaries and Interpretations*, edited by Kenneth B. Himes, 175–90. Washington, DC: Georgetown University Press. 2005.

Laurent, Bernard. 2010. "*Caritas in Veritate* as a Social Encyclical: A Modest Challenge to Economic, Social, and Political Institutions." *Theological Studies* 71 (3): 515–44.

Laurentin, René. 1972. *Liberation, Development and Salvation*. Maryknoll, NY: Orbis Books.

Lebret, L. J. 1966. "Commentary on *Gaudium et spes*." In *La Chiesa nel mondo contemporaneo: Commento alla costituzione pastorale: "Gaudium et Spes,"* edited by H. de Riedmatten et al. Brescia: Queriniana.

Leclercq, J. 1934. *Leçons de droit naturel, II: L'État ou la politique*. 2nd ed. Namur, Belgium: Wesmael-Charlier.

Lernoux, Penny. 1979. "The Long Path to Puebla." In *Puebla and Beyond: Documentation and Commentary*, edited by John Eagleson and Philip Scharper, 3–27. Maryknoll, NY: Orbis Books.

Levertov, Denise. 1991. *Evening Train*. New York: New Direction Books.

Lewis, Thomas, Fari Amini, and Richard Lannon. 2001. *A General Theory of Love*. New York: Vintage Books.

Limbaugh, Rush. 2013; http://www.rushlimbaugh.com.

Lio, Ermenegildo. 1969. "*Povertá (Theol morale).*" In *Dizionario del Concilio Ecumenico Vaticano Secondo*, edited by Salvatore Garofalo. Rome: Vatican Press.

Lonergan, Bernard. [1972] 1990. *Method in Theology*, vol. 14 of the *Collected Works of Bernard Lonergan*. Toronto: University of Toronto Press.

———. [1957] 1992. *Insight: A Study of Human Understanding*, vol. 3 of the *Collected Works of Bernard Lonergan,* edited by Frederick E. Crowe and Robert M. Doran. Toronto: University of Toronto Press

Longley, Clifford. 2014. *Just Money: How Catholic Social Teaching Can Redeem Capitalism*. London: Theos.

Lovelock, James. 1988. *The Ages of Gaia*. Oxford: Oxford University Press.

Malley, François. 1968. *Le Père Lebret: L'économie au service des hommes*. Paris: Cerf.

Malone, Mary T. 2014. *The Elephant in the Church: A Woman's Tract for Our Times*. Dublin: Columba Press.

Manne, Robert. 2015. "*Laudato Si'*: A Political Reading." *Atlantic,* July 1, 2015; https://www.themonthly.com.

Marshall, George. 2014. *Don't Even Think about It: Why Our Brains Are Wired to Ignore Climate Change*. New York: Bloomsbury.

Marzani, Carl. 1982. "The Vatican as a Left Ally?" *Monthly Review*, July–August.

Masse, Benjamin L., ed. 1966. *The Church and Social Progress: Background Readings for Pope John's Mater et Magistra*. Milwaukee: Bruce.

Mattai, Giuseppe. 1969. "Commentary on *Gaudium et spes*." In *Commentary on the Documents of Vatican II*, vol. 5, edited by Herbert Vorgrimmler, 1049. London: Burns and Oates; New York: Herder and Herder.

Mayer, Jane. 2010. "Covert Operations: The Billionaire Brothers Who Are Waging a War against Obama." *New Yorker*, August 30; http://www.newyorker.com.

McClarey, Donald R. 2011. "BOMFOG & Towards Reforming the International Financial & Monetary Systems in the Context of Global Public Authority." *American Catholic: Politics and Culture from a Catholic Perspective* (online), October 27; http://the-american-catholic.com.

McDonagh, Francis. 2014. "More Good Samaritan than Marx and Engels." *Tablet*, August 2, 2014, 14–15.

McDonagh, Sean. 2004a. *The Death of Life: The Horror of Extinction*. Dublin: Columba Press.

———. 2004b. *An Open Letter to the Vatican on Genetically Engineered Food*. London: Columban Faith and Justice Office.

———. 2006. *Climate Change: The Challenge to All of Us*. Dublin: Columba Press.

———. 2009. Untitled articles in *The Universe*, February 1, 8, 15, 22; March 1, 8, 15, 22, 29; April, 12, 19, 26; May 17; June 7, 14, 21, 28; July 5, 19, 26; August 2, 9, 16, 23, 30; September 6, 13, 20, 2009; November 22, 29; May 10, 2010. (Only the relevant articles in the series have been listed here.)

McDonagh, Sean, and Donal Dorr. 2008. *Unless the Grain of Wheat Shall Die: The Moral and Theological Case against Terminator Seeds*. London: Progressio.

McDougall, Heather R., and Stephen McDavid. 2014. "Go Global, Innovate! Training Social Entrepreneurial Leaders." *Journal of Leadership Studies* 8 (2): 46–51.

McGovern, Arthur F. 1980. *Marxism: An American Christian Perspective*. Maryknoll, NY: Orbis Books.

McGregor, Bede. 1977. "Commentary on *Evangelii Nuntiandi*." *Doctrine and Life* 27 (3/4): 53–97.

McKibben, Bill. 2011. *Earth: Making a Life on a Tough New Planet*. New York: St. Martin's Griffen.

McLoughlin, Nellie. 2004. *Out of Wonder: The Evolving Story of the Universe*. Dublin: Veritas.

Merle, Marcel, ed. 1967. *Les Églises chrétiennes et la décolonisation*. Paris: Armand Colin.

Mich, Marvin L. 2005. "Commentary on *Mater et magistra (Christianity and Social Progress)*." In *Modern Catholic Social Teaching: Commentaries and Interpretations*, edited by Kenneth B. Himes, 191–216. Washington, DC: Georgetown University Press.

———. 2011. *The Challenge and Spirituality of Catholic Social Teaching*. Maryknoll, NY: Orbis Books.

Michaelson, Jay. 2015. Online article in *Boston Globe*; http://www.cruxnow.com.

Miller, Amata. 1991a. "Catholic Social Teaching—What Might Have Been If Women Were Not Invisible in a Patriarchal Society." *Journal of Justice and Peace* 3:51–70.

———. 1991b. "On the Side of the Poor: Evolution of a Stance." In *Shaping a New World: The Catholic Social Justice Tradition, 1891–1991*, edited by Network. Washington, DC: Network.

———. 1991c. "The Centennial Encyclical—*Centesimus Annus*." In *Shaping a New World: The Catholic Social Justice Tradition, 1891–1991*, edited by Network. Washington, DC: Network.

Miller, Raymond J. 1947. *Forty Years After: Pius XI and the Social Order: A Commentary*. St Paul: Radio Replies Press.

Miller, Vincent. 2011. "Is the Idea of a Global Government Agency Radical?" *NCR* online, October 28; http://ncronline.org.

Mindell, Arnold. 1995. *Sitting in the Fire: Large Group Transformation Using Conflict and Diversity*. Portland, OR: Lao Tse Press.

Miranda, Jose Porfirio. 1980. *Marx against the Marxists: The Christian Humanism of Karl Marx*. Maryknoll, NY: Orbis Books.

Moeller, Charles. 1969. "History of the Drafting of Text of *Gaudium et spes*." In *Commentary on the Documents of Vatican II*, vol. 5, edited by Herbert Vorgrimmler. London: Burns and Oates; New York: Herder and Herder.

Molony, John. 1991. *The Worker Question: A New Historical Perspective on Rerum Novarum*. Melbourne: Collins-Dove; Dublin: Gill and Macmillan.

Monbiot, George. 2014, "There Is an Alternative." *Guardian* December 8, 25.

Moody, Joseph N. 1953. *Church and Society: Catholic Social and Political Thought and Movements 1789–1950*. New York: Arts.

Murphy, Charles M. 1983. "Action for Justice as Constitutive of the Preaching of the Gospel: What Did the 1971 Synod Mean?" *Theological Studies* 44:289–311.

———. 2007. "Charity, Not Justice, as Constitutive of the Church's Mission." *Theological Studies* 68:274–86.

Murray, John Courtney. 1952. "The Church and Totalitarian Democracy." *Theological Studies* 13:525–63.

———. 1953a. "Leo XIII on Church and State: The General Structure of the Controversy." *Theological Studies* 14:1–30.

———. 1953b. "Leo XIII: Separation of Church and State." *Theological Studies* 14:145–214.

———. 1953c. "Leo XIII: Two Concepts of Government." *Theological Studies* 14:551–67.

———. 1954. "Government and the Order of Culture." *Theological Studies* 15:1–33.

Naudet, Jean-Yves. 2011. *La doctrine sociale de l'église: Une éthique économique pour notre temps*. Collection du Centre d'Éthique Économique. Aix-en-Provence, France: Presses Universitaires d'Aix-Marseille.

Nell-Breuning, Oswald von. 1936. *Reorganization of Social Economy: The Social Encyclical Developed and Explained* (English ed. prepared by Bernard W. Dempsey). Milwaukee: Bruce.

———. 1969. "Commentary on *Gaudium et spes*." In *Commentary on the Documents of Vatican II*, vol. 5, edited by Herbert Vorgrimmler, 326–27. London: Burns and Oates; New York: Herder and Herder.

———. 1970. "Social Movements" and "Socialism." In *Sacramentum Mundi* 6:98–116. New York: Herder and Herder; London: Burns and Oates.

———. 1986. "The Drafting of *Quadragesimo Anno*." In *Readings in Moral Theology No. 5: Official Catholic Social Teaching*, edited by Charles Curran and Richard McCormick, 60–68. New York: Paulist Press.

Nicholas, Jeffery. 2011. "Local Communities and Globalization in *Caritas in Veritate*." *Solidarity: The Journal of Catholic Social Thought and Secular Ethics* 1 (1).

Nolan, Albert. 1986. "The Option for the Poor in South Africa." *CrossCurrents* 36:17–27.

Nordhaus, William D. 2015. "A New Solution: The Climate Club." Review article of *Climate Shock: The Economic Consequences of a Hotter Planet*, by Gernot Wagner and Martin L. Weitzman. http://www.nybooks.com.

Novak, Michael. 1982. "'Creation Theology'—John Paul II and the American Experience." *This World* 3:71–88.

———. 1989. *Catholic Social Thought and Liberal Institutions*. Oxford: Transaction.

———. 2009. "Pope Benedict XVI's Caritas." *First Things Online*, August 17.

Nussbaum, Martha, and Amartya Sen, eds. 1993. *The Quality of Life*. Wider Studies in Development Economics. New York: Oxford University Press.

OECD Report, *Focus on Inequality and Growth*, December 9, 2014; http://www.oecd.org.

O'Boyle, Edward J. 2010. "*Caritas in Veritate*: Pope Benedict XVI on Development." *ITEST Bulletin* 41 (1): 1–14.

———. 2011. "Social Justice: Addressing the Ambiguity." Mayo Research Institute, 1–27; http://www.mayoresearch.org.

O'Brien, David J. 1991. "A Century of Catholic Social Teaching: Contexts and Comments." In *One Hundred Years of Catholic Social Thought: Celebration and Challenge*, edited by John A. Coleman, 13–24. Maryknoll, NY: Orbis Books.

O'Brien, David J., and Thomas A. Shannon, eds. 1977. *Renewing the Earth: Catholic Documents on Peace, Justice, and Liberation*. Garden City, NY: Doubleday Image.

O'Hanlon, Gerry. 2010. *Theology in the Irish Public Square*. Dublin: Columba Press.

———. 2014. "Catholic Social Teaching and Inequality." *Working Notes [of Jesuit Centre for Faith and Justice]* (Dublin) 75 (December): 22–26.

———. 2015. "Catholic Social Teaching and Housing." *Working Notes [of Jesuit Centre for Faith and Justice]* (Dublin) 75 (May), 26–31.

Ormerod, Neil. 2008. "The Argument Has Vast Implications: Part II of *Deus caritas est.*" In *Identity and Mission in Catholic Agencies*, edited by Neil Ormerod, 67–81. Strathfield, New South Wales, Australia: St. Paul Publications.

Orsy, Ladislas. 2014. "Francis' New Order." *Tablet*, June 21, 12–13.

Orobator, Agbonkhianmeghe. 2010. "*Caritas in veritate* and Africa's Burden of (Under)development." *Theological Studies* 71:320–34.

Pabst, Adrian. 2010. "Modern Sovereignty in Question: Theology, Democracy and Capitalism." *Modern Theology* 26 (4): 570–602.

Pagola, José Antonio. 2009. *Jesus: An Historical Approximation*. Miami: Convivium.

Pakenham, Thomas. 1991. *The Scramble for Africa, 1876–1912*. London: Weidenfeld and Nicolson.

Panksepp, Jaak. 1998. *Affective Neuroscience: The Foundations of Human and Animal Emotions*. New York: Oxford University Press.

Pennings, Ray. 2010. "Work and Love in the Global Village: Responding to *Caritas in Veritate*." *Review of Faith & International Affairs* 8 (4): 69–73.

Piercy, Marge. 1985. *Woman on the Edge of Time*. New York. Fawcett.

Piketty, Thomas, 2014. *Capital in the Twenty-first Century*. Cambridge, MA: Belknap Press of Harvard University Press.

———. 2015. "A Practical Vision of a More Equal Society." *New York Review of Books* 62, no. 11 (June 25–July 8, 2015): 26–29. (A lengthy review of Atkinson 2015.)

Pope, Stephen J. 2008. "Benedict XVI's *Deus caritas est*: An Ethical Analysis." In *Applied Ethics in a World Church: The Padua Conference*, edited by Linda Hogan, 271–77. Maryknoll, NY: Orbis Books.

Potter, George Ann. 1988. *Dialogue on Debt: Alternative Analyses and Solutions*. Washington, DC: Center of Concern.

Price, Vera. 1991. "A Feminist Look at Catholic Social Teaching." *Doctrine and Life* 41:123–29.

Quade, Quentin L., ed. 1982. *The Pope and Revolution: John Paul II Confronts Liberation Theology*. Washington, DC: Ethics and Public Policy Center.

Renouard, Cécile. 2010. "Relational Capitalism: Justice and Gift in Corporate Activities according to *Caritas in Veritate*;" http://www.stthomas.edu.

Rhodes, Anthony. 1973. *The Vatican in the Age of the Dictators, 1922–45*. London: Hodder and Stoughton.

Rohr, Richard. 2011. "The Cosmic Christ" in The Catholic Corner. https://www.youtube.com.

Robertson, James. 1985. *Future Work: Jobs, Self-Employment and Leisure after the Industrial Age*. Aldershot, UK: M. T. Smith.

Rostow, Walt W. 1960. *The Stages of Economic Growth: A Non-Communist Manifesto*. New York: Cambridge University Press.

Ruether, Rosemary Radford. 1983. *Sexism and God-Talk: Towards a Feminist Theology*. Boston: Beacon Press.

Ryan, John A. 1935. *A Better Economic Order*. New York: Harper.

Ryan, Liam. 1991. "The Modern Popes as Social Reformers." *Furrow* 42:87–100.

Ryan, Maura A. 2010. "A New Shade of Green? Nature, Freedom, and Sexual Difference in *Caritas in veritate*." *Theological Studies* 71:335–49.

Sachs, Jeffrey D. 2015. "The Great Gift of 'Laudato Si'." *America, National Catholic Review*, July 6.

Sachs, Wolfgang. 1991. "The Economist's Prejudice." *Aisling Magazine* 4:59–63.

Sandoval, Moises. 1979. "Report from the Conference." In *Puebla and Beyond: Documentation and Commentary*, edited by John Eagleson and Philip Scharper, 28–43. Maryknoll, NY: Orbis Books. 1979.

Saunders, Peter. 2010. *Beware False Prophets: Equality, the Good Society and the Spirit Level*. Edited by Natalie Evans. London: Policy Exchange.

Savignat, Alain, ed. 1956. *Relations humaines et société contemporaine: Synthèse chrétienne directives de S.S. Pie XII*. Fribourg, Switzerland: St. Paul.

Schindler, David L. 2006. "Charity, Justice, and the Church's Activity in the World." *Communio: International Catholic Review* 33:346–67.

———. 2010. "The Anthropological Vision of *Caritas in veritate* in Light of Economic and Cultural Life in the United States." *Communio: International Catholic Review* 37 (4): 558–79.

Schindler, D. C. 2010. "Enriching the Good: Toward the Development of a Relational Anthropology." *Communio: International Catholic Review* 37 (4): 643–59.

Schooyans, Michel. 1991."*Centesimus Annus* et la 'sève généreuse' de *Rerum Novarum*." In *De "Rerum Novarum" à "Centesimus Annus,"* edited by Pontifical Council for Justice and Peace, 27–72. Vatican City: Pontifical Council for Justice and Peace.

Schore, Allan N. 1994. *Affect Regulation and the Origin of the Self: The Neurobiology of Emotional Development*. Hillsdale, NJ: Lawrence Erlbaum Associates.

Schotte, Jan P., ed. 1982a. *From Rerum Novarum to Laborem Exercens: Towards the Year 2000 (Symposium)*. Vatican City: Pontifical Commission for Justice and Peace.

———. 1982b. *Reflections on Laborem Exercens*. Vatican City: Pontifical Commission for Justice and Peace.

Schuijt, Willem J. 1969. "History of the Text of *Gaudium et spes*." In *Commentary on the Documents of Vatican II*, vol. 5, edited by Herbert Vorgrimmler, 339. London: Burns and Oates; New York: Herder and Herder.

Schultheis, Michael J., Edward P. DeBerri, and Peter J. Henriot. 1987. *Our Best Kept Secret: The Rich Heritage of Catholic Social Teaching*. Washington, DC: Center of Concern; London: CAFOD.

Schumacher, E. F. 1974. *Small Is Beautiful: A Study of Economics as if People Mattered*. London: Abacus; New York: Harper and Row, 1989.

Schüssler Fiorenza, Elisabeth. 1983. *In Memory of Her: A Feminist Theological Reconstruction of Christian Origins*. New York: Crossroad; London: SCM.

Segundo, Juan Luis. 1985. *Theology and the Church: A Response to Cardinal Ratzinger and a Warning to the Whole Church*. Minneapolis: Winston Press; London: Geoffrey Chapman.

Shannon, Thomas A. 2005. "Commentary on *Rerum novarum (The Condi-*

tion of Labor)." In *Modern Catholic Social Teaching: Commentaries and Interpretations*, edited by Kenneth B. Himes, 127–50. Washington, DC: Georgetown University Press.

Sigmond, Raimondo. 1966. "Commentary on *Gaudium et spes.*" In *La costituzione pastorale sulla Chiesa nel mondo contemporaneo: Introduzione storico-dottrinale; testo latino e traduzione italiano; esposizione e comment.* Turin, Italy: Elle di Ci.

Sirico, Robert. 2009. "*Caritas in Veritate:* The Pope on 'Love in Truth.' " *Wall Street Journal*, July 10; http://blog.acton.org.

Small, Garrick. 2011. "Connecting Economics to Theology." *Solidarity: The Journal of Catholic Social Thought and Secular Ethics* 1 (1): 1–14.

Sobrino, Jon. 1979. "The Significance of Puebla for the Catholic Church in Latin America." In *Puebla and Beyond: Documentation and Commentary*, edited by John Eagleson and Philip Scharper, 289–309. Maryknoll, NY: Orbis Books.

———. 1989. "Jesus, Theology, and Good News." In *The Future of Liberation Theology: Essays in Honor of Gustavo Gutiérrez*, edited by Marc H. Ellis and Otto Maduro, 189–202. Maryknoll, NY: Orbis Books.

Somerville, Henry. 1933. *Studies in the Catholic Social Movement*. London: Burns, Oates and Washbourne.

Staune, Jean, and Christopher Wasserman. 2010. "The Notion of Gift and Justice in Economics and Business." Paper at Rome Conference sponsored by Pontifical Council for Justice and Peace, February; http://www.stthomas.edu.

Stavrianos, Leften Stavros. 1981. *Global Rift: The Third World Comes of Age*. New York: Morrow.

Stiglitz, Joseph. 2002. *Globalization and Its Discontents*. New York: W. W. Norton.

Sullivan, Amy. 2011. "The Vatican's Radical Ideas on Financial Reform." *Time Swampland*, October 24; http://swampland.time.com.

Swimme, Brian, and Thomas Berry. 1994. *The Universe Story: From the Primordial Flaring Forth to the Ecozoic Era—A Celebration of the Unfolding of the Cosmos*. New York and San Francisco: HarperCollins. (Original ed. 1992.)

Tamez, Elsa. 1982. *The Bible of the Oppressed*. Maryknoll, NY: Orbis Books.

Théas, Pierre-Marie, et al. 1963. *Guerre révolutionnaire et conscience chrétienne*. Paris: Pax Christi.

Thomas, Scott M. 2010. "Catholic Social Teaching, Macintyre's Social Theory, and Global Development." *Review of Faith and International Affairs* 8 (4): 23–34.

Tian, Yunhe (Evelyn), and Wendy K. Smith. 2014. "Entrepreneurial Leadership of Social Enterprises: Challenges and Skills for Embracing Paradoxes." *Journal of Leadership Studies* 8 (2): 42–45.

Todaro, Michael P. 1977. *Economic Development in the Third World: An Introduction to Problems and Policies in a Global Perspective*. London: Longman.

Toniolo, Augustino Ferrari. 1966. "Commentary on *Gaudium et spes*." In *La costituzione pastorale sulla Chiesa nel mondo contemporaneo: Introduzione storico-dottrinale; testo latino e traduzione italiano; esposizione e commento*, edited by E. Guano et al. Turin, Italy: Elle di Ci.

Torres, Sergio, and John Eagleson, eds. 1981. *The Challenge of Basic Christian Communities*. Maryknoll, NY: Orbis Books.

Townsend, Nicholas. 2012. *Virtual Plater Module A: Living Life to the Full*. Birmingham, UK: Newman University College; http://www.virtualplater.org.

———. 2012. *Virtual Plater Module B: Public Responsibilities*. Birmingham: Newman University College; http://www.virtualplater.org.

Tripole, Martin. 1981. "A Church for the Poor and the World: At Issue with Moltmann's Ecclesiology." *Theological Studies* 42:645–59.

Tucci, Roberto. 1969. *Commentary on the Documents of Vatican II*, vol. 5, edited by Herbert Vorgrimmler, 267. London: Burns and Oates; New York: Herder and Herder.

UNCTAD. 1980. *Restructuring the International Economic Framework: Report by the Secretary-General of the United Nations Conference on Trade and Development to the Fifth Session of the Conference*. New York: United Nations.

Utz, Arthur Fridolin. 1963. *Die Friedensenzyklika Papst Johannes XXIII: Pacem in Terris*. Freiburg: Herder.

Vallely, Paul. 2013. *Pope Francis: Untying the Knots*. New York: Bloomsbury Academic.

Verstraeten, Johan, ed. 2007. *Scrutinizing the Signs of the Times in the Light of the Gospel*. Leuven, Belgium: Peeters/Leuven University Press.

———. 2011. "Towards Interpreting Signs of the Times, Conversation with the World and Inclusion of the Poor: Three Challenges for Catholic Social Teaching." *International Journal of Public Theology* 5 (3): 314–30.

Vidler, Alec R. 1964. *A Century of Social Catholicism*. London: SPCK.

Villain, Jean. 1953. *L'enseignement social de l'Église, t.I: Introduction, capitalisme et socialisme*. Paris: Spes.

von Pastor, Ludwig F. 1940. *The History of the Popes: From the Close of the Middle Ages*, vol. 31. London: Kegan Paul, Trench, Trabner.

Vorgrimmler, Herbert, ed. 1969. *Commentary on the Documents of Vatican II*, vol. 5. London: Burns and Oates; New York: Herder and Herder.

Walsh, Michael J. 1991. "Editor's Introduction." In *Proclaiming Justice and Peace: Documents from John XXIII to John Paul II*, new exp. ed., edited by Michael J. Walsh, xi–xxv. London: CAFOD/Collins.

———. 2012. "The Myth of *Rerum Novarum.*" *New Blackfriars* 93 (1044) (March): 155–62.

Ward, Barbara (Lady Jackson). 1967. "Editor's Commentary." In *Encyclical Letter of His Holiness Pope Paul VI On the Development of Peoples*, 1–22. New York: Paulist Press.

———. 1970. *The Angry Seventies: The Second Development Decade: A Call to the Church*. Vatican City: Pontifical Commission for Justice and Peace.

———. 1973. *A New Creation: Reflections on the Environmental Issue.* Vatican City: Pontifical Commission for Justice and Peace.

———. 1978. "Looking Back on *Populorum Progressio.*" *Doctrine and Life* 29:196–212.

Weigel, George. 2009. "*Caritas in Veritate* in Gold and Red: The Revenge of Justice and Peace (or So They May Think)." *National Review Online*, July 7; http://article.nationalreview.com.

———. 2011. "The Pope, Chaplain to OWS? Rubbish." *National Review Online*, October 24; http://www.nationalreview.com.

Weigel, George, and Robert Royal, eds. 1991. *A Century of Catholic Social Thought: Essays on "Rerum Novarum" and Nine Other Key Documents.* Washington, DC: Ethics and Public Policy Center.

Wilkinson, Richard, and Kate Pickett. 2010. *The Spirit Level: Why More Equal Societies Almost Always Do Better (with a New Postscript)*. London: Allen Lane.

Williams, Paul S. 2010. "Evangelicals, Pope Benedict, and the Financial Crisis." *Review of Faith and International Affairs* 8 (4): 65–68.

Williams, Raymond. 1976. *Keywords: A Vocabulary of Culture and Society.* Glasgow: Collins Fontana.

Williams, Rowan. 2015. "Embracing Our Limits: The Lessons of *Laudato Si'.*" *Commonweal* October 9, 13–15.

Williamson, Edwin. 1992. *The Penguin History of Latin America*. London: Allen Lane.

Wojtyla, Karol (Pope John Paul II). 1981. *Toward a Philosophy of Praxis: An Anthology*, edited by Alfred Bloch and Ceorge T. Czuczka. New York: Crossroad.

Zamagni, Stefano. 2000. "Humanizing the Economy: On the Relationship between Catholic Social Thinking and Economic Discourse." In *Catholic Social Thought: Twilight or Renaissance?*, edited by J. S. Boswell, E. P. McHugh, and J. Verstraeten, 149–69. Leuven, Belgium: Peeters/Leuven University Press.

———. 2010. "Catholic Social Thought, Civil Economy, and the Spirit of Capitalism." In *The True Wealth of Nations: Catholic Social Thought and Economic Life*," edited by Daniel K. Finn, 63–93. New York: Oxford University Press.

Zigliara. 1910. *Summa Philosophica III*, 14th ed. Paris: Beauchesne.

Index